THE FUNSTERS

By James Robert Parish

As Author

The Fox Girls*
The Paramount Pretties*
The Slapstick Queens
Good Dames
The RKO Gals*
Hollywood's Great Love Teams*
The Elvis Presley Scrapbook
    (& Supplement)
The Great Movie Heroes
Great Child Stars
Film Directors Guide: Western Europe
Great Western Stars
The Jeanette MacDonald Story
The Tough Guys*
Film Actors Guide: Western Europe
Hollywood Character Actors*
The Hollywood Beauties*

As Co-Author

The Emmy Awards: A Pictorial History
The Cinema of Edward G. Robinson
The MGM Stock Company: The Golden Era*
The Great Spy Pictures
The George Raft File
The Glamour Girls*
Vincent Price Unmasked
Liza!
The Debonairs*
The Swashbucklers*
The Great Gangster Pictures
The Great Western Pictures
Film Directors Guide: The U.S.
Hollywood Players: The Forties*
Hollywood Players: The Thirties*
The Great Science Fiction Pictures
The All Americans*
Leading Ladies*
Hollywood on Hollywood

As Editor

The Great Movie Series
Actors Television Credits: 1950–72 & Supplement

As Associate Editor

The American Movies Reference Book: The Sound Era
TV Movies

By William T. Leonard

As Co-Author

Hollywood Players: The Forties*
Hollywood Players: The Thirties*

Film Directors Guide: The U.S.

* Published by Arlington House

THE FUNSTERS

BY

JAMES ROBERT PARISH and WILLIAM T. LEONARD

WITH

GREGORY W. MANK and CHARLES HOYT

Research Associates:

JOHN ROBERT COCCHI and FLORENCE SOLOMON

ARLINGTON HOUSE·PUBLISHERS
NEW ROCHELLE, NEW YORK

Book design by Pat Slesarchik

Manufactured in the United States of America

Library of Congress Cataloging in Publication Data

Parish, James Robert
  The funsters.

  Includes index.
  1. Comedy films.   2. Comedians—United States.
I. Leonard, William T., joint author.   II. Title.
PN1995.9.C55P37   791.43'092'2   78-32095
ISBN 0-87000-418-2

For VICTOR MOORE
1876–1962

Acknowledgments

RESEARCH CONSULTANT:
DOUG McCLELLAND

RESEARCH VERIFIER:
EARL ANDERSON

Richard A. Braff
Eleanor Boardman D'Arrast
Howard Davis
Robert A. Evans
Morris Everett, Jr.
Film Favorites (Bob and Charles Smith)
G. Harold Hozey
Ken D. Jones
Milton Kenin
Albert B. Manski
Alvin H. Marill
Mrs. Earl Meisinger
Peter Miglierini
Joseph M. Paradin
Michael R. Pitts
Screen Facts (Alan G. Barbour)
Mrs. Peter Smith
Charles K. Stumpf
T. Allan Taylor
Vincent Terrace
Theatre Collection, Free Library of Philadelphia (Geraldine DuClow, Elaine Ebo)
Lou Valentino
Paul G. Wesolowski

And Special Thanks to Paul Myers, curator of the Theatre Collection at the Lincoln Center Library for the Performing Arts (New York City), and his staff: Monty Arnold, David Bartholomew, Rod Bladel, Donald Fowle, Maxwell Silverman, Dorothy Swerdlove, and Betty Wharton; and Don Madison of Photo Services.

Contents

In In the Navy *(1941)*.

Abbott & Costello

As Hollywood celebrated New Year's Eve on December 31, 1940, Universal Pictures was very close to terminating its 25 years of existence. The smallest of the *major* film factories, the lot faced bankruptcy. Money troubles had nearly mashed the studio several times in the past decade. In 1931 the *deus ex machina* appeared in the form of Bela Lugosi's *Dracula* and Boris Karloff's *Frankenstein*. In 1936 *Show Boat* with Irene Dunne and Allan Jones saved the day. In the later years of the Thirties, Universal had kept solvent via contractee Deanna Durbin. Now the studio required a commercial miracle to remain intact.

That is exactly what it found. A team of comedians—Bud Abbott, lean, snide, con-artist straight man, and Lou Costello, roly-poly, falsetto-voiced, hysterical clown. The duo came to Hollywood after triumphs in burlesque, radio, and Broadway and were featured as comedy relief in Allan Jones' *One Night in the Tropics* (1940). They stole the limelight and were promptly starred in *Buck Privates* (1941). The program picture, reputed to have cost only $180,000 to make,

grossed several million dollars over the years. It volleyed Universal back into feasible operation and turned Abbott and Costello into the number 3 box-office attraction in 1941. The team became an institution, their names synonymous with the World War II years when laughs and brisk visual entertainment were precious commodities. From 1941 to 1944 and then again from 1948 to 1951 they were among the top 10 cinema attractions in the United States. Their NBC network radio show was top-rated for years, and they scored powerfully on early television.

The comic heyday of Abbott and Costello ended in poor screen vehicles, much publicized bitterness between the partners, and endless regurgitations of their once-inspired routines on television. While the film work of the Marx Brothers and Laurel and Hardy has been elevated to greatness by cinema historians, it is only the masses who continue to adore the slapstick shenanigans of Bud and Lou. While there is hardly a television station in North America that does not play their repertoire of films on a weekly basis, and while their vintage TV series continues to make the round of syndication, it is still thought déclassé to find enjoyment in their inspired mayhem. They have yet to receive their proper critical due.

William "Bud" Abbott was born on Wednesday, October 2, 1895, in Asbury Park, New Jersey. His father, Harry, was an advance man for the Barnum and Bailey Circus, in which Bud's mother, Rae Fisher Abbott, was a bareback rider.* After four years at Coney Island's P.S. 100 (by this time Bud's parents had abandoned circus life to create the "Columbia Wheel," the first of the burlesque circuits), Bud worked at a variety of jobs. He was a Coney Island amusement-park pitchman, an assistant treasurer at Brooklyn's Casino Burlesque House, and, after a shanghaied stint aboard a Norwegian freighter for six months, a producer of tab shows that led to a position as a producer of sorts at Washington's National Theatre. Via his constant exposure to virtually every burlesque act in the country, Bud soon realized he was well equipped to perform the hoary routines himself. Thus he decided to leave the responsibility of management for the lucrative, freewheeling job of straight man in front of the footlights. In those days the straight man of an act was usually the better paid member of the team. Bud was soon in demand by many established burlesque comics who wanted him to feed them the laugh lines.

Meanwhile, Louis Francis Cristillo had been born on Tuesday, March 6, 1906, in Paterson, New Jersey. The son of an Italian immigrant (Sebastian) and an Irish-Italian (Helen Rege), Lou grew up in Paterson where his father worked for the Prudential Life Insurance Company.** During these years he became fascinated with motion pictures. Despite his chubby 5'4" frame, he was entranced with athletics and soon became a top-notch basketball player. After graduation he turned to boxing, until his aghast dad ended that sojourn.

At the age of 21, Lou and pal Gene Coogan boarded the first of several freight trains (intermingled with hitchhiking) that took them to California, where they hoped to break into the movies. By this time Lou had followed the lead of his brother, Sebastian (Pat), who for professional reasons (as a bandleader) had changed his surname to Costello. Lou Costello was soon disillusioned with Hollywood, forced to accept work as a carpenter's assistant on a studio work crew, later performing stunt and extra jobs. His most celebrated credits were performing action stunts for Dolores Del Rio in *The Trail of '98* and for Joan Crawford in *Taxi Dancer,* both 1928 MGM releases. Eventually discouraged by his lack of success, he abandoned Hollywood and worked his way back across the country. He talked his way into a job as a comic at the Lyceum Theatre in St. Joseph, Missouri. His whiny voice and remarkable prowess at pratfalls—all the more appealing due to his compactness—soon launched him onto the top burlesque circuits. He eventually headlined at Philadelphia's Shubert and New York's Orpheum theaters. By 1936 Lou was booked into the Eltinge Theatre on 42nd Street of New York City's Times Square—where comic Harry Evanson was appearing with a straight man named Bud Abbott.

Over the years the comedy team would invent an array of stories dramatically explaining the reasons for their teaming. The fanciful accounts ranged from Lou's straight man not showing up and Bud substituting for him, to Bud bailing Lou out of a gambling disaster. Actually, each admired the other's work. Ironically, New York City's Mayor Fiorello LaGuardia banned burlesque in May 1937, just when the new team of Abbott and Costello began clicking with audiences. But they managed to build a reputation in other cities. In the touring show *Life Begins at Minsky's,* they caused such an enjoyable commotion with audiences that they landed a 10-week engagement at Atlantic City's Steel Pier.* Graduating to still more refined bookings and routines, they appeared in Manhattan and Washington, D.C., and broke box-office records in 1938 at New York's Loew's State Theatre.

---

* Harry and Rae Abbott had four children: Harry Jr., Olive Victoria, Bud, and Florence.
** Sebastian and Helen Cristillo had three children: Anthony Sebastian (1902), Lou, and Marie Teresa (1911).

* The comedy team would return each year for an engagement (through 1946) out of gratitude for their success on the Pier. Their first visit to the Pier was with a minstrel show which they performed in blackface.

By this time Abbott and Costello were functioning so well in show business that they had long since stripped their act of blue humor. With the aid of writer John Grant, they perfected such routines as the classic "Who's on First?" which was a guaranteed crowd pleaser. They soon were hired to perform on Kate Smith's popular CBS network radio program, turning "Who's on First?" into a nationally acclaimed sketch. They quickly became regulars on Smith's show—eventually earning $1250 a performance—and this success led to their debut on the "legitimate" New York stage.

The show was *The Streets of Paris,* which opened at the Broadhurst Theatre on June 19, 1939. The two-act, 28-scene revue boasted a hodgepodge of acts, including comic Bobby Clark, Luella Gear, and the Brazilian bombshell Carmen Miranda. Jimmy McHugh, Al Dubin, and Harold J. Rome supplied the songs. The *New York Times* saluted, "Out of vaudeville and motion picture stage shows someone has had the wisdom to bring Lou Costello and Bud Abbott to town with some remarkably gutsy stuff. They belong to the traditional school of mountebanks that pairs a dazed clown with an abusive straight man, and throws water freely in its most inspired moments . . . pretty funny fellows in low-comedy antics." The raucous show ran for 274 performances, with audiences continually amazed at the ad-libs, vitality, and anti-Establishment approach provided by Abbott and Costello.

The motion picture industry was at a strange, transitional stage as Bud and Lou traveled westward. Laurel and Hardy, after several battles with mentor Hal Roach (largely induced by ambitious Stan), were soon to leave their producer for a dismal series of films at Twentieth Century-Fox and MGM that would destroy their lofty box-office standing. The Marx Brothers were approaching the end of their MGM stay, and the mirthful Ritz Brothers, whose wild-faced antics had won only limited approval from cinema fans, had left Fox after publicized contract battles with Darryl F. Zanuck over the quality of their vehicles.

Yet while the established screen comedy-team masters neared the end of contracts and appeal, the need for laughter to combat the growing gloom of World War II was at a high.

MGM offered Abbott and Costello $17,500 per picture to perform a routine or two in a Metro film. The team's manager, Eddie Sherman, was against this deal and was proved correct when Universal offered the duo $35,000 to play their routines in an upcoming screen musical. The song-and-dance film in question was being created by Jerome Kern, Dorothy Fields, and Oscar Hammerstein II. Allan Jones, Nancy Kelly, Robert Cummings, and Mary Boland were set to star in it. Before *One Night in the Tropics* (1940) had completed production, a dismayed Jones found that a good deal of the 82-minute running time had been reassigned by director Edward Sutherland to the ex-burlesque team. When the film was released, the *New York Times* would report that Abbott and Costello "stand out like logistical wizards." Universal signed the team to a 4-films-per-year contract at $50,000 a film plus 10 percent of the profits.

One success led to another. In the summer of 1940 the team became the replacement act for Fred Allen on his radio time spot. Then Universal decided to try the pair in a comedy of their own. In September of 1940 the United States Draft Bill had become an unhappy fact of life for the country's young men and the studio tapped the theme for *Buck Privates* (1941). Universal filmed the $180,000 picture in 20 days under the direction of fast-working Arthur Lubin. The result was a slick, attractively packaged bundle of entertainment.* (There were diverting musical interludes by the Andrews Sisters, studio contractees, who sang: "I'll Be with You in Apple Blossom Time," "You're a Lucky Fellow, Mr. Smith," and "Boogie Woogie Bugle Boy.") The comedy team's highlights included the famous routine where Bud teaches Lou close-order drilling, and a boxing match with fleshy Costello clearly outmatched. *Variety* reported how frequently "dialogue drowned in the audience uproar," and Abbott and Costello were suddenly the biggest thing in Hollywood. (The team would repeat their *Buck Privates* performance on "Lux Radio Theatre" on October 13, 1941.)

---

* John Grant who supplied special material for many of the early Abbott and Costello Universal outings stuck to the formula which proved so successful: the comedy pair would perform four to five of their antic routines and the wispy plot would be interwoven around the set pieces.

With Nat Pendleton
in Buck Privates
(1941).

Universal rushed their new stars into more streamlined comedies, all produced with typical studio economy. *In the Navy* (1941) set them loose in blue, with the Andrews Sisters and Dick Powell adding box-office potency. *Hold That Ghost* (1941), one of the team's all-time best films, added comedienne Joan Davis to the fray. *Keep 'Em Flying* (1941), yet another service comedy, offered a frenetic Martha Raye, recuperating from poor handling at Paramount, as twin sisters. At one point in the story, Lou tries to lure Martha into the Tunnel of Love with him.

COSTELLO: We could have a lot of fun in there. We'd get in a boat all by ourselves, and when we got to a place where it was dark and nobody could see us . . .

RAYE: Then what would we do?

COSTELLO: We could take off our shoes and put our feet in the water!

All their films were tremendous box-office hits and they found themselves third in the country's popularity charts, behind those great marquee attractions Mickey Rooney and Clark Gable. At this juncture, Abbott and Costello were re-courted by MGM who signed the pair to a contract by which they were paid $150,000 for one film a year and Universal received a like amount. Also Abbott and Costello began their own Thursday evening radio program. It premiered on October 8, 1941, over NBC with Paramount's Veronica Lake as a guest star. In the six-year run, regulars included Mel Blanc, Sid Fields, and Iris Adrian, with singers Marilyn Maxwell and Connie Haines, and announcer Ken Niles. On December 8, 1941, one day after Pearl Harbor and only 10 months after their first starring film, Bud and Lou placed their hand and foot prints in the celebrated cement slabs of Grauman's Chinese Theatre. At this point they were receiving $150,000 per picture from Universal plus 20% of the profits. For their radio program they earned $20,000 weekly, and $10,000 weekly for stage appearances.

Being schooled in burlesque, Bud and Lou often used film plots merely as background before which they could parade their tried-and-true routines. The practice would both make and break them. The director of their first five Universal films was Arthur Lubin.

He would later recall, "We usually had two cameras, a close-up for Lou, because he had such a doll face, and a close two-shot. I usually tried to have the camera on a dolly, so I could move with them. You couldn't keep them in one position. Lou was all over the place. He was a darling, chubby little guy. I would rehearse with them and would ask them not to give me everything, but just to give me where they were going to go. No one could direct their routines as well as they, because as they went into a routine, something would spark them, and they would add little things here and there.

"It was a joy, it really was, to work with them. They were fabulous."

In 1942 their popularity rose ever higher! (The public was unaware of the increasing squabbles arising between the two stars—over billing, over strength of contribution, etc.) In *Ride 'Em Cowboy* they donned Western duds and broke loose on a dude ranch that included cowboy hero Johnny Mack Brown, evil Indian Douglass Dumbrille, and such musical performers as Tip, Tap, and Toe, the Ink Spots, and Ella Fitzgerald. *Ride 'Em Cowboy* included the famous "Crazy House" sketch, in which Lou, needing relaxation, tries to sleep while in the environs there are a knife-throwing Indian and gun-battling cowboys, not to mention the swami who asks Lou if he would like his palm read (and then smears it with red paint).

The comedians' first MGM film was *Rio Rita* (1942), a haphazard confection which divides the screen time between the boys' antics and the singing of Kathryn Grayson and John Carroll. The *Hollywood Reporter* graciously noted, "They have the best comedy material they've had to date" in this one, the highlight of which was Lou being trapped in a washing machine. However, in typical Hollywood style, after Metro had fought so hard to obtain the screen services of Universal's bonanza, the studio refused to expend very much on the budget. At MGM, Abbott and Costello remained outsiders—Universal players who were beneath the consideration given to Metro contractees.

Back at Universal where the comedy teams of Olsen and Johnson and the Ritz Brothers were not faring especially well, Abbott and Costello played in *Pardon My Sarong* (1942). Abetting the team in this effort were William Demarest (as a flatfoot cop), Lionel Atwill (as a pirate chief), Leif Erickson (as a boastful native—"I biggest stinker of them all!"), and the saronged shapes of Nan Wynn and Marie "The Body" McDonald. Their fourth and final release of 1942 was *Who Done It?* An inspired murder mystery yarn set at a radio station, the film was the first of their features to give full reign to comedy without benefit (?) of musical interludes. By now the team of Abbott and Costello was number one at the cinema popularity polls.

As Bud and Lou became show-business legends with such follow-ups as Universal's *It Ain't Hay* (1943), *In Society* (1944), and *The Naughty Nineties* (1945, in which they performed "Who's on First?"), and MGM's *Lost in a Harem* (1944), the stars attempted to become legends offscreen as well.

They demanded and received royal treatment from Universal, soon earning a percentage of the profits on their pictures and luxuriating in lavish trailers on the lot, where they rested between soundstage scenes. Certainly the economy-minded lot never before tolerated the on-the-set behavior of contractees who indulged in poker games (which held up shooting) and practical jokes (which set the "tone" for the day). "I remember my last birthday with them," says director Lubin. "They filled a suitcase with condoms. For the leading lady, who had a birthday the same day, it was full of Kotex. A suitcase! As they opened it, the contents fell all over the floor!"

Abbott and Costello each bought clubs and restaurants as hopeful but ostentatious investments. They brought relatives to the Coast and supplied them with homes and jobs, gambled extravagantly in Las Vegas, and at the height of their success started to bicker. Soon they were competing not with outsiders but with each other. Each angled to outdo the other in acquiring the better home, the more fanciful luxury. When Bud purchased an Encino mansion, Lou bought a bigger one in Thousand Oaks. When Bud built a leviathan swimming pool, Lou managed to install a pool one foot longer and one foot wider. Lou would become incensed when fans mistakenly called him Abbott and openly insisted in front of his partner that he was the entire show. Lou began referring to his partner as "a jerk," "a caddie," and "a

With Ed Gargan in
Hit the Ice (1943).

punching bag." Once he poured a bottle of beer over Bud's head and cracked, "Now you look as wet as you act!" Occasionally Abbott would respond in amassed anger, as on the occasion when he grabbed a fire extinguisher and saturated his partner. According to witnesses at the fracas, an astounded, furious Costello sputtered, "Do that once more and I'll see you never work again. I'm your meal ticket." As the *New York Times* later explained in Abbott's obituary, "Their conflicts were serious. Mr. Abbott liked arguing, while Mr. Costello was just plain stubborn."

Still, for all their escapades (most of which were concealed from the adoring general public), Bud and Lou accomplished some very positive things. Both were dedicated family men. Bud had wed Betty Smith on September 17, 1918, and had adopted a son (Bud) and daughter (Vickie). Lou had wed Anne Battler in 1934 and had had three daughters (Patricia, Carole, and Christine) and a son (Lou Jr.—known as Butch). Both wives had been dancers who met their husbands on the burlesque circuits. The team tirelessly entertained troops (in California

and on the road), performed to raise money for many charities, and were credited with selling at least $80,000,000 worth of war bonds.

Perhaps the greatest tragedy to befall Costello occurred on November 4, 1943, when his one-year-old son fell into the swimming pool and drowned. Lou was notified only a few hours before he was to go on the air for his radio show. Despite their artistic and personal differences, the first person Costello reached to for support after hearing the grim news was Bud. In shock, Lou insisted on performing that night anyway (guest star Lana Turner was so upset she could hardly speak her lines above a whisper). Afterward, Bud and Lou raised the funds for establishing the Lou Costello Jr. Youth Foundation for Underprivileged Children. It was realized in 1947. To create it, Bud agreed after the tragedy not only to change the salary of the act from 60-40 (which he had received since the team's founding) to 50-50, but also to join Lou in equal participation to pay the costs of maintaining the foundation. (The $80,000 annual cost was absorbed by the city of Los Angeles in the 1950s.)

16

Besides the emotional traumas that almost demolished the phenomenally successful team,* Lou's health was a serious factor in their ability to function. In early 1943 he collapsed from rheumatic fever and was forced to recuperate in bed for nearly six months. (Bud carried on the radio show with substitute guests, Bert Lahr being a frequent visitor.) But somehow the boys managed to pull through, and in 1943 they earned a joint total of $789,628 from just their Universal salaries.

After placing in the top 10 box-office attractions of 1943 and 1944, the comedy team fell out of the prime listing. Weak vehicles such as *Bud Abbott and Lou Costello in Hollywood* (MGM, 1945—which ended their association at that studio) and *Little Giant* (Universal, 1946) kept their popularity scarcely at maintenance level. It did not help matters that astute Alex Gottlieb who had produced their prior Universal efforts had left the series, or that *Little Giant* and *The Time of Their Lives* (Universal, 1946) avoided having the boys play themselves (they were actual storyline characters!). As some analyzed the situation, the team had simply been trotting out its old material for too long, and audiences had better memories than filmmakers cared to believe. Abbott and Costello were becoming stale.

It was at this time that Universal, in financial peril, became Universal-International. The new head of production, William Goetz, was all for firing the team but was persuaded to give them another chance. Thus evolved *Buck Privates Come Home* (1946), an open example of cashing in on past triumphs. The ploy worked well enough.

In 1947 Abbott and Costello's radio program ended and it appeared that now they had run their career course. Then in 1948 Universal-International whipped up a box-office bonanza by resurrecting the horror characters of Count Dracula (Bela Lugosi), the Wolf Man (Lon Chaney, Jr.), the Invisible Man (Vincent Price), and the Frankenstein monster (Glenn Strange), and teaming them with the comedians for *Abbott and Costello Meet Frankenstein* (1948). The gambit worked wonderfully. Audiences howled at scenes such as the one in which lanky Abbott tries to assure rotund Lou that he has *not* witnessed Lugosi's rising from his coffin.

ABBOTT: Listen, *I* know there's no such a person as Dracula. *You* know there's no such a person as Dracula!
COSTELLO: But does *Dracula* know it?

Many deem it the best of all the Abbott and Costello features. Certainly it was the wildest adventure they ever filmed. (During production, the team brought pies in daily to fling at the crew and co-workers.)

The 1948 popularity polls placed them back in the top 10 attractions and they remained there for three more years. Yet the quality of their features went drastically downhill. Universal had never regained its enthusiasm for these comedians and there were constant battles over the proceeds from re-issues of prior Abbott and Costello features at home and abroad and the sale of home movie rights to segments of their various Universal feature romps. For their individual production companies, the team made two films: *Jack and the Beanstalk* (Warner Bros., 1952) and *Abbott and Costello Meet Captain Kidd* (Warner Bros., 1952). Each film was budgeted at approximately $450,000, with Bud being paid $200,000 to appear in the first and Lou's company keeping any profits from the feature, and the reverse on the second outing. *Jack and the Beanstalk* was the team's first color film; . . . *Meet Captain Kidd* featured a very hammy Charles Laughton as the infamous pirate. The screen partners hit a professional low with *Abbott and Costello Go to Mars* (1953), a cheap send-up of the then current science-fiction movie cycle. Meanwhile, Universal forced out more *Abbott and Costello Meet . . .* monster pictures, including . . . *the Killer Boris Karloff* (1949), . . . *the Invisible Man* (1951), . . . *Dr. Jekyll and Mr. Hyde* (1953, again with Karloff), and . . . *the Mummy* (1955). After that

* It was in 1945 that the team of Abbott and Costello split apart temporarily. The impetus for the long-brewing action was Abbott's hiring of a maid whom Costello had fired. Lou considered the action an affront and wanted to dissolve their partnership there and then. Calmer heads prevailed and the two players were urged to embark on their summer "in person" tour on the East Coast. Onstage the pair were their rollicking selves; offstage they spoke to one another only through intermediaries. The press played up the feud to the fullest extent. By the time Abbott and Costello returned to California, it was agreed that their tandem knockabout comedy would continue for some time to come.

film, their Universal contract expired, and it was not renewed. By then, the comedy team of Dean Martin and Jerry Lewis had long been enthroned as filmdom's best-loved pranksters.

While Abbott and Costello's movie career careened, the pair found steady work in television. On January 7, 1951, the duo became one of the guest hosts (others included Eddie Cantor, Bob Hope, Donald O'Connor, Jimmy Durante, and Martin and Lewis) of NBC-TV's "The Colgate Comedy Hour." They would appear regularly on the program until 1954, frequently reprising their standard routines. In 1952 they shot the first of 52 half-hour black-and-white episodes of "The Abbott and Costello Show," which premiered via Revue Syndication on December 5, 1952. With such regulars as Hillary Brooke, Joe Besser, and Sid Fields, the program provided the stars with ample opportunity to tape their well-proven material. (Lou made his brother Pat the nominal producer of the TV show, continuing the nepotism he had forced upon Universal in the mid-Forties when his father joined the payroll for a spell. Later Sebastian, Pat, and Lou's brother-in-law, Joe Kirk, were on salary for the team's radio program.)

By the time their film career tottered with the expiration of their Universal pact (1955), their video careers were in a similar state. They had to wait a year before a firm film offer materialized—the poor, independently made *Dance with Me, Henry* (1956). It was the comedians' last picture together.

It was in late 1956 that Costello and Abbott came to the final parting of their professional path. Sid Kuller produced and wrote a revue, *Miltown Revisited,* for presentation at the Sahara Hotel in Las Vegas. The team was paid $30,000 a week and, if successful, the revue would play Reno, Lake Tahoe, and then be sent on an eastern tour. However, at the second show on opening night, Abbott appeared onstage in a "glazed" condition, leaving an aggravated Costello to carry the routines himself. Only by the grace of their manager's diplomacy did the team survive the Sahara engagement. Thereafter they went their separate paths.

The press was informed that the main reason for the split was professional: Bud wanted to retire and Lou preferred to keep

With Charles Laughton in Abbott and Costello Meet Captain Kidd *(1952).*

working at his usual frantic pace. "I worried about Bud for 20 years," Lou admitted in a *TV Guide* interview at this time. "Would he be there for rehearsal? Would he make the airport on time? Did he know the new material?"

Reveling in a new career, Lou began as a regular visitor on "The Steve Allen Show" (at $7,500 per program), gave straight guest performances on 1958 episodes of "G. E. Theatre" and "Wagon Train" (as a down-and-out frontier type accused of murder), and teamed with Sid Fields in a Las Vegas act called "Minsky's Follies of 1958." Many who saw the Nevada show noted that Lou did not have his heart in his performance.* Costello then starred with Dorothy Provine in Columbia's low-budget *The 30 Foot Bride of Candy Rock* (1959). (Daughter Carole would have a brief bit in the picture. Years later daughter Chris would become a club vocalist.)

This film would be posthumously released (and quickly forgotten). A heart attack struck Lou on February 26, 1959. As he recuperated in Beverly Hills' Doctors' Hospital, a second attack killed him on March 3, 1959. Bud Abbott, who was suing his ex-partner for $222,465.19 in connection with their television show, appeared a very drawn man at the requiem Mass in North Hollywood four days later. Among those attending the services were Red Skelton, Joe E. Brown, Danny Thomas, Leo Carrillo, George Jessel, and Jerry Colonna. Abbott, overcome with despair, was reportedly inebriated at the tearful occasion. Costello was buried in a mausoleum at Calvary Cemetery near the final resting place of his son, Lou Jr. Later in 1959, Lou's mother, Helen, passed away.

Both entertainers had a history of battles with the Internal Revenue Service. Their manager, Eddie Sherman, recalled of their salaries, "They thought it would never stop. They spent it all each year, forgetting that they had a partner, Uncle Sam." Lou had settled a tax problem shortly before his death. Not long after Costello's funeral, the Internal Revenue Service faced Abbott with a demand for back taxes estimated at $750,000. The crushed performer, who had

settled into what he trusted would be a comfortable retirement, was forced to sell his home, property (including his wife's diamonds), and even his percentage in the Abbott and Costello films. But these drastic measures were not enough to meet the tax demands. He then made a plea for each of his old fans to send him a dollar so he might extricate himself from his awesome debt. It met with public indifference.

By the close of 1960, Bud had made peace with the IRS ("Today I don't owe the government a dime") and was living in a very modest tract home in California's Woodland Hills on Redwing Street, near the Motion Picture Country House. His lifestyle was in vast contrast to the palmy days when he was chauffeured about Hollywood in a custom-made Cadillac with genuine alligator upholstery. Returning to work, he tackled a small dramatic role on "G. E. Theatre" (April 16, 1961), playing the agent of club-comic Lee Marvin. The episode was filmed at Universal studios. It met with unimpressive results. Thereafter, Bud played a few club dates with comic Candy Candido (a former teammate of Jimmy Durante), with Candido performing an unabashed imitation of Lou. Abbott's only professional work after that was supplying his own voice for a series of 200 Abbott and Costello TV cartoons for Hanna-Barbera Productions in 1967.

It became publicly known in his last years that Bud was an epileptic, which he blamed for his drinking problem. From late 1964 (shortly before Universal released an uninspired compilation feature, *The World of Abbott and Costello*) until his death, he suffered several strokes. In 1972 he fell and broke his hip, which forced him to remain in a wheelchair for the rest of his days. Near the end, Bud was asking for onetime fans to write him letters of appreciation.

On April 24, 1974, Bud Abbott died of cancer in his Woodland Hills home, seven months after celebrating 55 years of marriage with his wife, Betty. On April 27 there were quiet services for the comedian at the First Christian Church in Reseda, California. His body was cremated and the ashes strewn over the ocean. His widow was forced to sell the Redwing Street house, with the proceeds going to the state of California for new tax claims.

---

* The Sahara management was so concerned about the poor business the revue was doing, it suggested a ballyhooed reunion of Abbott and Costello. However, Lou refused to split the $10,000 weekly salary 50-50; he wanted to pay Abbott only $500 a week. Their manager refused to insult Bud with such an offer.

The wacky world of Abbott and Costello.

On November 5, 1978, NBC-TV presented the telefeature *Bud and Lou*, starring Harvey Korman and Buddy Hackett. The *Los Angeles Times* reported: "Not surprisingly, Harvey Korman brings dignity to his Bud Abbott. The revelation is Buddy Hackett. The seemingly irrepressible clown gives a thoroughly disciplined, poignant performance as Lou Costello, making him an essentially warm and appealing man who nonetheless was an often tormented and trying individual. The scene in which Korman and Hackett handle the news of the death of Costello's baby really is a heart-wrencher." The *Hollywood Reporter* noted: "The film doesn't shirk the conflicts, disagreements, selfishness, and irre-sponsibility that eventually ripped the team apart and left them virtually penniless when they died." What the telefeature could not reproduce was the miracle of chemistry that the two late, great performers created when they appeared together.

In retrospect, nobody has ever called Abbott and Costello geniuses of comedy, but they were talented craftsmen whose antics appealed to the less-demanding natures of audiences. When they were operating at peaks of inspiration, they could be deliciously amusing in the broad realms of slapstick and verbal chicanery. They possessed the talent to make people laugh, a rare gift indeed.

20

Advertisement for TV movie *Bud and Lou* on NBC-TV *(November 15. 1978).*

Feature Films

One Night in the Tropics (*Universal 1940*)
Buck Privates (*Universal 1941*)
In the Navy (*Universal 1941*)
Hold That Ghost (*Universal 1941*)
Keep 'Em Flying (*Universal 1941*)
Ride 'Em Cowboy (*Universal 1942*)
Rio Rita (*MGM 1942*)
Pardon My Sarong (*Universal 1942*)
Who Done It? (*Universal 1942*)
It Ain't Hay (*Universal 1943*)
Hit the Ice (*Universal 1943*)
Lost in a Harem (*MGM 1944*)
In Society (*Universal 1944*)
Here Come the Co-eds (*Universal 1945*)
The Naughty Nineties (*Universal 1945*)
Bud Abbott and Lou Costello in Hollywood (*MGM 1945*)
Little Giant (*Universal 1946*)
The Time of Their Lives (*Universal 1946*)
Buck Privates Come Home (*Universal 1946*)
The Wistful Widow of Wagon Gap (*Universal 1947*)
The Noose Hangs High (*Eagle Lion 1948*)
Abbott and Costello Meet Frankenstein (*Universal 1948*)
Mexican Hayride (*Universal 1948*)

Africa Screams (*United Artists 1949*)
Abbott and Costello Meet the Killer Boris Karloff (*Universal 1949*)
Abbott and Costello in the Foreign Legion (*Universal 1950*)
Abbott and Costello Meet the Invisible Man (*Universal 1951*)
Comin' Round the Mountain (*Universal 1951*)
Jack and the Beanstalk (*Warner Bros. 1952*)
Lost in Alaska (*Universal 1952*)
Abbott and Costello Meet Captain Kidd (*Warner Bros. 1952*)
Abbott and Costello Go to Mars (*Universal 1953*)
Abbott and Costello Meet Dr. Jekyll and Mr. Hyde (*Universal 1953*)
Abbott and Costello Meet the Keystone Kops (*Universal 1955*)
Abbott and Costello Meet the Mummy (*Universal 1955*)
Dance with Me, Henry (*United Artists 1956*)

Lou Costello alone:
The 30 Foot Bride of Candy Rock (*Columbia 1959*)

Woody Allen

"I don't want to achieve immortality through my work. I want to achieve it through not dying."

With these words Woody Allen, the poor-soul schlemiel with the glasses, thinning mud-red hair, and shrimpy frame, has sought to dismiss the huzzahs of genius that serenade him today as cinema comedy's prime force. He insists, "People have always thought of me as an intellectual comedian, and I'm not. I'm a one-liner comic like Bob Hope and Henny Youngman. I do the wife jokes. I make faces. I'm a comedian in the classic style."

Still, whether he likes it or not, Woody Allen has earned the position of today's number one motion picture funnyman. He is a superb talent (albeit sometimes undisciplined) who writes, directs, and performs, producing box-office eruptions like *Bananas* (1971) and *Everything You Always Wanted to Know About Sex but Were Afraid to Ask* (1972), films which have become standards in revival theatre repertoires.

Beginning as a television writer and progressing to becoming a stand-up nightclub comic, Woody has also mastered the media of television, recordings, the Broadway stage (as writer and performer), and the world of prose (columns in The *New Yorker* magazine and several books of his wit). Whenever Woody is cornered and almost bullied into admitting he is a very, very talented man, he credits his success to his heroes: George S. Kaufman, the Marx Brothers, and Bob Hope. But as Groucho himself responded, "They say Allen got something from the Marx Brothers. He didn't. He's an original. The best. The funniest."

He was born Allen Stewart Konigsberg in the Flatbush section of Brooklyn, New York, on Sunday, December 1, 1935.* His father, Martin Konigsberg, worked at a variety of jobs, including stints as a waiter at Sammy's Bowery Follies of Manhattan and a jewelry engraver. His mother, Nettie (Cherry) Konigsberg, was a bookkeeper for a Brooklyn flower shop. Allen, who quickly obtained the convenient and welcome nickname of

* Allen once joked, "When the other kids learned my name, they'd beat me up. So I'd tell them my name was Frank, but they'd still beat me up."

23

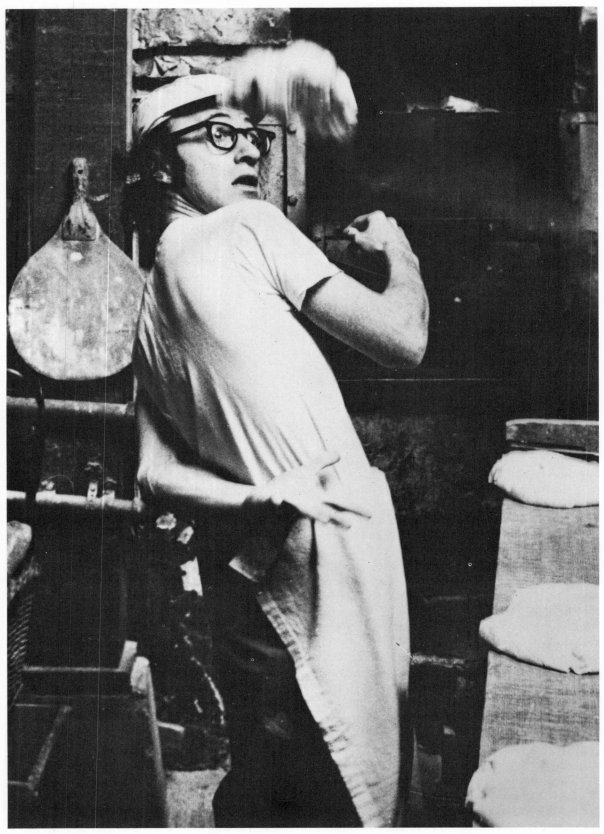

In Play It Again, Sam *(1972).*

Woody, attended P.S. 99 and Brooklyn's Midwood High School, where, he recalls, his scholarship "varied between below average and way below average."

From childhood, Woody was infatuated with comedy, especially the brand practiced by Groucho Marx and Bob Hope. Accordingly, he tried his skill at writing jokes and began sending his efforts to columnists Walter Winchell and Earl Wilson. To his amazement, the newsmen began using his one-liners in their syndicated columns. Wilson ran the first, "Woody Allen says he ate at a restaurant that had OPS prices—over people's salaries." His newspaper exposure won him a $25 weekly salary offer from publicist David Alber to write jokes that would be credited in show-business columns to such "wits" as Arthur Murray, Guy Lombardo, and Sammy Kaye, for the sake of their own publicity. Woody worked at the job for two years and estimates he created some 25,000 jokes in the unglorified ghost position.

Woody's creativity continued to find paying outlets. By the time he was 17, in 1953, he was an NBC staff writer, providing material for Peter Lind Hayes and Herb Shriner. In the meantime he enrolled at New York University, where his poor grades led to his quick dismissal. Later he matriculated at City College of New York where a similar fate awaited him. However, his poor showings as a student hardly hurt him professionally. He became a full-time comedy writer for NBC, cranking out material for such performers as Sid Caesar, Art Carney, Kaye Ballard, Buddy Hackett, Pat Boone, Carol Channing, Jack Paar, and the "Tonight Show." In 1957 the 21-year-old Woody won a Sylvania Award for a Sid Caesar TV show he wrote. He also earned several Emmy nominations, and by 1961 he was a $1,700 per week writer for the "Garry Moore Show."

Despite his success, insecurity-prone Woody soon began having misgivings about his job. "Writing for other comedians is a lifetime in a blind alley . . . there is no future in being a TV writer. You can hack around from show to show and you're always worried—is the comedian you're writing for going to be dropped because of bad ratings? And if he is dropped, you may find yourself moving 3,000 miles to the other coast to write for a new comedian. It's a rough business."

Hence, Woody was amenable to the wise suggestion of his manager, Jack Rollins, that he try entertaining *sans* the middleman and become a nightclub performer. Despite very frightening personal handicaps ("lack of confidence and fear of getting up in front of an audience"), Woody made his debut as an unpaid jokester at Greenwich Village's Duplex. The 5'5½", 120-pound bespectacled entertainer clicked with audiences and soon received offers to work (for money) at such posh clubs as the Blue Angel and the Bitter End. The *New York Times* recommended Woody to "anyone who is interested in watching a rising young comic develop into an established young comic." Audiences howled at some of the diminutive entertainer's more woesome tales:

> I keep having this birthday cake fantasy, where they wheel out a big cake with a girl in it and she pops out and hurts me and gets back in.
>
> *Or*
>
> My grandfather had a wonderful funeral. It was a catered funeral with accordion players and a buffet table, and there was a replica of the deceased in potato salad.
>
> *Or*
>
> My wife was an immature woman. I'd be in the bathroom taking a bath and she would walk right in and sink my boats.*

Woody's humor found a ready audience across the country in such popular night spots as Mister Kelly's (Chicago), the Hungry i (San Francisco), and the Crescendo (Los Angeles). On December 22, 1963, Woody appeared with Count Basie & His Orchestra at Carnegie Hall, and by the end of 1964 he was able to demand $10,000 for a single personal appearance.

Also in 1963 Woody made a 30-minute TV pilot, co-starring Alan Alda and Louise Lasser. It dealt with a group of improvisational comics who hope to appear on Ed Sullivan's TV show. *The Laughmakers* was never commercially telecast, but is now available for home viewing. Simultaneously, Woody be-

---

* In 1955 Woody had wed 16-year-old Harlene Rosen, a Hunter College student. Woody would recall, "For a while we pondered whether to take a vacation or get a divorce. We decided that a trip to Bermuda is over in two weeks, but a divorce is something you always have." They were divorced in 1960. She later became a teacher in Greenwich Village.

came popular with television audiences, guesting on the talk shows of Merv Griffin and Jack Paar. In July 1964 Woody replaced Johnny Carson as host for a week on the "Tonight" program and received terrific national response. At about this time he recorded two LP albums of his routines on the Colpix label. (The fact that his records never became good-sellers always baffled Allen, for he feels that they contain some of his best material.)

It was while appearing at New York's Blue Angel in 1964 that Woody received his first movie offer. Agent-*cum*-producer Charles Feldman interested Woody in writing and acting in a film to be called *What's New Pussycat?* which was to star Warren Beatty. Allen wrote three drafts. In the meantime, Beatty dropped out of the project. What was originally envisioned as a minor effort mushroomed into a major property. The result was the 1965 box-office winner that the *New York World-Telegram* labeled "a hurricane of hilarity." With location work in Paris, the episodic, slapstick venture boasted an impressive cast: Peter O'Toole, Peter Sellers, Romy Schneider, Paula Prentiss, Capucine, Ursula Andress, and Woody as the sex-hungry wardrober of a striptease house. Though his contribution to the wild proceedings was praised by all those involved in the filmmaking, Woody was very shy around the stars and spent most of his free time teaching himself new tunes on his clarinet.

Woody's next cinema effort was a shoe-string affair named *What's Up, Tiger Lily?* (1966), an American International release. Woody's delightfully unique concept was to take a 1964 Japanese film, *Kizino Kizi (Key of Keys)*, erase the soundtrack, reedit the picture, dub in English, add several new sequences, commentary, and the music of the Lovin' Spoonful, and create 80 minutes of what he termed "bottled in Bond spy drama." Wrote the *Saturday Review*, "After a spate of lengthy spectacles such as *Hawaii* that bit off considerably more than they could chew, I found myself not only pleased but grateful to comedian Woody Allen for a marvelously unpretentious little movie that sets its sights

In What's Up, Tiger Lily? *(1966).*

In **Casino Royale** *(1967).*

modestly, then scores bull's-eye after bull's-eye all the way. . . . Allen's sense of fun is at once low-keyed, far out, and hip."

Woody then moved into the major leagues with the expensive, if misguided, *Casino Royale* (1967), Columbia's $12,000,000 James Bond spoof. The overexpansive feature utilized five directors (John Huston, Ken Hughes, Val Guest, Robert Parrish, and Joe McGrath), a sterling roster of principals (David Niven, Peter Sellers, Ursula Andress, Orson Welles), and several guest stars (Deborah Kerr, William Holden, Charles Boyer, John Huston, Kurt Kasznar, George Raft, Jean-Paul Belmondo, Peter O'Toole), not to mention the location work in England, Ireland, and France. Woody appeared as the devious Jimmy Bond who turns out to be the head of SMERSH and winds up swallowing a bomb. He made a few, small contributions to the script, but the colossal production remained, in the words of the *New York World-Journal-Tribune,* "A relentless spoof. . . .

Casino Royale offers proof positive that the best of premises, talents, and initial ideas can, like the biggest of balloons, go phfft and collapse."

Meanwhile, Woody remarried on February 2, 1966. His bride was Louise Lasser,* who had understudied Barbra Streisand in Broadway's *I Can Get It for You Wholesale* (1962), had a bit in *What's New Pussycat?,* and would eventually emerge as the star of the 1976 TV hit series, "Mary Hartman, Mary Hartman." The couple set up house in a six-room brownstone in Manhattan.

Woody's next show-business target was the Broadway stage. Shortly after completing his role in *Casino Royale,* he scored as

* She was born on April 11, 1941 (or 1939), in New York City, the daughter of tax expert/author S. Jay Lasser. Besides appearing in the Woody Allen films *What's Up, Tiger Lily?* and *Take the Money and Run* (1969), she appeared on Broadway in the short-lived 1967 musical *Henry, Sweet Henry* and in a number of off-Broadway efforts, and in other movies, *Such Good Friends* (1972) and *Slither* (1973) among them.

the author of the play *Don't Drink the Water* (Morosco Theatre: November 17, 1966), produced by David Merrick. The comedy of a family of American tourists caught behind the Iron Curtain starred Lou Jacobi, Kay Medford (replacing Vivian Vance), Anita Gillette, and Anthony Roberts. It ran for 598 performances, and was eventually turned into a (mediocre) film with Jackie Gleason and Estelle Parsons. Allen's next Broadway play was *Play It Again, Sam* (Broadhurst Theatre: February 12, 1969). He not only wrote the comedy, but starred as Allan Felix, a Humphrey Bogart worshipper who is advised on his love troubles by the ghost of Bogart himself (impersonated by Jerry Lacy). Diane Keaton and Anthony Roberts provided the other lead characterizations. The *New York Times* reported, "Mr. Allen has the heart of a comedian and the tongue of a comic, and it is no bad combination. He makes *Play It Again, Sam* into a cheerful, virtuous romp, and, of course, he is joyous." The show ran for 453 performances. (Bob Denver replaced Woody in January 1970 for the remainder of the Broadway run.)

During the summer of 1969, while Woody was appearing in *Play It Again, Sam, Take the Money and Run* premiered. The film comedy starred Woody as Virgil Stockwell, a lifelong failure who becomes an inept thief. He directed and co-wrote (with Mickey Rose) the offbeat vehicle. The *New York Times* was impressed: "Woody Allen's *Take the Money and Run* is a very funny movie. The film is the cinematic equivalent to one of Allen's best comic monologues, a kind of cowardly epic peopled with shy FBI agents, cons who are wanted for dancing with mailmen, overanalyzing parents, and a lady blackmailer who has the soul of a Jewish mother—she likes to feed her victims good, hot meals . . . this is [Allen's] . . . first attempt at direction. The nicest surprise of *Take the Money and Run* is that it shows he has been able to complement visually the word-oriented humor of the writer-performer. . . . Allen has made a movie that is, in effect, a feature-length, two-reel comedy—something very special and eccentric and funny."

It was two years before Woody emerged on the screen again. During this period he and Louise Lasser divorced (1969), although they remained close friends. Of her he would say,

she is "brighter than I am, funnier than I am . . . the only person who can cheer me up."

Bananas (1971) was pure Woody Allen— wacky, slightly sick, and jam-packed with one-liners and sight gags. Again Woody directed and co-wrote (with Mickey Rose). Starred as the hero Fielding Mellish, Woody survived a childhood in which he frequently received shocks from his electric blanket (he was a bed wetter) and stole pornographic books in braille so he could rub the dirty parts. With location work in Puerto Rico and New York, a musical score by Marvin Hamlisch, co-stars including ex-wife Louise Lasser and sports commentator Howard Cosell, and a plot hinging on a South American revolution, *Bananas* was heralded generally as the most inventive and outrageous cinema nonsense since the palmiest days of the Marx Brothers.

Audiences were appreciative of such askew comedy scenes as Cosell officiating for the "Wide World of Sports" at the assassination of a Latin American dictator ("When did you know it was all over?") and the consummation of the hero and heroine's marriage. The *Washington Post* championed, "*Bananas* . . . is, in a word, hilarious. And the sooner you can arrange to see it, the better, since delighted and well-meaning friends are going to have a terrible time keeping the best lines and sight gags to themselves." There was, however, some dissension from critics who thought Woody's celluloid comedy had become too freewheeling and too often tasteless (his unsubtle spoofs at Christianity earned the film a "Condemned" rating from the Roman Catholic Church's Legion of Decency).

In late 1971 Woody began work on a PBS network special satirizing politics. The results were so controversial that the usually bold Public Broadcasting System shelved it. But there were two Woody Allen theatrical films in release in 1972. The first was the Paramount screen version of *Play It Again, Sam.* He adapted his play, with Herbert Ross directing. Woody, Diane Keaton, Anthony Roberts, and Jerry Lacy ("I never met a dame who didn't understand a slap in the mouth or a slug from a .45") repeated their Broadway roles. *Cue* magazine wrote, "Woody Allen is the funniest man working in films today.

What's more, his potential is such that he could conceivably prove to be one of the most important satirists films have produced." *Play It Again, Sam,* with its location filming in San Francisco, grossed $5,757,000 in distributors' domestic rentals at the box office.

The second 1972 release was *Everything You Always Wanted to Know About Sex but Were Afraid to Ask.* It owed little more than its title to Dr. David Reuben's bestselling tome. Woody directed and wrote this outlandish farce, which included seven* sketches: (1) "Do Aphrodisiacs Work?" with court jester Woody smitten with the queen (Lynn Redgrave), (2) "What Is Sodomy?" in which Gene Wilder falls madly in love with a sheep, (3) "Why Do Some Women Have Trouble Reaching an Orgasm?" wherein Woody and Louise Lasser, a married couple, discover that she can reach orgasm only in public places, (4) "Are Transvestites Homosexual?" in which plump Lou Jacobi gets his jollies capering in drag, (5) "What Are Sex Perverts?" wherein game-show host Jack Barry and contestants Pamela Mason, Regis Philbin, Toni Holt, and Robert Q. Lewis try to guess the sexual hang-ups of the visiting guest, (6) "Are the Findings of Doctors and Clinics Who Do Sexual Research Accurate?" with mad John Carradine imprisoning Woody and unleashing a giant breast later caught by our hero in a giant brassiere, and (7) "What Happens During Ejaculation?" featuring Woody as a reluctant spermatozoon who has to live up to the order "You took an oath to fertilize an ovum or die in the attempt." (Burt Reynolds and Tony Randall appeared in the sketch as technicians working to launch him on his way.)

Everything You Always Wanted to Know was Woody's biggest commercial hit to that point—it grossed $8,500,000 in U.S. and Canadian distributors' rentals—and many reviewers like Judith Crist found it "pure hilarity," "probably the best of Allen's superb brewings," and "the funniest sex comedy we've encountered to date." However, *Variety* described the film as "tasteless" and "disappointing," and some reviewers stated in strong language that they saw nothing amusing about Lou Jacobi in a smart dress or a scene of a sheep in a garter belt.

* There was an eighth sketch, edited out, featuring Woody and Louise Lasser as spiders.

Sleeper, Woody's comedy release of 1973, was co-written with Marshall Brickman. The concoction dealt with a Greenwich Village health-food store owner (Woody) who is frozen and launched into the year 2173. As the hero reflects, "There are two important things that come once in a lifetime: sex and death. But at least after death you aren't nauseous." Of this project, which once had been planned as a Vincent Price vehicle, memorable sequences include Allen's masquerade as a robot and his escape, with Diane Keaton,* in a rusty 200-year-old Volkswagen that starts up on the first try. *Films in Review* called Woody "the most inventive comedian in films" and termed *Sleeper* "his most cohesive and probably his funniest work to date. Although laced with rapid-fire verbal and sight gags, it has a unity, or approaches it, that his other films have lacked."

The equally elaborate *Love and Death* (1975) was directed and written by Woody and starred him as Boris Grushenko, a thinker in the days of the Napoleonic Wars who becomes an accidental war hero and ensuingly becomes aggressively cocky. In his postwar strutting Woody beds a countess. When she praises his lovemaking, he replies, "I practice a lot when I'm alone!" *Films in Review* hailed the costumed comedy as "a gem, a cockeyed, minor *War and Peace.*"

The following year witnessed the release of *The Front* (1976), a deliberately none too funny but deeply enthralling picture about the blacklisting of the Senator Joseph McCarthy era. The director (Martin Ritt) and the scripter (Walter Bernstein) were both blacklist victims, as were supporting players Herschel Bernardi (as a producer without the guts to fight the movement) and Zero Mostel (as the comic whom the blacklist drives to unemployment and suicide). Woody starred as a schnook who "fronts" for several black-

* The attractive Miss Keaton, who appeared as Mrs. Michael Corleone in *The Godfather* (1971) and *The Godfather: Part II* (1974), would gain tremendous acclaim for her interpretation of the death-seeking frequenter of *Looking for Mr. Goodbar* (1977). In the Seventies she had replaced Louise Lasser as the woman in Woody's life on- and offscreen. For a period when she and Woody *were* lovers, they shared quarters together in New York. Like Allen, she is hardly cocksure—"I just don't like the way I look and sound." Says Johnny Carson, "I think she's Woody's sister. Both of them are uncomfortable and withdrawn in a crowd. She's a free spirit—and her vulnerability is a good quality. She's honest about being what she is, and that's rare."

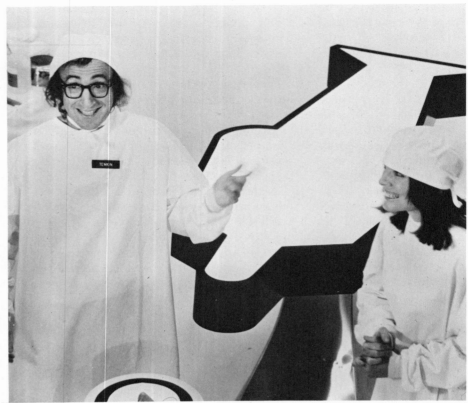

With Diane Keaton
in Sleeper (1973).

Second from left; in
Love and Death
(1975).

listed TV writers by posing, for a salary, as the author of their video scripts. He is eventually summoned before the investigating committee and his climactic words ("Fellas, I really don't think you have the right to ask me these questions. And furthermore, you can all go——yourselves") caused audiences to burst into cheers. The *Baltimore News-American* called *The Front* "a rare thing—an entertaining, commercial movie that should make you think about some serious things." At the Teheran International Film Festival in December 1976, *The Front* was named Best Feature of the Year.

Some audiences were quick to express displeasure with *The Front*. Woody Allen had come to mean a barrage of nonstop gags and quips to many people and they felt he had no right to fracture the successful formula. Woody disagreed. In an interview granted over a decade ago, he was already insisting, "Once you start to think about, 'Do the newspapers like me, or did the audience like me, or am I making enough money, or should I be doing this?' you are in trouble. The only important thoughts are: '*Am I being as funny as possible in as many different ways?*' Once you view the rewards too tantalizingly, you're dead. Then you start accepting and turning down jobs on the basis of how it affects your income tax. Then you might as well be working in Macy's, except that the money is better in this business."

The intellectually complex Mr. Allen also once stated, "All my films have been personal failures. This is not to say that an audience, not knowing the grandiose plans I had in mind when I undertook the project, can't go in and find something to enjoy. . . . But none of them leaves me with a good feeling. I finish them and I don't want to see them again. I can only see all the mistakes and embarrassing moments. I can't get to the point where they're a kick for me. . . . The only criticism that is meaningful to me—really meaningful—comes from a few close people. Diane [Keaton], who is a good friend of mine, probably is the most important to me in terms of criticism. . . . If I hand Diane a script and she tells me it is not a good script, it is more meaningful to me than what anyone else has to say."

Keaton highly approved of his next script, *Annie Hall* (1977). As with all Woody's lat-est films, it was lensed in complete secrecy (quite a feat considering it was shot mostly on New York streets) and did not have a title until a few weeks before it was finished. To quote one reviewer, the leading figure (Keaton) in *Annie Hall* is "a fresh-faced, slightly loopy innocent from the Midwest who eats her pastrami with mayonnaise, washes her face with black soap, and falls temporarily in love with a gloomy New York comic." That these characteristics were a close approximation of the real-life Miss Keaton and her relationship with Allen led many critics and filmgoers to assume that the picture was merely a catharsis of the love affair that had turned into a strong professional and platonic alliance. In explaining the movie's premise, Allen described, "I wanted it to be about . . . *real* people, *real* problems besetting some fairly neurotic characters trying to exist in male-female relationships in America, in 1977. So it turns out to be far more serious than anything I've ever tried before."

In detailing his rather unique relationship with United Artists Pictures, Woody states:

> . . . I have a nice simple gentlemen's agreement with the studio. The best of anyone, artistically. I've traded the idea of making millions and millions from them for my artistic control. For instance, I hate having my pictures shown on TV—everything sliced up with deodorant commercials—and they've agreed they won't allow that as long as my movies make a profit. Not necessarily a huge profit—none of mine ever have. [*Take the Money and Run* and *Sleeper* finally debuted on network TV in 1978.]
>
> UA doesn't get to approve scripts, my casting, anything. I just come to them with a movie which can be made for $2 million, at the very most $3 million, which is not a lot today. The movie will not be starring Barbra Streisand or Robert Redford—I have no real interest in working with stars—therefore it won't cost so much.

With the above firmly in mind, hardly anyone was prepared for the tremendous reception given *Annie Hall* when it debuted in late April 1977. "Never before has the diminutive comedian been so urbane, so open—so funny," wrote the *Hollywood Reporter*. "In his idiosyncratic, comic terms, what Allen is attempting here is not so much different from what his favorite director, Ingmar Bergman, did in *Scenes from a Marriage*. This film could be called *Scenes from a Relationship*. Allen and Keaton go through just about all the emotional changes one could expect from an intelligent contemporary couple, only in this case the anguish is masked by the surface bravery of Allen's wisecracking and Keaton's deft retorts."

In his praise of *Annie Hall,* the *New York Times'* Vincent Canby observed, "One of Mr. Allen's talents as a director is his casting. . . . Most prominent are Paul Simon as a recording industry promoter, Carol Kane as Alvy's [Woody Allen] politically committed first wife, Tony Roberts as Alvy's actor-friend, Colleen Dewhurst as Annie Hall's mother, and Christopher Walken as Annie's quietly suicidal brother. That's to name only a few."

It was Canby of the *Times* who realized:

Because Mr. Allen has his roots as a writer of one-liners and was bred in television and nightclubs, standing up, it's taken us quite a while to recognize just how prodigiously talented he is, and how different he has always been from those colleagues who also make their livings as he once did, racing from Las Vegas to the Coast to Tahoe to San Juan, then back to Las Vegas. Among other things, he's the first major American film maker ever to come out of a saloon.

For all of Mr. Allen's growth as a writer, director, and actor, *Annie Hall* is not terribly far removed from *Take the Money and Run,* his first work as a triple-threat man, which is not to put down the new movie but to upgrade the earlier one. *Take the Money and Run* was a visualized nightclub monologue, as freely associated as an analysand's introspections on the couch.

This also is more or less the form of *Annie Hall,* Alvy Singer's freewheeling self-deprecating, funny and sorrowful search for the truth about his on-again, off-again affair with a beauti-

ful young woman who is as emotionally bent as he is. The form of the two films is similar, but where the first was essentially a cartoon, *Annie Hall* has the humane sensibility of comedy.

By August 1977, four months after its initial domestic release, *Annie Hall* had grossed $19 million in 2,000 U.S. and Canadian engagements. It disproved the old theory that Woody's films were too sophisticated for "rural audiences." (*Annie Hall* would prove a prize-winning bonanza for Woody. Not only did the picture achieve prizes for Allen from the New York Film Critics, the National Film Society, the Directors Guild of America, and the British Academy of Film and Television Arts, but it engendered four Academy Awards: best picture, best direction, best original screenplay, and best actress. It lost in the Oscar sweepstakes only in the best actor rivalry to Richard Dreyfuss' performance in *The Goodbye Girl.* Publicity-shy Woody did not show up at the Oscar Awards. Instead he could be found playing his clarinet at Michael's Pub in Manhattan.)

With such spectacular results from *Annie Hall,* the press was eager to learn more details about Allen's next project, which started shooting in New York on October 17, 1977. The cast included Diane Keaton, Maureen Stapleton, Genevieve Page, E. G. Marshall, Sam Waterston, and Richard Jordan. One person who did not appear in this psychological drama was Allen. When asked if his new picture reflected his Ingmar Bergmanish sense of misery, the often-secretive star-comedian responded, "Not really. I don't say this with false modesty, but right now I'm faced with the pitfalls of half-baked ideas and derivative techniques. I'm feeling my way, just as when I was beginning as a cabaret comedian, I had a tendency to lean on people who had influenced me. I have to watch out for touches of other people in my work. This movie is an exploration, and I'm anxious to get it made so that I can take a look at it and see what I've done."

When *Interiors* opened in the late summer of 1978, audiences—although warned in advance—were not prepared that the film's tone would be so sombre. As *Variety* observed:

. . . this is stonefaced straight drama about death, art and the human condition. It is full of pain, angst and psychic suffering. There isn't a single joke in the script; not one scene is played for laughs. Except for two or three minutes when source music is heard in the background, the film uses no music. The opening credits, in plain typeface, come on screen over silence. . . . Watching this picture a question keeps recurring: What would Woody Allen think of all this? Then you remember he wrote and directed it.

The *New York Times'* Vincent Canby judged:

Rather than describe *Interiors* as his first serious drama, I think it's more precise to say that it's the first Woody Allen film that doesn't care to be funny. That's something else entirely. . . .

Interiors is not inaptly titled. From the opening sequence, a series of shots looking out at the sea from the sparely furnished rooms of a large, handsome Long Island beach house, it's apparent that we are to be given a film about emotional drain, unfulfilled longings and vaguely defined fears—things that are never easy to describe and always difficult to dramatize. Mr. Allen's characters are in the furious grip of making do. They are seized—and sometimes overcome—by the need to accommodate the commonplace. . . .

Though the movie looks beautiful, the elegant style occasionally works against it, showing it up. This happens in a striking close-up of Miss Keaton, sitting alone on a photogenically wind-swept ocean beach as she is supposed to be thinking sensitive poet-type thoughts. Yet the image is empty.

As was to be expected, the film appealed largely to the intelligentsia, while general filmgoing audiences were put off by the picture's stark seriousness. When confronted with the notion that *Interiors* actually was very negative, Allen defended his project:

When Diane [Keaton] and Marybeth Hurt embrace at their mother's funeral, these [criticizing] people say that it is a

meaningless gesture, a momentary thing, that a lifetime wall has been built between these girls. But I saw the ending in a more positive way; I felt there was hope for the sisters, that they had arrived finally at a point where they could communicate. You see, I'm the optimist. . . .

Even while embroiled in the complexities of making *Interiors* Woody was already planning his subsequent screen contribution. As he explained, "I have a really strong comic idea I'm working on with Marshall Brickman who wrote *Sleeper* and *Annie Hall* with me. I'll appear in it, and I think it's going to be very, very funny." The project, *Manhattan,* began shooting in New York on August 7, 1978. The cast, directed by Woody, features Allen, Diane Keaton, Michael Murphy, Mariel Hemingway, and Anne Hoffman. Meantime, the multi-talented Woody won first prize in the 1978 O'Henry Awards for the best American short story of 1976-77, entitled "The Kugelmass Episode."

Since Allen first gained fame, one of the more recurrent questions asked of the performer is why he continually plays losers who apparently reflect the actor's offscreen personas. Allen insists that (1) in *Sleeper* and *The Front* he did not play losers, (2) that the press has built up an image of Woody being the quintessential nebbish because it works journalistically, and (3) that the losers in *Play It Again, Sam, Love and Death,* and *Bananas* "were guys in a story on a screen, they weren't me." According to Allen:

Paranoia, anxiety, alienation, insecurity—these have *always* been very pregnant sources of comedy, you know. Sure I've used them, but never deliberately. Anybody who's funny, I'm convinced, is just born with that ability like an ear for music. And the way you present yourself, comedically, just happens.

The best comics—Chaplin, Bob Hope, Mort Sahl, Milton Berle—never sat down and said, "OK, I'm going to walk *this* way, move like *this*. I'll be *this* brand of buffoon." When you work, you simply do what *you* can to make people laugh. You develop your own style instinctively, without, I think, a lot of calculation. And ineptness is simply one of the great comic traditions.

Though the Woody Allen of the late Seventies has achieved the status of the most celebrated jokester of his generation and one of America's best filmmakers, he still remains very much the Woody Allen who first touched base with audiences in the early Sixties. "People tell me there are a lot of guys like me, which doesn't explain why I'm lonely," he laments. He continues to inform a worshipful public, "I'm afraid of the dark and suspicious of the light. I have an intense desire to return to the womb—anybody's."

Feature Films

What's New Pussycat? (*United Artists 1965*)
What's Up, Tiger Lily? (*American International 1966*)
Casino Royale (*Columbia 1967*)
Take the Money and Run (*Cinerama 1969*)
Bananas (*United Artists 1971*)
Play It Again, Sam (*Paramount 1972*)
Everything You Always Wanted to Know About Sex but Were Afraid to Ask (*United Artists 1972*)
Sleeper (*United Artists 1973*)
Love and Death (*United Artists 1975*)
The Front (*United Artists 1976*)
Annie Hall (*United Artists 1977*)
Interiors (*United Artists 1978*)
Manhattan (*United Artists 1979*)

Roscoe "Fatty" Arbuckle

Buster Keaton, the greatest screen comedian to rise to stardom in the Twenties, credited Roscoe Arbuckle with teaching him the mechanics, techniques, and magic of filmmaking. Keaton said, "I could not have found a better-natured man to teach me the movie business, or a more knowledgeable one." Ironically the pupil would far outdistance the teacher on the screen.

Arbuckle was a funny man whose approach to moviemaking floundered on a conviction that the average mind of the moviegoing public was 12 years old, a myth he mitigated after Keaton became part of his movie unit. At the time Keaton first appeared in front of Arbuckle's camera, the fat, happy comic was second only to Chaplin in world acclaim as a top comedy director and silent-screen comedian.

But as Hollywood's Golden Age of Comedy was beginning, the career of Arbuckle ended in an orchestration of blaring headlines, a national hue and cry of outrage, and three devastating trials for manslaughter. Although proven innocent and fully exonerated of the charges against him, he was banished from the screen.

Roscoe Conkling Arbuckle was born on Thursday, March 24, 1887, in Smith Center, Kansas. He weighed 16 pounds. When Roscoe was one and a half years old, the Arbuckle family migrated to Santa Ana, California. In 1895, at the age of eight, Roscoe made his stage debut as a pickaninny in Frank Bacon's Stock Company and was paid 50 cents a night. He toured the West Coast in a stock repertory company in 1902 and two years later Sid Grauman paid him $17.50 a week to sing popular songs in his San Jose vaudeville house. He left Grauman for a successful singing job at Portland, Oregon's, 1905 Fair where he met rubber-legged comedian Leon Errol. Errol persuaded the fat young man to join his burlesque company at Portland's Orpheum Theatre. When the Errol troupe went broke in Boise, Idaho, Roscoe joined John Burke's burlesque until, later, with burlesque comedian Walter Reed, he packaged his own unit to tour the Southwest.

On August 5, 1908, Roscoe married Araminta Durfee,* a chestnut-haired, witty girl he had met on a streetcar five months earlier. They were married on the stage of the Byde-a-While Theatre in Long Beach, California,

---

* Minta Durfee would be Chaplin's leading lady in his first Keystone comedies; and she had survived most of the original Sennett company when she died on September 9, 1975, at the age of 85.

With director Joseph Henaberry on the set of Brewster's Millions *(1921).*

where the blond, rosy-cheeked, ballooning (250 pounds), 5'8½" Arbuckle was on the vaudeville bill. Arbuckle's film debut was for Colonel Selig's Polyscope Company in a Tom Santchi one-reeler in 1909. During his brief initial venture into motion pictures, Roscoe made several Selig shorts including the one-reeler *The Sanitarium*. But he left the fledgling flickers to return to the stage.

Roscoe and Minta Durfee Arbuckle toured the West Coast, Hawaii, the Philippines, China, and Japan with the Ferris Hartman Musical Comedy and Comic Opera Company. The troupe's repertory included *The Campus* and Gilbert and Sullivan's *The Mikado*. Returning to Los Angeles, Roscoe found work as a plumber's helper and in brief stints in vaudeville. Deciding to try motion pictures again, he was hired by Mack Sennett. Sennett was looking for a fat comic to replace Fred Mace, who was leaving Keystone to form his own company. Arbuckle made his Keystone debut with Mace in an April 29, 1913, one-reel release, *The Gangsters*.

At a salary of $3 a day, Arbuckle was schooled in the Sennett college of slapstick. Mabel Normand persuaded Sennett to feature Arbuckle in two half-reel pictures, *Passions, He Had Three* and *Help! Help! Hydrophobia!* On June 13, 1913, Mabel and Arbuckle were first seen on the screen together in *The Waiter's Picnic*. The teaming of Arbuckle and Mabel Normand during the next three years became as popular as Vitagraph's pairing of fat, jolly John Bunny and scrawny, taciturn Flora Finch.

Sennett's Keystone comedies were based on manic movement, improvisation, and outrageous buffoonery in a mad, overly fast-paced world. By the end of 1913, Arbuckle had made 22 Sennett shorts, alternating as one of the Keystone Kops, and one gaining image identity in *Fatty's Day Off. Fatty at San Diego. Fatty Joins the Force.* and *Fatty's Flirtation*. He became the recipient of what would become a world-famous Sennett comedic ingredient when Mabel Normand, in a moment of improvisation, tossed a pie in his face in *A Noise from the Deep* (July 17, 1913).

By 1914 Sennett was permitting Arbuckle to devise and direct his own films: *Barnyard Flirtations, Chicken Chasers,* and *Where Hazel Met the Villain*. The larger-than-life Sennett comics were relegated into "types"

with ill-defined characterizations that transcended reality. From the mad mixture Arbuckle molded an image of an oversized youth in frenzied motion, who used his enormous weight for comedic effect *but* with astonishing agility. He would perform hilarious sight gags with precision and unusual dexterity. According to Gene Fowler (who chronicled the life of Mack Sennett), Arbuckle "could deliver a bake-over grenade [a pie] from any angle, sitting, crouching, lying down with a good book, standing on one leg, or hanging by his toes from a pergola." But Arbuckle never developed an identifiable character like Harold Lloyd's bound-to-succeed shy boy, Keaton's indomitable stoic battler against man, machines, and mayhem, or Chaplin's wily seriocomic tramp.

Once established at Sennett's barnlike ramshackle Edendale Studio, Roscoe brought wife Minta and his sister Nora's son, Al St. John, into the explosively comic world of Keystone. The Sennett clowns, with no established pattern or scenario for screen comedy, improvised on a premise or idea with frenzied low comedy. They combined this with frequently dangerous sight gags and wild chases that were executed with incredible speed and split-second timing.

By 1914 Arbuckle was writing, directing, and appearing in most of the nearly forty comedies he made for Keystone. The same year a new clown was first seen under the Keystone banner. With Charles Chaplin, the 285-pound Arbuckle appeared in *A Film Johnnie* (March 2, 1914) and, a week later, in *Tango Tangles*.

Subtle changes in Arbuckle's screen characterizations occurred during 1915. The alteration was most notable in a two-reel satire on divorce, *That Little Band of Gold*. Here the hefty comedian relied more on stressing a definable character through expert pantomime than on the rough, overblown, and frequently vulgar Sennett slapstick. With Mabel Normand, he continued the *Fatty and Mabel* series— *. . . at the San Diego Exposition* and *. . . Viewing the World's Fair at San Francisco*. In July three of filmdom's earlier pioneers—Sennett, David Wark Griffith, and Thomas H. Ince—organized Triangle Films. On November 14, Arbuckle's first two-reeler for the new company was issued. In *Fickle Fatty's Fall* he expertly flipped a pancake

With Edgar Kennedy and Louise Fazenda in Fatty's Tin Type Tangle *(1915).*

into the air and caught it unconcernedly on a spatula behind his back. In December, Triangle released two solid Arbuckle shorts: *The Village Scandal* and *Fatty and the Broadway Stars* (Sam Bernard, Weber and Fields, Joe Jackson, and William Collier Sr.).

Arbuckle's last year with Sennett (1916) produced the very amusing *Fatty and Mabel Adrift** and two final screen appearances with Mabel Normand: *He Did and He Didn't* and *The Bright Lights.* Production values on the Triangle comedies had exceeded the Keystone output, but Arbuckle had higher ambitions. On January 1, 1917, Arbuckle left Sennett to join forces with producer Joseph Schenck. Arbuckle was to head his own company, with a studio in New York City to be known as the Comique Film Company. He

had spent five months of 1916 making his final Triangle pictures at its New York studio and also at the old New York Motion Picture Company studio at Fort Lee, New Jersey. When he returned to New York to his own company, Al St. John and Alice Lake went with him. While in Manhattan Arbuckle met Buster Keaton and casually suggested that the vaudevillian drop by the studio to make a few scenes.

The "few scenes" started one of the screen's greatest comedians toward a career that would far outshine Arbuckle's. In fact, during Keaton's term with Arbuckle, the fat man's comedies would show a marked improvement with new inventiveness. But inculcated with Sennett's slapdash, slapstick theories, Arbuckle's screen work would remain relatively primitive compared with that of other later, more sophisticated funsters. Whereas Chaplin had already progressed to such classics as *Easy Street*, Arbuckle was

* A portion of *Fatty and Mabel Adrift* would be included in the compilation feature *When Comedy Was King* (1960).

38

still making such films as *The Butcher Boy* (1917), his first Comique Film.

Arbuckle's Comique comedies were extremely popular and Paramount was forced to nearly triple the number of prints of each two-reeler in circulation to meet exhibitors' demands. His fame soared worldwide and the baby-faced, bubbling personality was second in audience affection only to Chaplin.

The Butcher Boy was released on April 23, 1917, and like most of his two-reelers was composed of two unrelated parts. The *New York Dramatic Mirror* wrote, "Fatty appears as a conscientious but clumsy butcher boy whose frantic attempts to please his customers lead him into deeper and deeper disaster. The second reel is staged in a young ladies' boarding school, where the butcher boy arrives to meet his beloved, disguised as a coy but mammoth girl 'cousin.' The spectacle of Fatty as a kittenish young thing in ruffled pinafore and short socks and his efforts to behave as a young lady boarder should, will undoubtedly delight the Arbuckle fans. As for Arbuckle himself, exhibitors have discovered long ago that he is the best known proof of the fact that everybody loves a fat comedian."

Arbuckle's female impersonation was as funny as anything he ever created on the screen. John Bunny had provoked great laughter when he appeared on the screen disguised as a woman (in *Bunny's Dilemma* and other comedies) and Wallace Beery had had a successful career at Essanay as an oversized, unpretty, rambunctious maid named Sweedie. At the Keystone lot, Arbuckle had made a marvelously funny comedy, *Miss Fatty's Seaside Lovers* (1915), and continued his female masquerade in *The Waiter's Ball* (1916). Gerald Mast in *The Comic Mind* (1973) writes, "Arbuckle was a great drag performer who slipped into a dress in at least half of his own Comique comedies. The fat, smooth-faced, Kewpie-doll comedian was a delight in a dress, especially when he added his fat agility at mimicking a lady's mincing, flirtatious flutterings."

The Comique Film Company completed four* more comedies in New York's 48th Street Colony Studios and at a 174th Street studio. With the completion of *Coney Is-*

land—with Arbuckle in an outlandish woman's bathing suit carrying a ridiculously tiny parasol—the troupe moved to Long Beach, California, in October 1917. Their first comedy adventure there was called, appropriately, *Out West*. In the course of his California moviemaking, Arbuckle, like many of the major movie stars, made a Liberty Loan Bond short for Lasky-Paramount. It was released in 1918 and had him confronting the Kaiser and the "Clown Quince" in Berlin.

The combination of Arbuckle and Keaton sparkled successfully in the California-made comedies: *The Bell Boy; Moonshine; Goodnight, Nurse; The Cook; A Desert Hero; Back Stage; The Hayseed;* and, their final entry, *The Garage*.

Ever anxious to move up in the industry, Arbuckle persuaded Joseph Schenck to arrange with Paramount for the production of his first feature-length picture. *The Round-Up* was an adaptation of a Broadway play, which had starred another portly player, Maclyn Arbuckle (no relation to Roscoe), intermittently for several years. Arbuckle's 1920 feature-film debut presented him as "Slim" Hoover, sheriff of Pinal County, Arizona. *Motion Picture World* thought "his lovemaking was comic with graceless blunders, which he makes still funnier by his air of grave order," and found "his talent for flapping and drooping is exploited only to a limited degree." The big old-fashioned melodrama was disappointing and Roscoe never attempted another Western.

The Life of the Party, written by Irvin S. Cobb, was Arbuckle's second 1920 feature. It was reviewed by the *New York Times,* which judged, "Too long to hold its own all the way, it furnished many laughs because Fatty Arbuckle is often funny and always pleasant." The *Times* thought the overall playing was "probably broader and more given to slapstick than the story was." As Algernon Leary, winning the race for mayor, Arbuckle was proving himself capable of sustaining a well-defined comedy role. Of this feature another scribe wrote, "Arbuckle has long been *The Life of the Party* who needs neither makeup nor strained grimace to be amusing. He is just naturally funny!"

Although *Brewster's Millions,* Arbuckle's first 1921 feature release, was a popular and

---

* A fifth entry was *A Reckless Romeo,* which has long since disappeared from public view.

With Alice Lake and Buster Keaton in the short Fatty at Coney Island *(1917).*

financial success, *Motion Picture World* qualified its pleasure: "Roscoe Arbuckle, erstwhile Fatty, now a full-fledged comedian, while bound to please by sheer force of personality, works a little too hard in *Brewster's Millions* to be at his best. It is not at all necessary for him to interpolate any of the horse-play of farce in order to win in pure comedy. His expressive face is far more effective than his physical agility, and he need not fear to give larger development to other characterizations in his plays, if only for the sake of variety."

Paramount was delighted with the box-office returns from the Arbuckle features and kept him constantly in front of the camera for the first eight months of 1921. He was a delight as Franklin Pinney, a laundryman turned amateur detective, in *The Dollar-a-Year Man.* He garnered such praise as, "He puts over every good piece of business that comes his way with the deftness of a sleight-of-hand performer. When there is nothing provided by the scenario writer, he puts something of his own and makes a dozen laughs grow where the

A Paramount-Arbuckle Comedy

"IF SHE WON'T WASH THE DISHES CHOKE HER".

Roscoe "Fatty" Arbuckle
in
"Camping Out"

With Al St. John in Camping Out (1918).

In Out West (1918).

A GEORGE MELFORD PRODUCTION   A PARAMOUNT PICTURE

"I'LL HAVE TO PUT YOU
UNDER ARREST, JACK."

© FAMOUS PLAYERS-LASKY CORP., 1920.

With Tom Forman in The Round-Up *(1920).*

director would have been delighted to get one."

James Forbes' 1908 play, *The Traveling Salesman*, became Arbuckle's third 1921 release. As the salesman of the title, he gave a restrained performance that *Motion Picture World* said was the picture's strongest asset. "While it cannot be called Arbuckle's best picture, it makes an amusing vehicle for the corpulent star, affording him plenty of chances for a display of his unique style of funmaking."

Arbuckle in the role of Dr. Hobart Hupp, convinced he can rehabilitate criminals and reduce crime, occupied the footage of *Crazy to Marry*, released in August 1921. The photoplay gleaned comments like, "Good, clean fun! The rotund but agile Mr. Arbuckle creates a constant gale of merriment in this fast moving farce. It is far the best vehicle for the display of his particular brand of humor that has been given him up to date." The picture's biggest laugh was provoked by Arbuckle's leaping into a fountain to rescue a sup-

posedly drowning woman. By force his weight empties all of the water from the basin.

In a spurt of corporate economy, Jesse L. Lasky persuaded Arbuckle to make *three* feature-length comedies without a day's rest between them. Lasky admitted, "I don't know of another star who would have submitted to such extortionate demands on his energy. But Fatty Arbuckle wasn't one to grumble. There were no temperamental displays in his repertoire. He went through the triple assignment like a whirling dervish, in his top form. They were the funniest pictures he ever made."

The three pictures made on this marathon filming were: *Gasoline Gus, Freight Prepaid* (with location shots filmed in Chicago's stockyards), and *Leap Year*. A small portion of the moviegoing public saw *Gasoline Gus*. The two other features would be shelved, written off as a loss, and never released.

Exhausted from his nonstop work on Lasky's three feature pictures, Arbuckle refused Buster Keaton's invitation to spend

In Gasoline Gus
(1921).

Labor Day weekend aboard a yacht. Instead he motored to San Francisco where a suite of rooms had been reserved for him on the 12th floor of the St. Francis Hotel. In his party were actor-director Lowell Sherman and director Fred Fishback. Well stocked with bootleg liquor, the suite became open house for boisterous revels. The bacchanalian bash exploded when, on the following Friday, one of the *uninvited* guests, a minor actress named Virginia Rappe, died of peritonitis. A postmortem disclosure listed a ruptured bladder as a compounding cause. Doctors would later testify that the latter condition could have been caused by the promiscuous starlet's "certain ailment," syphilis.

Undaunted and unimpressed with the basic truths of the sordid affair, the police arrested Arbuckle for the rape and murder of Virginia Rappe. The charge, later reduced to manslaughter, was "founded" on a lurid tale of drunken rape, told to the police by Miss Rappe's companion, Maud Delmont. (Miss Delmont's unsavory reputation would be confirmed by a string of affidavits against her for excessive activities as an overly enthusiastic co-respondent in divorce proceedings. On December 18, 1921, she would be convicted of bigamy but would be released again to be the state's star witness against Arbuckle in the second of three trials.* Keaton prophetically called it "The Day the Laughter Stopped.")

The nation's headlines blared the orgiastic minutiae in front page coverage. Hollywood became synonymous with Sodom and Gomorrah. Women's Clubs of America arose in self-righteous indignation and the professional moralists, ever seeking new victims, raised a hue and cry for Arbuckle's scalp. The district attorney's office, reflecting the animosity then existing between the Bay City and Hollywood, announced, "Nobody can come to San Francisco and do a thing like this and get away with it." Arbuckle was prejudged, condemned, and vilified by the press. Once beloved, jolly "Fatty" became ridiculed

* In 1975 a putrid movie, *The Wild Party*, was released, starring James Coco and Raquel Welch. It was very loosely based on the Arbuckle case. Several years ago, plans were made for a Broadway musical, *Fatty*, to star Jackie Coogan. It never materialized.

and scorned as a "fat, sadistic slob." Even his weight was against him.*

Hollywood panicked. Studio heads banded together and formed the Motion Picture Producers and Distributors Association. To front their self-imposed regulatory codes and censorship, Will H. Hays, incumbent postmaster general in President Warren G. Harding's cabinet, was appointed. On September 11, Sid Grauman withdrew *Gasoline Gus* from his Los Angeles theatre. Arbuckle's comedies were banished from the screen nationwide.

The first trial resulted in a hung jury. While Arbuckle's second trial was being heard, Hollywood and the nation withstood another salacious scandal when on February 2, 1922, director William Desmond Taylor was found murdered.

In San Francisco the jury for the second Arbuckle trial was completely hung up on the confusing (and often perjured) circumstantial evidence. On April 12, 1922, Arbuckle was acquitted in a one-minute verdict. The jurors' statement in this third trial was a stinging indictment against the court and the professional moralists:

> We feel that a great injustice has been done him. We feel also that it was only our plain duty to give him this exoneration under the evidence, for there was not the slightest proof adduced to convict him in any way with the commission of the crime.
>
> He was manly throughout the case and told a straightforward story on the witness stand, which we all believed.
>
> The happening at the hotel was an unfortunate affair, for which Arbuckle, as the evidence shows, was in no way responsible.
>
> We wish him success and hope that the American people will take the judgment of fourteen men and women who have sat listening for thirty-one days to the evidence, that Roscoe Arbuckle is entirely innocent and free from all blame.

* On the country's newsstands, the September issue of *Photoplay* magazine carried an article by Adela Rogers St. John on Arbuckle. It was entitled "Love Confessions of a Fat Man" and stressed his views idealistically on women, revealing his awe and frequent fear of them, and his genuine respect for the opposite sex. But the article was poorly timed.

The judgment and exoneration were *only* legally effective. Hollywood studios would have no part of Arbuckle, feeling he had tarnished the illusionary aura of high standards of the film factories and had brought an end to Hollywood's age of deluded innocence. Will Hays' "pardon" of Arbuckle, with a plea that the man be permitted to work, was met with violent protests nationwide from moviegoers aflame by the wretched death of idolized leading man Wallace Reid on January 18, 1923, from advanced drug addiction.

In the summer of 1923, Arbuckle tried a comeback at a Chicago cafe. Cheered by a capacity audience, he said, "I thank you from the bottom of my heart. It's the first time I've had a real smile in a long time." But the National Federation of Women's Clubs continued their condemnation of the fat comic. With the exception of close friends—Keaton and James Cruze*—Arbuckle was anathema to Hollywood filmmakers and the acting community.

Minta Durfee and her brothers Harry and Arthur had supported Roscoe during the siege of the three San Francisco trials. But on December 31, 1923, she supposedly was granted a divorce from Arbuckle in Providence, Rhode Island, on charges of desertion in 1917.

In 1924 Arbuckle signed for a nationwide vaudeville tour and was enthusiastically received by audiences. While playing on a bill in Cleveland at the Bandbox Theatre he was impressed with a brash young comic on the program and recommended him to tab show producer Fred Hurley. Hurley signed Bob Hope for his *Jolly Follies*.

With Buster Keaton as best man and his wife Natalie Talmadge as matron of honor, Roscoe married Doris Deane. The ceremony took place on May 16, 1925, in San Marino, California, at the home of the bride's mother (Mrs. Charles R. Dibble). The ceremony was performed following a good deal of confusion relating to Minta Durfee's final decree not being legal in California until April 8. At any rate, Arbuckle's marriage to Doris Deane ended in divorce four years later.

Mack Sennett agreed to give Arbuckle work directing Keystone comedies, but in-

* Cruze had directed several of Arbuckle's features. For Cruze's *Hollywood* (1923) the director persuaded Arbuckle to appear as "a fat man in a casting office."

sisted he use the name of William B. Goodrich (Arbuckle's grandfather). When Keaton was in the initial preparations for a new production he engaged Roscoe to direct it. But the heavily drinking, nervous clown was unexpectedly irritable and overwrought. Keaton, reluctant to fire his close friend, convinced Marion Davies that William B. Goodrich would be excellent as the director of her forthcoming feature, *The Red Mill* (1927). (There is some evidence that Arbuckle did not complete this film, but was replaced by George Hill and other directors.) As Goodrich, he also directed Eddie Cantor's second feature picture, *Special Delivery* (1927).

Arbuckle then returned to the stage. He chose for his Broadway stage debut a revival of a 1910 comedy hit, *Baby Mine*. The farce had not weathered the years but the actor was applauded. "Mr. Arbuckle was given an extremely cordial reception last night when he made his first appearance shortly after the rise of the curtain. The applause continued for several minutes and after the second act he was forced to make a curtain speech of almost record length" (*New York Times*). His performance was regarded as more satisfactory than those of fellow cast members who included Humphrey Bogart and Lee Patrick. After 12 performances, the show closed.

The onetime star then turned to vaudeville. In between his stage outings he supervised Roscoe Arbuckle's Plantation Cafe on Washington Boulevard, outside Culver City, California. The club featured Roscoe "Fatty" Arbuckle and his Merry Gang in a Smart Set Revue plus dinner and dancing. The nightclub venture failed.

He continued headlining in vaudeville to enthusiastic audience response. In mid-1931 James R. Quirk headlined an article in *Photoplay* magazine, "Give Arbuckle a Chance!" But the pious and self-righteous lashed back in further outrage.

In May 1932 Roscoe headlined a bill at Broadway's Palace Theatre with Milton Berle, Jack Whiting, and Grace Hayes. For the Vitaphone division of Warner Bros. he started a series of talking shorts at their old Brooklyn studio in August. The first, *Hey, Pop!*, was well received and Arbuckle made personal appearances with the picture at Broadway's Strand Theatre. In the meantime, on June 21, 1932, he had married Addie Oakley Dukes McPhail.

Arbuckle completed several Vitaphone shorts,* ending with 1933's *Tomalie* (with his old sidekick Al St. John). It was a mildly amusing, if pedestrian, farce, in which he was more restrained and far less active than in his earlier comedies. He did resort to a sight gag he had used in 1919's *The Garage*. There was talk of Warner Bros. starring Arbuckle in a feature-length comedy. The renewal of his career, plus his happy marriage to Addie McPhail, seemed to lift him out of the morass of notoriety that had plagued him for years.

With the finish of his sixth Vitaphone short, Arbuckle celebrated his first wedding anniversary (a week late) on June 28. Early in the morning of Thursday, June 29, 1933, in his suite at the Park Central Hotel, his wife Addie discovered that he was dead. The rotund clown had died in his sleep of a heart attack. He was 46.

Funeral services were held under the auspices of the New York City BPOE Lodge No. 1 in the Gold Room (where Valentino had been viewed by thousands in 1926) of Campbell's Funeral Home at 66th and Broadway in Manhattan. Among the honorary pallbearers were Bert Lahr, Bert Wheeler, Leo Carrillo, and Gus Edwards. Interment was in a crypt at Forest Lawn Cemetery in California.

About Roscoe (no one called him "Fatty" who knew him) Buster Keaton said, "Arbuckle was that rarity, a truly jolly fat man. He had no meanness, malice, or jealousy in him. Everything seemed to amuse and delight him." He was also one of the screen's great laughmakers and gave the world bountiful joy and, above all, laughter.

* His other Vitaphone shorts of the period were: *Buzzin' Around* (1933), *How've You Been?* (1933), *Close Relations* (1933), and *In the Dough* (1933).

FEATURE FILMS

The Round-Up (*Paramount 1920*)
The Life of the Party (*Paramount 1920*)
Brewster's Millions (*Paramount 1921*)
The Dollar-a-Year Man (*Paramount 1921*)
The Traveling Salesman (*Paramount 1921*)
Crazy to Marry (*Paramount 1921*)

Gasoline Gus (*Paramount 1921*)
Freight Prepaid [The Fast Freight] (*Paramount 1921*) [unreleased]
Leap Year (*Paramount 1921*) [unreleased]
Hollywood (*Paramount 1923*)

Eve Arden

The Motion Pictures Annual Poll voted Eve Arden the best comedienne in films for six consecutive years: 1948–54. Chic, sophisticated lady Eve had few, if any, peers in comedy as the cool, caustic companion of many film heroines. Her ability to take any seemingly innocuous line and deliver it with vocal versatility of range soon placed her in great demand in Hollywood. Her dialogue delivery of being flippant or oozing with well-bred vitriol caused her to make many a supporting role into a picture's greatest asset. With a raised eyebrow and a withering or knowing glance, she could memorably mime her stock characterization of the liberated dame with all the answers.

Her talents far exceeded the mold into which Hollywood cast her. However, the "Eve Arden" type was good box-office. Although she longed to play the type of roles assigned to Irene Dunne, Rosalind Russell, and Carole Lombard, she never did. But her "Eve Arden" type, she played to the hilt!

Born on Friday, April 30, 1909, in Mill Valley, California, a suburb of San Francisco, she was the only child of Lucille (Frank) and Charles Peter Quedens. They named their daughter Eunice. When she was five years old, her parents divorced. Raised by her mother, Eve would later say, "She was very beautiful. I lost five years with a psychiatrist because of not being as beautiful as she." While attending Mill Valley Grammar School Eve won a medal, at age seven, from the WCTU Outdoor Art Club for reciting "No Kicka My Dog," a poem about an Italian immigrant succumbed to demon rum. Her determination to become a performer began with her fancied expertise as a dialectician and continued through her playing in *Dulcy* at Tamalpais High School, from which she graduated in 1926. That year she was hired by producer Henry Duffy in San Francisco for a walk-on part in *Alias the Deacon.* Billed as Miss Eunice M. Quedens, Eve was one of four female members of the Women's Welfare League.

Eve was attractive, blonde, had green eyes and a flashing smile, and was 5′9″ tall. Her height and angularity made ingenue roles impossible so she settled for character parts in Duffy's productions of *Meet the Wife, The*

With Audrey Long in Pan-Americana (1945).

Patsy (1927), and *Lombardi, Ltd.* (1928). (In the cast of the last show was Gale Gordon, much later to be her nemesis on the "Our Miss Brooks" series.) When *Lombardi, Ltd.* reached Duffy's El Capitan Theatre in Hollywood, Eve decided to test her talents in the new talking motion pictures. She signed for a one-picture deal with Columbia.

She was given the supporting role of a blonde songstress who lures Ralph Graves from his vaudeville-singer wife (Belle Baker). Regarding *The Song of Love* (1929), the *New York Times* noted, "Eunice Quedens makes Mazie quite lifelike." But the movie caused no great stir nor did it ignite Eve's film career.

Thereafter she joined a group of four players known as the Bandbox Repertory Theatre. They traveled in an old Ford playing the hotel-lobby circuits from Palm Springs to Del Monte. In 1933 she landed the small part of Marcia in MGM's *Dancing Lady*, starring Joan Crawford. Still billed as Eunice Quedens, Eve played a brief scene with a thick, phony Southern accent.

Leonard Sillman, who later made a career producing *New Faces* of various years, pulled together a brisk revue called *Lo and Behold* to play a one-week engagement at the Pasadena Playhouse. Sillman assembled a remarkable cast of young talent: Tyrone Power, Charles Walters, Kay Thompson, former opera singer Marguerite Namara, June Lang. Eunice Quedens was hired with the proviso that she change her name. She did—to Eve Arden. With Tyrone Power, Eve played a sketch of two statues coming to life in a park. The revue stayed three weeks in Pasadena then transferred to Hollywood's El Capitan Theatre for more performances. In the final week of the run Lee Shubert caught the show and agreed to sponsor the snappy, risqué revue on Broadway. The company went East to open *New Faces* (of 1934). The zestful cast now included Imogene Coca, Charles Walters, Nancy Hamilton, Roger Stearns, Sillman, and Henry Fonda, but not Eve. She had other commitments.

Eve signed for *Ziegfeld Follies of 1934*. Her Broadway debut took place on January 4, 1934, at the Winter Garden Theatre with Eve doing brief stooging and fill-in sketch parts. Her New York bow went virtually unnoticed, but she was paid $100 weekly. Her next Broadway assignment was *Parade* (May 20, 1935), a revue strewn with social consciousness and stinging reviews. Although the critics slaughtered the show, Eve made an impression with the aisle-sitters. *Variety* reported, "Another standout comes with Eve Arden, a Coast girl who wins rating as one of the cleverest of newcomers. Diction excellent, she displays versatility both in handling numbers and playing parts. . . . Miss Arden is very easy to look at. . . ."

Producer Max Gordon, impressed with Eve's versatility in *Parade,* thought she would be just right for the role of Elsa Maxwell in his upcoming production of Cole Porter's *Jubilee.* But when the sprightly, blonde young girl went to audition, Gordon was astonished at her youth. The role went to older, portly Maxwell-lookalike May Boley. Eve returned to the fold of the Shubert Brothers for *Ziegfeld Follies of 1936*, a production which ranks among the best editions of that revue format.

The supremely talented cast assembled for that version headlined Fanny Brice, Bob Hope, Gertrude Niesen, Hugh O'Connell, Harriet Hoctor, Josephine Baker, Edgar Bergen, Judy Canova, and others. Eve was placed in seventh billing and had several opportunities to display her versatility and talent. The show established Eve as a headline revue artist. One of the show's best songs, "I Can't Get Started with You," was sung to a hard-to-get Eve by Bob Hope. When the revue closed for the summer, Eve returned to the West Coast. Her mother died shortly after her return to California and Eve decided to make another attempt at motion pictures. When the *Follies* reopened in September 1936, burlesque queen Gypsy Rose Lee had replaced Eve.

Eve's agent, Arthur Landau (who had guided Jean Harlow's career), secured a screen test for her at Universal. They gave her a supporting role in Edward Everett Horton's comedy, *Oh, Doctor!* (1937). It was strictly a programmer. But the public became Arden-aware in her next film, because director Gregory LaCava permitted Eve and a few other supporting players to expand their minor roles into memorable bits. Eve's inspiration of using the company's cat, Henry, as a live fur neckpiece and her wisecracks to the feline companion caused audiences to notice

With Phyllis
Kennedy and Grady
Sutton in Stage Door
(1937).

the long-limbed blonde. This film, RKO's *Stage Door* (1937), helped to establish the mold for the Eve Arden type screen role.

Eve sailed through many freelance roles, resisting being tied to a stock studio contract. She built up an audience following doing a reverse, burlesque adagio dance with Ben Blue in Paramount's *Cocoanut Grove* (1938). She was George Murphy's love interest in *Letter of Introduction* (1938), and was prim, bespectacled Henrietta in RKO's *Having Wonderful Time* (1938). In 1939 she played four conventional supporting roles. If her personal notices were usually good, the pictures were not.

On June 29, 1939, she wed insurance agent Edward G. Bergen in Reno, Nevada. Her fifth and final screen role for the year was a decided step upward. She was cast as Peerless Pauline, the human fly, in the Marx Brothers' film riot *At the Circus*. The picture's most hilarious sequence involved Eve outwitting shyster lawyer Groucho by stashing stolen cash in her bra. The situation leads Groucho to observe, "The thing I like about you is that money doesn't go to your head."

Eve's first escapade with madcap comedy remains one of her most memorable scene thefts. It was a fine showcase for Arden and led to a return to Broadway. Producer Max Gordon watched her scenes with Groucho Marx on the set and signed her for his production of Jerome Kern and Oscar Hammerstein II's new musical.

Eve was delighted to be with her husband in their apartment at 10 Park Avenue and pleased with her role of Winnie Spofford in Gordon's *Very Warm for May*, directed and designed by Vincente Minnelli. Throughout the pre-Broadway tour the show was plagued with troubles, and when it opened in New York (November 11, 1939) it was found to be "excessively tedious and humorless." But Eve garnered good personal notices. The show collapsed after 59 performances.

While Eve was rehearsing a musical revue, *Two for the Show*, films she had made before her eastern trek began to appear. Warner Bros.' *A Child Is Born* (1940) cast Eve as brassy nurse Miss Pinty. In United Artists' *Slightly Honorable* (1940), she was seen as Pat O'Brien's secretary, a delightful comedy role that terminated in her being stabbed in the back. Meanwhile, *Two for the Show* opened (February 8, 1940) to modest enthusiasm. Eve's contributions to the production included satirized imitations of Marlene Dietrich and Gertrude Lawrence. She was lauded as "always vivid, throws herself into the broad comedy with lovely abandon." In mid-May 1940 Eve withdrew from *Two for the Show* and returned to Hollywood.

MGM's efforts to duplicate the huge success of Garbo's *Ninotchka* resulted in a Clark Gable-Hedy Lamarr vehicle entitled *Comrade X* (1940). But the copy, heavily directed by King Vidor, never recaptured the magic and wispy humor of the Garbo film. Eve played an American journalist flipping terse comments. For Herbert Wilcox's remake of *No, No, Nanette* (1940), starring his wife, Anna Neagle, Eve played one of philandering Roland Young's "protégés."

The year 1941 was Eve's most productive film season. She made 11 films. In MGM's *Ziegfeld Girl* she was Patsy Dixon, an experienced showgirl who knows all the answers and bestows them with pithy advice on fledgling showgirls. In Ernst Lubitsch's *That Uncertain Feeling* she was cast as an eager legal secretary (a part played by Clara Bow in the 1925 film version). Warner Bros. gave her the lead in *She Couldn't Say No*. It was a bottom-of-the-biller in which she performed beyond the merits of the script. As Joan Bennett's fan-dancing roommate in Columbia's *She Knew All the Answers*, Eve drained the part and walked off with the notices. She played Gabby Trent in *San Antonio Rose* and was Barbara in *Sing for Your Supper*, two mindless musical quickies.

On the other hand, Warner Bros.' well-made *Manpower* provided Eve with a splashy, tightly written role as a tough dance-hall hostess. She portrayed the brassy blonde clip-joint dame to perfection. Her scenes with star Marlene Dietrich were very effective and the part seemed tailor-made for Arden's glib delivery of lines. She returned to routine comedy as Red Skelton's overly efficient business manager in *Whistling in the Dark. Variety* found Arden "convincing" as Kate, an 1880s Texas saloon hostess in *The Last of the Duanes*. Her next picture, *Oblig-*

With George Montgomery in Last of the Duanes (1941).

ing *Young Lady*, gave her room to romp as a sophisticated newspaper reporter. Her final role of the year was as a hard-boiled musical comedy star in *Bedtime Story*. It was another instance where the supporting cast outshone the stars (Loretta Young, Fredric March).

Tired and a bit discouraged by the sameness of her film roles, Eve welcomed the opportunity to return to Broadway.* It was a new Cole Porter show, with dances by Charles Walters and book by Herbert and Dorothy Fields, based on a riotous mid-Twenties' comedy, *Cradle Snatchers*. It had the promise of being a great hit—and it was. Eve, Edith Meiser, and Vivian Vance played the three bored, middle-aged wives who hire three G.I.s for the weekend to provoke (they hope) jealousy in their spouses. Starring Danny Kaye, *Let's Face It* opened at the Imperial Theatre on October 29, 1941, to great acclaim. The musical lasted 547 performances. A tall, willowy blonde was Eve's understudy—Carol Channing.

The critics lauded *Let's Face It* and Eve received her share of the honors. The *New York Herald-Tribune* noted, "Miss Arden, who can be briskly and genuinely comic without even losing her cool beauty and engaging charm, is a player of great style and quality, and she is a complete delight in a not-altogether appetizing role." Playing opposite Danny Kaye would challenge the hardiest of actresses, critic Richard Lockridge acknowledged, but "Miss Arden is more than a match for him . . . she is a match for almost anybody." Eve accepted the glowing acclaim of press and public with her usual poise and wit. "Just imagine I, who am filled with human kindness, making a neat profit out of vitriol." She had few peers in the art.

Let's Face It gave Eve an amusing duet with Kaye, "Let's Not Talk About Love." With Edith Meiser and Vivian Vance, Eve harmonized "A Lady Needs a Rest." Eve was voted the best female lead in a musical for the season in the annual New York Drama Critics' Poll.

Back in Hollywood, with her husband away in the army for the duration of World War II, Eve entertained at servicemen's clubs. She continued her screen career in

---

* Originally, the leads had been offered to Milton Berle and Martha Raye; when they were unable to accept the parts, Danny Kaye and Eve were hired instead.

Republic's escapist *Hit Parade of 1943*. When Paramount filmed *Let's Face It* (1943) as a Bob Hope vehicle, Eve was the only member from the Broadway cast to repeat her assignment. She was joined by ZaSu Pitts and Phyllis Povah as the philandering wives and got to solo the song "Let's Not Talk About Love," the only one of Porter's numbers retained for the picture version. Arden then found a rewarding assignment in Columbia's *Cover Girl* (1944), starring Rita Hayworth and Gene Kelly. It was Eve's first Technicolor picture and she was splendid as chic, sophisticated magazine editor Cornelia "Stonewall" Jackson. Well produced and enhanced with a beautiful score by Jerome Kern and Ira Gershwin, the film won five Academy Award nominations and an Oscar for the musical scoring.

Joseph Fields' comedy of crowded wartime Washington, D.C., had been a tremendous Broadway success. Warner Bros. paid $250,000 for the screen rights to *The Doughgirls* (1944) and set about casting the film with a well-chosen group of their younger players: Ann Sheridan, Alexis Smith, and Jane Wyman. For the project's most colorful part, celebrated Russian sniper Natalia Moskoroff (played on the stage by Arlene Francis), the studio scheduled Faye Emerson. But Miss Arden wanted the juicy, comedic part. For the first time in her screen career, she agreed to a studio contract, a seven-year, three-pictures-a-year pact with Warner Bros. Although the contract generously gave her the privilege of accepting other assignments—including those from her beloved theatre—Eve would rankle under the arrangement. ("Whenever I get a yoke around my neck, I immediately start gnawing at it.") But she got to play Natalia Moskoroff, killer of 397 Nazis and winner of a goodwill mission to Washington, D.C., where she took short hikes to Baltimore, Maryland, and became a double-feature movie fanatic when not shooting pigeons off the hotel-room balcony.

Eve played the Russian for all she was worth. (The part remains one of her favorite screen roles.) However, she received oddly mixed critical comments such as, "Armed with a bad Gregory Ratoff accent and even shoddier mannerisms, she seems to be doing her utmost to shove U.S. movie treatment of the Soviets back to the *Comrade X* level." *Variety* described her as the vodka Dick Tracy in drag. But the *New York Herald-Tribune* claimed, "Fortunately Eve Arden does a first-rate piece of acting.... She is altogether the best player in the lot, giving the photoplay a breezy continuity which is rarely contributed to by the adaptation or the staging." She followed her rifle-toting Russian role with two clinkers: RKO's *Pan-Americana* (1945) and Universal's *Patrick the Great* (1945).

After playing a Broadway nightclub owner in Republic's *Earl Carroll Vanities* (1945), Eve returned to her home lot. There she was assigned one of her best roles, despite the industry's knowledge that she could pull the rug from under the feet of most stars with her notorious scene stealing. Joan Crawford's first starring role in a Warner Bros. picture, *Mildred Pierce* (1945), was vitally important to the former MGM star and she tested with each member of the hand-picked supporting cast. Eve's compatibility with Crawford paid off onscreen. Their scenes together were ex-

pertly professional. Eve's Ida was well written, if perhaps typical Arden fare. Thankfully it was blessed with succulent dialogue. At one point she cracks, "Alligators have the right idea.... They eat their young." Later she says to overly amorous Jack Carson, "OK, I'll give you some scrambled eggs ... but that's all. I hate to wrestle in the morning." Eve provided strong support as Crawford's confidante and best friend. She was also nominated for the Academy Award as Best Supporting Actress of the Year (her only entry in the Oscar sweepstakes), but lost to Anne Revere (*National Velvet*). Joan Crawford won the Oscar for Best Actress of the Year.

Eve's continued enchantment with the theatre found an outlet during the summer of 1945. She joined the Gryphon Players in La Jolla, California, a group comprising some of her best friends: the Gregory Pecks, the Barry Sullivans, and the Mel Ferrers. She had the opportunity there to play such roles as Marion in *Biography*, Amytis in *The Road to Rome*, and Mary Hilliard in *Here Today*.

With Don Brodie and Jack Carson in **My Dream Is Yours** *(1949).*

Back on the screen, Eve was seen in *My Reputation* (made in 1944 but not released until 1946). Arden was back to her stereotyped assignment, that of the star's best pal—here Barbara Stanwyck's. The tearjerker was well acted by all but presented no memorable markers in the sob-story genre. For Samuel Goldwyn's remake of the play *The Milky Way*, Danny Kaye was starred in the Technicolor musical version, *The Kid from Brooklyn* (1946). Eve had little to do as Kaye's fight manager's girlfriend.

On the Burbank lot she was lost as French chanteuse Gabrielle in Warner Bros.' "biography" of composer Cole Porter, *Night and Day* (1946). Ironically, the same year the *Motion Picture Herald-Fame* annual poll named her a star of tomorrow, after nearly 18 years on the screen. Universal's unlikely and overblown tale of Russian composer Rimsky-Korsakov, *Song of Scheherazade* (1947), had Eve in elaborate 1865 period costumes as Yvonne DeCarlo's mother. In MGM's mediocre *The Arnelo Affair* (1947), written and directed by Arch Oboler, she had another backup assignment.

The day after completing a bitchy role in Warner Bros.' *The Unfaithful* (1947), Eve was handed her biggest screen part (and one of her best) to date. She played the role of Olive Lashbrooke, a glib, nosy, gabby actress in Warner Bros.' film version of John Van Druten's rollicking stage success, *The Voice of the Turtle* (1947). She performed with a flamboyant flair that outshone the leads: a too slickly polished Eleanor Parker and a phlegmatic Ronald Reagan. Eve came off best and the critics were writing, "Certainly Eve Arden gives her best to the part of the other girl. Several times there are genuine laughs as she expertly takes the last ounce out of the role."

During the filming of her 1947 releases, Eve and her husband, Ned Bergen, now a Hollywood agent, discovered "we were both strangers." They separated in April and were divorced on July 27, 1947. Eve would fill the gap in her personal life by adopting two daughters: Liza (born in 1946) and Connie (born in 1948).

Eve had made her radio debut in 1936 on "The Ken Murray Show," was heard in 1938 on "The Russ Morgan Show," and during World War II was frequently heard on "The Danny Kaye Show." In 1945 Eve had succeeded Joan Davis on radio's "Village Store" variety show, and in September 1947 her vis-à-vis, Jack Haley, was succeeded by Jack Carson. The "Village Store" assignment seemed to be going well, and Eve was reluctant to accept the radio script of "Our Miss Brooks." (Shirley Booth, an actress of greater depth and warmth than Eve, had rejected the assignment.)

On Monday, July 19, 1948, "Our Miss Brooks" made its radio debut. Audience reception to the show was so successful that the CBS network signed Eve and the cast to a long-term deal. The humorous misadventures of Madison High School's half-hour regular series premiered on Sunday, September 10, 1948. Eve was cast as the zestful schoolmarm alive with unrequited love for a bashful biology teacher (Jeff Chandler) and trying to help a soprano-voiced, low I.Q. student (Richard Crenna), while coping with the excessively authoritarian nincompoop school principal (Gale Gordon). Reviews for the radio series were excellent and extolled Eve's deft comedy. Thanks to Eve's performance the character came alive as an amusing human being.

On screen she was seen in Universal's slow-paced *One Touch of Venus* (1948), which emasculated Kurt Weill's musical. In it she played a disappointed man-hungry female. She then was Chris in a low-case programmer for Warner Bros., *Whiplash* (1948). Jack Carson, Eve, and S. Z. Sakall were the studio's insurance for bolstering their production-line product. The boisterous trio were all in *My Dream Is Yours* (1949), one of Doris Day's earlier musicals. *The Lady Takes a Sailor* (1949) ill-used Jane Wyman and it remained for Eve's comedy relief to salvage the forced farce.

In 1950 Eve ground out a supporting role in Paramount's baffling and woeful tearjerker *Paid in Full*. In Universal's frequently entertaining *Curtain Call at Cactus Creek*, Eve was seen as Gale Storm's mother and for a change of pace had a song ("Waiting at the Church") to sing. She returned to Warner Bros. for its revised remake of *No, No, Nanette*, called *Tea for Two*. She was Pauline, Doris Day's man-prowling chum. The *New York Times* printed, "And Miss Arden glides through the picture dropping caustic

With Victor Francen in Night and Day (1945).

comments with an air that seems to say make what you will of the innuendos, bub. Miss Arden is good at this sort of thing—very good, indeed."

The chance to renew her love for the theatre and the opportunity to harvest a rich salary sent Eve eastward in the summer of 1950. The project was a straw-hat tour of Ruth Gordon's comedy, *Over Twenty-One*. A review of her performance at Princeton, New Jersey's, McCarter Theatre glowed, "The statuesque blonde's brassy humor, in the face of discouraging events, was a lesson, in spirit as well as acting. Her excellent timing, flawless delivery of punch lines and amusing facial contortions were a pleasure to the entire audience."

Eve returned to Hollywood in a seedy, dreary movie as Howard da Silva's wife in *Three Husbands* (1950). Although both Joan Crawford and Eve were excellent in *Goodbye, My Fancy* (1951), the successful play lost most of its glitter by a pedestrian screen adaptation. The bulk of the critical applause went to another of Eve's wisecracking good dames. But Eve was telling the press, "I'm sick of that wisecracking blonde. It's got so bad that I never go to my own pictures and even try to avoid looking at the rushes. They have just got to find someone else to play Eve Arden!"

Boston's Mutual Hall summer season opened June 2, 1951, and for the second week Eve Arden, starring in *Here Today*, proved to be a box-office bonanza. Her leading man for this summer tour was actor Brooks West, a graduate of the University of Texas. He had been seen on TV opposite Marie Wilson in the series "My Friend Irma." On August 24, 1951, Eve married Brooks West at a friend's home in Bridgeport, Connecticut, with her two daughters as flower girls. Eve and *Here Today* were encouraged to return to close the Boston summer theatre season for the week of September 10. However, the box-office response was so great that the show remained a second week.

Returning to the West Coast for her "Our Miss Brooks" radio show, Eve signed with Twentieth Century-Fox for the episodic and often very funny *We're Not Married* (1952), in which she was cast

With Joan Crawford and John Qualen in **Goodbye, My Fancy** *(1951).*

as Paul Douglas' "wedded, bedded, and bored wife."

"Our Miss Brooks" had been on the air for five seasons when on Friday, October 3, 1952, CBS debuted its teleseries. The show used the same cast from the radio series except for Jeff Chandler, who was replaced by Robert Rockwell as Professor Philip Boynton, biology teacher. The series became more popular on television than it had been on radio. *Variety*, reviewing the opening telecast of the show's second season, wrote, "The punch lines go to Miss Arden, from whom all laughs flow. She's a past mistress of the type of humor and can time a gag with the precision of some of the best comedy minds. Uniquely, too, she is lacking in warmth, humility, and sympathy, the cardinal virtues of the successful mime, yet overrides these liabilities as a straight trader in laughs that seems to have caught on. It would be fun to have had her as a schoolteacher."

In 1953 Eve made *The Lady Wants Mink*, a less-than-amusing comedy, for Republic. On September 17, 1954, she gave birth to her first child. Eve and Brooks called him Douglas. (In 1952 they had adopted a son, Duncan.) With their enlarged family, they purchased Ronald Colman's former home on Hidden Valley Road in Thousand Oaks, California, in which Eve could pile her many years' collection of early-American antiques.

Radio's "Our Miss Brooks" lasted seven seasons, until 1954–55, and continued as a television property through the 1956–57 season. After filming the 154th segment at the Desilu Studios, the series ended. Its ratings had waned badly in the final months. Yet in 1956 Warner Bros. brought *Our Miss Brooks* to the screen, directed by Al Lewis, one of the original radio scripters of the show. The film was ill-timed as the television series had just about run its course, and the public's disinterest was evident when the movie died at the box office.

"Our Miss Brooks" had consumed nearly a decade of Eve's career, but she gained national recognition for her work. In 1952 the Teachers College of Connecticut rewarded "her contribution toward humanizing the American teacher" with a plaque and she received the radio industry's "woman of the year" award. In the 1953–54 season Eve was nominated as television's outstanding female performer along with Lucille Ball, Dinah Shore, Loretta Young, and Imogene Coca. Eve won the Emmy Award for her portrayal of Connie Brooks. She received nominations in future years, but only her sparkling playing of the perky Miss Brooks brought her the Emmy. Radio critic John Crosby defined Eve's enormous popularity as the schoolteacher, "There just isn't anyone in the business who can handle feline dialogue as well as Miss Arden."

On September 17, 1957, Eve became widow Liza Hammond in another teleseries, "It Gives Me Great Pleasure." But the shaky show was constantly revised and the title eventually became "The Eve Arden Show." Nothing helped and it was withdrawn after 26 weeks. Eve rejected offers to return to the stage in *The Marriage-Go-Round* (Claudette Colbert played the role) and *The Pink Jungle*. (In the latter misfire, Agnes Moorehead would be signed for Eve's intended part as co-lead with Ginger Rogers.) A West Coast tour in *Auntie Mame* starred Eve, lasting from August to December 1958. Brooks West was cast in the touring comedy as Beauregard Jackson Pickett Burnside. Many found Arden too one-dimensional and abrasive in her interpretation of the volatile title role.

Otto Preminger offered Eve the role of Maida, James Stewart's wisecracking secretary in *Anatomy of a Murder* (1959). It was an undemanding, stereotyped assignment, but it was exposure in a big picture and Eve accepted. She popped up as a guest on various television shows such as "Meet Cyd Charisse" and "The Red Skelton Show," and on variety programs like those hosted by Perry Como and Dinah Shore. In 1960 she returned to her old home lot for *The Dark at the Top of the Stairs*. Arden was cast as Lottie, Dorothy McGuire's nagging sister, overly prejudiced and loud. Her playing was almost caricature and she never reached the poignant or desperate characterization of Eileen Heckart in the Broadway production or Joan Blondell in the national touring company.

Summer theatres were beneficial, and welcome, to Eve. In 1960 she and Brooks West toured the circuits in *Goodbye, Charlie* and the following summer they were back co-starred in *The Marriage-Go-Round*. A two-year sabbatical from show business took the

West family to live in London and then in the Italian countryside.

In 1965 Eve returned to the stage to play the mother-in-law in *Barefoot in the Park* in Atlanta, Georgia. During that summer she and Brooks toured in *Plain and Fancy* and *Beekman Place*. She returned to movie-making on a lesser level. In American International's addle-brained comedy *Sergeant Deadhead* (1965), she was a WAF lieutenant who sings "You Should've Seen the One That Got Away" and cavorts with such comedians as Fred Clark and Gale Gordon. Frankie Avalon and Deborah Walley were the film's romantic leads.

On June 13, 1966, Eve succeeded Carol Channing at the Shubert Theatre in Chicago in *Hello Dolly!* which she played for four months, winning the Sarah Siddons Award for the best female performer of the year in Chicago. On television she was seen in episodes of "Laredo," "Bewitched," "Run for Your Life," and "The Man from U.N.C.L.E."

A new series, "The Mothers-in-Law," starring Eve with Kaye Ballard debuted on September 10, 1967. The show lasted two seasons and was not the success of "Our Miss Brooks." Nonetheless, admits Eve, "The show could have gone on; our ratings were good, but Desi Arnaz was causing trouble so NBC said 'Forget it.'"

In 1969 she made the telefilm *In Name Only*, playing a chic matron. On May 20, 1970, she opened at the Hartford Theatre in Hollywood as the Scarsdale matron who dotes on her blind son in *Butterflies Are Free*. The comedy went on to a successful run in Chicago. But when the tour was to continue eastward, Eve retired from the project and was replaced by Gloria Swanson. Eve was next seen in two segments of "Love, American Style." She then signed for a pre-Broadway tour in a new play with Brooks West, but the summer tryout of *Natural Ingredients* indicated it was not for Broadway.

With Buster Keaton and Fred Clark in Sergeant Deadhead *(1965).*

With Reginald
Gardiner, Cesar
Romero, and Gale
Gordon in Sergeant
Deadhead.

Edna May Oliver, Helen Broderick, and ZaSu Pitts had played spinster-detective-schoolteacher Hildegarde Withers on the screen and the crime-solving teacher seemed a natural for television. Eve was cast in the title role and the pilot for the proposed series was telecast on March 4, 1972, as "A Very Missing Person." But the proposed teleseries never materialized. That fall Eve was excellent as the super-efficient marriage coordinator for Robert Young's four daughters in the telefilm, *All My Darling Daughters*. In May 1973, Eve was back on the stage in San Diego in a new comedy, *Under Papa's Picture*. She was blithely funny in 1974 as Sally Field's flamboyant aunt in an episode of the TV series "The Girl with Something Extra," and showed up that year in a video special, *Mother of the Bride*. Like many other Hollywood and television stars, Eve has found financial advantages in doing television commercials, most recently extolling the virtues of a margarine.

On Sunday, October 19, 1975, Eve played a radio soap-opera star who is poisoned and shot on an episode of the "Ellery Queen" television series. For the country's bicentennial, Eve did a TV "Bicentennial Minute" on John Quincy Adams. She also completed a

CBS-TV pilot for another proposed series, "Harry and Maggie," which was tossed away after a summertime airing. (Neither Don Knotts as a small-town hardware-store owner and widower nor Eve as his "flamboyant and sophisticated" sister-in-law was much liked by reviewers in this outing.) In addition, Eve slipped into costume and makeup for a segment of TV's "Masquerade Party," dressed as a clown celebrating New Year's Eve.

In December 1975 Eve and her husband left for Australia, where Eve played Lauren Bacall's sparkling role in the musical *Applause!* The grande-dame bitchiness of the Margo Channing part brought her great audience response. Although Eve had temporarily left the U.S., she could still be seen on domestic screens in the Walt Disney comedy *The Strongest Man in the World* (1975), wherein she added moments of professional humor to the broad farce. As Aunt Harriet, the director of Crumbly Crunch cereal, she "makes the most of her distinctive catalogue of grimaces and inflections" (British *Films and Filming*).

In the summer of 1976 Eve was appearing on stage at Chicago's Drury Lane North Theatre in *Under Papa's Picture*, and in March 1977 she turned up on an episode of

59

"Maude" (CBS-TV) as the free-spirited, outrageous Aunt Lola, who has a penchant for older men. When *Grease* (Paramount, 1978), starring John Travolta and Olivia Newton-John went before the cameras in mid-1977, Eve was on hand as the perplexed high-school principal. In keeping with her academic promotion from "Our Miss Brooks" days, Arden had an oncamera secretary, played by Dody Goodman. Eve got to perform some of her famous doubletakes, snap out a few acidulous remarks to her Rydell High students, and lift her heels in dance.

Since then, Eve has continued to be as professionally busy as ever. She played with *Grease* co-actress Stockard Channing in a stage version of *Absurd Person Singular* in Los Angeles; helped co-hostess *CBS: On the Air* (March 31, 1978); and, in the telefeature *A Guide for the Married Woman* (ABC-TV, October 13, 1978), she joined Cybill Shepherd, Barbara Feldon, and Peter Marshall in a tale of infidelity performed for laughs. Eve was seen as the Employment Lady.

Of her best-remembered role as Madison High School's favorite English teacher, Eve says:

It's amazing to me that I still can't get away from Miss Brooks. I don't mind any more. After all, I did enjoy playing her very much—there was a lot of me in that character. I think part of the show's appeal was that I managed to make Miss Brooks a human being. I had none of that frightened awe so many people have of teachers, and the reason for this was that my aunt used to have a lot of young teachers as friends. So when I was growing up, I knew teachers on a social basis and I was fond of them—I even combed their hair.

At first, though, it did bother me to be so strongly pinned to one series because the height of my ambition was always to create a role on Broadway, something that was all mine, the way Judy Holliday did in *Born Yesterday*. But, gradually, I came to realize that Miss Brooks was it, so I might as well relax and enjoy it.

With Annette Charles and John Travolta in Grease *(1978).*

FEATURE FILMS

As Eunice Quedens:
The Song of Love (*Columbia 1929*)
Dancing Lady (*MGM 1933*)

As Eve Arden:
Oh, Doctor! (*Universal 1937*)
Stage Door (*RKO 1937*)
Cocoanut Grove (*Paramount 1938*)
Letter of Introduction (*Universal 1938*)
Having Wonderful Time (*RKO 1938*)
Women in the Wind (*Warner Bros. 1939*)
Big Town Czar (*Universal 1939*)
The Forgotten Woman (*Universal 1939*)
Eternally Yours (*United Artists 1939*)
At the Circus (*MGM 1939*)
A Child Is Born (*Warner Bros. 1940*)
Slightly Honorable (*United Artists 1940*)
Comrade X (*MGM 1940*)
No, No, Nanette (*RKO 1940*)
Ziegfeld Girl (*MGM 1941*)
That Uncertain Feeling (*United Artists 1941*)
She Couldn't Say No (*Warner Bros. 1941*)
She Knew All the Answers (*Columbia 1941*)
San Antonio Rose (*Universal 1941*)
Sing for Your Supper (*Columbia 1941*)
Manpower (*Warner Bros. 1941*)
Whistling in the Dark (*MGM 1941*)
The Last of the Duanes (*20th Century-Fox 1941*)
Obliging Young Lady (*RKO 1941*)
Bedtime Story (*Columbia 1941*)
Hit Parade of 1943 (*Republic 1943*)
Let's Face It (*Paramount 1943*)

Cover Girl (*Columbia 1944*)
The Doughgirls (*Warner Bros. 1944*)
Pan-Americana (*RKO 1945*)
Patrick the Great (*Universal 1945*)
Earl Carroll Vanities (*Republic 1945*)
Mildred Pierce (*Warner Bros. 1945*)
My Reputation (*Warner Bros. 1946*)
The Kid from Brooklyn (*RKO 1946*)
Night and Day (*Warner Bros. 1946*)
Song of Scheherazade (*Universal 1947*)
The Arnelo Affair (*MGM 1947*)
The Unfaithful (*Warner Bros. 1947*)
The Voice of the Turtle (*Warner Bros. 1947*)
One Touch of Venus (*Universal 1948*)
Whiplash (*Warner Bros. 1948*)
My Dream Is Yours (*Warner Bros. 1949*)
The Lady Takes a Sailor (*Warner Bros. 1949*)
Paid in Full (*Paramount 1950*)
Curtain Call at Cactus Creek (*Universal 1950*)
Tea for Two (*Warner Bros. 1950*)
Three Husbands (*United Artists 1950*)
Goodbye, My Fancy (*Warner Bros. 1951*)
We're Not Married (*20th Century-Fox 1952*)
The Lady Wants Mink (*Republic 1953*)
Our Miss Brooks (*Warner Bros. 1956*)
Anatomy of a Murder (*Columbia 1959*)
The Dark at the Top of the Stairs (*Warner Bros. 1960*)
Sergeant Deadhead (*American International 1965*)
The Strongest Man in the World (*Buena Vista 1975*)
Grease (*Paramount 1978*)

With Joan Bennett in Twin Beds *(1942).*

Mischa Auer

Irrepressible, high-strung, beanpole Mischa Auer became Hollywood's mad Russian. He was a champion scene stealer who could purloin sequences from other players and stars as easily as he could play roles of phony nobility. Tall (6'2"), lanky Mischa became a comedian through a quirk of casting, but he developed into one of the zaniest, wildest comics to cross the screen. In the Fifties he explained how he emerged as a comedian:

"I was usually a leering villain, killed in the first reel. Fortunately, in 1936, Gregory La-Cava decided I might do as a phony artist, something between a gigolo and a dilettante, in his picture *My Man Godfrey*. That's when I hit the Hollywood mother lode. That one role made a comedian out of me. I haven't been anything else since. It's paid off very well. Do you wonder that I'm flattered when people say I'm mad?"

For the 10 years following *Godfrey*, Auer's soulful, slightly popped eyes and gangling frame were seen in a constant flow of good, mediocre, and bad comedies. His portrayals were uninhibited, wild, and frequently overplayed. However, his dour Russian face and diverting way of delivering lines saved many pictures from eclipse. His attitude toward life was typically Russian. He theorized that life was an unexpected dividend and refused to get upset about anything. He reveled in living and was infatuated with nonsense.

He was born Mischa Ounskowski on Friday, November 17, 1905, the son of a Russian naval officer who was killed in the Russo-Japanese War. His mother was the daughter of onetime czarist violinist Leopold Auer. During the Bolshevik Revolution Mischa and his mother became separated and he was consigned to Siberia with a large group of other children. Mischa later related his childhood experiences: "We were such a problem [the roaming begging children sent to Siberia] they finally sent us back to St. Petersburg to find our families. I found my mother by chance and we went to the South of Russia, to a town near the front which had been taken by the White Russians. There still wasn't enough to eat. I learned then that there are no morals, no conventions, when your stomach is empty. You'll even eat dead horses. We did."

With his mother, Mischa escaped to Constantinople. The swarm of escaping humanity living in unspeakable conditions had to cope with an outbreak of typhus. Mischa's mother, trained by the Red Cross during the war, tended to the plague victims. But within two weeks she was dead. Mischa buried the typhus-ravaged body of his mother with his own hands. The young boy finally made his way to Florence, Italy, where his grandfather located him and brought him to America.

Living in New York with his maternal grandfather, Leopold Auer, Mischa took his mother's maiden name when he entered the Ethical Culture School. He displayed little interest in school but developed a lifelong interest in music. His grandfather, a famous violinist, was the teacher of Jascha Heifetz and Mischa Elman. While at Ethical Culture School, Mischa begged for the role of François Villon in the school's production of *If I Were King*. With school behind him, Mischa haunted Broadway agents' offices. Finally he was engaged for the Actor's Theatre revival of Ibsen's *The Wild Duck* (1925), in which a very young Helen Chandler startled Broadway with her performance as Hedvig. Mischa, as a walk-on, played a bewhiskered old man. He was 20 years old. He did other bits with Eva LeGallienne's company and had four small roles in Walter Hampden's *Cyrano de Bergerac* (1925), for which he received $20 a week.

Mischa played a footman in the Actor's Theatre production of *Morals* (1925) for 40 performances, and on January 3, 1926, he was Slim in an experimental staging of a play, *Dope*, that played matinees only at Manhattan's 48th Street Theatre. The following month he signed with actress Bertha Kalich for a national tour as the company's leading juvenile. For the next year he toured with Mme. Kalich playing Max von Wendlowski in Hermann Sudermann's *Magda* and Nils Olrik in *The Riddle Woman*. The Kalich company reached the West Coast in January 1927. There Auer met Paramount director Frank Tuttle, who offered him a small role in Esther Ralston's *Something Always Happens* (1928).

Auer loved California and the motion picture medium but said it took him three years to make a living in Hollywood. "It's a wonderful country and you can live on oranges and credit, and have a car to boot!" He became one of the youngest actors in Hollywood to play character men of varying ages, usually the heavy or an exotic foreign role. Somehow he managed to eke out a living. He was a faithful Hindu servant killed early in *Inside the Lines* (1930) and in Ronald Colman's *The Unholy Garden* (1931) he played the first of his many celluloid pretenders to royalty, Prince Nicolai Poliakoff. His movie roles at this time were generally quite brief, but his imposing appearance was usually memorable. Tiffany advertised his portrayal of Duke Charles in its *Command Performance* as one of the best of his career.

Friendship with Mr. and Mrs. Frank Tuttle led to Auer's meeting a dress-shop owner, Norma Tillman, an attractive, self-sufficient all-American girl with one-quarter Indian blood in her veins. When Norma announced to her parents that she was going to marry the sad-eyed Russian actor, they asked, "In a country full of Americans, why do you have to pick a barbarian?" Mischa shrugged his shoulders and retorted, "Tell 'em that's why! A barbarian you don't pick up on every street corner." His screen career, still a composite of sinister Orientals and the like, did not produce an income to match his extravagant, lordly lifestyle. But Norma's business income helped to pay the debts that Mischa shrugged off with his usual, "What difference will it make a hundred years from now?" They married in 1931.

In any moment of crisis Mischa, like the Prince Mikail Alexandrovitch Ouratieff in the play *Tovarich* (a role Auer would later play in a Parisian stage revival in 1953), would get into bed and sleep soundly. While Norma dealt with bill collectors and held their home together, Mischa continued in nondescript, small roles. His parts ranged from the butler in the Barrymores' *Rasputin and the Empress* (1932) to villainous, sinister parts that could be clarified by their names— Abu Zeyd (*The Unwritten Law*, 1932), Kassim (*Dangerously Yours*, 1933), Sadik (*Wharf Angel*, 1934), Amil (*Stamboul Quest*, 1934), Suraj Ud Dowlah (*Clive of India*, 1935), Afridi (*Lives of a Bengal Lancer*, 1935)—to portraying a priest in *Cradle Song* (1933) and a monk in *The Crusades* (1935). He played the piano well and was typecast as a pianist in Lily Pons' *I Dream Too Much* (1935) and was one

With Nobel Johnson and Sojin in Something Always Happens *(1928).*

With Vera Reynolds,
Martha Mattox, and
Sheldon Lewis in
The Monster Walks
(1932).

of four international detectives in Carole Lombard's amusing *The Princess Comes Across* (1936). Lombard's next picture established Mischa as one of Hollywood's most irrepressible comedians.

The genre of screwball comedies had been nurtured by Frank Capra's multi-Oscar-winning *It Happened One Night* (1934). Other entries in the genre soon followed. None was wackier, better acted, or better directed than Gregory LaCava's *My Man Godfrey* (1936). Starring Miss Lombard and her ex-husband, William Powell, it became one of the all-time classic fun films. The story related the reformation of the wealthy, slightly demented Bullock family by a butler named Godfrey (Powell).

For the role of the mad Russian gigolo Carlo, LaCava cast Mischa, for the director had seen the actor provide hilarity with his wild antics at many Hollywood cocktail parties. Alice Brady played the scatterbrained mother of the Bullock ménage, a wacky matron who adopted protégés and acquired zany musician Carlo. It is the ever-hungry Carlo who constantly delights his sponsor with frequent outbursts of "Otchi tchornia!"

a song Mrs. Bullock prefers to "The Star-Spangled Banner" because the words are all the same and easy to remember.

Mischa's performance was a captivating delight and his leaping onto a sofa to imitate a gorilla became one of the picture's more memorable scenes. LaCava's sophisticated, outrageously funny film established Auer as a top screwball-zany who could spark duller pictures with his buffoonery. (He would repeat his role of Carlo on "Lux Radio Theatre's" broadcast of *My Man Godfrey* on May 9, 1938.) For the 1936 Academy Award contest, William Powell and Carole Lombard were nominated for Best Actor and Actress of the Year and, in the first year of the Best Supporting Players category, Alice Brady and Mischa were among the nominees. But in February 1937, when the Oscars were handed out, none of the *My Man Godfrey* company received them.

By this time the Auers were the parents of a two-year-old child. Mischa explained naming his son Anthony: "If he is a serious artist, he'll be Anthony Auer. If he is a swing player, he'll be Tony Auer. Artists and spices are always in demand, no matter who is in power."

Auer's screen appearances become showier. He gave an excellent performance as a radical in *Winterset* (1936) and was fine as a member of Gene Raymond's band in Lily Pons' *That Girl from Paris* (1936). While making *The Gay Desperado* (1936), director Rouben Mamoulian went to great lengths to explain to Mischa how to run like an Aztec Indian, which the latter was playing, and finally decided he should run like a gazelle. Grave-faced, Auer inquired, "Male or female?"

Mischa signed a long-term Universal contract and performed in *We Have Our Moments*. Wrote *Photoplay*, "Mischa Auer as a French sleuth is a panic." His studio loaned him out for an excellent performance as suave movie star Rinaldo Lopez in MGM's *Pick a Star* (1937), to play Dimitri in Warner Bros.' *Marry the Girl* (1937), and to appear as Prince Muratov in United Artists' *Vogues of 1938* (1937). Of his performance in the last film, *Photoplay* carped, "He mouths his way through the entire film." In Universal's *One Hundred Men and a Girl* (1937) Auer was a jobless piccolo player, pressing his screen image into joyous focus in an excellent film.

While filming *It's All Yours* (1938), in which he performed with the lovely Madeleine Carroll, a scene required his falling into water fully dressed. After four takes, the company left the set in hopeless laughter. "When I came out of the water for the fourth time the whole set was deserted. I wanted to laugh so much I forgot my lines." The picture was stolen by Mischa as the Baron Rene de Montigny. The *New York Times* reported, "It is certainly a fortunate thing that Mischa Auer has a loyal public. For if he hadn't—if the audience didn't chortle with devoted glee every time he so much as shrugs his shoulders or rolls his eyes in *It's All Yours*—that weightless bauble would be declined with thanks."

For French actress Danielle Darrieux's American film debut, Universal selected a light, sprightly comedy directed by Henry Koster. In *The Rage of Paris* (1938) Mischa was on target as a distraught waiter named Mike. During the filming the actor broke up director Koster, who found it hard to film close-ups of the wild Russian. Koster finally gave up, "Do it yourself, Mischa. I won't look. I have seen many actors do many things, but

In Three Smart Girls *(1936).*

this is the first time I have seen a man turning his face inside out."

Since *My Man Godfrey*, Auer had had showy if insubstantial roles. It remained for Frank Capra to give him a very meaty part in Columbia's expensively mounted *You Can't Take It with You*. Mr. Capra would recall of the casting, "To play the threadbare Russian, Kolenkhov, there could be no one gloomier than the fallen-faced picture of doom itself— Mischa Auer." Again, amidst a family of elaborate eccentrics, Mischa was a standout as the ballet master Boris Kolenkhov (played on Broadway by George Tobias). As the Soviet, Mischa wore a pointed goatee and a swirling cape. His stock answer to queries about the Monte Carlo Ballet, the Russian Revolution, and one of the family's daughters who is more inspired than talented for ballet was, "Confidentially, it *stinks.*"

Auer garnered laughs as Russian nobleman Bobenko in *Service de Luxe* (1938), an otherwise dreary picture salvaged by the expert playing of the supporting cast with little assistance from star Constance Bennett. Mischa, as an excitable belligerent playwright, separated the onscreen team of Jeanette MacDonald and Nelson Eddy in MGM's *Sweethearts* (1938). (The role could have been easily, and with greater finesse, played by Auer's fellow Russian, Gregory Ratoff.) For Universal's *East Side of Heaven* (1939) Auer played Nicky (wearing a boxer's bathrobe labeled "Moscow Golden Gloves— 1919"), getting the bulk of the laughs in this Bing Crosby picture. Mischa told the press, about scene-stealing Baby Sandy (Henville), "Bing and I fell in love with the kid, so we just let her have all the scenes. She'd have taken them anyway!" Auer would support Baby Sandy in two more features, *Unexpected Father* (1939) and *Sandy Is a Lady* (1940).

In 1939 Mischa made his first film with Marlene Dietrich. In *Destry Rides Again* he

With Charlie Ruggles, Joy Hughes, Constance Bennett, Vincent Price, and Helen Broderick in a pose for Service de Luxe (1938).

was Boris Callahan, who loses his pants in a poker game to the glamorous Marlene, leading to the battle royal between his wife (Una Merkel) and Dietrich. The following year he played a part-time magician and pickpocket, Sasha, companion to island-rover Marlene, in *Seven Sinners*. The same year he was cast as an unlikely cowhand, doubling as a medicine-show Indian and a Mexican matador Bolo, in the tongue-in-cheek comic Western *Trail of the Vigilantes*. His personal life was less successful than his film activities. He and his wife, Norma, separated and then she filed for divorce.

Mischa soon became a ladies' man about town, dating Maria Montez (under contract to Universal) and other lovelies. On screen he was Zolotov, Dietrich's former Russian lover, in *The Flame of New Orleans* (1941). He finished 1941 playing supporting roles in minor Universal programmers, including Maria Montez' *Moonlight in Hawaii*, but did add some hilarity to Olsen and Johnson's screen version of their stage insanity *Hellzapoppin*.

At the end of November 1941 Mischa was persuaded to return to the stage and to Broadway. While in New York he decided to rewed. One-half hour after receiving a call from the West Coast that his final divorce decree was signed and legal, he and radio singer Joyce Hunter applied for a marriage license on December 2, 1941. Two days later they were married at city hall by his honor the mayor, Fiorello LaGuardia. Mischa's grandmother, Mrs. Leopold Auer, and his close friend, Youka Troubetzkoy, were witnesses. The newlyweds honeymooned at Manhattan's Hotel Dorset and Mischa started rehearsals for a new Broadway musical.

The show, *The Lady Comes Across*, was one of the most ill-fated of the early Forties. England's Jessie Matthews, signed to star in the musical, had a nervous breakdown in Boston during tryouts and was replaced by Evelyn Wyckoff. The scenery and costumes

With Olsen and Johnson in Hellzapoppin (1941).

had been salvaged from a prior year's outing that never reached Broadway. But the talented cast (including Joe E. Lewis, Mischa, Gower Champion, and Wynn Murray) made a game effort to put across the Vernon Duke–John LaTouche score, with choreography by George Balanchine. The show opened on January 9, 1942, and closed the next night. Mischa received some very bad reviews. One critic observed, "Mischa Auer should stick to pictures, for stage work can only detract rather than enhance a talent that has so little variation and light or shade. Possibly out of desperation, he's finally clad in women's clothing, one of the oldest comedy tricks, and even there he doesn't achieve a humorous effect. Unfortunately there are no retakes in a stage musical comedy."

The year 1942 was not one of Mischa's shining seasons. Following the Broadway fiasco, he and his new wife did an extensive vaudeville tour. While on the road he learned that his ex-wife had committed suicide. By May 1942 Mischa and wife, Joyce, were back in Hollywood telling reporters about the discomforts of playing vaudeville. Referring to hecklers in the audience, he said, "I never had to think so fast in my life; I was like a prizefighter warding off blows from all sides. If you let them get your goat, you're through. So I just kidded them back and, after a while, I got to like it." If he sang, someone would shout for "Otchi tchornia," which had virtually become Auer's identification and theme song. Dialogue that missed the laughter mark was greeted by hecklers with "Confidentially, that steeenks!" His Hollywood fame had caught up with him. But he could not catch up with Hollywood.

By now the total screwball, pseudosophisticated zany that Auer played so often in films had begun to pale. New talents had arrived at other studios and had gained public approval. Escapist film fare ground out for a country at war veered from the requirements of a mad Russian and consequently Mischa's roles were less demanded. An excellent opportunity, however, did arise when he was assigned the standout Danny Kaye Broadway role in Paramount's filming of *Lady in the Dark*. The screen musical was begun in December 1942 but withheld from release until February 1944. The film did not live up to people's expectations, and there was much

disappointment in Ginger Rogers' pivotal performance, a far cry from the joyous interpretation given the part on Broadway by Gertrude Lawrence. And in the course of production, Mischa's role as the swish temperamental photographer was cut down to an oversized bit.

Photoplay appraised his screen work in RKO's *Around the World* (1943) as "Mischa Auer grows cornier by the Auer." But as the Russian waiter frenetically trying to retrieve a misguided bit of lingerie in *Up in Mabel's Room* (1944), Auer added some spots of hilarity.

Mischa's personal life, meanwhile, was having its rocky moments. He was expelled as vice president of the Russian-American Club of Los Angeles on December 7, 1944, because of his proclaimed support of Governor Thomas Dewey for President and his alleged derogatory remarks about the glories of Mother Russia. And his marriage was quaking.

The following year he shared comedy honors with June Havoc in a remake of *Brewster's Millions*. In the Ernst Lubitsch production *A Royal Scandal* (1945), ponderously directed by Otto Preminger, Mischa, as Captain Sukov, supported star Tallulah Bankhead. Before the year ended he made the press columns again when he chased a burglar from his home over a backyard fence. Mischa broke his leg. His final film of the year was Rene Clair's exceptionally well-paced *And Then There Were None*. The murder mystery was based on the Agatha Christie novel and play *Ten Little Indians*, providing Mischa with the role of Prince Nikki Starloff, who is killed in the first reel with a poisonous after-dinner drink.

Since movie offers were dwindling for Mischa, he returned to the stage. He joined the cast of *The Temporary Mrs. Smith*, written by Jacqueline Susann and Beatrice Cole and directed by Hollywood comic Billy Gilbert. The show opened on September 13, 1946, in Wilmington, Delaware. Two weeks later the play folded in Baltimore. Revised, the production tried out again, in Philadelphia in November 1946, then closed in Toronto. The show went through production and cast changes and finally opened in New York on December 25, 1946, retitled *Lovely Me*. It closed after 37 performances. The critics wrote of Mischa, "Auer plays his customary role, complete with manual flourishes, grimaces, and hokum."

Mischa made two minor films and then in the summer of 1948 did a summer theatre tour as the dictatorial producer in *Twentieth Century*, co-starring with Haila Stoddard. Subsequently he divorced Joyce Hunter, married Susanne Kalish, the daughter of a college professor, and left for Europe to make French films. In the summer of 1952 he again toured the straw-hat circuit in the United States, first in *Twentieth Century* and then in *The Happy Time*. The next summer he starred in *The Play's the Thing*.

His home was now in Salzburg, Austria, and he found work in Continental films and for Radio Free Europe. He appeared on the Paris stage in a successful revival of *Tovarich* (1953). After several French film flops, he was reunited with Marlene Dietrich on-camera. It was *The Monte Carlo Story* (1958), filmed in Rome; it was a rather boring comedy. For Brigitte Bardot's *Mam'zelle Pigalle* (1958), Auer once more played a ballet mas-ter. But neither the role nor the film in any way resembled the happier days of *You Can't Take It with You*.

He was cast as a Russian scientist in *Au Pied, au Cheval et Par Spoutnik* (1960), a bizarre French film. He was credited with offering a good straight performance. At about this time he became a resident of the Spanish fishing village Merbella. In 1962 he made two films in England: Orson Welles' complicated *Mr. Arkadin* and the not very funny naval farce *We Joined the Navy*, with Lloyd Nolan, in which Mischa played the colonel-president.

After a few more French films, Auer returned to the States to appear as Baron Popoff in the Lincoln Center Music Theatre's production of *The Merry Widow*. It opened on August 17, 1964, and ran for 40 performances. At last Auer's stage notices were good. The *New York Times* printed, "Mischa Auer is, after all, one of the great comics. Head down a little, jowls flapping, his ripe Marsovian accent rolling through the house, his eyes popping, he dominated the performance."

With Vittorio De Sica (right) in The Monte Carlo Story *(1957).*

The Merry Widow, starring Patrice Munsel, with Bob Wright and Auer, went on a road tour. As the season progressed, Auer's performance digressed until he was missing his lines; he had given up any pretense of playing the Marsovian character and was hamming it up, playing to the audience for laughs. But he carried the show, which ended its tour in Chicago in mid-January 1965.

It was in 1965 that Mischa was divorced by his third wife. On September 4 of that year he wed Elise Souls of Gloversville, New York. They returned to Europe and lived in Rome. Auer made two last films. The Christmas That Almost Wasn't (1966) would bore any child over six. In the Tony Curtis flop, Arrivederci, Baby! (1966), Mischa was seen briefly as Romeo.

Back in 1959 Mischa had suffered a heart attack. On March 5, 1967, he died in Rome from a second seizure. Yet another member of Hollywood's Golden Age had passed away.

In retrospect, madcap Mischa added a good deal of zest to many films during the Thirties. Though his brand of comedy, like that of many other screen humorists, has lost favor, Mischa Auer remains an integral part of the history of Hollywood comedy.

FEATURE FILMS

Something Always Happens (Paramount 1928)

Marquis Preferred (Paramount 1929)

The Studio Murder Mystery (Paramount 1929)

The Benson Murder Case (Paramount 1930)

Paramount on Parade (Paramount 1930)

Just Imagine (Fox 1930)

Inside the Lines (RKO 1930)

The Unholy Garden (United Artists 1931)

Command Performance (Tiffany 1931)

Drums of Jeopardy (Tiffany 1931)

Women Love Once (Paramount 1931)

The Lady from Nowhere (Chesterfield 1931)

The Yellow Ticket (Fox 1931)

Delicious (Fox 1931)

Murder at Dawn (Big Four 1932)

Rasputin and the Empress (MGM 1932)

The Monster Walks (Mayfair 1932)

Midnight Patrol (Monogram 1932)

No Greater Love (Columbia 1932)

Sinister Hands (Willis Kent 1932)

Drifting Souls (Tower 1932)

Beauty Parlor (Chesterfield 1932)

Scarlet Dawn (Warner Bros. 1932)

The Unwritten Law (Majestic 1932)

The Western Code (Columbia 1932)

The Intruder (Allied 1932)

Dangerously Yours (Fox 1933)

Sucker Money (Willis Kent 1933)

The Infernal Machine (Fox 1933)

The Flaming Signal (Invincible 1933)

Corruption (Imperial 1933)

Tarzan the Fearless (Principal 1933) [serial and feature]

After Tonight (RKO 1933)

Cradle Song (Paramount 1933)

Girl Without a Room (Paramount 1933)

Woman Condemned (Marcy Pictures 1934)

The Crosby Case (Universal 1934)

Wharf Angel (Paramount 1934)

Bulldog Drummond Strikes Back (United Artists 1934)

Stamboul Quest (MGM 1934)

Mystery Woman (Fox 1935)

Clive of India (United Artists 1935)

Lives of a Bengal Lancer (Paramount 1935)

Murder in the Fleet (MGM 1935)

The Crusades (Paramount 1935)

I Dream Too Much (RKO 1935)

The Adventures of Rex and Rinty (Mascot serial 1935)

We're Only Human (RKO 1936)

Tough Guy (MGM 1936)

The House of a Thousand Candles (Republic 1936)

One Rainy Afternoon (United Artists 1936)

Sons o' Guns (Warner Bros. 1936)

The Princess Comes Across (Paramount 1936)

My Man Godfrey (Universal 1936)

The Gay Desperado (United Artists 1936)

Winterset (RKO 1936)

That Girl from Paris (RKO 1936)

Three Smart Girls (Universal 1937)

We Have Our Moments (Universal 1937)

Top of the Town (*Universal 1937*)
Pick a Star (*MGM 1937*)
Marry the Girl (*Warner Bros. 1937*)
Vogues of 1938 (*United Artists 1937*)
One Hundred Men and a Girl (*Universal 1937*)
Merry-Go-Round of 1938 (*Universal 1937*)
Prescription for Romance (*Universal 1937*)
It's All Yours (*Columbia 1938*)
The Rage of Paris (*Universal 1938*)
You Can't Take It with You (*Columbia 1938*)
Service de Luxe (*Universal 1938*)
Little Tough Guys in Society (*Universal 1938*)
Sweethearts (*MGM 1938*)
East Side of Heaven (*Universal 1939*)
Unexpected Father (*Universal 1939*)
Destry Rides Again (*Universal 1939*)
Alias the Deacon (*Universal 1940*)
Sandy Is a Lady (*Universal 1940*)
Margie (*Universal 1940*)
Spring Parade (*Universal 1940*)
Public Deb No. 1 (*20th Century–Fox 1940*)
Seven Sinners (*Universal 1940*)
Trail of the Vigilantes (*Universal 1940*)
The Flame of New Orleans (*Universal 1941*)
Cracked Nuts (*Universal 1941*)
Hold That Ghost (*Universal 1941*)
Sing Another Chorus (*Universal 1941*)
Moonlight in Hawaii (*Universal 1941*)
Hellzapoppin' (*Universal 1941*)
Twin Beds (*United Artists 1942*)
Don't Get Personal (*Universal 1942*)
Around the World (*RKO 1943*)
Lady in the Dark (*Paramount 1944*)

Up in Mabel's Room (*United Artists 1944*)
Brewster's Millions (*United Artists 1945*)
A Royal Scandal (*20th Century–Fox 1945*)
And Then There Were None (*20th Century–Fox 1945*)
Sentimental Journey (*20th Century–Fox 1946*)
She Wrote the Book (*Universal 1946*)
For You I Die (*Film Classics 1947*)
Sofia (*Film Classics 1948*)
Futures Vedettes (*French 1950*)
Bachelor in Paris [Song of Paris] (*British 1952*)
Frou-Frou (*French 1955*)
En Effeuillant La Marguerite (*French 1956*)
Mannequins de Paris (*French 1956*)
Mam'zelle Pigalle [That Naughty Girl] (*French 1958*)
Tabarin (*French 1958*)
The Monte Carlo Story (*United Artists 1958*)
Nathalie [The Foxiest Girl in Paris] (*French 1958*)
Au Pied, au Cheval et Par Spoutnik (*French 1960*)
Mr. Arkadin [Confidential Report] (*Filmorsa Productions 1962*)
We Joined the Navy (*British 1962*)
Les Femmes d'Abord [Ladies First] (*French 1963*)
Dynamite Girl (*French 1963*)
The Christmas That Almost Wasn't (*Childhood 1966*)
Arrivederci, Baby! [Drop Dead, Darling!] (*Paramount 1966*)

With Jack Oakie in a publicity shot for Affairs of Annabelle *(1938).*

Lucille Ball

"Even in those *B* pictures, the only thing I really wanted to do was to make people laugh," states Lucille Ball, America's most beloved funny lady who somehow never really became a superstar in motion pictures. Before the premiere of "I Love Lucy" on the CBS-TV network on October 15, 1951, Lucy had labored for nearly 20 years in Hollywood film mills: a decorative bit player at Columbia, a serviceable ingenue at RKO, a gloriously gowned, tastefully lacquered, vocally dubbed attraction in some of MGM's glossier wartime products. But never did her screen work totally prepare the public for the red-headed dynamo who became videoland's most irresistible attraction.

Lucy's show-business endeavors span a half century, and her efforts have ranged from modeling to radio to the Broadway stage. Yet her familiarity as a television star has somehow limited (and overshadowed) her degree of success in these other areas. It seems that all other efforts pale before her 179 episodes of "I Love Lucy," 156 adventures in "The Lucy Show," and 144 entries of "Here's Lucy." When in the summer of 1974 Lucy announced her retirement from the TV series arena, *TV Guide* dubbed its Lucy cover story "End of an Era" and published the awesome "The Lucy Book of Records":

MOST SHOWS, CAREER: 495—179 episodes of the original "I Love Lucy," 156 of "The Lucy Show," 144 "Here's Lucy," and 16 specials.

TOTAL VIEWING TIME: 10 days, 15½ hours.

PAPER CRISIS: Lucy and company have used about two tons' worth for their scripts.

KIND TO ANIMALS: Lucy has worked with dozens of animals on her show, including lions, tigers, sheep, goats, penguins, porpoises, chimpanzees, horses, bears, cats, birds, pigs, and dogs of all descriptions.

CHARACTERS PLAYED: More than three dozen, including showgirl, ballet dancer, chauffeur, Indian, bricklayer, bullfighter, grape stomper (in a famous wine-making episode), fight manager, nurse, process server, saxophone player in an all-nun band, Martian, knight in armor, pool hustler, astronaut, softball player, Little League coach, cellist, drummer, violinist, ukulele player, kangaroo, pickle, and front end of a horse—usually with disastrous results.

COSTUMES DRESSED IN: More than 1,500, accounting for some 7,500 yards of cloth—enough to wrap a very sizable mummy (which Lucy has *not* played).

PICKLES BEEN IN: Countless, though one per episode would be fairly close. They include: being frozen, getting coated with chocolate, being starched, innumerable soakings, falling out of a helicopter, skiing down a flight of stairs, sliding down a fire pole, having knives thrown at her, getting hand-cuffed, and having a loving cup stuck on her head.

CELEBRITIES IMPERSONATED: At one time or another, Lucy has appeared as Harpo Marx, Charlie Chaplin, Tallulah Bankhead, and one-third of the Andrews Sisters.

EMPLOYMENT OFFICE: More than 3,000 actors, plus her son and daughter, have appeared on Lucy's shows in the past 23 years.

Unfortunately, complete records were not always kept in the early days of Lucy's career, and we must sadly report that such significant statistics as MOST BLACKED-OUT TEETH, CAREER, and CUSTARD PIES, PER EPISODE MOST THROWN are lost to history.

Serenaded by CBS-TV in 1976, with a special toasting her 25 years on the network, Lucy herself recently quipped in an interview, "Stardom came late, my children came late. It's like the first 20 years in Hollywood didn't even exist." But for a quarter of a century Lucille Ball reigned over the realm of television situation comedy, deposed in recent years by the emergence of explicit, humorous sordidness.

She was born Lucille Desirée Ball on Sunday, August 6, 1911, in Jamestown, New York, daughter of Henry Dunnell Ball (a telephone company worker) and his wife, Desirée Hunt. Mr. Ball died in 1915; Mrs. Ball remarried (to salesman Ed Peterson) but quickly divorced. She raised her daughter in Jamestown while working in a dress shop.

Lucy's first brush with entertaining came when her mother enrolled her at the Chautauqua Institution to take piano lessons. Though she never mastered the piano, Lucy became attracted to the idea of performing and embarked on a pursuit of stage success that would squelch the ambitions of almost anybody else. In 1926 she enrolled at New York City's John Murray Anderson–Robert Milton drama school. Her instructor's verdict was,

"Lucy's wasting her time and mine. She's too shy and reticent to put her best foot forward." Lucy's comment, "I was a tongue-tied teenager spellbound by the school's star pupil—Bette Davis." The drama school reject then decided to audition for stage work without a drama academy diploma, and in 1927 was fired from two different chorus lines: the third road company of *Rio Rita* and a pre-Broadway musical, *Step Lively.* Between these misadventures, the blonde, shapely Lucy (then using the nickname Montana) paid rent by working as a salesgirl, a soda jerk, and a model for artist Roger Furse, who delineated some revealing portraits of the aspiring actress in his Manhattan studio.

"My ambition wasn't high. I just wanted to work," recalls Lucy of these unpredictable days. With the new name of Diane Belmont, Lucy tried modeling—with more successful results. She became steadily employed as a Seventh Avenue dress model, and soon joined the lovely ranks of the Hattie Carnegie line, sometimes displaying several dozen outfits a day. This engagement led to an offer from Liggett & Myers, which was producing Chesterfield cigarette posters. The firm's national ad campaign led to Lucy appearing (in a bit, along with another aspiring hopeful, Ann Sothern) in *Broadway Thru a Keyhole* (United Artists, 1933). More important, it led to Lucy's being picked as one of the dozen "Goldwyn Girls," all imported to Hollywood to appear in *Roman Scandals* (1933), a Busby Berkeley-choreographed extravaganza starring Eddie Cantor.

Lucy herself has commented on the road she took from backup beauty to leading player: "I came out to Hollywood to do an Eddie Cantor picture with 12 or 14 showgirls, right? They had more experience, more money, knew their way around. Yet I made it and they didn't. Why? Maybe because they turned down more working jobs or social opportunities and I did just the opposite. As a result, I've never been out of work in this town except for two hours once between contracts."

The spunk and determination of the novice in competitive Hollywood were indeed remarkable. Following her negligible stint in *Roman Scandals*, Lucy managed to decorate the backgrounds of such 1934 Goldwyn productions as *Nana, Bulldog Drummond*

Strikes Back, and *Kid Millions* (another Cantor musical epic). She crashed the Fox gate to play in a number of bits in pictures such as the musical *Bottoms Up* (1934), invaded the Columbia Pictures lot for a spot in Frank Capra's *Broadway Bill* (1934), and remained at Columbia where she signed a player's contract in the fall of 1934.

Lucy's status at Columbia was hardly noteworthy. She did dumb blonde bits in the Three Stooges' short *Three Little Pigskins* and Leon Errol's two-reeler *Perfectly Mismated,* and then received screen billing—finally—in the feature *Carnival* (1935) in which she played a nurse. Lucy was delighted by her professional progress and sent for her family (mother, grandfather, brother, cousin) to join her in her new house in Hollywood Hills. They all arrived and almost simultaneously Columbia dropped her screen option.

However, with her usual fortitude and ambition, Lucy managed to interest high-class RKO in her motion picture potential. The studio which Lucy would later own placed the girl in its Little Theatre project and enrolled her in the acting classes of Lela Rogers (Ginger's mother). Good parts took a while to arrive: she had a bit as a model in Irene Dunne–Fred Astaire–Ginger Rogers' *Roberta* (1935), paraded through *The Three Musketeers* (1935), was a flower girl with one line in Astaire-Rogers' *Top Hat* (1935), played a girlfriend of Ginger in the Astaire-Rogers' *Follow the Fleet* (1936), and so on. Distraught at her lack of progress, Lucy returned to the East to join the cast of the Broadway-bound *Hey Diddle Diddle.* The lackluster show opened January 21, 1937, in Princeton, New Jersey, and closed in Washington, D.C., on February 13, 1937.

But her career perked up back at RKO. Lucy was assigned the role of wisecracking Judy Caulfield in the glittering screen version of *Stage Door* (1937) starring Katharine Hepburn and Ginger Rogers. Lucy responded well to Gregory LaCava's direction. The critics and the public responded well to Lucy, and RKO gave her a pay boost and some leading-lady assignments. She and young Ann Miller were the female leads in the Marx Brothers' unsatisfying *Room Service* (1938). She played the hooker who boards the plane headed for a crash landing in the headhunter-infested jungles of the popular *Five Came Back* (1939). Ball stooged for Kay Kyser and His Kollege of Musical Knowledge in *That's Right—You're Wrong* (1939). She stripped while singing (actually mouthing the words to) "Oh Momma, What Do I Do Now?" in *Dance, Girl, Dance* (1940). Here Lucy and Maureen O'Hara vied for Louis Hayward's attention. The *New York Herald-Tribune* labeled this Dorothy Arzner-directed feature "a springboard for the new star's rise." But it was more than that for Lucy; it was the locale for her first meeting with Desi Arnaz.

Arnaz* was in Hollywood to repeat the role he had played in the Broadway version of the

* He was born Desiderio Arnaz y de Acha on March 3, 1917, in Santiago, Cuba, where his father was mayor. The 1933 revolution put his father temporarily in jail and chased his mother and Desi to Miami. After odd jobs he joined a rumba band at the Roney-Plaza Hotel and later became a vocalist with the Xavier Cugat Orchestra. Then he formed his own band which toured. Later he was offered a leading part by George Abbott in the Broadway show *Too Many Girls.* This led to the offer from RKO, where he also played in *Father Takes a Wife* (1941), *Four Jacks and a Jill* (1941), and *The Navy Comes Through* (1942). He went to MGM for *Bataan* (1943) and after service in World War II was at Universal for *Cuban Pete* (1946) and then at Columbia for *Holiday in Havana* (1949).

In his autobiography, *A Book* (1976), Arnaz writes:

The first time that I saw Lucille Ball, she had just come from a stage where she had been filming *Dance, Girl, Dance* with Maureen O'Hara, in which they both played burlesque queens.

She had just finished a scene with Miss O'Hara, in which they had been in a big fight, and her hair was all over her face, she had a black eye and she was dressed in a cheap costume.

After she left, I asked, "Who the hell was that?"

"That's Lucille Ball," came the answer.

Later that afternoon at the studio, when I was going over some music with the band, I saw this girl come in. She was dressed in a pair of tight-fitting beige slacks and a yellow sweater, and had beautiful blonde hair and blue eyes.

I said, "Man, this is a hunk of woman!" And my companion, who'd been with me earlier, answered, "You met her today. That's Lucille Ball."

"That's Lucille Ball? She sure doesn't look anything like she did this morning."

"Hello," she said as she walked up to me.

I asked, "Miss Ball?" Like I wasn't sure I had met her before.

"Why don't you call me Lucille and I'll call you Dizzy."

"Okay, Lucille, but it's not Dizzy."

"Oh? How do you say it? Daisy?"

"No, Daisy is a flower, it's Desi—DESI."

The next few lines I used were the oldest in history—and the corniest. "Do you know how to rumba, Lucille?"

"No, I've never learned."

"Would you like me to teach you to rumba?"

And the rest is history. . . .

musical *Too Many Girls*. RKO was producing the film and Lucy was the leading lady. (Her two songs, "I Didn't Know What Time It Was" and "You're Nearer," were dubbed by Trudy Erwin.) The couple would later embark on a personal appearance tour to promote the picture, and they were soon very much in love. On November 11, 1940, 29-year-old Lucy married 23-year-old Desi in Greenwich, Connecticut (they later remarried in a Roman Catholic ceremony in California).

After the marriage Lucy returned to RKO where she was then earning (as Queen of the B Pictures) about one-half of the $100,000 per annum that Arnaz was reaping with his band engagements and recordings. Unexciting projects materialized for Lucy.* She was the femme stooge of Charlie McCarthy in *Look Who's Laughing* (1941) and the heroine of the oater *Valley of the Sun* (1942). But Carole Lombard, a pal of Lucy's, came to the rescue. She introduced Ball to Damon Runyon, whose story "Little Pinks" was about to become RKO's *The Big Street* (1942). Runyon thought Lucy would be fine as the bitchy golddigger Gloria who is knocked down a flight of stairs and crippled. Subsequently busboy Henry Fonda lavishes love on the ungrateful gal. Obviously dubbed vocals in her chanteuse sequences (courtesy of Martha Mears) did not discourage James Agee, leading U.S. film critic, from enthusing, "Pretty Lucille Ball, who was born for the parts Ginger Rogers sweats over, tackles her 'emotional' role as if it were sirloin and she didn't care who was looking." Lucy, as well as most everyone else, believed this personal acting triumph would boost her to top roles at the studio. Ironically, increasingly modest RKO decided it would be unable to afford her screen services any longer and allowed her option to lapse.

But MGM was interested in Lucy and she was signed to its stable of glittering stars. Situated in the former dressing room of recently departed Norma Shearer, Lucy made her Metro debut in the Ethel Merman stage role of *DuBarry Was a Lady* (1943). Her co-star was Red Skelton; her singing was again dubbed by Martha Meers. She replaced pregnant Lana Turner in *Best Foot Forward* (1943)—singing by Gloria Grafton; joined Ann Sothern and Marsha Hunt in a sequence with Frank Morgan in the revue *Thousands Cheer* (1943); paraded through the tedious musical *Meet the People* (1944) with Dick Powell, Vaughn Monroe, and Spike Jones; essayed another gorgeous wisecracker in the Spencer Tracy–Katharine Hepburn *Without Love* (1945); cameoed in *Abbott and Costello in Hollywood* (1945); and was a pink, beplumed, whip-cracking eyeful in the Fred Astaire "Bring on the Girls" number in *Ziegfeld Follies* (1946). In her best Metro showcase she played the role of Gladys Benton in *Easy to Wed* (1946)—a remake of *Libeled Lady* (1936)—with Van Johnson, Esther Williams, Keenan Wynn, and Lucy in the parts originally played by William Powell, Myrna Loy, Spencer Tracy, and Jean Harlow. It was a rousing romp for Lucy in which she mouthed the dubbed lyrics to the zesty "Continental Polka." But her position at MGM as a singing musical attraction who required constant dubbing wore on her ego.* She left the opulent lot after the unmemorable *Two Smart People* (1946) with John Hodiak.

For a time Lucy freelanced. She appeared as sex maniac bait in the thriller *Lured* (1947), returned to Columbia for one unfunny comedy, *Her Husband's Affairs* (1947), and then toured for 22 weeks in the Elmer Rice stage show *Dream Girl* (giving a superb performance). On radio Lucy could be heard in the very popular CBS series "My Favorite Husband" (July 1947–March 1951) with Richard Denning as her co-star. She cut up beautifully onscreen with Bob Hope in two Paramount releases: *Sorrowful Jones* (1949—a remake of *Little Miss Marker*) and *Fancy Pants* (1950—a remake of *Ruggles of Red Gap*).

In the meantime, a show-business phenomenon was formulating. In 1951 Arnaz began finalizing plans to create for himself and Lucy their own comedy series for the TV medium. Borrowing $8,000 he formed Desilu

* At one point when Barbara Stanwyck had rejected the role of stripper Sugarpuss O'Shea for Samuel Goldwyn's *Ball of Fire* (1941), Lucy was considered for this RKO release. Then Miss Stanwyck reconsidered, and Lucy was returned to programmer fare.

* Lucy was mentioned for the lead female role in *Yolanda and the Thief* (1945) opposite Fred Astaire, but Lucille Bremer won that role as she did the sequences opposite Astaire in *Ziegfeld Follies* (1946), another assignment possibility touted for Ball. It was Angela Lansbury who replaced Lucy as the club singer opposite William Powell in *The Hoodlum Saint* (1946).

With unknown
player, Kenny
Bowers (2nd from
left), and Tommy
Dix in Best Foot
Forward (1943).

In Lover Come Back (1946).

With Eddie Albert in The
Fuller Brush Girl *(1950).*

Productions, Inc., hired Lucy's writers (Jess
Oppenheimer, Madalyn Pugh, and Bob Carroll) from "My Favorite Husband," secured
Vivian Vance and William Frawley to play
the neighboring Mertzes, and contracted veteran cinematography wizard Karl Freund to
film the situation comedy. Arnaz then sold
the first show to sponsor Philip Morris ciga-
rettes. On Monday, October 15, 1951, the
half-hour program "I Love Lucy" premiered
on CBS.

Perhaps the most famous of all teleseries,
"I Love Lucy" became an American institution. Filmed before a live audience, the program won Lucy Emmy Awards in 1952 and
1955. (She has been Emmy-nominated 11
times in her TV career. She would later win
Emmies in 1966 and 1967 for her "Here's
Lucy" half-hours.) In November 1976 Lucy
spoke to the *New York Times* of her years
with the show:

"The believability of all our unbelievable
situations is what made it funny. It wasn't

just slapstick comedy. It was a new thing
called 'situation comedy,' which had a beginning, a middle, and a happy ending in which
we put all the pieces back together. . . .

"It wasn't my genius. It was the genius of
craftsmen behind the scenes, and rehearsing
over and over again until we had it down
perfect. Some people try to make perfection a
four-letter word, but it isn't. I learned that
from Buster Keaton—he told me never to
trust anybody else with my props—and my
writers. We had great identification with
millions of people who, whether they could
understand all the words or not, could tell
that the boss' hat was being knocked off.
They could identify with my problems, my
zaniness, my wanting to do everything, my
scheming and plotting, the way I cajoled my
husband. People identified with the Ricardos
because we had the same problems they had.

"Desi and I weren't your ordinary Hollywood couple on TV. We turned down those
scripts from the very beginning. We lived

Publicity shot with Desi Arnaz and James Mason for Forever, Darling (1956).

in a brownstone somewhere in Manhattan, and paying the rent, getting a new dress, getting a stale fur collar on an old cloth coat, and buying a piece of furniture were all worth a story.

"People could identify with those things—babysitters, traveling, wanting to be entertained, wanting to be loved in a certain way—the two couples on the show were constantly doing things that people all over the country were doing. We just took ordinary situations and exaggerated them. That's exactly it."

While "I Love Lucy" ran and ran, Lucy and Desi considered feature-film offers. They rejected a bid from Universal to star in *Policewoman*, but did agree to return to MGM for *The Long, Long Trailer* (1954). It was a situation comedy—albeit in widescreen and color—very much in the vein of their TV show; it grossed $4,291,000 in U.S. and Canadian rentals. In 1956 they filmed for MGM release the less-satisfying *Forever, Darling*, a fantasy with Lucy and Desi again playing spouses, this time with the presence

of angel James Mason who must safeguard their marriage.*

In 1957 Lucy and Desi sold the rerun rights to all the segments of "I Love Lucy" to CBS for $5,000,000, which they used to help provide the purchase price ($6,150,000) of the RKO lot. That fall Lucy, Desi, Frawley, and Vance (the latter two maintaining their distaste for each other) appeared in hour-long specials as their old characters. Meanwhile, tycoons Mr. and Mrs. Arnaz continued producing such shows as "Our Miss Brooks," "The Ann Sothern Show," "The Untouchables," "The Danny Thomas Show," and, much later, "Mission: Impossible" and "Star Trek."

The extra-marital romps of Desi had long been the topic of much Hollywood gossip by the time the world-famous couple separated officially on February 26, 1960. The divorce

* In real life Lucy had by now (after a number of miscarriages) become a mother. On July 17, 1951, Lucie Desiree was born (a cesarean); on January 19, 1953, Desi Jr. was born. It was decided before Desi Jr.'s birth to weave Lucy's pregnancy into the show and to make the offspring a character in the show (played first on camera by the Simmons twins and later on by Richard Keith).

decree was granted on May 4, 1960; each received half of Desilu. Lucy received the Beverly Hills home and $450 per month for child support. Desi was given the Riverside, California, ranch, and their Palm Springs hotel was placed in trust for their children.

In 1960 Lucy enjoyed one of her best screen roles opposite Bob Hope in United Artists' *The Facts of Life*. The duo played long-marrieds (to other spouses) who find adultery too much bother. On December 15 of that year Lucy starred in her first Broadway show, *Wildcat*, which opened at the Alvin Theatre with a Cy Coleman–Carolyn Leigh score and Keith Andes as her leading man. The reviews were lukewarm and Ball's singing was raucous and hoarse. The star found the eight-shows-a-week routine a terrible ordeal, especially when she had to carry the insipid showcase almost entirely herself. On April 20, 1961, the worn 49-year-old actress collapsed on stage, and *Wildcat* folded after 171 performances. The episode was a great personal expense to Lucy, who had invested several hundred thousand dollars of Desilu's money in it, as well as $50,000 of her own. The $165,000 in ticket refunds had to be provided largely from her own pocketbook.

One positive aspect of the *Wildcat* phase was that it introduced Lucy to her second husband, standup comedian Gary Morton (né Gary Goldapper). They wed on November 19, 1961, at New York City's Marble Collegiate Church, the Reverend Norman Vincent Peale presiding. Morton has since worked in a production capacity on his wife's programs, and played the Milton Berle-type comedian in the film *Lenny* (1974) with Dustin Hoffman.

In 1962 Lucy acquired Desi's share of Desilu for $3,000,000.* On October 1, 1962, she returned to CBS-TV with "The Lucy Show," playing a widow with two children. Vivian Vance was in the cast as was Gale Gordon. (William Frawley, who would die in 1966, had joined "My Three Sons.")

Lucy starred once again with Bob Hope in Warner Bros.' *Critic's Choice* (1963), a none too good film version of Ira Levin's Broadway

comedy with Henry Fonda. In 1967 she appeared with Art Carney in a blackout skit in Twentieth Century–Fox's *A Guide for the Married Man*. Also that year she sold her share of Desilu to Gulf & Western for a reputed $7,000,000. In 1968 she rejoined her *The Big Street* co-star Henry Fonda in a nice comedy, *Yours, Mine and Ours*, in which widowed Lucy (with eight children) contemplates marriage to widower Fonda (with 10 children). The picture had domestic gross rentals of $11,500,000. That year she also added her own children to the cast of "Here's Lucy." In 1971 Lucy transferred her Lucille Ball Productions from Paramount-Desilu to Universal Studios, where the lot has maintained her lavish bungalow as a stopover on its tourist tour.

When Lucy was named as the star of the cinema version of *Mame* (1974), the Broadway smash with the Jerome Lawrence–Robert E. Lee book and Jerry Herman score, it would appear that the crowning achievement to her cinema career was here at last. Nothing could have been further from the truth. In mid-1972 Lucy broke her ankle in a skiing accident, but maneuvered to have the Warner Bros. film delayed until she recovered. (She also had the scripts for her TV series written around her temporary impediment.)

In the course of filming *Mame*, Lucy also indulged in some "star behavior." She fired Madeline Kahn from the role of Agnes Gooch. A very lacquered, taut-faced Lucy was filmed with heaps of gauze over the camera lens in order to give the illusion of glamour. But when *Mame* was released—with direction by Gene Saks and leading roles filled by Robert Preston (Beauregard), Jane Connell (Gooch), and Beatrice Arthur (Vera Charles)—Lucy received the most derogatory notices of her career. She was further humiliated by publicized reports of her vanity during the production. Critics seemed to take great glee in dissecting her modest dancing and her unmelodic, husky-voiced singing. Since this debacle, the star has been protesting that she never wanted to play the part anyway. She even insists that the broken leg she strived so hard to overcome so as to save the assignment for herself was intentional: "I even broke my leg to get out of it. Angela Lansbury [the star of the Broadway musical version] should have been *Mame*."

---

* Desi would marry Edith Mack Hirsch in 1963. In 1965 he formed his own TV production company, Desi Arnaz Productions, Inc., which turned out "The Mothers-in-Law" series.

With Bob Hope in Critic's Choice *(1963).*

Along with the *Mame* unpleasantness came Lucy's announcement of retirement from the weekly TV airwaves. "I did the last three years of 'Here's Lucy' for the kids, but now that they're on their own, I kind of lack the incentive," she told *TV Guide*. When asked later if she missed the daily routine she so long pursued, Lucy replied, "I did at first. I cried a lot. I was very . . . very at loose ends. It took a lot to get me together. I missed Gale [Gordon] and I missed my arena and I loathed giving up my people who had been with me for so long. I was very unhappy about that. Very. And I still am. But the worst is over . . . the shock." The fall of 1974 came and the only Lucy shows on the small screen were the repeats.

Notwithstanding, Lucy is scarcely forgotten by anybody. On November 28, 1976, an excellent two-hour special honoring Lucy was aired over CBS-TV, featuring clips from the favorite episodes. It was produced by her spouse, Gary Morton, who conducted street polls to learn the most popular vignettes (Lucy's pantomime with Harpo Marx, her direction of John Wayne in a saloon fight scene, the birth of "little Ricky," the grape-stomping episode, etc.). Morton spent five and a half months delving into old footage (over a million feet of it). At the close of the program, Jimmy Stewart, Lucy's friend and neighbor (she lives at 1000 Roxbury Drive, he at 918), presented her with a plaque from the National Academy of Television Arts and Sciences, inscribed with the words, "Thank you for the greatest gift anyone can give us: Laughter." A teary Lucy thanked Stewart, the Academy, CBS, and her writers, directors, and craftsmen.* "And, I think most of all, I want to express my gratitude to you, the television audience, for allowing me to become a part of your lives. You've made it a very happy 25 years for me. And may I say—I love you all."

* The anniversary special contained specially taped tributes from many of her peers, including Vivian Vance, Danny Kaye, Dick Van Dyke, Dean Martin, Gale Gordon, Bob Hope, John Wayne, Carol Burnett—and Desi Arnaz.

The Lucy of today, eligible for full Social Security, keeps active in her craft. She guested on Danny Thomas' short-lived series "The Practice," and Dick Van Dyke's abortive variety hour, as well as filmed commercials for a national toy company and the Encyclopedia Britannica. She guested on Bob Hope's *All-Star Tribute to Vaudeville* (NBC-TV, March 25, 1977) and has continued with her occasional specials. *Guess Who's Coming to Dinner* (CBS-TV, November 21, 1977) was one of Ball's less-enticing special offerings, as she maneuvered through skits with Ed McMahon, Vivian Vance, Gale Gordon, and others (including a cameo by the President's mother, Mrs. Lillian Carter). Katie Kelly of the *New York Post* reported sadly, "The gags are old, the set-ups creak with age, and the timing is as far off as a broken clock. Even worse are the painfully obvious gags."

But an undaunted Lucy continues to be part of the current TV entertainment scene. When not guesting on the likes of the "Donny and Marie Osmond Show" or being a ringmaster for the *Annual Circus of Stars* (CBS-TV, December 5, 1977), she finds time to make the round of talk shows, or to be interviewed by Barbara Walters (CBS-TV, December 6, 1977). On the latter forum, Lucy admitted, "I can do funny things other people write down . . . but I don't *think* funny." Then there were six weeks of seminars on the art of comedy she conducted at Sherwood Oaks Experimental College in Hollywood in the spring of 1977. More recently, Lucy co-hostessed *TV: The Fabulous 50s* on NBC-TV on March 5, 1978, had her own CBS-TV special in November 1978 entitled *Lucy Comes to Nashville*, and was seen receiving the *Photoplay* magazine's Hall of Fame Award on an ABC-TV special (November 21, 1978).

How does she spend her free time? "Well, I stay home a lot. I've really gotten into the house and the house plants and taking care of my kids' houses, inside and outside—things I wanted to do for some time but didn't have time to do." For a long period, Lucy had curtailed her traveling to be near her ailing mother. On July 20, 1977, Mrs. Ball passed away at the age of 84, survived by daughter Lucy, son Fred (of Cottonwood, Arizona), a niece (Mrs. Cleo Smith), six grandchildren, and two great-grandchildren.

If Lucy had been pleased by the Dean Martin TV roast in early 1975 (which included Jack Benny's last public performance), she was ecstatic about being the first woman to receive the all-male Friars' Club Life Achievement Award. She was being honored "for her many contributions to the entertainment industry and particularly in celebration of her 25 years in television." On November 4, 1977, a thousand people gathered in the ballroom at the Beverly Hilton Hotel where Milton Berle was toastmaster of the event. Among the celebrities in attendance were George Burns, Jack Lemmon, Henry Fonda, Mary Tyler Moore, Sammy Davis, Jr., Gale Gordon, Carol Burnett, and Beverly Sills (the latter two performing a medley of blues and arias on the subject of "suffering womanhood"). In accepting the Award, Lucy stated, "It's been a hell of an evening for me, but I don't believe the half of it. There's no way I could be as wonderful as all these people have said. But I couldn't have an evening like this without really knowing that somewhere along the way I did something right. I do appreciate the things you've said so I will accept a third of them. Fair enough?"

These days, the husky-voiced, increasingly conservative Lucy looks back on it all with justifiable pride, but she exudes bitterness over the current state of movies and television. She recently told the *New York Times* she doubts "I Love Lucy" could weather the rating storm in today's sordid market: "I don't think people would buy it now. Too tame. If we were starting out now, how could we compete with all the sex and explicit language now on the air? Also, when we started . . . years ago, we were pioneering, and there wasn't all that much competition."

However, with a glint of optimism, Lucy told the *Times* interviewer, "Still, I could be wrong. The shows Desi Arnaz and I made are still being rerun, and three generations of people are watching them. Wherever they play, they still get the No. I ratings in their time slot. So, who knows?"

FEATURE FILMS

Broadway Thru a Keyhole (*United Artists 1933*)

Blood Money (*United Artists 1933*)

Roman Scandals (*United Artists 1933*)

The Bowery (*United Artists 1933*)

Moulin Rouge (*United Artists 1934*)

Nana (*United Artists 1934*)

Bottoms Up (*Fox 1934*)

Hold That Girl (*Fox 1934*)

Bulldog Drummond Strikes Back (*United Artists 1934*)

The Affairs of Cellini (*United Artists 1934*)

Kid Millions (*United Artists 1934*)

Broadway Bill (*Columbia 1934*)

Jealousy (*Columbia 1934*)

Men of the Night (*Columbia 1934*)

The Fugitive Lady (*Columbia 1934*)

Carnival (*Columbia 1935*)

The Whole Town's Talking (*Columbia 1935*)

Roberta (*RKO 1935*)

Old Man Rhythm (*RKO 1935*)

The Three Musketeers (*RKO 1935*)

Top Hat (*RKO 1935*)

I Dream Too Much (*RKO 1935*)

Chatterbox (*RKO 1936*)

The Farmer in the Dell (*RKO, 1936*)

Follow the Fleet (*RKO 1936*)

Bunker Bean (*RKO 1936*)

That Girl from Paris (*RKO 1936*)

Winterset (*RKO 1936*)

Don't Tell the Wife (*RKO 1937*)

Stage Door (*RKO 1937*)

Joy of Living (*RKO 1938*)

Go Chase Yourself (*RKO 1938*)

Having Wonderful Time (*RKO 1938*)

The Affairs of Annabel (*RKO 1938*)

Room Service (*RKO 1938*)

The Next Time I Marry (*RKO 1938*)

Annabel Takes a Tour (*RKO 1938*)

Beauty for the Asking (*RKO 1939*)

Twelve Crowded Hours (*RKO 1939*)

Panama Lady (*RKO 1939*)

Five Came Back (*RKO 1939*)

That's Right—You're Wrong (*RKO 1939*)

The Marines Fly High (*RKO 1940*)

You Can't Fool Your Wife (*RKO 1940*)

Dance, Girl, Dance (*RKO 1940*)

Too Many Girls (*RKO 1940*)

A Girl, a Guy, and a Gob (*RKO 1941*)

Look Who's Laughing (*RKO 1941*)

Valley of the Sun (*RKO 1942*)

The Big Street (*RKO 1942*)

Seven Days' Leave (*RKO 1942*)

DuBarry Was a Lady (*MGM 1943*)

Best Foot Forward (*MGM 1943*)

Thousands Cheer (*MGM 1943*)

Meet the People (*MGM 1944*)

Without Love (*MGM 1945*)

Abbott and Costello in Hollywood (*MGM 1945*)

Ziegfeld Follies (*MGM 1946*)

The Dark Corner (*20th Century-Fox 1946*)

Easy to Wed (*MGM 1946*)

Two Smart People (*MGM 1946*)

Lover Come Back (*Universal 1946*)

Lured (*United Artists 1947*)

Her Husband's Affairs (*Columbia 1947*)

Sorrowful Jones (*Paramount 1949*)

Easy Living (*RKO 1949*)

Miss Grant Takes Richmond (*Columbia 1949*)

A Woman of Distinction (*Columbia 1950*)*

Fancy Pants (*Paramount 1950*)

The Fuller Brush Girl (*Columbia 1950*)

The Magic Carpet (*Columbia 1951*)

The Long, Long Trailer (*MGM 1954*)

Forever, Darling (*MGM 1956*)

The Facts of Life (*United Artists 1960*)

Critic's Choice (*Warner Bros. 1963*)

A Guide for the Married Man (*20th Century-Fox 1967*)

Yours, Mine and Ours (*United Artists 1968*)

Mame (*Warner Bros. 1974*)

* Unbilled guest appearance.

In The Hollywood Revue of 1929 *(1929)*.

Jack Benny

"Jack Benny has a violin and talk. Mostly talk. He handles himself as though having played the small time."

The above critique was penned in the January 21, 1921, issue of *Variety*. Who could have visualized that 53 years later, the death of that "small-time" vaudevillian would cause headlines in *Variety*, occasion the largest funeral crowd in Hollywood's history, and move millions of people all over the world to mourn the star's passing.

Jack Benny proved to be the dean of American comedians: a radio institution, a vaudeville headliner, a television favorite, and a welcome (if not hugely successful) cinema personality. His reputed stinginess, vanity, and ego gave the world food for laughter for decades, even though the man himself was anything but the snooty, self-centered tightwad he performed so admirably. "Writers like to make me out a very complex, screwed-up guy. I'm a simple guy, a grateful guy . . . not a 24-hour-a-day clown . . . not a laugh machine . . . not a tightwad. I am surprisingly normal. I have never been to a psychiatrist, and I've only been married once. A fellow can hardly be more normal than that."

Nevertheless, this simple, grateful, normal man caused more laughter to sound in America than any of his peers (with the possible exception of Bob Hope). As actor Jesse White remarked when leaving Benny's funeral, "There's always been a Jack Benny. It's like being without a post office."

He was born Benjamin Kubelsky in Chicago on Wednesday, Valentine's Day, 1894, the son of Meyer Kubelsky and his wife, Emma (Sachs), Orthodox Jewish immigrants. He grew up—as all seasoned Benny fans know—in Waukegan, Illinois, where his dad ran a saloon and later a dry-goods store. Much of his youth (he quit school after the ninth grade at age 13) was spent alone as his parents were forced to scramble for a living. Like many boys in the ghetto, Benny (as he was called) took violin lessons. His ambition quickly became the concert stage. In an interview in the late six-

87

ties, Jack remembered what turns his early career had underwent:

"We-e-ell . . . when I was about 14, 15 years old in Waukegan, I used to play with dance orchestras. We would play in stores on Saturdays and maybe get a dollar and a half for the day. Then I studied and I went into vaudeville as a violinist. There was a woman pianologist—or whatever they called them—who sang and did talking, comedy songs. Her name was Cora Salisbury. She took me with her on the road. We did a violin and piano act—Salisbury and Benny. . . .

"Well, Cora's mother became very, very ill and she had to give up the stage. Soooooooh . . . I found another partner, a fellow by the name of [Lyman] Woods. That's how I have Benny as my last name—Benny is my right first name. We stayed together doing a violin and piano act until the First World War and then I joined the navy. . . .

"Then in the navy at Great Lakes, David Wolfe, who became a very dear friend of mine later, was the author of a couple of sailor shows for Navy Relief. And in this show I did my violin and piano act with Zef Confrey. But David Wolfe needed somebody to play the part of an admiral's orderly, who had only one or two comedy lines. He happened to see me and said, 'Hey, young fella, come over here!' (I was a young fella then.) And I read a couple of lines and he liked it, because the next day he added lines for me and by the time the show opened in Chicago in the Auditorium, I had practically the comic part of the show. Then I realized I could talk and get laughs. When I went into vaudeville again, I went back as a single act. But I always held the violin . . . did a lot of violin playing and just a little bit of talk. And then, gradually, I kept talking and less violin, until finally I dropped the violin entirely. If I wanted to have a finish for my act, I borrowed a violin from the orchestra."

As a single on the post–World War I vaudeville circuit, Jack billed himself as "Jack Benny, Aristocrat of Humor." Again, his reviews were not always tops; when he played the B. F. Keith Palace in New York, *Variety* reported, "Benny should lift his voice a bit for the rear of the house. It is possible to be overconfident. Benny becomes rigidly exclusive at times, eliminating all but the first rows in addressing his flip stuff." But

Jack worked hard at perfecting his timing, diction, and stage personality, and by the mid-Twenties, he was playing the New York Palace Theatre and heading touring vaudeville bills with Frank Fay, the Marx Brothers (whom he actually *followed* on certain bills), and singer Nora Bayes (with whom Jack had a quite serious romance).

In 1921, while touring with the brothers Marx, Jack was asked to accompany them to a Sabbath dinner in the Vancouver, British Columbia, home of the parents of 13-year-old Sayde Marks. The 27-year-old Jack was uneasy around the family's children and soon left, whispering to Zeppo, "Why did you bring me here with all these kids?" Almost six years later, Jack met the grown-up Sayde selling hosiery in the Los Angeles May Company department store and they were married on January 25, 1927.* Taking the stage name of Mary Livingstone, the new Mrs. Benny became part of Jack's act. (She disliked the pressure of performing on stage, but wanted to be near her traveling husband.) Jack himself was equally devoted to making the marriage viable. When his extensive trekking as a $1,500 per week headliner of Earl Carroll's *Vanities* became too much for Mary, he gave his notice, seeking less transient engagements. (During the late Twenties, Jack was a frequent performer in Manhattan. In May 1926 he was part of *The Great Temptations* revue at the Winter Garden Theatre, where he performed, among other items, a routine with Dorothy McNulty [later Penny Singleton] as his stooge. He was a frequent master of ceremonies at the New York Palace Theatre, and often headlined shows at this main temple of vaudeville.)

Jack's continued acclaim on the top vaudeville circuits eventually garnered him motion picture offers. In Culver City he made his feature film debut as the M.C. of MGM's *The Hollywood Revue of 1929* (introducing the famous "Wedding of the Painted Doll" number).** He remained at Metro for *Chasing Rainbows* (1930), but it soon became evident that Benny and Louis B. Mayer's studio had

* Years later the Bennys bought the Palm Springs abode of the owner of the May department store chain.

** Benny appeared in several short subjects: *Bright Moments* (Vitaphone 1929) delivering a monologue; and three two-reelers for Paramount in 1931—*A Broadway Romeo, Cab Waiting,* and *Taxi Tangle.*

As host of the short subject Songwriters Revue *(1929).*

little in common. For his final film of this period, Jack moved over to the humble portals of Tiffany Studios to star in the now long-forgotten opus *The Medicine Man* (1930). It proved that Benny was not destined to be a cinema romantic lead. However, at this juncture, Earl Carroll offered Jack the enviable position as leading comedian and master of ceremonies of his New York–based *Vanities* (New Amsterdam Theatre: July 1, 1930, 215 performances). Others in the show were Patsy Kelly and Herb Williams.

Perhaps the important night of Jack's career was that of May 2, 1931. Ed Sullivan invited the comedian to guest on his CBS radio variety program. Jack's legendary self-introduction was: "Ladies and gentlemen, this is Jack Benny talking. There will be a slight pause while you say, 'Who cares?'" Within weeks of that dry introduction Jack had his own radio show.* "The Jack Benny Program" was sponsored in its first year by Canada Dry (Chevrolet followed in 1933 and

---

* When Ed Sullivan initially requested Jack to perform on his radio show, Benny balked. "I don't know anything about radio." Sullivan replied, "Nobody does."

1934, and General Tire and Rubber in 1934); later JELL-O became Jack's long-standing sponsor, followed by Lucky Strike.

During his fledgling years in radio, Jack continued to appear in other media. In October 1934 he starred in a stage farce called *Bring on the Girls*, written by George S. Kaufman and Morrie Ryskind. He played a financial wiseacre in the comedy which poked fun at the New Deal. The show tried out in Washington, D.C., but never opened as planned in New York City. As later discussed, Benny's forays back into films were not hugely successful. It was his radio show which proved to be his mainstay.

For 23 years "The Jack Benny Program" aired at 7:00 P.M. on Sunday nights, winning consistently top ratings and the biggest laughs in radio.* Jack's thriftiness, his vanity—especially over his blue eyes—his tou-

---

* *Time* magazine would state of Jack's show, "Practically all the comedy shows owe their structure to Benny's conceptions. The Benny show was like a 'One Man's Family' in slapstick. He was the first comedian in radio to realize you could get big laughs by ridiculing yourself instead of your stooges."

With Patsy Kelly in Transatlantic Merry-Go-Round *(1934).*

pee,* his perpetual age of 39, and his self-illusions as a great violinist supplied both himself and his regulars with endless comic material. In fact, Jack was the first national radio star to allow his supporting cast to cash in on the best lines. He theorized, "The show itself is the important thing. As long as people think the show is funny it doesn't matter to me who gets the punch lines." Over the years the most popular regulars on Benny's show were Eddie Anderson as Jack's gravel-voiced valet Rochester; Phil Harris, Benny's bandleader who could never resist a rousing chorus of "That's What I Like About the South"; Don Wilson, the smooth-voiced announcer who took many a fat joke in jolly humor; Frank Fontaine, as John L. C. Sivoney; Mel Blanc, who vocalized such Benny institutions as Carmichael (the polar bear who guarded Jack's vault and reputedly devoured the gas man), the sputtering Maxwell automobile, the Mexican Si (who had a sister named Sue), and the train announcer ("Anaheim, Azusa, and Cuc-a-monga"). And of course Mary Livingstone Benny, who was

rushed into service at the microphone one evening when the scheduled actress failed to report; she stayed with the show for two decades. The program also frequently utilized Ronald Colman and his wife Benita Hume, Andy Devine, Sheldon Leonard, and Frank Nelson (of the famous "Yeeees?"); Frank Parker and Kenny Baker were among the tenors who preceded Dennis Day; and such writers as Sam Perrin, Milt Josefsberg, George Balzer, John Tackaberry, Bill Morrow, Jack Douglas, and Ed Beloin constructed the scripts over the years of the program.*

* Jack, whose own hair was gray and slightly thinning, only wore a toupee in his prime Hollywood films. Actually, it was Rochester who wore a toupee full-time.

* Where are the famous Benny regulars today? Eddie Anderson had a heart attack in 1958, suffered a stroke in 1966, and died on February 28, 1977, of heart failure. Don Wilson is a top executive at KMIR-TV in Palm Springs, California. Dennis Day runs a Santa Monica antique shop, still sings sometimes at hotels and nightclubs, and in the early Seventies toured in a road company of *No, No, Nanette.* Phil Harris, a Palm Springs real-estate tycoon, still appears occasionally in Las Vegas or on television, and is still wed to Alice Faye. Mary Benny, who never enjoyed performing ("Sundays became torturous for me"), retired in 1958, now looks after her husband's estate. In 1978 her biography *Jack Benny,* written with her brother Hilliard Marks and Marcia Borie, was published. Mel Blanc has his own Hollywood advertising agency and still delights in performing the voices of Bugs Bunny and other characters for the Looney Tunes cartoons.

On June 16, 1969, Jack wrote a guest article for columnist Hank Grant of the *Hollywood Reporter*, recalling his choices as the funniest bits on his show. Among them:

> HOLD-UP MAN: Your money or your life.
>
> JACK: (Long pause) ["In fact, one of my longest."]
>
> HOLD-UP MAN: Quit stalling—I said your money or your life.
>
> JACK: I'M THINKING IT OVER!
>
>   *   *   *
>
> MARY: Jack, why don't you stop being so stingy?
>
> JACK: Mary, I'm not stingy and you know it!
>
> MARY: You're not, eh? . . . Last year when you were going to have your appendix removed, you wanted Rochester to do it.
>
> JACK: I DID NOT. I merely asked him if he knew how.
>
>   *   *   *
>
> JACK: Well, Rochester, I've never heard you rave that much about any girl. Tell me, how beautiful is she?
>
> ROCHESTER: Do you want me to describe her to you?
>
> JACK: Yes.
>
> ROCHESTER: MR. BENNY—DID YOU EVER SEE A HERSHEY BAR WITH ALL THE ALMONDS IN THE RIGHT PLACES?
>
>   *   *   *
>
> JACK: Professor LeBlanc—do you think you can ever make a great violinist out of me?
>
> BLANC: I do not know. How old are you?
>
> JACK: Why?
>
> BLANC: HOW MUCH TIME HAVE WE LEFT?

As he feuded over the airwaves with Fred Allen (they actually admired each other greatly) and dispensed his "Well!" and "Now cut that out!" to hysterical response, Benny soon earned himself a weekly paycheck of $17,500, thereby inaugurating his long-time status as the world's top-paid comedian.

Jack's CBS radio program was broadcast from Hollywood and he became a happy mixer in the cinema colony. He and Mary were especially close with George Burns and Gracie Allen. Jack soon purchased a lavish mansion at 1002 Roxbury Drive, a fashionable lane of Beverly Hills where resided such names as Lionel Barrymore, Warner Baxter, and Thomas Mitchell. (Years later Lucille Ball would become Jack's next-door neighbor.) In 1936 the childless Bennys adopted a daughter, Joan Naomi. (Married three times, she is currently wed to producer Robert Blumofe. She supplied Jack with four grandchildren—Michael, Marai, Robert, and Joanee—on whom the star doted.)

While Jack served as a ceaseless professional target for jokes regarding his stinginess, egomania, and vanity, his real-life image was quite the opposite. People who worked on his show remained for years. Comedian friend Benny Rubin remembers that Jack actually saved some of his friends' radio programs from cancellation. "The sponsors wanted to throw George Burns and Gracie Allen off the air. . . . They also wanted to get rid of Eddie Cantor. This was back in '39. . . . Jack jumped in and made it his business to find out why. Then he took all the agency big shots to lunch. He told them George would stop trying to take control of the scripts and he pledged that Eddie's show would go back to its old successful formula. Both promises were kept and the shows—and the careers of Benny's friends—were saved."

It was, of course, only natural for radio personalities to have motion picture aspirations. And it was a constant source of anxiety and sensitivity to Jack Benny that, certainly in his opinion and generally from most standpoints, he never fully succeeded as a cinema personality. His work appeared promising in MGM's *Broadway Melody of 1936* (1935) in which he was amusing as a vitriolic gossip columnist who makes life messy for stars Robert Taylor and Eleanor Powell. Metro optioned him for another picture, *It's in the Air* (1935), in which Jack as a con artist requests assistance from ex-wife Una Merkel.

Then Paramount Studios placed an offer. That studio had a stable of pleasant radio performers under contract, including Bing Crosby and Burns and Allen. Jack's first picture there was *The Big Broadcast of 1937* (1936), in which he sported with Burns and Allen, Bob Burns, and Martha Raye. A half-dozen films followed at Paramount, most of which allowed Jack to lean on his radio-enforced mannerisms. He starred with Burns and Allen and Martha Raye again in the musical *College Holiday* (1936). One of his best screen showcases was *Artists and Models* (1937), in which he played a conniving boss; his cohorts oncamera were Ida Lupino, Martha Raye, Gail Patrick, and Judy Canova. The studio turned out a follow-up, *Artists and Models Abroad* (1938), with Joan Bennett as the leading lady and a backlot setting of Paris. *Man About Town* (1939) saw Jack trying to crash London society; he was flanked by Paramount players Dorothy Lamour and Betty Grable as well as radio pals Rochester and Phil Harris. *Buck Benny Rides Again* (1940) presented Jack in a Western setting, with Ellen Drew and Andy Devine joining radio regulars Rochester, Harris, and Dennis Day. (The real star of the proceedings was Jack's outlandish, 50-pound cowboy suit.) Benny's Paramount sojourn ended with *Love Thy Neighbor* (1940), a cinema exploitation of Jack's "feud" with Fred Allen, with Rochester assisting Jack and Mary Martin providing the songs. None of these entries

really contained the zing and flavor of Jack's radio show. Nevertheless, each film earned decent box-office returns and provided the radio program with endless opportunities for plugs.

Away from Paramount, Jack freelanced in films, still anxious to succeed on a large scale. His frequently insulted effeminacy* made him a natural selection for the starring spot in Twentieth Century–Fox's *Charley's Aunt* (1941), wherein Jack hilariously impersonated the relative ("from Brazil—where the nuts come from!") before the real aunt (Kay Francis) arrived. The comedy was a top grosser of the year. United Artists' *To Be or Not to Be*, the stylishly directed Ernst Lu-

---

* Regarding Benny's trademark walk, the comedian once noted, "Now, Bob Hope walks exactly the same way, but he cups his hands. Bob Hope walks like a headwaiter who is leading a guy to a good table." Benny program co-player Phil Harris quipped of his boss' prance and stance, "You know what, . . . you could put a dress on that guy and take him anywhere."

With Cecil Cunningham in Artists and Models *(1937).*

With The Yacht Club Boys in Artists and Models Abroad (1938).

With Fred Allen in Love Thy Neighbor (1940).

93

bitsch* black comedy, was Carole Lombard's last film (released after her untimely death). In it Jack was well-cast as the hammy Shakespearean actor ("What he does to Shakespeare we are doing now to Poland!" cracks one Nazi officer), though several critics opined that the familiar Benny vanity weakened the picture rather than strengthened it. More important, the combination of the pall cast by Miss Lombard's death and the film's offbeat handling of the Nazi theme prevented the production from being the box-office success that was anticipated.

Warner Bros.' *George Washington Slept Here* (1942) allowed Jack to parade his familiar mannerisms with the assistance of a top straight lady in the form of charming Ann Sheridan. Fox's *The Meanest Man in the World* (1943), with Priscilla Lane, boiled the Benny formula well, by casting Jack as a lawyer who decides the only way to success is by being a louse. In 1944 Jack turned in a violin-playing guest spot in Warner Bros.' *Hollywood Canteen*. The next year he starred in the (in)famous *The Horn Blows at Midnight*, with Alexis Smith and directed by Raoul Walsh. It is actually an amusing fantasy with Benny as an earthbound angel. That the film lost money would serve as a standard Benny joke for years afterward.

In United Artists' *It's in the Bag* (1945) he made a guest appearance, trading canards with Fred Allen.

ALLEN: Oh, Mr. Benny! I was expecting a much older man!

JACK: Yes. You may not believe this, but next year, I'll be old enough to vote!

This was Jack's last picture as a starring performer. Thereafter he appeared in a handful of films, but only in cameo guest appearances, and never made peace with himself over his failure to become a great cinema comedian. (Jack also tried his luck as a

---

* On working with Lubitsch in *To Be or Not to Be*, Benny would say, "No comic can be great in films without two things, a great story—which gives you a character to play—and a great director. I'm not knocking the people who directed me in the films in my early days, but truthfully, they couldn't come near a genius like Lubitsch. . . . His method of direction was perfect for me. He would act out the whole scene, and then he'd say, 'Now let's see how you'd do it.' He'd give me the movements and then let me do them my own way. And he was great. . . . If Lubitsch were to tell me to jump out that window, I'd jump."

cinema producer with *The Lucky Stiff*, 1949, a rather modest entry for United Artists starring Brian Donlevy, Dorothy Lamour, and Claire Trevor.)

During World War II, between his radio and cinema work, Jack managed to undertake five worldwide trips to entertain troops. In 1943 he headed a USO troupe through Egypt, the Persian Gulf, and Sicily. In 1949 Jack made a network change to CBS, for which the Columbia Broadcasting System paid him $1,356,000 (of which $1,030,000 went into income taxes). Cozy in his lucrative, long-successful medium of radio, Benny made the move to television with customary worries and reluctance.

His first CBS telecast was on October 28, 1950, abetted by his radio family (Mary Livingstone, Rochester, Dennis Day, and Don Wilson). He continued his radio show on a weekly basis until June 1954, when he decided to concentrate on the video medium with 20 half-hour shows a season. In 1958 Jack won the Emmy as television's finest comedian, and in 1960 "The Jack Benny Program" switched from an alternate-week basis to being a weekly feature in the CBS lineup. (One of his more intriguing jobs in this period was supplying an offcamera voice for the Warner Bros. cartoon *The House That Jack Built*, 1958, in which he made a cameo appearance at the finale.) On September 25, 1964, Jack returned to NBC, switching "The Jack Benny Program" to his old network. It ran a season (with only mediocre ratings) after which the 71-year-old comedian returned to TV regularly as a guest star, with his own prime-time specials, and doing commercials. Throughout this period he enjoyed successful nightclub engagements in New York, Las Vegas, and London. (In early 1963 and the summer of 1965 Jack played engagements on Broadway.)

Over the decades Jack's actual generosity became as legendary as his purported high-strung ego. During the Korean War he traveled some 30,000 miles to entertain combat forces. Starting in 1956 he embarked on the phase of his career that gave him the most pleasure—as guest artist with symphony concerts in order to raise money for orchestra pension funds. "Playing a violin with the Philharmonic or soloing with Leonard Bernstein at Carnegie Hall is like being alone on a

With Alexis Smith and Guy Kibbee in The Horn Blows at Midnight *(1945).*

desert island with Zsa Zsa Gabor and her boyfriend. You feel you're not needed." Nevertheless, he raised some $5,901,000 through his unpaid appearances with over 80 symphony orchestras.

On February 14, 1974, the perennially 39-year-old Jack turned 80. He was neither pleased nor proud. Recalls George Burns, "Sinatra gave him a party when he was 80 years old and it embarrassed him. He didn't mind being 79, but it bothered him to be 80. So six weeks before he died, we were sitting at the Hillcrest Country Club, and he said, 'I don't like being 80. It's an unlucky number.' And I said, 'Jack, you want to be 62 again? You got a great agent, Irving Fein. Call him up and he'll fix it.'"

But Jack did not laugh. He had reasons. Though he continued making personal appearances, rumors spread that the octogenarian suffered blackouts, which often made it necessary for stagehands literally to carry the star on- and offstage. Once onstage, the rapport of a live audience rejuvenated him.

However, Benny was beginning to tire. He complained of stomach pains, which many of his friends believed to be psychosomatic.

There were some sad episodes along the way. On October 19, 1974, Jack experienced a serious dizzy spell in Dallas, forcing him to cancel a performance at the Fairmount Hotel there. He was in fine form the evening of November 17, 1974, when he appeared at the Century Plaza to be inducted into the "Hall of Fame Awards" of the Television Bureau of Advertising. He quipped, "I had the feeling that eventually I would have been chosen, but not this soon in my career!" Yet, when he was to appear at the Beverly Hills Hotel on December 8, 1974, to receive the Louella O. Parsons Award from the Hollywood Women's Press Club, he felt so poorly that he had to leave the hotel before the ceremonies commenced. George Burns was a last-minute substitute to accept the award for his friend.

Jack's health continued to deteriorate so noticeably that, the week before Christmas, 1974, he underwent exploratory surgery. The verdict was inoperable cancer of the pancreas. Heavily sedated, the famed comedian returned to his home on Roxbury Drive. His agent released the sad news that the great man was dying. All over Los Angeles, radio stations asked listeners to "say a prayer for Jack Benny." His family and show-business peers, including Burns and Bob Hope, kept a vigil at Jack's bedside. Milton Berle later told the *Hollywood Reporter* of Jack's last conscious act: "His manager, Irving Fein, gave him a paper to sign, and told him two people wanted his autograph if he was up to it. Jack signed the paper, gave one autograph, and the pen dropped from his hand as he tried to sign the other." Shortly afterward, at 11:32 P.M. on Thursday, December 26, 1974, Jack Benny died.

International response to Benny's death was enormous. Tributes flowed in from all over the world, although none was quite as moving as Mary Benny's whimpered comment, "He never gave me one bad day; not one bad hour." The funeral service, conducted December 29, 1974, at Culver City's Hillside Memorial Park, was widely believed to be the largest Hollywood funeral since the death of Columbia Pictures mogul Harry Cohn.

Rabbi Edgar Magnin officiated at the Reformed Jewish ceremonies. George Burns and Bob Hope delivered the eulogies. In a black prayer shawl, Burns fought unsuccessfully to contain his tears. He said, "We're all good friends of Jack's. What can I tell you about Jack that you don't know? I've known Jack for 55 years, and I was very fortunate. He was very special to me. I can't imagine my life without him. I know I'm going to miss him very much." Hope, himself dabbing tears from his eyes, read a wire of condolence from President Gerald Ford, remarked that Jack Benny had brought "more sunshine to this world than Easter morning," and continued, "He didn't just stand on a stage, he owned it. For a man who was the undisputed master of comedy timing, you'd have to say that this was the time when Jack Benny's timing was all wrong. He left us much too soon. He was stingy to the end. He only gave us 80 years, and it wasn't enough."

The interment was private. Pallbearers Frank Sinatra, Gregory Peck, Milton Berle, Billy Wilder, Mervyn LeRoy, Irving Fein, Leonard Gershe, Frederick DeCordova, and Armand Deutsch carried the copper casket to the Hall of Graciousness at Hillside, near the graves of Al Jolson, William Goetz, Jeff Chandler, Harold Mirisch, and Eddie Cantor.

The Benny estate was valued at $5,852,025. The bulk was left to his widow, his sister, his daughter, and his four grandchildren. The Motion Picture and Television Fund also received a cash amount. (Mary Benny presented two of Jack's violins—worth over $100,000—to Los Angeles Philharmonic music director Zubin Mehta.) Benny's estate would appoint Irving Fein, Benny's long-time agent and friend, as representative for syndication of the 10 Jack Benny TV specials as well as representative for the use of the late comedian's name, voice, and likeness on radio and elsewhere.

Jack left projects he would never complete. An NBC-TV special was to be taped on January 11 and 12, 1975; and there was his role in the MGM film *The Sunshine Boys*, which had been previously postponed until his health improved. Pal Burns replaced him in the screen comedy, playing opposite Walter Matthau, and Burns won an Oscar doing so.

Jack Benny's actual professional farewell appearance came via the "Dean Martin Celebrity Roast" (NBC-TV) on February 7, 1975, in which he participated in lampooning Lucille Ball. His timing was as keen as ever, his canards ("If she wants to get over-exposed with all those TV reruns, I don't care!") beautifully delivered, and his presence a stunning reminder of just how potent—and irreplaceable—a comic giant he was.

Fittingly it is George Burns who has presented the most eloquent testimonial to Jack Benny: "A lotta great people died—Caruso, Jolson, Barrymore—but none of them got the newspaper space Jack Benny got. And the reason was not because he was the world's greatest comedian, but because he was the world's nicest man."

It was not generally known that Jack Benny suffered from diabetes in his later years. In Houston in May 1977 there was held the First Annual Jack Benny Memorial Pro-Celeb Tennis Tourney with the proceeds going to Diabetes Research. Dina Merrill was one of the masterminds of the event, which saw Benny's daughter Joan on hand for the court matches. In August of that year Merv Griffin hosted a tribute to Benny on his TV show; among his guests were Dennis Day, Phil Harris, Don Wilson, Mel Blanc, and Milt Josefsberg (long-time Benny scripter and the author of *The Jack Benny Show*, a detailed book on the comedian). On October 4 came the presentation of the first March of Dimes Jack Benny Memorial Award—to George Burns—at the Beverly Hilton Hotel. Special guest of honor was Mary Livingstone, with Bob Hope serving as master of ceremonies. Perhaps the nicest tribute to Benny occurred when CBS-TV in the summer of 1977 scheduled several of Jack's old half-hour TV shows for special telecasting. Richard F. Shepard wrote in the *New York Times*:

> It is a wonderful feeling to run across an old friend, one whom you haven't seen in years, and to find him looking great, just as he always did. . . . Jack Benny died two and a half years ago, but he left a very tangible heritage, recordings of his shows over the years.

> All of the marvelous shticks are here, all of them hyperboles that add up to silly and funny. The one arm crossing the chest while the other elbow rests on it and the hand strokes the chin and cheek as the head slowly turns away as if to say, 'You see how peculiar these other people are.' The eyes supplicating some overhead power for understanding. The perpetuation of his reputation as the world's champion stinter.

> This is vintage Benny, and if you liked it then, you will like it now.

FEATURE FILMS

The Hollywood Revue of 1929 (*MGM 1929*)
Chasing Rainbows (*MGM 1930*)
The Medicine Man (*Tiffany 1930*)
Transatlantic Merry-Go-Round (*United Artists 1934*)
Broadway Melody of 1936 (*MGM 1935*)
It's in the Air (*MGM 1935*)
The Big Broadcast of 1937 (*Paramount 1936*)
College Holiday (*Paramount 1936*)
Artists and Models (*Paramount 1937*)
Artists and Models Abroad (*Paramount 1938*)
Man About Town (*Paramount 1939*)
Buck Benny Rides Again (*Paramount 1940*)
Love Thy Neighbor (*Paramount 1940*)
Charley's Aunt (*20th Century–Fox 1941*)
To Be or Not to Be (*United Artists 1942*)
George Washington Slept Here (*Warner Bros. 1942*)
The Meanest Man in the World (*20th Century–Fox 1943*)
Hollywood Canteen (*Warner Bros. 1944*)
The Horn Blows at Midnight (*Warner Bros. 1945*)
It's In the Bag (*United Artists 1945*)
Without Reservations (*RKO 1946*)*
The Great Lover (*Paramount 1949*)*
Somebody Loves Me (*Paramount 1952*)*
Susan Slept Here (*RKO 1954*)*
Beau James (*Paramount 1957*)*
Gypsy (*Warner Bros. 1962*)*
It's a Mad, Mad, Mad, Mad World (*United Artists 1963*)
A Guide for the Married Man (*20th Century–Fox 1967*)

* Unbilled guest appearance.

With Wally Vernon in Always Leave Them Laughing *(1949).*

Milton Berle

If the myriad faces, phases, generations, and styles of comedy could be capsulized within one performer, he would have to be show business' famed jester Milton Berle. Many comedians devise, search for, and create an image that will reflect their special talent for a type of comedy: an underwriting of professional identification. Through years of constant performing, Berle's idiom became that of a flamboyantly brash, flippant, aggressive wise guy dominating the spotlight with seemingly inexhaustible energy and a wealth of talent. Characteristically, his stage persona would be vigorously seeking audience approbation in schizoid fashion. One upraised hand would be attempting modestly to quell audience applause while his other hand would be frantically beckoning more and more clapping.

His compulsion to inspire audience laughter frequently became frenetic and excessive, even to the extent of purloining other comedians' material. Ed Wynn once said Berle would steal anything; eventually, Berle turned his "borrowing" into part of his own comedic "shtick." Despite his detractors, Berle has survived in show business over 60 years. When other major entertainers were unwilling to face the grueling pace of a new medium, he leaped into the fray to earn the tag "Mr. Television."

Stage mothers have always been held in low esteem in show business. They are objects of vilification and snide comment. Yet, without them, the extent of their progeny's rise in the show-business world is a debatable question. For sheer dedication and life-consuming devotion, few of them have equaled Sarah Glantz Berlinger.

Sarah was the daughter of Polish-Jewish immigrant cobbler Henry Glantz. Her husband was Moses Berlinger, a gentle, kindly dreamer, the son of a German-born Jewish immigrant, Jacob Berlinger. Their marriage produced five children. Their fourth and last son was born on Sunday, July 12, 1908, at 68 West 118 Street in New York City's Harlem. They named him Milton.

Determined to harness the precocious talent of young Milton, Sarah discovered that some movie companies were paying youngsters $1.50 a day for extra work, so she hauled her six-year-old son to Fort Lee, New Jersey, where he was hired to be "saved" from a moving train by Pearl White in the Pathé serial *The Perils of Pauline* (1914). At Brooklyn's Vitagraph Studio, Milton had unbilled bits in short subjects like Mabel Normand's *The Maid's Night Out* (1911) and John Bunny's *Bunny's Little Brother* (who was actor Jay Dwiggins, not Milton) (1914). A trek to Hollywood resulted in Milton's appearance as a newsboy in *Tillie's Punctured Romance* (1914), with Charles Chaplin, Marie Dressler, and Mabel Normand. Between his shuttling back and forth from Coast to Coast, Milton had bits in Mary Pickford's *Rebecca of Sunnybrook Farm* (1917) and *Tess of the Storm Country* (1922), and a spot in Douglas Fairbanks' *The Mark of Zorro* (1920).

The flickers represented only a minor phase of show business. Without reluctance, Sarah accepted an offer from E. W. Wolf, who packaged kid acts for the vaudeville circuit. Milton joined the Philadelphia-based vaudeville show where he did an imitation of Eddie Cantor, sang popular songs, and bantered about. Over a four-year period the show kept the same format but changed its name from *Melody of Youth* to *The Rising Generation*, *Playmates*, *Ting-a-Ling*, and *Tid Bits of 1918*. Between shows Milton completed homework assignments for New York City's Professional Children's School. During these years in Philadelphia, the Berlingers' baby daughter, Rosalind Marianna,* joined Sarah and Milton, while sons Phil, Frank, and Jack remained in Manhattan with Moses.

Sarah's absorption in Milton's career dominated her life; her husband and the four other children had largely to fend for themselves. As the years passed, Mama triggered audience laughter, led applause, and glowed with pride over being Milton Berle's mother. She became the butt of other comics' jokes and won the sobriquet "Queenie." When Milton joined Elizabeth Kennedy in a successful vaudeville act, *Broadway Bound*, and was

---

* Rosalind died on May 19, 1977, in Los Angeles at the age of 64. She had left show business when she wed Dr. Charles B. Wigderson, whom she divorced in 1962. She was survived by a daughter, Diane, as well as by three of her brothers: Milton, Philip, and Jack. At one point in Milton's earlier career, Rosalind had created costumes for his stage appearances.

billed as Berle, Sarah suddenly became "Sandra" and the whole Berlinger family quickly became Berle, but never legally. Sandra's joy in her son was boundless when Kennedy and Berle opened the second half of the Palace Theatre's vaudeville show on May 21, 1921. It made all the stunts* she had engineered seem worthwhile.

Years on the Orpheum and Keith circuits promoted the act of Kennedy and Berle to a headliner. Someone once said, "Vaudeville will never die as long as Milton Berle is alive." Certainly he translated that once-robust form of entertainment into a rousing success on television. During his years in vaudeville Berle watched the various acts from the wings and absorbed most of the material that in later years his lively mind would recall—and use. He worked on the same bill with most of the great entertainers of the era, including the egocentric Frank Fay, who thought himself "the world's greatest comedian."

On December 29, 1924, Berle opened at Loew's State Theatre on Broadway, performing a 12-minute single act in the cinema's vaudeville show. His notices were improving and he was increasingly being booked into the vaudeville houses in the New York area. By the end of the Twenties and the beginning of the depressed Thirties, Milton was on a vaudeville tour with an act, *Chasin' the Blues*, on the Orpheum circuit, which took him back to Los Angeles.

His rise in show business was tremendously boosted in January 1932 when he was engaged by New York's Palace Theatre as master of ceremonies. He was held over for eight weeks. In May 1932 he hosted the Brooklyn Albee Theatre's vaudeville show starring Pola Negri, and the following week returned to the Palace on a bill headlined by Roscoe "Fatty" Arbuckle. During this period Milton made a few short subjects, among them Vitaphone's *Gags to Riches* and Educational's *Poppin' the Cork*.

---

* Among the ploys Milton's mother had her boy use were: deliberately getting out of step in the Baby Sextette number in the Shubert revival of *Floradora*, in which he made his Broadway debut on April 5, 1920; forcing him into Eddie Cantor's dressing room to perform his imitation of the banjo-eyed comedian; and, more unbelievable, shoving him onstage at one of Al Jolson's Sunday night Winter Garden concerts to sing "April Showers." That Jolson, a man who felt ownership of the spotlight, did not toss the brash youngster into the orchestra pit was remarkable.

On September 27, 1932, Milton was seen on Broadway in Earl Carroll's *Vanities*. He was modestly billed as "the rising young American comedian who has been the outstanding discovery of the present season and makes his first bow to the legitimate theatregoers." He was featured with Helen Broderick and English comedian Will Fyffe. The show lasted 87 performances.

In 1933 the performer was back in vaudeville headlining Loew's State with his own revue and by October was appearing at Times Square's Paramount Theatre with his show featuring fan-dancer Sally Rand. It was during this year that he became the hit of Chicago by being master of ceremonies for various stage shows there that headlined performers like Irene Bordoni, Peggy Hopkins Joyce, and Ethel Barrymore.

Mama Berle was overjoyed when her prize son returned to the legitimate stage in 1934. But *Saluta*, which opened on August 28, was a musical bomb. Brooks Atkinson noted in the *New York Times*, "It would be difficult not to like Mr. Berle as a gagster, although he does all that he can to discourage affection. Having immense enthusiasm and no discrimination at all, he runs the whole gamut from vulgarity to grossness in fine fettle, grinning at his own jokes. If someone would take Mr. Berle in hand and teach him the difference between cleverness and cheapness he would be voted a member of the theatre's liveliest entertainers." His playing of the lead, Windy Walker, did not advance his Broadway career.

The following year he toured in the Bert Lahr part in the musical revue *Life Begins at 8:40*. He aroused Mr. Lahr's ire, the latter stating that Berle imitated him in the road show. Now nearing 30, Milton made another stab at Hollywood. Although not handsome in the accepted movie sense, he had a rough flair and had developed a following with the public. He made a screen test for Samuel Goldwyn in October 1936, but it led to no contract. RKO, however, did sign him to a picture deal. They featured him in two misadventures, *New Faces of 1937* and *Radio City Revels* (1938). These releases were not harbingers of a promising screen career. Along the way RKO had considered Milton for the role of the resort camp master of ceremonies in Ginger Rogers' *Having Wonderful Time* (1938) and the part of producer Gordon

Miller in *Room Service* (1938); but the former assignment went to Red Skelton and the latter to Groucho Marx (after the Brothers had reconsidered accepting the leads in the adaptation of the stage hit).

It was during this California period that Milton became involved with an alcoholic movie starlet, by whom he says he had a son. (In later years the comedian would constantly refer to this child, stating he and the offspring have never officially met. Despite repeated press queries, Berle refused to reveal the name of the mother, who he says is still alive.)

Ever anxious to veer in any direction that might further his professional activities, Milton accepted all types of job offers. When Danny Kaye proved unavailable, Berle agreed to play the role of Arthur Lee in George Abbott's production of the comedy *See My Lawyer*. The show opened on Broadway on September 25, 1939, and ran for 224 performances.

In 1941 he tried Hollywood again and received good notices for his playing of Frosty (and sporting his newly reshaped nose) in Twentieth Century-Fox's *Tall, Dark and Handsome* opposite Charlotte Greenwood. Fox kept him on the payroll and he was effective as Nifty Allen, the obtuse manager of Glenn Miller's band, pursued by Joan Davis in *Sun Valley Serenade* (1941). He was in support of Jack Oakie, Linda Darnell, and George Murphy in *Rise and Shine* (1941), and bolstered Carole Landis' appearance in *A Gentleman at Heart* (1941). Berle was quite good as radio mystery solver E. H. Van Buren, verging on a nervous breakdown in *Whispering Ghosts* (1942). *Photoplay* found his performance as Moe Finkelstein in Otto Preminger's *Margin for Error* (1943) to be the film's outstanding feature: "He gives the performance of his career as the Jewish cop. His lines sparkle like icicles in the sun." It would remain Milton's best screen role.

Throughout this period Milton was beset with personal problems. On December 4, 1941, he had married Joyce Matthews.* She

* The Berle-Matthews marriage, at best, was stormy. The adoption of Victoria Melanie Berle (born September 2, 1947) promised to ease Joyce's erratic, suicidal behavior. It did not and on October 23, 1947, the Berles were divorced. On June 16, 1949, Joyce and Milton would remarry, but in less than a year, on March 30, 1950, they were divorced. Among her later husbands was Broadway entrepreneur Billy Rose.

With Jack Oakie,
Helen Broderick, and
Bobby Barber in
Radio City Revels
(1937).

With Wonderful Smith, Leon Belasco (rear), and Bob Reeves (cop) in Over My Dead Body (1942).

was blonde and beautiful and for 10 days had been the wife of Colonel Gonzalez Gómez, son of the Venezuelan dictator Juan Vicente Gómez. From the start of Milton's marriage there was contention between Mama Sandra and Joyce, each vying for his attention. Between coping with his dominating mother and mercurial Joyce on the one hand, and trying to tend to his career on the other, Milton was under a good deal of strain. His mounting hypochondria found surcease by embracing Christian Science, and for the next 20 years he followed the tenets of Mary Baker Eddy.

When Hollywood seemed to have no further need of Berle's services he parlayed an impressive return to Broadway. He became the first star to receive top billing over the *Ziegfeld Follies* which opened at the Winter Garden Theatre on April 1, 1943. The show enjoyed the longest run of any edition of the *Follies*, racking up 553 performances. Milton's success as the *Follies* star drew a mixed press. Ward Morehouse wrote, "Now, Berle is a fellow who can get in the hair of many a playgoer. Some may detest him; others want to slap him. Some may resent him. But the man is funny. At times, I thought, tremendously so. And it's Mr. Berle who sets the pace for this new *Follies*." Other reviewers thought Berle had substituted Minsky for Ziegfeld and that the Shubert production had little resemblance to any of Mr. Ziegfeld's *Follies* beyond the beautiful girls. Boston critic Elliot Norton, not fond of the onstage performer, had to admit that he had matured his comedy from the "brash, bold, insolent, slick, and self-satisfied, jeering wit of the Broadway cafe school" into something much finer. He added, "Milton Berle has come to love the audiences which he used to patronize in a callow way." Walter Winchell summed up the Berle talent, "Nobody likes Milton Berle—except his mother, and the public."

During the run of the *Follies*, Milton produced a play, *I'll Take the High Road*, which ran for only seven performances on Broadway. He later co-produced another stage flop, starring Paul and Grace Hartman, *Same Time Next Week*, which folded in Boston. During this period he was back on radio (never his true medium) in broadcasts of "Let Yourself Go" and "The Milton Berle Show." During 1945 he played to nearly 400 hospitals with a USO unit and that fall he returned to musical comedy.

Spring in Brazil opened at Boston's Shubert Theatre on October 2, 1945. The show featured Berle, Rose Marie, a deadly book, and unmemorable music. By the time the production reached Philadelphia, Milton was confiding to a bored audience, "If you think this is bad, you should have seen us in Boston!" With cast changes the show limped into Chicago and Berle was telling the meager audience, "Look out, we outnumber you!" The show, thankfully, closed in the Windy City on January 12, 1946. Berle cracked, "Business was so big, we sent the whole audience home in a taxi."

After the demise of the Brazilian fiasco, Berle returned to a part of show business in which he excelled—the nightclubs. His past successes at New York's Casino de Paree and Chicago's Chez Paree were preludes to his 51-week run at Nicky Blair's Manhattan club, The Carnival. Over subsequent years, whenever the job offers from TV or movies were scant, he would return to the club circuit. As he told reporters in 1974, "Give me a loud microphone and a good audience, and I'll stay on forever."

When Milton had been doing radio shows, one wag noted, "The trouble with Berle on the radio is that his personality comes through!" But in a different medium, television, his surging unharnessed talent and drive would have a commanding and historical influence.

Texaco's "Star Theatre" made its television debut on Tuesday, September 21, 1948, starring Milton Berle, *live* from Rockefeller Center in New York City. For the next eight years, Berle would romp like a whirlwind through videoland, milking laughs, playing fool and buffoon, trotting out aged routines, jokes, and gimmicks—anything for a laugh, even to parading in drag. His drive for perfection aroused ire in co-workers and performers, with resultant bad publicity. But Tuesday night in the United States became Berle's night and "Uncle Miltie" was king of the medium.

On January 27, 1950, the National Academy of Television Arts and Sciences gave him an Emmy Award as the year's "Most Outstanding Personality." On May 3, 1951, he made show-business history when he signed a 30-year contract with NBC-TV.

For an annual salary of $200,000 he agreed to restrict his television activities to the National Broadcasting Corporation. When his services were not required by NBC he was free to play club dates, accept sporadic movie roles, or, infrequently, star in stage productions. (Much later he would negotiate to end the contract which he found hampered his professional career.)

Just after Milton's initial TV success, Hollywood beckoned him westward. Warner Bros., eager to cash in on his new skyrocketing popularity, signed him for a picture during the show's summer layoff in 1949. Berle owned a small percentage interest in *Always Leave Them Laughing* (1949) and the part of Kid Cooper, a brash young comedian rising in show business, seemed made for him. He signed Bert Lahr to play the part of an older gagster. Soon the two funsters were in heated conflict. Milton had taken over the film's direction from director Roy Del Ruth, who was ill, and Lahr felt his role had been diminished. He called the assignment "one of the most unpleasant situations I've ever had in pictures." Berle strongly defended his position, contending Lahr was given proper treatment. The picture itself was no milestone in the advancement of screen comedy. When the movie opened in England, one reviewer reported, "He is a comedian for whom no joke is too old, and who can only be funny when surrounded with an apparatus of stage comic paraphernalia. Whatever his merits as a comedian, his place is clearly not the screen." Milton returned to New York and to television where he was still a kingpin.

A musical version of Booth Tarkington's *Seventeen* was co-produced by Berle. It opened in June 1951 for 182 performances and then toured. It was not a financial success. In the fall of 1951 Berle met an attractive former WAC captain and publicist for Sam Goldwyn. On December 9, 1953, Milton and Ruth Cosgrove were married in a private ceremony in the chambers of State Supreme Court Justice Morris Eder at the New York County courthouse. It was her third marriage. Among the witnesses were Mama Sandra and Berle's daughter Vicki. Before leaving for a three-week Miami Beach honeymoon, Ruth told reporters about her spouse, "He's a very funny man. He's one of the few comedians who is funny off TV as well as on.

He is also very sweet, very considerate, very kind and thoughtful."

The nagging guilt Berle felt from his mother's idolatry, which excluded his brothers and sister, always raised the question, "Did anybody really love me?" He found the answer in Ruth Cosgrove, who could cope with his vagaries and of whom he said, "She's a cool one. She can stop me at a glance or the lack of a glance. She has settled me down. I call her Rocky, because she's my Rock of Gibraltar." Ruth's strength was there when on May 31, 1954, Mama Berle died of a cerebral hemorrhage at New York's Essex House.

Recently Berle told newsmen, "Television didn't make me a star. I was a star long before television. What TV made me is unemployed." As the Fifties wore on, so did Milton; but the law of diminishing returns finally set in.* He was no longer the comedy king of television. Others, like Jackie Gleason, had already superseded him in the public's adulation. By the end of the decade he was regarded as a historic relic on the small screen and had long since passed from many people's thoughts. Occasionally he would make a resurgence in the medium with a brand-new (or so he said) format of video programming, but it proved to be Berle's old standby vaudeville-type show. Yet he was capable of offbeat performances, as when he gave an Emmy-nominated performance in the dramatic episode *Doyle Against the House*, shown on the "Dick Powell Theatre" on October 24, 1961.

It was Jerry Lewis who gave Uncle Miltie a new taste of moviemaking. He had a guest shot in *The Bellboy* (1960), filmed at the Hotel Fontainbleau in Miami Beach. In Marilyn Monroe's *Let's Make Love* (1960), Berle is seen briefly teaching Yves Montand a comedy routine. (Milton would later assert that at one period in his career he had a brief affair with Miss Monroe.)

During these difficult up-and-down career years, Ruth Berle faced her marriage with a good deal of fortitude. She told a reporter, "Being married to Milton is the hardest job I've ever had. He can be very difficult. He's a worrier who's never content. In the beginning

---

* Plans for Milton to produce and direct a film dealing with W. C. Fields and the *Ziegfeld Follies* were announced in mid-1956, but never materialized.

I found him childishly impossible. I had always been self-sufficient, accustomed to come and go as I pleased. Many times I resisted the urge to belt him one—and walk out." The marriage has survived. On December 31, 1961, the Berles adopted a four-day-old boy named Tony.

The success of MGM's *The Wizard of Oz* was not duplicated in the 90-minute animated-cartoon feature *Journey Back to Oz*, made in 1962 and shelved until 1970. Berle supplied the offcamera voice for the cowardly lion, a part played on screen in 1939 by his nemesis Bert Lahr. In another twist of fate, the summer of 1963 found Milton hitting the summer theatre stages in *Top Banana*. It was a revival of Phil Silvers' greatest stage success. Silvers freely admitted the character of the TV comic in the 1951 hit was unabashedly modeled after Berle. "I knew every flip gesture of Berle's, every ruthless smile. Milton was, shall I say, an impatient man. He had to have his laughs, and he didn't care where or how he found them." Berle was a

backer of that Broadway show and, with Mama, one of the heartiest laughers on opening night.

The year 1963 also provided Berle with one of his best screen roles. In Stanley Kramer's "comedy to end all comedy," *It's a Mad, Mad, Mad, Mad World*, he played J. Russell Finch, president of the Pacific Edible Seaweed Company, who joins the interminable chase after a fortune.

Far less heralded than his 1951 pact with NBC-TV was the May 21, 1965, alteration to the contract between the network and the former TV superstar. The performer took a 40 percent reduction in annual pay to gain his freedom to appear on other networks. But by 1965 the public's taste had changed from what it was in the early Fifties and there were few demands for his talents. He was reduced to appearing in a dismal half-hour game show, television's "Jackpot Bowling."

His roles in the movies were not a noticeable improvement. He and Margaret Leighton were the Kentons, mourning their pet

With Terry-Thomas in It's a Mad, Mad, Mad, Mad World *(1963).*

With Anthony Newley in Can Hieronymus Merkin Ever Forget Mercy Humppe and Find True Happiness? *(1968).*

dog, in the macabre, uneven *The Loved One* (1965). In another movie satire on the film industry, the deplorably sloppy *The Oscar* (1966), Berle showed that he could rise above mediocre material. He gave a finely etched dramatic portrait of Kappy Kapstetter, Stephen Boyd's astute talent agent, who is terminally ill. But Berle's playing of Anthony Quinn's business partner in *The Happening* (1967) pressed farce into doldrums. As pawnbroker Luther Burton, business manager of a group of incompetent, amateurish thieves, he was magnificently greedy and funny in *Who's Minding the Mint?* (1967). He had a minor role of a movie director in *Where Angels Go . . . Trouble Follows* (1968) and was unfortunately involved in Anthony Newley's distasteful ego trip, the film *Can Hieronymus Merkin Ever Forget Mercy Humppe and Find True Happiness?* (1968). Also that year he played a cameo part of a social director of a huge apartment complex designed for unmarried young adults. *For Singles Only* was very forgettable.

In 1968 Berle's daughter Vicki was married and Milton returned to Broadway after a 25-year absence. Herb Goodman's play *The*

Goodbye People opened on December 3 and closed on December 7. Actually, *The Goodbye People* was a decent play that simply did not register with the public. For Berle it was further proof of his ability to play a straight dramatic part. Clive Barnes (*New York Times*) wrote of Berle's emoting in *The Goodbye People:* "[He] rumbles around like an argumentative Yiddishe poppa, dispensing wisdom with indomitable indomitability, and making it sound like an epigram every time he clears his throat. Mr. Berle has fun and gives fun." Otis L. Guernsey Jr. (*New York Herald-Tribune*) thought that "one of the most poignant experiences of the season was Milton Berle's portrayal of an aged Coney Island concessionaire determined to do or die in making a comeback with a grand opening on the beach—in February—of a hot-dog stand."

Over the recent years Milton had played various summer stock engagements. He did *Never Too Late* in Las Vegas and *The Impossible Years* in Miami. In the summer of 1972 he was back on the straw-hat circuit in *The Last of the Red Hot Lovers.*

During the late Sixties and early Seventies, Berle was a very frequent guest on TV shows of all varieties. He capered on Lucille Ball's program, appeared on "Batman" as Louie the Lilac, mugged through "Love, American Style," and made several fine dramatic appearances ("Ironside," "Mannix," "The Bold Ones"). One of his best such performances was on the November 23, 1971, episode of ABC-TV's "Mod Squad" in which he was Uncle Bobo, a TV kiddie-show clown marked for murder. Berle's son had a role in the proceedings. Milton also gave a fine account of himself in such TV movies as *Seven in Darkness* (1969) and *Evil Roy Slade* (1971).

Berle showed no sign of slowing down in the mid-Seventies. In November 1974 his autobiography (written with Haskel Frankel) appeared. *Publishers Weekly* evaluated, "The most shockingly candid and humanly revealing story a superstar ever wrote. His book deserves curtain calls." The *New York Times* found, "An appealing, readable, unpredictable book—not that of a wise-guy comic but of a man trying to figure out how he got where he is." In the course of the soul-baring sensational confessional, Milton revealed that during a West Coast vaudeville engagement years before he had an affair with show-business-oriented evangelist Aimee Semple McPherson. In summing up the book, Tom Buckley (*New York Times*) observed, "In movies Mr. Berle was usually cast to type as a brash master of ceremonies, adept at applause milking and upstaging, ready to kill for a laugh or to die if he didn't get one, but not essentially very funny. Looking back, he says it hasn't been a happy life, and one can only agree."

When TV's new show "Vaudeville" premiered on May 26, 1975, it would be Milton Berle to initiate the series from Hollywood's Ritz Theatre. That summer Berle was also seen on the small screen (in drag) pitching commercials for a restaurant chain; the ad ended with a custard pie in his face. The pie should have been reserved for a picture released at that time, produced and directed by Israeli Menahem Golan. A biographical bomb, the film was based on the crime career of Louis Lepke Buchalter (Tony Curtis) and released by Warner Bros. as *Lepke*. One critic observed that the script was written in delicatessenese clichés and Berle's portrayal of Lepke's aged father-in-law was as unconvincing as his spongy old-man makeup.

An embarrassing appearance on Monty Hall's TV show "Let's Make a Deal" was made during rehearsals for Uncle Miltie's much-heralded return to Broadway in the summer of 1975. Contrary to immediate innuendo, the play, *The Best of Everybody*, was *not* autobiographical. Opening in Chicago on September 22, the play, starring Berle and Vivian Blaine, folded within two weeks. That same year he opened his nightclub act at Chicago's Regency Hyatt Hotel, parading his buffoonery for an hour that some found sensational and nostalgic. But *Variety* wrote, "Though a packed crowd received him with great affection, many seemed surprised to find their beloved Uncle Miltie struggling like an over-the-hiller. Quite simply, the old-wave one-liners and rejoinders he favors, many of them off-color, aren't funny anymore, and no amount of audience pestering is going to improve them."

But Berle remained undaunted. His compulsion to entertain and seek audience adulation took him to various midwestern college campuses, giving seminars on the mechanics of comedy (and to start writing a textbook on the subject). On November 23, 1975, Berle gave a polished, dignified performance as producer Jesse Lasky in the ABC-TV "Sunday Night Movie" *The Legend of Valentino*. He was one of the few sincere ingredients in the fatuous production.

On February 4, 1976, Berle glowingly did his "historic minute" for Shell Oil's TV Bicentennial series, and in subsequent months turned up on an assortment of talk and variety shows. He cannot bear the thought of retirement. "I work to live, I live to work. I lay around two or three weeks, and the fingernails come off. I've got to get up in front of an audience. . . . I've got to hear them laugh. It's hammy, it's corny, but it's true." (Work also helps to compensate for his enormous gambling losses. Berle, a compulsive gambler, estimates that he has lost $3.5 million in betting to date.)

In some somber moments, the legendary comedian will admit, "It is quite sad when you see that here's a guy who makes people laugh, and he doesn't get many laughs out of his own life." Regarding happiness, he confides, "I am content with my family and wife,

With Tony Curtis and Warren Berlinger in Lepke (1975).

and I live very comfortably. . . . But it's that extra something that I'm looking for . . . that I haven't found yet." But usually King Clown is always joking for the public. With a smirk and a chortle, he will insist on a TV game show, "At my age when I read racy fiction, it *is* science fiction."

The summer of 1976 found Berle headlining a show at the Latin Casino Club in Cherry Hill, New Jersey, teamed on the bill with George Jessel, The Ink Spots, and Donald O'Connor. He also toured the straw-hat circuit with Jack Gilford in *The Sunshine Boys* and was mentioned by filmmaker Stanley Kramer to co-star in a proposed film tentatively titled *The Sheiks of Araby* (which has yet to be made). He did have a cameo in that embarrassment of nostalgia, *Won Ton Ton, the Dog Who Saved Hollywood* (1976).

As the years pass, Berle's show-business activities seem to increase. In 1977 he made the rounds of the talk and quiz shows, and was special guest star on such TV variety

programs as "The Brady Bunch Hour" and "The Donny and Marie Osmond Show." For Frank Sinatra's Forest Hills, New York, concert show in mid-1977 Berle was second-billed; he later supported Steve Lawrence and Eydie Gorme in another appearance on the concert-club circuit. Milton also starred in "Sheila Levine," a CBS-TV pilot for a proposed series which did not sell. The test film, aired in August 1977, found Berle cast as a Broadway producer-songwriter who hires a marriage-bent assistant (Dori Brenner). It was all an unfunny mishmash. As part of his 1977-1978 TV season activities, Berle guested on "The Muppets," "The Love Boat," performed a special chore as the voice characterization of Uncle Claude in the NBC-TV animated special *The Lemming Condition*, based on Alan Arkin's book, and appeared as Morris Glickstein, a member of a synagogue involved in *Have I Got a Christmas for You.* Later came a network special *A Tribute to Mr. Television* (NBC-TV, March 26, 1978) in which, noted *The Hollywood Reporter.* "Berle himself is stage front center and funny throughout the majority of the night, thanks to the numerous scenes depicting his highlights. . . ." Needless to say, scarcely a week goes by that Berle cannot be seen on the small screen adding his raucous humor to a quiz/game/talk show program.

A few years ago, on October 13, 1973,* a gala Friars Club benefit dinner was given at the Beverly Hilton Hotel in California and was attended by 1,300 guests, including a glittering array of celebrities. The occasion was to honor Berle's 60 years as an entertainer. The bash was later televised as an ABC-TV special, "Show Business Salutes Milton Berle." The passing of time and reevaluation based on longevity were not lost on Berle. He reflected on his abrasive, early TV reputation and said, "Sure I did the whole bit with the chamois coat and the whistle and the yelling, but I was under a lot of pressure. I don't think I'm more mellow in the eyes of the audience. I'm still associated with flipness, brashness. Hoke, shtick, slapstick are still badly needed." Archbishop Sheen summed it up when he said, "With the way the world is going today, we'd be much better off with less throwing of bombs and more throwing of pies!" Mama Berle would heartily agree.

---

* On May 11, 1977, "Mr. Television" was honored with a huge stag roast at the Beverly Hilton Hotel in California, hosted by the Eddie Cantor Lodge of B'nai Brith. The occasion raised $25,000 for charity and proved once again what a sharp, if too-enthusiastic, raconteur Mr. Berle is.

FEATURE FILMS

The Perils of Pauline (*Pathé serial 1914*)
Tillie's Punctured Romance (*Keystone 1914*)
Lena Rivers (*Cosmo Feature Company 1914*)
The Little Brother (*Triangle 1917*)
Rebecca of Sunnybrook Farm (*Paramount 1917*)
The Wishing Ring Man (*Vitagraph 1919*)
Birthright (*Superior Pictures 1920*)
The Mark of Zorro (*United Artists 1920*)
Love's Penalty (*Associated First National 1921*)
Divorce Coupons (*Vitagraph 1922*)
Tess of the Storm Country (*United Artists 1922*)
Ruth of the Range (*Pathé serial 1923*)
New Faces of 1937 (*RKO 1937*)
Radio City Revels (*RKO 1938*)
Tall, Dark and Handsome (*20th Century-Fox 1941*)
Sun Valley Serenade (*20th Century-Fox 1941*)
Rise and Shine (*20th Century-Fox 1941*)
A Gentleman at Heart (*20th Century-Fox 1941*)
Whispering Ghosts (*20th Century-Fox 1942*)
Over My Dead Body (*20th Century-Fox 1942*)

Margin for Error (*20th Century-Fox 1943*)
Always Leave Them Laughing (*Warner Bros. 1949*)
The Bellboy (*Paramount 1960*)
Let's Make Love (*20th Century-Fox 1960*)
Journey Back to Oz [Back to Oz] (*Filmation 1962*) (voice only)
It's a Mad, Mad, Mad, Mad World (*United Artists 1963*)
The Loved One (*MGM 1965*)
The Oscar (*Embassy 1966*)
Don't Worry, We'll Think of a Title (*United Artists 1966*)
The Happening (*Columbia 1967*)
Who's Minding the Mint? (*Columbia 1967*)
Where Angels Go . . . Trouble Follows (*Columbia 1967*)
Can Hieronymus Merkin Ever Forget Mercy Humppe and Find True Happiness? (*Universal 1968*)
For Singles Only (*Columbia 1968*)
Lepke (*Warner Bros. 1975*)
Won Ton Ton, the Dog Who Saved Hollywood (*Paramount 1976*)

With Charlie Ruggles in publicity pose for Night Work *(1939).*

Mary Boland

America's capacity to laugh at itself has never been more evident than in the depths of the Great Depression. Caricature of human idiosyncrasies gained popularity in Hollywood's screwball comedy ventures, which reached their zenith during the Thirties. To maintain this genre the cinema used a roster of featured farceurs that included several well-trained stage actresses who deserted Broadway's light drawing-room comedies, minor dramas, and grim tragedies to brighten motion pictures with their expert clowning. Hollywood relegated these Broadway stars to perpetual feature status. But often they were so proficient that their performances considerably dimmed those of the top-billed stars, rescued many films from obscurity and boredom, and established them as vital box-office draws.

In this category, for instance, were Alice Brady and Billie Burke, each of whom brought to the screen huge talents nurtured and perfected in varied theatrical successes from musical comedy to stark drama. Hollywood shuttled them, with others, into the mold of the matronly zany. But rising above all the scatterbrained middle-aged matrons plying their craft on stage and screen was a handsome blonde. Although only 5'4", she was dominantly statuesque and possessed a refined speaking voice that swelled perfect diction into cackling cadence. Seemingly in a constant state of flutter, she created the screen's most memorable matron with a high gloss and ever professionally polished performances. Her name was Mary Boland.

In January 1880, actor William A. Boland left his Detroit home to fulfill a stock engagement in Philadelphia, taking his daughter and eight-months-pregnant wife, Mary Halton Boland, with him. On Wednesday, January 28, 1880, his second daughter was born, at 412 Edward Street in the then theatrical boarding-house section of Philadelphia. The newly arrived daughter was recorded in the Philadelphia Registry of Births as Marie Anne Boland. Returning to Detroit, Mr. Boland gave up the uncertainties of acting for a more lucrative job as an interior decorator, sent his daughters to the Sacred Heart Convent, and spent evenings reading Shakespeare and the classics to his

111

family, as he had done when courting his wife. (Mary, recalling her father's courtin' days years later, said, "Beaux aren't like that anymore. The light's so poor in rumble seats!")

When the younger Boland girl was 15 her father died and she entered show business as a chorus girl with Ward and Vokes. After stock seasons in Cincinnati and Nashville, she made her Broadway debut on August 28, 1905, as Dorothy Nelson in William C. de Mille's play, *Strongheart*, starring Robert Edeson. She abandoned Marie Anne and became Mary Boland. On May 8, 1907, she debuted in London at the Aldwych Theatre in the de Mille play and on September 2, 1907, she was back on Broadway as Dorothy Osgood in *The Ranger*, starring Dustin Farnum.* In September 1908 she signed with Charles Frohman to play Ethel Jennings in *Jack Straw*, starring matinee idol John Drew. For the next seven years Mary was John Drew's leading lady in a series of plays, *Inconstant George*, *Smith*, *A Single Man*, and *The Perplexed Husband*, and in 1913 was Hero to Drew's Benedick in *Much Ado About Nothing*. By the time she opened (October 10, 1914) in Edward Knoblauch's *My Lady's Dress*—playing six different roles—she was well established as a player of great ability and persuasion.

By 1914–15 many Broadway stars had been convinced to enter the film medium and Mary made her motion picture debut for Kay-Bee in the drama *The Edge of the Abyss*, with Willard Mack and Robert McKim. In February 1916, for her second film, *The Price of Happiness*, she reaped less than enthusiastic reviews for her playing of Bertha Miller. She was the wife of a shoemaker who delivers shoes to three friends and discovers her envy of them has been misplaced. After filming *The Stepping Stone* (1916) with Frank Keenan, Mary happily returned to the stage.

Although she had polished her stage acting through assorted shows with John Drew, had

---

* Years later Mary would recall, "When I began my career as an actress, theatre people were expected to keep away from the general public. In 1907 I had the lead in a play in London. Charles Frohman sent me back to New York on 12 hours' notice because he saw me twice dining at the Savoy Hotel. 'Do you expect the public to pay to see you, when they can see you every night at the Savoy?' he said. I guess that attitude stayed with me all my life."

appeared in repertory in Denver (in 1912), and had played in the farce *Sick-a-Bed*, Mary was not regarded as a leading comedienne. But Booth Tarkington's *Clarence* tilted her career. The Tarkington comedy was a huge hit when it opened in Atlantic City, New Jersey, on July 7, 1919; it stayed a month. It was expected that the show would be a big hit when it reached Broadway. However, Actors Equity called a general strike against the Producing Managers Association and in the front lines for Equity stood Mary, Marie Dressler, Ethel Barrymore, Ed Wynn, and Ralph Morgan. Mary predicted that by Labor Day the management-producers would concede "'cause they can't put on Broadway shows without actors." By early September the *Clarence* company started rehearsals and on September 20, 1919, the comedy opened at the Hudson Theatre. Overnight co-players Helen Hayes and Alfred Lunt became stars and Mary Boland was lauded as a newfound comedienne, playing Mrs. Wheeler, the mother of two lovable brats (Miss Hayes and Glenn Hunter). The show was an enormous success.

Before *Clarence* gave Mary's stage career new focus, she made a few more films. She was Sam Hardy's wife in *A Woman's Experience*, and had the title role in *The Prodigal Wife*, both 1918 releases. In *The Perfect Lover* (1919) she played opposite Eugene O'Brien. While still in *Clarence* she found time to star in the film *His Temporary Wife* (1920) with Edmund Breese. But none of these pictures did much toward establishing a flourishing film career for her. Mary's style was too vocal for the silent cinema.

After *Clarence* Mary was deemed a top Broadway star and would ply her craft almost exclusively on the stage. George Kelly's *The Torch Bearers* was the first play satirizing the "amateur theater" groups and was a bright, witty comedy that opened on August 29, 1922, and romped for 135 performances. As Paula Ritter, leading actress of the little-theater group, Mary was a constant delight. Alexander Woollcott wrote that she was an utterly delightful comedienne having a little glory all her own at the 48th Street Theatre. On August 30, 1922, Mary and Alison Skipworth would repeat their role of drama coach and aspiring actress in an excerpted second act of *The Torch Bearers* at vaudeville's famous Palace Theatre. (Thirteen years later Mary was still enthralled with Mr. Kelly's comedy: "I think if *The Torch Bearers* were done today it would be a great success. It came too early. It was brilliant." The same year, 1935, Fox filmed the comedy as the Will Rogers vehicle *Doubting Thomas*, with Billie Burke in Mary's meaty role.)

On November 26, 1923, Mary opened in what one critic aptly described as "the fattest and best comedy part ever handed an actress by an American writer . . . it fits her talents like the proverbial glove and will live in the memories of those who see her in it long after she has retired from the stage. As played by Miss Boland, the role is a classic." The part of Gertrude Lennox in Lynn Starling's farce, *Meet the Wife*, provided Mary with a joyous role, the type she would play frequently over the years.* The comedy ran on Broadway for 232 performances. Mary's performing sparkled and "seemed one of utter perfection" as a celebrity-seeking, twice-married matron who discovers she is a bigamist. Clifton Webb was equally lauded as her prospective son-in-law, giving a straight comedy performance that caused critics to suggest there was little reason for him to sing and dance again. Humphrey Bogart appeared in this offering as a "handsome and nicely mannered reporter."

Cradle Snatchers was a tremendous hit and ignited laughter for 332 performances after it opened on September 7, 1925, at Broadway's Music Box Theatre. As Susan Martin, one of three philandering middle-age wives (Edna May Oliver and Margaret Dale completed the trio) who acquire three college boys (Humphrey Bogart, Gene Raymond, and Raymond Hackett) as gigolos to provoke

* Over the years Mary would make a mini-career of *Meet the Wife*, although it was Laura LaPlante who played the lead in Universal's 1931 film. With Walter Connolly, Mary appeared on the Palace Theatre's vaudeville bill in December 1928 in a condensed version of the play to great ovation. (Reported one source, "Mary Boland has never been quite so broadly gushing, nor arranged flowers so assiduously as she does in this little piece.") Mary appeared in *Meet the Wife* at the Curran Theatre in San Francisco in the spring of 1941 and toured the summer theatre circuit in the East. In 1946 and 1947 she was again on tour as Gertrude performing one of the funniest telephone scenes ever seen on the stage. Her last fling with the role was at the one-night star-studded benefit performance for the ANTA Album on Sunday, May 6, 1951, at the Ziegfeld Theatre. She did a brief scene from the comedy.

jealousy in their preoccupied husbands, Mary was, again, in a role that permitted her free rein for her depiction of a silly acid-dripping matron. She was superb.

Like many funsters, Mary had a suppressed desire to play drama. The role of Mrs. Daisy Bowman in *Women Go on Forever* gave her the appropriate outlet. The play opened September 7, 1927, to run for 117 performances. In later years Mary would reflect on her unwise choice to play in a straight drama, "I had one once. . . . Lots of murders and full of plot. I'm sure that I helped kill it. People had never associated me with tragedy and I got many letters of complaint. They wrote that they'd come to see me to laugh and all that I'd given them was a gunman's boarding house." It was not one of Mary's glowing successes. But audiences did see a young actor named James Cagney in the role of Eddie.

Mary's next two plays were also out of tune with her image of eminent farceur. Her Rosalie West, collecting lovers while denying her husband a divorce in *Heavy Traffic* (1928), lasted 61 performances and *Ada Beats the Drum* (1930) had a shorter run.

Paul Osborn's *The Vinegar Tree* (1930) was tailor-made for Mary. She played the chic, witty, romance-riddled Laura Merrick on Broadway for 229 performances. Meanwhile, she returned to the screen, supporting Claudette Colbert in *Secrets of a Secretary* (1931), which was filmed at Paramount's Astoria, Long Island, studio by George Abbott. While still appearing in the Osborn play, Mary also made another bit of Paramount fluff, *Personal Maid* (1931), in which she was Gene Raymond's mother. Film critics were becoming aware of her "grand" performing.

Paramount, well attuned to hiring Broadway notables for the screen, signed Miss Boland to a long-term, expansively liberal contract that permitted her to retain her Broadway starring status. On February 17, 1932, undaunted, nonsinger Mary starred in her first musical comedy, *Face the Music*. With music by Irving Berlin, book by Berlin and Moss Hart, direction by acerbic George S. Kaufman, and staging by Hassard Short, the production was a thing of joy, cartooning Manhattan's politics, police force, and the Seabury investigation. The musical provided

Mary with a wonderful showcase as the fatuous wife of Police Sergeant Lockridge (Hugh O'Connell), who has bought a lucrative berth on the force. Critic Richard Lockridge reported, "It is always funny when Miss Boland is present and her musical comedy debut is one to be long remembered." Among Mary's prize bits in this show was riding an elephant with great aplomb and smugness while balancing an enormously outrageous headpiece. At another moment she is describing her vast collection of diamonds to another character, "On a clear day, you can see me from Yonkers."

After a road tour with *Face the Music* in early 1933, Mary left for Hollywood to begin her series of deftly drawn fluttery matrons for Paramount Pictures' West Coast facilities.

Brooks Atkinson's appraisal of Mary's work in *Face the Music* could also describe her film portraits of the middle-aged madame: "The venom she puts into her moments of shrewish indignation, the sticky unction of her philandering and the general club-lady excitability of her deportment are unconscionably sharp and funny."

Mary had appeared oncamera with veteran Charlie Ruggles in three films, including the episodic *If I Had a Million* (1932), before the studio really thought of the two players as a team. They were coupled in the delightful comedy *Mama Loves Papa* (1933), which *Photoplay* selected as one of the best pictures of the month and in which it found Mary "simply grand." Mary and Ruggles worked perfectly in tandem: she the dominant, selfish but lovable prattling creature, he the henpecked, peace-at-any-cost spouse. Together they would make fourteen films. The *New York Times* accurately detailed their screen image: "Miss Boland and Mr. Ruggles are unmatched on the screen as exponents of domestic comedy, and their work has a remarkable faculty for touching life. While you are laughing at the marital crises which they enact with such delightful accuracy, you have the uncomfortable feeling of seeing yourself mirrored on the screen."

In the fall of 1933 Mary worked for the first—and last—time under the direction of Cecil B. DeMille. The director's penchant for authenticity (and dangerous locations) begot a nervous, frantic cast shooting scenes in the dense jungles of Hawaii for an aptly named

epic, *Four Frightened People* (1934). Mary took a dim view of the illustrious DeMille's insistence on wallowing through wet, slimy jungles and repeatedly announced to all within hearing distance, "I wonder when that hilo-monster will let us finish the scene." Her natural, bright wit bolstered the dampened spirits of the cast and crew. At one point, after crawling for hours through the wet jungles of Waialula with Herbert Marshall, she asked, "Tell me, Bart, do you think the old-fashioned waltz is coming back?" *Four Frightened People*, which starred Claudette Colbert, Marshall, Mary, William Gargan, and Leo Carrillo, was an expensive dud that never recovered its cost. At any event, Mary's playing of the arrogant wife of a British official was well conceived.

Mary's closest brush with actual screen slapstick occurred in Paramount's hilariously funny *Six of a Kind* (1934). As Charlie Ruggles' wife Flora, Mary went off the brink of the Grand Canyon and was saved by a convenient tree. (The sequence required three days to film and Mary regarded it as the hardest scene she performed in pictures, including the DeMille fiasco.) Leo McCarey's expert direction helped to blend the variant styles of the all-star comedy cast: W. C. Fields, Alison Skipworth, Mary, Ruggles, and the zany team of George Burns and Gracie Allen.

If ever a role was unintentionally created for the talents of Mary Boland, it was that of the pretentious, socially conscious, flibbertigibbet Effie Floud in Leo McCarey's astute filming of *Ruggles of Red Gap* (1935). Once more Ruggles was her milquetoast spouse. The pair was surrounded by a superior cast which included: Charles Laughton, ZaSu Pitts, Roland Young, Maude Eburne, and Lucien Littlefield. One of the best of the many Boland-Ruggles screen ventures was the domestic comedy *People Will Talk* (1935), in which both players gave highly deft and humorous accounts of themselves as the Wiltons.

When Mary was offered the starring role in a new Cole Porter musical, she left Hollywood for her beloved Broadway. Producers Sam H. Harris and Max Gordon gave *Jubilee* a handsome production. Directed by Monty Woolley, it featured Mary, Melville Cooper, and June Knight, and in lesser roles Charles

With Claudette Colbert, Herbert Marshall, William Gargan, and Leo Carrillo in Four Frightened People *(1934).*

Walters, Mark Plant, and Montgomery Clift. Mary was the queen of a mythical kingdom who takes a brief respite from royalty. She sang "Me and Marie" with Cooper and joined vocalizers for two other Porter songs. Singing, as critic Robert Garland noted, was *not* one of Miss Boland's onstage attributes. But she carried it off with aplomb. And the show? John Mason Brown wrote, "Whenever Miss Boland is on the stage Mr. Hart's book proves to be enormously funny. She has never been seen to better advantage than she is as the stately queen who takes a few days off. She is breezy and lusty, gloriously ridiculous, and is possessed of a vitality and a comic skill which annihilate dullness. She is the one real comedian of the troupe, and the only one who knows how to project the broader values of a musical comedy with effortless assurance."

Brown's observation proved accurate. After playing her queenly role from October 12, 1935, to February 15, 1936, Mary became ill and was replaced by Laura Hope Crews. *Jubilee* folded on March 7, 1936. Max Gordon stated that her leaving the show brought on its early demise. Mary was ever the complete comedienne, Miss Crews was more the queen.

During the brief run of *Jubilee*, Mary was often interviewed by the press. She told reporter Ward Morehouse that she had never married and never would. "I've been alone too long. And maybe I'm one of the few people who don't mind being alone. I think I was once in love with Robert Loraine. I was playing with him, but he never spoke to me. I just peered at him constantly, and adoringly, from behind the scenery." Occasionally she would suggest to Charlie Ruggles that they might as well marry because everyone thought they were anyway. Mr. Ruggles shyly demurred. On this subject Mary informed the press, "Our love scenes are reserved for the screen. We never see each other out of the studio. I've never been at a party with Charlie, never even had a lunch or dinner with him. This isn't surprising when you consider that we neither one go about much. Charlie's one dissipation is going to the weekly fights. The height of my social gaiety is an evening at bridge."

After recovering from the strain of *Jubilee*, Mary returned to Hollywood. That August (1936) Paramount released a drama, *A Son Comes Home*, directed by E. A. Dupont. In it Mary made her only heavily dramatic screen appearance. Playing the owner of the Fisherman's Wharf Chowder House in San Francisco, she proves her long-lost son is not a murderer. One reviewer noted, "Switching from her usual high comedy to a role typical of the late Marie Dressler, Mary Boland deserves superlatives for a fine, convincing portrayal." But Mary was not emotionally geared to handle the pathos oncamera that came so easily to the late dowager MGM star. Miss Boland wisely returned to Ruggles and screen comedy.

Of the many Ruggles-Boland comedy entries, *Early to Bed* (1936) was one of their better efforts. Mary was delightful as Tessie Weeks, who browbeats Ruggles into marriage after a 20-year engagement. Mary played another comic role in *College Holiday* (1936) and then Paramount loaned her to Warner Bros. for *Marry the Girl* (1937). *Variety* termed the film "an addle-pated farce about a flock of screwballs" and *Photoplay* thought it was a "laugh riot." For Twentieth Century-Fox she was Ann Sothern's dim-witted mother in *Danger—Love at Work* (1937), a film heavily directed by Otto Preminger.

Before leaving Paramount, she made two last pictures with Ruggles, *Boy Trouble* and *Night Work*, both minor programmers for the 1939 film season. Right to the end, Ruggles was publicly fond of his frequent co-star. He found her "a dear, dear woman and a most clever woman" who knew her business of acting "just way down to the ground." Ruggles would later recall that during one of their joint picture-making efforts, Mary arrived on the set one morning after a champagne party the night before. She was reluctant to expose her eyes to the lights and camera, but decided against pleading as her excuse the champagne outing. Instead, she said the klieg lights hurt her eyes. When Ruggles reminded the actress that klieg lights had not been used for years, Mary bristled, "No? Is that so? Well, then, I'll have to think of something else!"

Perhaps no other screen part tested her mettle more than her role in MGM's *The Women* (1939). She had to compete for screen attention with Norma Shearer, Joan Crawford, Rosalind Russell, Paulette Goddard, Joan Fontaine, Lucile Watson, and Marjorie Main. Yet it was Miss Boland who offered the really memorable interpretation of Clare Boothe Luce's dialogue. She was the "silly, amiable, middle-aged" countess intent on "L'amour toujours, l'amour," despite a conviction that she had wed too many foreigners. (One spouse had pushed her off an Alpine mountain and her fourth husband, a French count, had laced her headache powders with arsenic.) The role was perfect for Mary, who offered a scintillating depiction of a pretentious, aging schoolgirlish romantic.

Mary remained at MGM to join with Nelson Eddy and Jeanette MacDonald in one of their lesser operettas, *New Moon* (1940). That same year at Metro she was the silly, greedy, marriage-obsessed mother of five daughters in the classy, polished production of *Pride and Prejudice*. She skittered precariously close to overacting as Mrs. Bennet. After run-of-the-flibberish roles in Republic's *Hit Parade of 1941* and Universal's *One Night in the Tropics*, both 1940 releases, Mary abandoned her Beverly Hills home and her hobby of orchid growing. She returned to the Broadway stage after a tour in *Meet the Wife*.

Directed by Eva LeGallienne and produced by the Theatre Guild, a revival of Richard Brinsley Sheridan's classic *The Rivals* co-starred Mary with Bobby Clark and Walter Hampden. The play opened on January 14, 1942. Clark and Boland were superb as Bob Acres and Mrs. Malaprop.* Mary had really been playing various malapropian ladies for years on the screen, but Mr. Sheridan's addled dame was waiting for her. Brooks Atkinson gushed in the *New York Times*, "And Miss Boland's whirling Mrs. Malaprop with a clacking voice is also enormously funny. Dressed in a billowing costume, with a bobbing headdress, she flounces through her demented dictionary of bungled English with a wit that is furious and spontaneous." The Sheridan revival lingered only 54 perform-

* During the pre-Broadway tour Mary suffered another one of her illnesses and was replaced for a time by Miss LeGallienne. The latter was then more convinced that Mary, never her choice for the part, had been playing the part too glamorously.

With Roger Imhof
and Burgess
Meredith in There
Goes the Groom
(1937).

With Ernest Truex in
Mama Runs Wild
(1937).

In New Moon *(1940).*

ances in New York. On March 2, 1942, the production opened at Chicago's Grand Opera House and Mary, pleading illness, abruptly withdrew from the cast. When she refused an examination by a Chicago doctor before leaving the show, Actors Equity fined her $500. Margaret Anglin replaced her. (Mary would reprise her manic Mrs. Malaprop for TV's "Masterpiece Theatre" in 1950.)

In 1943 Mary toured as Emily Welles in *Don't Mention It*, a prophetic flop. The next year she returned to filmmaking, accepting a subordinate role as the wealthy employer of Ida Lupino in *In Our Time*. Her comic bumbling added a note of levity to a rather heavy romantic drama set in wartime Poland. Supporting roles in Laurel and Hardy's *Nothing but Trouble* (1944) and Monogram's *They Shall Have Faith* (1944) were less than distinguished.

Early in 1947 Mary was persuaded to return to the stage in a new play, *The Greatest of These*, directed by Eddie Dowling and reuniting her with her stage gigolo from *Cradle Snatchers*, Gene Raymond. The show opened in Detroit in mid-February 1947 and closed a month later in Chicago. Also that year she appeared in a dismal flop about the housing shortage, *Open House*. She greeted visitors to her dressing room with, "Oh, my dears. Isn't this terrible!" in tones usually reserved for announcing the Lincoln assassination.

Mary shuttled between her home in California and the Essex House in New York City. In 1948, while in California, she played the mal-de-mer mother of a five-son acrobatic troupe (headed by Cesar Romero) in MGM's *Julia Misbehaves*. She joined Charlie Ruggles for their first stage venture together, starring with him on the West Coast in a new comedy, *One Fine Day*.

Her last screen appearance was in a cheaply made New York-shot programmer, *Guilty Bystander* (1950), in which she colorfully played a blowsy harridan, Smitty. On

February 5, 1951, Mary was seen with Fritzi Scheff and Melville Cooper in *Mlle. Modiste*. After 45 performances in a mild comedy, *Lullaby* (February 1954), Mary was never again seen on Broadway.

She spent her last years collecting antiques, playing bridge, and pursuing her beloved hobby of gardening. Occasionally she would appear on television: she joined with E. G. Marshall and Carmen Matthews on "Armstrong Circle Theatre" in 1954 for *The First Born* and the next year she played Mama on "Best of Broadway" in its adaptation of *The Guardsman*, starring Claudette Colbert and Franchot Tone.

Mary remained mostly out of the news for the next decade. Then on Wednesday, June 23, 1965, she was found dead in her Essex House suite. She had died in her sleep at age 85. After a viewing held at a Manhattan funeral home she was interred the next Monday at Forest Lawn Cemetery in Glendale, California. Only 30 people attended the service.

In Hollywood's gallery of comediennes, Mary Boland shines with shimmering brightness. Once when asked her valuation of the dizzy dame she portrayed on the screen, Mary said, "Women laugh their heads off at her. And the funny part of it is that they never think they're at all like her. I've heard them say, 'Isn't that Mrs. Smith to the life!' and, 'If that isn't Mrs. Jones to a dot!' They call her everybody but themselves!" Asked if she would call her screen character a perfect fool, Mary winced, "No one is perfect!"

FEATURE FILMS

The Edge of the Abyss (*Triangle 1915*)

The Price of Happiness (*Triumph-Equitable 1916*)

The Stepping Stone (*Kay-Bee–Triangle 1916*)

A Woman's Experience (*Bacon-Backer Foursquare Films 1918*)

The Prodigal Wife (*Screencraft Productions 1918*)

The Perfect Lover (*Selznick 1919*)

His Temporary Wife (*W. W. Hodkinson 1920*)

Secrets of a Secretary (*Paramount 1931*)

Personal Maid (*Paramount 1931*)

The Night of June 13th (*Paramount 1932*)

Evenings for Sale (*Paramount 1932*)

If I Had a Million (*Paramount 1932*)

Mama Loves Papa (*Paramount 1933*)

Three-Cornered Moon (*Paramount 1933*)

The Solitaire Man (*Paramount 1933*)

Four Frightened People (*Paramount 1934*)

Six of a Kind (*Paramount 1934*)

Melody in Spring (*Paramount 1934*)

Stingaree (*RKO 1934*)

Here Comes the Groom (*Paramount 1934*)

Down to Their Last Yacht (*RKO 1934*)

Pursuit of Happiness (*Paramount 1934*)

Ruggles of Red Gap (*Paramount 1935*)

People Will Talk (*Paramount 1935*)

Two for Tonight (*Paramount 1935*)

The Big Broadcast of 1936 (*Paramount 1935*)

A Son Comes Home (*Paramount 1936*)

Early to Bed (*Paramount 1936*)

Wives Never Know (*Paramount 1936*)

College Holiday (*Paramount 1936*)

Marry the Girl (*Warner Bros. 1937*)

Danger—Love at Work (*20th Century-Fox 1937*)

Mama Runs Wild (*Republic 1937*)

There Goes the Groom (*RKO 1937*)

Artists and Models Abroad (*Paramount 1938*)

Little Tough Guys in Society (*Universal 1938*)

Boy Trouble (*Paramount 1939*)

The Magnificent Fraud (*Paramount 1939*)

Night Work (*Paramount 1939*)

The Women (*MGM 1939*)

He Married His Wife (*20th Century-Fox 1940*)

New Moon (*MGM 1940*)

Pride and Prejudice (*MGM 1940*)

Hit Parade of 1941 (*Republic 1940*)

One Night in the Tropics (*Universal 1940*)

In Our Time (*Warner Bros. 1944*)

Nothing but Trouble (*MGM 1944*)

They Shall Have Faith [Forever Yours] (*Monogram 1944*)

Julia Misbehaves (*MGM 1948*)

Guilty Bystander (*Film Classics 1950*)

In Be Yourself *(1930).*

Fanny Brice

Funny girl. Funny lady. She was both. She was also the greatest Jewish ethnic comedienne ever to set the world laughing. Fanny was an unprecedented original. Only Barbra Streisand, who played Fanny onscreen in the spectacular *Funny Girl* (1968) and the less lustrous *Funny Lady* (1975), has succeeded in capturing some of the theatrical brilliance that was Fanny Brice. A part of Miss Brice's genius was the ability to wring pathos from an audience while turning tears of sorrow into tears of hysterical laughter. Singing a ballad or a torch song, Miss Brice could hold the spotlight as well as Helen Morgan or Ruth Etting. Her name became so synonymous with Ziegfeld's *Follies* that there was, as columnist Marjorie Farnsworth rightly observed, "a prevailing conviction that a *Follies* wasn't authentic without Fanny."

Her theatrical and private lives were pervasively dedicated to honesty. Producer Ray Stark, who married Fanny's daughter Frances and produced the stage and screen versions of *Funny Girl* and the screen sequel, *Funny Lady*, remarked, "There was no aura of theatre about Fanny offstage—but she brought it onstage with her, and it was tangible even behind the zaniest of antics, the pride, the dignity, and the strength with which she lived her personal life. She asked no favors, and the audience knew it. She was willing to work for everything she got."

Fanny lived the way she wanted to live and never the way people constantly suggested she should. The star admitted, "I made most things happen for me. If they were good, I worked to get them. If they were bad, I worked just as hard." She disagreed with Nora Bayes' advice to her to love the audiences. "If you love your work you need not worry about loving your audience, because you'll do that unconsciously, and they will see it."

Illusions Fanny left to the magicians. Reality she lived with her entire life, combined with an almost overwhelming interest in people. Although she could recall to the penny salaries she had made in obscure vaudeville dates, her acceptance of people rarely veered to classification. While frying smelts in her kitchen—she loved to cook— Fanny was unimpressed when a friend dropped in for luncheon with Edward, Prince of Wales. Names frequently eluded her nimble mind. Once when introducing her third husband, bantam Billy Rose, she got no further than "I'd like you to meet my husband, Mr...., uh, Mr...." Conversely, Fanny had total recall of the names of early teachers and classmates, obscure chorus girls passing into and out of the *Follies*, remote and brief social engagements, and, above all, the one great love of her life, Nicky Arnstein.

Fanny was born on the crowded Lower East Side of New York City, on Forsythe Street on Thursday, October 29, 1891. Her mother was Rose Stern, an immigrant from a small village outside Budapest, Hungary. Her father, Charles Borach, was a French-Alsatian Jew, worked as a saloonkeeper, and was known in the neighborhood as "Pinochle Charlie." Rose became the family's mainstay when Charlie bolted, raising her family (including son Lew a year younger than Fanny) in an eight-family tenement house she purchased on St. Mark's Avenue in Brooklyn.

At 13, Fanny made her first stage appearance. In an amateur-night contest at Brooklyn's Keeney's Theatre she sang "When You Know You're Not Forgotten by the Girl You Can't Forget." While busily picking up tossed coins, she gave her first audience an encore, "If the Man in the Moon Was a Coon." From Keeney's she graduated to a "slide singer" at the 83rd and Third Avenue nickelodeon. Determined on a theatrical career, she kept her promise to an Irish neighbor, John Brice, that she would use his last name professionally. She became Fanny Brice. The Borach family—like the Berlinger family, when Milton became Berle—immediately changed their surname to Brice.

One-night stands in *A Royal Slave*, in which she was an alligator, ended with the show in Hazleton, Pennsylvania. The long-legged, big-footed Fanny was discouraged. (Before the alligator bit she had been fired from rehearsal of a George M. Cohan–Sam Harris musical.) She next landed a job with Hurtig & Seamon's Transatlantic Burlesque Shows. Years later Fanny recalled, "They'd never even sniffed salt air but they made several rough crossings of the Gowanus Canal." Another burlesque show, Max Spiegel's *College Girls*, was saved for Fanny

by a fellow East Sider, Irving Berlin.

Frantic for a specialty number she assured Spiegel she already had, Fanny appealed to songwriter Berlin for help. He gave her a Jewish comedy song, "Sadie Salome," singing it to her in a Jewish dialect. Fanny later said that *had* the dialect been Irish, she would have become an Irish comic. "I had never had any idea of doing a song with a Jewish accent. I didn't even understand Jewish, couldn't talk a word of it. But, I thought, if that's the way Irving sings it, that's the way I'll sing it." Fanny was a huge success; dialect phrasing of songs became one of her important career mainstays.

In 1909 when *College Girls* played northern New York State and Springfield, Massachusetts, Fanny was pursued by barber Frank White. When the amorous Mr. White asked Fanny to marry him she could think of no good reason why she should not. So she married him because, "God, he smelled nice!" and "Christ, I loved everybody in those days!" Mother Rose tried to have the marriage annulled but in Philadelphia the persistent lilac-scented barber caught up with his reluctant bride. Being alone with the sweet-smelling White intensified Fanny's determination to retain her virginity. But the ploy of consuming a pineapple to fend off her husband was a lost cause. Two years later she decided a divorce from Mr. White was in order. The lark was dissolved by the courts.

Florenz Ziegfeld, ever seeking new talent, witnessed Fanny's performance in *College Girls* and signed her for his *Follies. Ziegfeld Follies of 1910* opened on June 20, 1910, and Fanny's singing of "Lovey Joe" brought an audience demand for 12 encores. Ziegfeld had a new star, one he could *never* glorify as he would such beauties as Peggy Hopkins Joyce, Marilyn Miller, Gilda Grey, Billie Dove, and Gladys Glad. However, he discovered a towering talent for comedy, an irrepressible mimic and farceuse second to none. She was capable of stirring an audience to tears in a song he made her sing that would become virtually her theme song, "My Man."

Ziegfeld's extravaganza for 1911 featured Fanny, and that year she met a man whose destiny reshaped her life. Their relationship would have destroyed a woman without Fanny's courage, fortitude, and, above all, unending sense of humor.

Norway-born Julius Wilford Arndt Stein, alias Nicky Arnstein, was a handsome, charming man with whom Fanny fell hopelessly in love. Fanny's acceptance of his shattered 1906 marriage and his wife's refusal of divorce led her into an unconventional design for living until 1918, when she became Mrs. Arnstein.

Meanwhile, on February 6, 1913, Fanny opened in *The Honeymoon Express*. The show starred Al Jolson, Yancsi Dolly, and Gaby Deslys, with Fanny as Marcelle, a domestic. It ran for 156 performances. When the show closed she and Nicky sailed for London. Fanny made her London debut at the Victoria Palace Theatre and was a great success. Eventually she replaced Anna Held at the London Opera House in the revue *Come over Here*. With the outbreak of World War I, Fanny and Nicky returned to the States and Fanny made her debut at Broadway's vaudeville Palace. Her debut there was greeted with rousing notices.

Years later one-man woman Brice analyzed this dramatic period of her life. "I never really loved but once. I could never understand when people say they have been in love two or three times. That first love, that's the last one, it takes everything in. I think love is like a card trick. After you know how it works, it's no fun anymore." It took Fanny a long time to discover just how it worked. On June 28, 1915, Nick was sentenced to two years in Sing Sing Prison for grand larceny. Fanny pawned her jewelry to pay for a defense lawyer and for the next two years she made weekly trips to the prison at Ossining, New York.

Fanny returned to Ziegfeld to open in his *Follies* on June 12, 1916, at the New Amsterdam Theatre. One of the highlights of the revue was her devastatingly funny lampoon of silent-screen vamp Theda Bara. The following June Fanny was back on the New Amsterdam stage in the 1917 edition of Ziegfeld's *Follies*, her second outing with W. C. Fields and Will Rogers. It was the *Follies* debut of an ambitious, wide-eyed comic, Eddie Cantor, with whom she dueted "Just You and Me." On August 23, 1918, Fanny tried straight farce with George Sidney, Smith and Dale, and Vera Gordon in a flop, *Why Worry?*

It was at this time that she finally married Nicky Arnstein. Daughter Frances Brice Arnstein was born on August 12, 1919, in Huntington, Long Island, where Nick had bought a house (according to Fanny, the only thing he ever bought). Fanny told Irene Castle, when the latter was expecting her first child, birth was relatively simple—"like pushing a piano through a transom."

Fanny returned to Ziegfeld for his *Midnight Frolics* on the Amsterdam Theatre Roof. Then on February 21, 1920, the nation's newspapers gave front-page coverage to Arnstein, naming him the "mastermind" in a plot to steal five million dollars of Wall Street securities. Besieged by the press, lawyers, and the law, Fanny parlayed their constant questioning with admirable fortitude and humor. "Mastermind?" she quipped. "He couldn't mastermind an electric bulb into a socket!"

Throughout the next several years, she never missed a performance, retained her composure and fount of humor, and wheeled and dealed with gangster Arnold Rothstein for $75,000 set for Nick's bail. She hired top criminal lawyer William Fallon to defend her husband. While Nick was in Washington awaiting trial, she gave birth to their son, naming him William (after Fallon). Three weeks after her son's birth she was back rehearsing for another *Follies* because "somebody has to pay the rent." In the interim she had bought the five-story, 20-room former Colgate mansion on West 76th Street in Manhattan.

Ziegfeld's 1921 *Follies* opened on June 21, 1921, to become one of the most memorable of his many extravagances. Raymond Hitchcock, W. C. Fields, and Fanny were extremely funny in the travesty "Lionel, Ethel and Jack" [Barrymore], as was Fanny burlesquing "Camille" as "a bad woman, but awful good company." But for all the edition's excellence it was Fanny who glorified the production with her unleashed clowning and her singing of the classic "Second-Hand Rose" and the *Follies'* most memorable torch song.

Maurice Yvain's French torch song "Mon Homme" had been set to English lyrics by Channing Pollock. With Fanny's life a daily headline, Ziegfeld saw an analogy in the heartbreaking cry of the song's lost love and the unrelenting public laugh-clown-laugh posture of Mrs. Arnstein. Five-foot, six-inch Fanny walked onstage at rehearsal to sing the song done to the teeth in a clinging black dress, draped with a bright, red shawl. A flaming red wig covered her natural light brown hair, accentuating her lively green eyes. Fanny thought she looked as radiant as French star Mistinguett, whom Ziegfeld had imported to sing the song but had returned to Paris after one audition.

Fanny's appearance horrified Ziegfeld. He accused her of looking like female impersonator Bert Savoy. He then ripped off her wig and shawl, and while Fanny watched, frightened and bewildered, he next ripped her black dress to near shreds. He smeared dirt from the stage over her arms and legs and repeated the dusting process on the tattered dress. He surveyed what he had wrought and said, "Now, now, sing it!" With arms folded, devoid of dialect, Fanny sang "My Man." Countless audiences would be moved to tears before she sang it for the last time. In MGM's *The Great Ziegfeld* (1936) the dramatic rehearsal scene would be recorded on film, with Fanny as herself and William Powell as Florenz Ziegfeld.

In between *Follies* engagements Fanny would make an occasional return to the Palace Theatre, where she was billed as "the girl who sweeps all before her like a tidal wave." On December 1, 1924, she switched from Ziegfeld to her old friend Irving Berlin for his fourth annual *Music Box Revue*. She played Eve to Bobby Clark's Adam and Madame Pompadour to Clark's Louis XV for 184 performances.

Fanny, ever aware that comedy was a fleeting thing and that people remembered the performer who brought them to tears, yearned to be a dramatic actress. Impresario David Belasco signed Fanny to star in a dreadful play he had co-written with Willard Mack called *Fanny*. It opened on September 21, 1926, for 63 performances. As Yiddish vamp Fanny Fiebaum of Horseblanket, Arizona, Fanny posed no threat to Bernhardt, Duse, Hayes, or her good friend Ethel Barrymore.

A year before, in 1925, *Vanity Fair* magazine had nominated Fanny to its Hall of Fame, "because, from the humblest beginnings on the East Side of New York, she came to be acclaimed as the best comedienne on the musical comedy stage; because she made the trial of Nicky Arnstein, her husband, one of the most diverting on record; because she is a financial genius of high rank; and, finally, because her mastery of pathos, mingled with her extraordinary sense of the comic, has brought her to stardom for the very serious producer Belasco."

That same year, on December 22, 1925, Nicky Arnstein was released from Leavenworth Prison, his two-year sentence reduced by 72 days for good behavior. The never-calm marriage continued its withering course. Although Fanny had magnificently withstood the trials, headlines, and living on the nation's front pages through Nick's criminal caprice, his extramarital affairs following his prison release convinced her that divorce was the only answer. She left for Paris with Norma Talmadge, returned, and on September 12, 1927, in Chicago circuit court, filed for divorce. She charged him with adultery and her complaint stated that her remodeled nose (rearranged four years earlier by plastic surgeon Dr. Henry J. Schireson) alienated her husband's affections.

On November 21, 1927, Fanny opened at New York's Palace Theatre; she stopped the show but refused to grant the audience's demand that she sing "My Man." She auctioned off the furnishings at her home at 306 West 76 Street and resettled in an apartment in the East 60s. By this time she had become Billy Rose's favorite companion.

Fanny made her film debut in a short subject at Paramount's Astoria Studios in a concoction of stage acts called *Night Club* (made earlier but not released until 1929). It had a flimsy story line written by Katherine Brush and the "test" featured, besides Fanny, Ann Pennington, June Walker, Tamara Geva, Pat Rooney, and Donald Ogden Stewart. But it was for Warner Bros. that Miss Brice made her feature-picture bow. The studio signed her to star in *My Man* (1928) and advertised it as a "Vitaphone Masterpiece—From Shop Girl to Show Star—a tender, heart-tugging story of a girl who won the hearts of millions after she lost the love of her man [Guinn 'Big Boy' Williams]." *Photoplay* found her acting and screen personality less than compelling, but praised her singing of the title tune, "Second-Hand Rose," "I Was a Floradora

In My Man *(1929).*

Baby," "I'm an Indian," and two schmaltzy songs (with lyrics by Billy Rose): "If You Want the Rainbow You Must Have the Rain" and "I'd Rather Be Blue with You Than Happy with Somebody Else."

One of the picture's brighter moments was Fanny's recitation of the ribald narrative, "Mrs. Cohen at the Beach." But Fanny emerged on the screen larger than life. Her healthy vulgarity and outrageous burlesques seemed close to excessive in front of a camera. But she delighted in "having my picture taken and getting paid for it." To the press she confided, "The only thing I feel at all sure about is that I shouldn't be in more than one picture a year. Seeing me oftener than that would probably make audiences think they were seeing an educational picture and say, 'Ain't nature wonderful?' I'd hate to have my face grow on them. And, anyway, I'm not sure now that it is my face. They've fixed it to suit themselves, my hair, my eyes, my nose, my mouth, and my cute little horse-

shoe dimple, till I look in the mirror and ask myself, 'Who's your friend?'"

After *My Man*, Fanny was next seen on stage in Earl Carroll's *Fioretta* (February 5, 1929). Her co-stars for 111 performances were Leon Errol and Lionel Atwill. Most of this carnival in Venice belonged to the brisk, risqué humor of Fanny, who tabbed the show as one "with a lot of words, and none of them funny." Her boisterous playing of the Marchesa Vera di Livio garnered the bulk of critical praise. Four days after the opening of *Fioretta*, Fanny and bantam Billy Rose were married by New York's ubiquitous Mayor James J. Walker in the city hall. While Fanny was making her second feature-length picture, Nicky Arnstein married heiress Isabelle McCullough on October 18, 1929.

United Artists' *Be Yourself* (1930) was generally dismissed as "just another movie." The *New York Times* passed it off with, "It makes the most of sound in a noisy way. It is decidedly rowdy, with a few laughable se-

125

quences and a generous supply of flip patter. Miss Brice conducts herself with her usual display of energy." As nightclub singer Fanny Field, managing a punk prizefighter (Robert Armstrong) to the championship, Fanny sang four songs (lyrics by Billy Rose), the best of which was "When a Woman Loves a Man." She recorded this number and the funny, dialectal "Cooking Breakfast for the One I Love" for Victor Records. (Most of Fanny's famous songs, plus her monologue "Mrs. Cohen at the Beach," were recorded by Fanny through the years.)

If Hollywood did not know what to do with Fanny's talents, Billy Rose was sure that he did. He presented her, George Jessel, and Hal Skelly in a "Helluva High-Toned Revue!" which was absurdly titled *Cornbeef and Roses*. The show tried out in October 1930 in Philadelphia. The outraged press wrote, "The producer's name is Rose. He's a Rose that does not smell so sweet!" Rose changed the title to *Sweet and Low*, substituting James Barton for Skelly. It ran on Broadway for 184 performances.

Revised and restocked with fresher sketches (and costumes designed by Brice), *Billy Rose's Crazy Quilt* opened on May 19, 1931, on Broadway. It starred Fanny, Phil Baker, and Ted Healy, and featured Fanny's younger brother, gambling-loving Lew Brice. After the Broadway run of 79 performances, the show took to the hinterlands, playing one-night stands. It eventually produced a quarter of a million dollars for Rose and had the country singing the show's song hit, "I Found a Million Dollar Baby in a Five and Ten Cent Store." Rose felt he had escaped the consuming shadow of being Fanny Brice's husband.

Billie Burke was the titular producer of the 1933–34 edition of the *Ziegfeld Follies*. It returned Fanny to glorified gaiety and permitted her to showcase her inestimable talent for satire. She appeared as Baby Snooks (with Eve Arden as her mother) and stopped the show as fan-dancing Countess Dubinsky. As a lark for producers/directors/scripters Ben Hecht and Charles MacArthur, she appeared in an unbilled cameo in a hotel lobby scene for *Crime Without Passion* (1934), shot at Paramount's Astoria, Long Island, studio. In 1935 Fanny moved to Beverly Hills and appeared weekly on radio as Baby Snooks. Meanwhile, Billy Rose was preoccupied with elephants and Jimmy Durante in his Hippodrome Theatre spectacle *Jumbo*.

Although her numbers "Yiddle on Your Fiddle" and the teary "My Man" were highlights of Metro's *The Great Ziegfeld* (1936), Fanny appraised her work in the film: "I wasn't sure of myself—I didn't relax—because it was a new medium. I was confused much of the time. And that isn't the right way to make people laugh." When the picture was completed, Fanny returned to Broadway.

She opened at the Winter Garden Theatre on January 30, 1936, in her last *Ziegfeld Follies*. Brooks Atkinson wrote in the *New York Times*, "If the 1936 edition offered nothing but Fannie [sic] Brice, most of us would feel sufficiently grateful. Here you see her up to all sorts of flamboyant Bricean mischief—stretching her mobile mouth a hundred different ways to draw comedy out of her material, rolling those eloquent eyes, fairly engulfing the whole show. The coarse elegance she contrives for the upper-class English of Ira Gershwin's 'Fancy, Fancy,' the infuriating temperament she puts into 'Baby Snooks Goes Hollywood,' and the grotesqueness of her burlesque of revolutionary dancing ('Rewolt!' she screams with her wicked eyes crossed) are Fanny in top form."

Fanny and the *Follies* were virtually one. When a severe cold resulted in a loss of voice, the management closed the show for two nights. It was the first show she missed in 20 years and this version of the *Follies* would be her last appearance on Broadway.

For MGM she was third-billed in a passably amusing musical featuring Judy Garland, *Everybody Sing* (1938). She played a screwball Russian maid named Olga. If Fanny was the picture's biggest asset, the *New York Times* still bristled. "Nobody has any right to try and foist upon us a cut Brice, robbed of those incomparably subtle touches of vulgarity for which Fanny is noted and widely beloved. As a Russian servant in a mad household of stage people whose waning fortunes are retrieved by Judy (that's the whole story), she sometimes manages to be funny, but never Fanny. And it's Fanny we care about!"

That same year, on October 1, 1938, Fanny filed for divorce. It was her first public comment on Billy Rose's highly publicized

With Allan Jones in Everybody Sing *(1938).*

romance with swimmer Eleanor Holm Jarrett. In her suit she charged desertion the previous year but refused to discuss the situation. She dismissed reporters with, "All I have to say is in the complaint." Meanwhile, back in Hollywood, MGM announced Fanny for a role in Josef von Sternberg's *New York Cinderella*. But that celluloid misadventure was reassigned to director Frank Borzage. Several of the originally named cast were dropped (Fanny, Walter Pidgeon, Ina Claire, and Adrienne Ames) and the film was finally completed by W. S. Van Dyke II in 1940 as *I Take This Woman*. It was hardly worth the effort.

Fanny was back in the national headlines again in 1939 when she sued Twentieth Century–Fox for invasion of privacy for using much of her life story (Ziegfeld star marries con man) as the basis of its *Rose of Washington Square* (1939). The superficial musical film had a good performance from Al Jolson and a pedestrian one from Tyrone Power, and Alice Faye's singing of "My Man" in no way endangered fonder memories of

Fanny. Fox settled Fanny's $750,000 suit out of court, but Nicky Arnstein was awarded $25,000 in an earlier settlement.

Ensconced in a lovely Beverly Hills home, Fanny took to enjoying life on a simpler basis. (At one point, Nick Arnstein sought to return to her life, but she refused him, convinced he would never change. He would die on October 2, 1965.) Her taste and flair for decorating fascinated many of her friends, and with little persuasion she decorated their homes—for no fee. Her insatiable search for knowledge, culture, and improvement continued throughout her life until her knowledge and impeccable taste became sought and respected. Despite her cultural attainments, her flavorsome, earthy repartee—often spiced with scatological stories—never disappeared. Fanny sprinkled four-letter words without blinking an eye.

Many regretted that so great a talent as Fanny should be "wasted" on the "Baby Snooks" radio show, but the comedienne was content mostly to rest on her laurels. She did make one more screen return. In 1946 she was

seen in MGM's *Ziegfeld Follies*.* In the elaborate revue-type proceedings she played Mrs. Edelman, who is trying desperately to retrieve her winning sweepstakes ticket which she had given to landlord William Frawley for the balance of her rent. Again she appeared too explosive on the screen, whereas on stage, her frenetic, boisterous exhibition would have rocked the house.

Thereafter, Fanny restricted her entertainment activities to "Baby Snooks." There was talk of dramatizing her life story for the stage or films, or both, and her personal choice to play the role was Joan Davis. But the project never came to be in her lifetime. In her final

* Another sketch, "The Burglar" with Fanny as Baby Snooks, Hanley Stafford as her long-suffering father, and B. S. Pully as the intruder, was cut from the release print of *Ziegfeld Follies.*

years she spent hours dictating her life story into a recording machine, helped on the project by writer Goddard Lieberson. The recording sessions became the basis of *The Fabulous Fanny* by Norman Katkov, published in 1952.

Five days after she suffered a cerebral hemorrhage, Fanny Brice died on Tuesday, May 29, 1951. Her two-million-dollar estate was left to her children by Nick Arnstein, William and Frances, and to Frances and Ray Stark's children, her adored grandchildren: John, Peter, and Wendy Stark.

With her death, a great star and a marvelous trouper was gone. One can only dwell with joy on how great Fanny would have been as Dolly Levi in *Hello, Dolly!* But she was no longer among us to set the land to laughter—and occasionally to tears.

128

FEATURE FILMS

My Man (*Warner Bros. 1928*)
Be Yourself (*United Artists 1930*)
Crime Without Passion (*Paramount 1934*)*

The Great Ziegfeld (*MGM 1936*)
Everybody Sing (*MGM 1938*)
Ziegfeld Follies (*MGM 1946*)

* Unbilled guest appearance.

With Helen Foster in Painted Faces *(1929).*

Joe E. Brown

His mouth was compared to the Grand Canyon, the entrance to the Holland Tunnel, and other national apertures. But nature's quirks, although contributory to comedic effects, do not necessarily make a comedian. Beyond the physical must be a deeply imbedded talent fleshing out a distinct individuality with which an audience can identify. As it was to other famous clowns, laughter was a serious business to Brown, who could mingle pathos with guffaws and, most important, retain an audience's sympathy and support while demolishing life's tragedies with buffoonery. He was also a warm, outgoing human being. This quality was apparent to a public that supported his comedy for many years, and the use of this talent propelled him into one of Hollywood's top money-making stars.

Contractor Mathias Brown and his wife, Anna Evans Brown, had two sons, John and Michael, when on Thursday, July 28, 1892, a third was born. He was named Joseph Evan (after his maternal grandfather Evan Evans) Brown. The family moved from Holgate,

Ohio, after the birth of Joseph, to Toledo, Ohio, and by 1904 the Brown family had increased by two more sons and two daughters. But only six children remained at home. Young Joseph, called Evan, had joined the Sells and Downs Circus in 1902 with a tumbling act called The Five Marvelous Ashtons. By 1904 the group had become part of the John Robinson Circus. The Ashtons also played vaudeville and were booked into the Haymarket Music Hall in San Francisco.

On April 18, 1906, the young tumbler was awakened by rumblings. The crashing buildings were just one aspect of the great earthquake which left the Bay City deluged with the world's "damnedest finest ruins." Evan escaped to Oakland by tugboat.

In July of that year, as the unnamed member of the Bell-Prevost Trio, Joe opened in a trampoline-acrobatic act at Coney Island's Henderson Music Hall. With Frank Prevost he became the other half of "The Prevost Brothers" and Frank encouraged him to inject comedy into their acrobatic routines. The act was booked into a burlesque show, *Ideals*.

131

During the summer layoffs Joe wrangled his way into playing baseball, a sport in which he excelled, with semiprofessional teams. The stage act later became known as Prevost and Brown, and Joe was tagged "The Corkscrew Kid." One contemporary reviewer noted that "he is the only acrobat in the world now doing a double-body twist and back somersault in one leap." *Variety* noticed Brown, "Looks like real comedy acrobatic turn that needs but little to make the big time. . . . He has a sneeze and laugh, both funny as worked by him, and several other mannerisms good for comedy purposes."

Prevost and Brown played the Pantages and Orpheum vaudeville circuits, including Manhattan's Palace. During his coast-to-coast travels on the show circuits Joe met Kathryn Frances McGraw. On December 24, 1915, they were married in New York City's city hall by Alderman Smith. The union became one of the most endearing and durable in show business and, certainly, Hollywood.*

Following his first "single" act in the burlesque show, "Sporting Widows," Joe was offered the lead in an established legitimate musical comedy on Broadway. In *Listen Lester* he was set to replace leading man Hansford Wilson. The night scheduled for Brown's legitimate Broadway debut also proved to be the evening the Actors Equity strike erupted. When the conflict between producers and actors ended in September, Joe joined the *Listen Lester* company for a road tour which stopped in Washington, D.C.

It was on October 4, 1920, that he opened on Broadway at the Court Theatre in *Jim Jam Jems*. Included in the cast were Frank Fay, Ned Sparks, and, doing a riotous broken-down automobile act, Harry Langdon. When the production was booked for an extensive road tour, only Joe E. was left to headline the show and it became his. His notices were good and he was developing as a comedian, devising bits of business such as opening his wide mouth to speak, pausing, and delivering the line in a whisper. He perfected an eccentric dance by falling into the orchestra pit (onto a trampoline) and bouncing back onstage with total composure. It was a gimmick he employed in several shows.

Following his stardom in *Jim Jam Jems*, he was signed as one of the stars of the third edition of *The Greenwich Village Follies* (1921) with Irene Franklin and Ted Lewis. Two more editions of *The Greenwich Village Follies* followed and on December 25, 1924, he opened on Broadway in *Betty Lee*, which featured Gloria Foy and Hal Skelly. It was in this period that Joe E. decided laughter was indeed a serious business and he studied hard to gauge laughs and to develop a warm rapport with audiences. After a subsequent road tour of *Betty Lee*, Joe E. was back on Broadway in *Captain Jinks* (1925), a musical revamping of *Captain Jinks of the Horse Marines*. Walter Winchell reported of the season's best musical, "Mr. Brown, whom I have enjoyed in other musical comedies, was never better than he was last night, and if space permitted I would like to go on applauding him." About his role as Hap Jones in the show, Brown explained, "A real comedian should be able to get laughs with his manner or speech, his facial expressions and his gestures, as well as with the lines he delivers. By studying my role I have managed to insert tricks of speech and expression and, as a result, the audiences laugh at lines not intended to be particularly funny."

Twinkle Twinkle (1926) starred Brown in a Broadway musical satire on motion pictures. After its New York run, it enjoyed a national road tour and wound up in Los Angeles in October 1927. Brown's fascination with motion pictures had resulted in several screen tests at Fort Lee, New Jersey, and Paramount's Astoria, Long Island, studios without success. (He had made a Vitaphone one-reel short subject, *Don't Be Jealous.*) Now he was determined to badger his way into pictures.

Director Ralph Ince, after seeing a performance of *Twinkle Twinkle*, signed Brown for a

* At the time Joe told his bride-to-be, "It looks like our wedding journey will have to be a subway ride. But some day we'll have a real wedding in a church." Joe kept his promise and on their 25th anniversary they were "remarried" at Hollywood's St. Thomas Episcopal Church. The second wedding was a family affair. Their son Joe LeRoy (who would become general manager of the Pittsburgh Pirates baseball team in 1955) was best man. Donald Evan Brown (their firstborn son, December 25, 1916) gave the bride away, and adopted daughters Mary Elizabeth Ann and Kathryn Frances served as flower girls. A few years later they "married" for the third time, the last ceremony performed by a Roman Catholic priest to reestablish Mrs. Brown's position within her own Catholic religion.

film he was then making, *Crooks Can't Win* (1928). It was a silent picture and Brown made his feature-film screen debut as newspaper reporter Jimmy Wells. Ince had to do a lot of convincing to persuade Joe E. that he could play drama and that his blue-eye slits would photograph adequately.

Ince also directed Joe as Twisty in *Hit of the Show* (1928), in which he dies of heart failure after the final curtain. For his third film at FBO, he appeared as a timid lion tamer who is fatally mauled by a king of the jungle in *The Circus Kid* (1928). Most of Brown's work in *Take Me Home* (1928), starring Bebe Daniels, was left on the cutting-room floor. He then made two pictures with actress Belle Bennett, famous for her interpretation of the screen's *Stella Dallas*. Brown was a vaudeville headliner in *Molly and Me* (1929) and was a novelist in their second, *My Lady's Past* (1929). Both of these silent pictures had talking sequences.

Warner Bros.' splashy Technicolor picture *On with the Show* (1929) featured Betty Compson and Ethel Waters and was advertised as the FIRST, 100% ALL TALKING, ALL SINGING, ALL NATURAL COLOR motion picture. The studio was impressed with Joe's work as Ike in this the-show-must-go-on tale. He would soon become a regular on the Burbank lot. When Warner Bros.-First National remade Marilyn Miller's Broadway hit musical, *Sally* (1929), they used the stage star to re-create her lead role. Joe E. Brown was Connie. The *New York Times* found his work good and said, "Mr. Brown's humor may not be especially light, but it is funny and is helped along by good lines."

After another melodrama at Tiffany-Stahl, *Painted Faces* (1929), Joe returned to Warner Bros. to play Charlie Ruggles' stage role in *Song of the West* (1930), a celluloid version of the Oscar Hammerstein–Vincent Youmans' flop musical *Rainbow*. When the unpromising feature was completed at its Lone Pine, California, location, Joe left for the East for one of his periodic "In Person" vaudeville tours. These outings became an annual event for the next five years.

It was Warner Bros.' *Hold Everything* (1930) that catapulted Joe to screen stardom. It was derived from Bert Lahr's Broadway hit and the stage clown was furious that the studio had not hired him for the role.* *Variety* enthused of the film, "*Hold Everything* is probably the best comedy picture Warners has turned out since talking came in . . . the basic point of the picture being Brown. On the strength of this effort he of the wide grin grabbed himself a long and sweet starring contract with Warners. Which should make it an event for Bert Lahr. The latter has now made two people—himself and Brown."

With the rousing success of *Hold Everything*, Warner Bros. gave Joe E. Brown a lucrative long-term contract. Within a year he had bought a home in Beverly Hills, enrolled his sons in California's Urban Military School, and begun sponsoring a youngster named Mike Frankovich (who later became a star football player for UCLA, a prominent film producer, and the husband of actress Binnie Barnes). When Joe and his wife Kathryn went east for a personal appearance tour they played Chicago. While there they visited The Cradle in Evanston, Illinois, and adopted a baby girl, whom they named Mary Elizabeth Ann. A year and a half later they adopted a second daughter from The Cradle, naming her Kathryn Frances.

Between raising children and opening his home to waifs, lodgers, and friends, Joe's popularity gained throughout the world with his screen performance in Warner Bros.' *Top Speed* (1930). His performance in *Maybe It's Love* (1930) caused the *New York Times* to

---

* The infuriated Mr. Lahr wrote a letter to the editor of *Variety* charging that Joe E. Brown was a "Lifter" and had copied his performance in the stage show. He stressed damage to his reputation and possible future detriment of his (Lahr's) future in talking pictures. Adding insult to injury, several critics thought Brown was better in the part than Lahr had been on the stage. The feud would continue for years, fanned onward by Lahr. Brown wisely remained quiet—at least, publicly.

This was not the first time Brown had been involved in a show-business feud. In vaudeville, on radio, and elsewhere, he had frequently employed a monologue about a drunken mouse that pugnaciously decides to fight the big cat. Baby-face, whimpering-voice comic Bert Wheeler claimed ownership of the tale and over an unbelievable stretch of years the controversy raged, wallowing in a mass of news copy far exceeding its worth. The conflict lasted right through to Wheeler's death in 1968 when the newspapers trotted out the feud for another bombardment. As *Variety* would recollect, "Bert Wheeler originated it but, because of radio's wide impact, Brown first became identified with it via the airwaves. This seemed to have clouded Wheeler's identity with the story. It was more of a 'delivery' type of gag, and both Brown and Wheeler did it well, in a baby-squeaking voice. . . ."

report, "His comedy was infectious. Joe E. Brown, whose mouth on the screen appears to have something in common with the Grand Canyon, is hilariously funny." His notices continued to applaud his outrageous comedy in *Going Wild* (1931), an otherwise dull affair. *Sit Tight* reunited him with his *Hold Everything* co-star, Winnie Lightner, and he played Jojo the Tiger Boy. His agility almost salvaged *Broad-Minded* (1931) and his bashful botany student who wins a relay race bolstered *Local Boy Makes Good* (1931).

George M. Cohan and Ring Lardner's classic comedy of a rookie baseball pitcher, *Elmer the Great*, seemed tailor-made for Brown to indulge his love of baseball with his ability to portray the amiable idiot. (The very different Walter Huston had played it on Broadway in 1928 for 40 performances.) Between shooting schedules he first played Elmer on the stage at San Francisco in 1931. He would later tour in the show and as late as July 1940 was playing *Elmer the Great* at the Cape Playhouse in Dennis, Massachusetts.* Elmer would remain Brown's favorite role and he filmed the rib-tickling play for Warner Bros. in 1933, repeating his performance on "Lux Radio Theatre" in October 1936.

Meanwhile, Brown was back on the stage at San Francisco's Alcazar Theatre in the comedy *Square Crooks*, with Jane Darwell and Jason Robards, after completing a mixture of slapstick firefighting and baseball in the movie *Fireman Save My Child* (1932). The studio kept its screen comic busy, unmindful that his career could suffer from overexposure. He was next seen in a version of George S. Kaufman's *The Butter and Egg Man*, this time filmed as *The Tenderfoot* (1932). Many of the Brown comedies provided a testing ground for promising talent, and in 1932 Ginger Rogers was his ladylove

in a surprisingly funny picture, *You Said a Mouthful* (1932), cast in the film at Brown's request after their pleasing teaming in *The Tenderfoot*.

Joe continued registering laughter in *Son of a Sailor*, based on a sketch, *The Gob*, by Paul Gerard Smith that Joe had purchased for use in the 1923 edition of *The Greenwich Village Follies*. After *A Very Honorable Guy* (1934), which Joe felt was a bad picture, he left for a four-month tour of the Orient with Mrs. Brown. He told the press he wanted to be out of the country when the film was released. Thereafter, studio head Jack L. Warner would not speak to him for six months.

The Circus Clown (1934) provided Joe with a familiar background and six stitches in his arm from an overly friendly lion. *Six Day Bike Rider* was tabbed "several laps short of being the perfect comedy," but with *Alibi Ike* (1935) Joe was back in fine fettle, with Olivia de Havilland as the love interest, in another amusing baseball tale. In Busby Berkeley's *Bright Lights* (1935) Brown drew on his early stage training to play Joe Wilson, a burlesque clown rising to headliner status. The *New York Times* found the film a surprise and added, "The best thing about his performance is the creation of an attractive, believable, and well-rounded character."

When Warner Bros. decided to film Shakespeare's *A Midsummer Night's Dream*, to be directed by Max Reinhardt (who had staged the Hollywood Bowl production in September 1934) and William Dieterle, the studio enlisted most of its stock company in a merry, if not always wise, casting of the roles. Mickey Rooney was signed to reprise his Bowl performance as Puck and Warner convinced Brown that he should play Flute, the bellows-mender. When the critical verdicts were tallied, the consensus was that the film was something less than a masterpiece. However, individual performances were singled out as exceptional: one was Joe E. Brown's perceptive playing of Flute, a role he freely admitted he knew nothing about.

Brown's last three Warner excursions were hardly up to snuff, although his playing of Alexander Botts in *Earthworm Tractors* (1936) was richly funny. His final studio film was *Polo Joe* (1936), for which he learned the game—and how to manipulate a horse—until he became expert, as shown in a 10-minute

* *Time* magazine covered the 1940 play date. It reported, "Star of the revival was shovel-mouthed, small-voiced Joe E. (for Evan) Brown, who has played the role before, both on the stage and in the movies, as a plausible and funny Elmer. Marvelous to witness was the enthusiasm with which he tore through food at each performance. In the course of an hour and a half as Elmer, he consumes a slice of ham, a batch of fried potatoes, four griddle cakes with syrup, a piece of pie, two cups of coffee, two apples, half a grapefruit, a glass of orange juice, two doughnuts, a slice of toast and a bit of shad roe. Only recently released from a Los Angeles hospital where (after an auto accident) he spent over six months in a cast with a broken back, Brown was in fine digestive fettle, managing his stage eating with no aid from bicarbonate."

With Winnie Lightner in a pose for Sit Tight *(1930).*

short subject made in 1941, *Polo with the Stars.*

After leaving Warner Bros., Joe made a series of unmemorable comedies for RKO, MGM, Columbia, and Paramount, including *$1,000 a Touchdown* (1939), in which he teamed with large-mouthed Martha Raye. It was an awful affair that helped neither of the mouthy players' sagging careers. His trademark yowl and bag of laugh-provoking gimmicks had slowly lost favor with a public constantly discovering change in entertainment and in comedy. Fast-rising Bob Hope, Red Skelton, and others were replacing Hollywood's erstwhile top comedians. The comedy programmers Brown was less and less frequently churning out in Hollywood provided neither challenge nor professional pride. He returned to the stage.

In the summer of 1940, after playing *Elmer the Great* and doing a WOR radio broadcast of *Lady in the Moon,* he joined Mildred Natwick and Dorothy McGuire at the end of the season in George Kelly's *The Show-Off*

at Bucks County Playhouse in New Hope, Pennsylvania. Mid-year 1941 found Brown appearing for the Civic Light Opera in Los Angeles and San Francisco in the role created by the late Robert Woolsey in a revival of *Rio Rita.* The Bert Wheeler part was played by Peter Lind Hayes. During the run of this production, Brown indulged in some strenuous acrobatics and broke a wrist, continuing, however, with the wrist in a cast and the same acrobatics. Later in the summer, he starred with Helen Chandler in *The Show-Off* in San Francisco and in 1942 made a cross-country tour in the play. (Brown would conclude each performance of the show with fifteen minutes of "spontaneous" story-telling to the theatre audience. For many it was hard to say which was better, Brown as the abrasive Aubrey Piper or Brown as Brown.)

With the outbreak of World War II his sons, Don and Joe, volunteered for service in the U.S. Army Air Corps. On October 8, 1942, before the curtain rose on *The Show-Off* in

With Donald Dillaway in
The Circus Clown *(1934).*

Detroit, Joe received a call from the Army Ferry Command in Long Beach, California. Joe happily accepted it, expecting the call since Don was soon to be transferred to Australia. Not expected was the news that his son Captain Donald Evan Brown had been killed in a plane crash during a routine training flight. After Don's funeral in California, Joe was determined to use his gift of comedy to brighten the far reaches of the war zones. He gave of himself unsparingly to the war effort as an entertainer. In January 1942 he was the first entertainer to go to the South Pacific, as he had been the first performer to venture into Alaska to entertain troops. Wherever G.I.s served was his destination. They all became his sons.

His odyssey took him to Pacific outposts, Burma, China, Teheran, India, North Africa, and Italy. Joe E. Brown brought welcome laughter, taking pride in never using a blue or dirty story to provoke laughs: a credo he observed throughout his career. He received

the Bronze Star,* and commendations from President Franklin D. Roosevelt; and General Douglas MacArthur awarded him the Asiatic-Pacific service ribbon for his "meritorious service." In California the Brown home was a perpetual open house to all servicemen.

After the war Hollywood had nothing to offer him, but producer Brock Pemberton saw in Brown a warm human being who would be a perfect choice to head the road company of Mary Chase's Pulitzer Prize-winning, record-breaking Broadway hit, *Harvey*. (Marion Lorne was his co-star.) Pemberton overrode objections that Brown would clown up the part. His faith in Joe was verified after the road company opened in Columbus, Ohio. The press verified, "Brown gave a magnificent performance, straight and sincere. He has what show people call the

* The only other civilian to receive the award was reporter Ernie Pyle.

136

'heart' for the role." Toward the end of 1945 the *Harvey* company reached San Francisco where the scheduled nine-week stand was extended to 13.

During the long run of *Harvey* on Broadway, various "guest" stars subbed for vacationing lead Frank Fay. For the last 20 weeks of the New York stand, Joe played the lead in *Harvey*. In early 1949 he embarked on another road tour. He would usually end the performance with an impromptu bit of patter aimed at the audience and would tell his "little mousie" story. Joe played Elwood longer than any other player, including Fay, and had great success in the role in Australia.

During the run of *Harvey*, Joe was honored by the city of Toledo, Ohio, when December 7, 1945, was proclaimed "Joe E. Brown Day." The University of Toledo presented him with an honorary Master of Arts Degree. In 1949 he would also receive an honorary degree from Bowling Green University for "his philosophy of life, epitomized in 'love, learn and laugh.'" *Harvey* became the crowning achievement of Brown's career and he continued to portray Elwood P. Dowd in December 1955 at Millburn, New Jersey, and on the summer theatre stages in 1959. In the 15 years he delighted audiences in *Harvey*, he maintained the same professional, placid playing of the part without slapstick, gimmicks, or clowning.

Brown's next Broadway appearance was unexpected. In March 1951 Lloyd Nolan started rehearsals for the musical *Courtin' Time*, but during the strenuous road tryout, Nolan developed acute laryngitis and the show closed in Philadelphia in May 1951. Joe was rushed into rehearsal as Nolan's replacement and the production struggled into Broadway's National Theatre on June 13, 1951, to last a meager 37 performances. One of the few joys that took place during the run occurred when General Douglas MacArthur visited Joe backstage one evening. He told reporters, "There isn't a man, in uniform or

With Lyda Roberti in **Wide Open Faces** *(1938).*

With Judy Canova, John Hubbard, and Gus Schilling in Chatterbox (1943).

With Agnes Moorehead in Show Boat (1951).

out, who has done more for our boys than Joe E. Brown."

In MGM's colorful remake of *Show Boat* (1951) Joe was excellent as Cap'n Andy coping with his shrewish wife (Agnes Moorehead) and life upon the *Cotton Blossom*. He ventured into television doing guest spots and in 1952 began a once-a-month telecast of "Circus Time." He was also seen on "Schlitz Playhouse" in a video version of *Meet Mr. Justice* (1955) and on "Screen Director's Playhouse" in *The Silent Partner* (1955). For Michael Todd's epic *Around the World in 80 Days* (1956) Joe did a cameo bit as the stationmaster. That year his autobiography (as told to Ralph Hancock), *Laughter Is a Wonderful Thing*, was published. (Several years before, in 1944, Joe had written *Your Kids and Mine*.)

For those who had observed and enjoyed Joe's performing over the years, it was no surprise that he stole the show in Billy Wilder's *Some Like It Hot* (1959), a vehicle ostensibly for Tony Curtis, Jack Lemmon, and Marilyn Monroe. Brown was marvelously droll as eccentric millionaire "playboy" Osgood Fielding determined to marry Jack Lemmon masquerading as a dame. Oblivious to Lemmon's declaration that he is a *man*, Brown, grinning from ear to ear (a very wide expanse), tossed off the film's famous tag line, "Well . . . nobody's perfect."

Brown would reprise Cap'n Andy of *Show Boat* for the Civic Light Opera season, opening in Los Angeles on August 15, 1960, and closing in San Francisco on November 5, 1960. He would appear as Cap'n Andy once again—in New York at the City Center. The new version opened on April 12, 1961, for 13 performances; it was Brown's final New York appearance.

Stanley Kramer's *It's a Mad, Mad, Mad, Mad World* (1963) was an overly long Cinerama exercise in silent-screen slapstick that will remain memorable as the film that brought together the largest assortment of Hollywood's great comedians within the framework of one picture. Joe played a brief bit as the "Orator." The Kramer experiment, plus an appearance in the Vincent Price-Boris Karloff-Peter Lorre *The Comedy of Terrors* (1963), finished his screen career. In April 1964 he was seen on ABC-TV's "The Greatest Show on Earth" in the episode *You're All Right, Ivy*. It proved to be his last media performance. The combination of a heart ailment, a stroke, and the debility of advanced age forced Joe to remain in retirement.

Death took no holiday during the month of July 1973. It claimed the lives of such show business folk as George Macready, Wally Westmore, Robert Ryan, Lon Chaney, Jr., and Veronica Lake. On Friday, July 6, the day following Betty Grable's funeral, Joe E. Brown died at his Brentwood, California, home.* He was 80 years old. A funeral Mass was held at St. Martin of Tours Church the next day in Brentwood. On Monday, July 9, Joe E. Brown was buried in Forest Lawn Cemetery in Glendale, California. His wife, two daughters, son Joe, eleven grandchildren, and six great-grandchildren survived him.**

Joe always enjoyed relating the comment of a six-year-old child. After seeing one of his screen comedies, the young boy asked his mother, "Mommy, when Joe E. Brown dies, will he go to heaven?" When the mother confirmed the possibility, the child marveled, "Golly, Mommy, won't God laugh!"

---

* In the early Sixties a disastrous fire in the hills above Hollywood totally wiped out a million-dollar community of homes. Among them was Burt Lancaster's and Joe E. Brown's. At that time it was reported that Kathryn Brown's priceless collection of first editions of children's books was destroyed. Not long before Joe's death there was a report that thieves had broken into the home in which the Browns had resettled. By that time, Brown had round-the-clock nurses. Kathryn confronted the thieves, telling them to take what they wanted, ". . . but if you harm Joe, I'll kill you." This may even have stopped them from their intended purpose.

** Kathryn Brown died in a Los Angeles nursing home on March 23, 1978, at the age of 81. She had been ill for a long period.

FEATURE FILMS

Crooks Can't Win (*FBO 1928*)
Hit of the Show (*FBO 1928*)
The Circus Kid (*FBO 1928*)
Take Me Home (*Paramount 1928*)
Molly and Me (*Tiffany-Stahl 1929*)
My Lady's Past (*Tiffany-Stahl 1929*)
On with the Show (*Warner Bros. 1929*)
Sally (*First National 1929*)
Painted Faces (*Tiffany-Stahl 1929*)
Song of the West (*Warner Bros. 1930*)
Hold Everything (*Warner Bros. 1930*)
Top Speed (*Warner Bros. 1930*)
The Lottery Bride (*United Artists 1930*)
Maybe It's Love (*Warner Bros. 1930*)
Going Wild (*Warner Bros. 1931*)
Sit Tight (*Warner Bros. 1931*)
Broad-Minded (*Warner Bros. 1931*)
Local Boy Makes Good (*Warner Bros. 1931*)
Fireman Save My Child (*Warner Bros. 1932*)
The Tenderfoot (*Warner Bros. 1932*)
You Said a Mouthful (*Warner Bros. 1932*)
Elmer the Great (*Warner Bros. 1933*)
Son of a Sailor (*Warner Bros. 1933*)
A Very Honorable Guy (*Warner Bros. 1934*)
The Circus Clown (*Warner Bros. 1934*)
Six Day Bike Rider (*Warner Bros. 1934*)
Alibi Ike (*Warner Bros. 1935*)
Bright Lights (*Warner Bros. 1935*)
A Midsummer Night's Dream (*Warner Bros. 1935*)

Sons o' Guns (*Warner Bros. 1936*)
Earthworm Tractors (*Warner Bros. 1936*)
Polo Joe (*Warner Bros. 1936*)
When's Your Birthday? (*RKO 1937*)
Riding on Air (*RKO 1937*)
Fit for a King (*RKO 1937*)
Wide Open Faces (*Columbia 1938*)
The Gladiator (*Columbia 1938*)
Flirting with Fate (*MGM 1938*)
$1,000 a Touchdown (*Paramount 1939*)
Beware Spooks! (*Columbia 1939*)
So You Won't Talk (*Columbia 1940*)
Shut My Big Mouth (*Columbia 1942*)
Joan of the Ozarks (*Republic 1942*)
Chatterbox (*Republic 1943*)
Casanova in Burlesque (*Republic 1944*)
Pin-Up Girl (*20th Century–Fox 1944*)
Hollywood Canteen (*Warner Bros. 1944*)
The Tender Years (*20th Century–Fox 1947*)
Show Boat (*MGM 1951*)
Around the World in 80 Days (*United Artists 1956*)
Some Like It Hot (*United Artists 1959*)
The Comedy of Terrors (*American International 1963*)
It's a Mad, Mad, Mad, Mad World (*United Artists 1963*)

George Burns & Gracie Allen

George Burns, waggishly described as "Hollywood's most promising newcomer" after his Oscar-winning performance as Al Lewis in *The Sunshine Boys* (1975), is today so energetic and legendary a show-business figure that he almost overshadows the over-30 years he spent as the coolly exasperated, cigar-smoking straight man to Gracie Allen in exchanges like the following:

BURNS: Did you ever go to school?
ALLEN: Oh yes, I did.
BURNS: Well, what school did you go to?
ALLEN: I'm not allowed to tell.
BURNS: (after a well-timed pause): You're not allowed to tell?
ALLEN: The school pays me $25 a week not to tell.

Yet for all the accolades George Burns has achieved in the dozen or so years since his wife's passing he still insists, "I tell you I had nothing to do with our success. It was all Gracie. I was strictly a sn all-timer."

For 20 years the team of George Burns and Gracie Allen was a radio institution in the United States, winning the loyalty of 45,000,000 listeners and reaping $9,000 in weekly salary at its peak. They also added to the color of 14 feature films, carried 14 short subjects, and were a top-rated CBS television program for seven seasons. The 30-year career that began in vaudeville ended in 1958 when Gracie officially retired because of poor health. Though she passed away in 1964, her spouse puffs on, playing Las Vegas, performing one-man shows, guest-starring on television, writing his memoirs, and still insisting, "I never would have been a star without Gracie."

He was born on Monday, January 20, 1896, at 95 Pitt Street on New York's Lower East Side, the ninth of the Birnbaums' 12 children (seven sisters, four brothers).* His father died when he was six, and shortly after son Nathan, unhappy with his name, took the tag of George. He would later adopt the surname Burns because he was one of the two boys

* The other children were: Morris, Annie, Isadore, Esther, Sarah, Sadie, Mamie, Goldie, Sammy, Theresa, and Willie.

In a pose for We're Not Dressing *(1934).*

constantly identified as poachers of coal from the Burns Brothers coal trucks. After attending P.S. 22 (he left after the fourth grade for economic reasons*) he became involved in a variety of enterprises. He won his first professional engagement at age 12, singing with the Pee Wee Quartet. He later became a dance instructor at Brownsville's Bernstein and Burns Dancing School. This establishment was soon closed by the police, who labeled it a den for delinquents.

Next he joined vaudeville courtesy of Fry and Company (he was the "Company"). Then came a spell as part of Browns and Williams, a 15-minute "Singers, Dancing and Roller Skating" act. For the group's first performance at the Imperial Theatre on Manhattan's 116th Street, George greeted the audience with a rendition of "Augustus J. McCan Was a Henpecked Married Man." His next job, for 36 weeks, was performing in a ballroom-dancing act with Hannah Siegal, whom George would rename "Hermosa Jose" (after his favorite cigar of the moment). The teaming produced more than he bargained for—his first marriage. "Her father wouldn't let me take her out of town. Well, I loved show business, so I married her. She was never too crazy about me. About four years ago I looked her up in New York. She introduced me to all her friends as her ex-husband. I thought that was nice. When I was her husband, she wouldn't spit on me."

George and Hannah–Hermosa Jose were divorced as soon as the 36-week junket ended. George, undaunted, continued his career, playing vaudeville houses as part of Burns and Links, Burns and Garry, and Burns and Lorraine. When Billy Lorraine (who toured with George billed as "Two Broadway Thieves") gave his notice, George sought a new partner. Though he had worked as a solo (under such names as Jimmy Delight, Billy Pierce, and Jed Jackson), he feared working as a single. As he explained, "I tried it once for three days in a Hoboken theatre. After the first day I was fired."

In those childhood years when George was stealing coal, Gracie Ethel Cecile Rosalie

* On November 23, 1977, Burns received an honorary diploma from P.S. 22. The diploma recognized Burns' "life" credits earned during his many decades in show business. "Now that I've graduated," Burns joked, "I'll be able to make a living."

Allen was born in San Francisco on Saturday, July 26, 1902 (usually given as 1906 in publicity releases). Her father, Edward Allen, was a minstrel song-and-dance man. At the age of three and a half, little Gracie debuted as the fourth of the Allen Sisters (Pearl, Hazel, Bessie, and Gracie). She also had a brother named George. Gracie was educated at San Francisco's Star of the Sea Convent School. Later she rejoined her three sisters in vaudeville and still later, at 18, she joined the Larry Reilly Stock Company. Her specialty was playing colleens. Even in those early days Gracie had a keen sense of professional tactics. When Reilly refused to meet her billing demands after she proved to be an audience pleaser, she quit. Thereafter Gracie enrolled in a secretarial school. She was attending its sessions when mutual vaudeville friends introduced George and Gracie at Union Hill, New Jersey. George was impressed and took Gracie on. The team first played the Hillstreet Theatre of Newark, New Jersey, at $5.00 a day in late 1922.

The team was not an immediate hit, but Gracie was. As George remembers, "When we started, I was the funny fellow and she was the straight woman. I wrote the act—well, actually, I stole it from the Billy Whizbang and College Humor joke books—so naturally I gave myself the best lines. But the audience giggled at Gracie's questions, because she had a funny delivery, and no one laughed at my answers. I could tell right away there was something between Gracie and the audience, a great rapport. They found Gracie's character. So I gave her all the funny lines and I asked the questions."

"They loved her," attests Burns. "You know, there was nothing sexy about Gracie, no big bust or anything like that. She was just a dainty, nice, darling Irish girl with blue-black hair and a quick delivery and great, great style." For a time George would express his exasperation with Gracie's onstage dumbness by blowing cigar smoke in her face. But he soon learned the audience would not tolerate it. The audience felt very defensive about the cute little screwball. George learned a cardinal rule, "You couldn't touch Gracie."

After three years as an act, Burns and Allen were married on January 7, 1926, by a justice of the peace in Cleveland. Six weeks later they were playing New York's Palace Theatre on a Keith's contract. Their act became known as "Dizzy," named for Gracie's endearing dumbbell, a characterization she had honed to perfection. In 1929 the team scored a major success at London's Victoria Palace and at the Empire Theatre in Glasgow. They followed these sessions with a popular 26-week engagement on BBC radio. Before leaving England the couple was sought to replace Fred and Adele Astaire as the leads in the London stage version of *Funny Face*. They had to decline because of a prior commitment waiting at Manhattan's Palace Theatre. As fate would have it, they never did a Broadway show.

Also in 1929 Burns and Allen made their first movie. George tells the story. "Our big break came when Fred Allen was supposed to make a short film out on Long Island and he got sick.

"Somebody called us and said we'd make $1,700 if we replaced him. Well, we were making about $400 a week then, so we went there the next morning. The movie was supposed to take place in a room that didn't fit us. We were very young then and had a 'flirtation act,' a street-corner act. Well, we wanted to make the material we had fit the room, so we improvised.

"They started the camera rolling and Gracie went in and began looking under ashtrays and in the drawers and I followed her in and said, 'What are you looking for?' She said, 'The audience.' So I said, 'The audience is right there, right in the camera.' Then I said, 'We're supposed to talk for nine minutes. If we do that, we get $1,700. Can you talk for nine minutes?' She said, 'Ask me how my brother is.' So I did and she began to talk. Nine minutes later she was right in the middle of a joke and I looked at my watch and said, 'You can't finish that. The nine minutes are up.' Then I looked into the camera and said, 'Ladies and gentlemen, we just made $1,700,' and that was the film." The title— *Burns and Allen in Lambchops*, a Warner Bros. Vitaphone short of 1929.

Meanwhile, the team's success on stage kept mounting. On Halloween night 1931 Burns and Allen were part of a special Eddie Cantor–George Jessel show at Broadway's Palace Theatre. The original two-week run was extended to a sold-out engagement

through New Year's Eve. During the turn Cantor signed Gracie to guest on his radio program for Chase and Sanborn Coffee. Cantor read George's straight-man patter. The following week Gracie and George debuted on Rudy Vallee's radio show.

In the meantime, Paramount executives had viewed *Lambchops* and signed the stage team to perform in short subjects at the Astoria, Long Island, studio. The first of the batch was *Fit to Be Tied* (1930). Most of the entries were modifications of their proven vaudeville materials. The studio also hired the couple to make personal appearances at movie houses in conjunction with special features and premieres. In the course of a three-year period, the pair would film 13 shorts for Paramount.*

But it was on radio where the team would really click with the public. On February 15, 1932, Burns and Allen joined the Guy Lombardo Orchestra as the headliners of CBS radio's "The Robert Burns Panatela (Cigar) Program." The program was a media first as the comedy team was often in one location while the Lombardo musicians were in another. The show became an immediate favorite, and enjoyed tremendous publicity in 1933 when Gracie began her on-the-air search for her long-lost brother. For 10 days Gracie, via instructions from CBS writer Bob Taplinger, interrupted other radio shows to ask assistance in locating her relation. Meanwhile, the network publicity department manufactured lots of publicity to back up the gimmick. The height of the ruse occurred when Gracie went to the NBC studios where Rudy Vallee was broadcasting. NBC mandated that Gracie not mention her now famous brother. But Rudy did, and an outraged NBC took the show off the airwaves. In the meantime, her real brother George, a San Francisco accountant, had to go into hiding.

After two years of sharing the microphone with Lombardo and musicians, the duo won their first solo radio show. It was ABC's "The Adventures of Gracie," which aired each Wednesday night at 9:30. Over the years, the

* The 12 other shorts were: *Pulling a Bone* (1931), *The Antique Shop* (1931), *Once Over, Light* (1931), *One Hundred Percent Service* (1931), *Oh My Operation* (1932), *The Babbling Brook* (1932), *Patents Pending* (1932), *Hollywood on Parade #2* (1932), *Your Hat* (1932), *Let's Dance* (1933), *Walking the Baby* (1933), and *Hollywood on Parade #12* (1933).

show gained such popular regulars as Dick (later Richard) Crenna as Waldo and Mel Blanc as the delightfully morose character known as the Happy Mailman. For some time George and Gracie were heard not as husband and wife characters but as boy and girl. And then, of course, there was the famous sign-off for the program:

BURNS: Say goodnight, Gracie.
ALLEN: Goodnight, Gracie.

George and Gracie thrived on their hard-won celebrity status. While based in New York, they lived at the Essex House on the 22nd floor and later moved to a triplex apartment at the Lombardy. In August 1934 the performers adopted (from Chicago's "Cradle" Home) Sandra Jean Burns, and on September 27, 1935, they adopted blond, blue-eyed Ronald John Burns. A $200,000 trust fund was established for each child. Burns and Allen eventually "went Hollywood" and moved into a huge mansion at 720 Maple Drive in Beverly Hills (where George still lives). Neighbors over the years included Hal Roach, Harry Ritz, and Louella Parsons.

The team's great radio success caused Paramount to reevaluate the performers, and soon Burns and Allen were promoted to feature films. Their first was *The Big Broadcast* (1932), with such company as Bing Crosby, Kate Smith, and Cab Calloway & His Orchestra. Other *Big Broadcasts* sparked by the nonsensical routines of Burns and Allen were the editions *of 1936* (with Crosby, Ethel Merman, Amos 'n' Andy, and the Vienna Boys Choir), and *of 1937* (with Martha Raye, the orchestras of Benny Goodman and Leopold Stokowski, and an old vaudeville pal of George's named Jack Benny). Twice oncamera they confronted the entertaining mayhem spawned by W. C. Fields. In the all-star *International House* (1933) (with Calloway, Rudy Vallee, Stuart Erwin, Franklin Pangborn, Bela Lugosi, and Peggy Hopkins Joyce) W. C. turns from a confrontation with zany nurse Gracie and sneers, "What's the penalty for murder in China?" In *Six of a Kind* (1934), which featured Fields' famous pooltable routine, George and Gracie were joined in their antics by such funsters as Mary Boland, Alison Skipworth, and Charlie Ruggles. In 1937 Paramount loaned them to RKO, where they danced, sang, and bantered with a

Ginger Rogers-less Fred Astaire in *A Damsel in Distress* (a stiff but beguiling Joan Fontaine played the non-singing, hardly-dancing heroine).

In total, the couple made 12 Paramount features, employed by the studio as a popular ingredient of the breezy entertainment of comedies and musicals for which the lot was noted. As a husband-and-wife team (or for that matter a male-female act) they were unique in Hollywood, where most of the comedy pairs were of the same gender. As a team, their last Paramount picture was *College Swing* (1938) in which "dumb" Gracie is tutored by none other than Bob Hope. Their studio tenure concluded with the screwball entry *The Gracie Allen Murder Case* (1939), in which Gracie starred sans George.

After leaving Paramount (which had taken on a new executive regime and was cleaning shop), the team signed a one-shot deal with MGM. They were poorly used as forced comedy relief in *Honolulu* (1939), an Eleanor Powell musical. Once again Gracie proved how versatile she was: joking, singing, and demonstrating her capacity for nimble tap dancing. It proved to be their last joint picture, although Gracie did accept offers to solo in two MGM features: *Mr. and Mrs. North* (1941—she was Mrs., and William Post Jr. was Mr.) and *Two Girls and a Sailor* (1944). In the latter, a June Allyson-Gloria DeHaven-Van Johnson starring vehicle, Gracie was among a colorful supporting cast which included Jimmy Durante, Lena Horne, Virginia O'Brien, Buster Keaton, and the bands of Harry James and Xavier Cugat. The multitalented Miss Allen performed the splendid mock-serious rendition of "Concerto for Index Finger," led in the rendition by Albert Coates, conductor of the London Symphony Orchestra. But this wound up Gracie's participation in the cinema. Speaking for the team, she later explained, "We gave up making movies because we hated to get up at 6:00 A.M., we hated makeup, and we hated learning lines."

Indeed, the cinema was *not* the perfect medium for Burns and Allen. George was not nearly as photogenic when a young man as he was when older, and their humor was always more auditory than visual (slapstick). In addition, Gracie was not a very energetic performer; radio was not a very

With Lee Kohlmar in
Love in Bloom *(1935)*.

With Samuel S. Hinds in The Big Broadcast of 1936 *(1935)*.

146

With Harold Nicholas in The Big Broadcast of 1936.

With Martha Raye in The Big Broadcast of 1937 (1936).

With John Payne, Martha Raye, Bob Hope, Florence George, Ben Blue, Betty Grable, and Jackie Coogan in a pose for College Swing *(1938).*

demanding medium. "Radio was like stealing money," says George. "You didn't even have to open a door. You just stood there, held a piece of paper in your hand, and you read it. You wouldn't even open a window. You'd say, 'How's the weather?' and a sound man would open a window and you'd say, 'Oooooh, it's cold out, close the window,' and the man would close the window. You did nothing and you got paid for it. And everybody was in the top 10 because there were only eight acts!"

At times, Gracie would perform stunts to boost the show's ratings. In 1940 she campaigned for political office as a member of "The Surprise Party." At one point in that decade their ratings declined and they lost their sponsor. George discovered the problem—they were still playing boy-girl instead of man-wife. The adjustment was made and their ratings recovered promptly. At their peak, the team earned $9,000 weekly the easy

way. Their undemanding work schedule allowed George to golf and indulge his passion for bridge, while Gracie reveled in gin rummy and canasta. Much of their social time was spent with Jack Benny and wife Mary Livingstone, another rare example of a husband-and-wife team working in tandem in 1930s and 40s Hollywood.

When television began its commercial development, it was only natural that Burns and Allen would segue into the new medium. "The George Burns–Gracie Allen Show" debuted on October 12, 1950, over CBS-TV. It was performed live every other week, with regulars Bill Goodwin (their radio announcer), Bea Benaderet (as neighbor Blanche Morton), and Hal March as her husband Harry. (The last was replaced by Fred Clark who in turn was replaced by Larry Keating. Harry Von Zell later took over Goodwin's chores.) After two years the video show became a weekly outing and in all appeared for seven years. Many of the 282 half-hour episodes, some of which featured son Ronnie, are still playing in syndication across the country. (Screen Gems purchased the negative rights to the series from Burns for a reported $4.5 million fee.)

By 1958 Gracie had tired of the demanding television routine of waking at 5:00 A.M., studying script lines, and working a seven-day week. She announced her retirement (which merited a *Life* magazine cover story in September 1959). George could not quit show business. "Hell, I was too young to retire. When I was 65, I had pimples." Instead, he returned to the TV lineup with NBC-TV's "The George Burns Show" (debuting October 21, 1958), played Las Vegas with such female partners as Carol Channing and Ann-Margret (his protégée), guested on major TV variety shows, and later headed the short-lived teleseries "Wendy and Me" on ABC as of September 14, 1964 (Connie Stevens was Wendy).

Shortly after he began production on the "Wendy" series, Gracie suffered a heart attack. On August 28, 1964, she died, with George at her side.* Most obituaries gave her age as 58. (George says he never knew how old she really was.) She was buried in a mausoleum at Forest Lawn Memorial Park. It took Burns a long time to recover from the shock. He remembers, "When Gracie died, I was very upset and couldn't sleep. We had twin beds the last years she was alive because she had a bad heart. So finally I decided to change over and sleep in her bed, and it worked. There was something warm about that."

Actually, since Gracie's death, George has worked very steadily in television and in club engagements (frequently with Lisa Miller). He suffered another serious emotional blow when his dear friend Jack Benny (with whom he lunched daily at the Hillcrest Country Club) died of cancer in December 1974.

George and Bob Hope were to deliver the eulogies at the funeral, but George was able only to mumble a few words: "What can I say about Jack Benny? I've known him for 55 years. . . . [sobbing] I can't imagine my life without him," and here he broke down completely and Hope took over.

But George was able to pay tribute to his friend in a grand way. MGM had wanted Benny to co-star with Walter Matthau in *The Sunshine Boys* (1975), which Neil Simon had adapted from his Broadway play. Upon Benny's death, George replaced him, cast as Al Lewis, the slightly senile ex-vaudevillian who comes out of retirement to appear one more time with his old partner Willy Clark (Matthau)—and they hate each other.

It was George's first feature film* since 1939, when he filmed *Honolulu* at the Culver City lot. He quipped, "They liked me so much, they asked me to do another one." Though he had undergone open-heart surgery just a year before the production, George amazed everyone with his vitality and showed up the first day of shooting with the entire script (everybody's part) memorized. "He's like a kid," marveled Matthau. "He's one of the most enthusiastic, considerate, terrific, entertaining men I've ever worked with." (It was strong testimony from a star known for his problems with co-stars.) When *The Sunshine Boys* opened as the Christmas 1975 attraction at Radio City Music Hall, business was fabulous and *Newsweek* magazine saluted, "If George Burns didn't exist, Neil Simon might have had to invent him—and in a sense he has." The Academy of Motion Picture Arts and Sciences voted George the Best Supporting Actor of 1975. The beaming comedian accepted his Oscar from presenters Linda Blair and Ben Johnson. He termed the honor "a beautiful moment" and added, "If you stay in the business long enough and get to be old enough you get to be new again." (He was voted 1975's "Star of Tomorrow" by the National Association of Theatre Owners.)

George Burns shows no signs of slowing down. On Sunday, March 1, 1976, he appeared at New York's Carnegie Hall, where onstage he reminisced and sang his beloved

---

* In his autobiography, *Living It Up* (1976), George would relate, "You know, lots of times people have asked me what Gracie and I did to make our marriage work. It's simple—we didn't do anything. I think the trouble with a lot of people is that they work too hard at staying married. They make a business out of it.

"When you work too hard at a business you get tired; and when you get tired you get grouchy; and when you get grouchy you start fighting; and when you start fighting you're out of business."

* In 1954 Burns was in two Columbia short subjects: *Hollywood Grows Up* and *Hollywood Fathers*. In the latter he plays checkers with son Ronnie.

With Walter Matthau in The Sunshine Boys *(1975).*

vaudeville songs.* On October 15 at the Beverly Hilton Hotel the Friars Club of California toasted George at their 30th anniversary dinner. Among those offering tributes was Milton Berle saying, "George gave me a great piece of advice [when I started at the Palace Theatre in 1931]. He said, 'Milton, don't make the band laugh. Make the audience!" Phil Silvers recalled the friendly hints Burns had provided him when the "top banana" first joined MGM in 1939. Burns sang "I'll Remember This Night the Rest of My Life" and finished with "That's the Only Way to Go." Reported *Variety*, "At 80 Burns still knows how to leave them wanting more."

Having completed a summer concert-club tour—highlighted by a command performance for Princess Margaret at the Palladium—and an engagement in Las Vegas, the energetic Mr. Burns on December 1 provided viewers with his first TV special in 17 years. The *Hollywood Reporter* assessed of this 60-

minute CBS-TV offering, "The producers have wisely allowed the 80-year-old entertainer to dominate his own show, and, as he chats with his live audience or sings cleverly risqué songs from a bygone era, the magic of this man for all media shines through. Guests [Madeline Kahn in a Gracie Allen routine; Walter Matthau, Johnny Carson, Chita Rivera, and the Osmond Brothers] come in, as they must, to play off their host or do their own numbers, but the focus is on the man with the cigar-chomping charisma."

Also in December 1976 his autobiography *Living It Up or They Still Love Me in Altoona* was published. *Variety* enthused, "Pick it up anytime, start reading anywhere and laugh! And when you've read it all, in any order, you've had an eccentric but lucid rundown on the many lives of George Burns." In contrast, Howard Teichmann in the *New York Times* snapped, "When a man resolves to put the story of his life into print his readers have the right to know the depth of his feelings, the insights he has toward himself and his fellow creatures. They may still love him in Altoona, but it is my opinion that it is far, far better to listen and watch George

---

* George summed up his relationship with Jack Benny by saying, "I always told Jack he was the world's greatest violinist and he always told me I was the world's greatest singer. That was the secret of our friendship—we never lied to each other."

Burns than to read him." Nevertheless, the public endorsed the book which sold very well.

George returned to the big screen in Warner Bros.' *Oh, God!* (1977). Burns was cast as the Lord (without cigars), who wears tennis shoes and a fishing cap, and selects a Tarzana, California, supermarket manager (John Denver) to disseminate the message that "what we have down here can work." The *New York Times* noted, "As directed by Carl Reiner, *Oh, God!* is an uneasy amalgam of inconsistent attitudes, without enough humor or zaniness to divert attention from its questionable premise. But Mr. Burns is amusing even when his material is substandard." The *Hollywood Reporter* observed, "Burns, of course, dominates the proceedings with his low-keyed, laid-back interpretation of the title role. It's a bit more mannered, a bit more forced than his work in *The Sunshine Boys*, but then, not many of us get to play God* these days." Despite the very mild critical response to the telefeature-style film,

---

* Groucho Marx played a gangster named "God" in Otto Preminger's would-be comedy *Skidoo* (1968).

Oh, God! did impressively well at the box office.

On October 4, 1977, George was the recipient of the first March of Dimes Jack Benny Memorial Award. At the celebrity-studded dinner at the Beverly Hilton Hotel, Bob Hope served as chairman and toastmaster. Among the name performers attesting to George's acts of kindness over the years were Frank Sinatra, Alan King, and Ann-Margret.

In what has become an annual event, Burns returned in a CBS-TV special on November 23, 1977. His guests included Bob Hope, Gladys Knight and the Pips, The Captain and Tennille, and Ann-Margret (who dueted with Burns for "Do You Believe Me?"). George provided a soft-shoe routine and sang "Give Me the Moonlight, Give Me the Girl" which he first introduced in vaudeville in 1905. *Variety* observed, "There is a metronome built into the head of every great comic that makes comedic gold out of base material, and few do it better than George Burns. There's no other way to account for the step-by-step risibility that Burns got out of a vaude-era monolog about a randy waitress in a theatrical hotel. . . ."

In Oh, God! (1977).

151

In Sgt. Pepper's Lonely Hearts Club Band *(1978).*

Reaffirming that he is always available for an offbeat assignment, George joined with Peter Frampton, the Bee Gees, and Paul Nicholas for Universal's *Sgt. Pepper's Lonely Hearts Club Band* (1978). It proved his point that he has no intention of retiring. Explains Burns, "In what other business can a guy my age drink martinis, smoke cigars, and sing? I think all people who retire ought to go into show business. I've been retired all my life." Before making this musical film, Burns had made a guest appearance in MGM-TV's telefeature *The Comedy Factory* (1978). He played a comedian who gives a benefit performance to raise funds for a failing nightclub owned by Jack Albertson.

Although *Sgt. Pepper* proved to be a major disappointment when released in mid-1978, Burns received some nice reviews. "George Burns is the sole oasis of calm as the bemused small-town mayor who narrates this assault on the senses" (*The Hollywood Reporter*). Thereafter he continued his busy moviemaking pace. He provided a brief narration/introduction for George C. Scott's film *Movie Movie* (1978) and then played opposite 13-year-old Brooke Shields in *Just You and Me, Kid* (1979). Burns was cast as a retired vaudevillian and radio performer. Next on his agenda is a planned sequel to *Oh, God.* Along the way, the seemingly tireless entertainer guest-starred on an episode of CBS-TV's "Alice" (January 1, 1978), and on a Goldie Hawn video outing (CBS-TV, March 1, 1978) he joined the ex-"Laugh-In" star in a rendition of "Some of These Days" and some softshoe dancing. Not to permit any breathing spells, he did voice-over radio commercials for a Los Angeles bank, and for the state of Washington he performed some conservation commercials. "You know," quipped Burns, "I'm really quite an authority on energy conservation. A man of my age doesn't get to be a man of my age unless he uses his energy wisely."

Despite his continuing acclaim, George remains a basically humble man. In *The Sunshine Boys* he revealed publicly for the first time his bald pate; after a night out, he laughs, "I come home, take off my toupee, and put it on its block. The block looks great and I look lousy." As he told *Celebrity* magazine recently, "Nostalgia is my soul food, and I've got enough of it to spread fond remembrances, recollections, and memorabilia from one coast to the other. And don't think the kids today aren't yearning for something deep, fond, and personal to hang their hats onto. Nothing will ever replace warm memories."

Certainly nothing could ever replace George's memories of Gracie. He confided to Rex Reed in a 1975 interview, "Gracie didn't marry me because I was a sex symbol. We were in show business and we made each other laugh. That's why it lasted 38 years. We slept together, ate together, dressed together, and worked together and never had a fight. It was a partnership and a friendship too. And she knew everything. The only thing I ever felt guilty about was a telegram we got in vaudeville. It was from Flo Ziegfeld, and he was out front, and that was one of the nights I blew smoke in Gracie's face and he hated my guts. So he sends me a cable saying, 'I'll pay $200 for the dame, $100 for the act.' I never read it to her. I told her it was from some of the boys at the Friars Club. Before she died, I said, 'Gracie, I got a confession to make. Remember that cable we got that time in vaudeville?' And she said, 'You mean the one from Ziegfeld?'"

Feature Films

The Big Broadcast (*Paramount 1932*)
International House (*Paramount 1933*)
College Humor (*Paramount 1933*)
Six of a Kind (*Paramount 1934*)
We're Not Dressing (*Paramount 1934*)

Many Happy Returns (*Paramount 1934*)
Love in Bloom (*Paramount 1935*)
Here Comes Cookie (*Paramount 1935*)
The Big Broadcast of 1936 (*Paramount 1935*)
The Big Broadcast of 1937 (*Paramount 1936*)

College Holiday (*Paramount 1936*)
A Damsel in Distress (*RKO 1937*)
College Swing (*Paramount 1938*)
Honolulu (*MGM 1939*)

Gracie Allen alone:
The Gracie Allen Murder Case (*Paramount 1939*)
Mr. and Mrs. North (*MGM 1941*)
Two Girls and a Sailor (*MGM 1944*)

George Burns alone:
The Solid Gold Cadillac (*Columbia 1956*) [narrator]
The Sunshine Boys (*MGM 1975*)
Oh, God! (*Warner Bros. 1977*)
Sgt. Pepper's Lonely Hearts Club Band (*Universal 1978*)
Movie Movie (*Warner Bros. 1978*)
Just You and Me, Kid (*Columbia 1979*)

Judy Canova

JUDY CANOVA: When I was four years old, my father took me to the zoo.

HE: What happened?

JUDY CANOVA: They rejected me.

Such exemplifies the verbal humor of Judy Canova, the energetic comedienne who managed to portray the American hillbilly with so much flavor that she became a headliner of Broadway and Hollywood. The braided pigtails, the oafish ankle boots and sloppy socks, the checkered blouse, and the billboard smile became a popular landmark to World War II audiences. While she was grinding out her frenetic films at Republic and Columbia in the Forties, she also emerged as a top favorite radio personality, headlining a very popular comedy program for many years.

Long before the country humor of shows like "The Beverly Hillbillies," "Petticoat Junction," and "Green Acres" was scoring high rating points on television, Judy had demonstrated the adulation and profit to be derived from exhibiting hillbilly antics. Unlike her successors, Judy rarely offended with her hi-jinks. Instead, she is a fine example of a performer who grew and matured within the framework of a certain characterization without boring the public, the press, or herself.

She was born Juliette Canova in Starke, Florida, on Monday, November 20, 1916, the daughter of Joe (a cottonbroker) and Henrietta Perry Canova (a former concert singer turned housewife). There were three older children, Anne, Zeke, and Pete, all of whom would work with Judy in show business. In the Twenties, Anne, Zeke, and Judy became the Canova Cracker Trio on WJAX in Jacksonville, Florida. Judy, the most outgoing of the group, was soon sidelining in amateur shows, talent programs, and any other outlet she could find for her extroversion. Unfortunately, her looks did not keep pace with her glamorous ambitions. She rationalized later, "I thought it was terrible that I didn't look like Clara Bow or Evelyn Brent. But no matter how I tried, I didn't. So one day, I got smart and not only accepted my lack of glamour, but made the most of it."

With Fortunio Bonanova in Hit the Hay (1945).

Anne and Zeke Canova had attended the Cincinnati Conservatory of Music, and Judy hoped to study there too. However, her father died in 1930, and the resultant decline in the family's income forced her to abandon this dream. Instead, Judy and her mother moved to New York City, where Judy studied tap dancing with Tommy Nip. Then it was back to Florida, where Judy earned a salary teaching contortion dancing at Orlando's Ebsen School.

However, Judy was determined to succeed as a performer, not as a coach. When she had saved some money from her teaching, she returned to New York. This time she was more successful. Along with Zeke and Anne, she won a job at Jimmie Kelly's Club and later at the Village Barn. It was in these engagements that she introduced her cornpone character to Gotham audiences. It was a twist few entertainers had ventured successfully in Manhattan. Judy carried it off so well that Rudy Vallee used her in a spot on his radio show. This job in turn led to a regular spot on orchestra leader Paul Whiteman's CBS radio program. Judy remained with Whiteman for a year, introducing her songs and jokes to a whole new audience. In her spare time, she traveled in vaudeville packages, trying to build her name to the extent that it would earn offers from the more prestigious producers. It worked.

A Broadway offer came. On December 13, 1934, Judy—with Anne, Pete, and Zeke—opened along with Lou Holtz, Phil Baker, Mitzi Mayfair, and Martha Raye at New York's Hollywood Theatre in the revue *Calling All Stars*. Judy's big moment was a sketch called "Last of the Hillbillies," in which she adapted the song "If It's Love" to her country style. The show ran for only 36 performances.

Calling All Stars had been backed by Warner Bros. When the revue folded the studio summoned Judy, Pete, Anne, and Zeke to Burbank to join the studio payroll. In her first feature, *In Caliente* (1935), Judy performed what remains her most memorable screen moment. In that musical hodgepodge featuring choreography by Busby Berkeley, songs by Harry Warren, Al Dubin, Mort Dixon, and Allie Wrubel, Winifred Shaw performed the soon to be famous "Lady in Red" number. Within the segment Judy did a

takeoff on it and Miss Shaw. In Spanish sombrero and absurd expression, Judy appeared in the midst of the routine—a startling surprise after a series of lovely chorus beauties—and nasally yodeled her version of the torch song. Later in the film the four Canovas performed a brief spot of hillbilly music, but it was Judy's burlesque of "The Lady in Red" which remained with audiences.

Filmgoers had been enthusiastic about Judy's irreverent bit in *In Caliente*, but her follow-up films at Warner Bros. did nothing to consolidate her position. *Broadway Gondolier* (1935) was a Dick Powell vehicle with the Canova family performing very briefly as a specialty act. Realizing that Judy was more promising as a solo player than as part of a troupe, Warner Bros. next gave her a featured role. The film was *Going Highbrow* (1935) with Guy Kibbee and ZaSu Pitts. Judy had the part of Annie, a rather dumb waitress. In Judy's words, the role was "not so hot." Thereafter, the studio dropped the Canova clan from the contract roster.

The Canovas returned to New York, where Judy was lucky. Without her family, she was signed to play in *Ziegfeld Follies of 1936* (Winter Garden Theatre: January 30, 1936). The revue boasted a Lee Shubert production, Ira Gershwin lyrics, and a cast that included Fanny Brice, Josephine Baker, Bob Hope, and Eve Arden. The *New York Sun* reported, "Judy Canova endangers the stability of the Winter Garden with her parodies." The play ran for 115 performances before closing for the summer. When it reopened that fall, Judy was no longer part of the production.

In the meantime, on the strength of her *Follies* work, Judy engineered a radio contract with NBC/WJZ radio, for a program entitled "Ripling Rhythm Revue." It provided parts for her family. The show was on the air for the 1936–37 season, but then Hollywood bid again, this time Paramount Studio. By now Pete Canova had entered business management, but Judy, Anne, and Zeke all trekked back to Hollywood. The studio placed them in *Artists and Models* (1937). Only Judy received a feature role (Anne and Zeke performed within the act) as Toots. She performed the specialty number "Pop Goes the Bubble," a farce of bubble-bath songs with Judy capering in a one-piece bathing suit. Within the fragmented story line, Judy

With Gordon Westcott in Going Highbrow *(1935).*

played the drab roommate of Ida Lupino. The star of the proceedings was Jack Benny and a featured performer in the outing was Martha Raye, Judy's confrere from Broadway's *Calling All Stars.*

About this time an ambivalent aspect of the Canova personality emerged. She became involved in a publicized ruckus with performer Edgar Bergen, who was then having outstanding success as the ventriloquist mentor of dummy Charle McCarthy on radio's "Chase and Sanborn Hour." Judy asserted that she was "breaking" her clandestine romantic engagement to Bergen because of his "obsession" with his dummy. Bergen's response to the situation was, "It was a terrible blow to me that Judy Canova should break our engagement without me being informed of the engagement or even becoming acquainted with her." What made the rhubarb all the more perplexing was that Judy was wed at the time. Her husband was Robert Burns, a New York insurance man, whom Judy had married in Maryland in 1936 with a complete lack of publicity.

Meanwhile, Judy joined Paramount players Betty Grable and Larry "Buster" Crabbe in *Thrill of a Lifetime* (1937). Judy was cast as the man-hungry clumsy sister of Eleanore Whitney and Johnny Downs, and is dated by Ben Blue. She also sang with Anne and Zeke. But Paramount saw no profitable slot for the Canovas, and again their film option was dropped.

The Canovas toured vaudeville where they built a strong following, played a two-week engagement at London's Cafe de Paris, and then performed for 13 weeks with Edgar Bergen on his NBC radio "Chase and Sanborn Hour" in 1938. On May 3, 1939, the Canovas appeared on an experimental NBC television program.

Judy achieved true success when she opened on Broadway in *Yokel Boy* (Majestic Theatre: July 6, 1939). The comedy's cast included Phil Silvers (in his Broadway debut), Buddy Ebsen, Dixie Dunbar, and Anne and Zeke Canova. As the hillbilly who becomes an overnight movie star, Judy won sterling reviews. The *New York Times* complimented, "A rowdy mixture of Beatrice Lillie and other comediennes along parallel lines in the general direction of Fannie [sic] Brice, this one pretty much puts the summer in its place. As 'Catherine the Great' she tells the legend of that Lady of the Russians, in 'Jukin,' she interprets the South, with 'Comes Love' she shows that she can look at an honest sentiment, face to face. Quite a girl on the whole." *Yokel Boy* would run for 208 performances. For a third time Hollywood studios made overtures.

Republic Pictures, under the rule of Herbert J. Yates, was enjoying financial success thanks to its array of cowboy stars (Gene Autry, Roy Rogers, and sometimes contractee John Wayne) and its action-packed serials. Yates made an offer to Judy, and the actress shrewdly accepted. She reasoned she had a better chance to shine on a lot underpopulated by stars.

Her debut picture for Republic was *Scatterbrain* (1940), a variation of the *Yokel Boy* success. Canova was cast as Judy Hall, a hillbilly who becomes a movie starlet, washes her kitchen floor on roller skates with brushes tied to them, and sings (shouts) "Benny the Beaver (You Better Be Like That, Yeah, Yeah)." On its own modest terms, the film was well received by the public and the press. The *New York Daily News* enthused, "The gags are good, the situations funny, and Judy Canova herself a riot in her first starring role for the screen."

Her next assignment under the five-year Republic pact was *Sis Hopkins* (1941), previously filmed in 1919 as a Mabel Normand vehicle. She was cast with Charles Butterworth, Jerry Colonna, and relative newcomer Susan Hayward. Judy displayed an amazing vocal versatility, performing selections ranging from an aria from *La Traviata* to Frank Loesser–Jule Styne's "It Ain't Hay." When the reviews were again fine, her stardom appeared assured.

Now a star, she told reporters of her hopes to play romantic parts. "I'll bide my time. One of these days they'll deliver me a leadin' man and then watch this kiddie show them how to really pitch woo for the movies." After Republic paid $5,000 for the film rights to *Yokel Boy*, Judy had an artistic disagreement with her studio employers and was replaced in the screen version by Joan Davis. Judy climaxed

her behavior of this period when MGM made an offer for her film services. She replied, "I don't want any more big studios for a while. You get lost." Meanwhile, she renegotiated her Republic contract so that she became part owner of her feature films.

Throughout the early Forties Judy worked as a popular character star. At Republic she starred in *Puddin' Head* (1941), with Francis Lederer, Raymond Walburn, and Slim Summerville in support. *Sleepytime Gal* (1942) found her cavorting in a deep freeze, falling off a fire escape, eating five soap-filled cream puffs, and singing some songs. *Chatterbox* (1943) displayed her in tandem with wide-mouthed Joe E. Brown and the two worked well together. *Sleepy Lagoon* (1943) offered Dennis Day as her leading man. These pictures were hardly top vehicles, but, rather, nimbly packaged properties to showcase Judy's vivacious cornpone persona. On loan-out to Paramount, she found *True to the Army* (1942) a bit more prestigious; it was a loosely constructed remake of Bing Crosby–Miriam Hopkins' *She Loves Me Not*. In this effort she was top billed over Allan Jones, Ann Miller, and Jerry Colonna, playing tightrope walker Daisy Hawkins. In the course of the 76 minutes of screen time, Judy escapes gangsters by masquerading as a soldier at an army camp. There are the expected jokes as she visits the physical examination room, the mess hall, and the rifle range.

Actually, like her more sophisticated rival Joan Davis, Judy began scoring her main success on radio. On July 6, 1943, "The Judy Canova Show" began airing as a CBS summer replacement for Al Jolson. Regulars on the show included Ruth Perrot as Aunt Aggie (later replaced by Verna Felton), Ruby Dandridge as Geranium the maid, Sheldon Leonard as taxi driver Joe Crunchmiller, and Mel Blanc as Pedro. The radio show also featured the Bud Dent Orchestra, with which Judy sang the famous sign-off song, "Goodnight, Sweetheart." On January 6, 1945, Judy moved over to the NBC radio network, where her ratings climbed in a new Saturday night spot.

Judy's pact with Republic soon lapsed and she moved bases to Columbia, where she starred in a trio of releases: *Louisiana Hayride* (1944), *Hit the Hay* (1945), and *Singin' in the Corn* (1946). All three films were really

In Puddin' Head (1941).

With Ernest Truex, Ruth Donnelly, and Dennis Day in Sleepy Lagoon (1943).

silly ventures which revealed no new facets of the superior Canova talent. Again radio remained her forte. By 1946 she had climbed within the top 10 rated comedy programs in the country, a remarkable achievement.

Throughout the late Forties, Judy was steadily employed on her radio show, with occasional recording sessions and some personal appearances. Her program reached an estimated 18 million enthusiastic listeners weekly. In 1951 Herbert J. Yates recalled her to his declining Republic Studio where Judy played in six programmers starting with 1951's *Honeychile* and ending with 1955's *Lay That Rifle Down*. In addition, she guested on the burgeoning television medium, appearing on November 2, 1952, on "The Colgate Comedy Hour." In April 1954 she played a three-week engagement at the Hotel Sahara in Las Vegas.

By 1955 her film contract and radio show had expired. Since then, Judy has worked sporadically, which is a sad waste of a major talent. She guested on a March 17, 1958, episode of "The Danny Thomas Show" on CBS-TV, and made her dramatic TV bow on a May 29, 1960, entry of CBS-TV's "Alfred Hitchcock Presents." In the stark half-hour drama, *Party Line*, Judy eschewed most of her famed comedy tricks to turn in a solid dramatic performance. In 1958 she recorded an LP album for Coronet Records, "Judy Canova—Country Cousin—Sings," and in 1960 she returned to films in MGM's *The Adventures of Huckleberry Finn*. She was the sheriff's wife and played a single scene which *Variety* called "potentially a memorable one." She made two pilots in the Sixties, "Tallie" and "Li'l Abner," but neither one sold as a video series.

More recently Judy has ventured from her San Fernando Valley home to accept professional work. In 1970 she appeared in another TV pilot, "The Murdocks and Mc-Clays," which did not sell (but did air over ABC-TV on September 2, 1970), and in December 1971 she joined June Allyson and Dennis Day in a touring package of *No, No, Nanette*, playing the mugging role of the maid Pauline (accomplished in the Broadway revival of 1969 by Patsy Kelly). She was then professionally inactive until she accepted a cameo spot on the September 20, 1974, episode of "Police Woman."

With Andy Clyde in Carolina Cannonball *(1955).*

For a lady who has always spoofed her appearance, Judy has quite an impressive marital record. Her 1936 marriage to Robert Burns collapsed in a divorce in 1939. On June 14, 1941, she wed army corporal James Ripley in Honolulu. He was reputedly an old friend from Florida and was arrested on their wedding night for being AWOL. The marriage was annulled quickly. On March 14, 1943, Judy wed Chester England, who became a cosmetic manufacturer and the father of their daughter Julietta (born: August 1944). The couple divorced on February 24, 1950. Later that year Judy took her fourth husband, Filiberto Rivero, a Cuban importer. They had a daughter, Diana, born in 1953.* The Riveros were divorced in 1964. Rivero, who had become a Los Angeles radio and television personality, is now deceased.

* Diana made her debut at the age of five months in her mother's Republic movie, *Untamed Heiress* (1954). She appeared in the film *The First Nudie Musical* (1976) in a clothed role, and in mid-1976 was a regular on Dinah Shore's summer variety TV show. Other video appearances have included "Ozzie's Girls," "Happy Days," "Chico and the Man," and "Soap."

"I don't have to work. Fortunately I put the money away when it was coming in," vows Judy, today a wealthy lady with ample real-estate investments who resides mostly in the San Fernando Valley. Of her general show-business inactivity, Judy says, "This has happened to me again and again. I get times when I just like being lazy. Then I get started working again and I get going like crazy."

Judy has been in an energetic mood in recent years. She appeared as Aunt Vivian in a Joy dish detergent TV commercial, attends assorted nostalgia conventions, and has plans to write her autobiography and prepare a cookbook. In 1976 she was cast in the New World's release *Cannonball*, as Sharma Capri, the mother of an oafish country-western singer. In the film she was the backseat driver involved in a hell-bent car trip from California to New York. In 1977 she was seen on an episode of the TV comedy series "Love Boat."

Obviously the effervescent funster has a great deal still to offer upcoming generations of audiences.

FEATURE FILMS

In Caliente (*Warner Bros. 1935*)
Broadway Gondolier (*Warner Bros. 1935*)
Going Highbrow (*Warner Bros. 1935*)
Artists and Models (*Paramount 1937*)
Thrill of a Lifetime (*Paramount 1937*)
Scatterbrain (*Republic 1940*)
Sis Hopkins (*Republic 1941*)
Puddin' Head (*Republic 1941*)
Sleepytime Gal (*Republic 1942*)
True to the Army (*Paramount 1942*)
Joan of Ozark (*Republic 1942*)
Chatterbox (*Republic 1943*)
Sleepy Lagoon (*Republic 1943*)

Louisiana Hayride (*Columbia 1944*)
Hit the Hay (*Columbia 1945*)
Singin' in the Corn (*Columbia 1946*)
Honeychile (*Republic 1951*)
Oklahoma Annie (*Republic 1952*)
The WAC from Walla Walla (*Republic 1952*)
Untamed Heiress (*Republic 1954*)
Carolina Cannonball (*Republic 1955*)
Lay That Rifle Down (*Republic 1955*)
The Adventures of Huckleberry Finn (*MGM 1960*)
Cannonball (*New World 1976*)

Eddie Cantor

Florenz Ziegfeld's theatrical genius found expression in opulent presentations of beautiful women arrayed in sensuous costumes set against stunning backgrounds. To pace his renowned *Follies*, the great producer engaged singers for his shows. In addition, despite his dim view and ambivalence toward them, he hired a notable group of clowns, comics, and comedians who were paid to distract onstage from the theatrical glorifying of the American girl.

Ziegfeld's clown corps became one of the prime highlights of his *Follies*, even though he often relegated their hilarious bits, stints, and sketches to "filler" status in the proceedings. From the *Follies* emerged such towering comedic talents as Bert Williams, Leon Errol, W. C. Fields, Fanny Brice, Ed Wynn, and Will Rogers. There was also a 5'7" bundle of nervous, inexhaustible energy known as Eddie Cantor.

Within the concept of comedy, Cantor, in the strictest definitive sense, was not a comedian nor, like Ed Wynn, an inspired clown. He neither created a lasting comic image, like the individually unique W. C. Fields, Jimmy Durante, and Leon Errol, nor established a permanent reputation as a brilliant wit and humorist, like Will Rogers. Eddie was basically a song-and-dance man who vigorously pursued comedy through topical jokes, sketches, and musical plays. His constant stage image was that of the banjo-eyed, frightened little-man-what-now syndrome of triumph over adversity. He performed with deadly seriousness, making it all seem much funnier than it probably was. His expert timing of jokes was equaled only by Bob Hope's.

Cantor's status as a superior song-and-dance man was illusionary. No hoofer, he could prance across a stage with admirable agility, patty-caking his hands in a whirl of distracting perpetual motion and selling a song with accomplished timing and ease. Despite the fact that his singing voice was not of a high range or a distinctive caliber, his 30 years of recordings grossed high sales, which exceeded those of many other show-business greats.

With Baby Quintanilla in Forty Little Mothers *(1940).*

Hearing today such standards as "Dinah," "Ida," "If You Knew Susie," "You'd Be Surprised" (his top-seller), "Mandy," and his memorable "Makin' Whoopee," one recalls one of America's greatest entertainers.

During the Thirties Eddie was a leading radio star (and in the early Fifties he would be a big name on early prime-time television). His signature song, "I'd Love to Spend This Hour with You," became as identifiable as Kate Smith's "When the Moon Comes over the Mountain" or Bing Crosby's "Blue of the Night." Ever alert to, and an encouraging sponsor of, new talent, Cantor introduced singers Deanna Durbin, Bobby Breen, and Dinah Shore on his radio show. Later he helped the career of Eddie Fisher and others. His philanthropic and charitable work rivaled that of any figure in the performing arts.

On Sunday, January 31, 1892, a son was born to Russian Jewish immigrants Michael and Maite (Minnie) Iskowitch in a crowded tenement flat over a Russian tearoom on Eldridge Street. The city was Manhattan and the area was the teeming poverty-plagued Lower East Side. Minnie died in childbirth a year later and violin-playing dreamer Michael succumbed to pneumonia the following year. Orphan Isidor Iskowitch was raised by his maternal grandmother, Esther Kantrowitz. At age 62 she provided food and shelter for him by peddling wares from door to door and, later, by managing her own employment agency.

Izzy's schooling was sparse at best. When he won a top prize of $5 under the name of Edward Cantor for his impersonation of contemporary show-business folk at Miner's Bowery Theatre Amateur Night, he was headed for an entertainment career. As Eddie Cantor he made his professional vaudeville debut at the Clinton Music Hall teamed with Dan Lipsky. The latter became Cantor's lifelong friend and proxy and would become the future vice president of Manufacturers Trust Company in Manhattan.

There were ups and downs in Cantor's early career years. A $15-a-week job with Frank B. Carr's burlesque unit, *Indian Maidens*, left Eddie stranded in Shenandoah, Pennsylvania, on Christmas Eve 1908. Later at Carey Walsh's Coney Island saloon Eddie found work as a singing waiter, accompanied

by an ebullient ragtime piano player named Jimmy Durante. A booking of 16 weeks, at $20 weekly, had Cantor doing a single in a circuit of four vaudeville houses owned by ex-furriers Adolph Zukor and Marcus Loew and two brothers escaping the pharmaceutical business, Joseph and Nicholas Schenck. Cantor was assured of an additional tour of the Zukor-Loew-Schenck People's Vaudeville Company circuit *if* he altered his act. What he changed was his makeup. He experimented with burnt cork and blacked up and behind the usual minstrel face mask. The gimmick worked and soon he was on his way to success. He became the featured stooge with the headlining team of Bedini and Arthur and was playing Hammerstein's Victoria Theatre on Broadway.

After two years with Bedini and Arthur, Cantor signed with Gus Edwards to be featured in his *Kid Kabaret* in 1912. The Edwards troupe included Lila Lee, Eddie Buzzell, Gregory Kelly, Georgie Price, and George Jessel. The *Kid* act was enormously successful. Two years later Cantor left the part of a black butler in Edwards' aging juvenile stint to marry his childhood sweetheart, Ida Tobias, the belle of Henry Street.

In Brooklyn on June 9, 1914, Eddie and Ida were married and they sailed to England on their honeymoon. After about a week, Cantor teamed with Sam Kessler for a week's engagement at London's Oxford Theatre and joined Charlot's revue *Not Likely*. There he stopped the show with his song, "I Love the Ladies."

The newlyweds returned to the States on July 29, 1914, and Eddie teamed with straight man Al Lee in a vaudeville act, *Master and Man*. Cantor and Lee roamed the two-a-day bills for nearly two years. Then in the early spring of 1916 Earl Carroll told producer Oliver Morosco, "This fellow ought to be good for our show. He sings songs like nobody's business and covers that stage like liquid fire." The show was to be produced on the West Coast. Al Lee was not interested in leaving the East. But Eddie had more responsibilities. On March 31, 1915, the Cantors' first child, Marjorie, had been born.

Oliver Morosco's production, *Canary Cottage*, featured Trixie Friganza and Charles Ruggles. Cantor had a minor role as a black chauffeur, to which he added bits of unscheduled business and pert asides. He also sang "It Ruined Mark Anthony" and was the hit of the show at its San Diego opening. He remained with the Morosco musical for five months but grew restive to return to Broadway and to his family, now enlarged with the birth on April 27, 1916, of their second daughter, Natalie.

Returning to New York, Cantor was given a "one-night tryout" by Florenz Ziegfeld in his *Midnight Frolics* atop the New Amsterdam Theatre. He opened his act by enlisting the services of several ringsiders. He asked "Diamond Jim" Brady, William Randolph Hearst, and Charles B. Dillingham to hold cards from a flash deck high above their heads. Eddie meanwhile launched into a raucous rendition of the song, "Oh, How She Could Yacki, Hicki, Wicki, Wacki, Woo!" All the while the three worthies continued to pose with the playing cards, reluctant to spoil his act. Ziegfeld was delighted. Cantor remained on the roof for 27 weeks. The Great Glorifier finally summoned him to play in the 1917 *Follies* at $400 weekly.

Ziegfeld's newest *Follies* opened for a run of 111 performances on June 12, 1917. The cast included Bert Williams, Will Rogers, W. C. Fields, and Eddie Cantor, who dueted the song "Just You and Me" with Fanny Brice. Eddie's great triumph was saddened by the death of his beloved grandmother who died on his birthday, January 31, 1917. Cantor thereafter was an impressive member of the 1918 *Follies* and by the time the 1919 edition was trying out in Atlantic City, Eddie had become the father of a third daughter, Edna (June 10, 1919).

The 1919 *Follies* remains one of the most memorable of Ziegfeld's spectacles because of Irving Berlin's lovely song "A Pretty Girl Is Like a Melody." In a minstrel scene Cantor played Tambo, and Van and Schenck introduced the delightful tune "Mandy," which would later be adopted by Eddie. But on August 6, 1919, the Actors Equity strike hit Broadway and Cantor became one of the cause's champions. His actions incurred the wrath of Ziegfeld. In 1920 the Cantor family moved from the Bronx to suburban Mount Vernon, and Eddie opened in *Broadway Brevities of 1920*. (Ironically, Cantor was a substitute for Ed Wynn, whom the Shuberts refused to rehire because of his leadership in the actors' strike.)

The Shuberts starred Cantor for the first time in *The Midnight Rounders* (1921)* in which he did a hilarious sketch of a pull-'em-off-the-street Jewish tailor convincing a customer to buy an ill-fitting suit. Pieced out with new sketches and much the same format, *Rounders* evolved into *Make It Snappy*, which opened on Broadway on April 13, 1922.

Then Ziegfeld reentered the stage star's life. He proposed that Eddie be the lead in a "book" show called *Kid Boots*. The comedy opened on New Year's Eve 1923 and Eddie was pure delight in the title role as a Florida golf caddie and a golf-club bootlegger. Cantor's often-used osteopath skit was reworked to accommodate the comedy of Jobyna Howland's bravura playing of Dr. Josephine Fitch with Cantor as the subject. Eddie's belief was that physical comedy was always a sure-fire laugh getter, and he brought that tenet to his shows and later to his films. When *Kid Boots* completed its long tour in 1926, Eddie went to Hollywood. Jesse L. Lasky had purchased *Kid Boots* for $65,000 with Cantor as the star.

Frank Tuttle's Paramount film version of *Kid Boots* opened on Broadway at midnight, Saturday, October 9, 1926. Eddie was there in person, backed by George Olsen and His Orchestra. For six weeks' work on the picture Cantor was paid $3,000 weekly. His personal appearance with the well-received film grossed him $7,500. The success of Cantor's feature-film debut was aided immeasurably by the playing of lovely Billie Dove and vivacious Clara Bow.**

Paramount signed Cantor for another film. *Special Delivery* (1927) was based on a hokey story by Eddie and the presentation of it was not helped by the poorly paced direction of William Goodrich (otherwise known as Roscoe "Fatty" Arbuckle). The picture was stocked with such players as William Powell, Jobyna Ralston, Paul Kelly, and Mary Carr.

---

* While touring in *The Midnight Rounders*, Ida presented Eddie with their fourth child whom they named Marilyn. She was born on September 16, 1921.

** In 1911 Eddie, along with George Jessel and Truly Shattuck, had made an experimental talking picture, *Widow at the Races*, for Thomas A. Edison. In 1925 Cantor had appeared in a short subject for DeForrest Photofilm Company.

However, the studio was unimpressed with the final results and failed to fulfill its announced intention of starring Cantor in a film version of Rodgers and Hart's *The Girl Friend* and in another comedy called *Help.* Neither film was made.

On August 16, 1927, Eddie returned to the New Amsterdam Theatre for his last *Follies,* and on October 8, 1927, his fifth and final daughter, Janet, was born. Small wonder that Will Rogers sent Eddie a telegram, "If you want a boy call Western Union," or that Eddie named his California residence, "Cantor's Home for Girls." Throughout the years Eddie would garner publicity on the fathering of five daughters. In fact, on December 31, 1939, the "Screen Guild Radio Theatre" satirized his paternal accomplishment with Cantor coping with his female brood (impersonated by Joan Blondell, Bonita Granville, and Martha O'Driscoll).

When the *Follies* closed Eddie joined Ruth Etting in a musical called *Whoopee,* based on the 1923 stage hit *The Nervous Wreck* which had starred Otto Kruger. In it Eddie was a confirmed hypochondriac entangled in an elopement from an Arizona Indian reservation. The show premiered in Pittsburgh in November 1928 with Miss Etting stopping the show with "Love Me or Leave Me." Cantor was in top form as the persistent invalid and Ruby Keeler was on hand (temporarily) as the featured dancer. *Whoopee* opened at the New Amsterdam Theatre on December 4, 1928, for a record run of 379 performances.

The stock-market crash of 1929 seriously dented the Cantor resources. He recounted his tribulations in an amusing short book, *Caught Short,* which became the basis of an MGM film with Polly Moran and Marie Dressler.

Eddie's health was unsteady during the run of *Whoopee* because he had extended his talents to a breaking point. Not only was he performing on the stage but he also made two short subjects at Paramount's Astoria, Long Island, studio, *Ziegfeld's Midnite Frolics* and *That Party in Person.* In addition to the shorts, Eddie reprised his rib-tickling tailorshop sketch in Ziegfeld's Technicolor screen production, *Glorifying the American Girl* (1929). Thereafter, the overworked performer appeared in other one-reelers at Astoria, including *Cockeyed News* and *Insur-*

ance. He was being hailed as a real cinema bet and the only possible screen rival of Al Jolson.

In June 1930 Eddie announced he was retiring from the stage. As he explained, "I've enough money and I've reached the peak of a theatrical career. Why shouldn't my family and children enjoy my companionship? Why should I worry about the responsibility of an entire company, so that even if I'm feeling sick I must go on when my doctor thinks a rest wouldn't hurt me? What does a performer work for? Only two things—money and applause. If I still want to remain before the public how long does it take to make a picture? In two or three months I can make one and then I'm through for the rest of the year to do as I darn please." Thus Eddie said goodbye to Broadway and hello to Hollywood.

Samuel Goldwyn and Florenz Ziegfeld produced a (two-color) Technicolor version of *Whoopee** in 1930. The United Artists release was well received, and judged superior to the stage production. *Photoplay* felt that Cantor was "one of the funniest men ever seen on the screen." It was probably his shining hour.

A lucrative contract with Samuel Goldwyn started with Cantor's *Palmy Days* (1931). It was a zestful farce, co-written by Cantor and greatly enlivened by Charlotte Greenwood, who joined Cantor in another reworked version of his osteopath skit. *Time* magazine reported, "Eddie Cantor belongs to the school of clowns whose humor derives from ineffectuality; a certain eccentric excitability makes him sometimes hilariously funny. His gaiety is without grace; it lacks the thin, almost horrible insanity of the Marx Brothers and it is seldom frankly pathetic, like Chaplin's. He is a culprit from a comic strip and no one would be surprised if, when something hit him on the head, it gave the sound of 'plop' or 'zowie!'"

Eddie returned to New York City after *Palmy Days* for a series of benefits with his old friend George Jessel. From the enthusiastic reception at those benefits, the two former Gus Edwards alumni consolidated

---

* In mid-1977, a new negative was struck of the feature for showing at a Los Angeles theatre; it has been out of circulation since 1933 (never having been shown on TV), save for a brief theatrical showing in 1971 with a print borrowed from a Czechoslovakian archive.

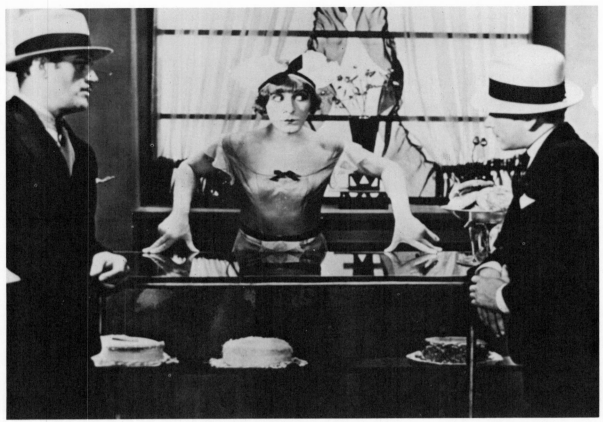

With Harry Woods and George Raft in Palmy Days *(1931).*

material for a spectacular engagement at the Palace Theatre, including in their show the team of Burns and Allen. Prior to the Cantor-Jessel Palace opening on October 31, 1931, the theatre was forced to operate two box offices to accommodate ticket demands. The original two-week engagement was extended to New Year's Eve.

Leo McCarey's *The Kid from Spain* (1932) was superior in many ways to *Palmy Days.* Eddie's bright playing of an ersatz bullfighter was uproarious, helped immeasurably by the deft playing of Lyda Roberti. For the production Mr. Goldwyn was acclaimed as "the Florenz Ziegfeld of the movies."

For Cantor's annual screen outing in 1933, George S. Kaufman and Robert E. Sherwood wrote a ribald farce that projected Eddie into ancient Rome as the taster to Emperor Valerius (Edward Arnold). A fine cast included Gloria Stuart, David Manners, and Ruth Etting, plus Busby Berkeley's dances against a lavish Goldwyn production. Its climax was

a *Ben-Hur*-type chariot race. *Roman Scandals* was a resounding hit.

Goldwyn's 1934 Cantor extravaganza had Eddie as a tugboat worker on the Brooklyn waterfront inheriting a massive fortune from his Egyptologist uncle. *Kid Millions* presented Ethel Merman and Warren Hymer as the chiselers while Ann Sothern and George Murphy (in his film debut) supplied the romantic interest. Then came 1936 and Eddie's film career hit a stalemate with his starring role in *Strike Me Pink.* The story by Clarence Budington Kelland was deemed more suitable to the talents of Harold Lloyd. For their efforts, Cantor, Ethel Merman, and Sally Eilers received little tribute.

To many it had become clear in the mid-Thirties that filmmakers were offering and audiences were demanding a brand of screen humor different from what Cantor could or would provide. By 1936 any pretense that Cantor was a major musical screen contender was dashed by the devastating competition

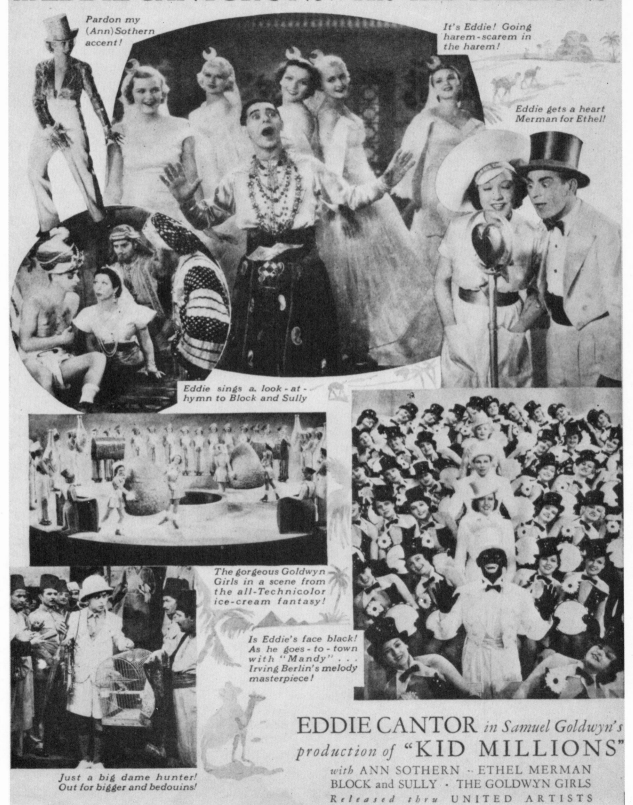

Advertisement for Kid Millions *(1934).*

from the other studios. Accordingly, Eddie and Sam Goldwyn parted their contractual ways.

Cantor's ever busy life had not been relegated solely to motion pictures. He was one of radio's top stars,* headed the Screen Actors Guild, was president of the Jewish Theatrical Guild, and was an indefatigable sponsor of charities—he helped to initiate the March of Dimes, for example. As the star would recall, "President Franklin D. Roosevelt, a victim himself, wanted my help in raising funds to fight infantile paralysis. I thought for a moment and said, 'Let's not ask for dollars or big donations. Let's ask the whole nation to send in dimes. Let's have a March of Dimes on your birthday.'"

For Twentieth Century-Fox in 1937 Eddie made *Ali Baba Goes to Town*, in which he played a tramp caught up in an Oriental movie set and dreaming he rescues old Baghdad with Roosevelt's New Deal programs. Gypsy Rose Lee was Baghdad's sultry sultana. The zany film did not have the anticipated impact on the public, and industry interest in promoting Cantor's screen future diminished further. In 1939 MGM announced plans to star Cantor and Eleanor Powell in *Girl Crazy*, but litigation over screen rights was alleged to have postponed the picture. (In 1943 MGM would film the musical with Mickey Rooney and Judy Garland.)

A French comedy, *Monsieur Petiot,* was the basis of Metro's *Forty Little Mothers* (1940), featuring Eddie in the straight role of a college professor harboring an abandoned baby. The deadly, winsome semidrama was redeemed neither by the presence of Judith Anderson in the cast nor by Busby Berkeley's slushy direction. For the Broadway premiere of the picture, Cantor and George Jessel headed the Capitol Theatre stage show.

For what would prove to be Eddie's final appearance in a Broadway play, he starred in *Banjo Eyes* (December 25, 1941). It was a musical version of the very successful stage hit *Three Men on a Horse*. Cantor was cast as the timid greeting-card writer adept at picking winning racehorses. To a new generation Cantor was a newly discovered musical comedy great. He danced, sang, and pranced about the stage in blackface, straw hat, and white-rimmed glasses. He was assisted in the proceedings by June Clyde, Audrey Christie, and, in a very minor role, Jacqueline Susann. Surprisingly, the show lasted only 126 performances.

With the outbreak of World War II, Cantor threw himself tirelessly into entertaining troops and, as he had done in World War I, selling enormous quantities of war bonds. At one point in his continual charity work he hosted an exhaustive 24-hour radio marathon which netted some $41 million in sales of war bonds.

It was in 1943 that Cantor returned to the screen. Warner Bros.' all-star musical *Thank Your Lucky Stars* was strung with cameo roles on a thin story line. Within the framework of the wispy story, Cantor played both studio tour guide Joe Simpson and himself. Many thought it was too much of Cantor in one film. He again appeared as himself in another wartime-geared release, *Hollywood Canteen* (1944). That year he produced and starred in a cavalcade of vaudeville, RKO's *Show Business*. It was a modestly budgeted effort but showed Eddie and co-star Joan Davis to good advantage. The duo did a mildly amusing burlesque of Anthony and Cleopatra, and in the *Ziegfield Follies* finale Eddie reprised his "Makin' Whoopee" song.

Continuing in his producer's capacity, Eddie turned to Broadway. In the autumn of 1945, with Nat Karson, he packaged a stage musical based on the legendary *Nellie Bly*. The show featured Victor Moore and William Gaxton with blonde, luscious starlet Marilyn Maxwell in the title role. Road tryouts of the show failed to shake its obvious flaws and it lasted two weeks on Broadway after its January 21, 1946, opening.

In 1948 Cantor returned to producing for RKO. *If You Knew Susie* again paired him with ebullient Joan Davis. But this last starring film was no accomplishment.

* Cantor was one of the first major Broadway stars to be heard on radio; on January 6, 1929, he was on CBS' "Majestic Theatre of the Air," along with Ruth Etting. A guest performance on Rudy Vallee's radio show in February 1931 started him on a long top-rated radio career. In April 1936, for example, Cantor signed a year contract with Texaco to star on its show at $7,000 a program. At one point in his radio career, Cantor tried to compete with Jack Benny's very popular Sunday night radio show, but after switching to a time slot opposite Benny and losing in the ratings, Cantor returned to his mid-week air time. Cantor tried to bow out of the situation "gracefully" by announcing, "It's unfair to ask the American public to choose between two of their favorites. . . ."

With Virginia Field
Ali Baba Goes to
Town (1937).

With Dennis Morgan
and Joan Leslie in
Thank Your Lucky
Stars (1943).

*With Joan Davis,
Allyn Joslyn, and
Harry Harvey in*
If You Knew Susie
(1948).

In 1952 Cantor would appear as himself in Warner Bros.' uninspired *The Story of Will Rogers*. The same studio, in an effort to capture audiences enthralled with *The Jolson Story* and *Jolson Sings Again*, turned out *The Eddie Cantor Story* (1953). In this "assembly-line success story" Eddie appeared in an epilogue with his wife, Ida. At the end of the film, which has Keefe Brasselle playing the star (for which Eddie dubbed the singing), Eddie is seen after a showing of the film. He tells the movie audience, "I never looked better." The *New York Times* benevolently noted, "He [Cantor] is not only talented, but kind!"

The early days of commercial television saw a good number of ex-vaudeville and burlesque stars rule the medium with their well-honed comedy routines. Eddie Cantor had a four-year run (1950–54) on "The Colgate Comedy Hour," during which time he trotted out his famous routines and, especially, the many songs he had either introduced or become identified with through his long theatrical career. He hosted ABC-TV's "Eddie Cantor Comedy Theatre" in 1955. On

October 18, 1956, he gave a telling performance in the straight seriocomic role of Morris Seidman in conflict over social and political issues with his son (Farley Granger) in "Playhouse 90's" *Seidman and Son*.

In his later years the veteran performer received many testimonials and awards. At the annual Academy Award fete for 1956, Eddie was presented with an honorary statuette for distinguished services to the film industry. The special Oscar was merited for Cantor's vigorous work benefiting screen players during his tenure as head of the Screen Actors Guild and his many diversely dedicated services toward the general welfare of the industry.

Cantor's last stage appearances were at Carnegie Hall in New York City on March 21 and September 30, 1950, in *My Forty Years in Show Business*, and in 1951 and 1952 in *An Evening with Eddie Cantor*. On January 31, 1952, the State of Israel Bond Committee sponsored a gala Eddie Cantor 60th Birthday Party in the grand ballroom of New York's Hotel Commodore in appreciation of his strenuous and rewarding efforts in selling bonds for Israel. The event was memorialized in a published booklet, *I'm Glad I Spent Those Sixty Years,* in which Cantor briefly reviewed his career and philosophical doctrines,* and tersely described his pride in the Jewish accomplishments and contributions in behalf of the American way.

On Sunday, June 7, 1953, Eddie and Ida Cantor celebrated their 39th wedding anniversary, reenacting their marriage ceremony on national TV. Cantor's famous protégée, Dinah Shore, served as matron of honor. The ushers were Ralph Edwards, Jack Benny, and George Jessel. On August 8, 1962, two years before the Cantors' golden wedding anniversary, Ida died of a heart attack. The loss of his beloved wife overwhelmed the star, com-

* These attitudes were reflected upon in Cantor's books *The Way I See It* (1959) and *As I Remember Them* (1963).

pounding his great personal grief over the death of daughter Marjorie in 1959. Marjorie had served as his secretary and confidante for years.

Long since retired, Cantor received in 1964 a Presidential Citation from President Lyndon Johnson for his services to the United States and to humanity. Since a serious heart attack in 1953 the comedian's health had been slowly deteriorating. Shortly after seven on Saturday evening, October 10, 1964, he died of a sudden coronary occlusion at his home in Beverly Hills.

Death was in a shockingly festive, devastating mood in mid-1964. Gracie Allen had died on August 28, followed by Harpo Marx on September 28, to be joined by Eddie Cantor on October 10—three famous funsters who lavished laughter on a world sorely in need of it.

FEATURE FILMS

Kid Boots (*Paramount 1926*)
Special Delivery (*Paramount 1927*)
Glorifying the American Girl (*Paramount 1929*)
Whoopee (*United Artists 1930*)
Palmy Days (*United Artists 1931*)
The Kid from Spain (*United Artists 1932*)
Roman Scandals (*United Artists 1933*)
Kid Millions (*United Artists 1934*)
Strike Me Pink (*United Artists 1936*)

Ali Baba Goes to Town (*20th Century-Fox 1937*)
Forty Little Mothers (*MGM 1940*)
Thank Your Lucky Stars (*Warner Bros. 1943*)
Hollywood Canteen (*Warner Bros, 1944*)
Show Business (*RKO 1944*)
If You Knew Susie (*RKO 1948*)
The Story of Will Rogers (*Warner Bros. 1952*)
The Eddie Cantor Story (*Warner Bros. 1953*)

With Jackie Coogan in The Kid (1921).

174

Charles Chaplin

Throughout the world he was hailed as the screen's "King of Comedy," "the world's foremost artist," comedy's "Everyman," and "the one universal man of modern times." The 5'4½" Englishman became a legend within his lifetime. George Bernard Shaw regarded him as "the only genius developed in motion pictures."

In his September 3, 1949, essay, "Comedy's Greatest Era," for *Life* magazine, critic James Agee sought the essence of Chaplin's screen supremacy: "Of all the comedians he worked most deeply and most shrewdly within a realization of what a human being is, and is up against. The Tramp is acentrally representative of humanity, as many-sided and as mysterious as Hamlet, and it seems unlikely that any dancer or actor can ever have excelled him in eloquence, variety, or poignancy of motion . . . the finest pantomime, the deepest emotion, the richest and the most poignant poetry are in Chaplin's work."

The voluminous praise showered on Chaplin reached its apex in early 1975. Pushed in a wheelchair into the huge ballroom of Buck-

ingham Palace three months before his 86th birthday, the renowned comedian was named Knight Commander of the Order of the British Empire by Queen Elizabeth II. He became Sir Charles Chaplin. A month later, in the United States, he was among the first 10 creators and performers* who "entertained American audiences and enriched the nation's culture" to be inducted into Entertainment's Hall of Fame. A month before his 87th birthday, in March 1976, Queen Elizabeth II of England awarded the clown prince of comedy a trophy and a place of fellowship in the British Academy of Film and Television Arts.

Within his lifetime, Chaplin had risen from the wretched poverty of London's slums to a station of world acclaim and regal entitlement as the screen's greatest comedian.

Hannah Hall was the daughter of an Irish (County Cork) cobbler and a Spanish gypsy

* The nine others were: D. W. Griffith, George Bernard Shaw, Judy Garland, George Gershwin, Irving Berlin, Tennessee Williams, Katharine Hepburn, Laurence Olivier, and Eugene O'Neill.

mother. She became known in London as Lily Harley, a music-hall soubrette. She married Jewish bookmaker Sidney Hawkes and moved to Cape Town, South Africa, where in 1885 her son Sydney was born. The following year Hannah divorced Hawkes. In London she married the French-Jewish but anglicized Charles Chaplin.* On Tuesday, April 16, 1889, at 8:00 P.M., on East Lane in the Walworth section of London, their son Charles was born. He was named after his vaudevillian father and given the middle name Spencer for his paternal uncle.

A year after the birth of Charles Spencer Chaplin, hard-drinking baritone Mr. Chaplin left his family. Hannah was forced to support her offspring and it was a tough struggle. In 1894, at age five, young Charles, substituting for Hannah who had become ill, made his stage debut singing a coster song, "Jack Jones." Hannah was later confined to the Cane Hill Insane Asylum and her sons were sent to the Lambeth Workhouse. Mrs. Chaplin was in and out of Cane Hill for varying periods while Charles and Sydney attended Hanwell Residential School. Two years at Hern Boys' College completed Charlie's education.

In 1897, the year Charlie became a member of a music-hall clog-dancing act, "The Eight Lancashire Lads," his father died of alcoholism in London's St. Thomas Hospital. Mr. Chaplin was 37. Thereafter, Hannah returned to the asylum and Sydney joined the Royal Navy. Charlie was on his own, living by his wits in the streets of London's slums. Later his "Little Fellow" on screen would closely identify with his real-life Oliver Twist experiences.

On January 15, 1900, three months before his 11th birthday, Charlie made his professional London stage debut at the Hippodrome in *Giddy Ostend*. He landed a tour of 48 weeks playing the pageboy Billy in *Sherlock Holmes* and newsboy Sammy in *Jim, the Romance of a Cockney*. Along the way he toured the English provinces in the play *Rags to Riches*. In the Duke of York's Theatre production of *Peter Pan*, Charlie was one of the wolves.

Producer Charles Frohman engaged Charlie to repeat his *Sherlock Holmes* page-

boy role with William Gillette in a newly written curtain raiser, *The Painful Predicament of Sherlock Holmes*. When *Clarissa*, the show for which it was a teaser, failed, Gillette revived *Sherlock Holmes* and retained Chaplin as the pageboy. After that, Charlie had a long run in a vaudeville act, *Casey's Court Circus*, and did a single in burlesque as "Sam Cohen, the Jewish Comedian."

Sydney returned from the navy and became a member of Fred Karno's famous music-hall company. At 17 Charlie joined the Karno troupe in a slapstick burlesque sketch, "The Football Match." Karno signed the younger Chaplin for a year at four pounds a week, and in 1909 he played Paris' famous Folies Bergere with the Karno troupe. On October 3, 1910, he made his American stage debut at New York's Colonial Theatre in Karno's *The Wow-Wows. Variety* succinctly noted, "There was at least one funny Englishman in the troupe and he will do for America." In a later American tour Chaplin did his famous full-dress drunk bit falling out of a theatre box and annoying the performers. It was in Karno's *A Night in an English Music Hall** that Mack Sennett and Mabel Normand saw him perform at Manhattan's American Music Hall. During this Karno period of developing his art of pantomime and swinging slapstick tricks, Charlie also learned to play the violin and cello.

In the fall of 1913, Adam Kessel, one of Sennett's Keystone film company backers, wired Chaplin on the road, asking him to join the movie studio. Charlie left the Karno troupe and early in December 1913 reported to Sennett's studio in Glendale, California. His first one-reeler for Keystone was *Making a Living* (February 2, 1914), in which Minta Durfee (wife of Roscoe "Fatty" Arbuckle) was his leading lady. In his second Sennett effort, the half-reel comedy *Kid Auto Races at Venice*, the Tramp character emerged that would sustain the bulk of his screen career.

Chaplin's Tramp was a sartorial contradiction. To baggy pants were added a tight coat over his slight shoulders, an undersized derby hat, and oversized shoes worn in opposition to the actual size of his feet. This tattered elegance was embellished with a

---

* Sydney at the age of four would be given his stepfather's surname of Chaplin.

* Arthur Stanley Jefferson, later famous as Stan Laurel, was his understudy.

In Making a Living *(1914)*.

small black toothbrush moustache, and given a flexible cane. Later the costume begat the man. Accepting adversity with a resigned shrug of his shoulders, flourishing the cane with nonchalance or as a handy weapon, he developed an inimitable but highly "imitated" shuffling walk. In moments of frequent chase, he would whirl teeter-fashion around a corner, extending one leg for balance.

If the Tramp developed as an underdog, he was also rife with human frailty. Buster Keaton would later observe, "Chaplin's Tramp was a bum with a bum's philosophy. Lovable as he was, he would steal if he got the chance." Mack Sennett would recall, "It was a long time before Chaplin abandoned cruelty, venality, treachery, larceny, and lechery as the main characteristics of the Tramp." In later years Chaplin would say of humanity, "The human race I prefer to think of as an underworld of the gods. When the gods go slumming they visit the earth."

Mabel's Strange Predicament (1914) was the first of several one-reelers he made with Mabel Normand. Although he gleaned a good deal of comedy nuance and timing from Mabel, he was dissatisfied with her brief directorial efforts. He then persuaded Sennett to let him write and direct his own comedies. Of the 35 Keystone comedies Chaplin made for Sennett, he wrote and directed over 20 of them. But it was the first Sennett-directed feature-length comedy *Tillie's Punctured Romance* (1914), starring Marie Dressler, that brought Chaplin international fame.

Essanay offered Chaplin 10 times his Keystone salary to make his own comedies for their release. After *His New Job*,* the first Essanay two-reeler and made in Chicago, Charlie moved his operations to California. He made a guest appearance in "Bronco Billy"

* Gloria Swanson played a stenographer.

Anderson's one-reel Western *His Regeneration*, and hired blonde Edna Purviance to be his leading lady in the four Essanay comedies he would make at Niles, California. He later moved his facilities to Los Angeles, where he completed his contracted 14 Essanay comedies. One of the best was the four-reeler *Charlie Chaplin's Burlesque of Carmen* (1916). After *Police*, Chaplin left Essanay to accept Mutual's $670,000 offer.*

Charlie made a dozen two-reel comedies for Mutual in a new Hollywood studio, Lone Star, over a period of 18 months. The Mutuals were well made and included such classics as *The Floorwalker*, *One A.M.*, *The Rink*, and *Easy Street*. His last Mutual comedy, *The Adventurer*, was a fast-paced classic that became one of his most popular comedies; it represented the apex of his Mutual period. He gradually built up his own company of players: Eric Campbell, Albert Austin, Henry

* After Chaplin left Essanay, the studio assembled a 1918 release called *Triple Trouble*. It was composed of bits from *Police*, *Work*, and an abandoned Chaplin picture, *Life*.

Bergman, Bud Jamison, Billy Armstrong, John Rand, and Leo White, plus subsequently famous directors Wesley Ruggles and Lloyd Bacon. Cameraman Roland Totheroh started with Chaplin on his first Essanay comedy and remained with him for 37 years.

With the rise of Charlie's fame came a host who tried to imitate him on the screen. Essanay imported famous French screen comic Max Linder* to fill, unsuccessfully, the Chaplin void. Harold Lloyd freely admitted basing his "Lonesome Luke" screen character on Chaplin. Charlie's other obvious imitators were Billy West, Billie Ritchie, and Mexican actor Amador, billed as Charles Aplin. (Chaplin would sue the last one and win a judgment against him in 1925.)

In October 1917 Charlie began his own studio in Hollywood at the corner of LaBrea and Sunset Boulevard. He also signed a million-dollar contract to release his pictures through First National. After the completion of his first picture, *A Dog's Life*, he made an

* Chaplin later admitted Max Linder had great influence on the development of his own comedy.

In *The Adventurer* (1917).

In A Dog's Life *(1918)*.

exhaustive tour with Mary Pickford, Douglas Fairbanks, and Marie Dressler to open the U.S.'s Third Liberty Loan Bond Drive.

While making his hilarious war comedy, *Shoulder Arms*, in the summer of 1918, Charlie met a blue-eyed blonde actress named Mildred Harris. She was 16 years old and had been in pictures longer than Chaplin.

Mildred and Chaplin were wed on October 23, 1918. Her first pregnancy (which had hastened her marriage) turned out to be false, but in the summer of 1919 she gave birth to Chaplin's first son, who lived for only three days. The mismatched marriage was doomed from the start. Matters were not helped when Mildred insisted upon pursuing her film career under the auspicies of Louis B. Mayer.* The latter hoped that by promoting her as Mildred Harris Chaplin he could gain extra box-office revenue. Chaplin accosted Mayer in April 1920 at Los Angeles' Alexandra Hotel and invited the bantam mogul to take off his glasses. Mayer obliged and knocked Chaplin into a potted palm.

Before the Harris-Chaplin divorce on November 19, 1920, Charlie kidnapped his production of *The Kid* (1921) to prevent the film

* Mildred Harris' last shining hour was in Cecil B. DeMille's *Fool's Paradise* (1921). Thereafter, she played leads in a group of programmers throughout the Twenties. She drifted into vaudeville and burlesque, and sang in second-rate cafes until her death in 1944.

from being attached in the community property divorce settlement. *The Kid* became one of Charlie's more enduring screen classics and launched Jackie Coogan as a major silent-screen star. The comedy-drama verified Charlie's ability to handle drama as well as comedy. Chaplin made a guest appearance in his friend Douglas Fairbanks' picture, *The Nut* (1921), and ended his Associated First National contract with the memorable four-reel *The Pilgrim* (1922).

Mary Pickford, Douglas Fairbanks, D. W. Griffith, and Chaplin formed their own studio to produce and release their own pictures. The creation of United Artists in 1919 inspired the comment, "The lunatics have taken over the asylum." For his initial contribution to the alliance (once he had completed his First National contract), Chaplin decided to present his onetime paramour and long-time leading lady Edna Purviance in a modern drama. *A Woman of Paris* (1923) was sophisticated and established a pattern for later intimate screen dramas. It was a critical success, made a star of Adolphe Menjou, and ended the career of Edna Purviance.*

* Miss Purviance later made *The Education of a Prince* in France. In 1926 Chaplin starred her in his *A Woman of the Sea*, directed by Josef von Sternberg. After a preview he shelved the feature. The actress retired on a pension from Chaplin which continued until her death in 1958.

With Henry Bergman (wearing beard) and Albert Austin (in frame) in Shoulder Arms *(1918).*

Charlie's libidinous pursuits ranged from actresses May Collins, Claire Windsor, and Pola Negri to a romantic interlude with sculptress Clare Sheridan and a joyous affair with famous beauty Peggy Hopkins Joyce. As the comedy king prepared what would become his most famous film and a cinema masterpiece, *The Gold Rush* (1925), he signed an unknown young girl for his leading lady. Using the professional name of Lita Grey, she had been "The Flirting Angel" in *The Kid* and a maid in Chaplin's *The Idle Class*. Scottish-Spanish Lillita McMurray was dark and vivacious but neither photographed well nor displayed much evidence of any acting talent. But the 16-year-old was to become Mrs. Charles Chaplin.

On November 24, 1924, in Empalme, Mexico, Charlie wed Lita Grey. On June 28, 1925, a son, Charles Spencer Chaplin, Jr.* was born, and on March 30, 1926, a second son, Sydney Earle Chaplin, was born. The second Chaplin marriage was over almost as soon as it started. While Charlie sought solace in the charms of Marion Davies, Lita began sensational, headline-making divorce proceedings that have seldom, if ever, been equaled even in Hollywood.** On August 22, 1927, Lita was granted a divorce, custody of her sons,

* Charles Chaplin, Jr. (with N. and M. Rau) published *My Father, Charlie Chaplin* in 1960. He was found dead in his grandmother's Hollywood home on March 20, 1968. He died of a massive pulmonary embolism after a long history of alcoholism.

** Lita Grey Chaplin's 42-page divorce complaint, filed on January 10, 1927, was a sizzling document that sold thousands of copies. It was further expanded into a book, *Chaplin vs. Chaplin*, published in 1965. In 1966 Lita published *My Life with Chaplin*, "an intimate memoir," written with Morton Cooper. In this book she states Charles Chaplin Jr. was actually born on May 5, 1925, but she and the baby were kept hidden away for nearly two months and the doctor falsified the birth certificate to read June 28. Chaplin was afraid that a baby born less than six months after his marriage and with the mother only 16 would ruin his career.

Lita, more recently a Beverly Hills department-store saleslady, has lately reflected, about Chaplin, "He was undoubtedly the greatest comedian in the world, but personally he had no sense of humor at all. Charlie's conversation was not witty, he didn't tell jokes, and he never found it easy to laugh at his own behavior. In a way, he wasn't living in this world with real people—he was living in his own world on the screen. . . . Charlie was probably worth $15 million when he married me. But on one occasion I ran up a drugstore bill of $35 or $36, and the man who handled Charlie's business affairs warned me he'd have to tell Mr. Chaplin if I didn't watch it. . . . And once I offered to end our disastrous marriage for $10,000 and child support—but Charlie refused. I think he was always worried about being broke again."

and a $200,000 trust fund for the offspring, plus a $600,000 settlement.

The Gold Rush remains as one of the silent screen's greatest pictures.* It is filled with such fondly recalled sequences as Charlie's famous New Year's Eve party to which no one comes, the delightful "dance of the rolls," the dinner of boiled shoe and laces, and the thrilling teetering of the cabin on an icy cliff. The picture added to Chaplin's mounting millions in income. It also demonstrated that the magical Charlie, unlike Roscoe "Fatty" Arbuckle and Mabel Normand, was able to survive the various scandals during his career.

Chaplin gave *The Circus* a lavish production. Although the silent feature was completed at the end of 1926, his involvement in Lita Grey's divorce litigation prevented its release until January 1928. During the filming of the picture his mother Hannah, whom he and Sydney had brought over from England in 1921, died. *The Circus* was a financial success and was one of 1928's 10 best films. At the first annual Academy Award banquet (May 16, 1929) Charlie was awarded an honorary statuette "for versatility and genius in writing, acting, directing, and producing *The Circus*." In another of 1928's best pictures, King Vidor's *Show People* (MGM), starring Marion Davies and William Haines, Chaplin had a brief scene with Miss Davies and appeared with other stars in a luncheon sequence.

Warner Bros.' *The Jazz Singer* (1927) made even the most skeptical observer realize that talkie features would soon be here to stay. But Chaplin resisted the trend. He insisted that the worldwide appeal of his "Little Fellow" would be destroyed by dialogue. He was probably right. He later wrote, "But I was determined to continue making silent films, for I believed there was room for all types of entertainment. Besides, I was a pantomimist, and in that medium I was unique and, without false modesty, a master. So I continued with the production of another silent picture, *City Lights*." Nearly two years later Chaplin spent three months composing a score for the picture and synchronizing it on

* Georgia Hale replaced Lita as Chaplin's leading lady in *The Gold Rush*. In 1942 Chaplin would reissue his masterpiece with a musical score composed by him and add an amusing soundtrack to the film; he read the narration.

With Merna Kennedy and Henry Bergman in The Circus *(1928).*

film. The prestigious motion picture opened on February 6, 1931, on Broadway to glowing praise for one of Chaplin's finest motion pictures. Virginia Cherrill, a strikingly beautiful blonde, was Chaplin's leading lady as the blind flower girl.

Three years later Chaplin, still maintaining screen silence as the last unvocal major star, started another *silent* picture. Charlie's statement on man's mechanization was called *Modern Times* (1936). For all of its several remembered scenes and the Chaplin-composed score that included the haunting song "Smile," it was a flawed entry. It suffered from Chaplin's intense political observations and a dimmed likeness to Rene Clair's *A Nous la Liberté* (1931), a brilliant satire on the machine age. But *Modern Times* did have Chaplin talk-singing on film (a nonsense song) and offered a striking performance from Paulette Goddard, a beautiful, vivacious young actress. It was a tribute to Chaplin's tutelage that he presented her

gamine role with such great care and saw to it that her acting technique was polished. With *Modern Times* in release Chaplin left on a world tour with Miss Goddard. Somewhere between Los Angeles and Singapore she became Mrs. Charles Chaplin. (In her ultimate divorce decree, she would list Canton, China, as the site of the 1936 nuptials.)

Charlie's inevitable full-fledged entry into the speaking screen was ill-timed. For his true talking-picture debut he wrote a satire called *The Great Dictator.* In it he played a dual role—Adenoid Hynkel, dictator of Tomania, and a meek Jewish barber. The controversial picture pointed up the oft-mentioned physical resemblance of Adolf Hitler to Chaplin. In the dual part, Chaplin gave a performance of stunning virtuosity. The feature contained the now famous sequence of Chaplin's dictator engaging in a bubble dance-ballet with a globe of the world and a zesty performance from Jack Oakie as the Mussolini-like tyrant, Benzino Napaloni.

182

To end the film there was a mawkish, impassioned six-minute speech read by Chaplin. The sermon on democracy detracted from the plunging satire, although outside the critical arena it was widely quoted and applauded.

But by the time *The Great Dictator* was released on October 15, 1940, Hitler's madness had passed beyond ridicule, and Charlie's satire met with a good deal of stern resistance from many sources. *Time* magazine summarized the film, "Almost everybody will have to see this picture because it is Chaplin's first in four years. Almost nobody will ever want to see it again—as people still want to see *The Kid* and *Shoulder Arms*." On the other hand, *The Great Dictator* was nominated for Academy Awards as the Best Picture of the Year, Best Actor (Chaplin) of the Year, and Best Supporting Actor (Oakie) of the Year. The Oscars went elsewhere. The New York Film Critics Award for 1940's Best Actor of the Year went to Chaplin. He refused it.

Unlike Chaplin's other leading ladies, Paulette Goddard achieved screen stardom on her own in Bob Hope's *The Cat and the Canary* (1939) and *The Ghost Breakers* (1940) and in *The Great Dictator* (playing the Jewish girl Hannah). As a Paramount star she went on to become one of the leading sex symbols of the World War II era. In June 1942 she divorced Charlie after a year's separation.* Paulette won a divorce decree *in absentia* in Juarez, Mexico. The following month Chaplin unwisely injected himself into world controversy by demanding that England and the United States open a second front in support of Russia's war effort.

While his political presumptions were decried in the press, he created further headlines by his involvement with a star-struck Brooklyn girl, formerly befriended by millionaire Paul Getty. In June 1941 Chaplin was grooming the 22-year-old aspiring actress

* Bachelor Charlie found solace with actresses Hedy Lamarr and Carole Landis.

With Chuck Hamilton, Stanley "Tiny" Sanford, Bobby Barber, Harry Wilson, and Walter James in Modern Times *(1936).*

As The Great Dictator
(1940).

Joan Barry for the lead in his projected screen project *Shadow and Substance.* The picture was never made but l'affaire Barry was headlined in the papers for a long time. In a devastating paternity suit, she stated that during her Chaplin tutelage she underwent two abortions before the birth of her daughter, Carol Ann, on October 2, 1943. Chaplin remained remarkably calm. The ensuing trial, in which the federal government became strangely involved, finally exonerated Chaplin. Even more strange, despite his submitting to a blood test and the impressive medical testimony to support the contention that he was *not* the father of Miss Barry's child, he was ordered by the California court to support Joan Barry's daughter.

During the several years of headlines, Charlie remarried. Oona O'Neill, the daughter of playwright Eugene O'Neill, was another candidate for the lead in the projected *Shadow and Substance.* She was 18 when on June 16, 1943, 54-year-old Chaplin married her in the home of a justice of the peace, Clinton Pancoast Moore, in the village of Carpinteria, outside Santa Barbara, California. On July 31, 1944, their first child, Geraldine, was born, followed on March 6, 1946, by son Michael John and later by daughters Josephine and Victoria.

If *The Great Dictator* had removed Charlie some degrees from his famous Little Tramp, *Monsieur Verdoux* (1947) completed the process. Some deem the macabre comedy of a modern Bluebeard the cleverest film he made. There was no controversy about Martha Raye's highly comedic performance. But there was a good deal of dispute about the film's philosophy that an individual who commits single homicides will be condemned by society, while governments are allowed to commit mass murder in war ("Numbers sanctify"). The film was attacked by the press and the public, and was more banned than booked.

His last American-made motion picture was *Limelight* (1952)* in which he played a declining music-hall star named Calvero. The picture's finest moment is the teaming of Buster Keaton and Charlie in an all too brief but hilarious music-hall bit. *Limelight* benefited by Chaplin's lovely score—which included the hit song "Eternally"—and a fine performance by Claire Bloom in her film debut. But the noncomedic, sentimental drama was called a self-indulgent, overblown exercise. Some said his playing of the clown Calvero brimmed with a "false humility that is integral to the film's unpleasant egotism." Other comments were generous: "One might as well criticize a rose for having thorns as condemn *Limelight* for its faults; it is a kind of cinematic poem about humanity, and if it does not scan mathematically, it touches the heart with its dramatic images of longing" (Otis L. Guernsey Jr., *New York Herald-Tribune*).

With the completion of *Limelight*, Chaplin and his family sailed for England on the *Queen Elizabeth*. While at sea he learned that he would be barred from reentering the United States. It seemed that the U.S. attorney general had forbidden his return to the U.S. without an investigation concerning his "Communistic sympathies and moral turpitude."

At the Paris premiere of *Limelight*, Charlie was given the rank of an officer of the French Legion of Honor and made an honorary member of the Société des Auteurs et Compositeurs Dramatiques. The Chaplin family settled in the Swiss village of Corsier, above Vevey. There son Eugene was born and later the Chaplins became the parents of Jane, Annette, and Christopher.

A King in New York was a bitter comedy made by Chaplin in 1957.** The often embarrassing picture was a feeble satire on the anti-red McCarthy era and had Chaplin appearing as the ex-king of a nameless country who comes to Manhattan for sanctuary and soon realizes that America is "insane." The film was finally released in the U.S. in December 1973. Like the 1952 government charges against Charlie, the strident protests of his *King* seemed rather foolish.

In 1959 Chaplin assembled a compilation, *The Chaplin Revue*, containing three of his First National films: *A Dog's Life*, *Shoulder Arms*, and *The Pilgrim*. Chaplin narrated the film and composed an exceptionally fine score.

For some strange reasons (above and beyond their box-office appeal) Chaplin chose to star two noncomedy players, Sophia Loren and Marlon Brando, in a comedy, *A Countess from Hong Kong* (1967).* Son Sydney again played the juvenile lead, and daughters Geraldine, Josephine, and Victoria made cameo appearances as did Chaplin himself (as a seasick steward). In England, the British *Monthly Film Bulletin* tersely commented on the long-winded, poorly directed film: "The saddest thing about this wan romantic comedy is that there is absolutely nothing to say about it."

In 1972 amidst much publicity and all-is-forgiven sentiment, Charlie returned to Hollywood to accept personally a special award from the Academy of Motion Picture Arts and Sciences. The Chaplin Award ("for the incalculable effect he has had in making motion pictures the art form of the century") was the highlight of the 44th Annual Academy Awards. It helped to compensate for the exclusion of his name from Hollywood Boulevard's "Walk of Fame" in 1960.

As Chaplin reached his late 80s his health deteriorated greatly. In 1976 he suffered a stroke and was mostly confined to a wheelchair. On April 16, 1977, when he celebrated his 88th birthday, his wife and their eight children were all gathered at the Chaplin home for the occasion. Monica de Montel, Charlie's former secretary, said at the time, "He is in his own little world now. His life has run its path." No longer had the Little Tramp plans of reactivating *The Freak*, a whimsical story about an angel coming to earth. He had

* Chaplin's son Sydney played the romantic lead in the picture, son Charles Jr. was a clown in a ballet sequence, and Geraldine, Michael, and Josephine appeared in one scene.

** Michael Chaplin performed well in *A King in New York*. In 1966 Michael's book *I Couldn't Smoke the Grass on My Father's Lawn* was published. Two years before, in 1964, Charles Chaplin published *My Autobiography*, a massive account of his life, career, and philosophy. For Richard Patterson's film documentary, *The Gentleman Tramp* (1975), Laurence Olivier read passages from Chaplin's *Autobiography*. Walter Matthau supplied the narration in addition to appearing in special filmed segments with Chaplin.

* At one time in the late Thirties, Chaplin planned this project as a vehicle for Paulette Goddard and himself.

written it years before for Victoria, but shelved it when she wed circus performer Jean-Baptiste Thierry in 1971. Chaplin's last published book in the United States was *My Life in Pictures* (1975) for which he wrote lengthy captions for the many photographs highlighting his long career.

At 4:00 A.M. on Christmas Day of 1977 Charlie Chaplin died peacefully at his Switzerland home. His wife Oona and seven of their children were at his bedside. (Geraldine was making a film in Madrid at the time.) Lady Chaplin informed a caller that day, "All the presents were under the tree. Charlie gave so much happiness and, although he had been ill for a long time, it is so sad that he should have passed away on Christmas Day." (Charlie's final public appearance had been when he attended a circus show in Vevey in the fall.) Chaplin was buried in the cemetery at Corsier-sur-Vevey on Tuesday, December 27. A brief Church of England service, consisting of commitment prayers, was held at the private funeral.

A bizarre episode occurred on March 2, 1978, when the body of Charlie Chaplin was stolen from its grave. A tremendous amount of publicity ensued, but it was not until some 12 weeks later that his body was recovered and reburied in a concrete vault in the small cemetery at Corsier-sur-Vevey. Apprehended were two refugees from Poland and Bulgaria who had stolen the 300-pound oak coffin and buried it in a cornfield 10 miles from the village. Their plans for a $600,000 ransom had gone afoul. The Chaplin family remained silent during the strange situation and only Oona, a few of the Chaplin children, and Gino Terni, the family butler, attended the reinterment. A much less publicized event during this period was the abandonment of plans for a life-size bronze statue of Chaplin to be erected near his birthplace in Lambeth, South London. The Greater London Council's Art Committee vetoed the idea for two reasons: the cost and the fact that Chaplin had "deserted" London in 1910 to rebase in America.

Meanwhile, Chaplin's death caused renewed interest in his movie output. Several of his feature films and compilations of his shorts were leased to a home video cassette distributor, and *A Woman of Paris* received national art-house release in the United States. Reported Vincent Canby in the *New York Times:* "The film is not only a treasure in itself—witty, sophisticated and often beautifully funny, though it means to be 'serious,' as Chaplin says—it's also a rare opportunity to see what Chaplin is like as a filmmaker when he is not contemplating his own image. *A Woman of Paris* is immensely entertaining, but, more important, it's an inside report on the essential Chaplin talent that, in the films in which he is also a star, seems so closely bound to the performer's personality we can't easily tell where one starts and the other leaves off." Also rushed into release was a "new" documentary, *The Gentleman Tramp,* devoted to the life of the comedian; Laurence Olivier, Walter Matthau, and Jack Lemmon supplied the offscreen narration.

Of the many tributes and eulogies engendered by Chaplin's death, perhaps the most perspicacious salutation occurred in a *New York Times* editorial:

> . . . Charlie was always in a class of his own. His was one of those precious talents that bridge the gap between

popular and highbrow art. Three generations of audiences have joined in laughter at the Little Tramp and recognized that in laughing at that jaunty figure, we laugh at our common predicament, the commotion we cause and the indignities we suffer trying to come to terms with the vagaries of the world.

Whatever Charlie Chaplin's political or personal predilections, they did not matter much then and do not matter at all now. What does matter is the finesse with which he eats a boiled shoe in *The Gold Rush* and attempts to eat corn on the cob from the assembly-line food-feeder in *Modern Times;* his triumph over the bully, with the help of a gas lamp, in *Easy Street;* his ballet with a globe of the world in *The Great Dictator.* What matters is the poignant ending of *City Lights,* when the girl who has regained her eyesight first sees the funny-looking little fellow to whom she owes so much. The feelings they continue to evoke in movie theaters around the world will be Charlie Chaplin's undying eulogy.

FEATURE FILMS

Tillie's Punctured Romance (*Keystone 1914*)
  (TV title: Charlie's Big Romance)
Charlie Chaplin's Burlesque of Carmen (*Essanay 1916*)
The Kid (*Associated First National 1921*)
The Nut (*United Artists 1921*)*
A Woman of Paris (*United Artists 1923*)*
The Pilgrim (*Associated First National 1923*)
Souls for Sale (*Goldwyn 1923*)
The Gold Rush (*United Artists 1925*)

The Circus (*United Artists 1928*)
Show People (*MGM 1928*)
City Lights (*United Artists 1931*)
Modern Times (*United Artists 1936*)
The Great Dictator (*United Artists 1940*)
Monsieur Verdoux (*United Artists 1947*)
Limelight (*United Artists 1952*)
A King in New York (*British 1957*)
A Countess from Hong Kong (*Universal 1967*)*

* Unbilled guest appearance.

The comedian.

Charley Chase

The greatest mystery of Charley Chase's prolific but obscure screen career is its *apparent* lack of mystery. The neglect that Chase as a performer suffered during the Forties and early Fifties can be explained by the lack of flamboyance and exaggeration in his screen persona and by the absence of real tragedy in his personal life. Unlike Buster Keaton, Ben Turpin, and others, Chase never made the transition to cameo player in feature-length comedies. His domain was strictly the two-reeler, and he appeared in only six full-length motion pictures (and one serial) in his entire career.

When James Agee wrote his famous essay on silent comedy which appeared in *Life* magazine in 1949, the astute critic neglected even to mention Chase. It was not until filmmaker Robert Youngson began producing his series of well-exploited compendiums that Chase enjoyed a renaissance. Within *Laurel and Hardy's Laughing Twenties* (1965) the narrator enters into a lengthy digression (illustrated by a Charley Chase short that is extraneous to the compilation's subject) about how sad it is that the two-

reeler's greatest star, Chase, should be so forgotten four decades later. In other compilations (*When Comedy Was King, The Golden Age of Comedy*, and *Four Clowns*) Youngson took pains carefully to edit material to demonstrate why Chase deserved to be on equal footing with Keaton, Laurel and Hardy, and perhaps even Charlie Chaplin himself. Had these compendiums not appeared at a time (the Sixties) when audiences' sensibilities were geared to television domestic comedy, it is unlikely that the Chase revival would ever have taken place.

The type of two-reeler exploiting the plight of the average man was Chase's forte, and new generations of filmgoers felt very much at ease watching him cavort through assorted domestic traumas. After all, they had been watching similar, if a little more sophisticated, fare on the small screen for years.

He was born on Friday, October 20, 1893, in Baltimore, Maryland, to Charles and Blanche Thompson Parrott.* Little has been discov-

* There was an older brother, James, born in 1892. He would die on May 11, 1939, having had a fascinating career as both motion picture actor and director.

ered about the specific details of his childhood or education other than that several years were spent performing in vaudeville and burlesque and even on Broadway before he made his way to Hollywood in 1914. There he found work with the Al Christie filmmaking unit at Universal before teaming up with Mack Sennett during film comedy's most inspired and fruitful period.

As an actor (using the name Charley Chase), his work for Sennett amounted to little more than extra-work and bit roles, supporting the likes of Charlie Chaplin and Fatty Arbuckle. He even appeared in the feature *Tillie's Punctured Romance* (1914) with Chaplin, Mabel Normand, and Marie Dressler, a motion picture which proved to be the vanguard of burgeoning American screen comedy. But as Chase lacked a gimmick in physical appearance (he appeared too normal and dapper for knockabout comedy), Sennett made little use of his skills as a comedian.

Nevertheless, the Sennett film factory proved to be an excellent training ground for the young actor. Like both Chaplin and Arbuckle, Charley became interested in the technical side of the new medium, and would co-direct several comedy shorts with Ford Sterling and Arbuckle. For these pictures he used his real name, Charles Parrott. Among the stars he directed were Bobby Vernon, Chester Conklin, Gloria Swanson, Hank Mann, and Wallace Beery in film shorts like *Hearts and Sparks*, *His Father's Footsteps*, *The Hunt*, and *His Pride and Shame*.

After achieving full rank as a director with Sennett, Charley departed abruptly to join Fox Films as a comedy director. But in 1916 most other studios' comedies were but pale attempts to duplicate Sennett's distinguished screen mayhem. The somewhat arrogant young Chase found that Fox's stable of movie comics was decidedly second-string compared to Sennett and his stable, and that most of the comedy material was provided by parodying recent screen successes.

From 1916 until the early Twenties Chase pursued the career of full-time director at Fox, Paramount, and Universal, apparently having abandoned his original intention of becoming a motion picture comic. Among his films during this period were several early collaborations with Oliver Hardy, including *The Handy Man*, *Bright and Early*, *The Straight and Narrow*, *Playmates*, and *Hop the Bellboy*. He also directed Mr. and Mrs. Carter DeHaven (Gloria's parents) in a series of two-reel comedies for Paramount and guided Lloyd Hamilton through *April Fool* (1920) and *Moonshine* (1921) at Educational Films.

Since most of these early pictures have unfortunately vanished into dust, it is impossible to assess their value. But in the days of early silent comedy, the role of the director was a thankless one, and Chase had little opportunity to work with first-rate comedy talent since most studios were all too quick to concede comedy kingship to the Sennett facilities. Nevertheless, his array of comedy shorts did permit Charley to perfect and develop many of his comedy ideas. Then too his experience as a director would be important to his years as a screen funster. It was around this time that Chase's brother James, working under the name of James Parrott, also came to Hollywood and began a prestigious directing career of his own.

It was filmmaker Hal Roach who came to Chase's professional rescue. He founded the only Hollywood comedy unit ever to rival Sennett's for popularity and innovation. Having inherited some money, Roach began his studio in 1915 with Harold Lloyd (a comic to whom Chase has frequently been compared) as his central star. Most of Roach's other contract comics were character figures like Billy Bevan and Snub Pollard, who were generally supporting players in the Lloyd comedy series. When Lloyd left the Roach unit in the early Twenties to investigate the possibilities of the feature film (as Chaplin had done), Roach attempted to promote Pollard and Bevan to star status. He assigned Chase (who used the name of Charles Parrott) as director-general of the studio. Here Chase found the necessary spirit of comic improvisation that had been so badly lacking at the other California studios. His only difficulty at this period was that his career frequently collided with that of his brother James, who was directing two-reelers and even appearing as an actor under the name of Paul Parrott in short subjects with Snub Pollard.

The flexibility as writer, director, and actor required of full-time employees at the Roach lot explains Charley's appearance in *Her Dangerous Path*, a 1923 Roach serial (in seven parts). He turned up in the Western *The King of the Wild Horses* (1924) as Edna Murphy's brother. Both he and Miss Murphy received billing *beneath* Rex the Wonder Horse. Perhaps his participation in these straight parts whetted his desire to return to performing. Thus in 1923 Chase began the most famous phase of his career, starring in a batch of one- and two-reelers for Roach, some of them directed by his able brother, James.

It may have been something of an exaggeration on Robert Youngson's part to claim that Chase was at one time the most popular comedy short star of the Twenties. But it is possible to understand the novelty of his appeal. Whereas Chaplin, Turpin, Pollard, and the Keystone Kops represented the extraordinary, and in some cases the grotesque, Chase hit upon the notion of domesticity in his screen comedy. He became the frequently brash and self-assured young man in a cultural background of the kind imaged in the novels of Sinclair Lewis. The screen type that Chase developed lacked the pathos of shyness that Harold Lloyd discovered could sustain the physical gags for the length of a feature.

In his book *The Silent Clowns* (1975) Walter Kerr perhaps best sums up Chase's virtues and predicament: "Charley Chase could be counted on to fill out a release schedule with a steady supply of more than acceptable two-reelers. But there was no pushing Chase beyond a sprightly domestic base, or toward features; his trim face and manner had no fairy-tale excess in them, no line to invite a caricaturist's ballooning, no mystery to be wrestled with. He would always be at his best as a faintly fussed Mr. Normal. . . . He was trapped between the arbitrary gagging of his Sennett origins and the sheer, not unattractive, ordinariness of his appearance."

Nevertheless, Charley's comedies were very frequently excellent. They provided a training ground for directors like Leo Mc-Carey and paved the way for the more conventional—and successful—plots of TV situ-

In His Wooden Wedding *(1925).*

ation comedies of the Fifties. Such Chase entries as *His Wooden Wedding, Bromo and Juliet, Mighty Like a Moose, Innocent Husbands,* and *Forgotten Sweeties* contain remarkably subtle domestic situations which would not seem to lend themselves to the pantomime of silent comedy. But through the slick pacing of directors James Parrott and Leo McCarey, the shorts work quite effectively. Then too, attractive leading ladies like Martha Sleeper and Katherine Grant contributed to the credibility of the situations. Unlike the occasional wives or girlfriends in the Laurel and Hardy comedies, the spouses in Chase films were presented sympathetically and rarely emerged as shrews.

Although small-town comedies like *Family Group* (1928) and *Movie Night* (1929) are typical of Chase's best-remembered offerings, complicated Grustarkian plots like *Long Fliv the King* (1926) come across quite well because of Chase's impeccable comic taste. If later critics would attack Charley for his alleged lack of comic "uniqueness," his adaptability as a performer was certainly greater than that of many of his contemporaries.

In 1929 Charlie made his talkie debut on loan-out to Universal in one of his rare excursions into the feature-length film. *Modern Love,* in which he co-starred opposite Jean Hersholt and Kathryn Crawford, was an awkward part-talkie combination of music, comedy, and romance. It was based on the "chestnut" (even for the Twenties) of the couple that must keep their marriage secret for professional reasons. Chase was first-billed as the romantic lead, but a surprising number of the film's occasional comic possibilities were given to Hersholt (as the visiting European nobleman). Charley did have an opportunity to sing ("You Can't Buy Love") and it was the first of many occasions in which his surprisingly well-trained singing voice would be a part of his screen work.

Back at the Roach studio, Chase began his series of talkie shorts. Although he was apprehensive about the advent of sound and its effect on screen comedy, his new work frequently surpassed the quality of his silents. His good friend Billy Gilbert reported that Charley "felt uncomfortable in talking pictures; his great forte was pantomime and a funny way of handling his body." Gilbert

With Carl Stockdale (left) in the short subject All Teed Up *(1930).*

192

With Edna Marion in a
MGM short (c.1930).

The star adrift in a
comedy short of the
30s.

was referring to Chase's Paul Lynde-like twitchiness.

But if anything, sound provided greater scope for Charley's characterizations. With the advent of commercial sound, the Roach lot expanded its stock company of players and was now releasing its product through MGM. Among the new additions to the Chase unit over the next several years were Thelma Todd, Billy Gilbert, Muriel Evans, Constance Bergen, Betty Mack, Andrea Leeds, Julie Bishop, Charlie Hall, Del Henderson, and the Ranch Boys (Jimmy Adams, Marvin Hartley, and Frank Gage). In addition, Charley took up direction of many of the entries himself: *Midsummer Mush* (1933), *Four Parts* (1934)—in which he played quadruplets—and *Nurse to You* (1935), to name a few. He also directed ZaSu Pitts and Thelma Todd in *The Bargain of the Century* (1933), possibly the best entry in their comedy series.

The advent of sound also encouraged more experimentation at the Roach unit. In addition to adding songs (some composed by Chase himself) to the shorts, several entries were expanded to three reels. (These latter pictures—*Dollar Dizzy*, 1930, *High C's*, 1930, and its sequel, *Rough Seas*, 1931—often betrayed their padding.) *The Tabasco Kid* (1932), in which Charley plays a Mexican bandit, and *Nature in the Wrong* (1933), a gloriously funny spoof of Tarzan, revealed that Charley was capable of some very inventive surrealistic humor when liberated from his usual suburban setting.

Although he confined most of his activities to Roach shorts, Charley did make two important features for the producer during the Thirties. In what today would be regarded as a cameo role, he appeared as Laurel and Hardy's fellow lodge brother in that team's most famous talkie, *Sons of the Desert* (1933). It was an offbeat performance as an unsympathetically loud-mouthed Babbitt figure. (One can only wonder what filmmaker Preston Sturges might have made of Chase as a member of the Quail and Ale Club in *The Palm Beach Story*, 1942.) In 1936

In Hasty Marriage *(1931).*

194

With Laurel and Hardy in Sons of the Desert *(1933).*

Chase played a more sympathetic character role as J. Willoughby Klum in *Kelly the Second* (1936). Although raucous Patsy Kelly was ostensibly the lead, Charley's performing nicely softened Miss Kelly's brash antics.

Of Charley's performance in that picture, Donald W. McCaffrey in his book *The Golden Age of Sound Comedy* (1973) wrote, "The most skilled acting in the picture, however, can be seen in Charley Chase's Doc Klum. Deftly, the actor produces excellent scenes of comic pretension and frustration. Bragging about his pugilist, Cecil Callahan (Guinn 'Big Boy' Williams), Doc gets involved with gangster Ike Arnold (Edward Brophy) who fixes fights. It may be that Chase's 'fall guy' portrait—a man who is on the receiving end of a joke—was not the kind of characterization which writers could use as a protagonist. Perhaps, too, the personality may not have had enough box-office appeal for the studios to place him as a lead in features. But looking with the perspective of a critic three decades removed, I wish they had at least tried."

Indeed, one other attempt to star Chase in a feature—*Neighborhood House* (1936)—was deemed so disastrous that after previews Chase had to re-edit the picture into a two-reeler, and an abrupt one at that. Roach's increasing interest in the more lucrative feature film, and the failure of *Neighborhood House*, caused Chase and Roach to terminate their association in 1936.

The year 1936 was a critical one in Charley's life. The indifference of critics to *Kelly the Second* and his belief that he should remain with short subjects led Chase at the last moment to reject the comedy lead in George Stevens' *A Damsel in Distress* (1937). One can only speculate on whether his role was the one eventually played by Reginald Gardiner or whether his part was rewritten to accommodate George Burns and Gracie Allen.

At any rate, Chase would never leave the two-reel comedy field. After appearing as master of ceremonies for MGM's motley Technicolor short *Hollywood Party* (1937),

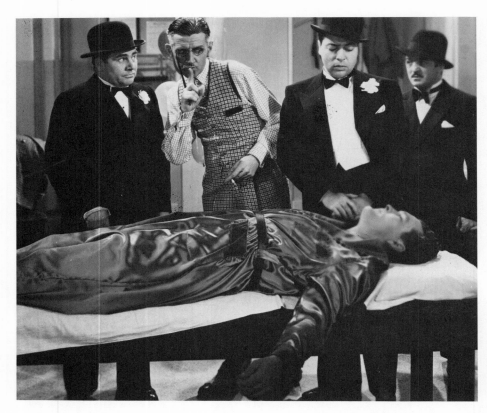

With Ed Brophy,
Harold Huber, Jack
Raymond, and Guinn
"Big Boy" Williams
(on table) in Kelly
the Second (1936).

Charley signed a contract to make two-reelers for Columbia Pictures. In addition to starring in a series of domestic comedies with Ann Doran (she regards him as "one of the overlooked greats in the comedy field"), Chase directed the Three Stooges, Andy Clyde, and Smith and Dale in comedy shorts.

The high quality so typical of the Roach entries was maintained in Chase's Columbia output. However, by 1940 the spontaneity seemed to be evaporating from the short-subject product. But not so with Chase. In one of his last pictures, The Heckler (1940)—in a cast which included Dorothy Comingore, Bruce Bennett, and Robert Sterling—Charley demonstrated that he would risk playing an unsympathetic character in order to explore new comedy areas. Rather than situation, the comedy was based on a "type" of person, the poor sport, suggesting something of the "Pete Smith Specialties" at MGM.

Of Chase's private life, too little is known. Most is conjecture. Actor Billy Gilbert once suggested that Chase and his wife, Babe Ettinge, had an "arrangement" for most of their marriage, revealing that they were separated, although he would visit her and their

two daughters (in Palm Springs on week-ends). Chase also suffered from a drinking problem, although this clearly did not affect either the quality or the enormous output of his work. His doctor warned him about excessive drinking, but the actor would not listen. He died abruptly of a heart attack on June 20, 1940, at the age of 47. He was survived by his widow and children, each of whom has married (Mrs. James Prishaw and Mrs. Donald Harris).

It is fascinating to speculate on the roles that Charley might have played had he lived and had he decided to leave the diminishing field of the short subject. At the time of his death he was negotiating to star in Worth a Million for the Shuberts on Broadway. Imagine Chase as Don Ameche's stuffy rival, Albert Van Cleve; in Ernst Lubitsch's Heaven Can Wait; or as Herbie Hawkins, the detective-story addict of Alfred Hitchcock's Shadow of a Doubt. In his own way he would have been as effective as Joe E. Brown playing the Tommy Manville–like millionaire in Billy Wilder's Some Like It Hot. One can only wonder at the missed opportunities as one enjoys the wonderful heritage of Chase's short subjects.

196

FEATURE FILMS

Tillie's Punctured Romance (*Keystone 1914*)
Her Dangerous Path (*Pathé* serial 1923)
The King of the Wild Horses (*Pathé 1924*)
Modern Love (*Universal 1929*)

Sons of the Desert (*MGM 1933*)
Kelly the Second (*MGM 1936*)
Neighborhood House (*MGM 1936*)

With Jack Oakie in She Wrote the Book (1946).

Joan Davis

In the late Forties, when Barbra Streisand was still a toddler, the legendary Fanny Brice was asked by the press who her personal choice was to portray her life on stage or in the movies, or both. "There's one dame that could play me," answered Fanny without hesitation. "That's Joan Davis."

Joan Davis was indeed a perfect selection to portray the unglamorous, somewhat clumsy, inexhaustibly talented Fanny. Miss Davis was one of the Thirties' most popular comediennes, usurping the position of Patsy Kelly as Twentieth Century–Fox's number one comic lady. On one occasion an entranced reviewer from the *New York Times* described Joan to his readers as "a strange female curtain climber, with a trick of punching herself in the jaw and a curious resemblance to Olive Oyl in the cartoons."

In the Forties Joan would become an enduring star of radio and in the next decade claim fame with a TV series. In whatever medium she performed, she was a master of slapstick, song, and comic inflection. In her comic offerings she was one of the first

women to employ successfully the art of self-depreciation (brought to a full boil later by Phyllis Diller). Davis would lacerate herself with insults, throw herself against inanimate objects, or do whatever was necessary to show an amused audience that she was indeed disgusted with her (professional) oafish self. As Joan once reflected, "Laughs are based on other people's misfortunes—it's awful, isn't it. A good fall always gets a laugh."

What made Joan even more fascinating as an enduring performer was the high degree of intelligence that lay beneath all of her apparent lowbrow buffoonery. Today there may be a Joan Rivers, a Phyllis Diller, a Ruth Buzzi, or a Lily Tomlin to amuse TV and club audiences. But in the Thirties through the Fifties there was Joan Davis, who combined in one individual the best performing aspects of all these later-day funsters.

She was born Madonna Josephine Davis on Saturday, June 29, 1907, in St. Paul, Minnesota. Her father, LeRoy, was a train dispatcher; her mother, Nina, was a housewife. At three the future star was capering in local church socials and at six was signed by the Pantages Theatre circuit, billed as the "Toy Comedienne" and "Cyclonic Josephine Davis." When stage work was not available, the youngster returned to school in St. Paul. Despite her sporadic attendance, she graduated as class valedictorian from Mechanic Arts High School.

Completing her formal education, she took an $8 weekly job at the local five-and-dime, where her work at the goldfish department foreshadowed her future absurdities. (She would ask customers if they wanted the fish wrapped as a gift!) Eventually she accepted the inevitable that she must be a part of show business. She ran off to join the rapidly failing vaudeville circuits, this time playing summer camps and amusement parks when no other engagements were available. Though professional life was often far from pleasant, Joan would later recall her years of "life in a suitcase" as the backbone of her success. "Most of the good comedians on the screen today started out in vaudeville. And I think that's the only way in which one may learn the important business of timing one's act to get the best laugh return. After you'd been on the vaudeville circuit grind for a couple of years, facing all sorts of audiences, you developed a 'feel' for the comedy situations that carried you through."

Searching for a straight man for her act, Madonna Josephine—now billed as Joan Davis—teamed with veteran Serenus (Si) Willis. They not only worked well together, but also fell in love. They married on August 13, 1931, in Chicago, and honeymooned on the road. A daughter, Beverly, was born on August 6, 1933.

Like most comics hoping to escalate their career prestige and income, Joan hoped to gravitate to the movies, the medium which was plunging vaudeville into deeper and deeper oblivion. In early 1935 the team's nomadic wanderings placed the Willis family in Los Angeles. Joan invited all her old vaudeville pals to a party and requested Mack Sennett to attend. She unabashedly performed one stunt after another to impress the aging filmmaker. It worked. Joan was hired to perform in Sennett's last celluloid effort for Educational Pictures. *Way Up Thar* (1935) was a 20-minute short subject in which Joan sang "Comin' Round the Moun-

tain," "I'm Gonna Get Married," and "That's Why I Stutter." For good measure she included her falling-dishes routine and made a large number of contorted comic faces. Joan later recalled the filming experience: "It ran for a day and a half, including all night. Buster Keaton's mother played my mother in it. I was so worn out before I was through. I told Si: 'If this is the movies, get me out of them. I've aged so since yesterday that I won't match in the rushes.'"

Way Up Thar may have been an enervating experience, but it did win Joan some industry notice. Thereafter she appeared in Paramount's *Millions in the Air* (1935), a forgettable musical satire in which she sang "You Tell Her Because I Stutter." She got the assignment as a favor to director friend Ray McCarey. The angular, lanky Miss Davis then signed a stock contract with RKO Pictures. At the time it seemed a great break, but Joan managed to appear only in a 1936 effort, *Bunker Bean*, as a zany telephone operator. After four months the RKO contract was terminated by mutual consent. It was at this juncture that Willis and Davis encountered their most resounding failure: a stint at New York's Palace Theatre where they flopped with audiences. They quickly were booked into the far less prestigious Academy of Music on Manhattan's 14th Street, and then toured some of the surviving, less-demanding vaudeville houses.

However, Joan's life was in for a great alteration. Darryl F. Zanuck had ambitious plans to promote the newly formed Twentieth Century-Fox studio into a major contender to MGM. He planned a series of flip, fast-paced musicals to lure Depression audiences to the box office. Joan, on a return junket to the Coast, managed to secure a Fox player's contract, after pushing and pleading for a screen test. With the Fox lot boasting few already established major stars, save for Warner Baxter and Loretta Young, Joan was in a good position to accomplish her ambition: to elevate herself from a specialty act in the lot's offerings to a cinema comedienne of top ranking.

Joan's emergence on the Hollywood scene was propitiously timed. Feminine mayhem on the screen was then a popular, if rare, commodity. Martha Raye was becoming the rage at Paramount with her raucous comedy,

200

and had somewhat prepared audiences for the type of scatterbrained, frenetic versatility that Joan displayed. In 1937 Joan appeared in 11 Fox releases, supporting such studio contractees as Jane Withers, Alice Faye, Tony Martin, the Ritz Brothers, Sonja Henie, and Tyrone Power. On camera Davis would sing, dance (everything from ballet to Spanish fandangos), gawk, grimace, and perform a number of athletic, awesome pratfalls.

When Joan appeared in the Henie-Power confection *Thin Ice* (1937), as the leader of an all-girl orchestra (and singing "My Swiss Hill Billy" and "I'm Olga from the Volga"), the *Brooklyn Daily Eagle* hailed her as "indescribably funny." The reviewer added, "Mere words do not quite catch the quality of Miss Davis' brand of humor. Superficially it is slapstick, but on second consideration, it appears to be a super-sophisticated distillation of the most elegant type of humor. The comedienne goes directly to the heart of her material in an almost savage manner without once sacrificing method to mugging. You'll have to compare Miss Davis with the obvious Miss Raye to see how good she is."

Joan appeared also in 1937 in such diverse assignments as the bedpan-juggling nurse in *The Great Hospital Mystery*, as an incongruous mantrap in the Ritz Brothers' *Life Begins in College*, and as Walter Winchell's Girl Friday and Bert Lahr's romance in *Love and Hisses*. While she appeared to be simply pulling out all the joke stops in these frenetic celluloid assignments, she was actually a very disciplined performer. She told reporters, "Even with 'hokum' comedy, which looks so natural, you need to study and study. One little slip of a finger, one slightly different expression on the face may make all the difference between getting a laugh or a shrug." She also estimated that it required approximately 500 feet of film to photograph one of her trademark pratfalls.

In 1938 Fox determined to showcase Joan a little more discriminately. Studio head Zanuck told the press, "Before this year is out, Miss Davis will have won number-one ranking as a comedienne." Her first 1938 release, *Sally, Irene and Mary*, had her as part of a trio (along with Alice Faye and Marjorie Weaver) of manicurists looking for

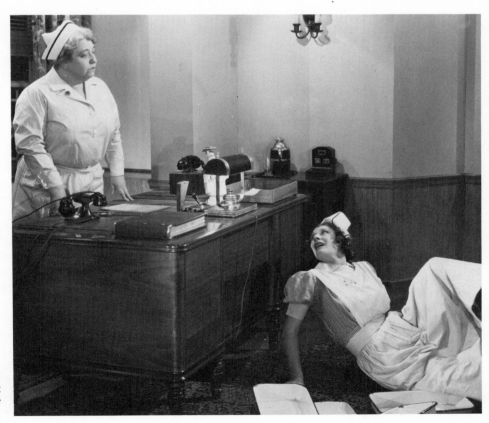

With Jane Darwell in The Great Hospital Mystery *(1937).*

show-business celebrities and matrimonial prospects. Joan agilely performed a big apple dance, sang "Who Stole the Jam?," performed "Help Wanted—Male," and with beefy, accented Gregory Ratoff dueted "I'm a Gypsy." *Josette* was a poorly received musical, despite the presence of Don Ameche, Robert Young, and Simone Simon in the cast (with Bert Lahr again as Joan's romance). But *My Lucky Star*, a twinkling Sonja Henie musical on ice, had Joan and Buddy Ebsen as an acrobatic team.* She was even better in *Hold That Co-ed*, a delight that cast Davis as Lizzie Olsen, a tomboy who is a master of dropkicking and flying tackles. In the cast was a declining John Barrymore, and *Variety* reported, "Miss Davis is a near panic all the way, either on or off the football field, and her presence, plus that of Barrymore, saves the picture." The comic highlight was Joan racing downfield to score a winning touchdown—while being repulsed by a hurricane wind! Her last 1938 film, *Just Around the Corner*, was a Shirley Temple entry, and Joan joined Shirley, Bert Lahr, and Bill "Bojangles" Robinson in a song-and-dance number.

During her infrequent free periods from the Fox soundstages, Joan would embark on a series of live stage appearances. But it did not distract her from the career fact that Fox was not promoting her standing into the top ranks that she felt she deserved. To complete her contract she appeared in 1939 in three studio pictures. *Tail Spin* found her as a grease-monkey crony of aviatrix Alice Faye. In *Day-Time Wife* she was a reception clerk briefly spotted oncamera between the romantic love-and-fight scenes of Tyrone Power and newcomer Linda Darnell. In *Too Busy to Work* she was billed eighth: the stars were Jed Prouty, Spring Byington, and the other regulars of the Jones Family series.

In 1940 Davis appeared as a comic maid in *Free, Blonde and 21* (a sequel to *Hotel for Women*, but without Linda Darnell), a pratfalling lovelorn in *Manhattan Heartbeat*, and a good-time gal in *Sailor's Lady*, an unflavorful quickie. *Variety* termed her "one of the cast's lone redeeming features" in 1941's *For Beauty's Sake*, which starred Ned Sparks and Marjorie Weaver. Joan completed her

---

* While singing the duet "Could You Pass in Love?" Buddy and Joan mistimed a stunt, Ebsen fell on her, and Joan wound up in the hospital.

Fox tenure with the well-mounted *Sun Valley Serenade* (1941), which featured Sonja Henie, John Payne, the Glenn Miller Orchestra, and Milton Berle, with whom zany Joan was to be infatuated in the picture. When her Fox contract came up for renewal, Joan declined to sign for another term.

In August 1941 Joan guested on Rudy Vallee's NBC "Sealtest Village Store" radio program. She rated such favorable response that soon she became a regular on the show. Meanwhile, onscreen she was priceless as Camille Brewster, a radio "scream specialist" in Universal's Abbott and Costello box-office bonanza, *Hold That Ghost* (1941). She and pudgy Lou Costello were such a delightful pair—especially in the slapstick waltz-rhumba they performed—that it was unfortunate they never again worked together in a film. (Joan would have been a good alternate for the role[s] of the twins Martha Raye later played in Abbott and Costello's *Keep 'Em Flying*, 1941.)

Thanks to her Fox films and her more recent radio work, Joan was established as a star comedienne who could and did demand $50,000 per film. She worked through the early Forties in a mixed bag of media efforts at various studios. She commuted to such studios as Columbia for *Two Latins from Manhattan* (1941), *Kansas City Kitty* (1944), etc., and was hired by Universal for such entries as *He's My Guy* (1943) and *She Gets Her Man* (1945). Eddie Cantor was a great admirer of Joan's talent and cast her in his *Show Business* (1944) at RKO, the same studio where she made *Around the World* (1943). Over at Republic she replaced Judy Canova in the film version of Canova's stage success, *Yokel Boy* (1942), when the latter proved too contractually demanding. In 1944 Joan signed a two-picture-a-year contract with both RKO and Universal, her salary elevated to $75,000 per picture.

Even more impressive, however, was Joan's radio work. By 1943 Rudy Vallee had joined the U.S. Coast Guard and Joan became the co-star (with Jack Haley) of the Sealtest radio program. One trade paper reported, "The show not only survived, it developed," and Joan soon became entrenched as radio's top comedienne. Within a year she jumped to starring in one of the five top-rated comedy radio shows. By 1945 only Bob Hope and

*With Sonja Henie
and Buddy Ebsen in
My Lucky Star
(1938).*

*With Lou Costello
in Hold That Ghost
(1941).*

203

Fibber McGee and Molly had topped her in radio popularity. In September of that year she defected from the NBC to the CBS network, replacing Burns and Allen in a prime Monday evening spot, 8:30 to 9:00. The sponsor was the United Drug Company, which signed Joan to a whopping $1,000,000 term contract.

While Joan remained active in motion pictures throughout the late Forties (including a reteaming with Eddie Cantor at RKO in 1948's *If You Knew Susie*), the weekly medium of radio remained her forte. In the summer of 1949 she began a new program, "Leave It to Joan," sponsored on CBS by the American Tobacco Company. The show fully gave sway to the self-depreciating humor that had become Davis' profitable stock-in-trade:

DEPARTMENT STORE MANAGER: I thought you'd do well in ladies' dresses.

DAVIS: I haven't done too well in them so far.

MANAGER: What color is your hair?

DAVIS: On top, or at the roots?

MANAGER: I'll put you in the exchange department. I can't think what harm you'll do there.

DAVIS: I'll think of something.

MANAGER: I've never been so insulted in all my life.

DAVIS: Oh, you must have been.

The format of Joan as a salesgirl, creating total havoc, suited her comedy style perfectly. She reaped an $8,250 weekly salary for her efforts.

Joan's work in motion pictures continued in the Fifties, but it was a sporadic affair. She returned to her old lot, Twentieth Century–Fox, for *Love That Brute* (1950), and was billed below Paul Douglas, Jean Peters, Cesar Romero, and Keenan Wynn. Then she supported Ginger Rogers and Jack Carson in Universal's overblown farce, *The Groom Wore Spurs* (1951). The finale to her 45 (all black and white) feature films was the rather slapdash *Harem Girl* (1952), churned out by economy-minded Columbia.

But then on October 15, 1952, Joan conquered a new medium—television. With herself as production head and star, and ex-husband Willis (they divorced on December 8, 1948, the marriage sorely tried by the

energy Joan poured into her career) as head writer, and Jim "Mr. Magoo" Backus as co-star, "I Married Joan" began a 98-episode, three-year run. With Backus as her usually dignified judge husband, Joan was free to cavort in the sort of comic mayhem that became the trademark of Lucille Ball ("I Love Lucy") and Gale Storm ("My Little Margie"). As producer and star, Joan told the *New York Morning Telegraph* of her woefully frantic daily pace: "I've made a lot of movies under all sorts of conditions, but the work was never anything like this. For nine months a year you never stop. . . . I practically live at the Hollywood studio where our shows are filmed. I even sleep there on Thursday nights instead of driving to my home, which is only 30 miles away. We have our final rehearsals on Thursday—shoot the program the next day. . . . Part of the week you're working on three programs at the same time, making your first study of the script to be shot next week, looking at the rushes of the film shot yesterday and sitting in on the final cutting of the show before that." Beginning with the November 4, 1953, episode, Joan's daughter Beverly became a regular on the show, the 21-year-old miss playing her 46-year-old mother's *younger sister*.

When "I Married Joan" left the small screen on April 6, 1955,* it marked the virtual end of Joan's career. In 1956 she signed a long-term deal with the ABC-TV network, but save for a pilot about the first woman astronaut, no work materialized. Actually, Joan had driven herself so furiously during her life-long career that she was beginning to feel the toll of all the pressures. Joan remained close to her Bel Air and Palm Springs homes. At one point she admitted to the press, "If show business has been good to me, it has also robbed me of many things. I'd have liked a college education, the chance to travel, and time for friends. Show business cost me my first beaux and it eventually cost me my marriage."

Save for a few rare guest spots on television variety shows, Joan's name was out of the show-business headlines. But, along the way, there were a few unpleasant episodes that did get recorded by the press. In 1959 she filed an assault and battery charge against

---

* Davis had made a few other appearances on TV, such as in *The Psychopathic Nurse* episode of "Soundstage" on NBC-TV on June 25, 1954.

With Paul Douglas, Arthur Treacher, and Peter Price in Love That Brute (1950).

With Jay C. Flippen and Leon Belasco in Love That Brute.

boyfriend Harvey "Bud" Stock, claiming he had hit her. Also that year she filed a suit against a Honolulu beauty salon, alleging it had spilt bleach in her eyes in 1954.

The years of exertion and drive exacted their toll on Wednesday, May 24, 1961. Joan had complained of back pains the night before, and her mother rushed her to Palm Springs' Desert Hospital—where she died of a heart attack at 3:00 A.M. A requiem Mass was held at St. Paul the Apostle Church in Westwood, with interment at Holy Cross Cemetery. Joan left a million-dollar estate, but no will.

A tragic postscript occurred on October 24, 1963. Joan's daughter, Beverly, who had something of a show-business career (she appeared in *Some Like It Hot*, 1959, had been a regular on "The Barbara Whiting Radio Show," and in 1962 appeared in the revue *Chips Off the Old Block* in Los Angeles), apparently fell asleep while smoking in the bedroom of her Palm Springs house. A pre-dawn fire killed Beverly, her

two sons, and her grandmother (Joan's mother). Gone were all the survivors of the late comedienne.

When in 1941 Joan declined to re-sign with Twentieth Century–Fox, she remarked, "In my heart, I feel I am so much more than a screwball." However, Joan emphasized the screwball element of her personality for the majority of her life. She epitomized the all-giving, short-lived comic performer. As she remarked rather stoically near the end of her life, "I've been afraid all along that I just wouldn't be funny or pretty enough for the long-time big time. I've kept going on a mixture of gall, guts, and gumption. Faith, too—I've hung onto faith until now I realize that every heartbreak has been a stepping stone."

Perhaps the greatest tribute to Joan's array of comic talents would be the often-heralded (but never materializing) return of her tele-series to the syndication circuit and more frequent showings of her features to new generations of TV watchers.

FEATURE FILMS

Millions in the Air (*Paramount 1935*)
Bunker Bean (*RKO 1936*)
The Holy Terror (*20th Century-Fox 1937*)
On the Avenue (*20th Century-Fox 1937*)
Time Out for Romance (*20th Century-Fox 1937*)
Wake Up and Live (*20th Century-Fox 1937*)
Angel's Holiday (*20th Century-Fox 1937*)
You Can't Have Everything (*20th Century-Fox 1937*)
The Great Hospital Mystery (*20th Century-Fox 1937*)
Sing and Be Happy (*20th Century-Fox 1937*)
Thin Ice (*20th Century-Fox 1937*)
Life Begins in College (*20th Century-Fox 1937*)
Love and Hisses (*20th Century-Fox 1937*)
Sally, Irene and Mary (*20th Century-Fox 1938*)
Josette (*20th Century-Fox 1938*)
My Lucky Star (*20th Century-Fox 1938*)
Hold That Co-ed (*20th Century-Fox 1938*)

Just Around the Corner (*20th Century-Fox 1938*)
Tail Spin (*20th Century-Fox 1939*)
Day-Time Wife (*20th Century-Fox 1939*)
Too Busy to Work (*20th Century-Fox 1939*)
Free, Blonde and 21 (*20th Century-Fox 1940*)
Manhattan Heartbeat (*20th Century-Fox 1940*)
Sailor's Lady (*20th Century-Fox 1940*)
For Beauty's Sake (*20th Century-Fox 1941*)
Sun Valley Serenade (*20th Century-Fox 1941*)
Hold That Ghost (*Universal 1941*)
Two Latins from Manhattan (*Columbia 1941*)
Yokel Boy (*Republic 1942*)
Sweetheart of the Fleet (*Columbia 1942*)
He's My Guy (*Universal 1943*)
Two Senoritas from Chicago (*Columbia 1943*)
Around the World (*RKO 1943*)
Show Business (*RKO 1944*)

Beautiful but Broke (*Columbia 1944*)
Kansas City Kitty (*Columbia 1944*)
She Gets Her Man (*Universal 1945*)
George White's Scandals (*RKO 1945*)
She Wrote the Book (*Universal 1946*)
If You Knew Susie (*RKO 1948*)

Make Mine Laughs (*RKO 1949*) [stock footage]
Traveling Saleswoman (*Columbia 1950*)
Love That Brute (*20th Century-Fox 1950*)
The Groom Wore Spurs (*Universal 1951*)
Harem Girl (*Columbia 1952*)

With Bob Denver in Did You Hear the One About the Traveling Saleslady? (1968).

Phyllis Diller

In Hollywood, the God-given and cosmetically enhanced faces and forms of many ladies have resulted in stardom. Such physical perfections as Greta Garbo's cheekbones, Marilyn Monroe's derriere, Betty Grable's legs, and Jane Russell's bustline have been exploited to win legions of fans. On the other hand, some ladies have employed their physical imperfections for salary-earning yocks. Marie Dressler and Edna May Oliver utilized their offbeat facial looks, Martha Raye has her cavernous mouth, and even the 1970s' highly touted pop songstress Cher has allowed her prominent nose to be slandered by partner/ex-husband Sonny Bono, for the sake of audience laughter.

And then there is Phyllis Diller.

In an almost miraculous show-business footnote, Phyllis Diller has taken a rubbery face, an unfortunate figure, and a nausea-inducing taste in "style" and whipped them together with an irresistible sense of humor. As a result she has become one of the most popular and well-paid of present-day comediennes. While less than attractive women have always been a pitied breed in the eyes of Hollywood commercializers, Phyllis garnished her naturally odd appearance with frightful wigs and bizarre costumes. She became the first successful, completely self-depreciating female comic in show business.

"I never made *Who's Who* but I'm featured in *What's That?*"

"If I were a building—I'd be condemned."

"Most people get a reservation at a beauty ranch—I was committed!"

"I'm looking for a perfume to overpower men—I'm sick of karate."

"At night, everything either comes off or out."

These are some of the witticisms that have helped to earn Phyllis astronomical salaries and a prime status in the profession of laughmakers.

Phyllis Diller was born in Lima, Ohio, on Tuesday, July 17, 1917, the only child of insurance sales manager Perry Marcus Driver and his wife Frances Ada (Romshe) Driver. While attending Franklin Grammar School and the local Central High, Phyllis early recognized her attraction to boys—and to comedy. She discovered she could get laughs "when I was in grade school. It sounds like I was a troublemaker, but it wasn't that at all. I was always a pro—even as a little teeny kid. I was an absolutely perfect, quiet, dedicated student *in* class. But outside of class I got my laughs. I've always been able to control myself and be disciplined and follow the rules. . . . There are people who have absolutely no way of shutting themselves up. You've seen them on the TV panel shows. . . . This doesn't happen to me because I have a great sense of timing and a sense of when to speak, when not to speak, and so it was a professional attitude toward comedy right from the start . . . when I was simply doing it for kicks and had *no idea* that I would ever become a comic. It was just a natural thing." Meanwhile, her parents, hoping to develop her into a more well-rounded individual, had her take violin, saxophone, voice, and dance lessons.

After high school graduation in 1935 Phyllis attended Chicago's Sherwood Music Conservatory, hoping to become a professional concert pianist (an ambition realized in recent years). She later studied at Northwestern University and Bluffton College, where she won campus notoriety for her nude prancing through dormitory halls with her hair in curlers and a rose in her teeth as she performed a takeoff on stripper Gypsy Rose Lee. Obviously by this point Phyllis had realized that she would never be a conventional lady, although the rigors of her parents' discipline and a fear of violating too drastically the norms of everyday life caused the burgeoning iconoclast a good deal of emotional grief over succeeding years.

Phyllis' studies ended when she met 26-year-old Sherwood Anderson Diller, who romanced and married her (an elopement) on November 4, 1939, in Kentucky. The couple moved to Ypsilanti, Michigan, where the first child, Peter, was born on September 22, 1940. As Sherwood became a real-estate agent and later an airline inspector at Alameda Naval Air Station, Phyllis played housewife, producing babies ("I was like the Easter Bunny, ready to lay 'em like eggs"), and living a drab life she described as "strictly pabulum, diapers, Drano, and no money." (The other Diller children are: Sally, born November 17, 1944; Suzanne, March 8, 1946;

Stephanie, October 9, 1948; and Perry, February 3, 1950.)

Phyllis traces her early exodus from this ho-hum existence (and at times the Dillers' finances and survival chances were indeed bleak) to religion. She recalls taking a walk and going past a church. "Something forced me to go into that church. As I slid down in a pew in the back, I heard the minister reading and I've never forgotten the words: 'Whatsoever things are true . . . whatsoever things are pure . . . think on these things. . . . ' They seemed to be addressed directly to me, as if God himself were giving me a message."

Determined to tap her talents (wherever they might lie), Phyllis became an advertising copywriter for Kahn's Department Store in Oakland, California, moving on to become a continuity writer for Oakland's KROW radio and head of merchandising and press relations for KSFO radio in San Francisco. She also, when not tending to her family's needs, began performing locally. "I was married . . . a suburban lady and I had been doing things for church groups, for little Kiwanis groups, for the navy—Alameda Naval Air Station, they had a little thing for the sailors. They'd invite me and give me 17 bucks and a live turkey. . . . Don't ever accept a live turkey! Gee, they're mean—mean sons-of-bitches!" It was husband Sherwood, himself moving about from one modest job to another, who encouraged Phyllis to audition for more prestigious spots and to assert her own needs, even at the expense of ministering to her large family.

After 10 months of practice with drama coaches and study of the techniques of her favorite stand-up comedians (Milton Berle and Bob Hope), Phyllis auditioned at San Francisco's Purple Onion club. That famous club was becoming the mid-Fifties' testing ground for such new comedians as Mike Nichols and Elaine May, Mort Sahl, the Smothers Brothers, and Milt Kamen. On March 7, 1955, Phyllis made her $60-a-week debut. She was disappointed with the result. "I still had a thousand things to learn," she recalls, and she met some unavoidable resistance. "Being a woman, right away you walk out to almost total rejection. Almost nobody wants you to be a female comic, and they give you a lot of static just because of your sex. . . . Men have this silly, witchy, witchcrafty attitude that a woman who is a comic has lost her femininity. Now it's not necessarily so." Despite her problems, Phyllis' collection of jokes and banter with the audience, borrowing furs for comic props, clicked, and she tallied a total of 89 weeks at the Purple Onion. (She would make annual returns to the club for several years thereafter.)

Meanwhile, Phyllis added to her media exposure, writing a column for the *San Francisco Examiner* as "the homely friendmaker" ("I had a phone call from a Peeping Tom. He asked me to pull my window shades down!"). With her husband serving as her business manager, Phyllis began touring the national nightclub circuit. In 1959 in Washington, D.C., Bob Hope saw her act. "He popped up from his table, caught me behind a pillar, and told me I was just great. You wouldn't possibly know what that meant to me." That same year, she recorded her debut LP album, "Wet Toe in a Hot Socket." (It was to be the first of many comedy recordings; in later years she would sing on some LPs.) Shortly afterward she appeared on the late-night Jack Paar NBC-TV talk show. By the close of 1961 she had revisited the Paar program over 30 times. One-of-a-kind Phyllis with the raucous laughter and self-depreciating humor had become a well-known personality.

It was easy to pinpoint Phyllis' audience appeal. Her almost militant flaunting of her assorted unattractive aspects, bedecked in ratty furs, frightful wigs, and a collection of grotesque outfits (about 500 in all), moved *Time* to describe her as "something that, by its own description, looks like a sackful of doorknobs." Many nonbeautiful people who saw her perform cheered Phyllis for her brutal self-parodies. Her cigarette holder (she does not smoke—the cigarette is a painted stick), her coarse laugh ("aah ha ha haaa"), her horror stories of husband Fang* ("Fang brought home a dozen flowers—three bottles of Four Roses." . . . "When Fang wants a hot meal, he knows where he can go." . . . "Fang applied to the SPCA for a divorce—claims he married a dog!"), and her

* On Fang, "I call him that because he has only one tooth in his old head and it's two inches long. The first time I met him I set fire to it. I thought it was a Lucky Strike." Phyllis has always maintained that Fang was, and is not actually based on, her first husband and she has continued to make jokes about Fang since her 1965 divorce from Sherwood.

good-humored tales of her inefficiency as a housekeeper and wife made her one of America's most popular comediennes. (A decade later diminutive Joan Rivers would use a variation of this klutzy-me attention-grabber to build her comedienne reputation.)

Phyllis was soon making the rounds of the major television variety shows (Bob Hope, Perry Como, Andy Williams) and game shows ("First Impression," "Picture This," "Play Your Hunch") touted as an oddball freak, much as singer Tiny Tim would be in the mid-Sixties. On November 28, 1963, Phyllis starred in a Thanksgiving evening ABC-TV network special, *The Phyllis Diller Show*, and on September 19, 1964, Diller became the emcee of ABC-TV's short-lived "Show Street," a low-budget lead-in to Saturday night's top-budgeted "Hollywood Palace" show.

However, for all her success in these assorted media, Phyllis really wanted to make motion pictures. This was one ambition of hers that was conventionally American. In Warner Bros.' *Splendor in the Grass* (1961), a romantic period drama starring Natalie Wood and Warren Beatty, Phyllis had played a bit assignment as nightclub hostess Texas Guinan. The tiny role scarcely merited her notice in film reviews. Later she toured in stock packages of *Dark at the Top of the Stairs* (1961), *Wonderful Town* (1962), and *Happy Birthday* (1963), often promoted rather as a freak attraction than as an actress. Her next film assignment proved to be a dud. *The Fat Spy* (1965), an independently produced venture starring Jack E. Leonard (in a dual role), made little dent in the film marketplace. Phyllis played the part of Camille, a cosmetics manufacturer out to snare a fountain-of-youth formula. Others in the oddball assemblage were Brian Donlevy, Jayne Mansfield, and rock "artists" Jordan Christopher and The Wild Ones. *Variety* yawned, "*The Fat Spy* is from dudsville. . . . The story erodes around a Florida island but someone must have lost the script." Phyllis was at least given credit by the reviewer for playing her role "credibly"; she later explained, "I was very anxious to make movies. My agency came up with it. It was unbelievably bad."

About the time of making *The Fat Spy*, Phyllis on September 3, 1965, divorced her husband of 26 years, citing general indignities. Sherwood was ordered by the court to pay a token $1.00 per month child support. Phyllis later reflected on the union, "I had been married more than 20 years, yet I knew six weeks after my wedding that the marriage was a mistake. I stayed married because I had been raised by a mother who insisted that divorce was wrong and that one should stick it out and have children despite unhappiness. So I tried to keep the marriage together. My first husband was tremendously handsome, with a high I.Q., an inventor type who always was ahead of his time. But he was a nervous wreck, and couldn't do anything practical. But I have to be grateful to him. Look what he did for me."

Thirty-four days later, on October 7, 1965, Phyllis remarried. The groom was 49-year-old Warde Donovan, a minor actor and singer who had appeared with Phyllis on television and in nightclubs. Donovan quickly began playing at the role of being a star's husband. While Phyllis apparently was bound to Donovan by some sort of love chemistry, they soon began the first of 38 separations before divorce in 1975 ended their domestic skirmishes.

Though *The Fat Spy* was an embarrassment to all concerned, Phyllis was soon signed by her idol and friend Bob Hope to a five-picture contract. Had the deal occurred a few years earlier, Phyllis might have benefited greatly from her association with the ski-nosed comic. However, in the late Sixties, many critics had become bitterly harsh toward Hope, angered by his "hawkish" politics concerning the Vietnamese conflict, and took out their rancor on his film and TV efforts. (Granted, the quality of Hope's output had dropped considerably since his cinema heyday in the Forties.)

In *Boy, Did I Get a Wrong Number!* (1966) Phyllis played Lily, Hope's madcap maid, who helps him hide French sexpot Elke Sommer from the eyes of wife Marjorie Lord. The picture was innocuous slapstick, punctuated with sex-oriented cracks. It was rather compactly directed by comedy veteran George Marshall and boasted a quite funny climactic chase with Phyllis on a motorcycle. However, the press went to great lengths to pan the effort. *Time* reported, "As Hope's mop-topped maid, Phyllis cleans up the house,

dirties up the jokes, and delivers her own brand of kitcheny self-deprecation. There is never the slightest doubt that her next job will be a sellout nightclub engagement in Las Vegas, and any viewer who thinks that's funny may be able to swallow the whole wretched show." (Nevertheless, there was a film audience for this type of fare and the movie did sufficiently well in release.)

Also in 1966 Phyllis lent her talents to Embassy's *Mad Monster Party*, providing the voice for a puppet likeness of herself and singing a song, "You're Different." She also quipped with the puppet versions of famous horror characters (to Dracula, "Don't kiss! You always leave marks"). The principal puppet was Baron Frankenstein, his voice provided by none other than Boris Karloff. The film did not receive full release until 1969.

While hoping for the best with her cinema career, Phyllis signed with the ABC network to star in her own teleseries. The result was "The Pruitts of Southampton," which debuted on September 6, 1966, with Phyllis as Phyllis Poindexter Pruitt and a supporting cast that included Gypsy Rose Lee (a neighbor), Grady Sutton (a butler), Reginald Gardiner (an aged uncle), and later Richard Deacon (as a financial advisor). Reaction to the bizarre situation-comedy show was less than ecstatic. "Last night's introduction was totally inept slapstick that only made one appreciate all over again the artistry of Lucille Ball" (*New York Times*). Some revamping was done, including a new show title ("The Phyllis Diller Show"), but there was little evident improvement. The half-hour comedy program lasted but one season. A year later Diller returned to weekly television via NBC's "The Beautiful Phyllis Diller Show" (debuting September 15, 1968). It was videotaped in Hollywood. The variety-style format was no better a package for Phyllis, and the last entry aired on December 22, 1968.

Phyllis' cinema work may not have won her critical accolades but it was apparent to industry sources that her unique presence did a good deal to instill financial life into Bob Hope's gaggle of films. *Eight on the Lam* (1967) was produced by star Hope, had Phyllis and Jonathan Winters in chief support, and boasted the charms of Shirley Eaton and

In Boy, Did I Get a Wrong Number! *(1966).*

Jill St. John. George Marshall again directed and there was another chase scene for audience distraction. Once again Diller was Hope's employee, this time Goldie, a baby-sitter-housekeeper. This time the *New York Times* alerted its readers, "But the woman of the day is Miss Diller, as a raucous baby-sitter, streaking through the picture like a berserk comet, every hair standing on end." Audience appreciation of the lowbrow production caused *Eight on the Lam* to gross $3,000,000 in distributors' domestic rentals. Also in 1967 Phyllis played in *The Silent Treatment*, a hodgepodge of such comics as Rowan and Martin, Jerry Lewis, Wally Cox, Rose Marie, Paul Lynde, and such nostalgia veterans as Jackie Coogan, Gene Autry, George Raft, and Rudy Vallee. The picture, with no spoken dialogue, was never released.

Universal thought it could tap box-office revenue from Phyllis' array of comic talents. In *Did You Hear the One About the Traveling Saleslady?* (1968), it co-starred her with television favorites Bob Denver ("Gilligan's Island") and Joe Flynn ("McHale's Navy"). Phyllis' husband, Warde Donovan, had a bit role in the proceedings. As Agatha Knabenshue, Phyllis sold player pianos in the West of 1910, scaring the populace and wildlife by recurringly hoisting her skirts à la Claudette Colbert of *It Happened One Night.* Of this disappointing vehicle *Variety* lamented, "Miss Diller is an excellent comedienne, though in pictures, her one-liner forte must be complemented by other adroit comedy elements, generally missing here."

The Private Navy of Sgt. O'Farrell (1968) was another Hope-United Artists outing, with Phyllis as Nurse Nellie Krause in the South Pacific of World War II. Her best scenes came in a dream (nightmare!) of co-star Jeffrey Hunter, in which he envisions Phyllis as Eve and then Cleopatra. Despite the usual critical barbs, the film grossed $2,400,000 in U.S. and Canadian distributor rentals.

213

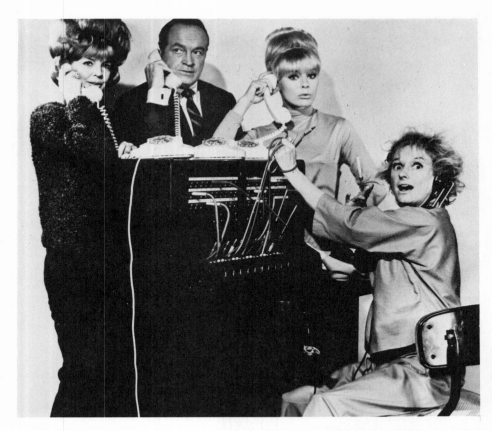

With Marjorie Lord, Bob Hope, and Elke Sommer in a publicity pose for Boy, Did I Get a Wrong Number!

With Larry Blake, Jonathan Winters, and Robert Foulk in Eight on the Lam (1967)

214

With Shirley Eaton in Eight on the Lam.

In Did You Hear the One About the Traveling Saleslady?

A serious turnabout in characterization came in the black-humored fantasy *The Adding Machine*, released by Universal in 1969. It allowed Phyllis to fulfill the dream of most any funmaker, to play a serious role—seriously. She was cast as Mrs. Zero, the nagging wife of a man (Milo O'Shea) who murders his boss when he is replaced by a computer. Phyllis won some splendid reviews for her stark performance. *Motion Picture Daily* reported, "Miss Diller is in command of what she is doing all the way, exemplified by a five-minute scene midway through the film and the last she appears in. O'Shea, on the morning of his execution, is visited by his wife, eagerly anticipating the martyrdom of notorious widowhood. It's a difficult posture to bring off comically, and she does it adroitly. The short sequence highlights an otherwise listless enterprise." Unfortunately, the poorly distributed *The Adding Machine* inspired no producer to offer Phyllis more quality assignments. She temporarily abandoned her hopes of major success in the movies, continuing with her club, television, and recording sessions.

In January 1970 Phyllis enjoyed a new career episode, playing the role of Dolly Gallagher Levi in the Broadway version of *Hello, Dolly!* Succeeding Carol Channing, Ginger Rogers, Martha Raye, Betty Grable, and Pearl Bailey (and preceding Ethel Merman), Diller stuck to the musical comedy script and won warm audience reaction, though most critics were skeptical. Clive Barnes of the *New York Times* assessed, "She sings a lot better than I feared a cabaret artist might, she mugs affectionately to her audience, and keeps things going. Even so, when Dolly comes down that staircase, call it charisma, call it chutzpah, call it what you like, but she either has it or she hasn't. For me, Miss Diller hasn't." Phyllis recalled the two-month stay with the musical as "one of the most glorious things I ever did as far as my satisfaction [was concerned]. . . ." (The engagement cost her $200,000 in delayed club dates and she lost a battle with producer David Merrick to have spouse Warde Donovan signed to play Horace Vandergelder in the show. Richard Deacon filled that co-starring post.)

With Milo O'Shea in The Adding Machine *(1969).*

In 1971 Phyllis earned most of her publicity not by performing, but by undergoing plastic surgery on her face. "Warde kept telling me I should have my nose fixed. It was broken when I was young and I always had trouble breathing. But I kept putting it off until one day I saw myself on the taped 'Sonny and Cher Show,' and I looked dreadful. I took a long look at myself in the mirror and started thinking old. That's no good. Even makeup can improve you only so much. So I went to Dr. Franklin Ashley, a top Beverly Hills plastic surgeon who has done many stars. Most of them prefer to keep their facelifts a secret, but I say that's like trying to hide your pregnancy. The experience wasn't very comfortable, but it was worth it. Rather than just have my nose done, I had remakes of everything—eyes, eyelids, chin, cheeks. Now I not only can breathe again, correctly, but I love my new look." (Some show-business pundits insisted that Phyllis had cut off her nose to spite her career, since her strange look was her professional trademark.)

Phyllis' satisfaction with her appearance has led her to try some self-satisfying endeavors in the Seventies.* In 1971 she appeared as a concert pianist with the Pittsburgh Symphony Orchestra. "I practiced every day for 17 years," she says, "but then I didn't play for 30 years. Now I want to play well. I listen to classical music at home and I practice every day. Even on the road there's always a piano in the room." Her basic repertoire currently is Beethoven's Piano Concerto No. 1 and Bach's Inventions Nos. 1 and 8. Since her debut as a classical pianist, Phyllis has appeared with the symphony orchestras of San Francisco, Dallas, and Detroit, averaging 10 appearances yearly. Sometimes she plays for benefits (as did Jack Benny with his famous Stradivarius violin).

Besides regular guest spots on television and lucrative nightclub visits, Phyllis infrequently makes a film appearance. She made a cameo appearance as herself (and a pretty bitchy self too) in *The Sunshine Boys* (1975). More recently she made a guest appearance

in *The Great Balloon Race*, shot in Florida with Terry Moore and Jayne Mansfield Jr.

It was in early 1975 that Phyllis and Warde Donovan finally divorced. "We had a great settlement," she laughed. "I got the house and I gave him the gate." Phyllis appears disinterested in future nuptials. "I think 35 years of ball and chain is enough for any woman."

Though Phyllis' nightclub routines continue to be sellout affairs, her material can be somewhat "rough" for the more-sophisticated audiences. For example, in August 1976 she entertained at the annual Pacific National Exhibition in Vancouver, British Columbia, at the special "golden age" day. About one-third of the 6,000 spectators departed before her 40-minute routine was completed. The early leavers complained that Phyllis was "too dirty." Lamented one senior citizen, "All she talked about were breasts and knees, sex and Kleenex. I didn't come here to listen to that." But for more ribald-inclined audiences elsewhere, Phyllis can do little wrong.

In 1976 she was going full force. Her *Phyllis Diller's Marriage Manual* was published, she was an interviewee on Beverly Sills' TV talk show, and she returned to Las Vegas for yet another successful club date. *Variety* reported:

> She zaps her usual characters in a rata-tat that brings equally wild and rotten visions to the mind. Her japed subjects are given the killer-Diller treatment. The let-up comes at last when she trots to the keyboard for a bit of Bach noodling with conductor Peter Daniels playing the other grand piano, a quick concerto-type round again with Bach losing out profoundly and a chirp of "Before the Parade Passes By" finish.

Never one to lose out in the publicity marathon, Phyllis' most recounted newspaper stunt of the year was her arrival at London's Heathrow Airport walking her "invisible dog" through the airport's lounge. It was an instant attention-getter. Winding up the year, she appeared at the New Drury Lane Theatre in Chicago in the comedy *What Are We Going to Do with Jenny?*

On the social scene in 1977, Phyllis was reported first dating Minneapolis businessman Keith Lalli and, later in the year, was

---

* She and Milton Berle performed in a pleasing episode on ABC-TV's "Love, American Style" in November 1971. They are a married couple who try to take separate vacations but jealous Milton follows her to Florida. Before long he is cavorting in drag as a maid, and later appears as a continental lover, complete with black wig and moustache.

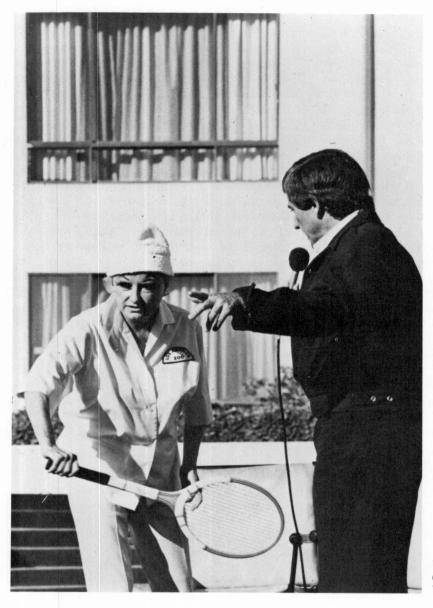

With Merv Griffin at Caesar's Palace Hotel in Las Vegas (1974).

noted as dating actor Taylor Williams, and, then, Jim Murray. She found time to reign as Queen of Argus at the annual Mardi Gras in New Orleans (February 21-22), guest on an assortment of TV game shows, and make appearances on such video variety programs as "Sha Na Na," "The Muppet Show," and "The Gong Show." Thereafter, she popped up on TV in such diverse outings as NBC-TV's "CHiPs" program, a guest appearance on "America 2Night" teleseries, and a role, along with Conrad Bain, Tom Smothers, and Misty Rowe, in the feature film *It's a Pleasure Doing Business* (1979), which was filmed on location in St. Louis.

One of the more interesting revelations of the year was that long before author Alex Haley gained fame via his book and TV series of *Roots*, he had written a biography of Phyllis. It seems that back in 1955 he was a struggling freelance writer stationed with the Coast Guard in San Francisco and Phyllis was then an emerging, but still obscure comedienne. Not long after they met, Haley requested Phyllis to allow him to write a book about her life. She replied, "Honey, I'm not big enough yet that a magazine big enough to do me any good would want my story . . . and, if I were, you're not big enough yet as a writer that they would want you to

218

write it. So let us stay in touch and keep faith and one day we will see this happen." Six years later, the *Saturday Evening Post* had Haley prepare a profile of her. When the two met for the interview sessions, Diller said, "Baby, we made it!" Later on, the two agreed to work on the biography which was to be entitled *From Sink to Mink*. However, after the project was completed, the publisher decided not to publish it. Haley returned the $4,000 advance.

It seems unlikely that the energetic, ambitious Phyllis can ever relax long enough to consider slowing down her pace. In analyzing her amazing career to date, Phyllis has her own theory: "There are two things important to success in any field. The first is belief in yourself, the second is never allowing yourself to be discouraged. Of course, there is a third ingredient: tireless effort and continuous work."

As to reviewers who have compared Diller's talents to those of Martha Raye, Lucille Ball, and Eve Arden, Phyllis reasons, "I think I have been more influenced by men. Now, let me tell you why. None of those girls are. Those girls . . . are all comic actresses. Therefore, they always work within a framework as a character. I am a true . . . female stand-up comic. Therefore I could be likened most to Bob Hope—who was always my idol—and I have just automatically studied him. There is a great similarity in our delivery and the way we work."

And so Phyllis Diller continues to reap rewards as the queen of self-deprecation, a status that has remained very lucrative *even* in the new age of woman's liberation, and the emergence of Mary Tyler Moore, Beatrice Arthur, Jean Stapleton, and Nancy Walker as the top TV comediennes.

FEATURE FILMS

Splendor in the Grass (*Warner Bros. 1961*)
The Fat Spy (*Magna 1965*)
Boy, Did I Get a Wrong Number! (*United Artists 1966*)
Mad Monster Party (*Embassy 1966*) [voice only]
The Silent Treatment (*1967*) [unreleased]
Eight on the Lam (*United Artists 1967*)
Did You Hear the One About the Traveling Saleslady? (*Universal 1968*)

The Private Navy of Sgt. O'Farrell (*United Artists 1968*)
The Adding Machine (*Universal 1969*)
The Sunshine Boys (*MGM 1975*)*
The Great Balloon Race (*1976*) [unreleased]
It's a Pleasure Doing Business (*TCA Pictures 1979*)

* Unbilled guest appearance.

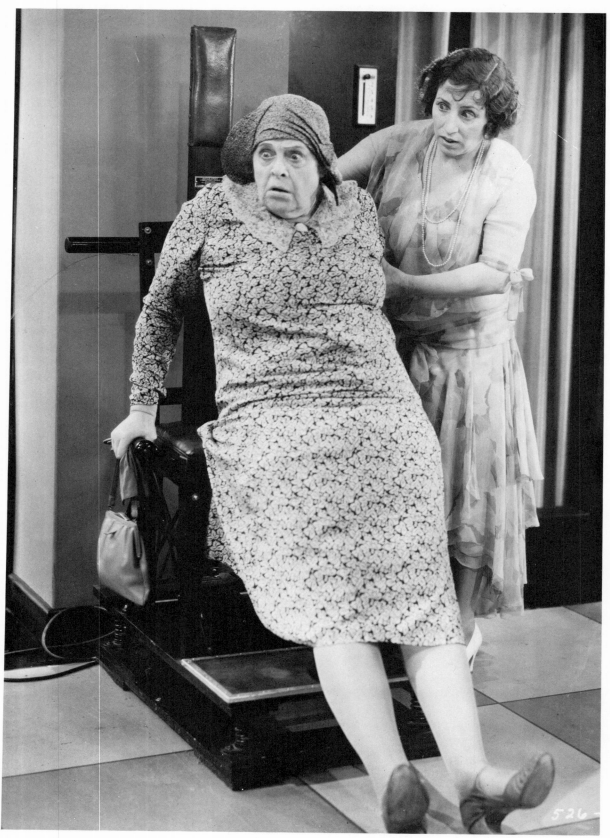

With Polly Moran in Reducing (1931).

Marie Dressler

When a new star arose in Hollywood, nearly always he or she possessed at least two qualities: youth and beauty. Within the screen's cosmos, Marie Dressler was an anachronism. At age 61 she became one of the movies' greatest stars. Moreover, advancing years had neither transformed her mug of a face into stateliness nor improved her over-stuffed figure. But she was extremely talented and very much beloved.

Harold Lloyd called her "the greatest comedienne of this generation, [who] made age a beautiful thing on the screen." Director George Cukor observed, "She was the biggest star of her time." Will Rogers, in a nationwide radio tribute, admitted, "Marie Dressler is the real queen of our movies. And we can say that conscientiously because she is. There's been nothing—nothing like her career has developed in our whole movie picture industry, or on the stage either, for that matter." Filmmaker Frank Capra capsulized: "There was only *one* Marie Dressler!"

She was born Leila Koerber on Tuesday, November 9, 1869, in Coburg, Ontario, Canada. She was the second of two daughters of former German Crimean War officer Alexander Rudolf Koerber* and his English-Irish wife, Anne Henderson. At age five Leila made her first audience laugh by falling from a pedestal while impersonating Cupid in a Lindsay (Ontario) church pageant. When the Koerber family relocated in Saginaw, Michigan, the ambitious, outsized young girl made her professional stage debut at the Teutonia Opera House. She appeared as Cigarette in *Under Two Flags* as adapted by Richard Ganthony, her sister Bonita's husband. Leila used the name of a deceased aunt, Marie Dressler, as her professional name. She appeared with Maurice Grau's Grand Opera Company as Katisha in *The Mikado*. The next three years she was in some 40 operas with the George Baker Opera Company, playing servant girls or queens or, occasionally, even kings.

During all these years, as in her childhood, Marie was constantly on the move. As she

* Years later Marie would add "Von" to the family's surname, thinking it made her background seem more grand.

later said, "When I started touring with show companies, wherever I hung my hat became home." As for coping with her lack of formal education she explained, "My brain is like a sponge. It just can't help soaking things up. Sometimes I wish it wouldn't do such a good job of it."

On May 28, 1892, Marie made her Broadway stage debut at the Fifth Avenue Theatre. She was Cunigonde in a musical, *The Robber of the Rhine*, with a libretto by Maurice Barrymore. The father of Lionel, Ethel, and John wisely persuaded 5'7", green-eyed, brown-haired Marie to become a comedienne. After singing engagements at the Bowery's Atlantic Gardens and at Koster and Beal's, Marie supported Lillian Russell in several opéras bouffe. The two contrasting women became good friends and, when they were seen together in public, observers used to call them "Beauty and her Beastie."

After playing Mary Doodle, a sextuple widow in *Madeleine of the Magic Kiss*, Marie tested the classics as Mrs. Malaprop in *The Rivals*, with Dan Daly and William Collier. A year earlier she had been seen as Isabella, queen of Spain, in the show *1492*. The part of Flo Honeydew of the music halls in *The Lady Slavey* (1896) further established the unlovely, talented comedienne, and in 1897 she played Dotty Dimple in *Courted into Court* from coast to coast. For 192 performances she was Viola Alum in *The Man in the Moon*.

By the turn of the century Marie was headlining in vaudeville, playing in a sketch with Adele Farrington. At one point in her vaudeville career composer Jerome Kern was her piano accompanist. It was in 1900 that she wed actor George Hoppert (a.k.a. Huppert or Hoeppert) in Elizabeth, New Jersey. Marie would later write of this failed union, "It didn't work out, the thrill soon vanished and, after a year or two, we realized there was no basis for companionship." During their marriage, Marie gave birth to a girl who died during infancy. A few years later the marriage was dissolved and Marie thereafter generally avoided talking of Hoppert or of their dead child.

On Christmas night, 1900, Marie returned to Broadway as the lead in *Miss Prinnt*. In *The King's Carnival* (as Anne, queen of Spain) she sang "Ragtime Will Be My Finish." During the run of *The Hall of Fame* she played a hilariously overly plump Juliet to Sam Bernard's Romeo. Joe Weber (of the famous team of Weber and Fields) signed Marie for his merry musical romps *Higgledy-Piggledy* and *Twiddle-Twaddle*. In Weber's satire *The College Widower*, Marie was Tilly Buttin'—a halfback.

On October 28, 1907, Marie made her first London stage appearance, at the Palace Music Hall. Back in the States she played Gladys DeVine in *The Boy and the Girl*, with Barney Bernard, and made such Edison cylinder recordings as "Rastus, Take Me Back," "I'm A-Goin' to Change My Man," "He's My Soft-Shelled Crab on Toast," and "I'm Looking for an Angel (Without Wings)." On May 5, 1910, Lew Fields presented Marie on Broadway in *Tillie's Nightmare*, a farce with music. The farce became Marie's greatest theater success and she would play Tillie Blobbs, the boarding-house drudge, on and off for several years. She made herself and the show's hit song, "Heaven Will Protect the Working Girl," a national success. In September 1910 she recorded the working girl's lament on an Edison cylinder, singing with her usual abandon. *Tillie* saved Marie both financially and professionally.

On Broadway she produced and directed *Marie Dressler's All Star Gambol* (March 10, 1913). Although her travesty on *Camille* was acclaimed, the show failed and she found a warmer reception for her theatrical effort in San Francisco. In the Bay City she had also met a young writer, Frances Marion, later one of Hollywood's best scenarists. In the late Twenties Miss Marion would almost single-handedly salvage Marie's sagging career.

America's first feature-length silent comedy was Mack Sennett's *Tillie's Punctured Romance*, based on Marie's stage character, Tillie. Sennett's bold experiment in producing a six-reel slapstick comedy in 1914 was insured by signing Marie Dressler as its star. He also employed his clown corps from Keystone, headed by Charles Chaplin and Mabel Normand. Marie entered with great zest into the wild low comedy and fast-paced slapstick, giving a rousing characterization as the innocent, ballooning country girl, Tillie. The picture—still being shown today and enjoyed—was well received and greatly helped the careers of both Chaplin and Mabel Normand.

Marie, hoping to find a new career in the moving-picture arena, made a follow-up to the Sennett hit, *Tillie's Tomato Surprise* (1915). *Motion Picture World* glowed over the Lubin release, "Miss Dressler is, as far as I know, without a peer anywhere. The picture is a litany of laughs." The *New York Dramatic Mirror*, aware that Marie was then 46, said, "For a woman her age, thrown head first from an auto, jumping into a moving freight train, jumping off the train into a pile of goose feathers, it is executed with the nonchalance of an athletic young girl—and she is laughably funny." Marie made several more *Tillie* adventures, but as two-reelers: *Tillie's Day Off, Tillie's Divorce Case, Tillie's Love Affair, Elopement,* and *Night Out.* Late in 1916 Frances Marion wrote another comedy for Marie, *Tillie Wakes Up,* released by World Pictures in January 1917. Marie was abetted by Johnny Hines, an excellent foil for her blundering, elephantine antics. (Marie also made other short subjects: the two-reel *The Scrublady,* 1917, for Goldwyn, and *The Agonies of Agnes* and *Fired,* both two-reelers for World, in 1918.)

With the first Sennett feature showing in theatres, Marie returned to Broadway in December 1914 in a straight farce, *A Mix-Up,* she had rewritten and directed. Bert Lytell was her leading man. The play lasted 88 performances. Marie exhorted the audiences to "smile awhile; and while you smile, others smile, and soon there'll be miles and miles and miles of smiles." It was a homily that had to bolster her trying life with James H. Dalton, a red-faced, red-headed entrepreneur with whom she had fallen in love back in 1907 when he was her manager and had persuaded her to perform in London.

It was determined Dalton who convinced her to produce *Philopena* (a revamped version of *Higgledy-Piggledy*) and *The Collegettes* in London. Both shows flopped and pushed Marie perilously close to bankruptcy. Dalton also urged her to form the Marie Dressler Motion Picture Company, which became involved in litigation in 1918 with World Pictures when Dalton confiscated the short subjects Marie had made for World Pictures distribution. Her film company had a brief life.

Although the record is unclear it seems at one point that Marie thought she had married Dalton. Later she discovered the marriage was a fake. Dalton's wife refused to divorce him, but Marie remained with him through a debilitating stroke. She had to sell her Windsor, Vermont, home to make ends meet, but somehow she saw to it that Dalton received superior medical attention. When Dalton later died, Mrs. Dalton and her adult children emerged to claim the man's remains. Marie was ignored. About her years with Dalton, Marie wrote, "I got both thrills and companionship, also an incredible amount of joy, compounded largely of sacrifice and serving and suffering."

During the late Teens Marie had toured the country selling Liberty Loan Bonds and giving impassioned speeches. She also made a patriotic short, *The Cross Red Nurse.* Along with Douglas Fairbanks, Mary Pickford, and Charles Chaplin, she stopped in Washington, D.C., during a bond-selling drive and made a great impression. Chaplin slipped on a hastily built temporary platform. He grabbed Marie for likely support and both clowns tumbled through the railing atop the assistant secretary of the navy, Franklin Delano Roosevelt.

Marie, with Ethel Barrymore, Ed Wynn, and Mary Boland, was one of the leading firebrands of the Actors Equity strike of 1919. She sponsored the chorus-girl contingent and carried banners reading "No More Pay—Just Fair Play." She worked indefatigably for the benefit of the performers who eventually won their cause.

In the Twenties, Marie, nearly down but not out, found it much harder to obtain decent show-business roles. She was in a 200-performance run of *The Passing Show of 1921* and played for 126 performances in *The Dancing Girl* (1923). On October 19, 1925, she headlined the Palace Theatre's "Old Timer's" vaudeville unit with Cecilia Loftus, Emma Trentini, May Irwin, and Marie Cahill and was held over a second week. After over 30 years, Marie Dressler and Broadway parted. She would never return.

By early 1926 Marie was in a strained financial state and was convinced her show-business years were gone forever. She talked of becoming a housekeeper at a Long Island estate or of trying to find backing to open a restaurant in Rome or Paris. According to cinema historian DeWitt Bodeen it was Nella

Webb, a noted astrologist, who advised Marie to sit tight, for something good was about to happen to her. And it did.

Director Allan Dwan hired Marie for two days' work in Olive Borden's *The Joy Girl* (1927), filmed on location in Palm Beach, Florida. It was not much of a comeback, but it was a start. Then Frances Marion, aware of Dressler's plight, found a story by Kathleen Norris in Metro's story department. She developed it into a scenario for Polly Moran—and for Marie, persuading MGM executive Irving Thalberg that only Marie could play the beer-guzzling Ma Callahan, the wary but warm friend to Moran's Mrs. Murphy. Marie arrived in Los Angeles on March 7, 1927, and registered at the Ambassador Hotel. The picture proved to be bright and witty and played to the hilt by the new team of Dressler and Moran. But the Hibernians, the Roman Catholic Church, and various Irish brotherhoods and other organizations raised a brouhaha about *The Callahans and the Murphys* (1927). MGM quickly ordered cuts in the film to appease the protesters. Finally, it was forced to withdraw the comedy from distribution. At 58 Marie was again unemployed.

Friends came to the rescue. She won a small but showy role in Constance Talmadge's *Breakfast at Sunrise* (1927). During this period Marie returned to the stage where for $150 she played the Queen Mother in Edward Everett Horton's Los Angeles stock production of *The Swan*. Back at Metro, Marie was reunited with Polly Moran in Frances Marion's adaptation of the comic strip *Bringing Up Father* (1928). She gave a vividly etched performance as Marion Davies' overbearing, bitchy mother in *The Patsy* (1928). Dressler's last silent picture was *The Divine Lady* (1928) which had sound effects *only*.

By 1929 Marie had been given a stock contract at MGM and as such was in the studio's *The Hollywood Revue of 1929*. In this her first talkie she was cast as an improbable seductive Venus rising from the sea in a ballet burlesque. With Polly Moran she sang "For I'm the Queen," with Moran and Bessie Love did the number "Marie, Polly and Bess," and provided a nosegay of nostalgia with a Gay Nineties song, "Strolling Through the Park One Day." For Al Christie, Marie and her cohort Polly Moran made a funny two-reel comedy, *Dangerous Females*

(1929), released by Paramount. The two women played the sisters Bascom, who mistake an innocent man for a wanted criminal. The "girls" were howlingly funny.

Rudy Vallee's *The Vagabond Lover* (1929) was dismissed by the *New York Times* except for Marie Dressler's effective comedy: "Miss Dressler is really funny as Mrs. Whitehall, who can't control her expressions of glee during fleeting moments of triumph over Mrs. Tod Hunter. She simulates the abandon and the speech of one to the manner born and toys with a chiffon handkerchief." Marie's "toying" with anything could steal a scene from the most camerawise performer. Her massive presence, her mugging, and her impromptu bits of business magnetized audience attention. *Chasing Rainbows* (1930) was Metro's unfulfilled hope to recapture the success of its *Broadway Melody*. It remained memorable only for one of its songs ("Happy Days Are Here Again") and Marie Dressler's comedy.

Frances Marion again interceded for Marie at Metro when casting started for the talkie screen version of Eugene O'Neill's *Anna Christie* (1930). Dressler's screen test convinced director Clarence Brown and producer Irving Thalberg that she would be fine as Marthy Owen, the drunken waterfront hag. The O'Neill play was vastly important to MGM. The picture would be Greta Garbo's talkie debut.

The great Swedish actress made the transition from silence to sound by beautifully playing the role of Anna. But it was the haggard, beer-soaked deposed mistress of her father who dominated. Dressler's characterization of Marthy (with the squashed, lopsided hat) emerged as one of her finest screen portraits. Although Garbo was lauded for her performance, it was Marie who received the lion's share of critical acclaim. As a follow-up of sorts, MGM cast her as wealthy Hettie Brown doing another low-comedy drunk scene for William Haines' *The Girl Said No* (1930).

When United Artists filmed *The Swan*—retitled *One Romantic Night* (1930) for the screen—Marie repeated her stage assignment as Princess Beatrice. Despite her comic performance, the film was dull.

Caught Short (1930) started a rollicking series of MGM comedies teaming Dressler

In The Hollywood Revue of 1929 *(1929)*.

and Polly Moran. Polly was usually the comedy foil for the more assertive low-comedy (laced with pathos) playing of Marie. Their four co-starring vehicles followed variations of two middle-aged, battling, lovable close friends caught up in resolving mundane crises and meddling in the lives of their offspring. Critics deplored the slapstick, thinly plotted comedies as a waste of two great talents. But the films did create explosive laughter, and audience response to the pictures was tremendous.

Caught Short featured the world of high finance and a comic routine involving a Murphy bed. The girls worked hard for laughs in *Reducing* (1931) and with *Politics* (1931) they hit their peak. *Photoplay* told its fans, "If that Dressler-Moran team doesn't cure your Depression-blues, it's time to see a doctor." Dressler was a constant delight as the vociferous widow Hattie Burns, who organizes a housewives' strike, closes the town's speakeasies, and reforms the state of politics by running for mayor. The last team-

ing of Dressler and Moran was in *Prosperity* (1932), which was below their previous adventures. Marie was cast as the president of a small-town bank who defeats the Depression and saves her depositors.

Meanwhile, Marie continued to appear in other Metro ventures. With her old theatre friends Fay Templeton, William Collier, De-Wolf Hopper, and Weber and Fields, Marie started an MGM musical early in 1930, a revue known as *The March of Time*. But after extensive shooting on Metro's planned revue of 1930, the picture was largely junked. (Portions of it would be used for the eventual banal *Broadway to Hollywood*, 1933, but none of Marie's material remained.)

In Norma Shearer's *Let Us Be Gay* (1930) Marie solidified her growing reputation as "The Thief of the Talkies." She gave a bravura performance as the sardonic dowager Mrs. Boucicault. *Time* described it as an almost perfect realization of casting and direction and said "it is distinguished by some wonderful acting by Marie Dressler." After *Let Us Be*

225

With Tom McGuire and Claire DuBrey in Politics (1931).

Gay Marie was given a role measured to her talents by Frances Marion. It was the part of a waterfront proprietress of a downgraded boarding house on Cannery Row at San Pedro harbor. This flamboyant seedy dame was named Min.

Min and Bill's (1930) greatest asset was the team of Marie Dressler and Wallace Beery—their first role together. The two far-from-young troupers tore up the screen in a six-minute battle that remains one of the most riotous battles of the sexes on film. Once seen, you could not easily forget Min pursuing her fisherman-sweetheart, Bill, flailing an axe, and hurling everything in sight (including a potty) at him, while terrified Beery helplessly growled two words, "Awww, Min!" Critics generally found the film distasteful and its tragicomic overtones ill-tuned to the stars' talents. But the public adored the film and its lead personalities. Audiences agreed that it was a tour-de-force role for the 61-year-old Dressler.

On November 10, 1931, the Academy of Motion Picture Arts and Sciences awarded Marie Dressler an Oscar as the Best Actress of the Year for her *Min* performance. At the banquet Marie reveled in her new, rarefied status. She acknowledged the years of devotion of Frances Marion by saying, "You can be the best actress in the world and have the best producer, director, and cameraman, but it won't matter a bit if you don't have the story."

Thereafter, Frances Marion again supplied a story that displayed Marie's capacity to extract tears and laughter from an audience. In *Emma* (1932) she was the loyal housekeeper of widowed inventor Jean Hersholt, accused of murdering her employer after their marriage. Dressler added strength to the tearjerking aspect of *Emma* through sheer warmth and humanity. The *New York Times* acknowledged, "The sympathetic and brilliant performance of Miss Dressler is one of the outstanding achievements of the screen and one of the finest character studies that have come to the screen." *Emma* won Marie a second Academy Award nomination as Best Actress but she lost to Helen Hayes of *The Sin of Madelon Claudet.*

With screen mate Polly Moran, Marie was one of several MGM stars featured in the one-reel short *Jackie Cooper's Christmas* (1932).

226

But Marie's health was failing. In the summer of 1931 an operation disclosed an inoperable malignancy. Marie was not told. Despite her slowly deteriorating physical condition, she continued filmmaking.

In *Tugboat Annie* (1933) she teamed with Wallace Beery for the second and final time.* Mervyn LeRoy, borrowed from Warner Bros. to direct the feature, recalled that Dressler could work only three hours a day, but that "she was always a lady, always kind and considerate. Her constant pain showed in her face and bearing but never in her professionalism when the camera was rolling." The rigorous location scenes were filmed in the harbor of Seattle, Washington—a strenuous assignment for a woman her age who was slowly dying of cancer.

Despite her physical problems, Marie was in top form in *Tugboat Annie*. She was the captain of the decrepit tugboat *Narcissus*

---

* Although they only made two features together with joint scenes, the combination of Dressler and Beery was deemed one of the screen's best. Beery would later be matched with crow-voiced Marjorie Main for seven MGM programmers.

who rescues her son's (Robert Young) captured steamer and copes with her trouble-prone husband (Beery)—"who never struck me except in self-defense." *Time* magazine enthused, "It is entirely because of the presence in its cast of an old lady whose preposterous career makes the happy ending in *Tugboat Annie* seem comparatively realistic and whose flamboyant character makes the people she impersonates seem pallid reflections of herself. What makes Marie Dressler's performances invariably exciting is the fact that even when they are careless impersonations they are brilliant records of her own robust and friendly personality." While *Time* found one of Marie's most dependable talents to be the flexing of her facial muscles (into a close approximation of a weary basset hound), Mervyn LeRoy said that although her face was not a thing of beauty, it was alive and easy to photograph.

In March 1933 shooting began on MGM's *Dinner at Eight* (1933), derived from the Broadway hit. George Cukor drew lively performances from an all-star cast. Marie gave a poignantly stunning performance as

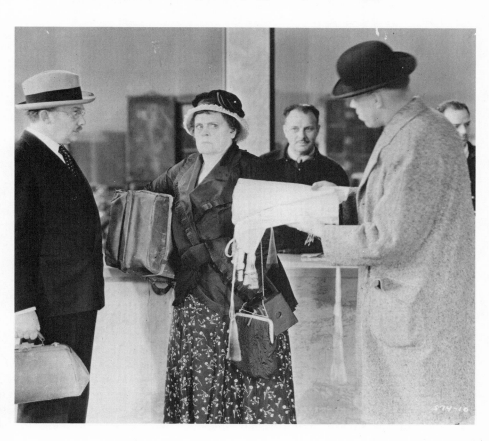

With Jean Hersholt, Ed Piel, and Jack Pennick in Emma (1932).

Publicity pose in 1932.

the faded, once-great stage actress Carlotta Vance. Director Cukor, discussing Marie's performance of the aging, romance-prone actress, stated, "She acquired a kind of peculiar distinction, a magnificence. She was a law unto herself. She'd mug and carry on, which she did in this picture, but she knew how to make an entrance with great aplomb, great effect."

Marie sailed through *Dinner at Eight*, in which she and past co-star Wallace Beery had no joint scenes. The final sequence remains a classic. Platinum blonde Jean Harlow, braless in a white satin gown, sets Marie up for one of the best curtain lines ever heard on the screen. Harlow announces that she has read a book (which shocks Marie) and that the author said machinery was going to take the place of every profession and function. Marie, with a flourish and an appreciative once-over of the Harlow structure, consoles,

"Oh, my dear. That is something you need never to worry about!"

Marie's 64th birthday on November 9, 1933, was celebrated with a national radio broadcast from one of MGM's largest sound stages. It was attended by 700 guests and memorialized with a scroll of greeting containing an impressive list of signatures, headed by those of President and Mrs. Roosevelt. A cake 500 pounds, eight feet tall, and six feet in diameter added to the gala. Will Rogers, Lionel Barrymore, and other close friends made speeches of praise in her honor. Louis B. Mayer, who adored the old actress and was one of the few who knew she had terminal cancer, rejoiced in the tributes accorded his favorite MGM star.

MGM adapted the Broadway play *The Late Christopher Bean* (derived from a French play) into *Christopher Bean* (1934). Marie was admirably cast as the lone protector of

228

her former lover's (Bean) painting. She refuses to part with the artist's portrait of her, now that he has become posthumously famous. The role of Abby was another of the growing, finely drawn screen portraits created by Marie Dressler. It was also her last.

Louis B. Mayer persuaded Marie to take a long rest following the completion of *Bean*. She left Hollywood and the home she bought in Beverly Hills in 1932 to reside at a nursing home in Santa Barbara, California. There, on July 28, 1934, at 3:25 P.M., Marie Dressler died. She was 64.

Following the viewing at the Wee Kirk o' the Heather chapel, Marie was buried in Forest Lawn's most honored mausoleum, the "Sanctuary of Benediction," near producer Irving Thalberg. MGM, following the unanticipated sparkling reaction to the Dressler-Harlow scene from *Dinner at Eight*, had planned to co-star them in a Louis Bromfield story, *Living in a Great Big Way*, and had penciled Marie in for the starring title role of

Mrs. Van Kleek, proprietress of a South Seas hotel. Neither film was made. A sequel to *Tugboat Annie*, reuniting Dressler and Beery, was also planned and, unfortunately, never realized.

Her autobiography, *Marie Dressler: My Own Story* (as told to Mildred Harrington), was published posthumously in November 1934. It revealed some intriguing facts.*

Perhaps *Photoplay* offered the finest final tribute to the "grand old lady of the movies":

If you ever saw Marie Dressler on the screen, she went straight to your

---

* Marie actually did win a beauty prize during her lifetime. At an early Twenties Newspaper Women's Club of New York Ball, Will Rogers was forced to select a "queen" from among a bevy of beauties. He spotted Marie Dressler in the audience and gave her the award. She accepted the unlikely accolade, saying, "After figuring out at an early age that I never could be a beauty and must therefore become a comedienne, it seems to me most odd that at the end of some 30 years as a funny woman, I should now be presented with a beauty prize!"

With Madge Evans in Dinner at Eight *(1933).*

heart. That was because the shining qualities that made her so beloved by everyone who knew her personally were revealed—every word, gesture, and facial expression were in her film interpretations.

FEATURE FILMS

Tillie's Punctured Romance (*Keystone 1914*)
  (TV title: Charlie's Big Romance)
Tillie's Tomato Surprise (*Lubin 1915*)
Tillie Wakes Up (*Peerless-World 1917*)
The Joy Girl (*Fox 1927*)
The Callahans and the Murphys (*MGM 1927*)
Breakfast at Sunrise (*First National 1927*)
Bringing Up Father (*MGM 1928*)
The Patsy (*MGM 1928*)
The Divine Lady (*First National 1928*)
The Hollywood Revue of 1929 (*MGM 1929*)
The Vagabond Lover (*RKO 1929*)
Chasing Rainbows (*MGM 1930*)

Anna Christie (*MGM 1930*)
The Girl Said No (*MGM 1930*)
One Romantic Night (*United Artists 1930*)
Caught Short (*MGM 1930*)
Let Us Be Gay (*MGM 1930*)
Min and Bill (*MGM 1930*)
Reducing (*MGM 1931*)
Politics (*MGM 1931*)
Emma (*MGM 1932*)
Prosperity (*MGM 1932*)
Tugboat Annie (*MGM 1933*)
Dinner at Eight (*MGM 1933*)
Christopher Bean (*MGM 1933*)

Jimmy Durante

If imitation is the sincerest form of flattery, James Francis Durante is the world's most flattered performer. Establishing originality in comedy identifiable with one performer is a rarity. To combine that talent with a bond of love and respect between performer, audience, and fellow players exceeds even the rare identification. The Cyrano of comedy, strutting like a stiff-legged penguin, waving his copious nose above a broad, infectious smile, while slaughtering the Queen's English, has delighted generations of fans.

Bartolomeo Durante emigrated from Salerno, Italy, and settled on the Lower East Side of Manhattan. He then sent for his mail-order bride, Rosa. Shortly after Rosa's arrival they were married and became the parents of Michael, Albert, Lillian, and James Francis. The last named was born on Friday, February 10, 1893, delivered by an Italian midwife in the Durantes' three-room apartment behind Bartolomeo's barbershop at 90 Catherine Street. Baby James was baptized at St. James Catholic Church on Oliver Street.

James attended Public School 114 to the seventh grade, although he says, "I was trown outuh duh winduh in second grade and never came back." His great interest was piano. At 10 he began studying the piano in earnest and in later years would be rated one of the best white ragtime pianists in America. At 15 he was playing ragtime at parties, Bowery gin mills, and between bouts at a prizefighting arena. His first professional job arrived two years later, playing piano at Diamond Tony's Oceanic Walk joint in Coney Island. By the end of the summer he was banging out his ragtime rhythms on Chinatown's Doyers Street at the Chatham Club. He returned to Coney Island the following summer. "Ragtime Jimmy" accompanied the singing waiters at Carey Walsh's Oceanic Walk spot, the most ambitious being a short, big-eyed waiter, Izzy Iskowitch, who became Eddie Cantor.

Upon organizing the Durante Original Jazz Novelty Band, Jimmy played the Alamo Club in Harlem on 125th Street, and then alternated between the Alamo and the

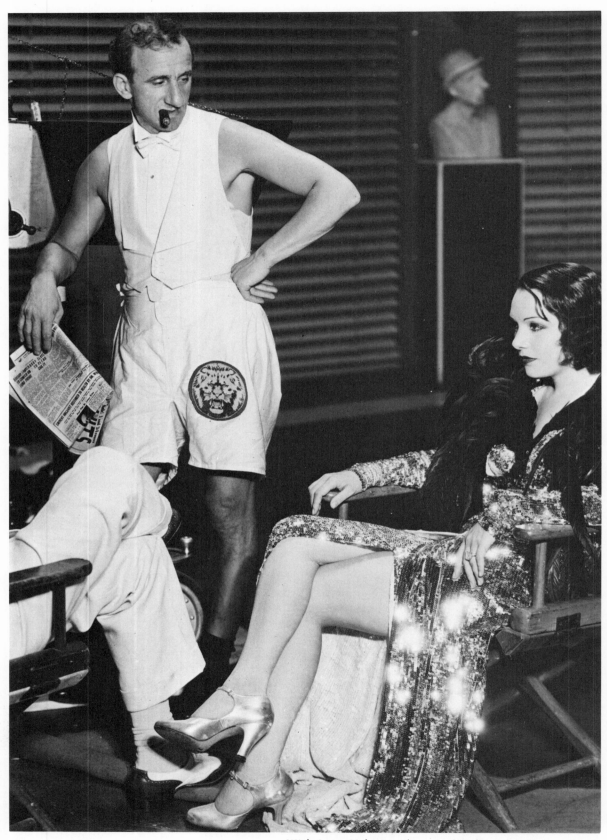

With Lupe Velez on the set of Hollywood Party *(1934).*

management's Coney Island College Inn for the next seven or eight years.* At the Alamo he met singer Maud Jeanne Olson, whom he wed on June 19, 1921, at St. Malachy's Roman Catholic Church. More important to his future, he also met a young Jewish dancer, Eddie (Jacobs) Jackson, and, in 1923, a suave soft-shoe dancer, Louis Finklestein, known professionally as Lou Clayton. Meanwhile the 49th Street club, the Nightingale, hired Durante and his Dixieland band. Headwaiter Frank Nolan later convinced Jimmy to open his own club and he found a likely spot at 232 West 58 Street in Manhattan. It became the Club Durant. (Lack of funds erased the e.)

The Club Durant soon became *the* speakeasy in New York City, packed with writers, gangsters, society, nouveaux riches, and fellow entertainers, all marveling at the wild antics and offbeat performing of the new team of Clayton, Jackson, and Durante. *Variety*'s Sime Silverman tagged them the "Three Sawdust Bums." Damon Runyon lauded them in print, "I doubt if a greater cafe combination ever lived," and other columnists heralded them as the "Three Musketeers of Broadway." By January 1923 the Club Durant was padlocked by federal agents for Prohibition violations. The trio thereafter enlivened several of the more posh Manhattan entertainment spots, all managed by the "mob."

Durante's distinctive approach to comedy developed during the club engagements as did his songwriting aptitude: "Jimmy, the Well Dressed Man," "I Ups to Him and He Ups to Me," "A Dissa and a Datta," "Who'll Be with You When I'm Far Away?" "I Can Do Without Broadway, but Can Broadway Do Without Me?" and his "national anthem," "Inka Dinka Doo." With Jimmy's fractured English-ragtime, Clayton and Jackson's dancing, and a wild sketch entitled "Wood"— in which the trio came close to demolishing nightclubs—they became Broadway's darlings. While appearing at the Rendezvous Club, Clayton (always the act's business manager) hired a young singer, Ethel Zimmerman, and changed her surname to Merman. Holdover engagements at the Palace Theatre and Loew's State Theatre in vaude-

ville led to Florenz Ziegfeld's contracting the trio for his production of *Show Girl.*

Show Girl, with music by George Gershwin and Vincent Youmans, and Jimmy Durante, opened at the Ziegfeld Theatre on July 2, 1929. Ruby Keeler had the title role and Harriet Hoctor performed a stunning ballet of Gershwin's "An American in Paris." But the hit of the show was "Schnozzle" Durante,* who convulsed audiences with the inane poem "I Got a One-Room House," delivering the stanzas in a dead seriousness that Robert Benchley compared to "the best cuckoo I ever heard." The *New Yorker* magazine exclaimed, "Clayton, Jackson, and Durante are the comedians. Having regarded them in their various nightclubs with something little short of idolatry for years, I can't write of them dispassionately. It seems to me that Jimmy Durante has the funniest face on earth, and there's a quality of high, wild burlesque in everything the three do which is irresistible."

When *Show Girl* completed its 111-performance run, Clayton, Jackson, and Durante were signed by Paramount for $50,000 to appear in the Ben Hecht and Charles MacArthur-scripted *Roadhouse Nights* (1929). The trio began working on the picture in November 1929 at Paramount's Astoria, Long Island, studio. During the month's shooting required for their roles, they appeared twice daily at Broadway's Palace Theatre and nightly at the Silver Slipper club. *Photoplay* wrote of his film debut as Daffy in *Roadhouse Nights*, "Jimmy Durante is immense in the Roadhouse sequence. Watch this Durante!" Within the feature the trio performed three of Jimmy's songs: "Everything Is on the Up and Up," "Everybody Wants My Girl," and "Hello, Everybody, Folks."

In the fall of 1930 the trio started rehearsals for Cole Porter's Broadway-bound musical *The New Yorkers*, which opened on December 8, 1930, at the Broadway Theatre. Several of the rave reviews crowned Durante with laurels. Robert Benchley reported, "I am already on record in the Library of Congress as being completely a victim of any of Mr. Durante's efforts, including the aspirate straightening of his tie or the sudden twirling

---

* Recordings made by Durante and his New Orleans jazz-style band have become collectors' items.

* Lou Clayton nicknamed Durante "Schnozzola."

on his heel to face his imaginary accusers; all that I can add now is an expression of wonder, entirely mixed with awe, that a man who started out as the greatest of all madmen should grow increasingly better as his fame and adulation spread."

The New Yorkers would be the last professional appearance of the Clayton, Jackson, and Durante trio. They brought down the house with their "Wood" routine, piling the stage with anything they found made of wood while Jimmy strenuously orated the bountiful blessings lavished on America by wood. The trio, after convulsing audiences in the Porter musical, continued playing nightly at the Silver Slipper Club. When the show closed, Jimmy was offered a five-year contract with Metro-Goldwyn-Mayer and left for the West Coast with his wife Jeanne.

Cast as "Schnozzle"* in William Haines' *New Adventures of Get-Rich-Quick Wallingford* (1931), Jimmy stole the picture. *Photoplay* enthused, "This boy Durante, by the way, is knocking Hollywood for a row of dialogue writers and is going to be one of the

---

* In 1933 Durante would apply for a copyright on his nickname, "Schnozzle."

big shots all over the country before many feet of film have passed through the camera." But Metro next assigned him as singer Lawrence Tibbett's Marine pal in an improbable, trite script, *The Cuban Love Song* (1931).

Metro executive Irving Thalberg was vastly amused by Durante's humor and teamed him with Buster Keaton (on the decline) in three dismal comedies: *The Passionate Plumber* (1932), *Speak Easily* (1932), and *What! No Beer?* (1933). Durante was the one redeeming feature of the pictures. Keaton's golden screen era had deteriorated with the talkies, personal problems, and alcohol. As cinema historian Arthur Knight would later observe, "Durante's natural style was volatile, explosive. It was Durante, not Keaton, that the talkies wanted. Jimmy Durante is a veritable fury of activity, magnifying every emotion until it becomes a parody of itself." Years later, Keaton, recalling the Durante period, warmly congratulated Jimmy for being completely professional, never upstaging him or trying to steal scenes during the making of the three films.

Between the Keaton comedies, Jimmy gave a good performance as Abe Schilling, a Pro-

With Buster Keaton in a pose for What! No Beer? *(1933).*

234

hibition agent who loses his life to save Robert Young, in *The Wet Parade* (1932). Durante was then loaned to Paramount for one of his best screen roles, as Charley Cooney, the medicine-show partner of George M. Cohan, in *The Phantom President* (1932). Cohan's talking-picture debut (in a dual role) was salvaged by the zany performance of Jimmy. It was he who capped the political musical satire by announcing, "A depression is a hole, a hole is nuthin', and why should I waste my time talkin' about nuthin'?"

Marion Davies' *Blondie of the Follies* (1932) was one of her better screen efforts, enhanced by a hilarious burlesque of Garbo in *Grand Hotel*, while Durante laughably slaughtered the John Barrymore role. The *New York Times* noted, "Jimmy Durante pops in irrelevantly for three minutes or so, which is long enough for him to break up the show. He sings one of his 'disa and data' songs, heaps vigorous and naughty scorn on his imaginary enemies and does a mad impression of John Barrymore in which Marion Davies figures as Greta Garbo." In *Hell Below* (1933), Jimmy as the ship's cook fought a kangaroo. He made two MGM programmers and then returned to Broadway.

Strike Me Pink began life with a quick death in October 1932 as *Forward March*. Songwriters Brown and Henderson reconstructed their revue, enlisted the services of Lupe Velez, Hope Williams, and Jimmy "Schnozzle" Durante, and opened the show as *Strike Me Pink* (March 3, 1933). It lumbered along for 105 performances. Most critics loathed the production, but felt Durante was as wonderful as ever. Richard Lockridge wrote about Durante's contribution to the show, "Nothing tires him. After squandering his energy in countless directions, slapping the furniture and pounding the stage he is still bursting with energy at the curtain. His metabolism must be perfect. Ebullient Jimmy! A herd of wild elephants could not crash through a show more passionately." The *New York Times'* Brooks Atkinson called Durante the Cyrano of Clowns and the show's greatest asset.

For his starring role in *Strike Me Pink* Jimmy received $3,000 weekly. He split his salary with Clayton and Jackson, although they were not in the musical revue. Despite

his becoming one of America's foremost clowns, this warm, lovable man always regarded himself as part of the trio of Clayton, Jackson, and Durante. Eventually Clayton hung up his dancing shoes to become Jimmy's business manager and Jackson became the star's companion and personal retainer. In later years Durante included Eddie Jackson in his nightclub and television acts, shuffling and singing "Bill Bailey, Won't You Please Come Home?"

Metro farmed Durante to United Artists as fight manager Knobby Walsh in a surprisingly good film exercise of Ham Fisher's comic strip *Palooka* (1934). Once again Durante proved he could create a warm, funny, well-rounded character. He easily walked off with the picture. *Palooka* was also noteworthy for an airing of Durante's self-written "Inka Dinka Doo," which would become virtually his theme song.

MGM permitted Jimmy to accept "Chase and Sanborn's Radio Coffee Hour" at $5,000, and this audio assignment brought him increased fame. However, the studio was not doing right by the comedian oncamera. A monumental mishmash called *Hollywood Party* (1934) had the studio assembling most of its stock comics: Laurel and Hardy, Lupe Velez, Charles Butterworth, Ted Healy, and the Three Stooges, plus Polly Moran.* Jimmy burlesqued the prevalent Tarzan craze as Schnarzan the Shouting Conqueror. Later in 1934 Durante would make his last picture for MGM for a while. But *Student Tour*, like RKO's *Strictly Dynamite* (1934) and Columbia's *Carnival* (1934), did nothing to help the comedian's faltering screen career. MGM's mismanagement of his cinema outings had nearly eradicated the star's status with the public.

On May 14, 1935, the *Hollywood Reporter* printed, "Jimmy Durante, who is washed up at MGM, is returning to New York to be featured in Billy Rose's production of *Jumbo*." In the Ben Hecht–Charles MacArthur play, the comedian was cast as illiterate press agent Claudius "Brainy" Bowers. It became his best characterization on stage or screen. *Jumbo* was colossal, and after

* Jimmy's wife Jeanne also appeared as "herself" in the film. Durante and Polly Moran headlined the Capitol Theatre's stage show in New York on March 13, 1934, after completing *Hollywood Party*.

With Dickie Walters, Lee Tracy, and Sally Eilers in Carnival *(1934).*

many tribulations it opened on November 16, 1935, at the enormous Hippodrome. The massive musical comedy extravaganza was nearly overpowering, but Jimmy and Big Rosie (playing the elephant Jumbo) stood out. Durante had one of his singularly funny deliveries when in the course of the story a sheriff, foreclosing the circus, accosts Durante as he leads Big Rosie from the ring. The law enforcer demands to know what he is doing with the elephant. Bewildered, belligerent James astonishingly bellows, "What elfin!?"

During the 233-performance run of *Jumbo*, producer Billy Rose conceived the idea of a Tuesday night radio series, "Jumbo," broadcast from the Hippodrome Theatre over NBC. It featured Durante, Gloria Grafton, Donald Novis, and Arthur Sinclair. When *Jumbo* ended its engagement on April 18, 1936, Billy Rose was still praising Durante's bravery: "I've known many comedians who would do anything for a laugh. But Durante is the only one I ever heard of who risked his life night after night in order to bring down the house in what I think was the biggest jolt in the

funny bone a Broadway audience ever got." On his back, Durante permitted Big Rosie to walk back and forth across his prostrate frame and place one huge hoof on his stomach. Frank "Bring 'Em Back Alive" Buck told Durante he would not do the stunt for a million dollars. To be truthful, Durante's confidence in Big Rosie's devotion occasionally wavered. Once he told Rose, "I know an elfin never forgets—what the hell has it got to remember?"

A stage tour of Dublin, Glasgow, and Liverpool also took Durante to London's Palladium where he scored a tremendous show-business hit. (He was amusingly billed on the Palladium's marquee as Jimmy "Schozzle" Durante—"The Hollywood Lover.") While in England he also played the role of Johan J. Whistler in the British feature *Land Without Music* (1936), a Ruritanian affair with opera singer Richard Tauber and American actress June Clyde.

Cole Porter's *Red, Hot and Blue* (October 29, 1936) presented a billing problem for Vinton Freedley. The solution came in a billing resembling a railroad-crossing sign

"X" for Jimmy Durante-Ethel Merman with up-and-coming comedian Bob Hope forming the base. But it was Jimmy's show. Richard Lockridge discovered Durante had never been funnier. The three stars rose above the ponderous book. With Merman to belt out the Porter songs, and Durante and Hope to enliven the comedy, the show lasted 183 performances. During the six-week run in Chicago Jimmy played a nightclub engagement at the Chez Paree and then returned to Billy Rose's Manhattan club, Casa Manana, working with a vaudeville team, Long and (Danny) Kaye.

Hollywood was still not sure what to do with the volatile Jimmy and used him for *mere* comedy relief in a trio of features: *Start Cheering* (1938), *Sally, Irene and Mary* (1938), and Shirley Temple's *Little Miss Broadway* (1938). The Big Nose returned to Broadway to co-star again with Ethel Merman, this time in Arthur Schwartz's musical *Stars in Your Eyes* (February 9, 1939). The Hollywood satire was adequately received for 127 performances. Merman and Durante stopped the show with the duet "It's All Yours."

As the new decade began the only offer from Hollywood came from Herbert J. Yates of Republic for Jimmy to play Cornelius J. Courtenay in a Gene Autry oater, *Melody Ranch* (1940). Durante had never been on a horse and was lashed to the saddle for the filming. He commented about the experience, "I'd never rode a horse and the horse never had been rode. So we both started out on even terms. It was a catastrastroke!" During this period he was under much pressure in his personal life. He was paying bills for Clayton's various hospitalizations and coping with his wife's constant unhappiness over the demands of his profession—and her unbridled jealousy of Lou Clayton.

Ray Bolger, Jane Froman, and Ilka Chase starred with Jimmy in the spring of 1940 in Broadway's short-lived revue *Keep Off the Grass*. In 1941 Durante was back on the screen, first in Warner Bros.' low-class *You're in the Army Now* (with Phil Silvers and Jane Wyman) and then in Warners' meritorious version of *The Man Who Came to Dinner*, giving a sparkling performance as Banjo (a caricature of Harpo Marx). Then Clayton arranged a contract for Jimmy's weekly appearance on the "Camel Caravan" radio show and negotiated another MGM contract. The new studio pact called for one picture a year over a five-year period and it liberally permitted him to perform in other media.

While Jimmy was in New York City for radio broadcasts (and also performing at the Copacabana nightclub) his wife Jeanne died, on February 17, 1943. He returned to California for her funeral and burial at Mountain View Cemetery in Arcadia. Back in Manhattan he completed fourteen weeks at the Copacabana. Then, in the spring of 1943, he was teamed on radio with a young master of ceremonies named Garry Moore. "That's My Boy" Moore was a literate, educated conversationalist, in marked contrast to Jimmy, who slaughtered the syntax. Moore's on-the-air efforts to improve the Durante English were squelched with, "You teach me to say dem woids right an' we're both outa job." The radio program became a national hit. Jimmy would sign off weekly with his compelling sentimental and mysterious curtain line, "And goodnight, Mrs. Calabash, wherever you are." In 1966 he addressed the National Press Club and revealed that the mysterious Mrs. Calabash was his first wife, Jeanne.

Durante's roles in the Forties at MGM were a vast improvement over his Thirties efforts at that studio. He was a delight in *Two Girls and a Sailor* (1944) utilizing his old routine, "Everybody Wants to Gets inta da Act!" As Andrews in MGM's *Music for Millions* (1944) he introduced Irving Caesar's wild song "Umbriago." Durante's zany clowning remained unchanged. He was still screaming at the orchestra to "Stop da music," staging mock warfare on the musicians, and, basically, doing the same set pieces developed many years before. But he performed them still with great flourish, and to a new generation they seemed iconoclastic, fresh, and inventive. The business produced more hilarity than ever before. In October 1945 Durante was immortalized in concrete when Sid Grauman pushed the famous Schnozzola into wet cement in the patio of his Chinese Theatre in Hollywood.

MGM's *Ziegfeld Follies* (1946) had nearly as much footage excised from the final print as was shown on the screen. Durante's song, "You've Gotta Start Off Each Day with a Smile," and his sketches, "Death and Taxes"

With Jose Iturbi and Margaret O'Brien in Music for Millions *(1944).*

(with Edward Arnold and Kay Williams) and "The Pied Piper," plus a routine with Lucille Ball and Marilyn Maxwell, were cut from the overlong revue film. In the released *Follies* Durante never appeared.

But he did claim audience attention in *Two Sisters from Boston* (1946), with June Allyson, Kathryn Grayson, and his friend, tenor Lauritz Melchior. (Durante always announced his pal as "Laurence Melcure.") *Photoplay* judged him "downright wonderful" in this screen venture. Bosley Crowther (*New York Times*) wrote that Jimmy "boldly but benignly runs away with the show. He fumes and tirades through the film, banging tunes out of his piano and badgering the husky chorus girls. And he also plays tender godfather to the two sisters who come down from Boston with all the drive and paternal authority of a longshoreman handling bales with care. There is a very strong sentiment on Broadway, with which this writer heartily agrees, that the Honorable James Durante is

the funniest man in the world—and the sweetest personality in Metro's *Two Sisters from Boston.*"

After the New York City premiere of *Two Sisters from Boston* in June 1946, MGM rented the old Silver Slipper Cafe. For the last time the trio of Clayton, Jackson, and Durante entertained—all night.

He was lauded for playing the New Utrecht High School janitor in *It Happened in Brooklyn* (1947) and then completed location shooting on an Esther Williams splash, *This Time for Keeps* (1947). While the great clown underwent intestinal surgery, Bob Hope, Frank Morgan, Red Skelton, and other show-business stars substituted for him on his radio show and there was a massive outpouring of love and sympathy from around the world. When he recovered Jimmy continued his club dates and broadcasting, and made another Esther Williams Technicolor musical, *On an Island with You* (1948). After his Metro contract expired, Durante would remain in Hollywood to play in Eagle Lion's *The Great Rupert* (1950), about a performing squirrel, and in *The Milkman* (1950), a tepid flick in which he taught Donald O'Connor the basics of milk delivery.

On September 12, 1950, his beloved Lou Clayton died after months of struggling with cancer. Prior to his death Clayton arranged for Durante's television debut. In October 1950 Jimmy returned to New York City where his first television show originated with guest star Donald O'Connor. The following spring the comedian was presented with the George Foster Peabody TV Award and *Motion Picture Daily*'s television poll named him TV's Best Performer. On February 5, 1953, he received 1952's television Emmy Award as the Best Comedian of the Year. His physical, outrageous comedy routines were naturals for television and one of his most delightful guests was opera diva Helen Traubel. Appearing in armor and carrying a spear, she seemed fully prepared to launch into her operatic role of Brünnhilde, when Durante gasped, "Holy smoke. She's been drafted!"

On screen Jimmy did a song-and-dance bit (unbilled) with Bob Hope in *Beau James* (1957). The same year he received a standing ovation from the United States Senate while he sat quietly (believing he was unobserved) in the visitors' gallery. On October 8, 1956, Durante had announced his engagement to showgirl Margie Little. Two years later, December 14, 1960, at St. Malachy's Roman Catholic Church in New York City (where he had married Jeanne), James Francis Durante, age 67, was again a bridegroom.* The next winter the Durantes adopted a baby girl, the California Superior Court having decided his age was not a factor. The judge told the lovable clown, "Jimmy, I've seen you perform. You are young at heart." Flanked by godmother Louella Parsons and godfather Danny Thomas the baby was christened Cecilia Alicia and nicknamed Che-Che. (Now an active teenager, she remains the delight of Durante's life.)

Durante performed a cameo in *Pepe* (1960) and the next year made an Italian feature *Giudizio Universale* (The Last Judgment). In 1962 he returned once more to MGM soundstages. This time the occasion was *Billy Rose's Jumbo*, a diluted version of the play. (Back in the Forties, Metro had planned to film it with Durante and Frank Sinatra starred.) Although Doris Day and Stephen Boyd were the top-billed performers in the release, it was Jimmy and comedienne Martha Raye who gave the dreary production its few lively moments. Durante's last screen appearance was as Smiler Grogan (who literally kicks the bucket) in Stanley Kramer's Cinerama-process comedy, *It's a Mad, Mad, Mad, Mad World* (1963).

In mid-1966 Durante guested on Lucille Ball's TV series; on November 6, 1966 he was Humpty-Dumpty on the TV special *Alice Through the Looking Glass*, and the next year he turned up on "Bob Hope Chrysler Theatre" in *Murder at NBC*. For good friend Desi Arnaz he appeared on the producer's series "The Mothers-In-Law" in 1969, involved with that show's amusing co-stars Eve Arden and Kaye Ballard. For the December 5, 1971, TV outing *Frosty the Snowman*, the inimitable Durante voice could be relished as he performed narration chores. Along the way he co-starred with the Lennon Sisters in a successful teleseries (ABC, 1969-1970) and continued making recordings.

Having survived a series of strokes, Durante, now in his 80s, will not likely be making any more professional appearances.* Equally distressing, his special capacity to entertain defies replacement or duplication. Imitators are poor substitutes; as Durante once observed, "I advise any comic—they never get anywhere imitating anybody. There's never been an imitation that ever got to be a big star, that I know of." And, he added, he never knew an entertainer that got anywhere using off-color material. He never did.

---

* For the entertainer's 83rd birthday, some 800 persons gathered at the Beverly Hilton Hotel to pay tribute to Durante on November 19, 1976. The banquet raised more than $100,000 for a Jimmy Durante Pavilion at the Villa Scabrini Home for the Aged in California. Danny Thomas and Robert Alda were the masters of ceremonies for the gala. Among the celebrities attending were Gregory Peck, Fred MacMurray, Glen Campbell, Pat Boone, and Tony Bennett. Durante, confined to a wheelchair, responded to the assorted stage acts with applause and a tip of his trademark hat. More recently (September 25, 1978), the CBS-TV series "People" did a special tribute to Durante.

---

* For years Durante had also been dating actress Betty Jane Howarth.

With Doris Day, Martha Raye, and Stephen Boyd in Billy Rose's Jumbo *(1962).*

With Mickey Rooney and Sid Caesar in It's a Mad, Mad, Mad, Mad World *(1963).*

Many comedians are far from lovable as private persons. Durante has been a glowing exception. Louis Sobol once said, "The bare mention of his name engenders a feeling of warmth." Press agent Richard Maney capped the man's standing within his profession: "You never hear anybody pan Durante—and that's *rare* in show business." Billy Rose, always a Durante booster, vowed that Durante was the best-loved guy in the business.

FEATURE FILMS

Roadhouse Nights (*Paramount 1929*)

New Adventures of Get-Rich-Quick Wallingford (*MGM 1931*)

The Cuban Love Song (*MGM 1931*)

The Passionate Plumber (*MGM 1932*)

The Wet Parade (*MGM 1932*)

Speak Easily (*MGM 1932*)

The Phantom President (*Paramount 1932*)

Blondie of the Follies (*MGM 1932*)

What! No Beer? (*MGM 1933*)

Hell Below (*MGM 1933*)

Broadway to Hollywood (*MGM 1933*)

Meet the Baron (*MGM 1933*)

Palooka (*United Artists 1934*)

George White's Scandals of 1934 (*Fox 1934*)

Hollywood Party (*MGM 1934*)

Strictly Dynamite (*RKO 1934*)

Student Tour (*MGM 1934*)

Carnival (*Columbia 1934*)

Land Without Music [Forbidden Music] (*British 1936*)

Start Cheering (*Columbia 1938*)

Sally, Irene and Mary (*20th Century-Fox 1938*)

Little Miss Broadway (*20th Century-Fox 1938*)

Melody Ranch (*Republic 1940*)

You're in the Army Now (*Warner Bros. 1941*)

The Man Who Came to Dinner (*Warner Bros. 1941*)

Two Girls and a Sailor (*MGM 1944*)

Music for Millions (*MGM 1944*)

Two Sisters from Boston (*MGM 1946*)

It Happened in Brooklyn (*MGM 1947*)

This Time for Keeps (*MGM 1947*)

On an Island with You (*MGM 1948*)

The Great Rupert (*Eagle Lion 1950*)

The Milkman (*Universal 1950*)

Beau James (*Paramount 1957*)*

Pepe (*Columbia 1960*)

Giudizio Universale [The Last Judgment] (*Italian 1961*)

Billy Rose's Jumbo (*MGM 1962*)

It's a Mad, Mad, Mad, Mad World (*United Artists 1963*)

* Unbilled guest appearance.

241

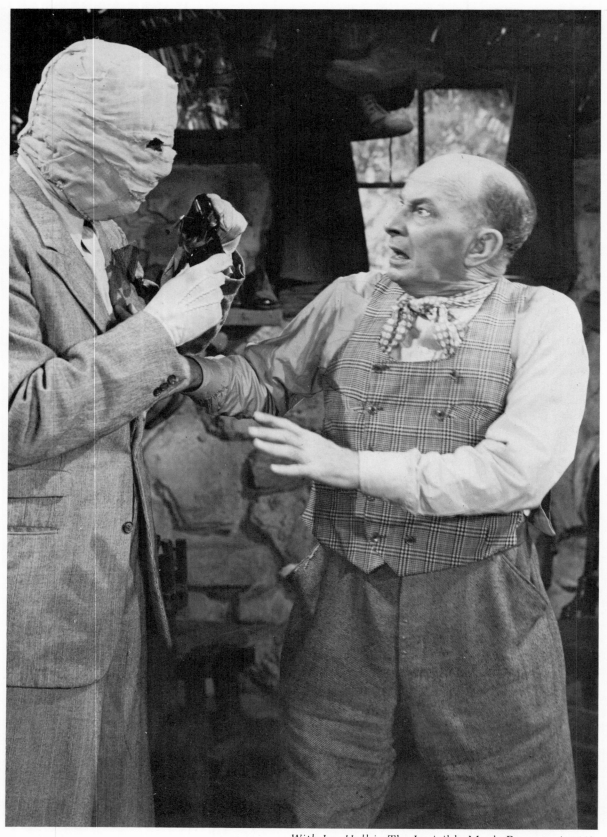

With Jon Hall in The Invisible Man's Revenge *(1944).*

Leon Errol

Comedic variance ranges from the joke-tossing comic, the talented comedian enlivening a script, to the outrageously costumed clown. Perhaps the rarest of the breed, however, is the funnyman who, without the props and the material of the others, is distinctively, and instinctively, funny. Ben Turpin, Lou Costello, Harry Langdon, and W. C. Fields were funnymen who established an instantly recognizable comedic logo. Another was Leon Errol.

Errol's loose ankles and rubber legs constantly threatening imminent collapse were his professional trademark. It helped to reinforce his frequently played guise of the willful, joyous inebriate. During his performing he utilized his entire body for laughter and perfected an outraged double take to rival those of the masters, Edward Everett Horton and Jack Oakie, and a "slow-burn" bit equal to Edgar Kennedy's. Although he specialized in playing careening souses,* Leon could, like most of the famous comedians, immerse himself in a comedy role and create a solid characterization.

Leon Errol was born in Sydney, Australia, on Sunday, July 3, 1881, to Elizabeth Adams Errol and government inspector Joseph Sims Errol. One of five children,* Leon was sent to St. Joseph's College and matriculated as a pre-med student at Sydney University. His interest in advancing medicine was overshadowed by his fascination for writing for and appearing in college variety shows. His first appearance was as a "red-nose" comic in baggy pants and outsized shoes in an operetta he had written for the college amateur group. Mr. Errol soon realized the futility of further education for Leon and gave his blessings to his son's driving ambition to become a professional performer.

Leon toured Australia and New Zealand with Paul Martinetti, and then joined a circus as a clown, bareback rider, and animal trainer. Later he spent a season playing

---

* Errol once said, "Why, I have followed drunks for blocks and blocks just to see how they acted. Most of the time was wasted, because most drunks act the same. But now and then I found a little business that I could use."

* Leon had two sisters and two brothers, one of whom took the professional name of Trav Royle and became a symphony orchestra conductor.

Shakespearean repertory (including portraying the nurse in *Romeo and Juliet*) with George Rignold's company. Later he played the celebrated drunk Eccles in *Caste*. After a season with the Sydney Stock Company, Errol migrated to America, to San Francisco. He played in the Bay City beer halls as an eccentric dancer and pantomimist. The reason for his silence on stage was that the management was convinced his Down Under accent was too perplexing for audiences. Eventually Leon drifted into burlesque. By 1905 he was managing a burlesque house in Portland, Oregon. While there he hired an aspiring fat boy eager to learn the business. The youth was Roscoe "Fatty" Arbuckle.

In the spring of 1906 Errol's traveling burlesque troupe went broke in Boise, Idaho, and the Australian returned to San Francisco. On April 18, 1906, he was playing comic opera when the San Francisco earthquake and fire erupted. An offer from producer John Cort for a season of musical comedy stock in Salt Lake City provided an opportunity to head eastward, away from the ruins and havoc and toward Broadway. Later with a burlesque unit (*The Lilies*) he had written and directed, Errol invaded New York as the leading red-nose, low comic. Abe L. Erlanger caught the ribald show at the Columbia Theatre, paid $15,000 for Errol's release from the burlesque show, and signed him as the lead in a proposed musical, *The Primrose Path*. The Erlanger musical was never produced but Florenz Ziegfeld Jr. took over his contract and cast him in the *Ziegfeld Follies 1911* that opened on June 26, 1911, to run 80 performances.

Featured with Fanny Brice, Bessie McCoy, the Dolly Sisters, and the remarkably talented Bert Williams, Leon (teamed with Williams) virtually stole the *Follies*. Errol and Williams reduced audiences to helpless laughter in the riotous sketch "Upper and Lower Level," with Errol as a very drunken Major Waterbrush. Errol's dancing partner in the show, Stella Chatelaine, was Mrs. Leon Errol.*

Ziegfeld next put Errol in the role of the president of the Purity League in *A Winsome*

* At the time of her death on November 7, 1946, the Errols had been married thirty-nine years.

Widow (April 11, 1912), which ran for 172 performances. For his *Follies* roles of 1912, 1913, and 1914, Errol won the title "Rubber Legs"; he also continued to be teamed with Bert Williams and with expert dancer Stella Chatelaine. In the Ziegfeld stage glorification of 1915, Errol impersonated Rip Van Winkle and again delighted audiences by exploiting his collapsible structure in the character "Constant Bunn." The lanky comedian was a true standout in a company that boasted Ed Wynn, W. C. Fields, Bert Williams, Ina Claire, and George White.

Charles Dillingham and Florenz Ziegfeld's *The Century Girl* (November 6, 1916) was overly opulent and contained a cast including Elsie Janis, Hazel Dawn, Frank Tinney, and Sam Bernard. Leon directed many of the sketches and was prominent in his own stage spots. He made a delightful Mad Hatter in an *Alice in Wonderland* sketch. The show ran for 200 performances. On June 7, 1917, Errol was featured with Irene Bordoni in Raymond Hitchcock's starring revue, *Hitchy-Koo*, which Errol, with Julian Mitchell (director of several *Follies*), also staged and continued into a 1918 edition. In August 1918 *Theatre* magazine said Errol was "the cleverest man on Broadway, a red-nose comic, a classic of inebriety!"

In March 1919 Errol made his first London stage appearance, at the Hippodrome Theatre in *Joy Belle*. He then returned to America to headline the bill at the Palace Theatre. The press greeted his return: "It is good to have him back on this side of the Atlantic. Nobody else can do the things he does quite as well as he does them and that the American public missed him was fully demonstrated at the Palace." The theatre billed Leon as "our foremost international comedian—just returned from taking London by storm."

Leon continued playing New York City's vaudeville houses until April 24, 1920, when Erlanger and Ziegfeld signed him for a new book show to showcase the lovely ballerina Marilyn Miller. Backed with music by Jerome Kern and Victor Herbert, *Sally* stayed on the boards for over three years. Errol as the hard-times waiter (actually the Grand Duke of Checkergovinia) was splendid and proved he could immerse himself into "character." In 1925 First National filmed the musical as a silent,* starring Colleen Moore, and imported Errol** to reprise his role of Connie. Critics found his performance "amusing" and that his ankles gave way at inopportune moments.

Remaining in Hollywood, he was in First National's *Clothes Make the Pirate* (1925) and was well cast as a timid mid-1700s Boston tailor who, though henpecked by his wife (Dorothy Gish), becomes the city's hero when his fantasies of being a notorious pirate are fulfilled. He captures a British frigate and the real buccaneer. As Tremble-at-Evil Tidd he "stalked, stumbled, glided, and flopped with his usual success." The *New York Times* thought that his portrayal of the meek tailor was "the mainstay of the production" and that his swashbuckling pirate well expressed that "the spirit is willing but the flesh is weak—especially about the ankles." On the other hand, *Photoplay* carped, "Resorting to one little trick that he used in *Sally*, Leon Errol does his utmost to try and amuse an audience. If you have seen Errol before, you've seen everything there is. If you haven't you may get a laugh out of his eccentric knees."

Leon returned to Broadway and starred in Ziegfeld's *Louie the 14th*. An adaptation from the German, with music by Sigmund Romberg, the play opened on March 3, 1925, for a run of 79 performances. *Time* reviewed the lavish pageant: "It outshines a Mardi Gras festival and the *Follies* combined. But unless the book had Mr. Errol's legs to uphold it, it could hardly stand on its own feet. . . . The tumbling Errol is the principal object of art in some extremely decorative snapshots of musical comedy France. The comedian seems a bit less springy than formerly, for constant falls have not taken the jar off his spine. But he is as potent as ever in his dipsy dizziness, his skittish gallop. Beneath his bald dome, his elastic face is still fluent with its infantile grimaces. Another Errol specialty vouchsafed is the cluttered, fumbling attempt to

gather an armful of packages. Ripe pantomimic art raises this above the level of the five-a-day variety. Mr. Errol's hands are beautifully pusillanimous."

For all the delights of his starring vehicle, *Louie the 14th* was forced to close on the road tour when Leon fell from a parallel bar and broke both of his expressive ankles.

By the end of 1926 Errol had returned to the screen, working in First National's *The Lunatic at Large* (1927). The wild scenario had Errol changing places with an inmate of a lunatic asylum. The *New York Times* noted, "Leon Errol is the stellar light in this comedy and he gives a performance that could hardly be improved upon by funmakers more experienced in acting before the cameras. Mr. Errol has a jolly time in one close-up making the pupils of his eyes move in opposite directions." While *The Lunatic at Large* was in release, Leon was back on Broadway in the musical *Yours Truly*, which opened January 25, 1927, to run 129 performances.* In 1928 he made an extensive road tour.

Errol's last Broadway play appearance was in Earl Carroll's *Fioretta* (February 5, 1929), reteamed with his *Follies'* co-star, Fanny Brice. The sumptuous "romantic Venetian musical comedy" enjoyed a 111-performance run. Errol was a drink-happy gondolier, described as staggering to and fro in his familiar and amusing displays of *delirium tremens*. Critic Robert Coleman acknowledged, "Leon Errol is at his best. His articulate limbs, his blustery speech, his droll smile, his sense of comedy all won him riotous applause."

With his broad, comic appeal, it was only natural that the movies should reclaim Errol for the blockbuster variety picture *Paramount on Parade* (1930). Leon appeared in the introductory sequence with Jack Oakie and Skeets Gallagher in a segment called "We're the Masters of Ceremony." He appeared later in a humorous sketch, "In a Hospital," with Helen "Boop-boop-de-doop" Kane.

Errol seemed to have hit his film pace in Paramount's lively *Only Saps Work* (1930).

---

* *Sally* was remade by First National as a 1929 Technicolor talkie starring Marilyn Miller, with Joe E. Brown in Errol's role.

** Errol had made his film debut in a two-reel 1916 comedy for Kleine, *Nearly Spliced*. In 1924 Leon played a minor role as the innkeeper in William Randolph Hearst's *Yolanda*, starring Marion Davies and made at Hearst's New York Harlem studio.

* During the run of *Yours Truly*, Errol was scheduled to star in an American screen version of the French musical comedy *Le Petit Cafe*. The project was eventually filmed by Paramount as *Playboy of Paris* (1930), with Maurice Chevalier. The boulevardier also made the French-language version, *Le Petit Cafe*.

The *New York Times* lauded Errol's clever performance as cunning kleptomaniac James Wilson, who picks pockets, robs a bank, etc. *Time* observed, "It is Leon Errol's picture and the best stretches are those in which, postponing as long as possible the moment for the next conference, he extemporizes while the camera watches. He is perfectly cast as a kleptomaniac." This analysis is a good description of Errol's comedic gifts: improvisation and ad-libbing, which he had done so well in the *Follies*.

England's beauteous Evelyn Laye's American film debut in United Artists' *One Heavenly Night* (1930) was greatly enlivened by Errol's playing of her erratic guardian, Otto, weaving through the musical on his accordion legs. The *New York Times*' critic described his performance as "Mr. Errol cooks up some fun by emulating a bull in a china shop. This wobbly legged comedian also has a fearful time trying to post a letter and he finally gives up the task as something too difficult for the ordinary mortal to do on the spur of the moment, so to speak." The "Mailing a Letter" routine was an Errol classic, which he included in a 1934 Columbia short, *One Too Many*. Bits of business Errol had perfected on various stages he utilized throughout his career. It was a common practice among comic greats.

Late in 1930 Errol returned to stage work in a road tour of the three-act straight comedy *Lost Sheep.* Then he came back to Paramount to team with flighty ZaSu Pitts as his long-suffering wife in *Finn and Hattie* (1931). As Finlay Pierpont Haddock, Leon fancied himself a wrestling expert only to be given a rough-and-tumble trouncing by a real expert. He had a further wrestling match against his brattish oncamera daughter (Mitzi Green). It gave the audience just what they wanted: plenty of laughs. For Warner Bros.' *Her Majesty, Love* (1931), Leon was reunited with his *Sally* co-star, Marilyn Miller. He deftly, and quite humorously, portrayed Miss Miller's suitor, Baron von Schwarzdorf, sporting an ever present monocle. Confronted by the likes

With Evelyn Laye and Vince Barnett in One Heavenly Night *(1930).*

*With ZaSu Pitts and Mitzi
Green in Finn and Hattie
(1931).*

*In the short subject
The Jitters (1938).*

of W. C. Fields, Ford Sterling, and Chester Conklin, Errol managed to garner many of the picture's largest guffaws.

Paramount cast Leon as Uncle Gilbert in its all-star *Alice in Wonderland* (1933) and paired him with Ethel Merman in *We're Not Dressing* (1934).

Feature pictures, however, offered Errol little other than supporting comedy relief roles. But within the framework of the more lowly two-reel comedy Errol found the best outlet for his considerable, versatile talents. From 1933 to 1951 Leon made some 100 short-subject comedies, freelancing for several studios before settling in at RKO. They were, for the most part, an impressive and lively series of two-reelers. Within the perimeters of the short comedy Errol would use his stock bits from the *Follies* and even his earlier burlesque period.* The stories invariably cast him as the philandering husband, caught in outrageous contretemps, and frequently drowning his problems in booze.

By the mid-1930s the series features had become box-office grossers that Hollywood could not ignore. The inexpensive formula features were ground out into the Forties with unrelieved tedium. Many of them were good, well-constructed, well-acted, and well-produced budget-minded products that found vast appeal among box-office patrons. RKO teamed volatile Errol and Lupe Velez (the Mexican Bombshell) in a series of eight Mexican Spitfire comedies, the first being *The Girl from Mexico* (1939). It was a nonsensical comedy that grossed well and so impressed studio head George Schaefer that he rushed a second feature, *Mexican Spitfire* (1939), into production.

For all the bombastic playing of the explosively active Lupe Velez, it was Leon who commanded the greatest audience attention and approval in the movie series, and it did a good deal to elongate Leon's Hollywood career. The entries also afforded Errol the opportunity to display his versatility by playing mild, down-to-earth Uncle Matt and his lookalike, stuffy English whiskey magnate, Lord Epping. Errol had a marvelous field day. The Errol-Velez combination was successful enough for Universal to borrow the duo for a Cuban brouhaha, *Six Lessons from Madame La Zonga* (1941).

Beyond the hilarious contributions to the profits of the *Mexican Spitfire* slapdash, slapstick Errol played minor roles in many features. But none of these showcased him the way his two-reel comedies and his roaring romps with Miss Velez did. He gave excellent support as the rival in W. C. Fields' *Never Give a Sucker an Even Break* (1941), delightfully played Cornelius V. Rensington III in a pleasant little comedy, *Gals, Inc.* (1943), and sparked a dual role in Universal's *Slightly Terrific* (1944).

The *Mexican Spitfire* property was running out of steam in the mid-Forties, yet might have continued had not Lupe Velez committed suicide on December 14, 1944. But within two years Leon was involved in another film series, Monogram's low-budget *Joe Palooka*. The comic strip was brought to life with Joe Kirkwood Jr. as the fighter and Leon Errol as his boxing manager, Knobby Walsh. (It was a role that had been wonderfully played with a good deal of verve by Jimmy Durante in United Artists' *Palooka*, 1934.) The seven-entry fight series ran from 1946 to 1950. The final entry, *Joe Palooka in Humphrey Takes a Chance*, became Errol's final feature film. On September 21, 1951, RKO released an Errol short that revived his zany *Mexican Spitfire* character, *Lord Epping Returns*. His last RKO two-reeler was released on December 21, 1951, *Too Many Wives*.

On October 11, 1951, Leon was admitted to Hollywood's Good Samaritan Hospital for a checkup. The next day, Friday, October 12, 1951, at the age of 70, he succumbed to a heart attack. On the following Monday funeral services were held at the Church of the Recessional, with interment at Forest Lawn Cemetery.

* His 1937 RKO short *Should Wives Work?* received an Academy Award nomination, but a *Crime Does Not Pay* MGM entry won the Oscar. In the late Forties RKO spliced together a mélange of earlier comedies, vaudeville turns, and musical numbers for a series of "feature" films. Their *Variety Time* (1948) included the previous year's Errol short, *Hired Husband*. The cast of that two-reeler included Dorothy Granger, his frequent leading lady, and another notable portrayer of debilitated drunks, Jack Norton. In 1949 another RKO potpourri, *Make Mine Laughs*, included Errol's comedy, *Beware of Redheads*. In 1951's *Footlight Varieties* Liberace, Jack Paar, and Red Buttons were featured with an excerpt from Errol's short *He Forgot to Remember*. The popularity of the RKO Errol comedies continued into the Fifties, when short subjects were in very low demand.

With Lupe Velez in Mexican Spitfire's Baby (1941).

With Walter Reed and Elisabeth Risdon in Mexican Spitfire's Blessed Event (1943).

With Helo Hattie in Follow the Band *(1943).*

With Elyse Knox a Joe Kirkwood Jr. in pose for Fighting Mad *(1948).*

FEATURE FILMS

Yolanda (*Metro-Goldwyn 1924*)

Sally (*First National 1925*)

Clothes Make the Pirate (*First National 1925*)

The Lunatic at Large (*First National 1927*)

Paramount on Parade (*Paramount 1930*)

Only Saps Work (*Paramount 1930*)

One Heavenly Night (*United Artists 1930*)

Finn and Hattie (*Paramount 1931*)

Her Majesty, Love (*First National 1931*)

Alice in Wonderland (*Paramount 1933*)

We're Not Dressing (*Paramount 1934*)

The Notorious Sophie Lang (*Paramount 1934*)

The Captain Hates the Sea (*Columbia 1934*)

Princess O'Hara (*Universal 1935*)

Coronado (*Paramount 1935*)

Make a Wish (*RKO 1937*)

The Girl from Mexico (*RKO 1939*)

Career (*RKO 1939*)

Dancing Co-ed (*MGM 1939*)

Mexican Spitfire (*RKO 1939*)

Pop Always Pays (*RKO 1940*)

Mexican Spitfire Out West (*RKO 1940*)

The Golden Fleecing (*MGM 1940*)

Six Lessons from Madame La Zonga (*Universal 1941*)

Where Did You Get That Girl? (*Universal 1941*)

Hurry, Charlie, Hurry (*RKO 1941*)

Mexican Spitfire's Baby (*RKO 1941*)

Moonlight in Hawaii (*Universal 1941*)

Never Give a Sucker an Even Break (*Universal 1941*)

Melody Lane (*Universal 1941*)

Mexican Spitfire at Sea (*RKO 1942*)

Mexican Spitfire Sees a Ghost (*RKO 1942*)

Mexican Spitfire's Elephant (*RKO 1942*)

Strictly in the Groove (*Universal 1943*)

Cowboy in Manhattan (*Universal 1943*)

Follow the Band (*Universal 1943*)

Mexican Spitfire's Blessed Event (*RKO 1943*)

Gals, Inc. (*Universal 1943*)

Higher and Higher (*RKO 1943*)

Slightly Terrific (*Universal 1944*)

The Invisible Man's Revenge (*Universal 1944*)

Twilight on the Prairie (*Universal 1944*)

Babes on Swing Street (*Universal 1944*)

She Gets Her Man (*Universal 1945*)

Under Western Skies (*Universal 1945*)

What a Blonde (*RKO 1945*)

Mamma Loves Papa (*RKO 1945*)

Riverboat Rhythm (*RKO 1946*)

Joe Palooka, Champ (*Monogram 1946*)

Gentleman Joe Palooka (*Monogram 1946*)

Joe Palooka in the Knockout (*Monogram 1947*)

Fighting Mad (*Monogram 1948*)

The Noose Hangs High (*Eagle Lion 1948*)

Variety Time (*RKO 1948*) [stock footage]

Joe Palooka in the Big Fight (*Monogram 1949*)

Make Mine Laughs (*RKO 1949*) [stock footage]

Joe Palooka in the Counterpunch (*Monogram 1949*)

Joe Palooka in Humphrey Takes a Chance (*Monogram 1950*)

Footlight Varieties (*RKO 1951*) [stock footage]

With Rita Moreno in The Lieutenant Wore Skirts (1956).

Tom Ewell

The distinction between the comic and the comic actor is a subtle one. It has to do less with the actor himself or his training than with the times and the recognition accorded by the public of a certain "type." Witness, for example, the "sudden" success of Carroll O'Connor in the role of Archie Bunker in TV's "All in the Family," or the brief cinema superstardom of Elliott Gould in the late 1960s. Eventually the actor has to outlive the comic moment if he is to survive.

Such is the case of Tom Ewell, who as the frustrated, conscience-stricken dupe had to cope with such celluloid sex symbols as Marilyn Monroe, Jayne Mansfield, Sheree North, Rita Moreno, and Ann Miller in the pre-sexual-revolution days of the mid-Fifties. As the innocent rube who had an enchanting way of arching his eyebrows, shuffling his hands into his pockets, and delivering a wry barb, Ewell was a major film personality for all too brief a spell. His time in the limelight faded and since then he has proven to be a very solid character actor.

Tom Ewell was born Yewell Tompkins in Owensboro, Kentucky, on Thursday, April 29, 1909. The son of Samuel* and Marline (Yewell) Tompkins, the red-headed youngster (nicknamed "Straw" for strawberry, the color of his hair) first became interested in the theatre at age six when he attended a performance aboard an Ohio River showboat. His parents' ambitions for his career future were more conservative than their son's. They attempted to direct him toward a career in law, even though young Yewell was actively interested in high school dramatics as a charter member of the Rose Curtain Players. (The parents hoped he would follow in the footsteps of his two grandfathers, who had both been prominent lawyers.)

Yewell attended the University of Wisconsin on a scholarship and was a liberal arts major. There his interest in the theatre increased and his penchant for the law diminished. He did attend the University of Wisconsin Law School for a year, but it was then apparent that the stage would always be his preferred vocation. As a member of a local

* Ewell once listed his father's occupation as "playboy."

253

stock company, the Wisconsin Players, young Tompkins made his professional debut on February 18, 1928, in a production of *The Spider* at the Park Theatre in Madison. That year Tompkins and another first-year law student, Don Ameche, decided to leave academics and seek a full-time career in show business.

From 1928 to 1931 the future comedian worked for several stock companies, appearing in over 50 productions. Among his assignments was a 1931 role in *Aren't We All* at the Park Theatre in Madison. When he felt confident enough, he moved to New York, arriving in Manhattan with only $50 in his pocket. He made the discouraging rounds of the casting offices. Not a handsome or even striking youth by any standards, his first two years brought no jobs on the stage. He did find other work: toy salesman at Macy's (where he worked with struggling Garson Kanin), sidewalk hawker, auctioneer, cigar-counter salesman, street photographer, dishwasher at a Bickford's coffee shop, elevator operator, and door-to-door salesman. If anything, this diverse catalogue of jobs taught him survival and resilience. His only dramatic work during this period was as a near extra on a "March of Time" radio broadcast and a one-line bit ("Welcome to New York, Miss Allen") on the Burns and Allen radio show.

Finally his luck changed—or so it seemed. Now billed as Tom Ewell, he had small parts in three short-lived Broadway plays. In *They Shall Not Die*, which debuted at the Royale Theatre on February 21, 1934, Tom had the role of Red in the drama based on the Scottsboro case. The play lasted only 62 performances, but it provided a recognizable credential. It was followed by equally brief parts in a series of largely unsuccessful plays: *The First Legion* (1934), *Geraniums in My Window* (1934), and *Deluxe* (1935). In the last he served as a stage manager, as well as playing the roles of a waiter and a character named Booth. Next came minuscule assignments in *Let Freedom Ring* (1935), and the role of Dennis Eady in *Ethan Frome* (1936). The most distinguished production with which he was associated during this period was *Dead End* (1935), but ironically his work on it was limited to the behind-the-scenes assisting of designer Norman Bel Geddes. Ewell

even found time to write two plays during this apprenticeship period. Of his own writing ability he would say, "My friends to whom I sent them were kind enough never to mention them."

Although his career was distinguished by appearances in box-office failures, there were a few pluses in his assignments. He succeeded Lamar King as Captain Tim in the extremely successful *Tobacco Road*, played Larry Westcott in the impressive *Stage Door* (1936), and was Dan in a touring company of *Brother Rat* during 1936–37. ("My wife," Ewell would later quip, "thinks every actor between 25 and 45 worked in *Brother Rat*.") After completing his trek in this comedy, Ewell embarked on an eight-month journey aboard a tramp steamer. He returned to Broadway to play Cornelius Hackle in Thornton Wilder's *The Merchant of Yonkers* (1938). The show struggled on for 39 performances before closing, but provided the genesis for *The Matchmaker* and *Hello, Dolly!* Equally dismal was a musical version of the often-filmed *Sailor Beware* called *Nice Going* (1939), which floundered despite a cast that included Mary Martin and Bert Wheeler.

No one could quibble about Ewell's fortitude. After a 111-performance stand in Judith Anderson's *Family Portrait* (1939) on Broadway, he embarked on a post-Broadway tour of *Key Largo*, which opened in Philadelphia on January 2, 1940. He had the role of Gage, played on Broadway by Graham Denton. This touring show brought Tom to southern California and provided a brief but premature screen career. He was promised a role in a picture that never materialized (a typical Hollywood occurrence). In desperation he turned to his old colleague of Macy's Department Store days—Garson Kanin. The latter was preparing a new film version of *They Knew What They Wanted* (1940). Kanin had scripter Robert Ardrey write a small role for Ewell into the scenario. He was given the part of a new hired hand, the friend of Karl Malden. But when this Carole Lombard–Charles Laughton RKO drama was released, Ewell could scarcely be seen oncamera. His bits had been excised from the print.

Most of Tom's first Hollywood experience consisted of collecting unemployment insurance, drinking gin with roommate Phillip

Coolidge, and lamenting over the lack of talent in films. This Broadway snobbism did not prevent Ewell from taking four days' work in *Desert Bandits* (1941), a Republic quickie that starred Don "Red" Barry. (Ewell would later recollect, "I did a Western in Hollywood, which I don't *think* got to New York. I was a cowboy, and whenever the action lagged, which it frequently did, I came on, horseless, and said, 'Somebody stole my horse.' The humor of this palled on me, for one.")

The humiliation of this California experience was quickly forgotten when Tom returned to New York and appeared in several—at least, prestigious—failures. He was Brother Galusha in *Susanna and the Elders* (1940) and Dick Brown in Philip Barry's *Liberty Jones* (1941). That December he had a lead in Oscar Hammerstein II's *Sunny River*, one of the lyricist's many solo, pre-Rodgers failures. Of this period Tom would assess, "I was always trying too hard in those days, trying to make something of every moment [onstage]. I knew I couldn't make people feel anything with the kind of roles I was getting so I'd try for laughs. I kept striving so hard to make everything count that I'd lose sight of the overall impressions." On another occasion Ewell admitted, "No matter how I tried convincing managers I was a funny fellow, I invariably finished up with a job as a modern Pagliacci." At least in the short-surviving *Sunny River* he received some recognition for having a penchant for creating comic moments.

These depressing failures on stage during which time he received little recognition from either critics or public were interrupted by a four-year term in the navy. There he served in a gunnery unit, eventually earning the rank of junior grade lieutenant. The sabbatical from the theatre provided Ewell with an opportunity to reevaluate his career. He returned to the stage in a pre-Broadway tryout of *Of All People*, which closed in Baltimore on December 22, 1945. Then he portrayed Huckleberry Haines (Bob Hope's old Broadway role) in the Civic Light Opera revival of *Roberta*, which played Los Angeles and San Francisco in 1946. Also in 1946 he was at the Biltmore Theatre for 118 performances of *Apple of His Eye*. That year he would marry for the first time. On March 18 he wed Judith Abbott, the daughter of Tom's former director, George "Brother Rat" Abbott. The marriage ended in divorce shortly afterward. He later married Marjorie Gwynne Sanborn, an advertising copywriter, on April 29, 1948, and they had a son, Taylor ("Tate"), born in 1955.

At long last Tom had a certified hit in *John Loves Mary*, which bowed at the Booth Theatre on February 4, 1947, for a run of 423 performances. As Fred Taylor, Ewell played opposite Nina Foch and won public and critical endorsement. For his performance he received the *Variety* New York Drama Critics Poll Award, the Clarence Derwent Award, and the Donaldson Award.

The success of the comedic *John Loves Mary* caused Hollywood to beckon—not to play in the Warner Bros. version of the play (Jack Carson inherited Ewell's role), but to appear on the MGM soundstage. Garson Kanin and Ruth Gordon had written a script for Katharine Hepburn and Spencer Tracy called *Adam's Rib* (1949). It provided four outstanding supporting parts for a quartet of screen "newcomers": Judy Holliday, David Wayne, Jean Hagen, and Tom Ewell. A good deal of audience and critical attention was diverted from the stars to Miss Holliday's smartly conceived interpretation of the scatterbrained wife standing trial for shooting her unfaithful spouse (Ewell). However, there were sufficient moments for Tom to shine oncamera. He is especially sharp when on the witness stand and being examined by attorney Tracy. He gives a deft portrayal of the male chauvinist, saying of his wife, "She's nuts, that's my complaint. I'd like to see her put away somewhere that she's all out of my hair." Reported the *New York Times*, "Mr. Ewell as the husband is deliciously droll, making of the loutish fellow a full-bodied character." Around this time, Tom narrated some comedy-travel short subjects. His offstage voice suggested a Robert Benchley quality for offhandedly delivering a gag line.

Despite his love for the theatre and his enjoyment of the country (he and Marjorie owned a Bucks County, Pennsylvania, home in the early Fifties), it was the films which provided him with a livelihood at this time. Most of the roles were best-friend parts that might have been rejected by Keenan Wynn. In

With Tyrone Power and Micheline Prelle in American Guerilla in the Philippines (1950).

1950 he supported Lana Turner in the turgid melodrama of models, *A Life of Her Own*, buoyed Tyrone Power's *An American Guerrilla in the Philippines* (as the embarrassing-obligatory comedy relief soldier from Idaho), and was in the background of Bing Crosby's *Mr. Music*.

His only part during this period that offered him any possibilities was that of Willie in a film based on Bill Mauldin's cartoons, *Up Front* (1951). But the potential pathos of the movie about World War II soldiers was diluted by veteran director Alexander Hall and his obsession with slapstick. Nevertheless, Bosley Crowther (*New York Times*) found praise for Tom's offering, "Mr. Ewell is lanky and dog-faced in the unloveliest sense of that phrase. He drawls in the weary cornfed accents that you would expect Willie to employ." A sequel, *Willie and Joe Back at the Front* (1952), was equally farfetched. Tom even found himself supporting Abbott and Costello in one of their lesser

vehicles, *Lost in Alaska* (1952), playing a suicide-bent prospector. (An excerpt from the film featuring Ewell's attempts to drown himself was seen in *The World of Abbott and Costello*, 1965.)

An almost obsessively busy actor, Tom found time between movie engagements to work on early network TV in episodes of such series as "Robert Montgomery Presents," "Lights Out," and "Studio One." In addition he was seen in stock in *The Male Animal* (1949), *John Loves Mary* (1951), *Harvey* (1951), and the pre-Broadway tryout of *Kin Hunter* (1951).

The year 1952 provided Tom with what was to be the high point of his professional career. Playwright George Axelrod had a new comedy to be cast and he remembered Ewell had played in *Small Wonder*, a 1948 revue he had written. Thus Tom was auditioned and given the lead of Richard Sherman in *The Seven Year Itch*, which debuted at the Fulton Theatre on November 20, 1952. In

256

what amounted to a two-hour monologue, Ewell received unanimous raves for this tour de force. He played to perfection a not-quite erring husband who speculates on the delicious prospect of adultery. For his part in the long-running (1,141 performances) show, he received the Antoinette Perry (Tony) Award and the Donaldson Award. Rarity of rarities, director Billy Wilder had the good taste to insist that Ewell repeat his acclaimed characterization in the film version made by Twentieth Century–Fox in 1955.

The picture was designed as an ideal CinemaScope, color vehicle for the increasingly difficult Marilyn Monroe. In the relatively small part of "The Girl," the object of Ewell's elaborate fantasies, she had star billing over Ewell (even though he was onscreen for the bulk of the running time). If the publicity for the picture celebrated Monroe (who can forget the image of MM in a white dress sensuously reacting to the breeze from a subway grill while Ewell watches admiringly?), the reviews for the film compensated Ewell for the press agents' slights. The *New York Daily*

Mirror observed, "Ewell is an extremely funny fellow whose pliable features and ungainly gait add to his natural humor. He's been kicking around for a long time and deserves this Hollywood success for his talents. And when you can 'steal' a picture from La Monroe's architecture—it's a tremendous accomplishment."

The Seven Year Itch proved to be one of the box-office smashes of the year (grossing $6,000,000 in domestic rentals). Fox, uncertain of what to do with Ewell's specialized, unvirile comic talents, rushed him into *The Girl Can't Help It* (1956) starring Jayne Mansfield, the studio's apprentice Monroe. Based on a Garson Kanin story, the picture has achieved an odd cult status in recent years since director Frank Tashlin has gained "respectability" from French critics. (The picture was even reissued theatrically a few years ago because of the number of rock 'n' roll stars doing cameos in the picture.) In the song-laden feature (17 rock 'n' roll numbers are interspersed) Tom was the alcoholic agent who falls for crow-voiced blonde

With David Wayne in Up Front *(1951).*

257

Mansfield, with Edmond O'Brien cast as her retired racketeer sponsor. *The Lieutenant Wore Skirts* (1956), also directed by Tashlin, teamed Ewell with Sheree North, the underrated Monroe rival at Fox. But this entry proved that Ewell, despite his recent screen successes, was uncomfortable in bedroom farces. Also in 1956 Tom went to MGM to join with Anne Francis and Ann Miller in *The Great American Pastime* (referring to baseball, not sex), a pleasant but tepid comedy.

Hollywood has rarely known what to do with an actor who is too accomplished to be merely a supporting player but is not handsome or young enough to be the conventional leading man. Thus after one more film—a Mickey Rooney mild comedy entitled *A Nice Little Bank That Should Be Robbed* (1958)—Ewell's Fifties' film career was over.

Fortunately, he was still in demand on Broadway. He played in the very offbeat *Waiting for Godot* in January 1956, during its Miami tryout. (When the show was recast for Broadway, E. G. Marshall was given Tom's role of Vladimir.) Then in February 1957 Tom had another comedy hit in *Tunnel of Love*, playing opposite Nancy Olson. *Time* reported, "Tom Ewell, though at times the quivering slave of direction, has always the wonderful look of an oaf with charm or a camel with problems." (When the vehicle was revamped as a Doris Day film in 1958, Richard Widmark was handed the Ewell part.) Rounding out the decade, he appeared again on Broadway in the short-lasting *Patate* (1958) with Susan Oliver, and played *The Gazebo* in stock in Colorado in 1959.

Always anxious for professional employment, Ewell was busy on television. Some of his Fifties' work in the medium was very impressive, such as the role of the desperate father trying to regain custody of his son in *Man on Fire*. (When this "Alcoa Hour" show of 1956 was turned into a feature film, Bing Crosby had the lead.) Also memorable were *The Case of Mr. Pelham*, directed by Alfred Hitchcock for his television anthology series in 1955 (Roger Moore did the film version), and a 1962 version of *The Four Poster* with Tammy Grimes, although it was evident by this time that the early scenes of the play, wherein he must play a young man, were beyond Ewell. Along the way Ewell worked on a situation comedy for TV, "The Tom

Ewell Show," another one of the "idiot father" programs that glutted the networks in the early Sixties. It lasted one thin season.

Tom had modest success in a play of skits entitled *A Thurber Carnival* (1960), suggesting that he would have been wonderful in a biography of Thurber. Two years later he resurfaced in Hollywood, but now categorized as a character actor. He was assigned the role of Abe in the listless Henry King production of *Tender Is the Night*, starring Jennifer Jones and Jason Robards Jr. (David O. Selznick, the star's husband and a consultant on the project, had wanted Montgomery Clift or Fred Astaire for Ewell's "friend" role.) Equally dismal was Fox's third edition of *State Fair* (1962), with Tom in the part created by Will Rogers. In the remusicalized version Ewell was surprisingly effective and certainly more credible than the film's younger stars (Pat Boone, Pamela Tiffin, Ann-Margret, and Bobby Darin). As a rural paterfamilias, a role that had nearly gone to his friend Don Ameche, Ewell got to sing "It's the Little Things in Texas That I Love" with musical star Alice Faye. But one can only wonder how Tom felt sharing the lime-light for the song number "More Than Just a Friend" with a prize pig. It was a sad decline from his days at the studio with Monroe, Mansfield, and North.

True to his astute prophecy that he would never find another role that would offer him the possibilities of *The Seven Year Itch*, Tom spent most of the Sixties working on plays that never made Broadway or closed after a few performances: *Thursday Is a Good Night* (with Sheree North and directed by his ex-wife Judy Abbott), *Christmas in Las Vegas*, and *The Armored Dove*. He also toured in established plays: *Life with Father; Take Her, She's Mine; You Know I Can't Hear You When the Water's Running; The Apple Tree*; and *Never Too Late* (playing opposite Nancy Carroll). With the advice of such talents as Billy Wilder, Marc Connelly, Garson Kanin, and Charles Laughton, Ewell assembled a one-man show—dealing with the best of American humor over the last 80 years—and took it on five transcontinental tours. He also guest-starred on such TV series as "Alias Smith and Jones," "The Man from Shiloh," "The Name of the Game," and "The Governor and J.J." One of his better-received ventures

With Alice Faye in State Fair *(1962).*

was a 50-minute radio show which debuted on NBC in September 1964. It co-starred him with his wife Marjorie in a program supposedly emanating from their Central Park West home (actually from a network studio) in New York City, in which program the husband-and-wife team did interviews, reviews, and commentary. Unfortunately, the program was unable to survive the declining days of radio.

When Tom eventually did return to the big screen in 1970 to play a racial bigot in the heavy-handed army comedy *Suppose They Gave a War and Nobody Came?* not enough people saw the picture to comment on the astounding amount of weight Ewell had added.* But two years later, when he was cast as a small-town deputy in *They Only Kill Their Masters*, most nostalgia buffs who

went to theatres to catch glimpses of such Forties' stars as June Allyson, Ann Rutherford, Edmund O'Brien, and Peter Lawford were particularly horrified not only by Ewell's physical appearance,* but also by his gravel voice, the combination of the two making him seem more Andy Devine than Tom Ewell.

To Find a Man, also released in 1972, was a teenage potboiler in which scripter Arnold Schulman updated his *Love with the Proper Stranger* thesis to meet the whims of the Seventies. Tom had the awkwardly written role of a New York abortionist.

The onetime star's last film to date was a cameo bit at the conclusion of the overblown remake of *The Great Gatsby* (1974). As a

---

* Ewell has long been a compulsive eater, unable to resist nibbling junk food when not preoccupied on stage, on camera, or asleep.

* On occasion the self-effacing Ewell will tell the story of the time he told Katharine Hepburn that he was being considered to interpret the life of Sinclair Lewis onstage. She replied, "Oh, I knew Lewis well. Without a doubt, he was the ugliest man I've ever seen. You'd be perfect for the part."

mourner arriving late to Jay Gatsby's funeral, he got to deliver the novel's "Poor sonovabitch!" punch line. When the film was shown on television a year after its disappointing theatrical release, such language was still deemed pretty strong. Thus the ABC-TV network excised Ewell's fragmented part completely.

Oddly enough, television has provided Tom with his steadiest work over the years. For a while he had a continuing role as Bill Lang in CBS-TV's soap opera "Search for Tomorrow" in the early Seventies (by which time it had become acceptable for former name stars to accept roles in the format drama). Ewell had featured roles in two TV movies, *The Spy Who Returned from the Dead* (1974) and *Promise Him Anything* (1975). Later he was a semiregular on the "Baretta" video series (NBC-TV, 1974-78), playing Robert Blake's constantly nibbling friend Billy.* More recently, Ewell turned up

* When the "Baretta" action series was being cast in 1974, the top contenders for the Billy role were, among others, Jack Oakie, Burgess Meredith, and Joseph Campanella. However, Blake's then wife, Sondra, had once worked with Ewell in stock and recommended him for the part. Star Blake said of his co-player, "I love 'im. When we're out there at three in the morning ready to start killing each other, he's always there with a warm hand or a line. He makes you feel the world is OK." In September 1977 Ewell was Emmy-nominated for Best

on an episode of ABC-TV's "Fantasy Island" playing a rusty burglar who yearns for a new caper.

Ewell and his wife, Marjorie, still retain a Manhattan apartment, as well as a home in Kentucky. When he is not professionally employed he resides there and works as director of State Park Theatrical Productions in Daviess County. He is also a gourmet cook (specializing in cookie making) and an inveterate horse better (with very bad luck). A quiet, conservative man, Ewell was one of those entertainers who stepped forward in 1976 to admit that he had been a heavy drinker. "I am an alcoholic and I guess will be until the day I die." He has not drunk in 30 years now, having become a member of Alcoholics Anonymous.

Although Ewell's persistent struggle in the theatre earned him the reputation of a survivor of his craft, the woeful expression that was the trademark of his comedy appearances may really be an extension of his personality. His ability to express frustration in the Fifties, worry in the Sixties, and weariness in the Seventies demonstrates that he is as flexible an actor as one is likely to find.

Supporting Actor in a TV drama series for his continuing role.

FEATURE FILMS

They Knew What They Wanted (*RKO 1940*)
Desert Bandit (*Republic 1941*)
Adam's Rib (*MGM 1949*)
A Life of Her Own (*MGM 1950*)
An American Guerrilla in the Philippines (*20th Century-Fox 1950*)
Mr. Music (*Paramount 1950*)

Up Front (*Universal 1951*)
Finders Keepers (*Universal 1951*)
Lost in Alaska (*Universal 1952*)
Willie and Joe Back at the Front (*Universal 1952*)
The Seven Year Itch (*20th Century-Fox 1955*)

With Don Ameche in Suppose They Gave a War and Nobody Came? *(1970).*

The Great American Pastime (*MGM 1956*)
The Girl Can't Help It (*20th Century-Fox 1956*)
The Lieutenant Wore Skirts (*20th Century-Fox 1956*)
A Nice Little Bank That Should Be Robbed (*20th Century-Fox 1958*)

Tender Is the Night (*20th Century-Fox 1962*)
State Fair (*20th Century-Fox 1962*)
Suppose They Gave a War and Nobody Came? (*Cinerama 1970*)
To Find a Man (*Columbia 1972*)
They Only Kill Their Masters (*MGM 1972*)
The Great Gatsby (*Paramount 1974*)

In You Can't Cheat an Honest Man *(1939).*

W.C. Fields

Too few funsters have retained their immortality through succeeding generations like W. C. Fields. Latter-day audiences continue to laugh and applaud the Great Man's dedicated coping with the human condition. They identify with his rebellion against the establishment and revel in his stalking of unsuspecting prey. They empathize with his aggressiveness and his belief that there is a sucker born every minute.

The comic world of Mr. Fields was inhabited by a suspiciously hostile population primed for immediate fleecing. One of his many memorable screen sequences exposed the Fieldsian approach to comedy and life. While dexterously shuffling a deck of playing cards, a brash innocent approached him to ask, "Is this a game of chance?" Fixing his vulpine eyes on the naive one, W. C. mumbled, "Not the way I play it!"

He was born in Philadelphia on Thursday, January 29, 1880. (Some sources list January 29, 1879, February 10, 1879, April 9, 1879, or June 29, 1879.) The exact location of his birth still remains unknown. However, a census of June 5, 1880, established that a child approximately five months old named William Claude Dukenfield was in residence with his parents at 6320 Woodland Avenue, Philadelphia.*

Fields' grandfather, an English cockney combmaker, arrived in the United States in November 1854 with his 13-year-old son, James Lyden Dukenfield. James served in the Civil War, had two fingers shot off at the Battle of Lookout Mountain, and on May 18, 1879, married Kate S. Felton in Philadelphia's St. George's Methodist Church. They named their firstborn son William Claude for his maternal uncle.

The blond-haired steely-eyed boy started to work at an early age. He taught himself to juggle and made his professional debut at 14 at the Plymount Park pavilion near Norristown, Pennsylvania. He modestly billed himself "Whitey, the Boy Wonder." At Atlantic

* After the death of his parents, Fields had gravestones erected in their memory. On his father's granite stone he had inscribed, "A Great Scout"; on his mother's marker, "A Sweet Old Soul."

City's Fortescue Pier he emerged as "W. C. Fields, the Tramp Juggler." He also doubled as a "drowner." The latter occupation was a gimmick used to attract crowds to a beer garden. As he later explained, "My work was very simple. All I had to do was to swim far out in the ocean, then flounder and scream for help. Lifeguards who worked for shows nearby would rescue me. Once I was brought to a pavilion, a crowd would gather. The waiters would immediately begin to yell their wares." The screen's foremost comic-confidence man had exemplary basic training.

At 18 Fields made his vaudeville debut in New York City at the Bowery's London Theatre. He later advanced to the Orpheum circuit and in February 1900 was doing his mute-tramp juggling act in England at London's Palace Theatre. On April 8, 1900, in San Francisco he wed chorus girl Harriet Hughes. The following year "Hattie" Hughes Fields joined her husband's juggling act for a triumphant tour of Europe. On July 28, 1904, their son, William Claude Fields Jr., was born. On August 28, 1905, "eccentric juggler" W. C. Fields made his Broadway stage bow in *The Ham Tree*. Fields' personal notices were glowing and continued through a long road tour in the musical vaudeville show.

William Claude Dukenfield had his name legally changed to William C. Fields on May 13, 1908, reducing it professionally to W. C. Fields. Although his name was legally altered, his floundering, briefly successful marriage was never legally terminated. Staunch Catholic Hattie steadfastly refused to give him a divorce. Their domestic life soon dissolved into a long series of quarrelsome, recriminatory letters.

A tour of Australia with his internationally known juggling act was cut short when producer Charles Dillingham cabled Fields to join the cast of Irving Berlin's *Watch Your Step*. After the show's opening tryout in Syracuse, New York, in November 1914 the management decided the revue did not require a juggler. Fields was dismissed. Luckily, Florenz Ziegfeld's perceptive talent scout, Gene Buck, was in the audience. He signed W. C. for the 1915 edition of Ziegfeld's *Follies*.

The *Ziegfeld Follies of 1915* opened at the New Amsterdam Theatre on June 21, 1915,

with a stellar cast that included Bert Williams, Leon Errol, Ina Claire, and Ed Wynn.* W. C. Fields convulsed audiences during the show's 104-performance run with his pool-table routine. The *Follies* provided Fields with a lush showcase for his uniquely offbeat routines. Much of his *Follies* material he wrote, injecting comedy into such sports as billiards, golf, and tennis. In his hilarious sketches, he often played the henpecked husband beset with a nagging, shrewish wife and bedeviled with badly behaved, belittling, brattish offspring.

Most of the authored *Follies* material later surfaced in his films, frequently modified or reworked. These set pieces, like his juggling, fumbling, hat tricks, and stalking aggressiveness, became standard Fields.

During his first *Follies*, Fields made his motion picture debut in *Pool Sharks*, a one-reel Gaumont-Mutual comedy release (September 19, 1915) utilizing his pool routine. At Flushing, New York, he made a Mutual-Casino one-reeler, released two weeks later. This entry, *His Lordship's Dilemma*, also featured comic Bud Ross. In *Dilemma* he drew from boyhood experiences as a runaway, street-wise hustler, conning free drinks and lunch from a bartender and performing his golf routine.

Ziegfeld's 1916 *Follies* provided Fields with his first major speaking part on the stage and a laughable encounter with the game of croquet. The 1917 edition cast him as a tennis player (winging tennis balls into the audience) and set him in a race for laughter against a new Ziegfeld draftee, Will Rogers. Ziegfeld's 1918 glorification featured Fields' intensely funny golf game.

W. C. was among the performers picketing in the Actors Equity strike of 1919. That December 21, with Fanny Brice, Gilda Gray, Sophie Tucker, and Roscoe "Fatty" Arbuckle, he brightened the *New York American's* Christmas Fund Show at the Hippodrome. In 1920's *Follies* his "The Family Ford" sketch had its first airing, with Fanny Brice as Fields' wife. In 1921 the two clowns repeated their roles in Fields' sketch "Off to the Coun-

* Also in the 1915 *Follies* was showgirl Bessie Poole, with whom Fields had an affair. In 1927 Miss Poole accepted a $20,000 settlement for signing an affidavit that her illegitimate child was not sired by Fields.

try."* With expert farceur Raymond Hitch-cock as "Lionel Barrymore," Fanny Brice as "Ethel," and W. C. as "Jack," the three comedians did a burlesque on *Camille.*

Fields deserted Ziegfeld to work for the competition in *George White's Scandals of 1922.* After Mr. White's outing W. C. was given a role in which he could flesh out a comic character within the framework of his first book show. It was a role tailored to those endearing qualities Fields raised to the level of art—the con man extraordinaire, Professor Eustace McGargle, in *Poppy.* The show opened on September 3, 1923, and ran for over 300 performances. Starring Madge Kennedy in the title role, the play featured W. C. and had him singing an act one solo, "Kodoola, Kodoola." Fields then returned to Ziegfeld's fold for a Broadway-bound revue, *The Comic Supplement,* which tried out and closed in Newark, New Jersey, in January 1925.

Fields had already made his feature-length film debut playing a drunken British soldier in the spectacle *Janice Meredith* (1924). But his real bow in the full-length picture field took place when D. W. Griffith transferred *Poppy* to the screen. The filmmaker hired Fields to re-create his stage role of the carnival faker. Made at Paramount's Astoria, Long Island, studio for United Artists release, the property was retitled *Sally of the Sawdust* (1925) with Carol Dempster in the title part. *Sally* still retains a good deal of charm. Fields' performance is a gem as he maneuvers his way through the role of being the foster father of an unknown heiress, juggling away and selling a phony talking dog to impatient suckers. W. C. would reprise his role to greater advantage in Paramount's *Poppy* (1936), and he repeated the assignment on "Lux Radio Theatre" in March 1938.

Less fortuitous was the comedian's second Griffith picture, *That Royle Girl* (1926). It was a lushy melodrama centered around Carol Dempster with Fields as "Dads" Royle, a drunken con man supplying sparse comedy relief. Allegedly it was Miss Dempster, Griffith's protégée, who convinced the director that the screen time of Fields detracted from her performance. W. C.'s scenes were thus reduced.

While the Griffith films were establishing no cinema milestones, Fields was performing in Ziegfeld's 1925 *Follies.* He delighted audiences with his sketches: "The Drug Store," "A Back Porch," "A Road-Joy Ride," and "The Picnic," the last co-written with J. P. McEvoy.

For the next two and a half years Fields pursued a mildly successful screen career. He was the bedeviled village druggist in *It's the Old Army Game* (1926), the inventor of an unbreakable automobile windshield in *So's Your Old Man* (1926),* and a self-styled financial wizard investing in oil wells in *The Potters* (1927). His playing of Pa Potter, office stenographer dabbling in stocks, drew critical praise. However, his broad playing of Elmer Finch in *Running Wild* (1927) was deemed excessive.

Paramount tried to establish a new screen comedy team with W. C. and veteran slapstick clown Chester Conklin. The three pictures pairing the two comics were not lasting joys. *Two Flaming Youths* (1927) was the first, and it boasted the presence of 10 other established comedy pairs culled from the stage, vaudeville, and pictures. The asorted duos included Paramount's own Wallace Beery and Raymond Hatton, and Clark and McCullough, Moran and Mack, Weber and Fields, and the Duncan Sisters. Beyond the title, *Tillie's Punctured Romance* (1928) had no relation to Mack Sennett's earlier feature with Marie Dressler, Charlie Chaplin, and Mabel Normand. *Fools for Luck* (1928) completed the Fields-Conklin trilogy.

On August 6, 1928, Fields returned to Broadway, starring in Earl Carroll's *Vanities,* which had a run of over 200 performances. It contained two of the comedian's best sketches, which he would use again and again. His "Stolen Bonds" was the basis of Fields' later Mack Sennett film short, *The Fatal Glass of Beer* (1933). It featured Fields croakingly singing the title song to a weeping Canadian Mountie and spouting the famous line, "It ain't a fit night out for man or beast," while stoically receiving a face full of prop

---

* Ziegfeld paid Fields a weekly salary of $700 plus an additional $100 for royalty payment on the use of the sketch.

* The talkie remake, *You're Telling Me* (1934), far outshone the silent version and would become one of Fields' classic sound features.

With Carol Dempster in Sally of the Sawdust *(1925).*

snow. His deliberate underplaying and mute acceptance of outrageous fortune made his comedy all the merrier. A second *Vanities* sketch written by and starring Fields was "An Episode at the Dentist." (It would become the basis of his two-reeler *The Dentist,* made for Mack Sennett in 1932.)

W. C. toured with the *Vanities* through 1929. He banked a goodly portion of his weekly salary of $3,500 in saving accounts under such pseudonyms as Charles Bogle, Ampico J. Steinway, Otis Criblecoblis, Felton J. Satchelstern, and Mahatma Kane Jeeves, *noms de plume* he also used for his later screenplays. Fields' frugality would have embarrassed Silas Marner.

Fields' last Broadway appearance was in *Ballyhoo* (December 22, 1930), which lasted for 68 performances. As Q. Q. Quayle he again paraded his set pieces from juggling billiard balls and cigar boxes to managing a transcontinental footrace and operating a drugstore. When *Ballyhoo* folded, Fields amassed his considerable savings and drove to California.

He made his talking screen debut in RKO's two-reeler, *The Golf Specialist.* In 1931 he was seen in a Warner Bros. Bobby Jones *How to Play Golf* series reel, *Hip Action.* (Also for Sennett Fields would make the short subjects *The Pharmacist* and *The Barber Shop,* both released in 1933.) W. C.'s first sound feature in Hollywood was *Her Majesty, Love* (1931) starring Marilyn Miller. Fields inherited the role played two years earlier by bubbling S. Z. Sakall in one of the first German-made talkies, *Ihre Majestaet Die Liebe.* As Miss Miller's uncouth, juggling, imbibing father, the performer managed to create a good amount of laughter.

It was at Paramount Pictures that Fields hit his stride in a series of films that not only were dominantly funny but also extended his basic characterization of the conniving con man, Professor Eustace McGargle. Usually his screen persona revealed an underlying, if reluctant, warmth. His plundering retaliation against humanity often seemed justified by the premeditation of his predators. His screen image was further improved with the disappearance of the deplorable black snip of a moustache stuck beneath his bulbous nose.

Million Dollar Legs (1932) was an insane comedy with Fields supervising Olympic games as president of mythical Klopstockia. In the episodic *If I Had a Million* (1932), the Fields segment has become classic, although the Charlie Ruggles-Mary Boland vignette is even better. In this multistoried film Fields is teamed with portly Alison Skipworth. They use his windfall of a million dollars to buy a fleet of jalopies and to hire a collection of thugs [to drive the cars]. Their aim is to gain retaliation against loathsome road hogs, the type of people responsible for the earlier demolition of Fields' roadster. After the picture was finished, Fields insisted on "buying" rights from writer Joseph L. Mankiewicz to the various bits of cooing dialogue he spoke oncamera to Miss Skipworth ("my little chickadee," "my little tomtit," etc.).

The ill-conceived *International House* (1933) occasioned little joy. However, Fields' scenes with the sultry former showgirl Peggy Hopkins Joyce evoked a few guffaws. During a part of the shooting of the picture W. C. slept peacefully in his dressing room through a series of earthquake tremors, more excitement than the picture produced. As Augustus Winterbottom of *Tillie and Gus* (1933), Fields was a cardsharp from Alaska now masquerading as a missionary. His aim was to claim an inheritance in America. He was fortified by Alison Skipworth as his estranged wife against the scene-stealing Baby LeRoy. The *New York Times* reported, "Insane as are the doings in this concoction, they succeed in being really funny. It is the sort of thing admirably suited to Mr. Fields' peculiar genius."

Lewis Carroll hardly had Fields in mind when he developed the character of Humpty-Dumpty for his *Alice in Wonderland*. But in Paramount's 1933 all-star screen version of the Carroll classic, W. C. emerged with probably the best performance in the picture. He stopped the show with his pool-table routine in Leo McCarey's *Six of a Kind* (1934). In *The Old-Fashioned Way* (1934) he as The Great McGonigle gave one

of his best comic performances, staging and appearing as the dastardly villain in a play-within-a-picture of the creaking melodrama, *The Drunkard*. He also performed his vaudeville juggling act herein, with his conceit over his expert juggling deflated by a well-aimed ripe tomato in his face thrown by Baby LeRoy.

Fields appeared as Mr. Stebbins, the prospective husband of fluttery ZaSu Pitts in *Mrs. Wiggs of the Cabbage Patch* (1934). Spouting flowery phrases to confused Miss Pitts, Fields was outlandishly funny. *It's a Gift* (1934) was based on a story by Fields (using the bogus name of Charles Bogle) and J. P. McEvoy. Many of the premises and scenes had been used in Fields' silent film *It's the Old Army Game,* especially the back porch scene and the anarchic picnic. In retrospect, it has been acclaimed his best film, although at the time of release it was dismissed as a "journeyman piece."

When Charles Laughton turned down the plum role of shifty, debt-drowned, impoverished but prolific father Micawber in *David Copperfield* (1935), producer David O. Selznick turned to W. C. It was conceded that Fields would be right for the social misfit, who, unlike most of the tale's many characters, reappears throughout the long narrative. Director George Cukor's tight reins reduced Fields' determination to embellish the role with juggling. But Cukor did allow the star to use his set piece of frantically searching for his stovepipe hat as it dangled on his upraised cane. The MGM feature was a great success. Most critics agreed that "W. C. Fields is a magnificent Micawber, reminding all that he is a good actor as well as the funniest of comedians."

Booth Tarkington's play *Magnolia* received its third Paramount filming with *Mississippi* (1935). It starred crooner Bing Crosby and blonde Joan Bennett in the romantic leads. W. C. was the tall-tale-spinning, imbibing Commodore Jackson. As captain of a riverboat he cheats at poker and blares such Fieldsian curses as "Mother of Pearl" and "Godfrey Daniels." His character is the one who observes that women are like elephants, nice to look at, but too much trouble to own. Blessed with a lovely Rodgers and Hart score, the feature was sparked by Fields' comedy.

With Jean Cadell, Freddie Bartholomew, and Elsa Lanchester in David Copperfield (1935).

Lurking behind his literary facade of Charles Bogle, Fields co-wrote with Sam Hardy *The Man on the Flying Trapeze* (1935). Here he was the badgered head of the family, who is gleefully vindictive but remarkably good-natured. Fields' paramour, Carlotta Monti, had a small part in this picture. (She would also be a member of the cast of Fields' *Never Give a Sucker an Even Break*, 1941.) In 1936-1937 Paramount announced Fields would co-star with Irene Dunne and John Boles in *The Count of Luxembourg*, a project which never came to be, nor did Fields star in *Don't Look Now*, another scheduled comedy that was abandoned. However, he did appear in *The Big Broadcast of 1938* which had Fields as twin brothers, S. B. Bellows and jinxed T. Frothingell Bellows, father of wide-mouthed, high-voltaged Martha Raye. The flimsy plot involved a transatlantic race between two ocean liners, had several amusing scenes for Fields, and featured Shirley Ross and Bob Hope (in his feature film debut) dueting "Thanks for the Memory." It was also

Fields' last Paramount picture. The studio no longer wanted to cope with the troublesome star and felt that his screen vogue had passed.*

The Fields legend is spiced with singular feats, not least his drinking exploits. His endless capacity for alcohol was incredible. A thermos of martinis became his standard offscreen prop on the set. He was cantankerous with directors, irascibly independent in establishing his own peculiar working schedules, and a notorious ad-libber who only occasionally managed to remain within the script's perimeters. This combination hardly endeared him to the studio management.

Rumor had it that he had once spiked Baby LeRoy's orange juice with gin. (One of his more publicized adages was, "I never drink

* Robert Lewis Taylor, one of Fields' biographers, succinctly expressed W. C.'s approach to filmmaking at the time: "His main purpose seemed to be to break as many rules as possible and cause the maximum amount of trouble for everybody."

anything stronger than gin before breakfast.") His frequent (and lucrative) radio performances, especially with Edgar Bergen and his dummy stooge Charlie McCarthy, played on Fields' passion for booze. Yet despite W. C.'s overindulgence, he was totally unsympathetic with and intolerant of anyone drunk. He also protested against local tales of friend John Barrymore's alcoholic revels. He vowed he intended to write a book, *Has Alcohol Taken the Place of Rover as Man's Best Friend?* because he was "enthralled by the muses."

Fields moved his comic equipment to Universal Pictures, where he was given a freewheeling hand as circus owner Larson E. Whipsnade in *You Can't Cheat an Honest Man* (1939), teamed with his radio chums Bergen and McCarthy. It proved to be Mr. Bergen and his wooden friend who garnered most of the praise for the better-than-average programmer. (Ironically, Fields had rejected a $150,000 offer from MGM to play the Wizard in *The Wizard of Oz*, 1939, because of his commitment to the Universal project.)

Inspired casting by Universal united W. C. Fields and Paramount alumna Mae West. Resourceful Miss West rewrote the script that eventually became a minor comedy classic, *My Little Chickadee* (1940). Onetime Mack Sennett director Eddie Cline was assigned to helm the picture. However, beyond the allure of its unique stars and the appeal of seeing them together in a Western burlesque, the picture was, in its direction, script, and production values, barely rewarding.

Miss West, a teetotaler, was aware of Fields' drinking habits on the set. Her contract specified that he had to abstain from his martini diet during the shooting of the film. One day as he encouraged several studio children to "go out and play in the traffic" and was boisterously entertaining a crowd of extras, Mae discovered he had indulged in liquid refreshments. She had him sent home. Notwithstanding, the picture was completed, and Fields is the itinerant snake-oil salesman and cardsharp Cuthbert J. Twillie, the individual who is duped into a fake marriage with Flower Belle Lee (West). The memorable closing scene switched each star's identify-

With Mae West in My Little Chickadee *(1940).*

With Gloria Jean in Never Give a Sucker an Even Break *(1941).*

ing gimmick; Fields tells Mae, "Come on up and see me some time," and West, from the corner of her mouth, retorts, "Yaaas, my little chickadee!"

In *The Bank Dick* (1940) the irreverent, irrelevant machinations of Egbert Souse (pronounced "Sow-Say") seem 90-proof Fields. Using prissy Franklin Pangborn as his comedy foil (and again beset with an obnoxious family), Fields ran riotous in the picture. He went even wilder in his original story (nom de plume Ottis Criblecoblis) *Never Give a Sucker an Even Break* (1941), in which Margaret Dumont (of Marx Brothers fame) helped the zany, far-flung narrative. Young singer Gloria Jean merited an award for playing Fields' niece in the picture, for two of the Great Man's growing gallery of human hates were adolescents and sopranos. She survived, but the picture's life was seriously critical.

Twentieth Century-Fox's multistoried, episodic digression of the fate of a tailcoat, *Tales of Manhattan* (1942), closed with a 22-minute segment. It starred W. C. Fields, featured Margaret Dumont and Phil Silvers, and was directed by Julien Duvivier. To decrease the running time of the picture, the entire Fields episode was cut from the final print. Fox's announced plan to issue the excised Fields tale as a short subject has never materialized.

Producer Billy Rose made an unsuccessful bid to get Fields to return to Broadway as star of a new musical revue. But W. C.'s physical deterioration was plainly visible in his face and the prospect of the stage chore was put aside. In 1944, at age 64, Fields made three escapist pictures geared to wartime entertainment. All were compilations of vaudeville stints thinly joined by wispy plots. Resorting to his old vaudeville routines, he played himself in *Follow the Boys* (1944), *Song of the Open Road* (1944), and *Sensations of 1945* (1944). His failing health did not interfere with his daily liquor consumption.

He defended himself against wide press criticism that his drinking ruined his film career by taking a full-page advertisement in the *Hollywood Reporter*, truthfully declaring he had never missed a performance in his long years on stage, screen, and radio. But his age and accumulated years of heavy drinking were taking their final toll.

On Christmas Day 1946, three minutes past noon, W. C. Fields died at the Las Encinas Sanitarium, in Pasadena, California, where he had been a patient for the past 14 months. His request for immediate cremation was ignored by his family. He was buried at Forest Lawn Cemetery. Two years after his death he remained in an unmarked grave. When a tombstone was erected, it bore his name and dates of birth and death. (It did not contain the legend, "I'd rather be here than in Philadelphia.") *Time* headed its obituary to the great clown as "Gentle Grifter," who was convinced that "everyone has a little larceny in his heart." *Life* properly observed that the character he created achieved contemporary greatness that "became a part of the American folklore."

Based on Robert Lewis Taylor's biography *W. C. Fields, His Follies and Fortunes*, a musical comedy called *W. C.* was unsuccessfully tried out in the summer theatres of 1971. Mickey Rooney surprisingly evoked an aura of Fields, but the book of the musical was conventional hokum. Bernadette Peters made an impressive Carlotta Monti in that outing. Miss Monti's own tome became the basis for the Universal movie *W. C. Fields and Me* (1976). Rod Steiger was cast as W. C. with Valerie Perrine as Fields' mistress of 14 years. In January 1976 Fields' family* filed a $7.5 million damage suit in Los Angeles against both Paramount and Universal. The

* On Friday, September 16, 1977, former F.B.I. agent (now a Philadelphia attorney) W. C. Fields III and his wife, Linda Weirerbach Fields, became the parents of a seven pound, 14-ounce boy born in Delaware County Memorial Hospital. The couple named their first born: W. C. Fields IV.

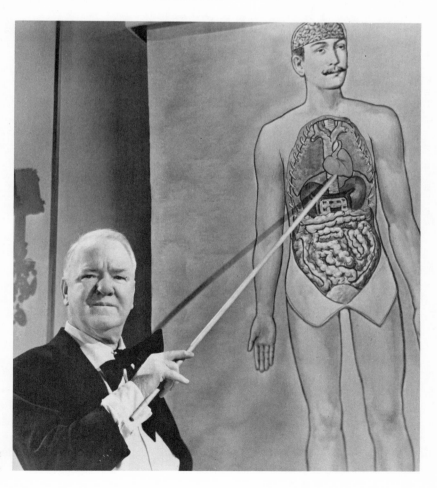

In the deleted sequence from Tales of Manhattan (1942).

In Follow the Boys
(1944).

plaintiffs charged the studios with breaches of contracts exceeding limitations of use of Fields' writings and performances, as well as Universal with "fraudulently fictionalizing and sensationalizing" Fields' life in its screen biography. The case has yet to be determined, but the critics and public alike quickly decided the movie was an overall dud.

On September 24, 1975, Fields was inducted into the Motion Picture Hall of Fame and Museum in Anaheim, California. His films continue to find new, appreciative audiences who are generally unprepared for his assault on civilization and who eagerly await his next caustic comment or wry, mumbling aside.

FEATURE FILMS

Janice Meredith (*Metro-Goldwyn 1924*)
Sally of the Sawdust (*United Artists 1925*)
That Royle Girl (*Paramount 1926*)
It's the Old Army Game (*Paramount 1926*)
So's Your Old Man (*Paramount 1926*)
The Potters (*Paramount 1927*)
Running Wild (*Paramount 1927*)
Two Flaming Youths (*Paramount 1927*)
Tillie's Punctured Romance (*Paramount 1928*)
Fools for Luck (*Paramount 1928*)

Her Majesty, Love (*First National 1931*)
Million Dollar Legs (*Paramount 1932*)
If I Had a Million (*Paramount 1932*)
International House (*Paramount 1933*)
Tillie and Gus (*Paramount 1933*)
Alice in Wonderland (*Paramount 1933*)
Six of a Kind (*Paramount 1934*)
You're Telling Me (*Paramount 1934*)
The Old-Fashioned Way (*Paramount 1934*)
Mrs. Wiggs of the Cabbage Patch (*Paramount 1934*)

It's a Gift (*Paramount 1934*)
David Copperfield (*MGM 1935*)
Mississippi (*Paramount 1935*)
The Man on the Flying Trapeze (*Paramount 1935*)
Poppy (*Paramount 1936*)
The Big Broadcast of 1938 (*Paramount 1938*)
You Can't Cheat an Honest Man (*Universal 1939*)

My Little Chickadee (*Universal 1940*)
The Bank Dick (*Universal 1940*)
Never Give a Sucker an Even Break (*Universal 1941*)
Tales of Manhattan (*20th Century–Fox 1942*) [deleted from release print]
Follow the Boys (*Universal 1944*)
Song of the Open Road (*United Artists 1944*)
Sensations of 1945 (*United Artists 1944*)

On the set of Oklahoma! (1955).

Charlotte Greenwood

Beauty and glamour have never been prerequisites for funsters. Often, quirks of physiogonomy have advantageously combined with soaring talent to create memorable images that fondly recall players who utilized nature's misadventures by capitalizing on, and even accentuating, them. Obesity underscored the comedy of John Bunny, Roscoe Arbuckle, and Jackie Gleason. Ben Turpin's cross-eyes were his fortune. Mr. Durante's publicized proboscis and Mr. Hope's ski nose became grist for gagsters. Joe E. Brown and Martha Raye emphasized large mouths, and Marie Dressler turned the ugly duckling syndrome into a Cinderella tale for senior citizens.

Lanky, awkward—but disguised with impeccable grace—Charlotte Greenwood harnessed her height (5'9½") to a towering success.* Her long arms and legs would flail about like an antic windmill and she would

* Years later (in 1950) Charlotte would confess to the press. "I capitalized on the gawky movements of my long legs and made a success on the stage. That cured my sensitivity. I haven't been sensitive about my height in 45 years."

defy physical restrictions by kicking her leg sideways overhead (she called it a "lift"), casually touching her toes with her fingertips and galloping about with the palms of her hands flat toward the floor. Later-day clowns Joan Davis and Cass Daley frenetically used their bodies for comedic acrobatics but no one has attained the disciplined, clowning grace and refined buoyant buffoonery of Charlotte Greenwood. During her over 50 years in show business she certainly verified her constant declaration that women are "never too tall."

Annabella Jacquet Higgins was married by the Reverend Joseph R. Moore at the Church of the Resurrection in Philadelphia on May 19, 1889, to Englishman Frank Greenwood. On Wednesday, June 25, 1890, at 1507 Reed Street in Philadelphia, Dr. John S. Pearson delivered Bella of her first child. They named the girl Frances Charlotte. A year later Frank left his family and Bella found employment in a local hotel, leaving her infant daughter to be cared for in the barbershop of her uncle, Jacob K. Higgins. The family moved to Boston, where one day Charlotte fell through a skylight, severing an artery in her upper arm. In later years Miss Greenwood would refer to her "scar a mile long, and it takes a lot of makeup to cover it when I have to wear an evening gown on stage."

When a warmer climate was advised for the growing, lanky child, the family moved to Norfolk, Virginia, where Charlotte attended school. At 11 she had reached her full height. After teachers discovered her rich contralto voice, she vows she sang "The Star-Spangled Banner" in every schoolroom except the basement. But academic pursuit little appealed to lanky Lottie, so she left school to earn a living and support her mother.

At 15 (and appearing much older) she made her way to New York City and show business. Referring to her beginnings, she recalls, "Having a natural contralto, I got an audition at the Metropolitan. The man said, 'Bring that voice back to me in 10 years.' But I had no money and I felt I should earn and take care of my mother. My first job was in the chorus of *The White Cat* at the New Amsterdam Theatre in New York on November 2, 1905. In the back line, of course. I never could be a front-row 'pony'—I'd have blotted all of them out!" Her first speaking part was as Lola in *The Rogers Brothers in Panama* (1907), and in 1908 she appeared with Sam Bernard in *Nearly a Hero*. With Eunice Burnham she formed an act, "Two Girls and a Piano." They played the vaudeville circuits, with a two-year engagement in Chicago. On Broadway in *The Passing Show of 1912* she gained recognition that disproved one obtuse critic's comment, "She's just a novelty—a cyclone, a whirlwind."

The "novelty" galloped on through 1913's *Passing Show*, and in 1914 Charlotte signed with producer Oliver Morosco for the second lead in Fritzi Scheff's *Pretty Mrs. Smith*. The Morosco association would last eight years, bringing Miss Greenwood her greatest theatrical success and her character identification, and would lead to her film debut.

Frank Lloyd directed Morosco's film production of the Lestocq comedy *Jane* (1915) with Charlotte in the title role. She was supported by her stage leading man, Sydney Grant. The Paramount release was reviewed by the *New York Dramatic Mirror*: "Miss Greenwood is probably the most grotesque of

the numerous Janes, beginning with [Miss] Johnstone Bennett—whom we have seen in the character; but the elongated Charlotte is always good for a laugh when it is handy. In this picture she confines her gymnastic eccentricities and facial grimaces to the character of the maid suddenly promoted to the mistress of the house and she makes Jane an amiable, if amusing, female." *Motion Picture World* found that "Miss Greenwood displays a keen sense of photoplay comedy in her portrayal of the servant who consents to pose as Shackleton's [Forrest Stanley] wife. Her facial expressions are varied and well judged and she never spoils an effect by unnecessary exaggerations. She was, in every respect, a fortunate choice for the character of Jane."

Had she remained active in pictures, Charlotte might well have become one of the silent screen's top clowns. But Morosco, with Elmer Harris, had written for her a new comedy for which Earl Carroll supplied music and lyrics. The musical farce opened a new career for the lanky Lottie until it seemed she would play nothing but Letty to her grave.

So Long, Letty opened at the old Burbank Theatre in Los Angeles late in 1915, and moved east to open on Broadway at the Shubert Theatre on October 23, 1916. The stage comedy provided Charlotte with a tailor-made role that she brilliantly played. She spouted such lines as, "Oh, men are peculiar. They spend their courting days telling us how unworthy they are, and their married life proving it!" She dueted the title song with Sydney Grant. Her playing of Letty continued to delight audiences on an extensive road tour, especially her closing number, "Here Come the Married Men," with its punch line, "If they are as faithful to their country as they are to their wives, God help the U.S.A.!" (When Robertson-Cole made the film version of *So Long, Letty* an unavailable Charlotte would be replaced oncamera by Grace Darmond.)

During the run of *So Long, Letty* Charlotte married the show's company manager, Cyril Ring. He was the brother of actress Blanche Ring and the brother-in-law of actors Thomas Meighan and Charles Winninger. On November 20, 1919, Charlotte starred in Morosco's production of *Linger Longer, Letty*; Olin Howland was her leading man and Ring supported. This comedy with music was a Cinderella tale of a family's ugly duckling who rises in the world and conquers her share of male attention.

Tempting offers from Hollywood perplexed her. "Pictures are no novelty in my young life," she reasoned. "When I first became a star in *So Long, Letty*, Mr. Morosco got me to appear in a photoplay called *Jane*, which he produced at his western studio. I did *Jane* while appearing in *So Long, Letty* and almost died. I'd no sooner close my pretty blue eyes than the alarm clock would call me to the movie studio. One thing at a time, if you please! That's going to be my motto. And that's where the problem comes in. I love to play Letty. The stage has been my playground as well as workshop ever since I was a kid breaking into the chorus under the eagle eye of Ned Wayburn."

A road tour in *Let 'er Go, Letty* terminated when Oliver Morosco and George V. Hobart revised Charles Klein's play *Maggie Pepper* for a fourth Letty vehicle. *Letty Pepper*, with music by Werner Janssen, lasted only 32 performances after its April 10, 1922, New York opening. Charlotte was prepared to start a repertoire of her Letty plays. "It looks as though I will have to keep on being Letty until I retire from the stage. Of course, each year I have a new play, but still Letty is always the central figure. I think that it would be a popular thing, say, to have one Letty one night and another the next. Just think, I soon would have a full week of Letties—one for each evening." But for the next 13 years, Miss Greenwood left Letty in the wings.

Her marriage had not been going well, and in the autumn of 1922 she left her Bayside, Long Island, farm and divorced Cyril Ring. She also became one of the stars of Irving Berlin's second *Music Box Revue*, which opened on October 23, 1922, to play 272 performances. She was a delight in the revue, highlighting the show with her dancing and singing of "I'm Looking for a Daddy Long Legs."

Hassard Short's Ritz Revue in 1924 provided a sparkling showcase for the Greenwood talent. Alexander Woollcott wrote, "But then there is Charlotte Greenwood. blowing through the show like a gale of fresh wind— the hearty, good-humored, likable Miss Greenwood, who plays one hilarious sketch

written by Norma Mitchell and Ralph Bunker. It is just the simple chronicle of a lady trying to take her bath while the iceman is calling and the telephones are ringing. Miss Greenwood makes it richly funny. This opinion is here recorded by one who has long cherished the conviction that the lanky comedienne is a first-rate actress who would do herself proud in a genuine comedy which did not require her meditatively to stroke the ceiling with her toe."

"Her Morning Bath" sketch from the *Ritz Revue* was the show's biggest laugh getter and in 1928-29 provided Charlotte with a rousing success on a Keith's-Orpheum vaudeville tour. In the *Ritz Revue* she also sang two numbers, "A Perfect Day" and "Too Tall," each a show stopper. The composer of the songs was an American, Martin Broones, whose music had a measure of success in England. After the closing of the *Ritz Revue*, Charlotte and Martin Broones ferried to Jersey City, New Jersey, and on December 22, 1924, were married in a civil ceremony performed by Judge Kincaid. The newlyweds honeymooned in Boston on tour with the *Ritz Revue*, and Charlotte was sporting a diamond-linked anklet from Mr. Broones. Years later, after the Brooneses had settled in Beverly Hills, Judge Kincaid was an occasional house guest of theirs and told a reporter, "Never have I seen two people so content, so absorbed in each other. It revives one's faith. Marriage is never a 'problem' with people like Charlotte and Martin."

Rufus Le Maire's Affairs, with music by Martin Broones, co-starred Charlotte Greenwood and Ted Lewis in March 1927. The show received mediocre notices but it did provide Charlotte with more material for vaudeville. She became one of the first "duplex" performers (if not the first) to play the Palace Theatre: a top-billed headliner appearing in the first *and* second halves of the bill. On June 1, 1927, she played a satirical sketch on the play *Gentlemen Prefer Blondes* from Le Maire's revue with former members of the cast, including Mr. Broones. In the star spot (next to closing) she sang a medley of her well-known songs, accompanied by her husband. When the play was held over for a second week, she was seen in the first half of the bill as a movie queen in the "Movieland" sketch from *Le Maire's Affairs*, and again with Broones she filled the star slot with songs and her eccentric dancing.

Following the Palace engagement the Brooneses left for California, where Charlotte filmed Margaret Mayo's stage success *Baby Mine* (1928). It was shot at MGM and featured the comedy team of Karl Dane and George K. Arthur. As Dane's ungainly wife Emma, "Charlotte Greenwood," the *New York Times* found, "endeavors to whittle up the fun by gymnastic activities and queer grimaces, some of which probably suit the peculiar humor of this photoplay." From the Culver City lot she moved to Warner Bros. to play Letty Robbins in a talking version that had little to do with the story line of *So Long, Letty* (1929). But the picture did afford her the opportunity to display the buoyant bag of Greenwood tricks and to sing the title tune and "My Strongest Weakness Is You." *Photoplay* said that Charlotte was the whole show and that "just to look at her boisterous antics is to laugh," while the *New York Times* reported, "The playful Miss Greenwood carries it along its frivolous route—romps happily through the film and does exceedingly well in her part of the light-headed wife."

In January 1930 Charlotte toured California in the comedy *She Couldn't Say No*, a play she later took to Australia with greater success. In April 1930 she was starring in a pre-Broadway tryout of *Mebbe*, which collapsed in three weeks. Thereafter she made two Educational talking comedy shorts, *Girls Will Be Boys* and *Love Your Neighbor*, and was seen on California's stages in *She Knew What She Wanted* and *Parlor, Bedroom and Bath*. She filmed the last-named farce in 1931 with Buster Keaton for MGM and *Photoplay* cited her effort as one of the month's best performances, based on her hilarious love scenes with the stoic Buster. She was critically applauded for her playing of Sally in MGM's *Stepping Out* (1931), and at the same studio was the maid abetting Robert Montgomery's charade as a butler in *The Man in Possession* (1931).

Samuel Goldwyn's *Palmy Days* (1931) cast 41-year-old Charlotte as predatory gymnast Helen Martin in hot pursuit of unlikely Eddie Cantor. With her blonde hair closely bobbed she whirled through the film creating madcap comedy and singing "Bend Down

Sister." *Photoplay* accurately called her "a grand funster." When MGM imported Bert Lahr to repeat his howling stage success, *Flying High* (1931), Charlotte was cast as his zany vis-à-vis. *Photoplay* declared, "Lahr and Greenwood are a comedy team second to none in talkies!" Unfortunately, they never made another film together.

In April of 1932 Charlotte was back on the stage; in San Francisco she performed in *The Alarm Clock*, a play with songs by Martin Broones. At the same time her performance on the screen in Fox's none-too-good movie *Cheaters at Play* (1932) was receiving hearty audience laughter.

Although Hollywood was offering her plenty of work, Charlotte was ever anxious for new accomplishments and fresh fields to conquer. Thus on October 31, 1932, she made her London stage debut at the Drury Lane Theatre in the musical *Wild Violets*, a sumptuous spectacle on a revolving stage. Soon Charlotte was the toast of the town. She remained in England to film *Orders Is Orders* (1933), with James Gleason, Cedric Hardwicke, and Ray Milland, for Gaumont-British. By October 1933 she was back at San Francisco's Alcazar Theatre giving a glowing performance in Sidney Howard's *The Late Christopher Bean*. Here she proved she could play a straight role and carry a show with the best of actresses.

The success of *Wild Violets* was not repeated when Charlotte returned to the Drury Lane Theatre in London on April 9, 1934, in Jerome Kern and Oscar Hammerstein II's musical *Three Sisters*. An adaptation of a French musical comedy, *Gay Deceivers*, with music by Martin Broones, fared better after opening at London's Gaiety Theatre in May 1935. The actress was feted by London society, and at a Mayfair party Lady Ravensdale advanced the theory that Charlotte's great talent had to come from a magnificent background. The Greenwood candor and wit acknowledged the compliment: "Yes, I have a wonderful background. I come from a long line of Philadelphia barbers!"

Letty awaited Charlotte's return to America in the fall of 1935 and nearly confirmed her past fears of a one-character career. "Someday I am afraid I will get a play about 'Letty' that will be taken as the one-and-only-Letty and then I'll have to stick to that one

With Cliff Edwards
in Stepping Out
(1931).

With Eddie Cantor in Palmy
Days (1931).

With Bert Lahr in Flying High *(1931).*

play for the rest of my natural theatrical life."
But on Monday evening, December 9, 1935,
she opened in San Francisco in *Leaning on
Letty.* It was a revision of the prior year's
Broadway success *Post Road,* which had
starred Lucile Watson. Long, lean, lanky
Letty had found the hit of her career.

As Letty Madison, an eccentric spinster
uncovering the perfect kidnapping crime,
Charlotte was superb. In the next two years
she would create a slice of theatrical history
for audience attendance and gross receipts,
shuttling from coast to coast in the play.
Audiences nationwide adored Letty and Miss
Greenwood gave them their money's worth
not only with an expert performance in the
play but also with what appeared to be an
impromptu song-and-dance routine following the show. Later in the run Percy Kilbride
was a replacement for the male lead, Taylor
Holmes.

As Letty she made one of the first backstage radio broadcasts over station WIP from

the Chestnut Street Opera House in Philadelphia. (During the 1945-46 seasons she
would have her own radio program, "The
Charlotte Greenwood Show.") *Leaning on
Letty* was equally successful in an Australian tour, and when Charlotte retired her gold-
producing Letty, she signed a film contract
with Twentieth Century-Fox.

Miss Greenwood became Fox's leading
character song-and-dance lead, enlivening
several of its assembly-line musicals. She
bolstered Linda Darnell's *Star Dust* (1940),
and she and Jack Oakie were Shirley Temple's ex-vaudevillian parents in Temple's last
Fox contract film, *Young People* (1940).
Temple, Oakie, and Greenwood, dressed to
the nines in top hat and tails, did a delightful
trio to the song "Tra-La-La." *Down Argentine
Way* (1940) was a Technicolor test of endurance for a talented cast against the overpowering Carmen Miranda, but Charlotte
held her ground and hit the mark with her
"Sing to Your Senorita" number. Press re-

leases announced the teaming of Charlotte "Legs" Greenwood and Milton "Nosey" Berle in Twentieth's *Tall, Dark and Handsome* (1941), and the two provided zesty comedy relief for an unheralded and rather pleasant musical. But a new movie team was *not* born.

Fox has made and remade *Three Blind Mice* (1938) so often under different guises that it has to be one of the studio's most profitable properties. In 1941 the oft-filmed tale of three girls in pursuit of millionaires was reconstructed as *Moon over Miami*, a Betty Grable–Carole Landis vehicle with Charlotte completing the triangle as their Aunt Susan Latimer, posing as their maid. She dueted the song "Is That Good?" with Jack Haley, got in a few high kicks, and joined the two blondes singing "Oh, Me, Oh, Mi-Ami." Although an unlikely bit of casting found her as the social-climbing, calculating wife of Charlie Ruggles in *The Perfect Snob* (1941), she carried the part off well.

Charlotte was filling roles that would once have been assigned to Fox's former musical comedy clown Joan Davis, who left the studio in 1941. The Davis wild slapstick subsided to a more mature yet freewheeling clowning projected by Charlotte. Both comediennes used their legs for comedic effect. Greenwood had masterful gymnastic control of her limbs, whereas Davis perfected the Leon Errol rubber-legs species (equally controlled). The uninhibited madcap flair for comedy smartly perfected by Davis was reduced to a more dignified matronly outburst by Greenwood. There was also a difference of almost two decades in their ages. But Charlotte more than bolstered the entertainment value of several less than entertaining Fox musical escapist pictures.

That she was also an effective dramatic actress was evident in her playing of Penny in *Home in Indiana* (1944). It was a performance Charlotte repeated with Walter Brennan, Jeanne Crain, and June Haver on "Lux Radio Theatre" in October 1944. Her expertise in playing farce was equally apparent in United Artists' remake of *Up in*

With Donald Meek, Linda Darnell, Roland Young, John Payne, and Mary Healy in Stardust (1940).

In a pose with Leonid Kinskey for Down Argentine Way *(1940).*

Mabel's Room (1944). The veteran performer admired Fox studio head Darryl F. Zanuck and it took a typically Greenwood turn. She presented him with a picture of a horse, because, she said, "Mr. Zanuck has been so nice to me, I wanted to give him my picture but was scared. He wouldn't want my mug in his office, among all those photos of glamour gals, I thought. In Australia they named a horse after me and sent me pictures showing her long legs bringing her in ahead of the other nags in the races. Knowing he was crazy about horses, I had one of the other Charlotte Greenwood framed and sent it to him. He was delighted with it."

After the mid-Forties the Hollywood film factories offered less-challenging and minor roles to Charlotte, so she returned to the stage. In the summer of 1947 she starred as Mama in a tour of the Broadway hit *I Remember Mama*. The run was another glowing tribute to her powers as a straight dramatic actress. Typically, the actress encored her evening performance with songs and dances. The San Francisco Drama Critics

Award went to Charlotte for her playing of Mama.

Oh, You Beautiful Doll (1949) was Miss Greenwood's final film for Twentieth Century–Fox. She was cast as Anna Breitenbach, the wife of S. Z. Sakall, in an ersatz film biography of composer Fred Fisher. The next year she was manhunting Mrs. Emelia Fielding in Universal's *Peggy*, a feature distinguished only by stock footage of Pasadena's annual Rose Bowl Parade.

But at age 60 Charlotte, an active Christian Scientist, still had plenty of vigor and starred in Cole Porter's new musical *Out of This World*. It had a pre-Broadway playdate in hometown Philadelphia as of November 4, 1950. She was greeted with great enthusiasm, which peaked with her second-act singing of the plaintive Porter song "Nobody's Chasing Me," punctuated with several of her unbelievably high kicks. As Jupiter's jealous wife, Juno, Charlotte was a constant joy. However, the romping Greek gods stumbled in the musical, and the Broadway critics received it with great reservation. (There were also protests against the scantily clad company of gods and goddesses, who were hastily given additional garments to cover their "near" nakedness.) After 157 performances *Out of This World* closed on May 5, 1951. Columbia Records released an original-cast LP album of the musical, the only Greenwood Broadway performance recorded.

The actress returned to her home on Rodeo Drive in Beverly Hills. Two years later Charlotte was back at MGM to play Esther Williams' mother, helping her to swim the English Channel, in *Dangerous When Wet* (1953). When Rodgers and Hammerstein II's milestone musical *Oklahoma!* was finally brought to the screen in 1955, Charlotte was an excellent choice for wise, staunch Aunt Eller.* She lent her lovely contralto voice to such songs as "The Surrey with the Fringe on

Top," "Everything's Up to Date in Kansas City," and "The Farmer and the Cowman." Her notices were justifiably the best of the entire cast. Her portrait of Aunt Eller would have been a glowing final fade-out of her film career. But in 1956 she resurfaced as Miz Tilbee in RKO's *Glory*, and then reprised Marjorie Main's rough Lucy role of *The Women* in MGM's uninspired musical remake called *The Opposite Sex* (1956).

On Wednesday, January 18, 1978, Charlotte died in Los Angeles at the age of 87, leaving no known survivors. (Broones had died on August 10, 1971.) In recent decades she had divided her time between caring for her Beverly Hills home and continuing her interest in the Christian Science religion. For many years she was a Reader in the church; in fact, when Doris Day adopted the Christian Science faith, Charlotte served in this capacity for her.

The Greenwood humor had amused many decades of audiences. Among her devout fans were several U.S. Presidents. She was the only actress ever to breakfast with the Chief

* Actually when Hammerstein II had been casting the part of Aunt Eller for the musical he had wanted Charlotte to play the stage role; however, her film commitments prevented her from joining the show which opened at the St. James Theatre on March 31, 1943, for a 2,212 performance run. Betty Garde thus became the Broadway Aunt Eller in *Oklahoma!*

With Walter Brennan in Home in Indiana *(1944).*

of State. The President was granite-faced Calvin Coolidge. Charlotte brought a huge guffaw from the taciturn gentleman when, after watching in astonishment the tremendous assortment of food being served at breakfast, she exclaimed, "My God, does this go on every day?" In 1940 Charlotte joined President and Mrs. Franklin Delano Roosevelt at a White House luncheon and they were delighted by her sparkling personality.*

* There is the anecdote concerning Charlotte and Groucho Marx, "Who else, one wonders, would go to a

Charlotte Greenwood's constant advice to young people concerned about their physical structure could underscore her standing in show business. "Think of a forest. There we always see one tree that is unusually tall. It stands its full height—and makes the whole forest seem more beautiful, doesn't it?" Miss Greenwood always stood majestically tall.

White House show, watch comedienne Charlotte Greenwood do a high kick that involved wrapping one leg around her neck, then turn to Mrs. Roosevelt and say, "You could do that if you'd just put your mind to it'?"

FEATURE FILMS

Jane (*Paramount 1915*)
Baby Mine (*MGM 1928*)
So Long, Letty (*Warner Bros. 1929*)
Parlor, Bedroom and Bath (*MGM 1931*)
Stepping Out (*MGM 1931*)
The Man in Possession (*MGM 1931*)
Palmy Days (*United Artists 1931*)
Flying High (*MGM 1931*)
Cheaters at Play (*Fox 1932*)
Orders Is Orders (*British 1933*)
Star Dust (*20th Century-Fox 1940*)
Young People (*20th Century-Fox 1940*)
Down Argentine Way (*20th Century-Fox 1940*)
Tall, Dark and Handsome (*20th Century-Fox 1941*)
Moon over Miami (*20th Century-Fox 1941*)
The Perfect Snob (*20th Century-Fox 1941*)

Springtime in the Rockies (*20th Century-Fox 1942*)
Dixie Dugan (*20th Century-Fox 1943*)
The Gang's All Here (*20th Century-Fox 1943*)
Up in Mabel's Room (*United Artists 1944*)
Home in Indiana (*20th Century-Fox 1944*)
Wake Up and Dream (*20th Century-Fox 1946*)
Driftwood (*Republic 1947*)
The Great Dan Patch (*United Artists 1949*)
Oh, You Beautiful Doll (*20th Century-Fox 1949*)
Peggy (*Universal 1950*)
Dangerous When Wet (*MGM 1953*)
Oklahoma! (*Magna 1955*)
Glory (*RKO 1956*)
The Opposite Sex (*MGM 1956*)

William Haines

Through the years Hollywood has endeavored to reflect the pulse and morality of each generation. Passage of the 18th Amendment to the Constitution at 12:01 A.M. on July 16, 1920, began the Roaring Twenties. While F. Scott Fitzgerald became the poet laureate of the era, Hollywood devised and created elements of the jazz age on film for a world to behold. The flapper emerged to be chronicled by John Held Jr., and the rah, rah collegian became a screen hero to escort her. Clara Bow, Colleen Moore, Joan Crawford, and others became the dancing daughters of the Twenties' flaming youth.

Of the assorted males hired to play the brash, perennial youth onscreen, no one created him better than William Haines. Flip, wisecracking Haines played variations of the same know-it-all type of role with great panache. He was the perpetual smart aleck making good, an extrovert often goaded into humility before winning the girl in the final reel. Haines' characters were harbingers of those later played by Lee Tracy, James Cagney, Pat O'Brien, Ben Lyon, et al., in the talkies when crisp, quick retorts became standard movie dialogue. Haines remained one of MGM's top stars for five years, and in a 1929 national exhibitors poll of money-making stars placed second (with 78 percent of the vote) to Lon Chaney.

Haines was born on Monday, January 1, 1900, at Staunton, Virginia, the oldest of five children (three boys and two girls). It was reasonable to the studio press department that he should be a graduate of Staunton Military Academy. His time at that eminent school was spent painting dormitory bedsteads for $6 a week during summer vacations from high school; he was not a student there, much less a graduate. At 14 Bill left his hometown to work in a powder factory on the James River at $200 a month. Later he moved on to a less profitable job as a clerk in a wholesale dry-goods house in Richmond, Virginia, where his family had relocated. In New York City he found employment with the Kenyon Rubber Company and then clerked in a Manhattan department store. While employed as assistant bookkeeper for

With Mary Brian in Brown of Harvard (1927).

the bond house of S. W. Strauss & Co., he submitted his photograph to a "New Faces" movie contest sponsored by Samuel Goldwyn Pictures.

Robert B. McIntyre, casting director for Goldwyn, persuaded Haines to leave his $20-a-week Wall Street job and embark for Hollywood. He and Eleanor Boardman, a lovely young girl from Philadelphia, had won the contest. Haines would later credit musical comedy actress and actor's agent Bijou Fernandez with his winning the prize. When Haines arrived at the Goldwyn studio he informed an astonished greeting commitee, "I'm your new prize beauty."

Bill's film debut was made in Goldwyn's *Brothers Under the Skin* (1922). He played a butler. Minor roles in other Goldwyn pictures followed, including playing a curate in Elinor Glyn's Ruritanian hit, *Three Weeks* (1924). When Goldwyn splintered from the newly formed corporation of Metro-Goldwyn, Haines went as part of the players' roster to M-G. He appeared as William Craig in Mae Murray's *Circe, the Enchantress* (1924) and made an impression on loan-out to Universal in *The Gaiety Girl*. For Metro-Goldwyn Haines was in *Wine of Youth* (1924), which featured Eleanor Boardman. With Miss Boardman and John Gilbert he registered in Louis B. Mayer's production of *Wife of the Centaur* (1924), directed by King Vidor, and he was killed as Rough Rider Lyman Webb in *The Denial* (1925).

Haines had not hit his stride as the fresh, breezy, overconfident comedian jazzing up the screen. At this time he was alternating between leading roles (as, for example, fireman Horatio Manly Jr. in Columbia's *Fighting the Flames*, 1925) and supporting roles (as in Norma Shearer's *A Slave of Fashion*, 1925). He had a dramatic spot as August in the Lon Chaney–Norma Shearer *The Tower of Lies* (1925), directed by Victor Seastrom. His biggest opportunity came when Mary Pickford selected him for her leading man in *Little Annie Rooney* (1925). Bill's exuberant manner was an able counterpart to Miss Pickford's rambunctious mixture of pathos and comedy. When he returned to his home lot, better parts awaited him. He was given Eddie Dowling's stage role in *Sally, Irene and Mary* (1925).

Despite being nearly overshadowed by Sally (Constance Bennett), Irene (Joan Crawford), and Mary (Sally O'Neil), Haines was effective as Mary's plumber sweetheart. There were plans in 1925 to film the hoary melodrama *The Span of Life* with Lon Chaney and Haines, but the idea was shelved. In John M. Stahl's *Memory Lane* (1926) William gave a solid performance as pretentious, overdressed Joe Field opposite Eleanor Boardman. In his next assignment for Metro, which had now become Metro-Goldwyn-Mayer, he found a role in which he could project his own personality, that of a good-natured, fun-loving, wisecracking youth.

The new version of *Brown of Harvard* (1926) was filmed in and around Boston and featured Mary Pickford's irrepressibly irresponsible brother Jack, and made a star of William Haines. The role of conceited, obnoxious Tom Brown gave Haines his first bout with the stylization of the often overbearing wisecracker he perfected on the screen. The film's success vastly enlarged the Haines' ego and the studio submerged him in a lesson in humility that would become a facet of his later screen characterization. Haines recalled the chastisement: "MGM did a wise thing with me. They put me in a little picture called *Lovey Mary* [1926] with Bessie Love as the star. I played a sort of musical comedy milkman. I still put my fingers to my nose when I think of myself in that one. It took the wind out of my sails completely. I couldn't be conceited as long as that picture was in circulation."

Tell It to the Marines (1926) starred Lon Chaney in one of his infrequent roles as a star without grotesque, disabling makeup. He was here a tough marine sergeant coping with a rebellious raw recruit, a former racetrack tout named "Skeet" Burns (Haines). The picture was a huge success, bringing critical praise to Chaney, Eleanor Boardman, Carmel Myers (as Haines' island paramour), and, especially, Bill, for his commendable work. *Photoplay*, perennially championing Haines, wrote, "This picture is going to do a lot toward making a star of William Haines." It did. Irving Thalberg personally liked Haines, who frequently served as escort to his sister Sylvia and who spent weekends with the Thalberg family at Lake Arrowhead.

With Lon Chaney and Claire McDowell in The Tower of Lies *(1925).*

Thalberg, stating his beliefs about the movie medium in a speech at the University of Southern California, noted the change in audience identification with the movies' heroes and heroines. He said that "William Haines, with his modern salesman attitude to go and get it, is more typical" of what contemporary audiences wanted on screen.

Haines was an inveterate practical joker and even Thalberg was grist to his mill. At a lavish costume party given by Marion Davies and William Randolph Hearst, Irving and Norma Shearer Thalberg appeared as West Point cadets. Billy Haines deliberately goosed Thalberg and, to calm the executive's outrage, quickly added, "Oh, pardon me, Irving. I thought you were Norma!"

Along with his flippant image Bill also became Metro's leading exponent of sports. *Slide, Kelly, Slide* (1927) became the harbinger (and one of the few money-makers) of several baseball pictures, and started Haines off on a career of varying exploits in the cinema sports world. As cocky, self-centered bush leaguer Jim Kelly, Haines had a field day. Partially filmed at New York's Yankee Stadium and at the Yankees' Florida spring training camp, the picture also featured professional baseball stars Irish and Bob Meusel, Tony Lazzeri, and Mike Donlin. But as Kelly, demoralizing the team with his self-enchantment and boasting he could "throw two balls at once and braid 'em," and pitching the Yankees to victory, Bill was just right.

From baseball he became smart-aleck shipping clerk Jack Kelly, winning a golf match in *Spring Fever* (1927) with Joan Crawford as his lady love. He again teamed with Crawford in *West Point* (1927), in which he was a cadet with problems. The *New York Times*, never a Haines admirer, wrote, "One might search the highways and byways of the United States and never find quite as preposterous a youth as the insufferable bounder in a picture glorying in the title of *West Point*." On November 5, 1928, Miss

Crawford was again Haines' screen love, when *The Smart Aleck* started shooting. Released in 1929 as *The Duke Steps Out*, Haines was robustly amusing as a prize-fighter.

One critic noted that Bill had added to his antic laurels in his recent pictures: "It has remained for William Haines to bring for the first time to Hollywood one true admixture of the sublime and the ridiculous; that curious undermining of comedy with a certain disarming humanity that is called Sob-Stuff when it veers—as it has always done before Haines—into the merely banal. Haines makes it genuine. For one thing, he does not take his cinema seriously. He kids gorgeously, he plays his drama with tongue in cheek, he romps thumb-to-nose with sacrilegious zest through the High Halls of Hokum; collegiate, irresponsible, smart-aleck, young. Perhaps it is this very lack of pomp which makes his sentimentality—when it does appear—so decent and fresh and bracingly true. It is a good thing to find in William Haines a comedian at last who keeps his pathos hard-boiled. It is a good thing for Hollywood."

Miss Crawford found Bill had great naturalness, charm, and an overwhelming sense of humor. He was fond of breaking up his leading ladies in a love scene yet he could and would be totally responsive to a serious turn in the plot. Joan and "Willie" became close friends and he frequently escorted her to premieres. Miss Crawford was among the first to recognize Haines' gift for decorating (he had decorated her Metro dressing room) and admired his sumptuously decorated home, where he hosted lavish parties.

The *New York Times*, continually harpooning Haines, commented on his polo-playing hero: "Another embodiment of audacity is introduced by William Haines in *The Smart Set.* This Tommy Van Buren is quite as impossible as any of Mr. Haines' previous portrayals, but, as this epic of insolence is chiefly confined to the polo field, he, in all probability, will amuse more people

With Joan Crawford in Spring Fever *(1927).*

than he irritates. He improves each shining instance by some further proof of his arrogance and impertinence. . . ." But the newspaper blast did concede his antics constantly aroused laughter in the audience. The audience, after all, had paid to laugh, and Haines certainly fulfilled their wish.

Telling the World (1928) amused little. Bill as a newspaper reporter went through the entire picture on a dead run. In those days Metro advertised the star's screen appearances in film trade journals as "The man you love to see—socked in the nose" and as "The smart aleck of the screen—its irrepressible wisecracker . . . the star who breezes through his pictures leaving a trail of laughter and huge enjoyment . . . the star that men, and women, adore . . . William Haines."

Offscreen, the six-foot, black-haired, brown-eyed Haines presented a problem to the imaginative studio press department. His fun-provoking personality made good copy but his insistence on remaining a "private person" prompted the dreamers of pulp to align him romantically over the years with the likes of Peggy Hopkins Joyce and Barbara LaMarr. Actually, he preferred the company of kindred spirit Polly Moran. Billy and Polly were good companions and later, in the Thirties, Billy was flippantly telling the press that they would soon marry.

The advent of sound in Hollywood prompted Irving Thalberg to add street noises, ringing telephones, and theatergoers' applause in Bill's *Excess Baggage* (1928), in which the actor was excellent as a juggler-acrobat performing a breakneck wire-walking act. *Show People* (1928), King Vidor's hardy satire on Hollywood, was probably Marion Davies' best picture and the first time Hearst consented (with Marion's approval) to her being co-starred in a film. Paired with Haines, the two expert comedians made *Show People* a thorough delight. Even the *New York Times* seemed impressed: "Mr. Vidor, who more than once has proved himself a wizard in handling players, has accomplished here the seemingly impossible, by eliciting a restrained performance from William Haines, who has knocked over the traces in a number of films. In *Show People*, he actually compels sympathy for the character." The feature further benefited from an exceptionally clever performance from Da-

vies and by the cameo appearance of several of Hollywood's top stars of the day: Norma Talmadge, Charles Chaplin, Leatrice Joy, Mae Murray, John Gilbert, and others.

Bill described MGM's entrance into talkies: "It was the night of the Titanic all over again, with women grabbing the wrong children and Louis B. [Mayer] singing 'Nearer My God to Thee.'" And it was Haines whom MGM selected to be its first major star to speak on the screen.

Alias Jimmy Valentine (1929) was made as a silent picture, reworked with "sound," and the last reel refilmed with dialogue. Bill's voice, considering the primitive recording techniques, registered with his personality. With Metro now geared for sound and the demanding new talkies, Haines' career continued. He played a comedy sketch with Jack Benny in *Hollywood Revue of 1929*, and an auto racer in *Speedway* (1929), partially filmed at the Indianapolis Speedway. In the summer of 1929 he started filming *Navy Blues*, in which he is a sailor on a two-hour leave. The *New York Times* noted, "Whether Mr. Haines is silent or audible, his portrayals are just about the same." At the end of November 1929 he started shooting *The Girl Said No* (1930), greatly assisted by Marie Dressler and Polly Moran. *Screenland* magazine wrote, "The star plays another of his cut-up roles that make the critics gnash their teeth and the audience chortle." Dialogue by Charles MacArthur helped the fun along in this entry.

Way Out West (1930) was a mixture of romance and slapstick with Bill as a side-show barker. *Remote Control* (1930), based on a mildly successful Broadway play, was refashioned for Haines, and *Time* remarked that his professional impertinence, disliked by most critics, was still highly salable to the public. Deemed risqué for 1931, *A Tailor-Made Man* had been a stage success for several years and was transferred to the screen in 1922 for the talents of Charles Ray, with whom Haines was often physically compared. Their acting images were far from similar. But the role of a pants presser flouncing into society in a borrowed dress suit gave Haines a meaty role that he played with noticeable restraint.

David Belasco's play *Dancing Partner* was the basis for Haines' *Just a Gigolo* (1931), in

With Josephine Dunn and Sam Hardy in A Man's Man *(1929).*

which he was Lord Robert Brummell. The critics found he played on a subdued level and well paced a cast of players far more experienced in the acting art than Billy H. But public response to Haines was fading. *Photoplay* admitted he was professionally slipping but thought his newest picture, *New Adventures of Get-Rich-Quick Wallingford* (1931), would reinstate him on the screen. The fan magazine observed, "It gives William Haines the best chance he's ever had for his special sort of ability. As Wallingford, he drops the usual smart aleck, wisecracking stuff and becomes sincere, human and enjoyable." But Jimmy Durante rated as many raves as Haines in this Metro picture. When the film premiered at Manhattan's Capitol Theatre on October 9, 1931, Haines appeared "In Person" on the stage performing a monologue and getting through a song, prior to the stage show featuring Milton Berle and his "Great Guns Show." Also that year he joined with many other Hollywood stars in performing in a fund-raising short subject for the National Variety Artists called *The Stolen Jools.*

Two comedy-dramas, *Fast Life* and *Are You Listening?* were completed in 1932. A still-ill Irving Thalberg was recuperating in Europe and the Metro climate was geared to new stars, newer story approaches, and the power mania of Louis B. Mayer. When a movie columnist openly suggested that Haines had homosexual tendencies, Mayer demanded the star's presence. The mogul reviewed the studio's contractual moral clause and gave Bill warning. This situation plus the fact that his two latest pictures created no box-office stampede led MGM to allow his contract to lapse. He was dropped from the Culver City galaxy of stars. Two minor films for Mascot in 1934 completed his film career. But resourceful William Haines had found an equally lucrative and, to him, far more rewarding career in interior decorating.

In 1936 director Dorothy Arzner had Haines design and dress the living-room set for Columbia's *Craig's Wife*, starring Rosalind Russell. Also in 1936 Haines made national headlines. Some 100 men and women,

With Esther Ralston and Conrad Nagel in The Marines Are Coming *(1934).*

calling themselves the "White Legion," attacked Haines and his companion Jimmy Shields near Manhattan Beach, California, over the Memorial Day weekend. The crowd smeared the men's car with rotten tomatoes and routed them, and 20 of their friends, out of town. Haines was perplexed over the attack and, with both eyes blackened, told reporters, "It was a lynch mob all right. Some wild, untrue rumors must have stirred them up. It might have been some sort of clan or secret organization."

Personal problems aside, his expertise in decorating and design, coupled with excellent taste, soon made him one of the country's top interior decorators. His clients included several of his former co-players, Leila Hyams, Joan Crawford, and Constance Bennett among them. And producers William Goetz, Nunnally Johnson, and Jack L. Warner had him refurbish their homes. He knew his new profession and was well versed in the vagaries of his former one, carefully adding plenty of mirrors to the homes of actors,

who, he said, were really vainer than the ladies.

Walter Hubert Annenberg was appointed ambassador to Great Britain in February 1969 and engaged William Haines to completely refurbish the U.S. ambassador's London residence. Previously Haines had spent five years redoing the Annenbergs' Cathedral City, California, home. The London project required many months to complete for 70-year-old Bill and his partner, Theodore Graber of Los Angeles.

Interviewed at the completion of the costly project, Haines told reporters, "I've been in and out of London eight times since February 23, 1969. It took nine months to finish to the hour." The whole mansion glistened from the entrance hall to the dining room, where paintings by the masters graced the walls. The Annenberg project was Haines' crowning achievement as a decorator.

Three years later, on December 26, 1973, William Haines died of cancer at St. John's Hospital in Santa Monica, California.

FEATURE FILMS

Brothers Under the Skin (*Goldwyn 1922*)
Souls for Sale (*Goldwyn 1923*)
Lost and Found (*Goldwyn 1923*)
Three Wise Fools (*Goldwyn 1923*)
Six Days (*Goldwyn 1923*)
Three Weeks (*Goldwyn 1924*)
True as Steel (*Metro-Goldwyn 1924*)
The Midnight Express (*Columbia 1924*)
Circe, the Enchantress (*Metro-Goldwyn 1924*)
The Desert Outlaw (*Fox 1924*)
The Gaiety Girl (*Universal 1924*)
Wine of Youth (*Metro-Goldwyn 1924*)
Married Flirts (*Metro-Goldwyn 1924*)
Wife of the Centaur (*Metro-Goldwyn 1924*)
A Fool and His Money (*Columbia 1925*)
Who Cares? (*Columbia 1925*)
The Denial (*Metro-Goldwyn 1925*)
Fighting the Flames (*Columbia 1925*)
A Slave of Fashion (*Metro-Goldwyn 1925*)
The Tower of Lies (*Metro-Goldwyn 1925*)
Little Annie Rooney (*United Artists 1925*)
Sally, Irene and Mary (*Metro-Goldwyn 1925*)
Memory Lane (*First National 1926*)
Mike (*MGM 1926*)
The Thrill Hunter (*Columbia 1926*)
Brown of Harvard (*MGM 1926*)

Lovey Mary (*MGM 1926*)
Tell It to the Marines (*MGM 1926*)
A Little Journey (*MGM 1927*)
Slide, Kelly, Slide (*MGM 1927*)
Spring Fever (*MGM 1927*)
West Point (*MGM 1927*)
The Smart Set (*MGM 1928*)
Telling the World (*MGM 1928*)
Excess Baggage (*MGM 1928*)
Show People (*MGM 1928*)
Alias Jimmy Valentine (*MGM 1929*)
The Duke Steps Out (*MGM 1929*)
A Man's Man (*MGM 1929*)
Hollywood Revue of 1929 (*MGM 1929*)
Speedway (*MGM 1929*)
Navy Blues (*MGM 1929*)
The Girl Said No (*MGM 1930*)
Free and Easy (*MGM 1930*)
Way Out West (*MGM 1930*)
Remote Control (*MGM 1930*)
A Tailor-Made Man (*MGM 1931*)
Just a Gigolo (*MGM 1931*)
New Adventures of Get-Rich-Quick Wallingford (*MGM 1931*)
Fast Life (*MGM 1932*)
Are You Listening? (*MGM 1932*)
Young and Beautiful (*Mascot 1934*)
The Marines Are Coming (*Mascot 1934*)

In It Should Happen to You *(1954)*.

Judy Holliday

"Do me a favor, will ya', Harry? Drop dead!"

Thus went the famous shrill line of one of the famous females of the American theatre and cinema—Billie Dawn, the blonde Galatea with the squeaky voice and streetwalker sashay of the comedy *Born Yesterday*. The outrageous character became flesh and blood via the remarkable talents of blonde, wide-eyed, pleasingly plump Judy Holliday, a luscious comedienne once hailed by *Time* magazine as "a major wonderment of the entertainment world." Miss Holliday would win an Oscar for her screen portrayal of Billie, sparkle in some Hollywood screen comedies, return to Broadway in triumph—and die of cancer at the age of 42.

Few women have blended femininity, intelligence, and comedic talent as charmingly as Judy Holliday. George Morris would write in a recent appreciation of the actress,

> She was a true original, a flawless comedienne who could switch from comedy to tragedy with a mere inflection in her voice. . . . She was able to perform endless variations with . . . [her voice], ranging all the way from the broadest comedy to the deepest pathos. . . . Judy Holliday was perhaps one of the most lovable personalities ever to appear on stage or screen. She radiated a warmth and generosity that continues to be irresistible when her films are seen today. . . . The actress was also blessed with a vulnerability that made her dumb-but-well-intentioned characters even more endearing.

Perhaps only Carole Lombard, Lucille Ball, and a handful of other ladies have ever matched Judy's performing magic. Since Holliday's tragic death in 1965, only a few have revealed more than a flash of her range of acting abilities.

She was born Judith Tuvim on Wednesday, June 21, 1922, in New York City's Lying-In-Hospital.* Her mother, Helen, a piano

* Tuvim is the Jewish word for "holiday"; hence the origin of Judy's professional surname.

295

teacher, had been watching Fanny Brice perform on stage when the labor pains began in earnest. Her father, Abraham, was a professional promoter and fundraiser who left his wife when Judy was six. However, he continued to keep a close relationship with his daughter.

The future star felt the urge of creativity early. When four, she danced about her home (Judy lived in an apartment with Helen and her Russian Jewish grandmother, Rachel) with such flair that her stage-struck mother* enrolled her in ballet school. As Judy grew older her ambition and intelligence became neighborhood legend. Judy would recall herself as "one of those precocious, obnoxious children who read *War and Peace*, Schnitzler, and Molière while my friends were going in for *The Bobbsey Twins.*" During her tenure at P.S. 150 and Julia Richman High School in Manhattan, she edited the school journal, won a prize for her essay "How to Keep the Streets, Parks, and Playgrounds of Our City Clean and Wholesome," acted in plays she wrote herself, and scored a walloping 172 on the city school I.Q. tests.

Rejected admission to Yale Drama School, Judy sought fulfillment after high school in the Broadway theatrical environs. Her first job was as a backstage "manager" for Orson Welles' Mercury Theatre. That post ended when she lost her calm during a crisis at the theatre's telephone switchboard.

A bit too tall (5'7") and certainly too plump (ca. 150 pounds) to squeeze into the tights of a Broadway musical chorine, Judy finally got her performing start in the late summer of 1938. According to the famous story, one rainy evening she was caught in a thunderstorm in Greenwich Village. She took shelter within the Village Vanguard nightclub and soon was engaged in conversation with the club's owner, Max Gordon. When he mentioned he was seeking fresh talent for his new entertainment spot, Judy at once thought of Adolph Green. She had met him the previous summer at a Catskill mountain resort when he was performing with a group called Six and Company. Judy had volunteered her help

* Judy's mother, Helen, was very suicidal and suffered several nervous breakdowns in later years. The dependence-independence relationship between Judy and Helen was exceedingly complex and a cause of great anguish to the actress throughout her adult years.

then. Now Judy and Green, along with Betty Comden, Alvin Hammer, and John Frank, put together an act which they auditioned for Gordon. He was pleased and soon The Revuers were performing in front of paid audiences.

Before long, The Revuers were the pet joy of the Manhattan intelligentsia, and success seemed imminent. According to Holliday's biographer, Lee Israel, it was at this time that Judy moved away from her mother and began living with a woman she had met during a summer holiday. Although the physical aspect of their relationship would end when Judy realized she sexually preferred men, the two women remained good friends.

By the time The Revuers had completed their Village Vanguard engagement, they were earning $250 a week and had been heard to good advantage on a 30-minute NBC radio show for some 32 weeks. The act moved uptown, playing such posh spots as the Rainbow Room (where they were unappreciated), and eventually ended up back at Max Gordon's basement club.

Later The Revuers decided to take their offbeat sketches to Hollywood, hoping the movies would beckon. They accepted an engagement at the Hollywood Trocadero Club.

Movie moguls and talent scouts did catch the act and were impressed—by Judy. "All the companies wanted her," remembers Adolph Green. "Nobody wanted us." Judy loyally refused all bidders, insisting that the group be signed in its entirety or not at all. Finally, Darryl F. Zanuck's Twentieth Century-Fox studio agreed. Fox assigned The Revuers to *Greenwich Village* (1944), a less than scintillating formula musical starring Carmen Miranda and Don Ameche. At that, the bulk of The Revuers' footage was pruned into the cutting-room wastebasket.

Via the technical jargon of the contract, Fox then dropped The Revuers but retained Judy (much to her dismay) on salary. In 1944's *Something for the Boys*, a Cole Porter Broadway musical distillation with Miss Miranda and a very young Perry Como, Judy, in welder's helmet, goggles, and overalls, had one line. "I knew a girl once named Marie who had Carborundum in her teeth and turned into a radio receiving set." After spewing that mouthful of wartime humor, Judy joined the

With Adolph Green, Betty Comden, and Alvin Hammer in Greenwich Village (1945).

cast of *Winged Victory* (1944), Fox's film version of Moss Hart's stage-hit serviceman show. Lon McCallister, Jeanne Crain, and Edmond O'Brien filled the major roles. Related Judy, "I played a Brooklyn pilot's [O'Brien] wife, but the way they made me up, I looked like his mother." *Winged Victory* was directed by George Cukor who would play an important part in Judy's later film career.

Fox soon decided that its once-promising new contractee was not living up to the expectations of such studio attractions as Betty Grable, Linda Darnell, Jeanne Crain, and Anne Baxter, or such novelty acts as Carmen Miranda and Charlotte Greenwood. The studio refused to reoption Judy for further films and she sadly returned to the East.*

Fortunately, things brightened professionally shortly after her return to New York. The

* Biographer Israel in her narrative of the life and times of Holliday reports that on one occasion Judy went to Fox studio head Darryl F. Zanuck, hoping to discuss the quality of and lack of roles she was receiving. It seemed Zanuck was far more intrigued with the actress' physical attributes. An angered Holliday, at that point, yanked out her studio-made falsies and shouted, "If you want them that badly, take 'em. *They're yours anyway!*"

actress won the role of Alice, a saucy hooker, in the comedy *Kiss Them for Me,* by Luther Davis (and based on the novel *Shore Leave* by Frederic Wakeman). The star was a pre-movies Richard Widmark. Judy detested the fluff and regarded her part as "moronic." But the *New York Times* reported, "By far the best performance of the evening . . . is that offered by Judy Holliday as a tramp who wanders into a hotel room, unashamed of what she can offer." *Kiss Them for Me* bowed at the Morosco Theatre on March 20, 1945, ran for 110 performances, and earned Judy a Theater World Award and the Clarence Derwent Award ($500) for Best Supporting Actress in a Play. However, Judy regarded this break as a fluke. No acting jobs materialized and she quickly used up the $500 Derwent prize money over the next six months as she lived (unemployed) in a furnished room with her mother.*

Meanwhile, Garson Kanin had written a play, *Born Yesterday.* The comedy concerned

* When Twentieth Century-Fox filmed *Kiss Them for Me* as a 1957 Cary Grant vehicle, buxom Jayne Mansfield inherited Judy's stage role.

an ambitious, crude junk dealer who hires an intellectual to coat the dealer's mistress—a former stage chorine—with a veneer of class. The original selection to play mistress Billie Dawn was mercurial Jean Arthur. Three days *before* the Philadelphia pre-Broadway opening, she "withdrew" because of illness. (Insiders insisted that Miss Arthur's legendary insecurity caused her to abandon the project.) Unwilling to suffer the loss required to postpone the show while a name performer mastered the demanding role, the management sought a quick understudy with a lot of bravery. They found Judy. Aided by many cups of black coffee, Judy was ready for the opening-night curtain in less than 72 hours after signing for the part. She won a huge ovation from the audience (those who had not turned in their tickets when it was announced that Miss Arthur was no longer among the cast) and the awe of her co-players. Her only comment on the momentous evening: "I don't remember a thing."

With Gary Merrill as her romantic tutor and Paul Douglas as her keeper, Judy opened in *Born Yesterday* at Broadway's Lyceum Theatre on February 4, 1946. She was a sensation. "As she plays the former chorine, no thought ever could have passed through her mind," wrote the *New York Times* of her "quite wonderful" portrayal; "as she learns about Sibelius and art, she clearly is headed for an intellectual salon of her own." Jack Benny was so enthralled with Miss Holliday's emoting that he never laughed the whole evening, and returned again for the purpose of enjoying the play. *Born Yesterday* continued on Broadway for almost four years, tallying 1,642 performances. Judy won a Donaldson Award for her irresistible portrayal.

Ever impressed by Broadway bonanzas, Hollywood began bargaining for the screen rights to *Born Yesterday*. Harry Cohn, despotic head of Columbia Pictures (some said Kanin based the junk dealer of the play on the bullying Cohn), beat out the competition,* becoming the first mogul to pay $1 million for a play. For two years speculation ran rampant as to who would play the plum role of Billie in the highly touted film version. Columbia tested 38 actresses, including Lucille Ball, Marie Wilson, Evelyn Keyes, Jan Sterling, and newcomer Marilyn Monroe. Studio superstar Rita Hayworth was regarded as the top contender for the part, although at one point Jean Parker (who was in a road company of *Born Yesterday*) was rumored as a likely candidate.

However, Kanin was adamant that Judy recreate her stage success. In his book *Tracy and Hepburn* (1971) the writer-director recalls that Cohn, who had seen the play in New York, refused even to test Judy. Kanin quotes Cohn as complaining, "Don't waste my money. You don't seem to understand. On the stage you can get away with a broad that looks like that, because the audience sits far enough away, but with the camera movin' in, she'd drive people out!" Cohn was, to a degree, quite correct, for Judy was battling her weight, a perennial foe that caused the sensitive girl to suffer much humiliation. (One night onstage during the *Born Yesterday* run, one of her costumes burst at the seams.)

Unable to persuade Cohn, Kanin took another course. He was co-scripting (with wife Ruth Gordon) the film comedy *Adam's Rib* (1949), an MGM Spencer Tracy-Katharine Hepburn vehicle in which the stars played husband-wife lawyers. The plot included a blonde floozie, Doris Attinger, whom Katharine defends (and Spencer prosecutes) for shooting and wounding her errant spouse (Tom Ewell). The Doris Attinger role contained ingredients similar to those of the Billie Dawn part. Kanin, Tracy, Hepburn, and director George Cukor all believed that Judy's performance in this part could win her the screen role of Billie.

At first Judy refused to play Doris. "I don't want to play a part where somebody calls me 'Fatso.'" But she finally agreed and was wonderful. *Newsweek* reported, "Judy Holliday (here from Broadway's *Born Yesterday*) gives a delightful indication of how the double standard can be discussed without double entendres," and the *New York Times* judged her performance "simply hilarious." (During production generous superstar Katharine Hepburn instructed Metro's publicity department to send out press releases saying that Judy was stealing the picture; the

---

* At one point, MGM was pondering the property as a vehicle for the screen team of Clark Gable and Lana Turner.

298

stratagem was hardly necessary.) She was paid $750 per week for six weeks.

On the strength of her *Adam's Rib* hit, Judy did indeed win the Billie Dawn role in Columbia's *Born Yesterday*. When the elated Judy reported to the studio to meet Cohn, the actress was wearing her most attractive outfit and best corset. But the crude boss walked around his new property, looked her over, and sneered, "Well, I've worked with fat asses before." The abashed Judy lost 15 pounds in the ensuing three weeks. Her new co-stars included William Holden as the tutor and Broderick Crawford (following his Oscar-winning performance in Columbia's *All the King's Men*) as the vulgar junk man. (Paul Douglas reputedly refused an offer to play in the film because he felt that Kanin "subordinated" his role to Judy's in the scenario.)

For a week before shooting began, the cast performed the show nightly for studio audiences to tone up for the filming. Columbia also sent the principals to Washington, D.C., for location work at the landmarks and museums Billie discovers in the film. With George Cukor again supplying his usual painstaking direction, the celluloid *Born Yesterday* was an enormous hit, grossing $4.115 million in the U.S. and Canada. *Time* reported, "Thanks largely to Actress Holliday's hilarious performance, the movie deserves to repeat the play's success. . . . Fortunately, Actress Holliday's mincing strut, Minnie Mouselike voice, and low-down genteelisms provide a delightful show of their own." After only two major motion picture roles Judy Holliday had become a major Hollywood star, earning $1,250 per week.

The year 1950 was a great one for powerful female performances in the cinema. The Academy of Motion Picture Arts and Sciences selected Anne Baxter and Bette Davis of *All About Eve*, Eleanor Parker of *Caged*, Gloria Swanson of *Sunset Boulevard*, and Judy of *Born Yesterday* to compete in the Oscar sweepstakes. Miss Davis won the New York Film Critics Award (for which Judy was also nominated), and Miss Swanson was selected the prize performer by the National

With Broderick Crawford and Howard St. John in Born Yesterday *(1950).*

Board of Review. But on March 29, 1951, it was Judy who won the Academy's gilded mannequin for 1950. She was not in Hollywood to receive her Oscar—Ethel Barrymore accepted for her—but in a Manhattan club with José Ferrer, who won that evening the Best Actor Oscar for his *Cyrano De Bergerac*, and Gloria Swanson. A few days later Judy called Ethel Barrymore on Tallulah Bankhead's "Big Show" radio program to thank her for accepting the award.

Although the proud owner of an Oscar and a seven-year Columbia Pictures contract, and the talk of show business, Judy refused to leap into the Hollywood lifestyle of parties and pool-equipped haciendas. She kept her antique-filled apartment at the Dakotas on New York's Central Park West, where she lived with husband David Oppenheim, a clarinetist and the head of Columbia Records' classical department, and their ash blonde spaniel.* The couple also enjoyed a farm in Monroe, New York, about 50 miles from Manhattan. When not accompanying her piano-playing husband on her orkon (half-oboe, half-piccolo), Judy toyed with inventions, including a special rack for storing phonograph albums (another commodity she collected enthusiastically, along with antiques).

Judy made it very clear that she would not tolerate being typecast as a dumb blonde. She refused lucrative offers to guest star on the Bob Hope and Edgar Bergen–Charlie McCarthy radio programs, because of the travel to the West Coast and the scripts. She would bristle whenever a fan would ask her to talk "in that voice." "The funny part of it is," Judy explained, "that it's always some bum whose own voice sounds l ike Mortimer Snerd's." Rather than accept another film offer immediately, Judy contracted to play Georgina Allerton in a limited engagement of *Dream Girl,* welcoming the job at New York's City Center because "Georgina is not dumb and she's not blonde. Maybe I'm making progress." The show opened September 9, 1951, and was a sellout during its 15-show engagement. Hollywood, meantime, had to turn its attention to promoting another blonde to dumb-sexy status—Marilyn Monroe.

After *Dream Girl* Judy returned to Hollywood, where she was assigned to another

* She wed Oppenheim on January 4, 1948.

Garson Kanin–George Cukor concoction, *The Marrying Kind* (1952). Aldo Ray was Judy's co-star in this comedy about a couple facing divorce.* Harry Cohn's delight with his star changed to fury when, a month before the release of her new picture, Judy was called by the House Committee on Un-American Activities to testify concerning past Communist involvement. When Judy appeared before the congressional panel in March 1952 she was well prepared for the ordeal. She charmed her interrogators and lamented her Red leanings of the past. In a mixture of part Billie Dawn and part Judy Holliday, she said, "I have been awakened to a realization that I have been irresponsible and slightly—more than slightly—stupid." (Later she would tell a friend, "I'm not proud of the defense, but I'm not ashamed either. I didn't name one single name. That much I preserved.")

But there were repercussions for Judy having been called to testify. A forthcoming TV series deal was cancelled, her current release *The Marrying Kind* was picketed, and she had to take a sabbatical from Hollywood. It was during this period, on November 10, 1952, that she gave birth to a son, Jonathan.

When her "past" had been forgiven, Judy returned to Hollywood and to Columbia Pictures. If that studio's contractual sexpots Rita Hayworth and Kim Novak were content to wiggle and pout through predictable romance yarns, Judy perplexed Harry Cohn and his staff. She insisted on a variety of roles that would prove she could do more than portray cute ignorance.

In 1954 she was seen in two Columbia releases. The first was *It Should Happen to You,* again courtesy of a Kanin-Cukor screen partnership, with Judy as flamboyant actress Gladys Glover who plasters her name and likeness on a huge billboard in Columbus Circle, New York City. Peter Lawford and Jack Lemmon (in his screen debut—he dueted "Let's Fall in Love" with Holliday) flanked her in this engaging entry. Next came *Phffft!* which, despite the title, was a solid comedy—again concerning divorce and again co-starring Lemmon. It was a shrewd study of titillation with Kim Novak in a Marilyn

* This mature study of a couple undergoing the ordeals and joy of marriage revealed the extent to which Holliday could maneuver both joyous and tragic moments on screen. It was a gem of a performance.

Monroe-like role. Lemmon recalls of Holliday, "Judy was very gracious and very sweet. She knew I was embarrassed and this was my first time around for this sort of thing . . . she was my girl—a sweet, wonderful, terrific lady." One night en route to dinner, Lemmon and Judy were driving over a remote San Fernando Valley mountain road when their car got a flat tire. Lemmon went running in frantic search of a service station, but could locate none in the deserted hills. Afraid that Judy would become hysterical alone in an immobile car at night on that frightening road, Lemmon rushed back to the car—and discovered that Judy had changed the flat herself and that her only concern was her dirty hands.

Also in 1954 Judy made her television debut on NBC network's "Goodyear Playhouse," starring in the episode *The Huntress* (February 24, 1954). In 1956 she completed her Columbia stay with two more features. In the first, *The Solid Gold Cadillac,* she was a small stockholder who takes on the board of directors of a large corporation. (The stage role had been designed for a much older female, but was especially revamped for Judy's talents. The film reunited her with *Born Yesterday* stage co-star Paul Douglas.) The second—and last for Columbia—*Full of Life,* found Miss Holliday as a very pregnant housewife, coping with Richard Conte as her husband and ultrarotund Salvatore Baccaloni as her excitable father-in-law. Richard Quine directed both these features.

Despite her continued success in films, Judy was devoted to New York and to the theatre. On November 29, 1956, she again became Broadway's favorite. Her old "Revuer" confreres Betty Comden and Adolph Green had long since become successful Broadway writers.* They wrote the book for *Bells Are Ringing,* a musical comedy with music by Jule Styne, direction by Jerome Robbins, and choreography by Bob Fosse. Judy played Ella Peterson, a good-natured Manhattan answering-service operator who cannot resist taking a very personal interest in her customers. The musical allowed her to sing 10 numbers, including "The Party's Over," "Just in Time" (a duet with co-star

* When Comden-Green's earlier Broadway hit, *On the Town,* was transformed into a 1949 MGM film, Judy, as a favor to her pals, dubbed in the voice of a sailor's date.

Sydney Chaplin), and her famous finale solo, "I'm Goin' Back (Where I Can Be Me)." The musical became a "hot" ticket, running over two years and playing 924 performances before going on tour. Judy won both the New York Drama Critics Award and the Antoinette Perry (Tony) Award for Best Actress in a Musical. (She defeated competition that included Julie Andrews' Eliza Doolittle of *My Fair Lady.*) Judy's perfectionist traits emerged in this show when, just weeks before closing in New York, she insisted on extra rehearsals to keep the cast from getting stale.

In 1957, during the Broadway run of *Bells Are Ringing,* Judy and her husband divorced. He soon rewed which upset her greatly. At the time she was deeply involved in an intense—mostly one-sided—relationship with co-star Sydney Chaplin who did not accompany her in the cross-country touring edition of the hit show (he was replaced by Hal Linden).

After the lengthy national tour, Judy was signed by Metro-Goldwyn-Mayer to recreate her role of Ella in the studio's $3-million cinema version of the musical, which was transformed into a comedy with music. (Many of the catchy songs used on stage to rivet audience interest while sets were being changed were deleted from the movie version.) Dean Martin (a substitute for Frank Sinatra) replaced Sydney Chaplin as her co-star. Though MGM gave the picture the deluxe treatment, with an Arthur Freed mounting and direction by Vincente Minnelli, Judy was the whole film. *Variety* wrote that Judy "steals the show with a performance of remarkable variety and gusto," and the *New York Herald-Tribune* reported, "With all due respect to an excellent cast, to the screenplay, and to the direction, the fact remains that the film, like the stage musical, seems essentially a reflection of Miss Holliday's boundless spirit." When released in 1960, the 127-minute entertainment package was another Holliday critical triumph. But it failed to win the kind of box-office reception for which MGM had hoped. Screen musicals were temporarily out of vogue, and so was Judy. Plans for her to star in *The Fanny Brice Story,* to be directed by George Cukor, were abandoned.

Still eager to prove her merits in a gutsy dramatic role, Judy accepted the lead in

With Neva Patterson, Arthur O'Connell, Paul Douglas, and Richard Deacon in The Solid Gold Cadillac *(1956).*

Samuel Taylor's *Laurette*, his adaptation of the life and times of the late, great actress Laurette Taylor (1884–1946). The offbeat casting of Miss Holliday in the demanding focal role was a mistake in judgment as was the venture itself. The show tried out at the Shubert Theatre in New Haven in late September 1960 and closed there on October 1, 1960. Plans for a Philadelphia run and a New York debut were cancelled.

During the New Haven ordeal with *Laurette* Judy had lost her voice during one performance. Frightened by the occurrence (and devastated by the audience's booing) she consulted physicians and later physical examinations revealed that she had breast cancer. At New York Hospital she underwent a mastectomy. The press was informed that she had a benign throat tumor.

It was in this period that Judy's love relationship with jazz saxophonist Gerry Mulligan (who would later wed Sandy Dennis) became most crucial. Not only did he keep her occupied with writing song lyrics

(one of which, "Christmas Blues," Dinah Shore sang on her TV program), but he became the guiding force in her unstable existence. It was very difficult for her to cope with recuperating from her operation, dealing with her mother, and her unhappy eight-year-old son.

At one point Judy hoped to star in a Broadway musical version of Anita Loos' *Happy Birthday*, a past Broadway hit which had starred Helen Hayes. That venture* unfortunately never came to pass. Meanwhile the Internal Revenue Service determined that Holliday owed the government over $99,000 in back taxes. As a result she lost the country home she had been so proud of, and the valuable early American antique furnishings, many of which she had personally restored.

When the producers of a Broadway-bound musical, *Hot Spot*, approached Judy about

* According to Anita Loos, Holliday had written some marvelous lyrics for the songs of the proposed musical *Happy Birthday*.

302

starring in their show, she could not refuse. She needed the money too badly. It had a book by Jack Weinstock and Willie Gilbert, with music by Mary Rodgers, and lyrics by Martin Charnin. Joseph Campanella, who had earned his reputation largely as a TV performer, was her co-star. As Peace Corps gal Sally Hopwinder, Judy was expected virtually to carry the musical herself. But the overweight star was not in the proper health to do so, especially with all the rewrites the floundering show was subjected to while being reshaped. When the production played Philadelphia, she performed with such hoarseness that she could scarcely talk; audience members in the balcony would shout "Louder . . . louder!" *Hot Spot* opened on Broadway at the Majestic Theatre on April 19, 1963, to very lukewarm notices. The *New York Times* lamented, "*Hot Spot* lets Miss Holliday down. You know it's in trouble when it requires her to do a routine in which she pretends to be three members of a State Department Reassignment Committee." The expensively mounted musical folded after

only 43 performances. (There was not even an original-cast album released.)

In what would be Judy's last two years, she was seen infrequently in public. The cancer had recurred and although her physician tried for a time to keep it from Judy, she eventually realized the full medical situation. On May 26, 1965, she quietly entered Manhattan's Mount Sinai Hospital. There on June 7, 1965, she died in her sleep at 5 A.M.

The hysteria surrounding Judy's funeral served as morbid testimony to her enormous popularity. When nondenominational services were conducted at the Frank E. Campbell Chapel at Madison and 81st Streets in New York City, some 400 people crammed into the building. Eight policemen and a sergeant were shoved and jostled by over 500 fans who rushed the entrance of the funeral home, hoping for last-minute admittance. On her closed mahogany coffin were an array of roses, peonies, and geraniums from friends such as Spencer Tracy, Katharine Hepburn, and Shelley Winters. Dr. Algernon Black, president of New York City's Ethical Culture

In Full of Life *(1956).*

303

Society, gave the eulogy, praising Judy's ability to portray "the uncommon good in common people."

After the service at Campbell's the coffin was transported to the Westchester Hills Cemetery near Valhalla, New York, for burial. Judy left the bulk of her estate—estimated at between $50,000 and $100,000—to her mother and 12-year-old son. Adolph Green received her cherished phonograph-record collection.

Judy Holliday was a very special talent and undoubtedly could have aged into a splendid character actress had she lived longer. While her blonde beauty and plumply curvaceous figure aided her campaign for celebrity, it was primarily her uncanny dramatic potential that was her top ally in show business. Director George Cukor, who was very close to Judy professionally and socially, recently spoke of her on the NET teleseries "The Men Who Made the Movies":

Judy Holliday was an extremely intelligent, intellectual person—very well educated, very highbrow, very musical, and she was unique. Some actresses are very talented and some actresses are talented and are artists. Judy Holliday was an artist as well. And it's a pity that she died so young because she would have done wonderful things. She showed you truth through comedy. There was a scene in *Born Yesterday* where just in a kind of a few steps you saw that she had been a chorus girl; that she had no talent, but she was a professional chorus girl. This is what an actor can do. And, then of course she was a master of comedy and subtlety, and of understatement. She was a brilliant actress . . . with the other pictures I did with her, I found her marvelous and modest and, in retrospect, infinitely touching.

FEATURE FILMS

Greenwich Village (*20th Century-Fox 1944*)
Something for the Boys (*20th Century-Fox 1944*)
Winged Victory (*20th Century-Fox 1944*)
Adam's Rib (*MGM 1949*)
On the Town (*MGM 1949*) [voice only]
Born Yesterday (*Columbia 1950*)

The Marrying Kind (*Columbia 1952*)
It Should Happen to You (*Columbia 1954*)
Phffft! (*Columbia 1954*)
The Solid Gold Cadillac (*Columbia 1956*)
Full of Life (*Columbia 1956*)
Bells Are Ringing (*MGM 1960*)

Bob Hope

The United States of America celebrated its 200th birthday during 1976. The year before, 1975, was the year of Hope. During the 75th year of the 20th century, Americans paused to honor a 72-year-old English-born comedian. His career has included vaudeville, theatre, radio, motion pictures, and television. These successes stretched through 31 years of globetrotting to keep a world laughing through three wars. The huge list of awards, citations, and honorary college degrees given to Bob Hope makes him the most honored member of his profession.

Early in 1975 Hope was named Entertainer of the Century, inducted into the Entertainment Hall of Fame, and selected by the first annual People's Choice Awards poll as the nation's favorite all-round male entertainer. In the spring the American Academy of Humor gave him its first Will Rogers' Humanitarian Award. On July 4 at Philadelphia's Independence Hall he received the Freedom Medal, previously awarded to only two other Americans: Presidents Herbert Hoover and Harry S. Truman. After over 50 years in show business, a two-hour telecast in 1975 commemorated his 25th anniversary in television. The silver anniversary telecast included highlights from Hope's quarter-century of televised laughter. It was distinguished by the reading of a unanimously passed Congressional Citation by United States Senators Stuart Symington and Edward Brooke.*

As a master of timing and of pertinent and impertinent commentary on the current social and political scenes, Bob Hope has no peers. Fortified with a staff of smart writers, the Hope monologue bristles with timely observations, zestfully delivered with a pungent punch line. His jests and one-line zingers may sear in truth or fancy, but they never cut, bruise, mutilate or turn purposely blue. Hope says the great monologuist Frank Fay served as a model of suave comic chatter. Bob has often been compared to the irreplace-

* President John F. Kennedy presented Bob Hope with a Congressional Medal in 1963. Only two other entertainers in America's history had received the distinguished award: George M. Cohan and Irving Berlin.

With Patric Knowles in Monsieur Beaucaire (1946).

able Will Rogers (who wrote all of his own material) in his perceptive pokes at political pomposities and pretensions.

For years Hope was a champion motion picture box-office draw. His briskly paced comedies were funny and enormously successful, and remain singularly unmemorable. These films will never threaten the classic comedies of Chaplin, Keaton, Lloyd, or even Langdon and W. C. Fields. Hope's screen persona was that of a reluctant, romantically bent hero battling adversity with brash quips. The seven *Road* musical adventures that Hope made with pals Bing Crosby and Dorothy Lamour remain pleasantly memorable despite their slight structure.

Grandfather Hope sired three daughters and fourteen sons, one of whom, William Henry Hope, a stonemason, married Avis Townes, the concert-singing daughter of a Welsh sea captain. William and Avis Hope settled in Standiforth Court, Eltham, England, some 10 miles from London, and produced four sons. On Friday, May 29, 1903, a fifth son was born. He was christened in the Church of England as Leslie Townes Hope. In March 1908, when the future Bob Hope was four years old, the family migrated from England to Cleveland, Ohio, where uncles Frank and Fred had already settled. The six Hope sons (Sidney, the youngest, had been born a few years before their Bristol, England, departure) were enrolled in Cleveland public schools. Son number seven, George, was the first and last of the Hopes' all-male offspring born in the former colonies.

Through Fairmount Grammar and Junior High Schools, young Les Hope was bedeviled by the transposition of his name to "Hopeless." After one and a half years at Cleveland's East High, he decided that show business had greater allure than academic pursuits. A local act with dancing partner Mildred Rosequist dissolved and he teamed with Lloyd Durbin. During an engagement at Cleveland's Band Box Theatre, Roscoe "Fatty" Arbuckle, who was heading the bill, spotted Hope. Arbuckle introduced the young entertainer to tab-show producer Fred Hurley, who signed Hope and Durbin for his *Jolly Follies*. Durbin's untimely death caused Hope to align with another Ohio dancer, George Byrne, in Hurley's *Smiling Eyes*. When the Hurley show folded, the team of

Hope and Byrne played several vaudeville grind houses in New York City and then were signed for a Broadway musical.

Sidewalks of New York (October 3, 1927) featured Ray Dooley and Smith and Dale. After the show opened, Hope and Byrne's specialty number with dancer Ruby Keeler was cut. Byrne was recast as East Side gangster Finger and Lester Hope was another hoodlum, Monk. One critic wrote, "Ray Dooley has something. Ruby Keeler has something. Bob Hope has something too, but you won't notice it if you sit back about five rows."

Hope retreated to vaudeville. He returned to Broadway on October 8, 1928, for 64 performances as Screeves the butler in *Upsa-Daisy*, billed as Bob Hope. Back in vaudeville he found a measure of success. However, the lure of Broadway theatre, especially a Ziegfeld-produced show, was compelling. Unfortunately, the Ziegfeld glow failed to keep a massive flop, *Smiles*, alive for more than 63 performances, despite the star combination of Marilyn Miller, Fred and Adele Astaire, and Vincent Youmans' song, "Time on My Hands." Virginia Bruce and Bob Hope were two unnoticed members of the chorus.

Bob returned to vaudeville with Louise Troxell as his stage stooge. One week he found himself on the bill following Leatrice Joy's star act at Proctor's 86th Street vaudeville house. Hope, aware of the extensive publicity given Miss Joy's divorce from the screen's then great romantic star, announced to a surprised woman in the front row, "No, lady—I'm not John Gilbert!" Keith's circuit offered him a three-year contract. With Al Boasberg's four-act vaudeville pastiche, *Antics of 1931*, Hope finally played Broadway's Palace Theatre. He also made a disastrous screen test for Pathé, teamed with Miss Troxell. Fortunately, the Palace Theatre stint led to his return to Broadway in a lusty if tasteless musical, *Ballyhoo of 1932*. He received fifth billing and in act two had center-stage for his monologue.

For his second appearance as master of ceremonies of the Capitol Theatre stage show, Hope was modestly billed as "the star of *Ballyhoo*." During his chore he tossed out quips on the current political scene and engaged in frivolities with the show's headliner, Bing Crosby. Neither performer could have known that December 2, 1932, on the Capitol stage would be the start of a lifelong friendship and working arrangement. While at the Capitol, Hope made his radio debut on Major Bowes' "Family Hour" and was invited to do a guest spot on Rudy Vallee's variety program.

In the fall of 1933 Hope was engaged for *Roberta* (November 18, 1933), a Jerome Kern musical. Hope was perfectly cast as Huckleberry Haines, leader of the California Collegian Orchestra (with Fred MacMurray on saxophone). The talented cast included George Murphy, Ray Middleton, Lyda Roberti, Sydney Greenstreet, and aging Broadway star Fay Templeton in her last role. The show, with its lovely, haunting score, would play for 255 performances.*

During the Broadway run of *Roberta* Hope's mother died of cancer. The following month, on February 19, 1934, Bob married a lovely performer, Dolores DeFina. (George Murphy had introduced him to her when she was singing as Dolores Reade at Manhattan's 57th Street club, the Vogue.) They were wed in Erie, Pennsylvania. While in the Kern stage musical Bob was signed for a series of six comedy shorts by Educational Pictures. He made one.

*Going Spanish*** was made by Al Christie for Educational Pictures at Astoria, Long Island. Then Walter Winchell printed Hope's appraisal of the short, "When they catch John Dillinger, the current Public Enemy No. 1, they're going to make him sit through it twice." Educational dropped his option for the five other comedies. He fared somewhat better at Warner Bros.' old Vitagraph studio in Brooklyn in a two-reel condensation of Cole Porter's *Fifty Million Frenchmen* with Dorothy Stone called *Paree, Paree*. For Universal, he made the 20-minute short, *Soup for Nuts*, released in June 1934. Hope appeared as the master of ceremonies in a nightclub

featuring various acts. Before he departed the Broadway scene, Hope would join comic Johnny Berkes in a series of two-reel Vitaphone shorts in 1935-36.

In the fall of 1934 Hope was back on Broadway in *Say When*, in which he zinged gags to the audience and overshadowed the show's star, Harry Richman. When the production collapsed after 76 performances, Hope completed a 15-week NBC radio contract. Then he and his wife Dolores took to the road on the vaudeville circuits. When he returned to Manhattan it was for the *Ziegfeld Follies*.

The 1936 *Follies* was a stunning spectacle overflowing with the talents of Josephine Baker, Edgar Bergen, Judy Canova, Gertrude Niesen, Eve Arden, and especially Fanny Brice. With Miss Brice, Hope played Daddy to her Baby Snooks. One of the *Follies'* delights was Hope's singing of "I Can't Get Started with You" to a very bored Miss Arden. By the time the show reopened after a summer hiatus, Hope had left to replace William Gaxton in Cole Porter's new musical, *Red, Hot and Blue!* (October 29, 1936). The comedian was somewhat lost in the stardust and powerhouse playing of his co-stars, Jimmy Durante and Ethel Merman. But Bob, with Miss Merman in tandem, stopped the show with Porter's lively song "It's De-Lovely." While playing in *Red, Hot and Blue!* Bob's father died, and in September 1937 Hope left for Hollywood.

Bob Hope's feature-picture debut was in Paramount's *Big Broadcast of 1938* (1937) as radio announcer Buzz Fielding, who deserts girlfriend Dorothy Lamour to rejoin his wife, Shirley Ross. With Miss Ross he dueted Ralph Rainger and Leo Robin's "Thanks for the Memory," which became a hit tune. It captured an Academy Award as the year's best song and some four decades later is still Hope's signature song. In 1938 Bob first appeared on the screen with Bing Crosby, in a Paramount golfing short, *Don't Hook Now*. Paramount tossed him into a couple of minor musicals opposite raucous Martha Raye as well as a reunion with Shirley Ross in *Thanks for the Memory* (1938).

In 1938 he was signed for Pepsodent's radio show. Competing with such radio favorites as Eddie Cantor, Jack Benny, Ed Wynn, and Fred Allen, young Mr. Hope soon captured a

* On September 19, 1958, Hope reprised his Huck Haines role with Anna Maria Alberghetti, Howard Keel, and Janis Paige in a 90-minute NBC-TV version of *Roberta*. He again played the role on November 6, 1969, in a TV color presentation taped on stage at the 392-seat Bob Hope Theatre of the Owens Fine Arts Center of Southern Methodist University in Dallas, Texas. (He had contributed $800,000 toward its construction.)

** The 1963 documentary *The Sound of Laughter* included a clip of a love duet with Bob and singer Leah Ray from *Going Spanish*. Three decades had not improved it.

With Shirley Ross in Thanks for the Memory *(1938).*

large national radio audience with his fast-paced and funny broadcasts. In 1939 he would place fourth in a national *Radio Daily* poll and in 1940 would be radio's top comedian. It was a position he maintained throughout the Forties. On his program he was ably assisted by clown Jerry Colonna and Vera Vague (Barbara Jo Allen), plus two croaking-voiced females, Brenda (Blanche Stewart) and Cobina (Elvia Allman). With the latter he made extensive personal tours in 1939 and 1940. Their radio show was strengthened by the singing of Judy Garland and, later, Frances Langford and Doris Day. Hope built up his stable of gag writers, who turned out a steady flow of copy for his expert, well-timed delivery.

Paramount refashioned the chills and spooky thrills of the play *The Cat and the Canary* as a Hope vehicle and the 1939 film became a box-office smash. It verified Bob's screen position as a comedy star. Hope was teamed with curvaceous Paulette Goddard in this offering and the studio reteamed them for another horror spoof, *The Ghost Breakers* (1940).

Bob was heard in the title role of *Elmer the Great*, with Ann Sheridan, on radio's "Screen Guild Theatre" in April 1940. That summer he made personal appearances at Atlantic City's Steel Pier and in major-city presentation houses. His first broadcast for Cecil B. DeMille's "Lux Radio Theatre" was in September 1940 in *Love Is News*, with Madeleine Carroll and Ralph Bellamy. But 1940's best news for Hope was at Paramount. The studio had been reworking a dusty melodrama as a possible vehicle for George Burns and Gracie Allen, later as a project for Fred MacMurray and Jack Oakie. Finally it was cast by the extremely fortuitous teaming of Bing Crosby, Bob Hope, and Dorothy Lamour.

The first of the fondly recalled *Road* pictures was *Road to Singapore* (1940). Whatever was left of the script that Paramount had altered with careless stitching, Hope and company embroidered with ad-libs and impromptu, uninhibited comedy. Victor Schertzinger defined his method of directing the picture by telling the principals, "All I have to do is start the camera. You'll take it from there." And they did!

With Bing Crosby in Road to Zanzibar *(1941).*

The *Singapore* road led to *Zanzibar* (1941) and on to probably the best of their turbulently funny travel-capades, *Morocco* (1942). The odyssey would continue on to *Utopia* (1945) and to *Rio* (1948). In the Fifties the unlikely and zany roads led to *Bali* (1952), and a decade later to *Hong Kong* (1962). But by the last two entries their journeys had grown perceptively tired. Yet the peregrinations were fun while they lasted.

In 1939 the Hopes, unable to have children, adopted an infant girl they named Linda. In 1940 they returned to Chicago's famous adoption agency, The Cradle, for a baby boy, Tony. In 1946 a third visit to Chicago brought two more children into the Hope family: Nora Avis and William Kelly Francis Hope.

Paramount altered Hope's *Road* itinerary with a series of brash comedies that, if not of lasting joy or nostalgic recall, were box-office winners. *Caught in the Draft* (1941) and *Nothing but the Truth* (1941) benefited from Hope-staffed gags. The studio then purchased Irving Berlin's stage hit *Lousiana*

Purchase (1941) for him. Although three of the show's Broadway stars (Victor Moore, Irene Bordoni, and Vera Zorina) were used in the elaborate Technicolor film set largely in New Orleans, Hope had to work very hard to obtain less than festive results.

Between Paramount features, Bob was heard on "Lux Radio Theatre" in *The Awful Truth* (with Constance Bennett), in *Mr. and Mrs. Smith* (with Carole Lombard), and in *The Bride Came C.O.D.* (with Hedy Lamarr). He made his first broadcast from a military base in March 1941 at March Field, California. It was the start of his legendary career that *Variety* tabbed "America's Number One Soldier in Greasepaint." At the 1941 Academy Award presentations for 1940 he was awarded a silver plaque "in recognition of his unselfish service to the motion picture industry."

Hope's earlier screen spoofs of the horror-film genre were topped by what the *New York Times* called "a fast and zig-zaggy thriller farce." *My Favorite Blonde* (1942) co-starred elegant Madeleine Carroll. The ski-nosed comedian would continue the popular spy spoofs with 1947's *My Favorite Brunette* (Dorothy Lamour), and a laughable 1951 lampoon with Hedy Lamarr, *My Favorite Spy*. A contrived and disappointing entry into the espionage satire was Sam Goldwyn-RKO's *They Got Me Covered* (1943),* for which Bob and Dorothy Lamour were borrowed from Paramount.

Cole Porter's *Let's Face It* had been a tremendous Broadway hit with Danny Kaye. Paramount brought the musical to the screen in 1943 with Hope and Betty Hutton (who was frequently heard on Hope's radio show) and it proved to be a rousing hit. Bob explained the complications of English currency to American troops in Paramount's 1943 short *Welcome to Britain*.** Goldwyn borrowed him again for RKO's *The Princess and the Pirate* (1944), an unfortunate debut in the costume-picture genre opposite Virginia

* The title of a gag-strewn Bob Hope book in 1941.

** With Crosby he dueted the song "Buy, Buy Bonds" in Twentieth Century-Fox's short *All Star Bond Rally* (1945), and he was one of many Hollywood stars in Paramount's two-reeler *Hollywood Victory Caravan* (1945).

Mayo. That same year the Academy of Motion Picture Arts and Sciences presented him with a life membership in the Academy for his many services to that organization.

Booth Tarkington's *Monsieur Beaucaire* (1946) was liberally laced with Hope's quips as a bumbling barber in the court of King Louis XV. The studio gave the offering lavish production values and exquisite sets, plus the lovely-to-look-at Joan Caulfield as Bob's leading lady. Hope's romps in the costume genre continued in a dreary 1954 concoction called *Casanova's Big Night*, which had been made in 1952.

The war years consumed more of Hope than his professional intrusions. His indefatigable entertaining of troops included combat areas of the European Theatre of Operations. In 1946 Dwight D. Eisenhower presented him with the nation's highest civilian honor, the Medal of Merit. The following year he made an appearance before King George VI at London's Odeon Theatre in a Command Performance. In 1948 he began an almost annual trek to headline the vaudeville roster of London's Palladium. When in 1948 Harry S. Truman astonished a great many by winning the presidential election, Hope sent

With Charles Arnt in My Favorite Brunette *(1947).*

311

him a congratulatory wire of one word—"Unpack!"

In 1948 came *The Paleface*,* one of the best Hope comedies, boosted by the presence of voluptuous Jane Russell and the Academy Award-winning song "Buttons and Bows." Paramount's remake of Shirley Temple's *Little Miss Marker* focused on Hope as racetrack tout *Sorrowful Jones* (1949), but the uniting of Damon Runyon and Bob Hope was ill-advised. Hope appeared uncomfortable within the Runyon mold, a fact even more reflected in the 1951 Runyon tale, *The Lemon Drop Kid*. Hope's *Sorrowful*, however, was a success, immeasurably helped by his asking Lucille Ball to co-star with him in the Runyon whimsy. The two great funsters would reprise their roles in *Sorrowful Jones* on "Lux Radio Theatre" on November 21, 1949.

The Hope-Ball screen team returned in Paramount's 1950 Technicolor musical remake of *Ruggles of Red Gap*. *Fancy Pants*, the fourth screen version of Harry Leon Wilson's comedy, groaned under deliberate slapstick

* Hope and Jane Russell, joined by Roy Rogers, appeared in a well-mounted sequel, *Son of Paleface* (1952), which was almost as funny as the original.

and a gagged-up plot. A more successful joint venture for the two masters of comedic timing was in *The Facts of Life* (1960). It was a delightful spoof on extramarital frustrations confronting a middle-age couple, who discover their unconsummated affair is not worth the trouble. Their last screen outing was an erratic adaptation of Ira Levin's stage hit *Critic's Choice*. The 1963 Warner Bros. version lost its satirical impact in a welter of mugging. Neither Hope (badly miscast as a theatre critic) nor Ball won laurels from critics or public for the misfire.

Hope had already conquered films and radio. On Easter Sunday, April 9, 1950, he made his first professional television appearance,* in *The Star Spangled Revue*, televised live from Broadway's New Amsterdam Theatre, with guest stars Beatrice Lillie, Douglas Fairbanks Jr., and Dinah Shore. During the telecast he dueted the popular song "Baby, It's Cold Outside" with Miss

* Hope had first tested television in the early Thirties and made the first West Coast commercial telecast for Lincoln automobiles in January 1947. In 1949 he had done his monologue on Ed Sullivan's TV show, "Toast of the Town."

With Jane Russell in The Paleface *(1948).*

With Marilyn Maxwell in
The Lemon Drop Kid *(1951).*

Shore. While appearing "In Person" at New York's Paramount Theatre in 1950 with Jane Russell, Hope discovered a fine but unknown singer, Anthony Domenic Benedecto. He invited him to the Paramount stage and renamed him Tony Bennett.

In 1952 Hope made an unbilled joke appearance with Bing Crosby in Cecil B. DeMille's *The Greatest Show on Earth.* He also won an Oscar that year. After years of brightening the annual Academy Awards as its only humorous master of ceremonies, the Academy presented him with a statuette "for his contribution to the laughter of the world, his service to the motion picture industry and his devotion to the American premise." In 1954 Hope's autobiography, *Have Tux, Will Travel,* was published.

Most comedians harbor suppressed desires to extend their talents to drama. In 1955 Hope ventured into the arena with a surprisingly well-rounded portrayal of former vaudevillian Eddie Foy in Para-

mount's *The Seven Little Foys.* The four Hope children had bits in the picture, which provided Bob with greater scope for performing than anything he had done previously on the screen. His precision hoofing with James Cagney (as George M. Cohan) was a joy to see.

The following year he tried sophisticated comedy in Paramount's screen version of the Broadway hit *King of Hearts.* It emerged as *That Certain Feeling* (1956), with Bob as a distraught comic-strip cartoonist. It was regarded as his most effective comedy in some time. One perceptive critic noted, "It offers the comedian an opportunity to build up a genuine characterization instead of relying merely on a series of wisecracks." The outing was enhanced by an unexpected light performance by Eva Marie Saint, by a droll George Sanders, and by relaxing, scene-stealing Pearl Bailey.

The kindest thing that could have happened to the British-produced *The Iron Petti-*

313

coat (1956) was scuttling. From the outset the witless imitation of Garbo's *Ninotchka* was beset with problems exceeding its worth. The grotesqueness of teaming Katharine Hepburn and Bob Hope was heightened by unveiled antagonism on the set between the two stars. Scripter Ben Hecht publicly disowned his script because Hope's gag-writing platoon had lacerated his work. Finally released by MGM, the picture was a disaster.

Manhattan's ubiquitous Mayor Jimmy Walker was the subject of Gene Fowler's biography *Beau James*. The 1957 screen version gave Bob another opportunity for a definite, straight characterization. But his portrayal of the politician was not projected as well as his Eddie Foy stint and he emerged more Bob Hope than James J. Walker. The picture's happiest moment was an unbilled appearance by Jimmy Durante, who joined Hope in a lively song-and-dance routine. The Walker screen biography was Bob's final Paramount picture. After 20 years as the studio's reigning comedian, his contract was not renewed in 1957.

At Columbia Studios he made a 40-minute documentary, *The Heart of Show Business*, with other top stars, and narrated by Cecil B. DeMille for Variety Clubs International. Hope wrote, produced, and co-starred with France's brilliant comedian Fernandel in *Paris Holiday* (1958). With Crosby, Ernie Kovacs, and Groucho and Chico Marx, he headed a promotional film for the *Saturday Evening Post* entitled *Showdown at Ulcer Gulch*.

For his own company, Hope Enterprises, Inc., Bob was a dim-witted salesman insuring Jesse James in an equally dim-witted United Artists release *Alias Jesse James* (1959). The same year he made an unbilled appearance in Danny Kaye's *The Five Pennies* and the Academy awarded him the Jean Hersholt Humanitarian Award. To round out the season he also received a special TV Emmy Award.

MGM's *Bachelor in Paradise* (1961) further displayed Bob's knack for sharp timing and terse, flippant delivery of dialogue. But he was miscast as a philandering writer of racy novels who is lustfully admired by a group of California suburbia wives. He was not helped by the unresponsive playing of his co-star, Lana Turner.

The Congress of the United States honored Hope in 1963 as "America's most prized ambassador of good will" and Simon and Schuster published his amusing book, *I Owe Russia $1,200.* In 1965 Hope received the first Gold Medal Honorary Award from the Academy of Motion Picture Arts and Sciences "for unique and distinguished service to our industry and the Academy." But his almost annual screen appearances from the mid-Sixties onward neither added to his stature as a comedian nor were they worth his time or the public's.

The 60-year-old Hope survived the safari *Call Me Bwana* (1963) to show up in MGM's *A Global Affair* (1964), which *Variety* kindly dismissed as a "lackluster romantic comedy." *I'll Take Sweden* (1965) was a sophomoric morass that produced "sadness at the sight of so seasoned a professional as Bob Hope engulfed by amateurish ineptitude." Bob received a box-office boost from using his protégée, zany Phyllis Diller, in three of his films: *Boy, Did I Get a Wrong Number!* (1966), *Eight on the Lam* (1967), and *The Private Navy of Sgt. O'Farrell* (1968). In the last Bob, at age 65, was the unlikely sergeant of the fiasco. In 1969 he made a tediously unfunny variation on the generation-gap ploy, *How to Commit Marriage*, which unfelicitously united Hope and TV's great, gargantuan comedian Jackie Gleason. Hope's last starring screen outing to date was *Cancel My Reservation* (1972), which again matched him with Eva Marie Saint as TV talk-show hosts. It received scanty bookings in theatres around the country. For years Hope and Bing Crosby had talked of making one more *Road* picture. However, with the death of Crosby in the fall of 1977, this dreamed-of project will never be. (Hope also has cherished the notion of directing a film based on the life of his late friend, columnist Walter Winchell.)

As part of his continuing crusade to entertain lonely troops away from home, Hope's first Christmas TV special emanated from Thiele, Greenland, in 1954. Guests Hedda Hopper, William Holden, Margaret Whiting, and Jerry Colonna helped to brighten the proceedings. On January 17, 1973, NBC televised his final one, the 1972 Christmas show, performed in Vietnam and Thailand. It represented the end of three decades of tirelessly taking laughter and joy to service personnel

In Call Me Bwana *(1963).*

the world over. In 1974 Hope published *The Last Christmas Show*, a detailed account of his combat-area odyssey that had started in 1943.

Hope has received many honorariums throughout his career, but the crowning one came on July 1, 1976, when Queen Elizabeth II of England made him an honorary Commander of the British Empire. (As an American citizen Hope will not assume the title accompanying the award.) He is the first American comedian to receive the royal honor.

Today Bob Hope is one of America's wealthiest men. But his insatiable drive to entertain persists. The lure of greasepaint and the applause of crowds are as vital to Hope as to Milton Berle, George Burns, and others for whom comedy and entertaining are the essence of their life. Explaining his

hectic schedule, Hope says, "I'd rather wear out than rust out."

On October 29, 1976, NBC-TV presented a two-hour salute to the comedian entitled *Hope's World of Comedy*, with clips culled from over 200 hours of video footage. On March 10, 1977, Hope was reunited with his 1936 *Red, Hot and Blue* co-star Ethel Merman to reprise the song "It's De-Lovely" on an ABC-TV *Salute to Cole Porter*. In the summer of 1977 Doubleday & Co. published his most recent memoirs (co-written with Bob Thomas) *The Road to Hollywood—My Forty Year Love Affair with the Movies*, a breezy, quip-laden account of the Hollywood Hope.

Bob continues to receive every award seemingly possible to give an entertainer (except the elusive Oscar). On June 15, 1977, he received the Father Flanagan Award for Service to the Young, Boys Town's most

315

With Tina Louise and Jackie Gleason in How to Commit Marriage *(1969).*

prestigious token of esteem. Via CBS-TV coverage, ex-President Gerald Ford in 1977 presented Hope with the People's Choice Award as the Favorite All Around Male Entertainer (for the third year in a row). Obviously, Old Ski Nose (as Hope is affectionately nicknamed) has become a legendary part of the American culture and conscience.

At the end of June 1977 his wife, Dolores, returned to show business, joining Bob's act at the Coliseum Theatre in Albany, New York. Besides his concerts, benefits, and recordings (he made a comedy album in 1976 entitled "America Is 200 Years Old and There Is Still Hope"), he found time for a wide array of TV appearances, including pitching commercials on the small screen for a leading gas company ("I've been giving America gas longer than they have").

The year 1978 seemed especially busy for Bob on TV: "The Bob Hope All-Star Comedy Tribute to the Palace Theatre" (NBC-TV, January 10, 1978) saluted vaudeville and had Hope in tandem with George Burns, Sammy

Davis Jr., Steve Lawrence and Eydie Gorme, and Carol Lawrence; "Bob Hope's Comedy Special" (NBC-TV, February 13, 1978) was telecast from Palm Springs and had Hope joining in the antics with Phyllis Diller, Glen Campbell, Raquel Welch, Flip Wilson, Andy Williams, and Telly Savalas; the "50th Annual Oscar Show" (ABC-TV, April 3, 1978) found Hope again as solo host; "Bob Hope All-Star Comedy Special from Australia" (NBC-TV, April 15, 1978) found Hope performing down under with Charo, Barbara Eden, and Florence Henderson; "Happy Birthday, Bob" (NBC-TV, May 29, 1978) was a three-hour marathon tribute to the veteran performer, with such diverse players as George Burns, John Wayne, Elizabeth Taylor, Lucille Ball, Fred MacMurray, Danny Thomas, Donny and Marie Osmond, Les Brown, and Dolores Hope offering their well wishes; "Saluting the 75th World Series" (NBC-TV, October 15, 1978) found the 75-year-old star kidding baseball; and on his annual Christmas outing (NBC-TV, December 17, 1978) Red Skelton was his special guest star.

Meanwhile, the comedian found time to accept the Beverly Hills Chamber of Commerce and Civic Association's annual Will Rogers Memorial Award and to guest star in *The Muppet Movie* (1979). In one recent tabulation it was noted that during a typical month in 1978 Hope had made 22 guest stage appearances in 22 cities coast to coast.

Not long ago Hope discussed his unique comedy style, which explains his genius as a showman.

> I think two things make it the distinctive [comedy] style it is. Versatility . . . the ability I have to do comedy in a tuxedo on one hand and wrestle a gorilla in a grass skirt on the other and be perfectly natural, not forced, in each case. It's very believable. I can perform for royalty and do slapstick oncamera. The other thing is timing. This is a crucial element in all comedy routines. It's a sixth or seventh sense. It's knowing when to let the audience have a moment to think, how long the moment will be, and when to pick up the action again. When to hit with the next line. At times I have good material and then sometimes there is *great* material. Tim-

ing is a thing that can be used to make the good material sound better than it is. I have to know how to snap the next line and cover it and move on. You have to get the idea over to the audience that there is a game of wits being played and they have to be alert or they'll miss something: It never fails.

When asked how he keeps himself feeling young, Hope replies,

> I exercise my mind by attempting to ad-lib jokes at least five or six times during each show, and I also change my show every night just to keep myself alert and not fall into a rut. And keeping up with the news is responsible for my continued success. I base my jokes on events that are fresh in people's minds. These are jokes they haven't heard before. I've been doing it for 30 years and it's one of the big secrets of keeping me in demand and keeping me young.
>
> There's therapy in doing this sort of work. I love to hear an audience laugh. I just can't get old when I hear that. When I make people laugh it means a hell of a lot to me.

FEATURE FILMS

Big Broadcast of 1938 (*Paramount 1937*)
College Swing (*Paramount 1938*)
Give Me a Sailor (*Paramount 1938*)
Thanks for the Memory (*Paramount 1938*)
Never Say Die (*Paramount 1939*)
Some Like It Hot (*Paramount 1939*)
The Cat and the Canary (*Paramount 1939*)
Road to Singapore (*Paramount 1940*)
The Ghost Breakers (*Paramount 1940*)
Road to Zanzibar (*Paramount 1941*)
Caught in the Draft (*Paramount 1941*)
Nothing but the Truth (*Paramount 1941*)
Louisiana Purchase (*Paramount 1941*)
My Favorite Blonde (*Paramount 1942*)
Road to Morocco (*Paramount 1942*)
Star-Spangled Rhythm (*Paramount 1942*)
They Got Me Covered (*RKO 1943*)
Let's Face It (*Paramount 1943*)

The Princess and the Pirate (*RKO 1944*)
Road to Utopia (*Paramount 1945*)
Monsieur Beaucaire (*Paramount 1946*)
My Favorite Brunette (*Paramount 1947*)
Where There's Life (*Paramount 1947*)
Variety Girl (*Paramount 1947*)
Road to Rio (*Paramount 1948*)
The Paleface (*Paramount 1948*)
Sorrowful Jones (*Paramount 1949*)
The Great Lover (*Paramount 1949*)
Fancy Pants (*Paramount 1950*)
The Lemon Drop Kid (*Paramount 1951*)
My Favorite Spy (*Paramount 1951*)
The Greatest Show on Earth (*Paramount 1952*)*
Son of Paleface (*Paramount 1952*)
Road to Bali (*Paramount 1952*)
Off Limits (*Paramount 1953*)

Here Come the Girls (*Paramount 1953*)
Scared Stiff (*Paramount 1953*)*
Casanova's Big Night (*Paramount 1954*)
The Seven Little Foys (*Paramount 1955*)
That Certain Feeling (*Paramount 1956*)
The Iron Petticoat (*MGM 1956*)
Beau James (*Paramount 1957*)
Paris Holiday (*United Artists 1958*)
The Five Pennies (*Paramount 1959*)*
Alias Jesse James (*United Artists 1959*)
The Facts of Life (*United Artists 1960*)
Bachelor in Paradise (*MGM 1961*)
The Road to Hong Kong (*United Artists 1962*)

Critic's Choice (*Warner Bros. 1963*)
Call Me Bwana (*United Artists 1963*)
A Global Affair (*MGM 1964*)
I'll Take Sweden (*United Artists 1965*)
The Oscar (*Paramount 1966*)*
Boy, Did I Get a Wrong Number! (*United Artists 1966*)
Eight on the Lam (*United Artists 1967*)
The Private Navy of Sgt. O'Farrell (*United Artists 1968*)
How to Commit Marriage (*Cinerama 1969*)
Cancel My Reservation (*Warner Bros. 1972*)
The Muppet Movie (*ITC 1979*)

* Unbilled guest appearance.

Edward Everett Horton

The screen's comedy genre has generated many extraordinary and capable laugh-makers whose presence in the mildest of diversions could assure audiences of some chuckles. They have enriched many thread-bare scripts with their deftly paced timing, studied mannerisms, and often outrageous mugging. The mere mention of their names evokes nostalgic smiles and remembered moments of mirth.

Long-faced, large-nosed, 6'2" Edward Everett Horton stood tall in the front ranks of players whose talent to amuse brightened the screen. His double take, double talk, and eternal bumbling, fumbling, and fretting over minor or imagined crises were usually expressed with a staid, prissy anxiety that gave way to an oblique if unbelieving piercing stare. He would augment his comic pose with various body gestures, all of which combined to emphasize constant frustration. He was a dedicated, constantly working performer whose career spanned seven decades on the screen and 64 years in show business.

Edward Everett Horton was born on Thursday, March 18, 1886, in Brooklyn, New York. His mother was Isabelle Diack Horton (who would live to the age of 102) and his father, for whom he was named, was foreman of the *New York Times* composing room. After graduation from Boys' High School in Brooklyn, Edward entered the Polytechnic Institute of Brooklyn, attended Oberlin College in Ohio, and then, without any burning ambition to become a professor, despite family encouragement, entered Columbia University. There he studied history and German and made his acting debut in a college show as an ungainly tall, corseted female.

Fascination with show business far over-shadowed academic pursuits, so the 20-year-old Horton left college to audition as a chorus boy in Broadway musicals. During one endurance test for the chorus line he found his untrained dancing ability immeasurably improved by avoiding the threatening over-sized feet of an equally unlikely chorus-line aspirant, Wallace Beery.

With May MacAvoy in The Terror *(1928).*

Edward survived back-row chorus jobs and then joined the Dempsey Light Opera Company on Staten Island in a repertoire of Gilbert and Sullivan comic operas. A year later, in 1908, he made his Broadway stage debut in a walk-on part in Louis Mann's *The Man Who Stood Still* (October 15, 1908). He became one of Mann's playing company, and on June 29, 1910, played a butler on Broadway in *The Cheater*. On January 22, 1912, he opened at the Liberty Theatre as Professor Del'Oro in *Elevating a Husband* and would make his last Broadway appearance for many years that September in *The Governor's Lady*.

Later in 1912 Horton joined the Orpheum Players at the Chestnut Street Theatre in Philadelphia at $25 weekly. With that excellent training group, he was given romantic and juvenile leads in a variety of roles. The parts ranged from the role of Sheriff Jack Rance in *The Girl of the Golden West* to that of the lover in *Three Weeks*. With stock companies in Portland, Maine, Brooklyn, and Elmira, New York, he perfected his stage training. By 1919 he had migrated to California to join Thomas Wilkes' Los Angeles Stock Company, as a replacement for leading man Lewis Stone.

Billed as Edward Horton, he made his film debut in April 1922 as the proprietor of a children's day nursery in Vitagraph's *Too Much Business*. He played the bank-teller lead in Vitagraph's *The Ladder Jinx* (1922) and was a newspaperman in that studio's *A Front Page Story* (1922). James Cruze's 1923 Paramount remake of *Ruggles of Red Gap* brought praise and prominence to Horton, who was well cast as the English butler transported to the American West by the uncouth nouveau riche couple (Ernest Torrence and Louise Dresser). Paramount's filming of the Broadway hit, *To the Ladies* (1923), was enhanced by the steady performance of Horton as the clerk. He then slipped into supporting roles, including playing Uncle Harry with Baby Peggy and Clara Bow in *Helen's Babies* (1924).

James Cruze gave the Broadway success *Beggar on Horseback* (1925) bright and imaginative direction. Edward was the composer who spends most of his time in Walter Mitty fantasies. He was ably helped by leading lady Esther Ralston and, in a dream

sequence, by Theodore Kosloff and Greta Nissen as the mythical prince and princess. The same year he was seen on the screen in the leading role of something called *The Business of Love* that Vitagraph had started filming in 1923 as *The Crash*.

With his brother George, Edward purchased over 20 acres of land in 1925 in the San Fernando Valley. The main house, where Horton's champagne breakfasts were acclaimed, overflowed a hilltop, growing in proportion to his career. The residence was filled to overflowing with his gathered antiques. Guest houses on the estate housed the Horton family: brothers George and Winter D. and their families, and sister Hannabelle Horton Grant and her family.* In later years F. Scott Fitzgerald rented one of the guest houses along Edward Everett Horton Lane in Encino, but found Horton's name for his estate, Belleigh (Belly) Acres, revolting.**

Edward alternated between stage and screen, becoming one of the few such talented members of the film colony. In 1923 his production of the play *Clarence*, in which he played the leading role, ran for 44 weeks. He soon was heading his own stage company at the Majestic Theatre in Los Angeles, managed by his brother, W. D. Horton. According to Kyle Crichton, writing in *Collier's* magazine, "A visit to L.A. without seeing Horton was accounted a social error in southern California." Meanwhile, onscreen he was seen in *La Boheme* (1926) with Lillian Gish and John Gilbert, was henpecked by Mae Busch in *The Nut-Cracker* (1926), and played opposite Laura LaPlante in the comedy *Poker Faces* (1926).

Besides his heavy stage schedule, Edward made several two-reel Paramount shorts in 1927: *No Publicity, Dad's Choice, Find the King,* and *Behind the Counter.* He also played the lead in Universal's feature *Taxi! Taxi!* (1927).

The specter of talkies created no trauma for the stage-trained Horton, and Hollywood signed him for its new, experimental, career-wrecking talking pictures. His first talkie venture was *Miss Information* (1928), a short with Lois Wilson. In *Call Again* (1928), a

* Horton never married but never lacked for "family."

** Several years later the state of California would purchase the bulk of Horton's estate for a freeway.

Paramount short, he played a young man having misadventures at a girls' school. That year he also performed the male lead in Warner Bros.' second all-talking picture, *The Terror.*

For the 1928–29 theatre season in southern California, Burns Mantle noted, "Edward Everett Horton has been almost uniformly successful as a producer of handsomely mounted plays with strong casts. His theater has been most conspicuous in drawing upon talent from the motion picture field which had previously earned its spurs in the 'legitimate.'" Horton's revival of *The Streets of New York* had a pleasing six-week run.

In Al Jolson's *Sonny Boy* (1929) Horton was an attorney. But for Warner Bros.' remake of *The Hottentot* (1929), he had the lead. Edward was meek Sam Harrington, afraid of horses and twisted into becoming a steeplechase rider. He headlined Warners' *The Sap* (1929) and was again top-billed in *The Aviator* (1929). The *New York Times* reported, "Mr. Horton upholds his reputation for being able to get more laughs out of slight facial contortions than most comedians."

During 1929 Horton also made a set of talking comedy shorts for Coronet: *The Right Bed, Trusting Wives, Prince Babby,* and *Good Medicine.* On stage, on Sunday, December 1, 1929, he produced *Among the Married,* co-starring himself with Florence Eldridge, and giving Mary Astor (who wanted to break into talkies) a supporting part.

With Patsy Ruth Miller, his leading lady in three former Warner Bros. comedies, Edward was featured as a timid bachelor in *Wide Open* (1930). The *New York Times* praised his playing: "It is difficult to analyze Mr. Horton's stumbling, groping, hesitant technique. He is, without overplaying in slapstick, perhaps one of the most consistently amusing comedians. In all his pictures he is cast in identical roles—the embarrassed, spineless creature who emerges finally as the glorified hero through a fluke of circumstances." All true. With slight variations, he would continue to play the bewildered, over-anxious nervous-Nellie-type character throughout his career. Frequently he would gasp an astonished "Oh, dear" with all the gravity of impending doom. It all gave rise to his being tagged the "male ZaSu Pitts."

The fledgling talkies set afoot a stampede of "talking" actors. The year 1930 saw the arrival at Warner Bros. of Joe E. Brown, who became the resident clown. To the other studios also came new talent from the New York stage, all a part of the Hollywood gold rush to find public acclaim. Edward was stage-oriented but an unlikely candidate for continued stardom. Reduced to supporting comedy roles, he became one of Hollywood's comedy mainstays and would maintain that position for many years.

Reflecting on the early phase of his Hollywood career, Horton would say, "The polite comedians in the silent days were handsome fellows. The other comics had their distinct peculiarities. Harold Lloyd had the glasses. Lloyd Hamilton was the goofy type. Buster Keaton had the dead pan. I wasn't handsome or funny looking—at least not funny enough. They couldn't make me out."

But as a supporting player he had few peers and was deemed by many to be a more versatile actor than, say, Frank Morgan or Franklin Pangborn. Horton's playing of Nick Potter in Pathé's classy *Holiday* (1930) was charming. (In 1938 he would again play Potter in the Katharine Hepburn–Cary Grant version.) In First National's Technicolor *Kiss Me Again* (1931) Horton ably supported Bernice Claire and Walter Pidgeon. As Douglas Fairbanks' valet, he nearly walked off with *Reaching for the Moon* (1931). *Photoplay* thought Pathé's *Lonely Wives* (1931) a "sheer side-splitting farce." And about Edward's dual performance as a lawyer and vaudevillian, the *New York Times* said, "It seems marvelous that the two persons on the screen can possibly be one and the same man." Lewis Milestone's tightly directed screen version of *The Front Page* (1931) had a sterling cast, not least of which was Horton as the chief feature writer for the *Tribune.* His playing of the dreamy, poetic, fussbudget newsman was well defined.

Benn W. Levy's comedy *Springtime for Henry* opened on Broadway on December 9, 1931, with Leslie Banks as the persistent, if aging, would-be roué. The show had a respectable New York run. When Edward found himself in need of a stage substitute for *Private Lives,* he persuaded Levy to let him produce and star in a West Coast production of *Springtime for Henry*, to complete his theatre season's remaining six weeks.

On May 9, 1932, Horton was again playing Henry in Los Angeles with Laura LaPlante as Miss Smith. The show thereafter moved to San Francisco. For the next two and a half decades, Horton would play Henry some 2,700 times from coast to coast in many towns where plays were rarely, if ever, seen. His lucrative annual outings as *Henry* brought him national fame, a pleasant salary, and one-third of the gross. With part of the profits Horton purchased a summer home in the Adirondack Mountains, near Glens Falls, New York.

Back on the screen Horton in 1933 was Maurice Chevalier's pal in *A Bedtime Story* (dominated by Baby LeRoy) and in *The Way to Love*. Ernst Lubitsch was one of Horton's favorite directors, and Horton was paced by the "Lubitsch touch" in a whitewashed, moribund screen translation of Coward's *Design for Living* (1933). When Lubitsch moved from Paramount to Metro to film the Chevalier-Jeanette MacDonald production of *The Merry Widow* (1934), he insisted upon Edward for the comedy lead. At the same time as he was working on the Culver City soundstages, Horton was in Paramount's fine farce, *Kiss and Make Up* (1934), with Cary Grant and Genevieve Tobin. In between these ventures, Edward managed to make trips to England, where he performed before the cameras in *It's a Boy* (1933), *Soldiers of the King* (1934), and *The Private Secretary* (1935).

The Fred Astaire-Ginger Rogers dance operas leaned heavily on comedians to brighten scripts. For *The Gay Divorcee* (1934) Edward was Astaire's bumbling lawyer pal and joined relative newcomer Betty Grable in a delicious dance routine, "Let's K-nock Knees." In probably the best of the Astaire-Rogers dancing reels, *Top Hat* (1935), Edward was again Fred's friend, this time as fussy show producer Horace Hardwick and with dry, acerbic Helen Broderick as his spouse. Horton's hilarious drunk scene and impeccable comedy did much to salvage the weak story line of the Gershwins' *Shall We Dance* (1937). For some viewers, Horton's playing of ballet impresario Jeffrey Baird was the highlight of this Astaire-Rogers outing.

In 1934 Fox had filmed *Springtime for Henry* but cast Otto Kruger as the philandering bachelor. The studio dismissed Horton with "You're not the type." Ironically the film version was a flop, while Horton would derive a good deal of popular and financial success from his stage trouping in the show. With Genevieve Tobin, Horton was again teamed in *Easy to Love* and *Uncertain Lady*, both 1934 releases. In 1936 the two farceurs would go to England to film *The Man in the Mirror*.

Despite his overexposure on screen, Edward still found himself in great demand by Hollywood filmmakers. Josef von Sternberg's exotic bore, *The Devil Is a Woman* (1935), extracted a silly characterization from Edward as the Spanish chief of police who blithely has miscreants shot. If that film was a disaster, his playing of worm-turning, civic-minded Dudley Dixon in *Your Uncle Dudley* (1935) restored his comedy status. *Photoplay* enthused, "Rally round, you Edward Everett Horton fans, here is his latest and one of his funniest, hot off the griddle." (Horton would reprise his *Your Uncle Dudley* role on "Broadway Theatre" for TV in December 1953.)

About his screen work Horton was telling the press, "I like the heavy dramatic stuff and always played it until I left the stage. In fact I'm still playing it, but on the screen they call it comedy. Not that I'm the village half-wit exactly, but something very close to that. I seem to represent the uncle who is—what shall I say?—not quite bright?"

Throughout the Thirties Horton continued to brighten many features with his wry delivery of lines, expressive face, and use of his body to punctuate his bumbling bewilderment. With first featured billing, Horton gave a sincere, professional performance as paleontologist Lovett in Frank Capra's *Lost Horizon* (1937). For Lubitsch's *Bluebeard's Eighth Wife* (1938) he was believable as Claudette Colbert's impoverished French aristocratic father.

The Forties continued his comedy relief roles. He gave a good account of himself as Ziegfeld's agent, Franz Kolter, in MGM's *Ziegfeld Girl* (1941). As incompetent, fussy celestial messenger number 7013 rushing Robert Montgomery to heaven by mistake, Edward was a delight in *Here Comes Mr.*

With Maurice Chevalier in The Merry Widow *(1934).*

Jordan (1941). He repeated the same role for the reworked musical version of the fantasy, *Down to Earth* (1947), which had been tailored to the talents of Rita Hayworth. A standout comic vignette of *Arsenic and Old Lace* (1944) was Horton's sedate, pompous Mr. Witherspoon arriving to escort the wacky, homicidal, if benevolent, Brewster sisters to his Happydale sanatorium.

Although Horton made theatrical road history with *Springtime for Henry*, he turned down a role that could have brought him Broadway glory when in 1944 producer Brock Pemberton offered him the lead of Elwood Dowd in *Harvey*. (Horton would later play Elwood in summer stock.) More gossamer was Edward's suppressed desire to extend his talent to drama. Thus in 1944 he found himself agonizing over his role in a hopelessly inane film version of Chekhov's *Summer Storm*. He mistakenly thought his casting would open up "a whole new career— no more double takes, but a serious actor with comic overtones." Like the picture, Horton's interpretation of the provincial

count who is infatuated with Linda Darnell met with little praise.

In 1945, following a revival of *Clarence* at Princeton's McCarter Theatre, Horton appraised his Hollywood career for writer Ward Morehouse: "I have my own little kingdom. I do the scavenger parts no one else wants, and I get well paid for it." (In the early Forties, Horton would tell interviewer Earl Anderson that he was never concerned about the size of a film role. His terms were $2,500 weekly with a four-week guarantee. If his part could be completed in a few days he still received $10,000.)

In the spring of 1949 Horton returned to touring the country's stages as Garry Essendine in Noël Coward's slight comedy *Present Laughter*, in which Clifton Webb had starred on Broadway two years earlier. He remained in the theatre for the next eight years, playing the Earl of Locharner in *Castle in the Air* in St. Louis, touring the summer stages in *Nina*, and returning to his perennial favorite, *Springtime for Henry*.

On March 14, 1951, Edward finally appeared in *Henry* on Broadway. Horton and the comedy fared well with the critics, although it lasted only 53 performances. By then Horton's performance had broadened, but he toned it down for New York audiences (his exaggerated mugging milked much laughter in the hinterlands). One critic expressed surprise that Benn Levy's spoof of moral rectitude had withstood the test of years: "*Henry* has never been more than an incredibly wispy trifle, an impudent conversation-piece for a quartet of characters, but the maestro of the petulant grimace has made it something peculiarly his own. As the middle-aged Lothario who tries moral reformation and finds it a snare and delusion, he can grow a belly-laugh out of a situation which only calls for a chuckle. Horton's *Henry* packs a lot of fun."

Television was a good showcase for Horton's talent. In the Fifties he was in telecasts of *Whistling in the Dark*, *The Front Page*, *The Canterville Ghost*, and *The Conventions and Mr. Miffin*. On "Best of Broadway" he re-created his role of Mr. Witherspoon, who accepts the Brewster sisters' kind offer of a glass of elderberry wine spiked with a pinch of arsenic, in *Arsenic and Old Lace*. On October 24, 1954, Edward played the role of Pablo in the telecast of an early Broadway musical, *Revenge with Music*, in addition to doubling as Harpo Marx's voice as the governor. For Max Liebman's television color special production of *The Merry Widow*, Horton was back ambassadoring for Anne Jeffreys in the title role.

In the course of the Fifties, Horton tried out several new plays in summer stock. In 1950 he tested *My French Wife* and, at Boston's Mutual Hall, *Uproar*. In 1954 he auditioned *The White Sheep of the Family* on the strawhat circuit. His only theatrical film work during the decade was in the unintentionally ridiculous spectacle *The Story of Mankind* (1957). Horton played Sir Walter Raleigh to Agnes Moorehead's Queen Elizabeth.

At the age of 74 the actor toured in the play *Not in the Book* and with Imogene Coca made

With Fred Astaire in The Gay Divorcee *(1934).*

With Eric Blore in a pose for Shall We Dance *(1937).*

an extensive one-night-stand tour in *Once Upon a Mattress.* He played the mute king that Buster Keaton also played on stage.

Frank Capra's uneasy remake of his sprightly *Lady for a Day* was freshly titled *Pocketful of Miracles* (1961). The forced comedy was blessed with exceptionally good performances by supporting players Peter Falk, Thomas Mitchell, Sheldon Leonard, and, as Apple Annie's (Bette Davis) imperious, smug butler, Edward Everett Horton. Rumors of an Academy Award for his butlering in *Pocketful of Miracles* were rampant. However, it was Peter Falk who was singled out for the nomination as Best Supporting Actor, a category prize won that year by George Chakiris of *West Side Story.*

Horton joined Stanley Kramer's clown caravan as Dinckler in *It's a Mad, Mad, Mad, Mad World* (1963). Edward's opening scene in *Sex and the Single Girl* as the staid publisher of a family magazine, now a racy scandal publication, was the film's best sequence. He made an extensive road tour in the musical *A Funny Thing Happened on the*

Way to the Forum in the role of Erronius. In June 1965 he played the Star Keeper in John Raitt's *Carousel* at Lincoln Center's State Theatre.

Television in 1965 added to Horton's fame. He played Mr. Fenwick, the company president on "The Cara Williams Show," in February of that year on CBS. And then came the series which allowed a new generation of viewers to discover Horton's comedic talents. In Forrest Tucker's "F Troop" (ABC-TV, 1965-67) Edward ran rampant as the funny Indian medicine man Roaring Chicken. His long face was naturally weathered and lined with wrinkles. However, his pursed, prissy lips, raised, inquisitive eyebrows, and piercing eyes belied his actual age. In typical fashion he undervalued his "F-Troop" role. "I don't think I'm adding too much to the hilarity of the program, but Roaring Chicken is an interesting old character."

The mid-Sixties found Edward teamed with the incomparable Hermione Gingold in a Broadway-bound musical *Dumas and Son,*

*With Kathryn Adams
and Raymond
Walburn in
Bachelor Daddy
(1941).*

With Linda Darnell in Summer Storm (1944).

which never left the West Coast. The two veterans were the only bright spots in the entire show. It was a marvel that an 80-year-old man and a 70-year-old woman were so head and shoulders above any of the younger people in the cast.

In Warner Bros.' misguided farce *2,000 Years Later* (1969) Horton was a TV culture show host. His last picture was Norman Lear's offbeat comedy *Cold Turkey* (1971), in which he played silent Hiram C. Grayson. This final screen appearance finds Horton's Grayson breaking wind in the back of a limousine. It was a scatological commentary on the film and perhaps on the low state to which Hollywood screen comedy had fallen.

On September 4, 1970, Edward was admitted to the Glens Falls, New York, hospital shortly after making his last live TV appearance on David Frost's afternoon talk show. Within a week he was able to return to his San Fernando Valley home, where he died on September 29, 1970, of cancer.

His final television role was on October 14, 1970, playing a crusty old physician on the series "The Governor and J.J." and his last video appearance was on December 7, 1970, on Johnny Carson's NBC-TV Special, *Sun City Scandals*, where he demonstrated for the last time his famous triple take. At 84, retirement had been out of the question: "Retirement? What's that? Technically, I am retired. But I know my weakness. If someone wants me to do a play, or a film, or a TV show, my nose twitches. I want to don greasepaint again, so—I say yes. When nobody asks me anymore then I'll settle down in Encino and really retire."

After Horton's death, Mayor Sam Yorty of Los Angeles paid tribute to the performer: "His many admirers and fellow actors will feel a void in the theater with his death, a particular void that cannot be filled because Edward Everett Horton was an actor of his own genre."

With Terry-Thomas in 2000 Years Later (1969).

FEATURE FILMS

Too Much Business (*Vitagraph 1922*)

The Ladder Jinx (*Vitagraph 1922*)

A Front Page Story (*Vitagraph 1922*)

Ruggles of Red Gap (*Paramount 1923*)

To the Ladies (*Paramount 1923*)

Try and Get It (*Producers Distributing Corporation 1924*)

Flapper Wives (*Selznick 1924*)

The Man Who Fights Alone (*Paramount 1924*)

Helen's Babies (*Principal 1924*)

Marry Me (*Paramount 1925*)

Beggar on Horseback (*Paramount 1925*)

The Business of Love (*Astor 1925*)

La Boheme (*MGM 1926*)

The Nut-Cracker (*Associated Exhibitors 1926*)

Poker Faces (*Universal 1926*)

The Whole Town's Talking (*Universal 1926*)

Taxi! Taxi! (*Universal 1927*)

The Terror (*Warner Bros. 1928*)

Sonny Boy (*Warner Bros. 1929*)

The Hottentot (*Warner Bros. 1929*)

The Sap (*Warner Bros. 1929*)

The Aviator (*Warner Bros. 1929*)

Take the Heir (*Big Four 1930*)

Wide Open (*Warner Bros. 1930*)

Holiday (*Pathé 1930*)

Once a Gentleman (*Sono Art-World Wide 1930*)

Kiss Me Again (*First National 1931*)

Reaching for the Moon (*United Artists 1931*)

Lonely Wives (*Pathé 1931*)

The Front Page (*United Artists 1931*)

Six Cylinder Love (*Fox 1931*)

Smart Woman (*RKO 1931*)

The Age for Love (*United Artists 1931*)

But the Flesh Is Weak (*MGM 1932*)

Roar of the Dragon (*RKO 1932*)

Trouble in Paradise (*Paramount 1932*)

It's a Boy (*British 1933*)

A Bedtime Story (*Paramount 1933*)

The Way to Love (*Paramount 1933*)

Design for Living (*Paramount 1933*)

Alice in Wonderland (*Paramount 1933*)

Soldiers of the King [The Woman in Command] (*British 1934*)

Easy to Love (*Warner Bros. 1934*)

Sing and Like It (*RKO 1934*)

The Poor Rich (*Universal 1934*)

Smarty (*Warner Bros. 1934*)

Success at Any Price (*RKO 1934*)

Uncertain Lady (*Universal 1934*)

Kiss and Make Up (*Paramount 1934*)

The Merry Widow (*MGM 1934*)

Ladies Should Listen (*Paramount 1934*)

The Gay Divorcee (*RKO 1934*)

The Private Secretary (*British 1935*)

Biography of a Bachelor Girl (*MGM 1935*)

All the King's Horses (*Paramount 1935*)

The Night Is Young (*MGM 1935*)

The Devil Is a Woman (*Paramount 1935*)

Your Uncle Dudley (*Fox 1935*)

In Caliente (*Warner Bros. 1935*)

$10 Raise (*Fox 1935*)

Going Highbrow (*Warner Bros. 1935*)

Little Big Shot (*Warner Bros. 1935*)

Top Hat (*RKO 1935*)

His Night Out (*Universal 1935*)

The Singing Kid (*Warner Bros. 1936*)

Her Master's Voice (*Paramount 1936*)

Hearts Divided (*Warner Bros. 1936*)

Nobody's Fool (*Universal 1936*)

The Man in the Mirror (*British 1936*)

The King and the Chorus Girl (*Warner Bros. 1937*)

Let's Make a Million (*Paramount 1937*)

Lost Horizon (*Columbia 1937*)

Shall We Dance (*RKO 1937*)

Oh, Doctor! (*Universal 1937*)

Wild Money (*Paramount 1937*)

Angel (*Paramount 1937*)

The Perfect Specimen (*Warner Bros. 1937*)

Danger—Love at Work (*20th Century-Fox 1937*)

The Great Garrick (*Warner Bros. 1937*)

Hitting a New High (*RKO 1937*)

Bluebeard's Eighth Wife (*Paramount 1938*)

College Swing (*Paramount 1938*)

Holiday (*Columbia 1938*)

Little Tough Guys in Society (*Universal 1938*)

Paris Honeymoon (*Paramount 1939*)

That's Right—You're Wrong (*RKO 1939*)

The Gang's All Here [The Amazing Mr. Forrest] (*British 1939*)

You're the One (*Paramount 1941*)

Ziegfeld Girl (*MGM 1941*)

Sunny (*RKO 1941*)

Bachelor Daddy (*Universal 1941*)

Here Comes Mr. Jordan (*Columbia 1941*)

Week-End for Three (*RKO 1941*)

Sandy Steps Out (*Universal 1941*)

The Body Disappears (*Warner Bros. 1942*)

I Married an Angel (*MGM 1942*)

The Magnificent Dope (*20th Century-Fox 1942*)

Springtime in the Rockies (*20th Century-Fox 1942*)

Forever and a Day (*RKO 1943*)

Thank Your Lucky Stars (*Warner Bros. 1943*)

The Gang's All Here (*20th Century-Fox 1943*)

Summer Storm (*United Artists 1944*)

Her Primitive Man (*Universal 1944*)

San Diego, I Love You (*Universal 1944*)

Arsenic and Old Lace (*Warner Bros. 1944*)

Brazil (*Republic 1944*)

The Town Went Wild (*Producers Releasing Corporation 1944*)

Steppin' in Society (*Republic 1945*)

Lady on a Train (*Universal 1945*)

Cinderella Jones (*Warner Bros. 1946*)

Faithful in My Fashion (*MGM 1946*)

Earl Carroll's Sketch-Book (*Republic 1946*)

The Ghost Goes Wild (*Republic 1947*)

Down to Earth (*Columbia 1947*)

Her Husband's Affair (*Columbia 1947*)

The Story of Mankind (*Warner Bros. 1957*)

Pocketful of Miracles (*United Artists 1961*)

It's a Mad, Mad, Mad, Mad World (*United Artists 1963*)

Sex and the Single Girl (*Warner Bros. 1964*)

The Perils of Pauline (*Universal 1967*)

2,000 Years Later (*Warner Bros. 1969*)

Cold Turkey (*United Artists 1971*)

Danny Kaye

In the 1944 Samuel Goldwyn screen musical *Up in Arms*, moviegoers had their first glimpse of an explosive, orange-haired package of singing, dancing, double-talking, face-making talent named Danny Kaye. A hard-working veteran of nightclubs and Broadway, Danny Kaye has since blazed through over three decades of delighting international audiences. Show business has rarely boasted a more potentially endearing entertainer. His cinema characterizations of such men as Walter Mitty and Hans Christian Andersen, his live stage performances, his Emmy Award-winning teleseries, and a special Academy Award for his unique talents testify to his status as one of the world's most beloved entertainers. In addition, Danny has accomplished a monumental amount of charity work, especially for UNICEF (United Nations International Children's Education Fund), and once said, "The long lines at the vaccination centers are probably the most rewarding tribute I have ever received for my peculiar ability to make funny faces."

All of which makes it quite perplexing that, within the entertainment industry, few per-formers are reputedly so abrasive as lovable Danny Kaye. Writers, fans, and fellow players have told tales over the years describing Danny as a reputed monster of ego and temperament. Kaye has become a classic example of the beloved public figure who in private life sometimes appears the very opposite of the cuddly imp he portrays perennially.

"I can never tell when a flight of fancy is coming on," says Kaye, born David Daniel Kominsky on the lower east side of New York City on Saturday, January 18, 1913. His parents were Russian Jewish immigrants who fled the pogroms of the czarist-ruled homeland. While Mr. Kominsky labored in the garment industry, his youngest son (there were two others) made funny faces for the neighbors. He attended Thomas Jefferson High School with the hope of becoming a surgeon, but dropped out a semester away from graduation to enter show business.

The early days were *not* encouraging. He became part of such acts as "Red and Blackie," "The Three Terpsichoreans," "La Vie Paree," etc., acts that zigzagged every-

In Knock on Wood *(1954)*.

where from private parties to the borscht circuit of the Catskill Mountain resorts to the vaudeville houses. But the employment was not always steady, and Danny found himself earning living expenses by working as a soda jerk, insurance clerk, etc. It was during these fledgling performing years that Danny adopted a more "American" name, Danny Kaye.

After a tour with fan dancer Sally Rand, Danny signed in late 1937 with New York-based Educational Pictures, producers of comic short subjects. He extraed in a few and played the lead in *Getting an Eyeful*, in which his dialect comedy shone, but the performer insists, "I'd rather forget all about them."

Kaye would also prefer to forget the London engagement he played shortly after leaving Educational Studios. He appeared with Nick Long Jr. at London's Dorchester Hotel. As he remembers it, "I was the most resounding failure that the London cafe set had ever seen. It was hopeless, and I struggled along for 6 or 7 weeks and they finally told me to take a walk."

Things improved when he returned to New York. He landed spots in two stage revues: *Sunday Night Vanities* and *The Straw Hat Revue,* the latter opening at the Ambassador Theatre on September 29, 1939, for a 75-performance run. The actor also scored at New York's plush La Martinique as a solo performer. In the midst of his rise to success, Danny Kaye married. His bride was Sylvia Fine, a composer who had written the specialty numbers ("Anatole of Paris," "Stanislavsky," "Pavlova") which had provided such winning material for Danny in *The Straw Hat Revue.* Kaye greatly admired his wife's talents, though he explained his attraction by quipping, "On our first date she ordered the 50-cent dinner. I was immediately impressed." On January 30, 1940, they eloped to Fort Lauderdale, Florida, and were wed. To please the bride's parents, they were remarried in a Jewish ceremony in Brooklyn on February 22, 1940.

Danny's monumental show-business break followed. While he was performing at La Martinique, Moss Hart visited the club and was so impressed by the vital versatility in front of the spotlight that he wrote for Danny the role of Russell Paxton, the chauffeur-photographer of the Kurt Weill-Ira Gersh-

win–Larry Hart musical *Lady in the Dark.* In rehearsals, Danny showed such promise, especially with the rapid-fire solo "Tchaikovsky," that the authors were forced to write the (soon to be famous) "Jenny" song to appease star Gertrude Lawrence. With a cast including Miss Lawrence, Victor Mature, Macdonald Carey, Bert Lytell, and Danny, *Lady in the Dark* premiered at the Alvin Theatre on January 23, 1941. The *New York Times* cheered, "Danny Kaye, who was cutting up in *The Straw Hat Revue* last year, is infectiously exuberant. . . ." His madcap delivery of "Tchaikovsky," in which he spit out the multisyllabled names of Russian composers in machine-gun fire fashion, earned him a spot in Ripley's "Believe It or Not." The play ran for a sold-out 162 performances before closing for the summer. When it reopened in September of 1941 for an additional 305 performances, Danny had left the show with many job bids from which to choose.*

MGM had offered Danny a $3,000 weekly contract, but Kaye declined. "I would work for much less, believe me, almost for nothing, if they would give me character roles and let me learn how to act," he explained. "But I know they would just put me in a specialty spot here and there and one bum picture would put me back two or three years. I'm very young. I've got lots of time. My wife doesn't want me to go into pictures for at least a year, and then as an actor and not as a specialty performer. . . ."

Acting on this professional wisdom, Kaye instead starred as Jerry Walker (accepting the role Milton Berle had rejected) in the Cole Porter musical *Let's Face It* (Imperial Theatre, October 29, 1941). The cast included Eve Arden, Vivian Vance, and Nanette Fabray and a score that allowed for special Sylvia Fine–Max Liebman material ("Fairy Tale") for Danny. The *New York Times* endorsed *Let's Face It* as "a wonderfully joyous musical show" and reported of Kaye's performance, "It is amazing. . . . Mr. Kaye conquered every ermine in the house last evening. . . . Although Mr. Kaye is a lean and likable virtuoso (who looks like a startled Julius

* Eric Brotherson replaced Kaye in *Lady in the Dark.* When the Paramount film version of the hit show was released in 1944, Ginger Rogers had the title role and Mischa Auer played a considerably toned-down copy of Danny's Russell Paxton.

Caesar, if you care), he does not swindle the other performers." Danny, however, was not above trying to "break up" his fellow performers. One night, while trying to "throw" co-player Benny Baker, his efforts backfired. "I gave him a straight line in double talk," Danny recalls, "but the startled expression on his face was so funny that he broke me up completely, and I forgot my lines for the next five minutes." Although it would be Bob Hope who would play the lead in Paramount's 1943 film version of *Let's Face It,* the show won Danny his first valid movie contract.

"While *Lady in the Dark* was running," remembers Danny, "Abe Glasgow, then my representative, told Sam Goldwyn there was a fellow in New York he ought to see. I played an effeminate role in the play and Goldwyn came, saw, and said, 'Why the hell did you bring me all the way to New York to see some fag?' . . . I must have been a good actor because Goldwyn really believed I was a fag." But, after Goldwyn saw Danny at a return engagement at La Martinique and learned of his success in *Let's Face It,* the producer changed his estimation. He signed Danny to a five-year, five-picture contract in 1943.

When Danny, rejected from World War II military service because of health problems, arrived in Hollywood, he felt, "I couldn't wait to get back to New York because California was supposed to be for the birds." Also, Goldwyn was toying with the notion of dying the redhead's hair blond (which he did) and having a plastic surgeon reshape Danny's nose (which he did not).

His first picture was *Up in Arms* with Dana Andrews, Louis Calhern, and 27-year-old Dinah Shore, as well as the Fine-Liebman tunes "Melody in 4-F" (borrowed from Broadway's *Let's Face It)* and "The Lobby Number," written especially for the film. When the motion picture opened in March 1944 at Radio City Music Hall, the *New York Post* printed, "In this, his first picture, Danny shoots the works. He brings to bear an amazing battery of talents, a dancer's grace, burlesque, satire, hands that talk, a voice of inhuman range, and a prodigious flexibility in achieving sudden change in face, spirit, and figure. . . . It's an experience like no other."

Danny immediately was accepted by the filmgoing public. (Some insisted he already

outshone MGM's red-headed funster, Red Skelton.) Kaye was young, fairly attractive, and was incredibly entertaining. Moreover, he could *act,* causing audiences not only to laugh but to feel. He also discovered he liked Hollywood. "You can get the same kind of excitement here that you can in New York," he allowed, and as he settled into the cinema colony, he accepted a CBS network offer to headline his own radio program. "The Danny Kaye Show" premiered in January 1945 with regulars Eve Arden, Everett Sloane, Jim Backus, and Butterfly McQueen. Goodman Ace directed the proceedings, with Sylvia Fine Kaye as the head writer. Though CBS was pleased with the program and wanted it to enter a second season, Danny asked for and received a release so he could concentrate on his film career.

Kept out of khaki by a bad back, Danny aided the war effort by raising some $1,000,000 worth of war bonds and traveling 32,000 miles to perform 98 special shows for servicemen. Meanwhile, Goldwyn, entranced with his newest star, mounted Danny's next feature with lavish production values, including color photography and the presence of those Olympian beauties, the Goldwyn Girls.

In *Wonder Man* (1945) Danny played twins—one a flashy nightclub singer, the other a timid bookworm. The *New York World-Telegram* reported, "Danny does a lot of his strange dances, he sings his hysterical double talk, he burlesques opera and concert singing, he screeches his way through some wild chases. He even pauses a couple of times to give a fleeting glimpse at an unsuspected talent for romantic acting." In 1946 Goldwyn's Kaye vehicle was *The Kid from Brooklyn*—adapted from Harold Lloyd's *The Milky Way* (1936)—in which Danny played Burleigh Sullivan, milkman turned boxer. His highlight in this amiable picture was his singing of the specialty number "Pavlova." "Those who may have supposed that Kaye was something of a one-man vaudeville act will be surprised to discover that he is a very accomplished actor in his newest film assignment," acknowledged the *New York Herald-Tribune.* "He makes a few excursions into his double talk takeoffs but for most of the time plays a straight comic role with infinite variety and humor." In both *Wonder Man* and

With Virginia Mayo in Wonder Man *(1945).*

The Kid from Brooklyn Danny co-starred with blonde beauty Virginia Mayo and tap-dancing Vera-Ellen. The latter film featured two of his regulars from his radio show, Eve Arden and Lionel Stander.

Offscreen, Danny's interviews revealed a personality that was both serious and flip. He said that his greatest virtue was "the way I make spaghetti—if you don't want to eat it, you can use a dish of it for rubber bands," and that his greatest ambition was "to have Lauren Bacall whistle at me." He explained to *Motion Picture* magazine: "People expect you to be funny all the time and never take into consideration the fact that you're a normal person and as much interested in world problems as they are. A group of people may be talking about something serious, but when I join them they change the subject as if I were Little Rollo who must be protected against the facts of life." Danny also admitted, "I'm very moody. For no reason at all I can get tangled up in the darnedest state of

the blues. And I have no patience." (This side of the Kaye persona would become more evident in later years.)

Kaye's best screen performance till then was the title role in *The Secret Life of Walter Mitty* (1947), in which he played Thurber's daydreaming hero, in love with Virginia Mayo and menaced by Boris Karloff. Though there was persistent criticism that the scenario enlarged Thurber's story out of its charmingly simple perspective, the post–World War II public loved the melodramatic adventures of Danny as the "ta-puccata-puccata-puccata" hero. His last feature with Goldwyn (and Miss Mayo—who moved on to Warner Bros. and James Cagney) was *A Song Is Born* (1948). It was a rather dull reshaping of Goldwyn's *Ball of Fire* (1941), which had provided a memorable teaming of Barbara Stanwyck and Gary Cooper. It was the only Goldwyn-Kaye entry *not* to feature special Sylvia Fine material. The reason was more private than professional. The Kayes were

With Eve Arden, Steve Cochran, Vera-Ellen, and Walter Abel in The Kid from Brooklyn *(1946).*

undergoing a trial separation at the time, Sylvia feeling Danny was accepting inferior material and Danny believing Sylvia was attempting to reverse the Svengali-Trilby roles ("Sylvia has a fine head on my shoulders," Danny would pun). On December 17, 1946, nine months before the separation began, the Kayes had become the parents of a daughter, Dena. Of *A Song Is Born* the best that could be said was that it offered some fine jazz work by Louis Armstrong, Benny Goodman, and Tommy Dorsey.

In 1948, free of his Hollywood contract, Danny—with Martha Raye on the bill—returned to London, playing an engagement that became legendary. It won him 100,000 fan letters a week and the tributes of England's top celebrities, including George Bernard Shaw, Winston Churchill, and the king himself. Danny recalls that when the royal family attended his performance (the first such time a royal entourage attended a vaudeville show that was *not* a Command Performance), "they visited me backstage for half an hour. I cracked jokes and the king cracked right back." The *London Daily Ex-*

press said of the Britishers' adoration of Kaye, "They brought out the fatted calf, roasted it, and served it to Danny Kaye on a red carpet." Once during the engagement Danny revealed his unflattering side when a group of distinguished physicians and psychiatrists visited him backstage. They inquired, "What is this magic you have with an audience?" Barked Danny, "I don't know what the hell you're talking about!"

In the late Forties Danny signed a long-term contract with Warner Bros., but appeared in only two films for the studio. *The Inspector General* (1949), a musical comedy of the Napoleonic era, had Walter Slezak and Elsa Lanchester in the character leads. Mrs. Kaye, with whom Danny had reconciled after returning from England, not only wrote eight songs for the film but also served as associate producer. In the latter capacity she had the best scenes of heroine Barbara Bates deleted. After Danny cameoed with such Warner Bros. stars as Errol Flynn, Joan Crawford, and Ronald Reagan in the Doris Day–Jack Carson feature *It's a Great Feeling* (1949), Danny left Warner Bros. A week later he

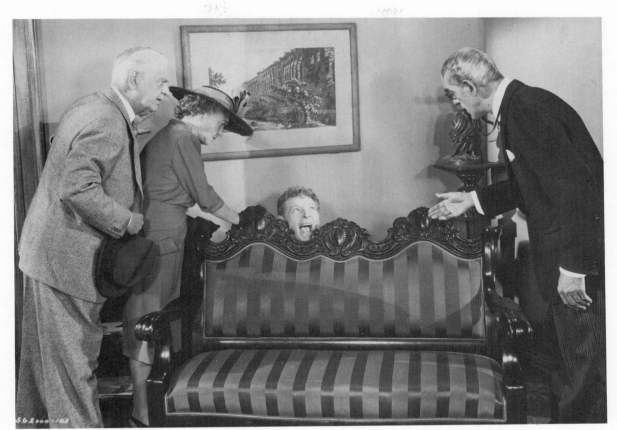

With Thurston Hall,
Fay Bainter, and
Boris Karloff in The
Secret Life of Walter
Mitty (1947).

With Joey Walsh in
Hans Christian
Andersen (1952).

337

signed with Twentieth Century–Fox. Already his restlessness and impatience with professional decisions were becoming very noticeable. He would make only one film for Fox, *On the Riviera* (1951), with Gene Tierney and Corinne Calvet, four Sylvia Fine songs, and the "Pop the Puppet" number in which Danny cavorted as a giant puppet.

Following a tour of Korea, where he performed for the troops, Danny signed a two-picture pact with his old mentor, Samuel Goldwyn. It resulted in his most charming screen performance, the title role in *Hans Christian Andersen* (1952), which Goldwyn produced as "a fairy tale about this great spinner of fairy tales." His enchanting characterization was Oscar-worthy but he was not even nominated. The music and lyrics by Frank Loesser and the adaptation by Jo Swerling and William Wyler (revised by Moss Hart) made it ideal entertainment for audiences of all ages. It grossed $6,000,000 in U.S.–Canadian distributors' rentals. His other Goldwyn project, a sequel to *The Secret Life of Walter Mitty*, was never made.

Throughout the Fifties Danny worked at a steady pace in a variety of media. With the writing/directing/producing team of Norman Panama and Melvin Frank, the Kayes formed Dena productions, which produced three films. *Knock on Wood* (1954) featured Danny as a ventriloquist, Sylvia Fine songs, and Michael Kidd choreography, and was shot in Europe. It remains Kaye's favorite feature. Plans for Kaye to star in the life story of Maurice Chevalier did not materialize, but he made *The Court Jester* (1956), an elaborate swashbuckling spoof with a sparkling cast which included Glynis Johns, Angela Lansbury, Mildred Natwick, and Basil Rathbone. For Danny's climactic duel with Rathbone, the latter, an expert swordsman, taught Danny the basics so the comedian could hold his own against him. But it backfired. As Sylvia Kaye would reveal, "Danny's mind works like a camera and he picks things up very quickly. Basil was well into his 60s when we did this film and Danny's movements were just too quick for him." The final Dena production, also for Paramount, was *The Five Pennies* (1959), a screen biography of trumpeter-bandleader Loring "Red" Nichols, with Danny in the leading role, Barbara

Bel Geddes as his wife, and an Oscar-nominated Sylvia Fine score.

Danny, in the meantime, accepted the offers of other producers. He replaced pneumonia-stricken Donald O'Connor in Irving Berlin's yuletide classic, *White Christmas* (1954). Kaye was matched with Bing Crosby, Rosemary Clooney, and his Goldwyn co-star Vera-Ellen. The film went on to gross over $12,000,000 in the United States and Canada alone, and remains a staple of TV showing at Christmas time. For MGM Kaye starred with Pier Angeli in *Merry Andrew* (1958), which the *New York Times* criticized as "a narrowly confined piece of comical contrivance," but of which *Time* wrote, "Fortunately, Danny, as always, transcends his material." The color comedy featured a delightful slapstick scene in which Danny, in an inflated ringmaster's costume, floats to the top of a circus tent.

The comedian was far more sober in his performance as Jacobowsky, the aging Jew fleeing persecution, in Columbia's *Me and the Colonel* (1958). With Curt Jurgens as the anti-Semitic officer and Nicole Maury as the heroine, the film was shot in France. It won Danny excellent reviews, but not box-office records. The *New York Times* noted, "Mr. Kaye plays the brave little fugitive with affection and sympathy . . . strikingly mindful of the old Chaplin in his wistful resignation and fortitude."

In Paramount's *On the Double* (1961), which Dena Productions produced in collaboration with Capri Productions, Danny enjoyed a supporting cast which included Dana Wynter, Margaret Rutherford, and Diana Dors. Kaye had the chance to impersonate a Gestapo agent, a Nazi pilot, Adolf Hitler, and Marlene Dietrich (singing "Cocktails for Zwei"), but many viewers were disappointed that the film was such an obvious repeat of elements from *On the Riviera* and *Knock on Wood*. Danny's last film for some time would be *The Man from the Diners' Club* (1963), for which he received surprisingly bad notices. The *New York Times* wailed that Kaye's "acting is so disordered, so frantic without being droll, so completely devoid of invention and spontaneity that he did no more than remind us, somewhat sadly, of that other Danny Kaye and what a terrible thing television has done to the comedy of the screen."

With Bing Crosby, Rosemary Clooney, and Vera-Ellen in White Christmas *(1954).*

A new Hollywood heavy named Telly Savalas stole what there was to steal of the film.

When not producing and starring in films, Kaye found the time to work in other media. On January 18, 1953, he opened at New York's Palace Theatre in "Danny Kaye's International Show." In May 1955 he returned to London's Palladium with great success. And on April 10, 1963, he opened "The Danny Kaye Show" at Broadway's Ziegfeld Theatre, supported by such talent as Senor Wences and the Johnny Mann Singers.

The performer also entered television. On December 2, 1956, he was the subject of the 90-minute documentary *The Secret Life of Danny Kaye,* aired on the CBS network and narrated by Edward R. Murrow. In October 1960 he presented his own CBS-TV special, and in 1963 he began an hour-long variety series, "The Danny Kaye Show." It ran for four seasons, won Emmy Awards for the show, director, and star, and earned a coveted Peabody Award. The show featured special guest stars each week, along with regulars Harvey Korman and Joyce Van Patten.

Additionally, Danny has accomplished a fantastic amount of charitable work. In the early Fifties he traveled hundreds of thousands of miles for UNICEF, visiting Burma, Korea, Thailand, Japan, and India. (Paramount would release a color documentary, *Assignment Children,* in 1955 detailing Danny's treks.) In 1957 President Eisenhower presented him with a special scroll honoring him as "Big Brother of the Year '56," and since then Kaye has done extensive work on UNICEF–sponsored tours.

With so many talents displayed, Danny Kaye was awarded a special Oscar statuette in 1955 "for his unique talents, his service to the Academy, the motion picture industry, and the American people."

Danny is so delightful an entertainer and so dedicated a friend to the needy that it is hard to understand or accept the nasty side of his nature that has occasionally surfaced over the past years. When he conducted the

With Curt Jurgens and Akim Tamiroff in Me and the Colonel *(1958).*

New York Philharmonic at Carnegie Hall (March 10, 1958), he turned to the audience at one point and remarked, "I don't know about you and I couldn't care less, but I'm having the time of my life." When Kaye began his weekly CBS-TV show, rumors of the star's ill-temper and a tyrannical nature ran rampant. A quite well publicized episode on the show concerned Danny's firing of a very young girl who had been appearing regularly at the close of each weekly show to chat coyly with him. Danny said she was losing the discipline required to perform. Unofficial versions stated that the star would not tolerate the fact that she was weekly upstaging him. Recently Dinah Shore, usually dripping honey-laden accolades about everyone and anyone, guested on TV's "Tonight Show." Guest hostess Helen Reddy asked Dinah if she had ever personally booked any of the guests on her video talk show. Replied Dinah, "Only once. My producer thought we should have Danny Kaye on the show. He said he knew Danny never did this kind of show, but

I had been with him in the picture and maybe if I called him. . . . So I got on the phone to Danny—but I never got past his secretary!"

Danny's most recent feature was *The Madwoman of Chaillot* (1969), an amazingly unentertaining offering despite its all-star cast. Katharine Hepburn had the title role and Danny was on hand as the Ragpicker, the one who delivers a satirical speech on the establishment. Danny would say later of this box-office dud, "Yah, I liked *The Madwoman of Chaillot*, but it wasn't a good movie. The audience wasn't able to tell where reality stopped and fantasy began."

On November 10, 1970, Danny returned to Broadway in the musical *Two by Two*, a loose adaptation of Clifford Odets' *The Flowering Peach*, with tunes by Richard Rodgers. As Noah, Danny sang, danced, aged backward from 600 to 90 and back again (Bible years), and delivered what for a time was the most vulgar line on Broadway, screaming at son Shem (Harry Goz), who has been saving fertilizer on the Ark to start a business, "Is that how you want the new world to begin? With a ton of sh——?" Actually it was a quite lovely play, and the *New York Daily News* judged, "There is a magnificent portrayal of Noah by Danny Kaye which goes deep into one's heart."

However, in February 1971 Danny tore a ligament in his left leg, and when it appeared the show could not continue its run without him, he returned in a wheelchair (as old Noah) and a crutch (as young Noah). It was no longer the same play. Danny's unorthodox behavior at the Imperial Theatre caused co-star Madeline Kahn to remember the play as "The Danny Kaye Show." He was soon deviating from the script to deliver ribald, prerehearsed ad-libs, going to ridiculous lengths to break up his co-players, singing out of tempo with the orchestra, and even partially undressing his wife Esther (Joan Copeland) on stage while doing a dance with her. Of course, many fans were captivated by the "impromptu" performance. Danny began

offering curtain speeches, saying, "I'm glad you're here, but I'm glad the authors aren't!" But many outraged patrons wrote letters of indignation to the *New York Times* after attending the play. Many autograph seekers were disillusioned when the lovable clown would charge out of the stage door nightly after the show to his waiting car, shrieking, "*No*, I will *not* sign autographs! Can't you people see I'm *sick*?" The play ran until late summer 1971.

"My life used to revolve only about my career, but a fellow can't live that way, work that way, all his life," said Danny a decade ago. "When you get into a position of some eminence in your profession you should be able to satisfy some of your other interests. I'm interested in flying, in cooking, in sports, in traveling." As such, the tireless Danny has become an expert pilot, a specialist in preparing Chinese cuisine, an honorary member of the American College of Surgeons, and the owner of real estate, a production com-

With Telly Savalas and Cara Williams in The Man from the Diners' Club *(1963).*

pany, and radio stations. He has also contributed to wounded Israeli freedom fighters and conducted symphonies for various charitable causes all over the world. More recently he made news when he was among five businessmen who purchased an American League baseball expansion team to begin play in Seattle's Kingdome in the spring of 1977. "Think of it," he said, "a guy who spent his youth watching the Dodgers play at Ebbets Field now owns his own baseball club. It's Walter Mitty time!"

With so many outside interests, Kaye's acting in recent years has been infrequent. In 1972 he appeared over ABC-TV in *The Enchanted World of Danny Kaye: The Emperor's New Clothes* and for the same network that year narrated the special *Here Comes Peter Cottontail.* On March 27, 1976, he played the kindly carpenter Gepetto and the wicked puppeteer to Sandy Duncan's Pinnochio in a CBS-TV special of Carlo Collodi's 1883 fable. Later that year, on December 12, he was Captain Hook to Mia Farrow's *Peter Pan* on NBC-TV, a new musical version with a Leslie Bricusse-Anthony Newley score that was taped in London. While the program received few critical endorsements (Mary Martin's 1955 TV version was too fondly remembered), many reviewers cited Kaye's effective work. "His scenes and songs glow with impudent wickedness" (*Hollywood Reporter*). (In March 1973 Kaye hosted the American Film Institute's Life Achievement Award Banquet honoring director John Ford.)

Danny explains his present lack of movie work by saying, "Movies are not like they used to be, times are not like they used to be, and most of all, I am not like I used to be." He returned to London's Palladium in 1955, but has not been back since. "Sure I could probably go back there and do the same routines and get a fine reaction. But it wouldn't be the same. There was something about that era that made it just right, and I would never be able to recapture what happened 20 to 25 years ago. It would be walking backward. Likewise, I don't want to go to Las Vegas; I've done that. Another television series? Those four years I did on CBS were among the most enjoyable of my life. But I wouldn't want to repeat. Nowadays I just want to do the things I want to do." He recently rejected the lead in the Broadway musical *On the Twentieth Century,* although he has agreed to film TV commercials for Polaroid's new instant movie system.

Now well into his 60s, Danny Kaye is most pleased about his 1975 record-breaking 65-city trip for UNICEF.* "I just learned that I've been accepted by the *Guinness Book of Records* for my Halloween trip last year. I flew my own jet to 65 cities in five days, traveling 17,000 miles and speaking at each stop."

---

* In May 1977 Kaye found time to perform as guest conductor for the Montreal Symphony Orchestra, raising $200,000 for the group's pension fund. Later that month he received an honorary degree of Doctor of Humane Letters at Colgate University.

FEATURE FILMS

Up in Arms (*RKO 1944*)
Wonder Man (*RKO 1945*)
The Kid from Brooklyn (*RKO 1946*)
The Secret Life of Walter Mitty (*RKO 1947*)
A Song Is Born (*RKO 1948*)
The Inspector General (*Warner Bros. 1949*)
It's a Great Feeling (*Warner Bros. 1949*)
On the Riviera (*20th Century-Fox 1951*)
Hans Christian Andersen (*RKO 1952*)
Knock on Wood (*Paramount 1954*)

White Christmas (*Paramount 1954*)
The Court Jester (*Paramount 1956*)
Merry Andrew (*MGM 1958*)
Me and the Colonel (*Columbia 1958*)
The Five Pennies (*Paramount 1959*)
On the Double (*Paramount 1961*)
The Man from the Diners' Club (*Columbia 1963*)
The Madwoman of Chaillot (*Warner Bros.- 7 Arts 1969*)

With Bobbi Shaw in Pajama Party *(1964).*

Buster Keaton

Though but 5'5", Buster Keaton was one of the giants of silent screen comedy. In popularity, box-office returns, and national fervor for proper placement, Keaton ran third, behind Chaplin and Lloyd. But unlike some of Chaplin's and Lloyd's comedies, Keaton's motion pictures have withstood the test of time.

Keaton's kinetic and inventive visual comedy was elaborately orchestrated to extract laughter. If his highly imaginative mind was devoted to perfecting sight gags at the expense of story and characterization, his career produced reels of film that became comedy classics of the screen.

Lloyd presented an eternally optimistic, bound-to-succeed image, and Chaplin offered the world a meddling, lovable, pathos-prone Tramp. In contrast, Keaton's great stone face registered pessimism to a world conspiring mechanically or historically against him. He was the screen comedian who accepted his fate with astonishing stoicism and struggled for survival.

Joseph Hollie Keaton, born in Dogwalk, Indiana, staked a claim in the 1889 Okla-homa Land Rush, but later abandoned pioneering to join a medicine show. While working with the Cutler-Bryant Medicine Show he eloped with the owner's daughter, Myra Edith Cutler, who performed as the soubrette-musician. Their son, christened Joseph Frank (Francis) Keaton, was born on Friday, October 4, 1895, in the hamlet of Piqua, Kansas.

At six months of age the baby plunged headlong down a flight of stairs. He was rescued by his parents' fellow performer, magician Harry Houdini, who told his astonished parents, "That's some buster your baby took." The nickname stuck. He became "Buster" Keaton and three months later, July 1896, made his stage debut by crawling out onto the stage to gaze, from between his father's shoes, at his first audience. Two years later Buster joined his parents' act.

The Three Keatons became headliners in vaudeville in the United States and England. Buster (made up into a pint-sized duplication of his father) and Joseph Sr. would stage a knockdown, dragout, slapstick free-for-all routine that earned Buster the tag "Human Mop." The act was often called "Buster,

Assisted by Joe and Myra Keaton." The youngster learned to take hazardous falls without injury, and to perfect his timing for greater laughs. Early on he discovered his deadly serious approach to the Keaton roughhousing (their act varied from one performance to the next with impromptu inventiveness) elicited louder guffaws from audiences.

Keaton later said, "I learned as a kid growing up with an audience that I just had to be that type of comedian. If I laughed at what I did, the audience didn't. The more serious I turned, the bigger laugh I got. So at the time I went into pictures, that was automatic—I didn't even know I was doing it."

His schooling was vaudeville with its rigid discipline. While performing and learning his craft, the Keatons were dogged by the child-protecting Gerry Society. The family act toured from coast to coast. When they played New York's Palace Theatre, Hammerstein's Victoria, and Tony Pastor's, they were hounded by the self-righteous Gerry group. When Buster turned 16, *Variety* carried an announcement, "Today, I am a Theatrical Man—Goodbye, Mr. Gerry!"

The Three Keatons had become five with the birth of Harry Stanley "Jingles" Keaton in 1900 and Louise two years later. But the act was disintegrating. Mr. Keaton's alcoholic battles and his long-running personal vendetta with theatrical impresario Martin Beck (head of the Orpheum vaudeville circuit) resulted in his abandoning The Three Keatons' act in February 1917. Buster was signed by the Shuberts for their *Passing Show of 1917.* By the time rehearsal got under way for the Winter Garden Theatre revue, Buster had relinquished the $250 weekly salary for a $40-a-week job in the flickers.

Keaton's casual meeting with Roscoe Arbuckle produced a Keaton visit to the Colony Studios on East 48th Street. There Joseph Schenck showed his wife's (Norma Talmadge) and her sister's (Constance) pictures. The same building housed Arbuckle's newly formed Comique Film Company. The mechanics and extensive potential range of the movie camera fascinated 21-year-old Buster. In an historical one-take shot, Keaton received a bag of flour in the face, marking his movie debut as the Village Pest in Ar-

buckle's two-reeler, *The Butcher Boy* (April 23, 1917).

Although Keaton would later credit his lifelong friend Arbuckle with teaching him the movie business, there was a marked improvement in the content of Arbuckle's two-reelers after Keaton became part of the unit. With his first screen appearance Buster introduced his singular sense of timing and rhythm and his vaudeville-learned discipline. He displayed an unhurried, unperplexed style amidst the frantic, often excessive playing of Arbuckle and the vapid Al St. John.

After making five two-reelers in New York, the unit moved to Long Beach, California, in October 1917. There they made five more two-reelers. Before the fifth comedy, *The Cook,* was released, Buster had been drafted into the United States Army's "Sunshine" Infantry Division. He returned to Hollywood after the war to make four more comedies with Arbuckle. Joseph Schenck opened in January 1920 the Keaton Studio, which gave Buster complete control and artistic freedom (and relief from the intricacies of management, for which he had little aptitude) to produce, write, and direct (with Eddie Cline) a series of two- and three-reel shorts for Metro release.

When Metro filmed the Broadway play *The New Henrietta,* it followed Douglas Fairbanks'* recommendation to co-star Keaton with imported, original star William H. Crane. Retitled *The Saphead,* the 1920 picture was highly successful and established Keaton as a comedy feature star. Despite the somewhat idiotic nature of Buster's screen character Bertie, he had several memorable moments in which he could exhibit his stoic acceptance of life's foibles. He accomplished this with what critic James Agee would term "Keaton's mulish imperturbability."

When Buster had made his film debut in *The Butcher Boy,* the second of the three Talmadge sisters, Natalie, was financial manager for Arbuckle's Comique Film Company. Their four-year romance culminated in marriage on May 31, 1921, at Norma's Bayside, Long Island, home. The newlyweds honeymooned by motoring from New York to California. In the closely knit Talmadge fam-

* Fairbanks had played Bertie Van Alstyne of *The New Henrietta* on Broadway, and used the character for his 1915 film debut in *The Lamb.*

ily, Mother Peg dominated the scene. Sons-in-law were acceptable as interlopers or, like Norma's husband Joseph Schenck, as benevolent sponsors. Buster called his first son, born on Friday, June 2, 1922, "Buster Jr." or Joe Keaton VII. But to the Talmadge clan Joseph Talmadge Keaton was "Jimmy." Buster would later admit he felt he had married not one girl but an entire family.

Following his marriage to Natalie Talmadge, Buster failed to convince Schenck that full-scale comedy features would be more successful than two- or three-reel short subjects. It did not matter to Schenck that Arbuckle had made his first feature comedy, *The Round-Up*, in 1920 and the next year embarked on a series of popular five-reel comedies for Paramount. Chaplin's *The Kid* and Lloyd's first feature, *A Sailor-Made Man*, were soaring 1921 successes. However, Schenck negotiated a deal with Associated First National Pictures to distribute 12 Keaton-produced comedy shorts.

Keaton's 1921-22 shorts were masterpieces of cinema comedy invention. *The Playhouse* was a brilliant fantasy in which Buster played many characters with alacrity. *The Boat* provided one of Keaton's finest moments with its launching scene in which Buster stands proud and erect on the prow as the boat immediately sinks. Sternly stone-faced, he holds his position and goes down with the boat; only his horizontal pork-pie hat remains afloat. His funny burlesque of equally frozen-faced Western star William S. Hart in *The Frozen North* was highlighted by the New York subway emerging in Alaska. The 11 First National releases (the contracted twelfth was never made) supported Keaton's craftsmanship as a sublime silent clown.

Metro released the first Keaton feature in August 1923. *Three Ages* pitted the hero (Keaton) against the villain (Wallace Beery) through six reels of cleverly interwoven tales of battle for love in the Stone Age, ancient Rome, and the modern day. The picture was basically three two-reelers which Keaton cut into episodic parallels resembling a satirical *Intolerance*.

On November 20, 1923, *Our Hospitality*, the second Keaton feature, was released. It was filmed on location around Lake Tahoe. The picture captures a nostalgic slice of America (1810-31) and is devoid of the pessimism and underlying bitterness of Keaton's other work. Based on the famous feuding families, the Hatfields and the McCoys (renamed Canfield and McKay), *Our Hospitality* became a Keaton family affair. Wife Natalie was the heroine, and, besides Buster, his father and his young son appeared in the feature.

Buster's second son, Robert, was born on February 3, 1924. The same year he tried to help his fallen friend, Roscoe Arbuckle, regain a foothold in the film industry. Buster hired the blacklisted comedian to direct his 1924 film *Sherlock, Jr.* under the alias of Will B. Goodrich. Buster's philanthropy was a disaster and he took over the directorial reins for his shortest (slightly over 4,000 feet) feature film. Yet it proved to be among his very best. Fifty-one years later critic Judith Crist would call *Sherlock, Jr.* her favorite Keaton feature, adding, "It is funny and witty, sweet and gay, and in its technical mastery proves that a half century ago Keaton was master of all there was to know—or has since been learned—about the essential magic of the motion picture."

Sherlock, Jr. cast Buster as a motion picture projectionist and an amateur detective. In the title role, he utilized all of his acrobatic expertise in a virtuoso display of technique perfected over the years. His stunts included racing along on the handlebars of a motorcycle (unaware he has lost his driver), being propelled through an open window, and running* atop cars of a moving train to grab a water-tower rope that emptied an avalanche of water which knocked him onto the tracks. The showing of *Sherlock, Jr.* in 1975 caused *New York Times'* Vincent Canby to assess, "The major portion of the film is an extraordinarily funny sequence, breathtaking in its control of screen technique, in which the dreaming Buster literally walks in and out of the movie he's projecting, trying very earnestly to interfere with the action and being not at all surprised by the fast cuts within the film that carry him from the desert to the seashore to snowy Alpine slope in less time than it takes to describe."

* He experienced one of his rare physical injuries in his career when he fractured his neck while performing this stunt.

In Sherlock, Jr.
(1924).

The *Navigator* (1924) was co-directed by actor Donald Crisp and by Keaton. It became one of Buster's favorite endeavors, and with a gross of over $2 million was his biggest financial success. He offered a deft, comic performance as ineffectual millionaire Rollo Treadway, adrift on an ocean liner. The assortment of masterful, technically exciting sequences bolstered his reputation as one of the comedy kings of Hollywood's golden age. The *New York Times* admired his performance, which was reflected in his sphinx-like face, saying, "The wildest emotions are reflected by an occasional upward turn of his right eyebrow."

His first of two 1925 features was *Seven Chances*, a fast-paced six-reel comedy enlivened by his first use of Technicolor sequences. He played lawyer James Shannon confronted by the number seven. He is set to inherit $7 million on his 27th birthday *if* he is married by seven o'clock on that day. In the course of his misadventures he is besieged by a monstrous army of predatory brides (including Jean Arthur), but the film concludes with his marriage to his sweetheart (Ruth Dwyer). In his second 1925 picture Buster

was saved by Brown Eyes, a cow that plunged into heat on location and held up production on *Go West* for 10 days. Neither of Keaton's 1925 releases compared with that year's classic Chaplin, *The Gold Rush*, or Lloyd, *The Freshman*.

Through the years Buster was aware of the style differences between himself and his closest comedic competitors, Chaplin and Lloyd. But he was astonished when the three of them were acclaimed cinematic geniuses and their celluloid work was termed "art" and their films "classics." Only Chaplin seriously accepted the mantle of proclaimed genius. Chaplin and Lloyd did far outdistance Keaton in handling their productivity; astutely, both retained control of their films and amassed huge fortunes. Keaton's profligate spending, disinterest in the financial structure of the studio (Joseph Schenck relieved him of such mundane anxieties), and mounting personal problems brought him to the brink of destruction.

Charles Ruggles had made a Broadway hit in *Mr. Battling Butler*, the 1923 musical version of a play by Brightman, Melford, and Furber. Keaton bought the screen rights to the original show and in 1926 played effete Alfred Butler, masquerading as the world's lightweight boxing champion. *Battling Butler* was amusing if not overly memorable.

At the end of 1926 the first of three films Keaton made for United Artists release was completed. *The General* (1927) was based on William Pittenger's *The Great Locomotive Chase*. "I took that page of history and I stuck to it in all detail. I staged it exactly as it happened," said Keaton. The poetic yet massive sweep of the picture would honor D. W. Griffith. The authenticity of detail and the superb photography are still impressive. Keaton, who co-directed the feature with Clyde Bruckman, offered an expansive performance as Johnny Gray, a rejected locomotive engineer who finally wins acclaim and a commission in the Confederate Army. He is the plagued soul who tries to save his Civil War locomotive (The General) and becomes involved in an epic chase on the railway.

The General was filmed in Oregon and boasts many outstanding sequences. In the course of the comedy he fires The General across the lines into Union territory (a gag he later reconstructed without a locomotive for Red Skelton's *A Southern Yankee* (1948). There is also a misfired cannon which inadvertently destroys a dam whose unleashed deluge destroys the Union Army cavalry. Throughout the chase and battle, Buster retains his calm dead pan. James Agee caught the wonder of Keaton's face, writing that it "ranked almost with Lincoln's as an early American archetype; it was haunting, handsome, almost beautiful, yet it was irreducibly funny."

College (1927) gave Buster an opportunity to extend his physical and acrobatic prowess as Ronald, a mama's boy and bookworm who disastrously attempts intercollegiate athletics finally to win "the girl." The character was more of a Harold Lloyd lineage than Keaton, but has many delightful moments. Buster's final independently produced film was *Steamboat Bill, Jr.* (1928). Although well received in many quarters, the *New York Times* thought it was "a sorry affair" and that Keaton gave an "impersonation of a specimen so brainless that his actions are pathetic." It was typical of how unappreciated Buster was in his time.

Against the advice of both Chaplin and Lloyd, Buster followed Joe Schenck's suggestion to abandon his studio to join MGM. Keaton later claimed it was the worst mistake of his career—and it was! At the Culver City studio he lost his productive autonomy and was digested into the Metro-Goldwyn-Mayer assembly line. Metro's first script for Keaton was *Snapshots*, revised by an army of gag writers into *The Cameraman* (1928).* While on location in New York City studio executive Irving Thalberg approved Keaton's idea to disregard the script. With director Edward Sedgwick, they shot several explosively laugh-provoking sequences that saved the picture. But his next, *Spite Marriage* (1929), was restricted to studio regulations and was a fiasco. It had the shortest run of any feature at New York's Capitol Theatre, where it was yanked, after five showings, on Saturday, March 24, 1929. Seen today it is remarkably funny and Dorothy Sebastian proved to be his best leading lady.

Buster was one of MGM's star roster fortifying *The Hollywood Revue of 1929* and, under Frank Reicher's direction, repeated his sequence for the German version *Wir Schaltzen Um Auf Hollywood.* For his "talkie" debut Metro concocted a whirling farce laced with music, *Free and Easy* (1930). The Hollywood background story cast Buster as a sap from Gopher City, Kansas. Unlike those of other silent stars, his voice, inexpressively flat and resonant, fitted his screen image. *Photoplay* overenthused that "Little Frosty Face makes his audible debut in a whizzing comedy that has everything." The picture was popular (as were most talkies then which starred a "speaking" silent star) and was financially successful beyond its worth. Anita Page's and Robert Montgomery's roles were played by Raquel Torres and Don Alvarado in Buster's Spanish version of the picture *Estrelladoes.* Subtitles were added for a French *Free and Easy* called *Le Metteur en Scene.*

Doughboys (1930), his second talkie, was the last picture over which he had any semblance of control. It resembled his early silent work, with several of the screen's funniest gags. The picture teamed Keaton

---

* *The Cameraman* was remade as Red Skelton's less funny *Watch the Birdie* (1950).

With Harold Goodwin, Sidney Bracy, and Marceline Day in The Cameraman *(1928).*

with Cliff "Ukulele Ike" Edwards and Sally Eilers, the luscious love interest, and was well received. He also made a Spanish version, *De Frente Marchen!*, with Conchita Montenegro and Juan de Landa.

Just as his screen career was slipping, so was his personal life. Rumors of divorce proliferated in the tabloids. Then there was the headline-making incident when actress Kathleen Key made a manic and unprovoked wild attack on the comedian in his dressing room. It cost him $10,000 when he fractured the woman's jaw. She stated that she had been "manhandled." *Parlor, Bedroom and Bath* (1931),* an aging farce, was revived by the comic talents of Buster and Charlotte Greenwood. But Keaton's appraisal of his professional and private life was accurate, "There I was sitting on top of the world—on a toboggan." The downhill plunge was fast.

Not sure what to do with Keaton, Metro teamed him with its new contract personality, effervescent Jimmy Durante.* Their four features together were resounding flops. The first was *The Sidewalks of New York* which was copyrighted in September 1931 but not released because it was considered so poor. They were paired for a second time in *The Passionate Plumber* (1932), which was, of all things, a reworked version of Jeanne Eagels' Broadway hit *Her Cardboard Lover*, with Buster cast in the unlikely role played by Leslie Howard on stage. The result was not as bad as it might have been. More than a year after it was originally shot, *The Sidewalks of New York* was released under the new title *Speak Easily*. It and *What! No Beer?* (1933) were terrible and Keaton looked poorly. After these films, the

* He made a German version of *Parlor, Bedroom and Bath* with Marion Lessing and Françoise Rosay, *Casanova wider Willen.*

* Buster has often been credited with working for Mack Sennett. But the closest he came to any association with him was in the two-reel short *The Stolen Jools* (1931), an all-star effort to raise funds for a tuberculosis sanatorium. Buster played a Keystone Kop.

screen teaming was forgotten. During the making of the last celluloid bomb, Keaton's personal problems, divorce, and drinking plagued him. He also received a letter from Louis B. Mayer informing him his services were no longer required by MGM.

On August 8, 1932, Natalie Talmadge Keaton received her interlocutory decree in the divorce suit. Without contest from Buster she received virtually everything he had accumulated in his show-business life, including their Beverly Hills home—a $300,000 Italian villa—and custody of their sons. She legally changed their surnames to Talmadge. Keaton's drinking led to confinement in a sanatorium. On January 8, 1933, he married nurse Mae Elizabeth Scribbens Hawley in Ensenada, Mexico. He told reporters in March that the secret marriage "may not be legal in the U.S. but it's okay in Mexico." When Natalie's final decree became effective on August 10, 1933, Buster was remarried to Mae at Ventura, California, on October 21, 1933. Two years later, on October 4, 1935, Buster and his second wife were divorced.

Hollywood offered Buster no work, but in France he filmed *Le Roi des Champs-Elysees* (1934). He went to England to film *The Invader* (1934), which was released in the U.S. in 1936 as *An Old Spanish Custom*. When he returned to America, Educational Pictures offered Keaton a chance to star in a series of two-reel comedies. Starting with *The Gold Ghost* and *Allez Oop* in 1934 and ending with *Love Nest on Wheels* in 1937, he made 16 pleasant, if undistinguished, shorts. At MGM he was in a 19-minute color two-reeler, *La Fiesta de Santa Barbara* (1936), with Gary Cooper, Harpo Marx, Robert Taylor, Ida Lupino, et al. On the Metro lot in 1938 he directed three one-reel shorts and served as gag writer on Clark Gable's *Too Hot to Handle*. The next year he began a series of 10 two-reel shorts for Columbia that continued through 1941. Over at Twentieth Century–Fox in 1939 he collaborated on two of the Jones Family series and appeared in *Hollywood Cavalcade*, belting Alice Faye in the face with a well-aimed custard pie.

With Dorothy Christy in Parlor, Bedroom and Bath *(1931).*

With Irene Purcell and Gilbert Roland in The Passionate Plumber *(1932).*

Keaton's personal life took an upturn in 1940 when he married dancer Eleanor Norris on May 29. He played minor roles in two RKO feature comedies that year and returned to the stage for a stint in *Charlot's Revue* for British War Relief. In the summer of 1941 Buster returned to the East Coast for his first appearance on stage in a straight play. He opened July 7, 1941, in *The Gorilla*, with former Hollywood comic Harry Gribbon, and continued on the summer stages in the play *Mr. and Mrs. North*. His work in Twentieth Century–Fox's multi-episode *Tales of Manhattan* (1942—with W. C. Fields and Margaret Dumont) was cut from the final print. But the next year (1943) he was seen on screen as Sir Cedric Hardwicke's assistant in RKO's all-star *Forever and a Day* (filmed in the autumn of 1941). He was fine as a bored bus driver taking his passengers for a joyride in Universal's fluffy comedy *San Diego, I Love You* (1944).

In 1946 Buster played a supporting role in Screen Guild's *God's Country* and the lead in a Mexican production, *El Moderno Barba Azul,* and had his original story "Lambs Will Gamble" adapted into a three-act play. The show did not survive its road tryout. Brief roles in a few other Forties features were augmented by serving as adviser or comedy consultant on two of Metro's Esther Williams entries and a pair of Red Skelton comedies. In June 1949 he returned East to play the lead in summer stock in the play *Three Men on a Horse.*

For Billy Wilder's beautifully executed *Sunset Boulevard* (1950) Keaton appeared as one of four bridge players (with silent stars H. B. Warner and Anna Q. Nilsson) at Norma Desmond's (Gloria Swanson) home. The ending of Chaplin's effective *Limelight* (1952) contains a treasured sketch between fallen music-hall comedian Calvera and his bumbling assistant. Buster was impeccably right as the pianist-stooge who is unable to control both the sheet music and the keyboard. There were flashes of his once great comic brilliance in the brief but effective appearance.

Television proved a bonanza for Keaton. He was a prized guest star on Ed Sullivan's variety telecast, with Ed Wynn (a good team), and on other major network telecasts. In England he played a straight dramatic role in *The Awakening*. Back in the U.S., on TV's "Best of Broadway" he was prim Dr. Bradley trying to sell his massive memoirs to Monty Woolley in *The Man Who Came to Dinner.*

The world's present and future generations owe a debt of gratitude to Raymond Rohauer, who in 1954, while manager of the Society of Cinema Arts in Los Angeles, came to Buster's aid. He helped the former star restore his decomposing nitrate films, and established a corporation through which Keaton would regain control of his productions. He later arranged for highly acclaimed European showings of the comedian's great silent comedies.

The first annual George Eastman Festival of Fine Arts at Rochester, New York, honored six of the silent screen's stars in November 1955. Lillian Gish, Mary Pickford, Mae Marsh, Harold Lloyd, Richard Barthelmess, and Buster Keaton were presented with gold plaques "for distinguished contri-

butions to the art of motion pictures." By 1959 the Academy of Motion Picture Arts and Sciences finally recognized Keaton by awarding him an honorary statuette "for his unique talent which brought immortal comedies to the screen."

Michael Todd cast Keaton as the train conductor, one of many cameo roles, in *Around the World in 80 Days* (1956). With money received from Paramount for the screen rights to his life story and serving as technical consultant on the picture, Buster bought a small home on one and a quarter acres in the San Fernando Valley. Unfortunately, *The Buster Keaton Story* (1957), despite Donald O'Connor's strenuous efforts trying to re-create Keaton, did not work.

For two seasons Buster toured the nation's stages in the musical *Once Upon a Mattress*. He starred in this 1960–61 showcase with Dody Goodman and with Mrs. Buster Keaton as Lady Mabelle. The critics reveled in Buster's mastery of pantomime, "Buster Keaton is perfection in the role of the mute king who takes delight in pinching the ladies of the court." Through May 1964, when he ap-

With Dorothy Appleby and Beatrice Blinn in the short subject Nothing But Pleasure *(1939).*

peared on a segment of "Burke's Law," he was seen on TV in several of the top network series programs.

His Sixties feature appearances were a mixed blessing. He had a brief role as a lion tamer in a musical version of *The Adventures of Huckleberry Finn* (1960). Hopes that the Canadian-made *Ten Girls* (1962) would bolster his career vanished when the film ended up unreleased. For Stanley Kramer's funsters convention, *It's a Mad, Mad, Mad, Mad World* (1963), Buster made a brief appearance as Jimmy the crook. While being acclaimed in Europe through Raymond Rohauer's restoration of his classic silent films,* Buster was appearing in minor, campy roles in a quartet of mindless programmers geared to the teenage trade in the United States. He filmed a series of short pictures in Canada: *The Railrodder, Buster Keaton Rides Again*, and *The Scribe*. In Italy he made *Due Marinese e Uno Generale*

(1965), which was released in the U.S. in 1967 as *War Italian Style*. His last screen appearance was as Erronius in *A Funny Thing Happened on the Way to the Forum* (1966).

On Tuesday, February 1, 1966, Buster succumbed to lung cancer. The twilight of his life was peaceful and he survived to witness a renaissance of his immeasurable contributions to cinematic art. At age 70 Buster's sagging, woeful face resembled a resigned basset hound but his energies and lively mind persisted. A year before his death he told reporters, "I have so many projects coming up, I haven't time to think about kicking the bucket." Following funeral services on February 4, 1966, Buster was buried in the Hollywood Hills Cemetery.

Recurring rediscovery of Keaton's screen canon has inspired volumes and many columns of intense critical rhetoric, all geared to qualifying and clarifying Keaton's proper niche in the history of screen comedy. Fortunately, his films are available for succeeding generations to enjoy, appraise, and reevaluate. They can discover anew one of the screen's greatest and most inventive laughmakers.

* Keaton's granite emotional control was reduced to tears in 1965 when at the culmination of the Venice Film Festival he appeared on stage following screenings of his films to receive a 20-minute standing ovation from fellow professionals.

FEATURE FILMS

The Saphead (*Metro 1920*)
Three Ages (*Metro 1923*)
Our Hospitality (*Metro 1923*)
Sherlock, Jr. (*Metro 1924*)
The Navigator (*Metro-Goldwyn 1924*)
Seven Chances (*Metro-Goldwyn 1925*)
Go West (*Metro-Goldwyn 1925*)
Battling Butler (*MGM 1926*)
The General (*United Artists 1927*)
College (*United Artists 1927*)
Steamboat Bill, Jr. (*United Artists 1928*)
The Cameraman (*MGM 1928*)
Spite Marriage (*MGM 1929*)
The Hollywood Revue of 1929 (*MGM 1929*)
Wir Schaltzen Um Auf Hollywood (*MGM 1929*) [German version of The Hollywood Revue of 1929]
Free and Easy (*MGM 1930*)
Estrellados (*MGM 1930*) [Spanish version of Free and Easy]

Le Metteur en Scene (*MGM 1930*) [Subtitled French version of Free and Easy]
Doughboys (*MGM 1930*)
De Frante Marchen! (*MGM 1930*) [Spanish version of Doughboys]
Parlor, Bedroom and Bath (*MGM 1931*)
Casanova wider Willen (*MGM 1931*) [German version of Parlor, Bedroom and Bath]
Buster Se Marie (*MGM 1931*) [French version of Parlor, Bedroom and Bath]
Sidewalks of New York (*MGM 1931*)
The Passionate Plumber (*MGM 1932*)
Speak Easily (*MGM 1932*)
What! No Beer? (*MGM 1933*)
Le Roi des Champs-Elysees (*French 1934*)
The Invader [An Old Spanish Custom] (*MGM British 1936*)
Hollywood Cavalcade (*20th Century-Fox 1939*)
The Villain Still Pursued Her (*RKO 1940*)

Li'l Abner (*RKO 1940*)

Tales of Manhattan (*20th Century-Fox 1942*) [deleted from release print]

Forever and a Day (*RKO 1943*)

San Diego, I Love You (*Universal 1944*)

That's the Spirit (*Universal 1945*)

That Night with You (*Universal 1945*)

El Moderno Barba Azul (*Mexican 1946*)

God's Country (*Screen Guild 1946*)

The Loveable Cheat (Film Classics 1949)

In the Good Old Summertime (*MGM 1949*)

You're My Everything (*20th Century-Fox 1949*)

Sunset Boulevard (*Paramount 1950*)

Limelight (*United Artists 1952*)

L'Incantevole Nemica [Pattes de Velours] (*Italian 1952*)

Around the World in 80 Days (*United Artists 1956*)

The Adventures of Huckleberry Finn (*MGM 1960*)

Ten Girls Ago (*Canadian 1962*) [unreleased]

It's a Mad, Mad, Mad, Mad World (*United Artists 1963*)

Pajama Party (*American International 1964*)

Beach Blanket Bingo (*American International 1965*)

Due Marinese e Uno Generale [War Italian Style] (*Italian 1965*)

How to Stuff a Wild Bikini (*American International 1965*)

Sergeant Deadhead (*American International 1965*)

A Funny Thing Happened on the Way to the Forum (*United Artists 1966*)

With Guinn "Big Boy" Williams in Kelly the Second (1936).

Patsy Kelly

Rambunctious, rough-and-tumble, wise-cracking Patsy Kelly was starring on Broadway when Hal Roach persuaded her in 1933 to go to Hollywood as ZaSu Pitts' replacement in a series of screen comedy shorts with Thelma Todd. The Todd-Pitts two-reelers had been popular and profitable. But Miss Pitts sought screen opportunities in features and Roach found in the uninhibited Patsy the perfect contrasting partner for lovely poised Miss Todd. The Todd-Kelly comedies were even more successful than the Todd-Pitts combine. One good reason for this commercial improvement was the incongruous pairing of cool, blonde, refined, and beautiful Thelma Todd with the raucous, loud Patsy. The latter's 5'3" frame tended toward plumpness. She had sparkling brown eyes and straight black hair which she wore casually, pushed behind near-Gablesque ears.

Her contract with Roach permitted assignments with other studios. Soon Patsy was adding zest and laughter to many Thirties features. Her expert timing and broad comedy antics, which brushed with slapstick, sustained and embellished many features.

Eventually she was reduced to an almost standard casting as an impertinent household servant, cook, or maid. Patsy's native Irish wit was undimmed by her screen domestic status. She averred, "I had a maid's costume that fit. They didn't have to get me a new outfit. They lent it from one studio to another."

John and Delia Kelly migrated to America from Ballinrobe, County Mayo, Ireland. John became a New York cop and settled his family in Manhattan on 62nd Street between 9th and 10th Avenues. Patsy, the sixth of the Kelly brood, was born on Friday, January 21, 1910, in Brooklyn. She was christened Sarah Veronica Rose Kelly. Her early years were noted for an incredible ability to be hit by automobiles without serious injuries or even abrasions and for an inordinate fascination for fire engines. The family nicknamed her "The Patsy." Years later Patsy admitted, "You know, if we'd had women's lib, I'd have been a fireman. That's what I wanted to be, and the local chief got hold of my mother and said she ought to get me off the streets." Mrs. Kelly heeded the man's advice. Knowing her youngest's innate talent for dancing, she packed her off to Jack Blue's dancing school.

At Blue's school Patsy enthusiastically learned tap dancing and became friends with another 10-year-old Irish girl, Ruby Keeler, who was from Nova Scotia. Two years later Patsy was teaching dancing to new arrivals at Blue's school and at 13 was earning $18 a week as a staff instructor. Her brother Willie had show-business aspirations and Patsy taught him to dance. When Willie was hired by Frank Fay's vaudeville act, Patsy went from Blue's 51st Street studio downtown to the famed Palace Theatre to coach her brother in his routines. Fay, watching the two of them working out, dismissed Willie and hired Patsy.

Frank Fay was a suave, attractive, red-headed Irishman who pioneered the status of master of ceremonies. Fay was also among the first of the stand-up sophisticated comedians and his style was later captured with greater success and nuance by Bob Hope and Jack Benny. Mr. Fay was also an egomaniac of gargantuan dimensions, a man of deep vanity and a memorable capacity for alcohol, a master of timing, and a person with few peers in the art of monologue. He was also a notorious ad-libber. Fay's Palace Theatre act included George Haggerty, Lew Mann, and the scraggy-haired Patsy. They were held over for 11 weeks.

Reflecting on her show-business initiation, Patsy said, "I started at the top and worked my way down. Fay was a great wit and I owe him a lot, but he could be cruel. He never had a script and would just spring lines on you. His tutelage was the most valuable in the world for an amateur. He nearly wore out your toes making you stand on them. He was apt to ad-lib all over the place. He might start talking about anything from pears to presidents. It always seemed to me that I was standing on the stage with my hand out—waiting for my cue to drop. I led with my chin because my knees were helpless." Years later, many of Patsy's biggest screen laughs were often ad-libs sprung from her early training with Fay, which schooling formidably combined with her own natural quick wit. While Patsy was with Fay, Frank would bawl her out *on stage,* and fire her several times a week. Yet she managed to withstand the fiery redhead's temper for

several seasons and made her Broadway stage debut when their successful vaudeville act was engaged for *Harry Delmar's Revels.*

Revels opened on November 28, 1927, on Broadway, featuring Frank Fay with Jeanne Hackett, Lillian Roth, and another vaudeville headliner team, Lahr and Mercedes, making their Broadway debut. Bert Lahr received the show's best notices. That rankled Mr. Fay, who deemed the ex-burlesque clown a low comedian. Interpolated into the revue was the hilarious "Tea Time" sketch Fay, Patsy, and Lew Mann had performed at the Palace. After 112 performances, *Delmar's Revels* left Broadway for a road tour. Patsy, feeling more at ease with the egocentric star, made the fatal error of addressing him as "Frank." He fired her on the spot. Less than a year later, Fay would marry former chorus girl Ruby Stevens, who attained stardom on Broadway as Barbara Stanwyck.

Meanwhile, Patsy signed with producer Charles Dillingham for a new Fred Stone show. But on August 4, 1928, Stone was critically injured in an airplane crash and his close friend Will Rogers offered to replace him. Rogers' heartwarming gesture captured the imagination of Broadway and the country. After a few weeks of rehearsal, the show opened at the Globe Theatre in New York on October 15, 1928. *Three Cheers* was a rollicking hit and Patsy's nimble wit was egged on by Rogers, a master at the art of asides and impromptu dialogue.

As Bobbie Bird, Patsy was paired in the show with comedian Andrew Tombes. *Time* magazine wrote, "Aside from Will Rogers, the best thing in *Three Cheers* is Patsy Kelly, who fixes her beady and inspired eyes upon a comedian and sings '[Because] You're Beautiful' in a scratchy voice." The show was Will Rogers' last Broadway musical and served to awaken critical acclaim for the talents of Miss Kelly. After 210 performances in New York, *Three Cheers* took to the road, closing in Pittsburgh on June 1, 1929.

A month later Patsy opened on Broadway in Earl Carroll's *Sketch-Book.* The show generously showcased her comedic talents as a maid, a factory flapper, a housewife, and a dueter of song—"Fascinating You"—with comedian William Demarest. *Sketch-Book* ran 400 performances and on July 1, 1930, Patsy transferred to Earl Carroll's eighth edition of his *Vanities*. In Earl Carroll's *Vanities* she was teamed with Herb Williams and Jimmy Savo and the great Jack Benny. When *Vanities* completed its 215-performance run, Patsy signed for what was heralded as "the great event of the theatrical year."

The "great event" was Al Jolson's return to the Broadway stage as master of ceremonies in *The Wonder Bar*. The musical carried an interesting story on which to hinge various vaudeville turns. Patsy was cast as an entertainer, Electra Pivonka, danced an ersatz tango with Jolson, and soloed a funny number, "The Dying Flamingo." The Parisian cabaret revue included lovely silent screen actress Claire Windsor and English comedian Arthur Treacher. Recalling the opening night, March 17, 1931, Patsy has said, "Jolson had an eye out for everything due him. His billing had to be 10 feet high. A half-inch too short and he'd explode. On opening night of *Wonder Bar*, I found him sitting out in the alley, crying, 'I won't go on! They are persecuting me!' I practically dragged him into the theater and the instant that spotlight was on him he forgot all his fears and tremors. But he had them!"

Wonder Bar was no great event. It folded after 76 performances, but played another year on the road (with a pair of wild Russians in the cast, Akim Tamiroff and Leonid Kinskey). Business was brisk, and after playing the show in San Francisco in April 1932, Patsy returned to her home base. She was back at the fabled Palace in a vaudeville bit opening April 24, 1932. In late summer she signed for a new Howard Dietz–Arthur Schwartz revue. It would be her first Broadway starring role.

Flying Colors had problems getting off the ground. There were the deplorable rehearsals, the replacement of then novice choreographer Agnes DeMille with Albertina Rasch, Norman Bel Geddes' alleged unsafe sets (one collapsed in Philadelphia during tryouts but no one was injured), and the nervous breakdown of producer Max Gordon. The show opened at Philadelphia's Forrest Theatre on August 22, 1932, starring Clifton Webb, Charles Butterworth, *and* Patsy Kelly. The cast included two delightful young dancers, Vilma and Buddy Ebsen, as well as Tamara Geva, Larry Adler, and Imogene Coca. Patsy

was a better foil for deadpan comedian Charles Butterworth than could be expected. Her singing of "Fatal Fascination" was a comedy gem. She was exceptionally funny in a "Bon Voyage" sketch in which she is "driven beyond human endurance, [and] turns savagely on the folks who have come to see her off."

But despite the cast's excellence, a delightful score, and Bel Geddes' imaginative staging, the show was a languid affair and failed to please the critics when it opened on Broadway on September 15, 1932. It lasted for 188 performances. While Max Gordon regained his health, *Flying Colors* lost its cost of $125,000.

Hal Roach's movie offer did not impress Miss Kelly. She told her friends she would be a flop. "Besides, I don't like 'em and I never did believe there was a place called Hollywood. Somebody made it up!" A more incongruous replacement for ZaSu Pitts could not have been found. When Patsy was informed of ZaSu's expertise in waving her helpless hands for comedic effects, Kelly came back with, "Maybe I can wave my ears!" Her first short* with Thelma Todd set her near slapstick style for the series. She was directed to act a clumsy cluck, fall from a stage into a bass drum in the orchestra pit, and be a real "Patsy." Kelly eyed director Gus Meins and cracked, "I think you've got me mixed up with Toto the Clown!" Mixed up or not, the Kelly-Todd comedies, starting with the September 1933 two-reeler *Beauty and the Bus* and continuing for 20 more shorts through January 1936, were fun. In many ways, they were more sparkling than the ZaSu Pitts–Thelma Todd two-reel output.

Patsy's enthusiasm and work in the Roach comedies blossomed and she was telling the press, "I'm supposed to make eight comedies a year, but I'm not very sure about the number. The average shooting time for one short is five days and they usually shoot two, sometimes three shorts in a row—so it's a little hard to keep track of them. I'm sure they could slip in an extra series of six on me and I'd never know the difference. With all this work you'd think I'd at least be rewarded with a little loss of weight. But no—I'm round

---

* While playing in *Wonder Bar*, Patsy made a one-reel Vitaphone short, *The Grand Dame* (1931).

and healthy as ever. There's a saying, you know, that 'you can't kill a Kelly.'" Patsy's success in the Roach comedies soon brought requests from major studios for supporting roles in top features. Her first feature was *Going Hollywood* (1933), with Marion Davies and Bing Crosby, in which she played an aspiring studio extra offering solace and a room to fellow player Marion. *Screenland* magazine wrote, "*Going Hollywood* has grand dialogue, and a knockout bit by the promising comedienne Patsy Kelly." The magazine also cited Kelly and Crosby for giving two of the month's best performances in the picture.

Apart from her short subjects, Patsy's comedic talents were given occasional bright display. She was Jean Harlow's pal in MGM's *The Girl from Missouri* (1934) and provided much needed comedy relief in the Al Jolson–Ruby Keeler starrer *Go into Your Dance* (1935). When Patsy's pal Marion Davies moved to Warner Bros. from Metro, Kelly joined her in *Page Miss Glory* (1935). Patsy joined with Alice Faye and Frances Langford as a trio "sister" singing act involved with George Raft in *Every Night at Eight* (1935). Fox's *Thanks a Million* (1935) provided Patsy with a showy role; it was an unusually good musical featuring Dick Powell, Fred Allen, Paul Whiteman & His Orchestra, and Ann Dvorak. Patsy and Dvorak dueted the song "Sugar Plum" in the proceedings. It was one of Patsy's best feature films.

The sudden, mysterious death* on December 16, 1935, of Thelma Todd shocked the

---

* In early 1937 Patsy would reveal to Sara Hamilton of *Movie Mirror* magazine, "You see, something, darned if I know what it is, has happened to me since I came to this crazy town. Everyone I loved, turned to, needed has gone, just like Thelma. It was Jean Malin, that swell New York actor and impersonator, first. I'd been a friend of Jean and his wife for years in New York. Then I went down to the Ship Cafe that night of Jean's appearance. I glanced up at the flashing sign over the door that said 'Jean Malin's Last Night' and as clearly as I'm hearing you, a voice said, 'Be careful. It *is* his last night.'

"He backed the car into the ocean off the end of the pier just one hour later. We all were submerged in the water. Adrenalin worked with me. It didn't with Jean.

"And then came Thelma. She gave me everything I needed. Got me on my feet. Gave me confidence and true friendship. And then she went.

"I had Ralph Farnum, my agent, left. He took me in hand, fought my battles, and gave me advice. He went, too, just a few weeks ago. I think he tried to tell me he was going for he kept advising me about investments, and the future. But Thelma is always near me."

film colony and Patsy lost a friend and co-star. Hal Roach teamed perky Pert Kelton with Patsy in a two-reel short, *Pan Handlers* (1936), but the combination of Kelly-Kelton did not succeed. Effervescent, blonde, charming Lyda Roberti was Roach's next selection to replace Miss Todd and the delightful Lyda worked well with Kelly in two of Patsy's last two-reelers in 1936. The new team was also in Roach's feature *Nobody's Baby* (1937), playing student nurses who solve a mystery and romance Robert Armstrong and Lynne Overman.

Fox was delighted with Kelly's work in *Thanks a Million* and continued borrowing her from Roach. She became virtually the comic female lead at a studio where she was *not* under contract. She was Gracie in a wilted Loretta Young–Robert Taylor feature, *Private Number* (1936), maintained her own zestful pace against such clowns as the Ritz Brothers, Ted Healy, and Adolphe Menjou in *Sing, Baby, Sing* (1936), and was the comic lead opposite Stuart Erwin in Fox's entertaining *Pigskin Parade* (1936). Studio head Darryl F. Zanuck recalled Kelly for her first starring feature-film role, as Molly Kelly backing boxer Guinn "Big Boy" Williams to the world championship in *Kelly the Second* (1936).

The phony but amusing feud between Walter Winchell and band leader Ben Bernie was carried over to the screen in Fox's *Wake Up and Live* (1937) and Kelly was cast as Winchell's girl Friday. Having a brief bit in the picture was a new screen comedienne, Joan Davis. When the less successful sequel to the Winchell-Bernie film was made, Davis inherited Patsy's role in *Love and Hisses*. By the end of the year Darryl Zanuck was telling the press, "Before this year [1938] is out Miss Davis will have won number one ranking as a comedienne." The multitalented Joan Davis soon replaced the sought-after Patsy in 20th's celluloid comedies. Her popularity at the box office would exceed Patsy's and even that of Paramount's Martha Raye.

Roach produced a giddy comedy that often sparkled with hilarity. *Pick a Star* (1937) was a travesty on Hollywood and Patsy was Nellie Moore, playing opposite Jack Haley, Mischa Auer, and Lyda Roberti. After appearing in Marion Davies' final film, *Ever Since Eve* (1937), Patsy played one of her

With Leo White, Eddy Conrad, Thelma Todd, and Rolfe Sedan in the short subject Done in Oil *(1934).*

first celluloid domestics. She was Rosa, the outspoken cook, in the Hal Roach–MGM zany *Merrily We Live* (1938), an attempt to duplicate the success (and almost the story) of *My Man Godfrey*.

By the time of *There Goes My Heart* (1938), producer Hal Roach was releasing his product through United Artists. In this film Patsy had a solid part as a shopgirl who befriends runaway heiress Virginia Bruce. *Photoplay* reported, "Patsy Kelly gets most of the laughs and manages to lift the show from the elegant Miss Bruce and the bewildered Fredric [March]." Kelly stayed on the United Artists' releasing charts with Sam Goldwyn's old-fashioned and dull *The Cowboy and the Lady* (1938). Gary Cooper and Merle Oberon had the top roles and Patsy played Oberon's cook. But even her comic antics, combined with Walter Brennan and Fuzzy Knight, could not enliven the ponderous and silly script.

When Twentieth Century–Fox decided to reuse the overworked play *The Gorilla* for a 1939 Ritz Brothers screen comedy, the com-edy trio quit, yet returned to fulfill their contract with unhappy results. Patsy played terrified Kitty but the whole cast was victimized by the script. She fared better in Hal Roach's *Road Show* (1941) being pursued by an Indian (George E. Stone).

Roach's successful *Topper* feature-film series continued with *Topper Returns* (1941) with Patsy stereotyped as the terrified maid. Roach then teamed both of Thelma Todd's filmmates, Patsy and ZaSu Pitts, in a mild comedy, *Broadway Limited* (1941). For RKO, Patsy was John Barrymore's press agent in *Playmates* (1941), remaining at that studio for a supporting role in *Sing Your Worries Away* (1942). She had been at Republic for *The Hit Parade of 1941* (1941) and returned there to appear in tandem with explosive Edgar Kennedy in John Wayne's *In Old California* (1942). *Photoplay* was stirred to remark, "Patsy Kelly and Edgar Kennedy are cute—Edgar is the cuter!"

In the spring of 1942 Patsy signed for a cross-country tour in a tabloid version of *Meet the People*. The "tab" version starred

361

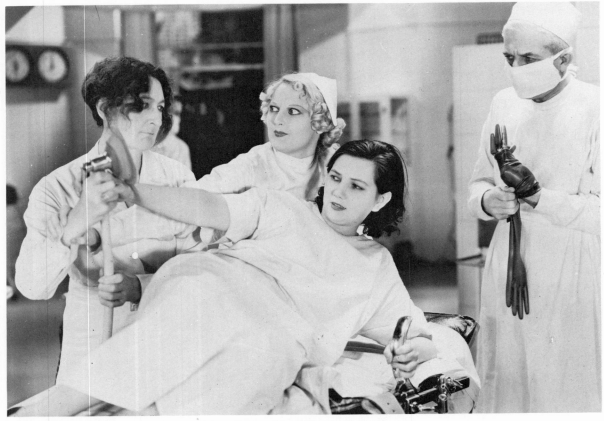

With Thelma Todd in the short subject Opened by Mistake *(1934).*

Patsy, Charles "Buddy" Rogers, and Joey Faye and played presentation houses to appreciative reception. In 1943 Patsy was on screen as Max Baer's wife in an RKO baseball mishmash, *Ladies' Day.* She then made two clinkers that year for Producers Releasing Corporation: *My Son, the Hero* and *Danger! Women at Work.*

By now Patsy's Hollywood days were over and she went into semiretirement to cope with "personal problems." She emerged in the summer of 1947 to join Bert Wheeler, Lou Holtz, Diosa Costello, and Barry Wood in *A Midsummer Night's Scream,* staged at Nicky Blair's Carnival in the Hotel Capitol at 51st and 8th Avenue in New York City. Summer stock provided occasional income and Patsy toured in *My Sister Eileen* and as Hildy, the tough cabdriver, in *On the Town.** The year

* Nancy Walker had created the role on Broadway. The two comediennes had a comparable out-of-the-corner-of-the-mouth wisecracking, gravelly voiced delivery and a basic rough-hewn comedic stance, although their ethnic background was different and Walker's talents are more extensive than Patsy's.

1950 found Patsy, along with Ilka Chase, Jimmy Dykes, and host Al Capp, on the CBS-TV game show "Anyone Can Win."

In the early Fifties, blowsy Patsy became a member of Tallulah Bankhead's household and accompanied her very close friend to Las Vegas for Tallulah's cabaret debut, serving as dresser, companion, and confidante. In the late summer of 1953 Patsy co-starred with Jack Albertson in a new revue, *High Time,* at the Grist Mill Playhouse in Andover, New Jersey, and was sustained by her guest-resident status at Miss Bankhead's home. About her pal Tallulah, Patsy said, "Having her for a friend was like waltzing with an atomic bomb. She was just tremendous. The energy of 20 truck drivers. She could be a lady of the world and mad as a March hare. She threw away better lines than Neil Simon ever wrote. She could swear so as to shake the building and would be a great and gracious hostess. Her idea of poverty was having to run her own tub. In all kinds of weak plays the magic of her name brought crowds to the theater. I was with her in *Dear Charles*. No masterpiece!"

Patsy played Madame Bouchemin in a 1955 road tour of *Dear Charles*. (Hilarious Alice Pearce had the role on Broadway.) It helped Patsy to see her way clear to overcoming personal problems and to making fresh inroads into the field of show business.

Patsy's generosity to friends over the years was rewarded in her leaner financial years when friends took care of her. In 1960 she was asked to play the maid-housekeeper-babysitter in the Doris Day–David Niven screen comedy *Please Don't Eat the Daisies*. The same year she was Gertrude, an actor's agent who is one of the plane passengers, in *The Crowded Sky*. She tried television, appearing in 1960 on the "Laramie" series. Over the next few years other small-screen outings occurred and in 1966 she was in the theatrical film *Ghost in the Invisible Bikini*, one of *those* beach-party pictures turned out by American International.

Each year there seemed to be a few guest appearances by Patsy on TV (in 1966 she was in the CBS-TV series pilot "My Son, the Doctor") and in films (she had a role in the inconsequential *C'mon, Let's Live a Little* at Paramount in 1967). She was in a major film in 1968 when she played Laura Louise, one of a coven of witches, in *Rosemary's Baby* (1968). Her astute playing of the overweight babysitter, who wears a pair of ominous thick-lensed glasses while knitting away at a sweater for the devil's offspring, made it obvious Patsy could play a serious character role. But Patsy refused to take anything too seriously. She cracked about the film, "I felt I should sprinkle holy water on the set!"

The year 1970 became the year of Kelly. She had one line in the opening segment of a new teleseries, "Barefoot in the Park," and did a cameo role in a deplorable waste of film for Warner Bros., *The Phynx*. Then her agent, Gloria Safier, landed her the showy comedy maid role in the revival of *No, No, Nanette*. Patsy went on a crash diet, and to compound her joy, her beloved Ruby Keeler had consented to return to Broadway in *Nanette*. After unbelievable tribulations throughout

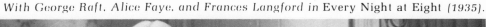

With George Raft, Alice Faye, and Frances Langford in Every Night at Eight *(1935).*

Advertisement for *Wake Up and Live* (1937).

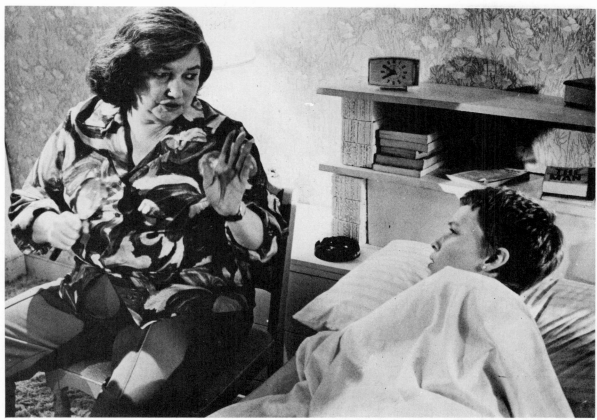

With Mia Farrow in Rosemary's Baby *(1968).*

the rehearsal of *No, No, Nanette* the show was taking shape, even if two songs ("My Doctor" and "Don't Turn Your Back on a Bluebird") written for Kelly were discarded. Imperturbable Patsy could not have cared less. She was not eager to sing in the show.

Pauline the maid of *No, No, Nanette* was a comic character Kelly could play with her eyes closed. She became one of the show's biggest hits. The "New 1925 Musical" opened in Boston to loud hallelujahs. Patsy recalled, "When people heard that Ruby and I were going into a revival of *No, No, Nanette,* what, they wanted to know, are you two old bags gonna do? You can hardly walk and you're gonna dance!" About opening night in Boston, "I got duck bumps. I heard a lot of banging out front and I said to Ruby, 'Let's get outta here, honey. They're coming to get us.'" The noise out front was the audience giving the inspired company a standing ovation, an occurrence that continued through the tryout tour of Toronto, Philadelphia, and Baltimore (on Christmas Day there, Patsy, billowing in

a Santa Claus suit complete with whiskers, passed out grab-bag gifts to the company).

No, No, Nanette opened on Broadway January 19, 1971, and thereupon began a phenomenal love affair between audiences and performers. The show won the hearts of everyone. For the hard-drinking, fun-loving Patsy it was a personal victory. Gone were such comments as "Is she still around?" and "I thought she was dead," which had preceded her casting. When the 25th Tony Awards were nationally televised from the Palace Theatre in New York on Sunday March 28, 1971, Patsy accepted the Award for the Best Supporting Actress in a Musical Play. It happened on the stage where she started in show business as a child stooging for Frank Fay.

Patsy accepted the award and used her time to praise her lifelong friend, "Without our beloved Ruby Keeler there would be no *No, No, Nanette.*" She concluded her acceptance speech with, "I'm going home now and faint."

Patsy was extremely funny as Pauline the maid. Columnist Earl Wilson would devote a newspaper spread to her in his *New York Post* slot, calling her "A Maid for All Reasons." He wrote, "Of all the stars named Kelly—and there have been Gene, Grace, Al, and Nancy—none is greater than Patsy who for a year and half has been making audiences roar as she plays a clumsy, lumpy, rebellious maid servant. . . ." He mentioned her cries of outrage when she had to answer the door, shouting, "You name it. I've cleaned it," and how on stage she was constantly threatening to quit her domestic's job to find one more suitable to her personality. In the show's finale, Kelly joined the company for a brief, shuffling soft-shoe routine. Frequently, out of the corner of her mouth she would mumble to her dear friend, "Eat your heart out, Ruby!" At 61 Patsy was rocking Broadway in her biggest hit. The show ran 861 performances and closed February 4, 1973.

Patsy was immediately cast as Mrs. O'Dare for Debbie Reynolds' *Irene.* Her playing in *Irene* was broad and she milked the role for all it was worth. But her outrageous camping of the part delighted audiences. Patsy remained with *Irene* from its opening at the Minskoff Theatre in New York on March 13, 1973, through the run (which saw Jane Powell replace Reynolds). On the long arduous road tour Patsy was rejoined by Debbie Reynolds and they concluded their stint in Southern California. During the summer of 1975, she toured again as Irene's broadly comic "mom," repeating the role yet again in November 1976 at the California Theatre of Performing Arts (in San Bernardino), teamed with Jane Powell once more.

Early in 1974 Patsy had made a pilot for a projected TV series, "The Cop and the Kid." She played Mrs. Murphy, the mother of a bachelor cop (Charles Durning). Patsy was enthusiastic about the series, which premiered on November 4, 1975, on NBC-TV to less than gaudy greetings. At the end of December 1975 Patsy left the touring company of *Irene* to continue her running role in the TV series. One reviewer acknowledged Patsy's great boost to the situation comedy, summing up the show with, "Kelly remains her own best tribute."

After the demise of "The Cop and the Kid" California-based Patsy made her first feature for Buena Vista, appearing in *Freaky Friday* (1976), starring Jodie Foster and Barbara Harris. Late in 1977 Patsy returned to the Walt Disney film studio to appear with Cloris Leachman and Barbara Harris in the Buena Vista release *North Avenue Irregulars* (1978). During recent years Patsy has found time to appear at various film-buff conclaves, seemingly thrilled that she is so affectionately remembered. More recently she has joined with Jean Kean for a comedy club act.

Someone once said about Patsy, "The little Irish comedienne knows just one thing. How to get laughs. It is more than a job. It is her life." Patsy's education was the stage. She learned from great performers, from the ego-laden Mr. Fay to Bert Lahr, of whom she said, "You'd learn your craft unless you were an absolute idiot. You'd learn more in five minutes on a stage with Bert Lahr than you could in five years of acting classes."

Of her re-emergence as an active performer, Patsy reflects, "In 40-odd years in show business—some of them I could do no wrong and some I could do nothing right—I haven't been so excited. It's a miracle. I think people are starved for happy endings. I know I was." Regarding her contribution to laughter over the years, she capsulizes, "Show business. I owe it everything. It owes me nothing."

FEATURE FILMS

Going Hollywood (*MGM 1933*)

The Countess of Monte Cristo (*Universal 1934*)

The Party's Over (*Columbia 1934*)

The Girl from Missouri (*MGM 1934*)

Transatlantic Merry-Go-Round (*United Artists 1934*)

Go into Your Dance (*Warner Bros. 1935*)

Page Miss Glory (*Warner Bros. 1935*)

Every Night at Eight (*Paramount 1935*)

Thanks a Million (*Fox 1935*)

Private Number (*20th Century–Fox 1936*)

Sing, Baby, Sing (*20th Century–Fox 1936*)

Pigskin Parade (*20th Century–Fox 1936*)

Kelly the Second (*MGM 1936*)

Nobody's Baby (*MGM 1937*)

Wake Up and Live (*20th Century–Fox 1937*)

Pick a Star (*MGM 1937*)

Ever Since Eve (*Warner Bros. 1937*)

Merrily We Live (*MGM 1938*)

There Goes My Heart (*United Artists 1938*)

The Cowboy and the Lady (*United Artists 1938*)

The Gorilla (*20th Century–Fox 1939*)

The Hit Parade of 1941 (*Republic 1940*)

Road Show (*United Artists 1941*)

Topper Returns (*United Artists 1941*)

Broadway Limited (*United Artists 1941*)

Playmates (*RKO 1941*)

Sing Your Worries Away (*RKO 1942*)

In Old California (*Republic 1942*)

My Son, the Hero (*Producers Releasing Corporation 1943*)

Ladies' Day (*RKO 1943*)

Danger! Women at Work (*Producers Releasing Corporation 1943*)

Please Don't Eat the Daisies (*MGM 1960*)

The Crowded Sky (*Warner Bros. 1960*)

The Naked Kiss (*Allied Artists 1964*)

The Ghost in the Invisible Bikini (*American International 1966*)

C'mon, Let's Live a Little (*Paramount 1967*)

Rosemary's Baby (*Paramount 1968*)

The Phynx (*Warner Bros. 1970*)

Freaky Friday (*Buena Vista 1976*)

North Avenue Irregulars (*Buena Vista 1978*)

In 1957.

Ernie Kovacs

"A very funny man was the late Ernie Kovacs, and never funnier than when he was playing a shtunk. Big, broad-shouldered, and vulgarly handsome, he had a way of swaggering up to some pitiful little twerp and sneering down at him as he sucked reflectively on a cigar the size of a fungo bat and stroked a big, black bushy moustache that seemed to demand insultingly: 'How zat for virility, ya hairless squirt?'"

Thus did *Time* magazine eulogize the comedian, weeks after the star fatally smashed into a telephone pole on Santa Monica Boulevard in Los Angeles on January 14, 1962. Kovacs certainly was a colorful asset to a series of Hollywood feature films from the late Fifties to his death, being effective as both comedian *and* actor. However, the cult of Kovacs aficionados tends to sneer at his film output and to register his celluloid (mis)-adventures as complete misfires.

Such was hardly the case. His performances in *Bell, Book and Candle* (1958), *Our Man in Havana* (1960), and *Five Golden Hours* (1961) make for rich, amusing entertainment and were warmly received by audiences. But, say his devotees, the big screen never offered Ernie the opportunities he found on television, in which he excelled with his creations of Percy Dovetonsils, the inebriated gay poet; Wolfgang Von Sauerbrauten, the German disc jockey; and Colonel Janos and His Kentucky Fried Paprikas, the Hungarian chicken mogul, among others.

He was born in Trenton, New Jersey, on Sunday, January 19, 1919, the second son (older brother, Tom) of Hungarian immigrants. He attended Trenton's Miss Bowen's Private School and Trenton High School, where his academics were unimpressive but his acting in high school dramatics a marvel. (He was especially fine as the pirate king in *Pirates of Penzance*.) Thereafter, Ernie managed to be accepted by the American Academy of Dramatic Arts in Manhattan, which he attended for two years. However, his acting training was cut short when an unfortunate blending of pleurisy and pneumonia sent him to Welfare Island as a moribund, presumably terminal case.

Fortunately, Ernie outlived the doctors' dire predictions. In 1941 he left the hospital ward and became the head of the Contemporary Players, a group of vagabonds who performed locally in and about Trenton, and who once played *Dr. Jekyll and Mr. Hyde* in an auditorium with only four customers. When the troupe folded, Ernie labored in a drugstore before winning an announcer's spot on Trenton's WTTM radio station. Over the next nine years, Ernie progressed from announcer to director of special events, winning a huge following. His devotees were enamored of his many on-the-air capers; in one Kovacs lay on a railroad track as a train approached so his listeners would know exactly how it felt to be run over by a train (he panicked, jumped up at the last minute, and left his microphone there—he had to buy the station a replacement). Other Kovacs stunts included standing vigil over a groundhog hole on February 2, and lying in a trench on a hunting reservation (bullets flying overhead) so his listeners would know how a rabbit felt being hunted.

In the midst of his rise to prominence—on August 13, 1945—Ernie wed Bette Wilcox, a dancer he met at a USO show. Ernie's mother, who had separated from her husband, moved in with the couple. The marriage produced two children: Bette Lee (born May 17, 1947) and Kippie (born January 5, 1949). The bitterly unhappy marriage ended in 1949 when Bette ran away. The ensuing years would feature assorted explosive episodes between the parents as each vied for custody of the children (who settled with Ernie eventually).

Needing a higher income to make ends meet, Ernie joined the Philadelphia TV station WPTZ, where he launched "Deadline for Dinner" (dubbed by Ernie "Dead Lion for Breakfast") on March 20, 1950. It was the start of a madcap array of video programs for Ernie, each show winning Ernie new fans who became quickly addicted to his offbeat humor and originality. NBC-TV network, of which WPTZ was an affiliate, placed Ernie on a national show, "Kovacs on the Corner" (with Edie Adams and Peter Boyle), which began January 7, 1951, and then on "It's Time for Ernie" (with Edie Adams and Hugh Price), beginning May 14, 1951. Sometimes Ernie was performing several television shows simultaneously.

Ernie's richly imaginative, unusual, and nonstop television work soon vaulted him to national prominence. On December 30, 1952, he began "Kovacs Unlimited," an 8-9 P.M. Tuesday spot on CBS-TV, opposite NBC-TV's Milton Berle. Regulars on the show were Edie Adams, Andy McKay, Trig Lund, and Peter Hanley. From August 29 to September 13, 1955, Kovacs was substitute host for Steve Allen on NBC-TV's "Tonight Show," later becoming the Monday and Tuesday alternate host from October 1, 1956, to January 22, 1957. From December 12, 1955, to July 27, 1956, he helmed NBC-TV's "The Ernie Kovacs Show" (with Edie Adams, Matt Dennis, Kenny Delmar, et al.), 10:30 to 11:00 A.M., Monday-Friday. And from July 2, 1956, to September 10, 1956, he was Sid Caesar's summer replacement on NBC. Ernie's humor was wild and slapstick while still appealing to the intellectual.* Like the Marx Brothers, he was able to utilize broad humor in so deft a manner that the highbrows were delighted. His stock of characters—like Percy Dovetonsils, J. Walter Puppybreath (a song seller), and Charlie Clod (a hopelessly clumsy Charlie Chan–like figure)—became very popular with the masses.

In a time of some miserably uninventive "entertainment" fodder on television, Ernie was unique in that he always played up— never down—to his audience. He would postulate in a *Life* magazine cover story, "The television audience of today is a sophisticated, alert, discriminating audience, quick to reject the inadequate. The picture of a nationwide audience holding its sides in ecstatic empathy as a smiling young man runs up and down the aisles kissing old ladies and handing out orchids to grandmothers is one that has been removed to the attic. . . ."

Meanwhile, Ernie wed again—Edie Adams,** a former Miss U.S. Television who

---

* The bulk of Ernie's early TV work is lost forever. Several years ago the New York–based networks junked most of the kinescopes of Kovacs' and many other performers' work.

** She was born Edith Enke in Kingston, Pennsylvania, on April 16,1927. She gained Broadway fame in 1953 playing in the musical *Wonderful Town*, cast as Rosalind Russell's fetching sister Eileen. In 1956 she played the fairy godmother in Rodgers and Hammerstein II's TV musical, *Cinderella*, and the same year she was back on Broadway as Daisy Mae in the musical *Li'l Abner*. On television she gained fame for her on-target imitations of Marilyn Monroe, the Gabor sisters, et al.

had studied opera at Juilliard. She had joined Ernie in his many early NBC adventures, and Kovacs soon fell in love with the blonde actress. They wed in Mexico on September 12, 1954. Not long afterward, Ernie finally obtained custody of his children. (They had been living in a rundown dwelling behind a restaurant where their mother was a waitress.) Edie often worked with her husband on television. When his success swelled, Ernie moved his family into a 17-room duplex apartment at 300 Central Park West in Manhattan. Ernie and Edie soon had a child of their own, Mia Susan, born on June 20, 1959.

An insomniac who passionately gambled, spent money, and smoked cigars, Ernie soon capped his reputation on January 19, 1957, when, as a half-hour replacement for Jerry Lewis, he headed NBC-TV's "Saturday Color Carnival—The Ernie Kovacs Show." The program was done completely silently, with Ernie portraying Eugene, a wide-eyed naive character who ever maintained his docile nature despite the indignities the world heaped upon him. The stunningly unique program won an Emmy and earned Ernie the best set of notices his work had yet received. *Life* magazine asserted that Kovacs was "the man most likely to rouse TV comedy out of its present unamusing rut." Also in 1957, the ever active Ernie wrote a novel, *Zoomar*.

On the strength of his Emmy Award–winning television spot, Ernie received an offer from Columbia Pictures to settle in Hollywood and make motion pictures. The bid was indeed tempting. It provided for $100,000 per film. This heightened income would allow Kovacs to begin to earn close to what he expended (he lavished a reputed $13,000 yearly on his favorite Havana cigars alone!). Kovacs accepted the deal and then purchased a plush, stately home at 2301 Bowmont Drive high in Coldwater Canyon. The "little farm" cost Ernie $100,000. Soon the dwelling was a $600,000 showplace with outlandish accoutrements such as a rotating driveway, upon which rested his plush white Rolls Royce.

His first assignment at Columbia was *Operation Mad Ball* (1957); the director was ex-actor Richard Quine and the stars were Jack Lemmon (a great Kovacs fan), Kathryn Grant, and Mickey Rooney. Ernie played Captain Lock, involved in a plot to throw a wild party on a military installation. (It was the first military-officer characterization for Ernie. Of his 10 feature films, he played a captain in four of them.) Unfortunately, the broad *Operation Mad Ball* was not a notable success.

Bell, Book and Candle (1958) was much better. Adapted from the 1950 Broadway hit, the witty farce of witchcraft starred James Stewart, a luscious Kim Novak, Jack Lemmon, Hermione Gingold, Elsa Lanchester, and Janice Rule. Ernie appeared as Sidney Redlitch, an alcoholic author whom warlock Lemmon helps write an exposé on Manhattan witches. Richard Quine again directed and this time Ernie won a nice set of reviews. *Variety* noted, "Kovacs drapes his character with dozens of fuzzy, funny touches." *Time* magazine endorsed, "Ernie Kovacs has some wonderful moments as a subnormal supernaturalist." Though Columbia overbalanced the story line to make the film a vehicle for its reigning sexpot, Kim Novak, the picture was still great fun and enjoyed healthy financial returns.

With his dark bearing, husky frame, and thick moustache, Kovacs was a natural to be a comic menace. He was at his best in *It Happened to Jane* (1959) as Harry Foster Malone, "the meanest man in the world." The comedy depicted Ernie waging war with lobster entrepreneurs Doris Day and Jack Lemmon. Kovacs is the villainous railroad owner who refuses to pay the hero and heroine the amount due them when his train fails to deliver their lobster shipment on time. *Films in Review* hailed *It Happened to Jane* as "a really exceptional comedy.... It could be the harbinger of a return to the Capra-like comedy-cum-Americana of the '30's." *Time* was less enthusiastic about the production, but raved, "Comic Kovacs turns a fairly unfunny script into a funny farce— the success story of a self-made monster." The *New York Times* remarked that his part was "deliciously played." Unfortunately, the film, also distributed as *Twinkle and Shine*, met an apathetic greeting from the box office. It was the third time Richard Quine directed Lemmon and Ernie together. Quine says today, "If Ernie had lived, the Lemmon-Matthau team might well have been Lemmon-Kovacs. They reminded me of a sophisticated

Laurel and Hardy." Indeed, it is not difficult to imagine Ernie in the role of Oscar Madison, infuriating Lemmon's prissy Felix Unger with his sloppy ways, in *The Odd Couple*.

While Kovacs labored in the cinema, he, of course, exhausted himself in other endeavors. He played in a short subject, *Showdown at Ulcer Gulch* (1958), with Edie Adams, Bing Crosby, Chico and Groucho Marx, Orson Bean, Salome Jens, and Bob Hope; guested on such NBC-TV shows as Perry Como's (October 1957), Eddie Fisher's (February 1959), "The Bob Hope Buick Show" (December 1959), the 1959 Oscarcast (April 6, 1959), his own special, *Kovacs on Music* (May 22, 1959), and the *Author at Work* episode (April 11, 1960) of "Goodyear Theatre." On CBS-TV he was seen in the "Playhouse 90" version (September 26, 1957) of *Topaze*, two episodes (October 19, 1958, and February 15, 1959) of "G. E. Theatre," a segment of the "Ann Sothern Show" (February 22, 1959), *The Salted Mine* installment (March 27, 1959) of "Schlitz Playhouse of Stars," and for the "Lucille Ball-Desi Arnaz Hour" entry *Lucy*

Meets the Moustache (April 1, 1960) he was the prime guest star. In the 1959-60 season he hosted the show "Take a Good Look" over ABC-TV (which boasted such regulars as Edie Adams, Cesar Romero, and Carl Reiner); in March 1961 he began hosting ABC-TV's "Silents Please," and as a follow-up to his 30-minute satirical "The Ernie Kovacs Show" (1958-59) over ABC-TV, he starred in "The New Ernie Kovacs Show" (1961-62) for the same network.

Kovacs also began making trips to Las Vegas, entertaining in the plush casinos with Edie as his co-star. The Nevada trips were primarily to appease his yen for gambling, which was becoming an increasingly costly addiction.

In 1960 Ernie played in five feature films. The first, *Our Man in Havana*, was a clever espionage comedy, directed with customary élan by Carol Reed and boasting a cast of Sir Alec Guinness, Burl Ives, Maureen O'Hara, Noël Coward, and Sir Ralph Richardson. Ernie was well showcased as Captain Segura, a Cuban chief of police. *Time* reported,

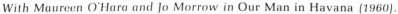

With Maureen O'Hara and Jo Morrow in Our Man in Havana *(1960).*

With Dick Shawn and Jack Warden in Wake Me When It's Over *(1960).*

"Funnyman Kovacs, a sort of Clark Gable with fangs, makes a perfect comedy menace, as smooth and slippery as a fresh-licked Havana cigar." Perfectionist Guinness was very taken by Ernie's comedy work, and at the time of Kovacs' death was said to be planning a film production with him.

Ernie then left Columbia temporarily for Twentieth Century–Fox, where he played Captain Charlie Stark in *Wake Me When It's Over* (1960), a service comedy directed by Mervyn LeRoy. This zany effort concerned Dick Shawn's plans to build a luxury hotel at his Far East station. It was not a top-caliber farce but was amusing and stocked with solid comedy actors, including Jack Warden, Don Knotts, and Robert Strauss. Back at Columbia Ernie found himself in a slick soap opera, *Strangers When We Meet* (1960). Star Kirk Douglas co-produced it with director Richard Quine. The film also offered Kim Novak, Barbara Rush, Walter Matthau, and Virginia Bruce (as Novak's mother). Ernie was Roger Altar, an eccentric author. The *New York Times* observed, "In his compara-

tively brief appearances, Ernie Kovacs strongly indicates once again that he is not only an eminent comedian, but also is an actor of stature who can even make his yearning for real love sound beautiful rather than banal."

Rounding out 1960, Ernie made a guest appearance in Columbia's cameo-laden *Pepe* (1960) starring Cantinflas, Shirley Jones, and Dan Dailey. He then returned to Fox for *North to Alaska*, a raucous actioner with Ernie as crooked gambler Frankie Canon ("surefire casting," judged *Films in Review*) who tries to swindle prospectors John Wayne, Stewart Granger, and Fabian out of their riches. The director was veteran Henry Hathaway; the romantic lead, Capucine.

Ernie's first of two 1961 releases was *Five Golden Hours*, an English-Italian production, released by Columbia and directed by Mario Zampi. It is perhaps the best cinema showcase for Ernie. It is a pungent black comedy with Kovacs as Aldo Bondi, a professional mourner and pallbearer who comforts wealthy widows. He meets his nemesis in the

With John Wayne and Capucine in North to Alaska *(1960).*

statuesque form of Cyd Charisse, a professional widow, who soon adds money-hungry Ernie to her fatality list. It was Ernie's brand of humor, especially the scenes in which he feigns insanity, hoping to obtain refuge in a sanatorium (where he meets George Sanders who has successfully accomplished the same stunt). But it was all before its time. *Saturday Review* sneered, "It's lucky the budget was kept low."

The last film of Ernie's life was *Sail a Crooked Ship* (1961) for Columbia. As "The Captain" Ernie was again a villain, this time menacing Robert Wagner, Dolores Hart, and Frankie Avalon; Carolyn Jones was his moll. Irving Brecher directed. Kovacs was allowed full rein to exercise his fancy, including performing a ball-bearing hand-rolling bit popularized by Captain Queeg (Humphrey Bogart) of *The Caine Mutiny. Time* wrote that the 88 minutes contained some large chunks of "fine hairy humor," but most reviewers declared that the film, in release at the time of Kovacs' death, was hardly a fitting swan song to his impressive screen career.

While many critics and audiences reacted favorably to Ernie's cinema persona, he himself held little affection for his screen work. At one point he placed an ad in a film trade paper reading, "No more @#/# captains." He insisted he was far happier in the television medium where sponsors allowed him to be more freewheeling with creativity and money. His first special for Dutch Masters Cigars—in April 1961—was budgeted at $11,174 and Ernie gleefully escalated the sum to $25,185.83 by air time.

This same outrageous disregard for moderation in living and spending stretched his private life out of proportion. When he and Edie performed in Las Vegas, the casino producers ordered that he be kept away from the gaming tables so he would not squander all his salary via gambling. He finally helped himself out of this habit. But by 1962 he was in dire straits with the federal government, owing back taxes amounting to some $400,000. Still, Ernie continued onward, indulging his and his family's every conceivable whim.

374

In the first days of 1962 Ernie was negotiating with Alec Guinness regarding a cinema production deal, and he was working on a comedy TV pilot for Screen Gems, "A Pony for Chris," with Buster Keaton. But it was all halted via one of Hollywood's most publicized tragedies of the Sixties. On Saturday evening, January 13, 1962, Ernie attended a party at Billy Wilder's apartment at 10401 Wilshire Boulevard and Beverly Glen. It was a christening party for Milton and Ruth Berle's new son, Michael.

Edie met him at the gathering. He had been working on the pilot all day and came in his white Rolls Royce. She drove from home in a white Corvair station wagon. Around midnight, Ernie left the party for PJ's, a Hollywood night spot. He took the station wagon rather than the Rolls, which he asked Edie to drive home. As he sped through the wet night, his car smacked the concrete triangle at Beverly Glen and Santa Monica Boulevard. It spun in a circle and smashed into a pole. Ernie fatally fractured his skull. He was found dead with a cigar a few inches from his hand.

Even at this early morning hour, news spread about Hollywood concerning Ernie's demise. Edie Adams refused to believe the tragedy until Jack Lemmon visited the morgue and sadly confirmed it for the widow. In the grand hysterical Hollywood style, mobs stood outside the Kovacs home on Bowmont Drive the next morning, screaming for a glimpse of the bereaved family and visiting celebrities.

Edie, as a strange last request, asked Jack Lemmon to place some cigars in Ernie's pocket before the burial. Lemmon would recall in David G. Walley's *Nothing in Moderation: A Biography of Ernie Kovacs* (1975):

> It was so awful and bizarre because there he was, how they had dressed him all up, and this pimply faced kid is there saying, "We're *terribly* proud, we *really are* of the job we've done. . . . I think he looks marvy. . . . I assume it will be open?" and I said, "No, it's gonna be closed." "Oh" and he's just looking at Ernie and beaming at the work he has

With Dennis Price in Five Golden Hours *(1961).*

done. Now I go to put the cigars in [but] I can't open [the pocket] up. It's tight, the clothes are form fitting. He's got it pulled in the back and everything else, and I'm trying to get the cigars in the pocket and I'm thinking, "Holy Jesus and now they're flaking all over the place." Now this guy [the pimply faced attendant] is going berserk. It was so bizarre and awful, and then I started to laugh because what else can you do? I said, "I can't believe this is happening." . . . I said I might have known it would happen with that now 'cause I know he was circling overhead and laughing his ass off.

On January 18, 1962, the funeral was held at the Beverly Hills Presbyterian Church, where the Kovacs children had enrolled in Sunday school. The funeral was attended by a fleet of Hollywood's major attractions, including Charlton Heston, Jack Benny, Samuel Goldwyn, Kim Novak, and Edward G. Robinson.*

Like so many of the talents of the cinema, the remains of Ernie Kovacs were buried at Forest Lawn, where his simple marker summed up succinctly the man, his life, and his comedy:

Ernie Kovacs   1919–1962
Nothing in Moderation

In the spring of 1977 Video Tape Network distributed a series of ten half-hour segments of "The Best of Ernie Kovacs" that were telecast over the Public Broadcasting System

stations. (They had previously been shown to great acclaim on the college network.) The rave reviews surprised even Kovacs' most loyal fans.

The *Hollywood Reporter* noted,

Inventive comedian Ernie Kovacs proved to be king of electronics wizardry from 1950 to 1962 and his zany video tricks have never been matched since. . . . Living up to expectations was always a breeze for this unconventional cigar-chomping clown and, judging from this new series, there will be no disappointment for old or new fans. The outrageously daring attitudes of Kovacs are still way ahead of 1970s TV.

In his opening introduction, Jack Lemmon warns the viewer "slow down your internal clock, it was a more leisurely time, you know"—a statement that is immediately contradicted by the pace and timing of the actual show. There are the wildly wacky sight gags; the running gags; the spoofs; the take-offs; the characters (like Percy Dovetonsils); the Nairobi Trio (as funny as ever); the playful surprises; and in each show, a mechanistic symphony with inanimate objects dancing to classical strains. No opportunity for comedy is missed, with even the credits spelled out with wit and imagination.

At the request of Kovacs' widow, Edie Adams, none of the sequences were altered or edited, which is just as it should be. . . .

John O'Connor (*New York Times*) pointed out, ". . . the fascination is constant as the series reveals the dazzling inventiveness that influenced all subsequent television comedy from 'Laugh-In' to 'Saturday Night Live.'"

In a study of Kovacs' TV work, Jeff Greenfield observed,

It isn't that Kovacs was a crusader—neither in these 10 half-hours nor any of his shows I can remember is there evidence of a single topical or political comment—but that he found in the treacle of broadcasting an irresistible target of opportunity ("Thank you for letting us into your living room," he said once in obeisance to the cliche of the day, "but

* Widow Edie Adams was burdened with woeful publicity, as she detailed how she was saddled with Ernie's tax and gambling debts—once estimated at $600,000. However, she not only survived the lamentations of the sob sisters, but also managed to pay off all the debts (some gambling pals tore up their accounts out of love for Ernie and Edie) by becoming the Muriel Cigars commercial chanteuse, and performing constantly on the road, on television variety shows, and in movies. Her friend Debbie Reynolds summed up her admiration for Edie recently: "It took her five years to pay it off. She raised their child and his two children and took care of his mother. She couldn't save a penny. She never got off the road. There was no one to help her but herself. Edie was the most courageous girl. My respect for her is limitless."

Edie Adams would later wed bandleader Pete Condoli (the ex-husband of Betty Hutton) and together they frequently tour in stock productions. The couple resides at the Coldwater Canyon estate Edie once shared with Ernie.

couldn't you have cleaned it up a little?").

And some of his wildest moments were cheerfully malicious abuses of the medium—with none of the "only kidding, folks" reassurances of a Bob Hope. When an early TV venture in Philadelphia was canceled—Kovacs was never a master of the rating—he devoted his last show to dismembering the set with an ax. In 1956, during a summer replacement show, he placed the character of deranged Hungarian chef Miklos Molman in a show very much like "Howdy Doody." Miklos swilled wine from a bottle, brandished a whip over the terrorized kiddies of the peanut gallery and with a huge pair of shears cut the strings of the bubbly puppet. To watch the bleary-eyed Miklos sweep the lifeless hunk of wood from the set was a moment of sweet revenge for any child of the 1950's.

Greenfield concluded,

Let Kovacs build to his point, and be satisfied at times with a smile instead of a belly-laugh. What you'll see is a demonstration of what can happen when television is placed in the hands of someone who was delighted and not petrified by the possibilities of the medium.

Comedian Chevy Chase applauded,

Ernie Kovacs was a video innovator. He knew that there was an intrinsic magic about television itself that should be explored. He not only dealt with existing reference points, he gave viewers new reference points. This is not to say that Kovacs' work never dealt with situations and routines familiar to television audiences. He could do a "sketch" in a restaurant setting as well as the next man. What is memorable about Ernie was his inclination to stay away from the familiar. He chose to break precedents whenever possible.

FEATURE FILMS

Operation Mad Ball (Columbia 1957)
Bell, Book and Candle (Columbia 1958)
It Happened to Jane [a.k.a. Twinkle and Shine] (Columbia 1959)
Our Man in Havana (Columbia 1960)
Wake Me When It's Over (20th Century-Fox 1960)
Strangers When We Meet (Columbia 1960)
North to Alaska (20th Century-Fox 1960)
Pepe (Columbia 1960)
Five Golden Hours (Columbia 1961)
Sail a Crooked Ship (Columbia 1961)

With Judy Garland, Jack Haley, and Ray Bolger in a pose for **The Wizard of Oz** *(1939).*

Bert Lahr

Should one day a compendium of classic comic screen performances be made, Bert Lahr's Cowardly Lion, following the yellow brick road in *The Wizard of Oz* (1939), would have to be near the top of the list. To imagine any other actor cavorting so brilliantly, or enhancing L. Frank Baum's neurotic lion with greater nuance of human foibles, is fantasy. In this memorable MGM film, Lahr's expert buffoonery revealed human complexities, fears, and anxieties, mitigated with pathos and a strong sense of survival. His singing of the song "If I Were King of the Forest" reached back into years of intense theatrical training. His background had made him expert at mouthing nonsense lyrics, elongating vowels, and slurring the most erudite couplets into almost inarticulate diction punctuated with a trilling vibrato. Strangely, within the structure and bravura performance of the courage-seeking lion, there was a great deal of Bert Lahr.

Training grounds for comedians today are almost as extinct as the dinosaur. The great comedians lacked formal, and often basic, education and sought their schooling within their chosen profession, learning their trade in the theatre, vaudeville, and burlesque. From the last-named rough-and-tumble school graduated Phil Silvers, Red Buttons, Jack Albertson, Jackie Gleason, Bobby Clark, Abbott and Costello, Joe E. Brown, Fanny Brice, and others, including Bert Lahr. They learned comedic timing, the catalyst of laughter, from years of testing material on audiences.

Irving Lahrheim was born on Tuesday, August 13, 1895, in the Yorkville section of New York City. His parents were Augusta Lahrheim and her decorator-upholsterer husband, Jacob. By 1900 the German-Jewish family had become four with the birth of a daughter, Cele. Until World War I, German would be spoken and read in the Lahrheim home. But with the outbreak of hostilities, the family became Americanized and Irving became "Bert."

At age 15 the future comedian left the Bronx's Public School 40 to join a kid act, "The Seven Frolics," and in a few years he was signed as "second comedian" on the quality burlesque circuit, The Columbia

Wheel. Burlesque was then a "family" show and a sterling basic training post for ambitious, embryonic clowns. Lahr's success in burlesque was bought with total dedication, intense training, and a frenetic drive to polish and perfect his trade. His ambition was to move on to the richer and more rewarding field of vaudeville.

With Billy K. Wells, who had signed him into burlesque, Lahr developed a comedy act, "What's the Idea?" in which he played a low-comic policeman. It was here he developed his famous gutteral "gnong, gnong, gnong," and was hilariously funny mugging outrageously and stopping a luscious lady from doing the "hootchy-kootchy." His partner was a lovely young woman, Mercedes Delpino, and they played the sketch in burlesque. After a full-season run in the burlesque show *The Best Show in Town,* they also became a team off stage. Bert gave Mercedes a ring and she was known as "Babe" Lahr. Their lives became their act. They never thought about the fact that they should legally wed.

After a nine-month stint in the naval reserve, Bert rejoined Mercedes for the burlesque shows *Folly Town* (in which young novice singer Jack Haley appeared) and *Rose-Land Girls* into 1921's *Keep Smiling.* Lahr and Mercedes took their "What's the Idea?" sketch to vaudeville, playing four years on the Orpheum circuit. They eventually turned their act into a headliner and brought it to New York City's venerable Palace Theatre. They had reached the big time. But Bert was constantly perfecting his Dutch dialogue, mangling the King's English into malapropisms, and striving to improve his personal and professional self. He was unsparing of himself and his partner.

Harry Delmar signed Lahr and Mercedes for his musical revue, *Delmar's Revels.* The show opened at the Shubert Theatre on November 28, 1927, and top-lined Frank Fay. It featured Lahr, Jeanne Hackett, and Patsy Kelly. The production ran for 112 performances. During this period Mercedes' erratic behavior offstage was a constant source of concern for Lahr. She became withdrawn, almost catatonic. She cropped off her beautiful black hair and was forced to wear a scarf to cover a near bald dome. Then she became pregnant. At Hoboken, New Jersey, in Au-

gust 1929, Lahr and Mercedes were officially married. Shortly after the wedding their son, Herbert, was born.

If Lahr's private life was chaotic, his professional life boomed. DeSylva, Brown, and Henderson's *Hold Everything* (October 10, 1928) was written for Lahr. As Gink Shiner, a punch-drunk sparring mate of a boxer who fights the champion and wins, he became a Broadway star. His broad, expansive comedy was oddly well meshed with the droll whimsy of delightful Victor Moore. Following the opening at the Broadhurst Theatre, Lahr was crowned by the press as the new comedy king of Broadway. St. John Ervine wrote in the *New York Morning Telegram,* "This man is funny. He can make old, tired stuff seem new and original. Mr. Lahr can obtain laughter by merely distorting his features." The reviews firmly entrenched Lahr as a Broadway name.

The musical also provided another spurt of theatrical brouhaha. Lahr badly wanted to play in the Warner Bros. film version of *Hold Everything,* but producer Vinton Freedley would not release him from his stage contract. After the release of the 1930 film, in which Joe E. Brown played Lahr's part of the dim-witted slugger, Bert fired off a volley of protest in a letter to *Variety.* He labeled Brown a "lifter," demanding redress for Joe's deliberate copying of his performance in the Hollywood film. The *Saturday Evening Post* did an article about the controversy and onetime Dutch comedian Sam Sidman joined the fray by asserting that Bert's burlesque-Dutch comic character was originally his—and that he had stolen it from Sam Bernard. (Throughout his career Lahr would lash out at any comedians he felt infringed his style. In 1962 he was victorious in winning a federal lawsuit against Adell Chemicals for having a duck imitate his voice in a TV commercial. If his objectives were righteous, his gnawing suspicions of piracy were often without foundation.)

George White's *Flying High* opened on Broadway on March 3, 1930. Lahr's bright playing of the cross-country airmail race pilot reaffirmed his hold on Broadway stardom. On April 27, 1930, he had to commit Mercedes to a Connecticut sanatorium, but the tragedy of his personal life disappeared when he leaped onto the stage. The George

White musical had several interludes of interest in Lahr lore. One was a scene involving his pouring Scotch into a test tube normally used for urinalysis. His comedic expertise overrode bad taste through a bewildered, befuddled appearance of innocence. Years later, he explained, "It's a matter of maintaining an air of innocence. You can do almost anything on stage, if you do it as if you haven't the slightest idea that there's anything wrong with what you're doing. Some comedians can do that particular thing, but a lot of comedians make it vulgar and dirty, and the audience won't accept it."

The *New York World-Telegram* review of the show said that "George White's new musical is chiefly remarkable for three items, Bert Lahr, a fat girl named Kate Smith, and a very physical medical joke. . . ." The second item, Kate Smith, was Lahr's leading lady and he felt her youth and inexperience detracted audience response from his comedy. During the show's 122 performances, Lahr fanned the feud with under-his-breath mutterings to Miss Smith. Her memories of *Flying High* would remain clouded by the unhappy experience.

Flying High provided Bert with the entree for his feature-film debut.* Made by Metro-Goldwyn-Mayer, it faithfully translated the musical. Bert came across larger than life. *Photoplay* enthused over his and Charlotte Greenwood's performance, "Lahr and Greenwood are second to none in talkies!" During the making of *Flying High,* the film ran over its eight-week production schedule. Louis B. Mayer treated Lahr to one of his "flag, mother, Metro, and God" sermons as a preamble to not paying him overtime to finish the picture as agreed in his contract. The Mayer manifesto soured Lahr (as it had many others) into a lifetime distrust and distaste for the high-powered Hollywood producers. He was happy to return to Broadway.

Florenz Ziegfeld's *Hot-Cha!* was the impresario's last extravaganza and it opened at the Ziegfeld Theatre on March 8, 1932. It starred Lahr, Lupe Velez, and Charles "Buddy" Rogers. The show was roundly panned, but Bert's playing of ersatz fearless matador Alky Schmidt was received better than the material. The cast took cuts in salary but the show closed after 119 performances.* Working for the great Ziegfeld became one of Lahr's glowing stage memories as was the illuminating experience of coping with the explosive, sensuous Miss Velez. Her erratic behavior (she rehearsed in the nude) and reluctance to bathe armed Bert with sufficient barbs to provoke the Mexican Spitfire into what Lahr called her "duck" laugh. Ed Sullivan's filmed Manhattan nightclub tour, *Mr. Broadway* (1933), included Bert and Lupe Velez among the celebrities.

In the summer of 1932 Lahr headed New York's Paramount Theatre stage show with Harry Richman, Eleanor Powell, and Sylvia Froos. In the fall he signed with mercurial George White to star with his friend Richman and Lily Damita in White's *Music Hall Varieties. Varieties* offered Lahr a departure from his low-comedy routines and allowed him to experiment with satire. He was hilariously successful in a takeoff ("Chanson by Clifton Duckfeet") on the sophisticated and elegant song-and-dance routines of Clifton Webb and riotously sang "Trees" while being pursued by a pack of dogs.

John Murray Anderson's production of *Life Begins at 8:40* (August 27, 1934) gave Lahr a glossy showcase to polish his comedy further, plus songs to sing by Harold Arlen and E. Y. Harburg. He starred with Ray Bolger, Luella Gear, and Frances Williams, with Brian Donlevy as Bert's straight man. The reviews were lavish, especially for Bert. His songs perfectly captured his comedic image, stressing his buffoonery and underscoring his projected humanized joker characteristics. As Harburg put it, "I could say so many things through Bert's voice that I couldn't with my own. All his reactions are those of a man society doesn't accept, but laughs at." Lahr's rendition of the number "Things" was a devastatingly funny travesty of a Metropolitan Opera baritone in concert. It was sung in a violent vibrato punctuated with declamatory, nonsensical lyrics. The bits of burlesqued business culminated in a well-aimed pie in the face.

---

* Lahr had appeared in the Vitaphone two-reeler *Faint Heart* made in the later part of 1929. On March 19, 1951, he would repeat his antic performance in *Flying High* on television.

* During the run of *Hot-Cha!* Bert made his radio debut on June 20, 1932. His contracted thirteen weeks dissolved after four. Although future guest spots on national radio shows were successful, this venture was not.

After headlining *George White's Scandals* in 1935 Lahr moved on to the revue *The Show Is On* (December 25, 1936), co-starred with Beatrice Lillie. The perceptive, perfectionist Vincente Minnelli "conceived, staged, and designed" a blockbusting, marvelous revue. It contained music and lyrics by most of America's top songwriting teams and sketches by the likes of Moss Hart and David Freedman. For constant worrier Lahr, Lady Peel, better known as Bea Lillie, was a godsend. Lahr would recall, "Working with Bea was one of my great experiences in the theater. We never had a cross word. I never saw her make one bad move. She was entirely professional." The unlikely stage team immediately became a mutual admiration society.

For his performance in *The Show Is On*, Lahr was lauded for his "Song of the Woodman" number, which has become a classic in the annals of great musical comedy performance. Here Bert showed again that the assured, pompous poised clown had matured into an eminent satirist. With each "chop, chop" of the lyric, Lahr was pelted with wood chips (or anything else conveniently wooden) from backstage. Bea Lillie once tossed a broom into the fray. On June 28, 1937, Willie and Eugene Howard replaced Bert in the show, which continued, but without the frenetic polished mayhem injected by Lahr. Bert went to Hollywood.*

The journey was hardly worth the effort. But Universal's mildly pleasant musical *Merry-Go-Round of 1938* (1937) did put onto celluloid his famous "Woodchopping" routine which he played with great fervor. The studio paid him an enormous salary for a one-picture deal. Then Twentieth Century–Fox signed him to a six-month contract and he was the peripheral comic support in *Love and Hisses* (1937) and *Josette* (1938). In *Just Around the Corner* (1938) he was teamed for a third time by Fox with Joan Davis and the

two played in support of Shirley Temple. George Cukor's astute casting of Bert in the role of Claudette Colbert's stage partner and adviser in Paramount's *Zaza* (1939) was inspired. It propelled Lahr into a phase of performing he later would perfect as brilliantly as he had comedy. *Photoplay* was as amazed as most of the industry over Lahr's work in *Zaza*. "Bert Lahr, with unsuspected dramatic talent, does a fine job in the role of Zaza's theatrical manager." Cukor was the first director to tone down the larger-than-life Lahr comedy that leaped from the stage onto film.

Bert built a home in Hollywood in Coldwater Canyon and lingered to make film history as the Cowardly Lion in *The Wizard of Oz* after Twentieth Century–Fox had dropped his contract. But despite the praise he received for the MGM Technicolor musical, MGM did not pick up an option on his services.

Meanwhile, Lahr's personal life had its own special intricacies. He was plagued by Mercedes' continued mental collapse, which saw her confined to a number of sanatoriums and homes. In 1931 the comedian had fallen in love with a lovely, blonde Cincinnati girl who had appeared in the chorus of several New York musicals. His romance with Mildred Schroeder was rocky, principally due to Bert's agonizing about his mentally disturbed wife, his inability to cope with his son, and the constantly gnawing anxieties about his career. In 1936, unable to get a decision from Lahr about their future, Mildred married attorney Joseph S. Robinson. By November 1936 front-page headlines were keeping the country informed of a love-thief triangle in which Bert was the baffled culprit. Mildred had left the attorney, and had moved to California where she was supported by Lahr pending her divorce. She received her freedom on October 4, 1937. A bond of annulment (and a large cash settlement to provide for Mercedes and her son) dissolved his first marriage. The traumas of his personal life eased when Bert married Mildred on February 11, 1940, before an Episcopal minister in Elkton, Maryland.

Eighteenth-century France would hardly have been prepared for Mr. Lahr but for Cole Porter. Bert's playing of Louis XV in *DuBarry Was a Lady* (December 6, 1939) was a gem of

* Ironically, despite his star status on Broadway, Lahr's low comedy was acknowledged by Hollywood only in comedy shorts, first by RKO in 1933-34 (*Hizzoner, Henry the Ape, No More West*) and then by Educational-Twentieth Century-Fox in 1936-37 (*Gold Bricks, Off the Horses, Montague the Magnificent, Whose Baby Are You?*). Perhaps one of the facts responsible for Hollywood deeming that Lahr lacked the necessary box-office appeal and/or talent for major promotion was that he faced the camera with the same intensity he used on stage. On film he was almost a caricature.

With Simone Simon, Georges Renavent, and Ben Bernie in Love and Hisses *(1937).*

comedic invention. Porter's lyrics were ribald, risqué, and funny, and their double entendres became grist for the Lahr gag mill, making the words far funnier than they might have read. He sparked "In the Morning, No" into a show stopper, exceeded only by his closing duet, "Friendship," with co-star Ethel Merman. Brooks Atkinson in the *New York Times* enunciated the Lahr comedy style: "He decorates the choruses with all sorts of old-time clowning—mugging, quick steps, and finally a series of nonsensical capers at random."

In March 1942 Lahr was part of a massive all-star Hollywood Victory Caravan that traveled cross-country and was feted at a White House luncheon hostessed by Mrs. Eleanor Roosevelt. On June 10, 1942, Lahr opened with Joe E. Lewis and Bert Wheeler for a brief run (two and a half weeks) in a vaudeville-style revue, *Headliners of '42.* Bert was back in front of the cameras for a programmer at RKO, *Sing Your Worries Away* (1942), and was Red Skelton's stooge in the MGM musical *Ship Ahoy* (1942).

Metro's *Meet the People* (1944), a film version of a highly successful California revue that had a mild success on Broadway, gave Bert the picture's biggest guffaw as a commander singing "Heave-Ho." But Hollywood, again, had been unable to harness the Lahr brand of comedy. Following the birth of his daughter Jane* on September 2, 1943 (his son and biographer** John had been born in Los Angeles on July 12, 1942), he sold his Cold-

* Daughter Jane is a sculptress and married to New York theatre reviewer Martin Godfried.

** *Notes on a Cowardly Lion* (1969). In November 1976 the Philadelphia Company presented *The Lion and the Lamb,* a play by Joseph M. Orazi, based on *Notes on a Cowardly Lion. Variety* reported of the actor who played Lahr, "Dan Strickler, without physical resemblance to the late comic, maintains a melancholy mien while attempting to simulate the Lahr sound. It's satisfactory in the straight dramatic sequences, but naturally misses Lahr's unique vocal style as a buffoon." Sherry Steiner appeared as Lahr's first wife, Mercedes. In late 1977 producer Joel W. Schenker announced plans to transform *Notes on a Cowardly Lion* into a Broadway musical. Shecky Green was mentioned as a candidate to star in the vehicle which might have a score by Jule Styne. "Bert Lahr, from burlesque to Beckett," said Schenker. "Think of that!"

With Joan Davis in Just Around the Corner *(1938).*

water Canyon home and took his family back East, where he became involved in an overblown Billy Rose extravaganza.

On December 7, 1944, at $24 tops (including champagne during intermission), *Seven Lively Arts,* Rose's packaged entertainment, opened. It was staged by Hassard Short, scored by Cole Porter, and star-billed Beatrice Lillie, Bert Lahr, Benny Goodman, Alicia Markova, and Anton Dolin. The opulent million-dollar-plus production had its world premiere in Philadelphia, where Miss Lillie tagged it the *Seven Deadly Arts.* The show was a typical Rose misadventure into lavish bad taste—especially in wartime. Only the huge advance sale of tickets kept the show alive on Broadway through May 12, 1945.

The play *Burlesque* had been a rousing hit on Broadway in 1927 with Hal Skelly and Barbara Stanwyck. On Christmas night 1946 Jean Dalrymple revived the Twenties hit with Bert Lahr as the burlesque comedian Skid and film actress Jean Parker

as his partner Bonny. In Lahr the writhing insecurities, lost affections, and internal problems of the clown character were given protean expression. Lahr had tested the show during the summer of 1945 and played the summer circuit again with the play in 1946, adding his reliable "cop" act from his own burlesque days. It worked. Arthur Hopkins (who had co-written the original play) directed the revival, with Lahr calling the pacing of the interpolated burlesque sketch and the songs he injected into the script.

When the revival of *Burlesque* closed on Broadway after 439 performances on January 10, 1948, Bert started an extensive road tour the following Monday. The play provided Lahr with several years of trouping, including a "Prudential Playhouse" telecast on January 2, 1951. In the summer of 1952 he reprised the show again on the stock circuit. He did put aside his successful play to film Milton Berle's *Always Leave Them Laughing* (1949) at Warner Bros. It was a fiasco that

384

was not improved with ill-disguised friction between the two comics. Both charged "foul" and countercharges of unprofessionalism continued many years.

The musical revue *Two on the Aisle* opened on July 19, 1951, at the Mark Hellinger Theatre, giving Lahr a dazzling return to the mainstream. He offered a gallery of comic portraits from a baseball player to Queen Victoria and cavorted through the revue for 281 performances. His onstage romping was buoyant despite his intolerance of co-star Dolores Gray. The same year another misadventure in front of the cameras was released, *Mr. Universe*. For MGM's least successful remake of the musical *Rose-Marie* (1954) Bert played Canadian Mountie Barney McGorkle, pursued by oversized Marjorie Main. In a picture that needed all the comedy relief it could find, many of the Lahr-Main scenes were discarded on the cutting-room floor.

Bert fared better on television. In the "Best of Broadway" production of *The Man Who Came to Dinner* (October 13, 1954) Bert was entertaining in the part of Banjo, and the following year he was effective singing "I Hate the Waltz" in the telecast of *The Great Waltz*, with Patrice Munsel and Keith Andes. For the prestigious "Omnibus" teleseries he did superior work in the telecasts of *School for Wives* and *Androcles and the Lion*. He made another stab at the screen in Universal's *The Second Greatest Sex* (1955), an updating of *Lysistrata*, starring Jeanne Crain.

Samuel Beckett's *Waiting for Godot* inspires most anyone's imagination and remains open to anyone's personal interpretation. It seemed an unlikely theatrical exercise for Bert Lahr but he was fascinated with the play and saw within Beckett's cryptic lines a vast array of human comedy always close to tears and clinging to hope. In the role of Estragon, Lahr found depths of meaning while admitting the whole eluded him. With Tom Ewell co-starred, *Waiting for Godot* opened and closed in Miami. But Lahr did not

With Lucille Ball in Meet the People *(1944).*

lose faith in the play. Recast, with E. G. Marshall now his co-player, *Godot* finally opened on Broadway on April 19, 1956. Its brief run gave Lahr his most satisfying stage experience. Kenneth Tynan's critique of Lahr's performance glowed with praise for a noble performance and audiences cheered his "beleaguered simpleton."

From Beckett, Lahr leaped into French farce in *Hotel Paradiso* (April 11, 1957), which he played with great éclat and abandon. The play marked Angela Lansbury's Broadway debut. He returned to familiar territory, the musical revue, co-starring with Nancy Walker in an unfortunate flop, *The Girls Against the Boys* (November 2, 1959). It is remembered for one hilarious sketch, "Hostility," which Lahr and Walker reprised on Ed Sullivan's Sunday night TV show. On "G. E. Theatre" (1959) Bert was very funny as the cigar-smoking, pink-winged fairy godfather in *Mr. O'Malley*. In 1960 he tackled the bard, William Shakespeare.

Lahr won the "Best Shakespearean Actor of the Year" award for his playing of Bottom in *A Midsummer Night's Dream* and Autolycus in *The Winter's Tale* with the American Shakespeare Festival. He found in the classics elements of his low burlesque comedy and dredged up his own intuitive sense of timing to make the parts work. In the summer of 1961 Bert was on the summer circuit playing Elwood Dowd in *Harvey* (a role he had also done on the summer stages in 1950). On September 18, 1961, he opened at the Bucks County Playhouse at New Hope, Pennsylvania, in a new play by S. J. Perelman. In *The Beauty Part* he played five different comic roles. He said that it contained "the funniest material I've ever had" and was distraught that the play, which opened on Broadway December 26, 1962, lasted only a brief time, despite a year of revising and polishing the Perelman work.

A rowdy, musical version of *Volpone*, reset in the gold rush Yukon, had Bert in the lead as *Foxy*. He had played the revitalized Volpone under the auspices of the Canadian government in Dawson City, Yukon Territory, in the summer of 1962.* The *Foxy* experiment opened at the Ziegfeld Theatre on February 16, 1964, to adequate reviews for the show and accolades for the star. *Time* lauded, "The whole show is as cheerful as any show ought to be which rejoices in the presence of the funniest man left alive." But for all Bert's clowning and mugging shamelessly, the show folded after 72 performances. In May 1964 Bert received the Tony Award for his playing of *Foxy*.

United Artists' homage to burlesque, *The Night They Raided Minsky's* (1968), was filmed on location in New York. For a faint brush with authenticity they engaged Bert Lahr to play aging Professor Spats, although Lahr never worked for the Brothers Minsky or appeared in their type of burlesque. It was his last performance. Two weeks after "completing" his Minsky assignment he died, on December 4, 1967.** The cause was cancer.

When he made the film *Flying High* in 1931, *Motion Picture Herald* wrote, "Bert Lahr certainly has done his bit for this 'make America laugh' movement. It is pure unadulterated farce with Lahr going at a terrific pace. Lahr, long a Broadway favorite, may not be well known to the country now, but this one should go a long way toward popularizing him in the provinces." *Flying High* missed the mark. But his Cowardly Lion in *The Wizard of Oz* remains for future generations to enjoy, and they can ponder his invitation to a bewildered world to "Put up your dukes! Put up your paws!"

* In Canada in 1962 he also made a film appearance in a monumental disaster that offered money and an opportunity to work with his old friend Buster Keaton. The film, *Ten Girls Ago*, died in Toronto and was never released.

** Lahr died before the much-beleaguered film was finished. A substitute for Bert was used; the stand-in Professor Spats was filmed mostly in dark shadows or from behind or, on occasion, from the waist down.

FEATURE FILMS

Flying High (*MGM 1931*)

Mr. Broadway (*Broadway-Hollywood Productions 1933*)

Merry-Go-Round of 1938 (*Universal 1937*)

Love and Hisses (*20th Century-Fox 1937*)

Josette (*20th Century-Fox 1938*)

Just Around the Corner (*20th Century-Fox 1938*)

Zaza (*Paramount 1939*)

The Wizard of Oz (*MGM 1939*)

Sing Your Worries Away (*RKO 1942*)

Ship Ahoy (*MGM 1942*)

Meet the People (*MGM 1944*)

Always Leave Them Laughing (*Warner Bros. 1949*)

Mr. Universe (*Eagle Lion 1951*)

Rose-Marie (*MGM 1954*)

The Second Greatest Sex (*Universal 1955*)

Ten Girls Ago (*Canadian 1962*) (unreleased)

The Sound of Laughter (*Union Films 1964*) [stock footage]

The Night They Raided Minsky's (*United Artists 1968*)

With Jonathan Hale in Blondie Brings Up Baby *(1939).*

Arthur Lake

There are few instances in American film history of actors submitting so willingly—even eagerly—to typecasting in a specific role as that of Arthur Lake in the part of Dagwood Bumstead. The acting demands of the characterization required him to appear almost continually bemused (some said stupid), clumsy, and regressively adolescent. It might have seemed a simple characterization, but few could have been so convincing in the role as Lake. Audiences appreciated how well he played the congenial bungler who managed somehow to emerge victorious over assorted domestic and career predicaments.

Between 1938 and 1950, baby-faced, agile Lake starred in 28 Blondie features released by Columbia, all loosely based on Chic Young's popular comic strip. It became a way of life for Arthur, with side excursions into radio and television to portray the same beloved, addled husband and father. For decades of entertainment seekers Arthur was best known as the inventor and consumer of the gastronomical nightmare (the Dagwood sandwich), as the arch-enemy of the post office (due to his repeated morning collisions with the mailman), and for being a walking adding machine (when totaling columns of figures, his head would gyrate like a computerized robot).

Although the low-budgeted black-and-white films never attained the popularity of the more polished Hardy Family MGM series, the Blondie movies were quite successful on their own. In fact, their reception at the box office insured that their stars—Arthur Lake and Penny Singleton (as scatter-brained Blondie)—would never escape association with these roles.

He was born Arthur Silverlake on Tuesday, April 17, 1905, in Corbin, Kentucky. From the very beginning he was a product of show business. His father and uncle had formed a circus acrobatic act called "The Flying Silverlakes." Arthur's mother, Ethel Goodwin Silverlake, had considerable stage experience. Feeling the act too dangerous, his parents would not permit Arthur or his sister Florence to participate in the big-tent gymnastics. However, young Arthur did toddle around backstage, getting a true feel of show business.

Till the age of 11 Arthur's education was supervised by Mrs. Silverlake. However, when the family settled in Detroit for a time, Arthur attended grade school there. Then the family moved to California where the 12-year-old Arthur was "discovered" by the movies. He was among the scores of children in the cast of Fox's *Jack and the Beanstalk* (1917) and *Aladdin and the Wonderful Lamp* (1917), both ventures co-directed by Sidney and Chester Franklin. There followed several uncredited bits in two-reel Westerns starring Franklin Farnum. During this period acrobatics were dropped from the family act and when the Silverlakes played vaudeville, Arthur joined the group in "Family Affair." At one point the family presented a capsulized production of *Uncle Tom's Cabin.*

The death of a relative provided a slight inheritance in Nashville, and the Silverlakes settled there. When Mr. Silverlake later died, the family returned to the stage. Reportedly, the Silverlakes were part of a car caravan playing one-night engagements until the auto burned up. Then they joined the tent-show circuit. Later Florence obtained a movie offer and the Silverlakes relocated, once again, in southern California. While waiting for a movie break, Arthur took a job pressing trousers at a Los Angeles cleaning establishment. Then Florence—who was developing a screen reputation as a daffy blonde—got her brother work at Universal.* As an arrogant, gawky teenager, he began his official motion picture career in a series of "Sweet Sixteen" two-reelers produced by Universal in 1924. It was at this time that his surname was shortened to Lake.

Even this early in his movie career, Lake was submitted to the typecasting that would characterize his adult career. Trade ads of the time promoted Arthur as one of the three top attractions of the Bluebird comedies. (The two others were rotund Charles Puffy and facial contortionist Neely Edwards.) The shorts did open up some opportunities for Lake in feature films, although he was

---

* Sister Florence would remain active in show business well into the Seventies, specializing in feisty old ladies on an assortment of TV shows: "Banyon," "Apple's Way," "The Mary Tyler Moore Show," etc.

always seen playing the same part. In Universal's *Sporting Life* (1925), starring Bert Lytell and Marian Nixon, Lake's bit as a collegiate did not even reach the billing stage. But this situation changed when he worked for veteran comedy director William Seiter in *Where Was I?* (1925) and *Skinner's Dress Suit* (1926), both starring dapper Reginald Denny.

More prestigious was Arthur's performance in Howard Hawks' *The Cradle Snatchers* (1927) at Fox. Based on the enormously successful Broadway comedy hit that had starred Mary Boland and a young Humphrey Bogart, Lake played the important role of Oscar, a bashful Swedish college student (performed on Broadway by Gene Raymond). Arthur becomes involved in the machinations of a trio of married flappers trying to make their husbands jealous. When Lake's character is "aroused" by his love mate, he demonstrates some basic caveman courtship methods.

Returning to Universal, Arthur reverted to playing the heroine's idiotic brother in both *The Irresistible Lover* (1927) and *The Count of Ten* (1928). Thereafter he again worked for director Hawks in *The Air Circus* (1928), a silent drama which had talking sequences, a music score, and sound effects, all courtesy of the studio's Movietone sound system. As Speed Doolittle, Arthur's swaggering conceit well served this early exploration by Hawks of macho mystique, failure, and redemption through sacrifice. Sue Carol played the heroine of the piece, with Heinie Conklin offering comedy relief. The film, which contained some outstanding aviation sequences, also contained Arthur's first talkie scenes. He demonstrated that his voice was adequate (at best) to the medium.

Even more impressive was his cameo appearance in the Colleen Moore–Gary Cooper tearjerker-romance *Lilac Time* (1928). Under George Fitzmaurice's sensitive direction, Lake in an unbilled part gave the best straight characterization of his career as a doomed aviator. It should have been enough to establish him as leading-man material, but such was not to be the case.

His next screen assignment proved to be his most career-progressing to date. He was assigned the title role in First National's adaptation of the successful comic strip

Harold Teen, created by Carl Ed. Produced by Allan Dwan and directed by a young Mervyn LeRoy, the film follows the misadventures of brash young high school student Harold Teen (Arthur resembled Ed's comic drawings of Harold as closely as he would resemble Dagwood Bumstead a decade later). The comedy depicted Harold's matriculation at a new high school and his becoming involved with the making of a sagebrush movie by the school drama club. Although the film suffered from all the clichés (the last-minute touchdown in the big football game, etc.), the breezy direction and the charm of Lake, Mary Brian, and Alice White made the feature a success. It established Arthur as an important juvenile lead.

Part of Lake's growing screen image was his whining and occasionally high-pitched voice. What began as a cute gimmick became a career deficit. One of Warner Bros.' musicals of the song-and-dance film craze of 1929 was *On with the Show* (1929). Seen today the entry is an embarrassment, one of those uneasy silent-to-talkie transitions that nervously attempt to embrace music, comedy, and melodrama in the same plot. An exception to the corniness of this backstage tale was Ethel Waters' sensuous rendition of "Am I Blue?" Joe E. Brown had the male lead, with Arthur cast as Harold, the juvenile in a tacky road company. He was required to sing the Harry Akst-Grant Clarke song "Don't It Mean a Thing to You?" His rendition was as painful as the corny plot.

Equally absurd (especially by today's standards) was *Tanned Legs* (1929), directed by Marshall Neilan for RKO, in which Arthur starred with June Clyde, Sally Blane, and Ann Pennington. *Photoplay* magazine insisted "this frothy musical comedy will thrill the Tiredest Business Man" (especially with glimpses of Miss Pennington's famous dimpled knees and June Clyde's legs). As for Arthur's appearance as Bill, the young hero of the beach-resort comedy melodrama, *Photoplay* noted, "Arthur Lake whoops gaily through the picture in his usual loose-limbed fashion."

Arthur seemed, if anything, to be the victim of the glut of college musicals that surfaced between 1928 and 1932 in Hollywood. The rash of campus roles offered him few opportunities except for a decreasingly engaging recap of his Harold Teen antics. Fox's *Cheer Up and Smile* (1930), which co-starred him with Dixie Lee and Olga Baclanova, is noteworthy today only for John Wayne's bit as Arthur's fraternity brother. Leo McCarey's *Indiscreet* (1931) at United Artists was potentially the most important of Arthur's films of this period. But this Gloria Swanson–Ben Lyon picture was not the major success anticipated, nor was Lake well received as the comedy relief. He had outworn his welcome on the screen and thereafter found it difficult to obtain movie work.

Bruce Cabot and Betty Furness were the stars of RKO's *Midshipman Jack* (1933), with Arthur in a supporting role as a plebe. In 1934 he and his sister co-starred in a Vitaphone musical short, *Glad to Beat You*. However, it did little for their careers. He was soon reduced to comedy character roles, sometimes little more than an extra. Some of his worst pictures were for minor companies— Steiner, Monogram, and Grand National. He was scarcely visible in Paramount's *True Confession* (1937), a big picture starring Carole Lombard and Fred MacMurray. Probably his best bit in this unfortunate period in his career was as the confused and exasperated elevator operator taunted by the ghostly Kirbys (Cary Grant and Constance Bennett) in Hal Roach's *Topper* (1937).

If his film career was in dire jeopardy, Lake managed a coup in his personal life. On July 24, 1937, he wed 18-year-old Patricia Van Cleve. She was the daughter of Rose Davies Van Cleve of Beverly Hills and of George Barnes Van Cleve of New York. More important, she was the niece of former film-star Marion Davies. The society wedding was sponsored by Miss Davies and her lover, newspaper tycoon William Randolph Hearst. The ceremony was officiated by the Reverend F. H. Avery, rector of St. Stephen's Episcopal Church.

Not too many months after the nuptials, Arthur's screen career took a dramatic upswing. Columbia signed him to star as harassed suburbanite Dagwood Bumstead in the first of the Blondie series, released in December 1938. Penny Singleton (replacing an ailing Shirley Deane) was his attractive, zany wife, Blondie. Gangling Arthur proved to be the perfect embodiment of America's most popular comic-strip character.

With Maude Eburne, Barbara Kent, and Gloria Swanson in Indiscreet *(1931).*

The first episode in the film series neglected the genealogy of the comic strip
(Blondie had been a flapper and Dagwood
was the son of a wealthy family that objected
to his marriage to her). Instead, the entry
found the Bumsteads and their child involved in typical domestic comedy plot situations with Arthur becoming increasingly
befuddled by his daffy wife. The critics were
generally far more kind than could have been
anticipated. ". . . it's all quite human in a
comic-strip way. The manner of telling and
the mood are more in the comic-strip style
than the story itself. These are perfectly
possible young people. . . . Arthur Lake is the
eager, ineffectual and slightly scatterbrained
Dagwood" (*New York Sun*). In her three-
star review, Wanda Hale of the *New York
Daily News* reported, "Arthur Lake, with his
unruly hair parted in the middle, makes you
really feel that the timorous Dagwood has
come to life."

So successful was the first of the Blondie
pictures (which cost only $85,000), that the
studio quickly capitalized on the property by
pushing it into a full-scale series. At best, the
Blondie pictures were inoffensive programmers that filled out the lower part of the bill.
The plots were necessarily more complicated
and involved the Bumstead family and dog
Daisy with haunted houses (*Blondie Has
Servant Trouble*), South American music
(*Blondie Goes Latin*), the World War II defense effort (*Blondie's Hero*), radio contests
(*Blondie Hits the Jackpot*), and femmes
fatales (*Blondie on a Budget*)—all situations
outside the simple domestic scope of the
strip.

Among the fledgling stars who received
early screen experience and exposure from
the series were Rita Hayworth, Lloyd
Bridges, Janet Blair, Larry Parks, and Robert
Sterling. Supporting roles were fleshed out
by such established players as Gene Lock-
hart, Hugh Herbert, Tito Guizar, Donald
Meek, Ernest Truex, Edgar Kennedy, Veda
Ann Borg, William Frawley, and Grant
Mitchell.

Variety was on mark when it reviewed the first Blondie film and judged that the "studio has hit paydirt." But strangely this same trade journal was off base when it reported on the July 3, 1939, 7:30 P.M. CBS broadcast of the first Blondie radio show. *Variety* stated, "The program is silly, lacking the power to persuade, replete with illusion-destroying plot liberties and absurdities. It is impossible—taking the first installment as typical—to predict anything but a minimum audience and a minimum engagement." But the summer replacement show was to last for 11 seasons, until 1950! During that time Lake played opposite four Blondies: Miss Singleton, Ann Rutherford (who went so far as to bleach her hair blonde for her tenure on the audio show), Alice White, and Patricia Van Cleve Lake.

By the early Forties the Blondie films had become so productionline-like that even the gentler critics began to carp. For example, in reviewing the entry *Footlight Glamour* (1942), the *New York Post* complained, "We do wish that Lake would quit whining through his role, but guess it's too late to say it."

If Arthur was the fumbling dad on screen, he was the proud papa off camera. On March 1, 1943, the Lakes became the parents of Arthur Patrick. At the christening held later that month, both godparent Marion Davies and cartoonist Chic Young were present. There was much publicity as to how the Lakes had redecorated their Amalfi Drive home in Santa Monica to accommodate the newest addition to the family. (Later daughter Marion would be born.)

It was ironic that the still very youthful Arthur was too old for military duty during World War II, but it was a traditional part of show business that he, a clown, should want to play more serious roles—well, at least, non-Dagwood screen assignments. He was paired opposite a young, svelte Shelley Winters in a grade B service comedy called *Sailor's Holiday* (1944), then played a radio engineer involved in a comedy murder mystery on his honeymoon in *The Ghost That Walks Alone* (1944). He was seen in a

With Penny Singleton in Blondie Goes to College (1942).

characteristically confused-male role as Jeff Donnell's spouse and Charlie Ruggles' son in a United Artists lark, *Three's a Family* (1944). The following year found Arthur playing a Joe E. Brown–type part opposite Dale Evans in the Republic musical comedy *The Big Show-Off*. Lake was seen as the shy, gentle pianist with Dale as the lovely miss who also works at the Blue Heaven Club. She sang three songs, backed up by Anson Weeks & His Orchestra. *Variety* labeled the film "a briefie that has its moments."

How did Lake feel about being internationally typecast as the all-American boob? He said in 1944, "When I'm not playing dopes, I don't work. My agent talked me into playing a straight character once. I played a no-account brother. I guess you could call me the villain. It was awful. I went back to my agent and said, 'Please—from now on I want to be a dope.'" Lake further analyzed, "The only time I eat regularly is when I'm playing dopes, so why should I yell about being typed. I'm grateful to Hollywood. Where else could I make as much money as I do?"

One eager reporter of the mid-Forties researched whether Arthur was as wacky off screen as on. Lake was prompt to volunteer that he had, for example, recently bankrolled a bar in Santa Monica. Six weeks later it closed. "The bartender drank up all the liquor." The amazingly astute actor then admitted, "I'm always completely mixed up in something but off the screen it isn't always so funny."

In both 1946 and 1947 four Blondie comedies were released—more of the same moaned the critics, but the public continued to endorse the quickie films. Every once in a while Lake would, contrary to his credo of accepting a good thing, bristle at his stock-in-trade. At such time his frustrated multi-creative dreams would push him into action. In 1938 he had composed a song ("Help, Help, I'm in Love") for United Artists' *There Goes My Heart*, and in 1948 he formed Arthur Lake Productions. His unit produced for Monogram Pictures a remake of the 1934 *Sixteen Fathoms Deep*. Top-billing himself above Lloyd Bridges and Lon Chaney Jr. (who had played the hero in the 1934 version and was now seen as the villain), Lake's heavy-handed comedy relief antics all but ruined the Ansco-colored film. It *might* have

been a fascinating semidocumentary on Greek sponge fishermen. The *New York Times* lambasted, "We could have been spared Arthur Lake's inane comedy . . . [and] woefully inept comedy techniques." It was to be the only film ever released by Arthur Lake Productions. (In 1950 Arthur did direct an unreleased documentary on Guatemala, but never pursued film directing after that.)

Like so many aspects of the American way of life after World War II, Hollywood was not the same anymore. The film industry was in a dire economical slump, and double-feature fodder was becoming an economical anachronism. Equally important, the public's taste had changed, and simple-minded fare (at least on theatre screens) like the Blondie segments fell by the wayside, as did most of the studio series. In 1950 when *Blondie's Hero* was released, Columbia Pictures called it quits with the Chic Young property. It was the sign of another era coming to a close.

At a loss of direction in which to guide his career, Arthur chose to enter a period of semi-retirement, although he did tour army camps with a series of skits and routines based on the Dagwood character. Then in the mid-Fifties, when television was dredging up all sorts of properties as possible series bonanzas, Arthur was corralled into starring in a video version of Blondie. The program debuted on NBC on Monday, January 4, 1954, with Pamela Britton in the title role. But since the half-hour show could not make up its mind whether to gear itself to kiddie or adult audiences, it only lasted until December 4, 1954. It was also very evident that Arthur was definitely too old for the part. (An attempt to revive the Blondie series in the late Sixties—with Will Hutchins in Arthur's role and Patricia Harty as Blondie—was equally unsuccessful.)

Arthur and Patricia Lake did have another go at television in the Fifties with a pilot for a series called "Meet the Family." The title of the entry indicates how derivative the program was of "Blondie." Lake's most recent fling in show business was as part of the Seventies' nostalgia boom, when in 1974 he and Penny Singleton were briefly reunited for a road company edition of *No, No, Nanette*.

However, business interests (including a small plastics manufacturing company) and

With Murray Alper, William "Bill" Phillips, Jack Rice, Joseph Crehan, Kernan Cripps, and Penny Singleton in Blondie's Secret *(1948).*

his family have occupied most of Arthur's time since 1950, and he has felt little need to return to films (even if there were offers). Besides having invested the finances from his picture career wisely, the Lakes inherited a considerable amount of money from the Marion Davies estate. The ex-movie star was particularly fond of the Lakes and even left Patricia a $600,000 cut sapphire necklace in her will.

Perhaps what is most unusual about the Arthur Lake of today is the way the role of the self-assured businessman seems at odds with the bungling bumpkin that so typified his cinema career.

FEATURE FILMS

Jack and the Beanstalk (*Fox 1917*)
Aladdin and the Wonderful Lamp (*Fox 1917*)
Sporting Life (*Universal 1925*)
Where Was I? (*Universal 1925*)
Skinner's Dress Suit (*Universal 1926*)
The Cradle Snatchers (*Fox 1927*)
The Irresistible Lover (*Universal 1927*)
The Count of Ten (*Universal 1928*)

The Air Circus (*Fox 1928*)
Lilac Time (*First National 1928*)
Harold Teen (*First National 1928*)
Stop That Man (*Universal 1928*)
On with the Show (*Warner Bros. 1929*)
Dance Hall (*RKO 1929*)
Tanned Legs (*RKO 1929*)
Cheer Up and Smile (*Fox 1930*)

She's My Weakness (*RKO 1930*)
Indiscreet (*United Artists 1931*)
Midshipman Jack (*RKO 1933*)
Girl o' My Dreams (*Monogram 1934*)
Silver Streak (*RKO 1934*)
Women Must Dress (*Monogram 1935*)
Orchids to You (*Fox 1935*)
I Cover Chinatown (*Steiner 1936*)
23½ Hours Leave (*Grand National 1937*)
Topper (*MGM 1937*)
Annapolis Salute (*RKO 1937*)
Exiled to Shanghai (*Republic 1937*)
True Confession (*Paramount 1937*)
Double Danger (*RKO 1938*)
Everybody's Doing It (*RKO 1938*)
Blondie (*Columbia 1938*)
There Goes My Heart (*United Artists 1938*)
Blondie Meets the Boss (*Columbia 1939*)
Blondie Takes a Vacation (*Columbia 1939*)
Blondie Brings Up Baby (*Columbia 1939*)
Blondie on a Budget (*Columbia 1940*)
Blondie Has Servant Trouble (*Columbia 1940*)
Blondie Plays Cupid (*Columbia 1940*)
Blondie Goes Latin (*Columbia 1941*)

Blondie in Society (*Columbia 1941*)
Blondie Goes to College (*Columbia 1942*)
The Daring Young Man (*Columbia 1942*)*
Footlight Glamour (*Columbia 1942*)
It's a Great Life (*Columbia 1943*)
Sailor's Holiday (*Columbia 1944*)
The Ghost That Walks Alone (*Columbia 1944*)
Three Is a Family (*United Artists 1944*)
The Big Show-Off (*Republic 1945*)
Leave It to Blondie (*Columbia 1946*)
Life with Blondie (*Columbia 1946*)
Blondie's Lucky Day (*Columbia 1946*)
Blondie Knows Best (*Columbia 1946*)
Blondie's Holiday (*Columbia 1947*)
Blondie's Big Moment (*Columbia 1947*)
Blondie in the Dough (*Columbia 1947*)
Blondie's Anniversary (*Columbia 1947*)
Sixteen Fathoms Deep (*Monogram 1948*)
Blondie's Reward (*Columbia 1948*)
Blondie's Big Deal (*Columbia 1949*)
Blondie Hits the Jackpot (*Columbia 1949*)
Beware of Blondie (*Columbia 1950*)
Blondie's Hero (*Columbia 1950*)

* Unbilled guest appearance.

Harry Langdon

The legend of Harry Langdon, like that of James Dean, is based on a remarkably slim volume of work: three outstanding star-oriented feature films. But access is more onerous to Langdon's silent comedies than to the three Dean-starring features. Too, Langdon's serviceable but undistinctive supporting work as a character actor in talkies would seem to negate the legend.

But the legend of greatness persists. And when perusing pictorial histories of the cinema and observing his elfin, petulant face staring helplessly from the pages, one comprehends not only the possibility, but also the essence, of his stardom and its uniqueness. Whereas most film personalities are stars because they transmit to their audiences the assurance of their survival, Langdon's celluloid survival was always suspect. In his Twenties work, Harry would survive within the story line *only* because of his "innocence" (director Frank Capra would call this the key to Langdon comedy), just as three decades later when "innocence" was passé, James Dean would survive on screen only by virtue of his "honesty."

Harry Langdon was born in Council Bluffs, Iowa, on Sunday, June 15, 1884. His permanently wistful countenance is perhaps explained by his doleful childhood. His parents were very poor, managing to eke out a bare existence for themselves as Salvation Army workers. At an early age Harry went to work selling newspapers; later he found employment as a sign painter. When he proved victorious in an amateur-night contest in Omaha's theatrical district, the young Langdon discovered that a theatrical career might be the means to his financial salvation. For a time he was a property man and occasionally an actor, with the Council Bluffs Stock Company. Then, still in his early teens, he left Iowa to join Dr. Belcher's Kickapoo Indian Medicine Show. Langdon performed a blackface act.

He was with the Gus Sun Minstrels and then in 1903 initiated an act called "Johnny's New Car," which has a breakaway car collapsing in front of a hospital. The novelty of the car as a means of transportation to turn-of-the-century audiences enabled this rather limited routine to be pleasant enough to sur-

The sad clown.

vive two decades of vaudeville audiences. Harry's partner (playing his shrewish wife) was Rose Frances Mensolf, who in 1903 eloped from the cast of the road company of B. C. Whitney's *Show Girl* to marry Harry. The 1922-23 season found Langdon writing and appearing on the circuit in an act entitled "After the Ball."

It was a primitive film record of the "New Car" sketch that filmmaker Mack Sennett used to introduce Langdon to his most gifted gag writers and directors (among them were Arthur Ripley, Frank Capra, and Harry Edwards). The Sennett company, perhaps jaded by the sophistication of their own car gags, were horrified by the "Old Man's" enthusiasm for the new comic. Reportedly, only Frank Capra perceived the dynamic potential of the comic. Curiously, in their autobiographies, both Capra (*The Name Above the Title*, 1971) and Sennett (*King of Comedy*, 1965) defer to each other as Langdon's motion picture discoverer. (Langdon's widow would state that it was Sennett who actually purchased Harry's contract from the minor league studio Principal Pictures in 1923.) Possibly, Capra's and Sennett's modesty was the result of each Frankenstein not wanting to take credit for the monster thus created.

In any event, under the direction of Roy Del Ruth, Erle C. Kenton, and Harry Edwards, pudgy Harry began his film career at Sennett's California studio with a series of two-reelers in 1924 that included *Picking Peaches, Feet of Mud, The Cat's Meow, Smile, Please,* and *Boobs in the Woods.* It was the restraint, understanding, and pervading taste of Capra which brought a unique "humanness" to Langdon's work, an aspect not present in the emoting of the other Sennett stock comics.

While the other Sennett funmakers of the time based their performances on caricature and overexaggeration, Capra conveyed to Harry the necessary virtue of sacrificing a gag for an effect. He also understood how vulnerable Langdon was as a comic. There were traits in Langdon, which did not bear deep analysis, that suggested other comics—Chaplin, Lloyd, Stan Laurel, Buster Keaton among them. Frank Capra, in his autobiography, with pardonable pride claims credit for assigning Langdon his uniqueness, "Harry'll be the Little Elf."

The rise and fall in Hollywood of Harry Langdon consumed a three-year period. The story is curiously suggestive of that time-worn play *Burlesque,* in which a burlesque comic rises to fame, gets a swelled head, discards those who helped his career rise, and then soon hits the skids.

At a time when critics were lauding Langdon's array of two-reelers for Sennett, and Harry was still heeding the advice of his directors, he decided to leave Sennett. His aim was to try his luck with feature films and First National offered him a contract. The decision was a professionally sound one, since he took Capra, Ripley, and Edwards with him. The result was three of the best feature-length comedies to emerge from the silent era.

Tramp, Tramp, Tramp (1926) found Harry as a young hobo who falls in love with the comely daughter (Joan Crawford) of an imperious shoe manufacturer. The latter is sponsoring a transcontinental walkathon and the vulnerable hero enters the ordeal. He is convinced that if he wins the contest he will win the hand of the heroine. In typical Langdon fashion, he does win the race but discovers that Crawford is engaged to another. But in his adventures he had met an attractive young lady and the two are reunited for the fade-out.

When *Tramp, Tramp, Tramp* was released in March 1926, *Photoplay* enthused, "This picture takes Harry Langdon's doleful face and pathetic figure out of the two-reel class and into the Chaplin and Lloyd screen dimensions. Not that he equals their standing yet, but he is a worthy addition to a group of comedy makers of which we have entirely too few. Langdon has graduated and this picture is his diploma." (Years later in judging this comedy classic, the British Film Institute's *Monthly Film Bulletin* would assess, "In trying to distil the essence of Landon's continuing appeal, one can perhaps point to his unprepossessing character's quite unjustified optimism. . . .")

The Strong Man, released in September 1926, also was directed by Frank Capra. This time around Harry is Paul Bergot, a Belgian soldier who after World War I moves to the United States in the entourage of Zandow the Great (Arthur Thalasso), a professional weight lifter. In the course of his travels, the

399

In Soldier Man
(1926).

woebegone hero finally finds the girl (Priscilla Bonner) with whom he had corresponded during the war. Only after he chases local bootleggers out of town does her father change his mind about the suitor's worth.

The critics applauded this full-length comedy. The *New York Times* approved: "Mr. Langdon's work in this production displays true ability, and it is to his credit that he is more effective in the more sober scenes than in the turbulent streaks." Reviewer Mordaunt Hall did note, "If Mr. Langdon would study psychology in constructing his narratives, his films would be more than mere laughmakers." Nevertheless, the *Times'* reviewer had to admit, "These interludes of fun, which are like short sketches . . . serve their purpose in stirring up gales of laughter. . . ." One segment that particularly amused critic Hall was the one "where Paul [Langdon], having had a bath the previous day, is suffering from a bad cold. He makes things uncomfortable for all the passengers on a bus, until finally the man near to him tears off Paul's porous plaster. Here one perceives cold cream mistaken by Zandow

for Limburger cheese, while Paul rubs the cheese, instead of cold cream, on his chest. Neither is the worse for the experiment in an hour or so."

Capra also directed *Long Pants*, which had its New York premiere on March 26, 1927. It was a curious example of whimsy. Harry's hero is presented as a teenage youth who is constantly daydreaming (picturing himself as a romantic Don Juan) and who nags his protective mother to allow him to be a real adult (symbolized by giving up his knee breeches for long pants). In *The Silent Clowns* (1975), author Walter Kerr observes that this gambit "takes something of the comedy away, for what was funny was a man behaving like a 13-year-old, not a 13-year-old behaving like one. Belief in the image is diminished as well, for what we see is still a man, pretending. The drift toward explicitness—generally, a drift toward defining Langdon as child rather than man—is risky; what had intrigued us, and had resisted our initial itch for an explanation, was now yielding to literalness, letting the composite crack." But then, suddenly in the course of the film, the scenario allows for Harry to be mature enough to wed. As Kerr has to admit in his chapter essay, "The transition is not accounted for; it is simply made. With it, the ambiguity is restored—late, but restored. Now Harry is free to confound us again with his impenetrability."

Although audiences were appreciative of the comedy interludes throughout *Long Pants*, the critics were still unsure of how to rank Langdon in the pantheon of screen comedians. *The National Board of Review* magazine chose not to make a decision, but to judge the film for its entertainment value: "The picture is replete with hilarious gags. . . . He is particularly funny when he sets out to shoot his bride with an old horse pistol after the pattern of the unscrupulous villain of whom he has been reading, as well as in the scene where he seeks to impress the adventuress with his skill as a bicycle rider."

On the other hand, the *New York Times'* Mordaunt Hall insisted, "Mr. Langdon is still Charles Spencer Chaplin's sincerest flat- terer. His short coat reminds one of Chaplin, and now and again his footwork is like that of the great screen comedian." As to comparison to other funster greats, Hall added, "Mr. Langdon has once again capitulated to his omnipotent band of gag men. It may be all very well for Harold Lloyd to rely on mechanical twists, but Langdon possesses a cherubic countenance which offers him a chance in other directions."

While the critics were evaluating Langdon and the public was adoring him, Harry was seeing to his own professional self-destruction. According to Capra, Harry was becoming exceedingly difficult to work with on the set. He was impressed by the critical interest in his screen comedy and was convinced he could match or even top the best efforts of Chaplin and the other greats. Recalls Capra, "'Pathos,' he'd scream at me, 'I want to do more pathos.'"

Langdon reasoned that no one could direct him better than he himself, so he abandoned

In Long Pants *(1927).*

Capra, Edwards, and Ripley to star in and direct his own feature film, *Three's a Crowd* (1927). Here he is a sad-faced tenement worker who finds inspiration in an attractive girl (Gladys McConnell). Later she weds another, not knowing of Harry's romantic interest in her. Thereafter she and her husband separate and amidst a snowstorm she finds refuge at Langdon's shack. There she has her baby. But soon her husband arrives to claim her and she and the infant leave with him, not knowing how much Harry loves her. Harry tries to cope with his latest calamity, with some comic results.

Three's a Crowd, while revealing some excellent moments and solid visual offerings (Capra and the usual team had worked somewhat on this project before being discharged), was basically a self-indulgent *Laugh, Clown, Laugh*-type effort. What had been pathos before in his screen works became merely pathetic in this attempt to duplicate Chaplin's *The Kid*. Langdon's foundering as a director became embarrassingly apparent to his fans through mismatched shots and sluggish pacing. Few comics—Chaplin excepted—have ever survived this sort of funnyman-and-child tragicomedy.

In what must be the most abrupt decline in cinema history, many critics who a few months before were comparing Harry to Chaplin and Lloyd were now dismissing him. "Harry Langdon," wrote *Photoplay*, "reaches for the moon in this and grasps—a feeble glowworm. . . . The result is an absurd, unbelievable story." The *New York Times'* Mordaunt Hall was less charitable: "It happens only too often in this present production that the bright bits are followed by a barrage of buffoonery that has about as much right in the narrative as a chimney sweep would have in a flour mill. . . ." Newspaperman Hall was far more impressed with the short-subject offering at New York's Strand Theatre where *Three's a Crowd* debuted on October 2, 1927. The short was the fifth of Will Rogers' motion pictures, entitled *In Switzerland and Bavaria*.

Moreover, *Three's a Crowd* signaled the beginning of Langdon's financial and marital woes, from which he would never recover. As an independent filmmaker, Harry was a failure. His $150,000 salary which he received for each full-length film was quickly devoured by overbudgeting. The disappointing returns of his subsequent 1927 pictures, *The Chaser*, which prematurely attempted to put Harry into domestic comedy, and the equally feeble spy comedy, *Heart Trouble*, completed his association with First National.

In a 1928 *Photoplay* interview with Theodore Dreiser, Harry's ex-boss Mack Sennett summed up both Harry's potential and the cause of his downfall: "Langdon suggests a kind of baby weakness that causes everybody to feel sorry for him and want to help him out. He's terribly funny to me. On the other hand, Langdon knows less about stories and motion picture technique than perhaps any other screen star. If he isn't a big success on the screen, it will not be because he isn't funny but because he doesn't understand the many sides to picture production. He wants to do a monologue all the time, he wants to be the leading lady, cameraman, heavy, and director all in one. So far in my experience that attitude has never proved successful." Later Sennett would say that Harry "was a quaint artist who had no business in business."

Perhaps finally humbled by his bittersweet screen experiences, Harry returned to short subjects, signing a contract with Hal Roach and MGM. Despite excellent production values and the frequent participation of talented Thelma Todd as Harry's co-star, the eight shorts released in 1929 and 1930 were *not* up to the quality of the prior batch for Sennett. There were two reasons for this: the uneasy period of transition in Hollywood between silents and sound, and the fact that Roach simply did not know what to do with or make of Harry the performer.

Harry's professional despondency was duplicated in his personal life. On July 5, 1929, he and Rose were divorced in a legal action costly to Harry. The next day a license was issued for Harry to wed Helen Walton of Toledo, Ohio. They were married a few weeks later. On March 14, 1932, in New Rochelle, New York, the court would grant the couple a separation. That summer the courts awarded Helen $21,078.57 for separate maintenance and $2,250 in legal fees.

Meanwhile his occasional work in feature films did not provide him with the proper showcasing to warrant a "comeback." In

In The Chaser *(1928).*

Michael Curtiz' *A Soldier's Plaything* (1930) he was billed first but merely served as comedy relief for leading man Ben Lyon. In *See America Thirst* (1930), a Prohibition gangster comedy for Universal, he was teamed awkwardly with lanky Slim Summerville. (It would be difficult to find two more disparate comedy styles than those of these actors.) Compounding his artistic plight, Harry's screen work did not provide him with sufficient financial compensation to meet the alimony demands. In 1932 he filed for bankruptcy with debts totaling $62,637 and assets of $700. The once-vain comic listed his profession as "unemployed actor."

In 1933 Harry began the long, humiliating "comeback" trail. He signed to make two-reelers for the low-budgeted Educational Pictures. On occasion Educational reunited him with Vernon Dent, his comic foil from the Sennett days, and Harry Edwards, his old director. The shorts were not among Harry's best, but they are the closest the talkies

would come to suggesting the spirit of the silent Harry Langdon since most of the emphasis was on slapstick. During this period he also made several shorts for Paramount Pictures. Perhaps his best work for that major company came in a 1933 *Hollywood on Parade* featurette, in which Harry appeared in a golfing sequence with Viola Dana and her golfer husband, Jimmy Thompson.

By the mid-Thirties, the prestige of comedy short subjects had greatly diminished. They were regarded as fillers for increasingly longer double features, and it was clear that they lacked the star-making power of the silent shorts. As a character actor, Harry returned—hesitantly—to feature films in *Hallelujah, I'm a Bum* (1933). The credits on the offbeat project were most impressive. Lewis Milestone was the director.* Rodgers

* Milestone replaced Harry D'Arrast as director of *Hallelujah, I'm a Bum.* D'Arrast could not get along with Jolson, especially when it was known that he had wanted Fred Astaire for the lead role.

and Hart wrote the score and the dialogue, which was conceived in rhyming couplets like *Love Me Tonight,* but which was without the resultant charm of that Maurice Chevalier–Jeanette MacDonald entry.

S. N. Behrman wrote the script for *Hallelujah, I'm a Bum* from a Ben Hecht story. The cast included Al Jolson (his first film in three years), Frank Morgan, Chester Conklin, Madge Evans, and Harry as Jolson's trash-picker enemy, Egghead. Sadly, when the film had to be drastically edited to conform to the complex rhyming dialogue, most of Harry's role was cut also. When released, the Depression-era politics of the film were deemed too bizarre for general audiences, and the picture proved to be a box-office failure.

My Weakness (1933), a Lillian Harvey musical for Fox, proved to be a more adroit comeback vehicle for Harry. Cast as Cupid, Langdon served as a Greek chorus for the art-deco musical, which also featured Lew Ayres, Charles Butterworth, and a guest appearance by Mickey Mouse. It suggested that despite Harry's advancing age, his very real talent still existed and it implied a surprising maturity and restraint as a character performer.

Despite the fact that his first two marriages had proven so costly, Harry remarried on February 12, 1934. His bride was Mabel Georgiana Sheldon of Portsmouth, England. They were married by the Reverend Karl P. Buswell at Trinity Presbyterian Church in Tucson, Arizona. Although Langdon had obtained a Mexican divorce from wife number two (Helen) on November 19, 1934, she would sue him for divorce in the United States. It was a situation which would cause the comedian further legal and financial problems. Harry and Mabel would become the father of Harry Jr. in January 1935. Their union was a stormy one: they divorced, remarried, divorced, and remarried (1938); along the way they became the parents of daughter Virginia.

Oddly enough, although Langdon's career would never regain the heights of his silent classics, there were still opportunities left in random cameo screen appearances. Columbia Pictures signed him for a series of two-reel comedies in 1934 and 1935. Some were directed by Arthur Ripley. From 1938 to 1944

Harry was steadily employed in Columbia short subjects.* Sometimes he was teamed with El Brendel. The shorts varied in quality. The studio obviously had no idea how to promote Harry for it switched him from domestic comedy to situation comedy to outright slapstick.

As for feature films, he made *Atlantic Adventure* (1935) for Columbia, in which he was seen as Lloyd Nolan's comic sidekick. *Variety* reported, "Harry Langdon as a news cameraman provides droll laughs and is a splendid comic foil." For British-Lion he played Otto Schultz in *Mad About Money,* with Lupe Velez and Ben Lyon. It was filmed in England in 1937 and released in the United States in 1938 as *He Loved an Actress.* In 1938 Langdon rejoined the Hal Roach studio, working primarily as a scriptwriter for Laurel and Hardy's *Blockheads* (1938), *The Flying Deuces* (1939), *A Chump at Oxford* (1940), and *Saps at Sea* (1940). Harry also worked on the script of Roach's *Road Show* (1941), a screwball comedy starring Adolphe Menjou and Carole Landis.

In 1938 Harry the actor made a cameo appearance in *There Goes My Heart,* playing a preacher who weds the romantic leads, Fredric March and Virginia Bruce. The bit occurred in the film's last 30 seconds. However, Langdon had been out of major features for so long that his "gag" appearance was meaningless to most moviegoers.

Roach, nevertheless, had sufficient confidence to co-star Harry with Oliver Hardy (then contractually separated from Stan Laurel) in *Zenobia* (1939). The film was well produced with an exceptional supporting cast: Billie Burke, Hattie McDaniel, Alice Brady, Jean Parker, and Stepin Fetchit. But its period humor about a circus elephant owned by Langdon who "adopts" a small-town southern doctor was too low-keyed to appeal to the usual Roach comedy audience. Too, although Langdon was not actually teamed with Hardy in this effort, his resemblance to Stan Laurel only underscored Laurel's absence. It is a shame that the picture was a failure because it was rather

* When the team of Olsen and Johnson left their hit Broadway show *Hellzapoppin'* in 1941, there was a rumor that Harry might replace Johnson in the lunatic revue show. However, Happy Felton won the assignment.

charming and both Langdon and Hardy were quite good in unusual assignments.

From that point on, Harry was consigned to the oblivion of poverty-row films. His cinema downfall paralleled that of Buster Keaton, but unfortunately, unlike Keaton, Harry never lived to see a renaissance of interest in his early movie work. It was perhaps a false vanity that permitted Harry to star in pictures like *Misbehaving Husbands* (1940), *All-American Co-ed* (1941), *Double Trouble* (1941), and *House of Errors* (1942). Unlike Keaton in his Forties film forays, Harry was either too old or too disinterested to try to re-create his best routines or to develop new ones. Sadly his presence was being drained for whatever name value remained. In *Spotlight Scandals* (1943) for Monogram, he was required to stooge in an unsympathetic part. In the East Side Kids comedy, *Block Busters* (1944), he had an extraneous role as an undertaker. By the time he had made *Hot Rhythm* (1944) even his now modest name value was meaningless.

Harry's last feature film was *Swingin' on a Rainbow* (1945), a Jane Frazee musical for Republic. Three days before Christmas 1945, Harry Langdon died of a cerebral hemorrhage. He was survived by his third wife, their son (now a commercial photographer) and daughter. His passing was little noted by Hollywood. Obviously, the film community was embarrassed by the demise of one of their greats who had been working for the past five years as a B-film supporting actor.

Harry was one of those noted in James Agee's 1949 essay "Comedy's Greatest Era," but by that time silent-screen comedy was merely academic and the only revival truly encouraged by that article was Chaplin's *City Lights,* in 1951. Nevertheless, in the late Sixties New York's Museum of Modern Art organized a retrospective of Harry's great silent pictures. Public response was strange: some were frankly puzzled by this unique, sensitive, and specialized talent; others felt that Langdon was on a par with Chaplin and Keaton. (Donald McCaffrey in *Four Great Comedians,* 1968, makes Langdon one of the subjects, along with Chaplin, Lloyd, and Keaton.)

Perhaps the best summation of Langdon's rather precious entertainment gift comes in Walter Kerr's *The Silent Clowns:* "Langdon at his best, and in the hands of men who understood better than he the indefinable impulse that moved him, was a genuine original, strangest by far of all the fantasists who walked real city streets. He must be looked on selectively today, with some sympathy for the lost language on which his furtive whisper depended."

FEATURE FILMS

Tramp, Tramp, Tramp (*First National 1926*)
Ella Cinders (*First National 1926*)*
The Strong Man (*First National 1926*)
Long Pants (*First National 1926*)
His First Flame (*Pathé 1927*)
Three's a Crowd (*First National 1927*)
The Chaser (*First National 1927*)
Heart Trouble (*First National 1927*)
A Soldier's Plaything (*Warner Bros. 1930*)
See America Thirst (*Universal 1930*)
Hallelujah, I'm a Bum (*United Artists 1933*)
My Weakness (*Fox 1933*)
Atlantic Adventure (*Columbia 1935*)

* Guest appearance.

Mad About Money [He Loved an Actress] (*British-Lion 1937*)
There Goes My Heart (*United Artists 1938*)
Zenobia (*United Artists 1939*)
Misbehaving Husbands (*Producers Releasing Corporation 1940*)
All-American Co-ed (*United Artists 1941*)
Double Trouble (*Monogram 1941*)
House of Errors (*Producers Releasing Corporation 1942*)
Spotlight Scandals (*Monogram 1943*)
Block Busters (*Monogram 1944*)
Hot Rhythm (*Monogram 1944*)
Swingin' on a Rainbow (*Republic 1945*)

In Berth Marks (1929).

Laurel & Hardy

I was driving down one of the streets in Hollywood and I made a wrong turn. . . . There's this cop on his motorcycle and he sees me. . . . He finally gets over to my car and asks to see my license. He looks at it and says, "What? You're Groucho Marx? Forget about the ticket I was going to give you! But I want to ask you one thing. . . . Why aren't there more Laurel and Hardy movies on TV?" I said, "Don't ask me! How the hell do I know?" And that's all he had to say, and he drove off on his motor scooter and left me alone.

—Groucho Marx

Today, these two derby-sporting comedians enjoy the greatest popularity and celebration of any comedy team in cinema history. When one ponders the less than top-drawer commercial status they possessed in their heyday, this is remarkable. The Marx Brothers had the highbrow appeal of being Broadway successes and prospered in films at plush Paramount and then at MGM. In contrast, Laurel and Hardy performed their classics on the madcap but humble Hal Roach lot, using improvisational technique in the earlier days. Abbott and Costello reigned at Universal, topping the Forties box-office polls and each drawing $10,000 weekly plus percentages of their films' profits. On the other hand, Stan and Ollie never enjoyed percentage deals in their filmmaking efforts and never earned more than $3,500 a week each at at their peak. Yet, in the overall view, no comedy team has ever inspired the laughs or the love that graced Laurel and Hardy in their lifetime—or in their posthumous fame.

"I was more or less a born comedian, I think. I can't recall a time I wasn't kidding around in class (or out of it)—and that, perhaps more than anything else, made me the dreadful student that I was!" recalled Stan Laurel. He was born Arthur Stanley Jefferson in Tynemouth, Ulverston (Lancashire), England, on Monday, June 16, 1890. His father, Arthur J. Jefferson, was an actor-comedian who became a theatre owner and manager. His mother, professionally known as Madge Metcalfe, was a singer-actress. After some less' than sterling academics at Ruther Glen School and Queen's Park Academy in Glasgow, Arthur left the classroom in 1905 to tend the box office of his father's Glasgow Metropole Theatre. By 1907 the lanky lad had weaved a great dream of becoming a comedian and joined Levy and Cardwell's Juvenile Pantomimes Company. He performed a "Golliwog" in *Sleeping Beauty*. After trouping with that company in the vaudeville sketch "Home from the Honeymoon," he toured as a "stable boy" in the play *Gentleman Jockey*, appeared in the Hal Reid melodrama *Alone in the World*, and then landed the starring spot in the Fred Karno Music Hall group's production of *Jimmy the Fearless*. This was presented at Manchester's Hippodrome Theatre in 1908.

In the Karno Company at the time was another young British comic by the name of Charles Chaplin. Laurel was so taken by Chaplin's talents that the former had no qualms about becoming understudy to the latter in the act "Mumming Birds" (in which Stan doubled as the routine's comic-singer). When "Mumming Birds," retitled "A Night in an English Music Hall," toured the United States in 1910 on the Sullivan-Considine vaudeville circuit, Stan continued in his capacity as standby for Chaplin.

In *The Laurel and Hardy Book* (1961) film scholar John McCabe quotes Stan as admitting, "I never had a chance to imitate him [Chaplin] on the stage because he played every show with Karno. Once for the hell of it at one of our little cast parties I announced that I was going to imitate the 'brilliant' Mr. Chaplin. Skeptical applause. First I tried his crazy look at the audience but I just wound up looking like a constipated giraffe—and you haven't lived until you've seen one of *those*. Anyway, the one thing I *could* do pretty well was that eccentric walk of his— the waddle with the cane which he was only then starting to do. So I didn't do too badly when I worked that, and I even got a laugh from *him* as well. That made me feel pretty good."

Stan soon returned to England, performing with a variety of partners in such acts as "The Rum 'Uns from Rome," "The Wax Works," and "Fun on the Tyrol." In 1912 his brother Gordon, manager of London's Prince's Theatre, maneuvered Stan into a job as a supernumerary in the Dion Boucicault play *Ben Machree*. The following year he returned to the States for another tour of "A Night in an English Music Hall." When he left the troupe this time, he remained in America playing the Keith vaudeville circuit as part of "The Keystone Trio," in which he performed a splendid Chaplin imitation.

In June 1916 he formed his own "Stan Jefferson Trio," in which he performed the sketch "The Crazy Cracksman." After this act disbanded, Stan met an attractive Australian singer-dancer by the name of Mae Charlotte Dahlberg (1888–1969), with whom he appeared in drag as an old falsetto biddie. The act clicked with audiences and Stan became so taken by his co-star (who could not obtain a divorce from her husband in Australia) that they decided to live together as a common-law couple. "It seemed one hell of a fine idea," Stan later recalled, though a bitter court battle would later take place when he attempted to extricate Mae from his life. Incidentally, it was Mae who, respecting theatrical superstitions, convinced Stan Jefferson that he was tempting fate by using a name with 13 letters. The act quickly became "Stan and Mae Laurel."

When Stan and Mae Laurel played the New York Hippodrome Theatre in 1917, Stan made his film debut in a one-reeler, *Nuts in May*, for Universal. Thereafter he contracted with the company's "Uncle" Carl Laemmle to star in a series of comic shorts called *Hickory Hiram*. When the character of Hickory failed to catch on with the public, Universal canceled its option on Stan's screen services. Thus when not touring with Mae in vaudeville, Stan would freelance in films. In one 1917 Metro two-reeler, *Lucky Dog*, Stan wrangled with a corpulent bandit. The heavy's name was Oliver Hardy. His first title-card words to Stan were, "Put 'em up, insect, before I comb your hair with lead!"

Norvell Hardy was born on Monday, January 18, 1892, the offspring of a well-to-do southern family. His father, named Oliver, was a local lawyer and politician. From his childhood, "Babe" (the famous nickname, courtesy of a hometown barber) loved to sing, loved to eat (he would always be sensitive about his weight problem), and loved to watch people. "Whenever I travel," he would confess, "I still am in the habit of sitting in the lobby and watching the people walk by—and I can tell you I see many Laurels and Hardys. I used to see them in my mother's hotel when I was a kid: the dumb dumb guy who never had anything bad happen to him—and the smart smart guy who's dumber than the dumb guy only he doesn't know it." Mr. Hardy did not approve of his son's fascination with people when it led to show-business leanings. Shortly after their homesick boy was brought tearfully home after running away to join a minstrel show, the family sent him to a military academy and later to the law department of the University of Georgia. But Babe's attraction to the stage and screen soon terminated his studies.

In 1910 he opened the first movie theatre in Milledgeville, Georgia. After three years of daily watching the antics of the film players, he ran off to audition for film companies. In 1913 he made his film debut with the Lubin studios of Jacksonville, Florida. (His first screen credit has yet to be documented.) He then proceeded to New York, where he worked for the Vim and Edison studios. Poetically, Babe, whose size seemingly doomed him to heavy assignments, pined for more admirable movie roles. He would compensate for his usual screen slobbery by becoming in real life impeccably groomed and an immaculate dresser. Off camera he loved to sing.

Though the comedians first worked together in 1917, nine years would pass before they officially evolved into a film team. In that time Stan had played in nearly 70 films, and had become a writer-producer-director of comedies on the Hal Roach lot, happier behind the camera than before it. Babe, meanwhile, had worked at the old Vitagraph Studios as a director, played in approximately 200 films, and metamorphosed from a heavy into a versatile character player. (He played the Tin Woodman in the 1925 version of *The Wizard of Oz*.) By the mid-Twenties he had a contract with Roach as one of the producer's "Comedy All Stars."

In 1926, Stan was directing *Get 'Em Young*, in which Babe played a butler. The hefty actor scalded his arm in a cooking accident; because a pay hike was promised, Stan replaced Hardy in the role. "When the picture was finished, Roach liked it," recalled Stan,

"and he asked me to write myself into the next one. By then Hardy was ready to go into the next picture, and I appeared with him in it." Their first film as a team was *Duck Soup* (1927), a two-reeler reworking of Stan's father's old vaudeville favorite sketch "Home from the Honeymoon." Thus began one of the cinema's most delightful acting matches.

On the wild Roach back lot, the stable of funsters raced through plots filled with flying pies, lethal wives, and giggly floozies. They would run amok in trains and automobiles, and at one time or another would plunge into the facility's man-made lake. Laurel and Hardy worked constantly amidst this organized and profitable chaos. The bumbling, pretentious Ollie, with his admonitory tie-twiddling, exasperated stares at the camera, and ever urbane manner (in the talkies he would say repeatedly on camera, "I am Mr. Hardy and this is my friend, Mr. Laurel"), was complemented by the gawky Stan Laurel. The latter boasted a simple-minded grin, Olympian eye blinks, and irresistible crying bouts whenever blamed for another's fine mess. Together they were wonderful. Despite the on-camera calamities, and no matter how upset they became with each other in their scenario misadventures, it was somehow always clear to the audience that these two contrasting lost souls would never wish to face a day without the other's company. As Roach himself later said, "Basically the Stan and Ollie characters were childlike, innocent. The best visual comedians imitate children really. No one could do this as well as Laurel and Hardy and still be believable. We always strived for that, and we sure must have succeeded—because the world is still laughing at them."

It is fascinating to note that the real teaming of Stan and Babe occurred on the eve of sound. While the transition in Hollywood would sap the vitality from the careers of such critics' favorites as Buster Keaton and (to a lesser extent) Chaplin, it did no damage to Laurel and Hardy. As filmmaker and critic Alberto Cavalcanti wrote in 1938 of the wrath of the sound era, "Laurel and Hardy took it calmly. They had not become so great in silent days that they needed to fear destroying the atmosphere by their voices. They modified their technique very little. They used sound with the same freshness and the same lack of pretension that they had brought to silent pictures. . . . When sound came in they were plain Laurel and Hardy, and as such they were the pioneers of sound comedy."

In their 105 joint short- and full-length films,* the proceedings were aided by a fleet of priceless supporting players: regal Anita Garvin, who never topped her hilariously decorous derriere-twitching after slipping and falling on a pie in *The Battle of the Century* (1927); Billy Gilbert, the volatile nemesis and purchaser of *The Music Box* (1932) classic, which won Stan and Babe an Academy Award for Best Short Subject; ever decadent Mae Busch, at her most deadly as the knife-wielding madwoman of *Oliver the Eighth* (1934); Edgar Kennedy, the masterful slow burner who suffered so beautifully as his car was demolished in *Two Tars* (1928); James Finlayson, baldpated, mustachioed Scotsman who could perform the most vio-

lent double take in Hollywood. And there were many others.

Unlike most major comedy performers, Stan and Oliver did not worry about over-exposure. They worked steadily, alternating between shorts and features that placed them in any background conducive to mayhem: including prison in *Pardon Us* (1931), the Foreign Legion in *Beau Hunks* (1931) and *The Flying Deuces* (1939), the World War I trenches in *Pack Up Your Troubles* (1932), the navy in *Our Relations* (1936—in which they played a long lost set of twins), and such costumed Ruritanian excursions as *The Devil's Brother* (1933—a.k.a. *Fra Diavolo*) and *The Bohemian Girl* (1936). They attempted to conquer the land of the sagebrush in *Way Out West* (1937) and in 1940 found themselves involved with the "veree" British in *A Chump at Oxford*. Most of the features were economically handled by cost-conscious Roach, who from 1927 to 1938 released his product through MGM. Occasionally the team would actually work for the Metro film factory, as when they provided comedy relief

* Regarded as the team's official tally by the Sons of the Desert, their international fan club.

With Jean Harlow in the short subject Double Whoopee *(1929).*

in *The Rogue Song* (1930), for which Lionel Barrymore had no idea of how to direct the team. They were among the unfortunate caught in MGM's *Hollywood Party* (1934), trading words and troublesome eggs with Lupe Velez, and *Babes in Toyland* (1934), in which many nursery-rhyme characters were delightfully re-created in front of some charming settings.

During their professional heyday in the Thirties, the offscreen Stan and Babe enjoyed a perfect working relationship—almost. Hardy had tremendous respect for his partner's artistry and he would settle every creative question with the response "Ask Stan." He was perfectly happy to allow his seemingly tireless co-worker to have the final say on their artistic output. While Stan would remain at the studio for long hours after the day's takes, developing gags and situations, Babe would be off to the golf course or racetrack. They rarely mixed socially offscreen. Stan related years later, "We had different hobbies. He liked horses and golf. You know my hobby—and I married them all!"

Indeed, in his prime Stan Laurel was quite a character. He was a sometimes abrasive egotist with a falsetto, startling horse laugh and a very roving eye for the ladies.* Outsiders to the film industry were surprised to learn that Stan was actually the extrovert, while Hardy was quiet, very courtly, and a stickler for clothes and sports. While some writers have sensationalized this gap in their

personalities by inferring that the men hated the sight of each other—grossly untrue—there were unpublicized flare-ups on the set from time to time. Veteran MGM camera technician Ralph Jansen would recall that a foul-tempered Stan once lambasted Babe as "a tramp living off the pickings I throw you. I'm the only one with talent. If you saw talent you wouldn't recognize it!" Hardy retaliated by calling Stan "detestable" and "hardly better than vermin." Jansen remembers that Stan's taunts at one juncture became so cruel that "I saw Hardy thump Laurel on the jaw on the set at MGM and all hell broke loose. We were all sworn to secrecy."

Despite these infrequent spats (mentioned *only* to allow that there were clashes from time to time, as there are in most long-term co-workers' lives) each comedian actually had great respect for the other. If Hardy deferred all questions on creativity to Stan, Laurel was well known to keep his eye ever on his partner when watching the rushes, never tiring of his comic nuances. The late director George Stevens once recalled, "One day I walked into the projection room at Roach's, and Stan was the only one there. He was watching some Laurel and Hardy rushes, and as he watched, he howled with laughter. I recall his feet were in the air; he was bicycling them furiously in a reaction of utter merriment. He knew what was good; there was no need for false modesty. He laughed especially at Babe, and that not only because Babe was such a superb comedian but because Stan had the chance that creative people get so rarely—of seeing his own ideas not only brought to life but brought to life more magnificently than he had ever dared to dream they would be."

It was, in fact, Stan's admiration for Babe's talents that caused the team to vacate the Roach lot. The producer had shrewdly kept both men on separate contract, thereby controlling their futures and safeguarding them from accepting another studio's offer. Stan argued strongly that Roach should sign them as a team—or not at all. Meanwhile, Roach was becoming increasingly upset by Stan's behavior and ambitions. The producer traced the team's revolt to their 1932 tour to Europe, where they were greeted, especially in England, with riotous enthusiasm. "Stan came back from England with a swelled head," said

---

* Stan's marital adventures were prime targets for the cinema gossipers. After leaving common-law mate Mae, Stan wed screen player Lois Neilson on August 23, 1926, in Los Angeles. A daughter, Lois, was born in 1928 and a son, Stan Jr., was born in 1930 (but lived only a few days). The couple separated in May 1933, reconciled, and then divorced on September 10, 1935. Next Stan wed Virginia Ruth Rogers in 1936; they were divorced the following year. His most volcanic mate was shapely Vera Ivanova Shuvalova, a Russian singer-dancer known professionally as "Illeana." They wed on January 1, 1938, rewed February 28, 1938, and then went through a third ceremony in the Russian Orthodox Church on April 28, 1938. That disruptive union dissolved in 1940. In 1941 he remarried Virginia Ruth Rogers; they were divorced in Yuma, Arizona, on April 30, 1946. He wed Ida Kitaeva Raphael in May 1946, and it was she who became his widow. At one point in lengthy distaff encounters, it required the Beverly Hills police to keep an ex-wife from making unpleasant telephone calls to Laurel's residence.

By comparison, Hardy's marital record was tame. He wed Myrtle Reeves in 1921; they divorced in 1937. His second and final spouse was Lucille Jones, whom he married in 1940.

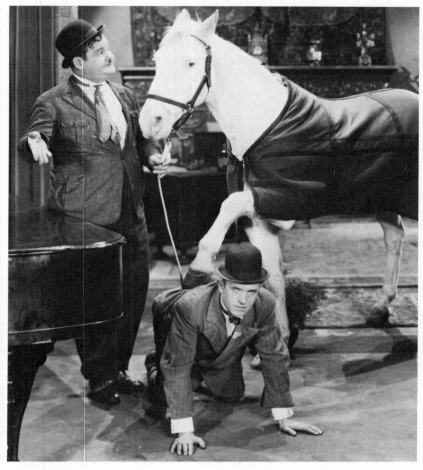

In Wrong Again *(1929).*

Roach. "He developed a Chaplin complex. He wanted to do everything—write, direct, and produce. And somewhere over there he picked up the idea that he was a real devil with the ladies."

In 1938* *Blockheads*, the team's last picture under their revised Roach contract, was released. Roach, who was moving his production facilities to United Artists, was not pleased with the results. He said that Stan "was having too much woman trouble then" to keep his mind properly on his work. Stan left the Roach banner, while Hardy worked out his contract by doing *Zenobia* (1939) with fading Harry Langdon. Freelancing, Laurel and Hardy rejoined for RKO's *The Flying Deuces* (1939). The same year they appeared live at the Red Cross benefit at the San

Francisco World's Fair in "The Driver's License Test," written by Stan. Next they signed a two-picture contract with Roach, filming *A Chump at Oxford* (containing Stan's amazing "double" role as an English scholar) and *Saps at Sea*, both 1940 releases.

The team hoped for the best as they entered the Forties. They toured the expiring vaudeville circuit in 1940 with "The Laurel and Hardy Revue," boasting a 65-member cast. In October 1941 they performed their "Driver's License Test" skit for Caribbean-located bases on a USO junket, joined by Ray Bolger, John Garfield, Jane Pickens, Benay Venuta, and Mitzi Mayfair. By this time they had signed a team contract at Twentieth Century-Fox (which had just lost the Ritz Brothers) and with MGM (where the Marx Bros. had been until recently).

Laurel and Hardy felt they had reason to be professionally happy. They did not. Both major studios painfully abused the comedians, supplying them with low-budgets,

---

* Stan wrote a pilot script, *The Wedding Party*, for a projected radio series. It was recorded before a live audience in 1938, with a cast that included Stan, Hardy, and Edgar Kennedy. The series, however, never materialized.

412

In Brats (1930).

In a pose for Bonnie Scotland (1935).

413

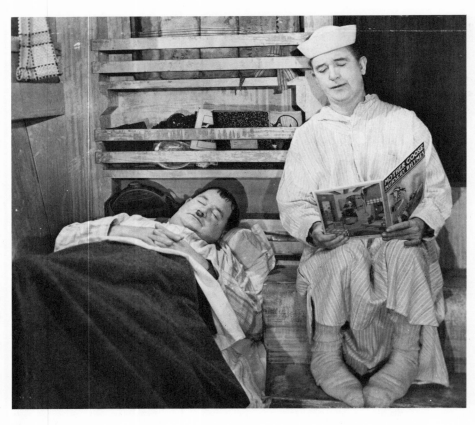

inappropriate materials, and shoddy promotion and distribution. Vivian Blaine, then a Fox contract ingenue, appeared with the men in *Jitterbugs* (1943) and recalls, "It was a B picture and Fox treated Laurel and Hardy as if they were B people." Their eight features of this period Stan later labeled "garbage." At the premiere of Fox's *The Bull Fighters* (1945), veteran stars, abashed at the tawdry results, reportedly held their noses.

It remains a great mystery why MGM and Fox treated the seasoned performers in such abysmal fashion. Certainly the wartime public had not grown indifferent to the talents of the team. In 1942 they joined the "Hollywood Victory Caravan," a war-bond-selling gaggle of Hollywood stars including Bing Crosby, James Cagney, Bob Hope, Cary Grant, Claudette Colbert, Joan Blondell, Merle Oberon, Bert Lahr, Groucho Marx, Joan Bennett, and Pat O'Brien. O'Brien relates in his memoirs, *The Wind at My Back* (1964), "With all of the greatest stars on hand, the greatest ovation and reception all across the country were always for Laurel and Hardy!" Nevertheless, film producers myopically overlooked their still-existing commercial appeal. Abbott and Costello, with their flip manner and racy, burlesque-school style, appeared to be the vogue and Laurel and Hardy had to sit on the sidelines. (In 1943 Laurel and Hardy made a one-reel silent Technicolor government defense short, *The Tree in a Test Tube.*)

On Valentine's Day 1947, Laurel and Hardy began a tremendously successful tour of the British Isles. They reprised "The Driver's License Test" and played a Command Performance in London on November 3, 1947. The sketch was also performed at Paris' famous Lido Club.

Upon their return to Hollywood, Babe played character roles in Republic's *The Fighting Kentuckian* (1949—as John Wayne's sidekick) and in Paramount's *Riding High* (1950). Finally a new joint film for the team developed—the disastrous *Atoll K* (sometimes called *Robin Crusoeland*—1951). "Nobody—and that includes the director and us—knew what the hell was going on," related Stan of the year-long production that featured a multilingual cast and French-Italian financing. It was a sad final feature for the aging team.

In the early 40s.

With Robert Emmett O'Connor, Joe Yule, David Leland, and Ray Teal in Nothing But Trouble *(1945).*

Yet, despite its failure and the mediocre quality of their Forties film work, Stan and Babe continued to draw almost hysterical response from audiences wherever they toured with their stage act. In 1952 they enjoyed a nine-month tour of the English music halls in the sketch "Night Owls." The next year they played their last professional engagement in a routine called "Birds of a Feather," written by Stan. It played an eight-month stand in British music halls. The duo also visited Cobh, Ireland, where they performed and received what perhaps was their most touching salute. "The love and affection we found that day at Cobh were simply unbelievable," recalled Stan. "There were hundreds of boats blowing whistles, and mobs and mobs of people screaming on the docks. We just couldn't understand what it was all about. And then something happened that I can never forget. All the church bells in Cobh started to ring out our theme song, and Babe looked at me, and we cried. . . . I'll never forget that day. Never."

Now in their declining years, Babe and Stan began fully to realize what they meant to so many people, and a very warm feeling for each other had developed. When television* began showing their films to enormous popularity in the mid-Fifties and thereafter (neither comedian received *any* residuals), Hal Roach Jr. delighted both men by planning to produce a four-hour-long TV special, to be called *Laurel and Hardy's Fabulous Fables.* The boys were to have complete artistic control. It was a dream come true. However, 10 days before shooting was to commence, Stan had a minor stroke. Before he could recover, Babe (who had dieted down to 180 pounds to get into shape) suffered a major one. Thus the special was canceled.

* The duo were the guests of Ralph Edwards on "This Is Your Life" in 1954. The show almost did not materialize because Stan balked at the prospect of appearing unrehearsed in anything. Babe managed to urge him on stage and both managed to look properly happy or wistful at the right moment.

416

Hardy's second wife, Lucille, would often roll her wheelchair-bound husband to the television set to watch the Laurel and Hardy films. The stroke prevented him from fully comprehending what was occurring on the small screen. "Look, Babe," Lucille would cry, while watching *Two Tars*, "look what you and Stan did to that poor touring car!" But Babe did not laugh, and on August 7, 1957, at the age of 65, Oliver Hardy died. Stan, who had been too ill to visit his ailing friend, commented, "What's there to say? It's shocking, of course. Ollie was like a brother. That's the end of the history of Laurel and Hardy." Stan was too sick to attend the funeral; his wife, Ida, attended in his place, as did Adolphe Menjou, Wallace Ford, Andy Clyde, Hal Roach, and several of the original Keystone Kops.

Stan Laurel outlived his co-star by seven and one-half years. He lived modestly at the Oceana Hotel in Santa Monica with his wife. Stan touchingly devoted his last years to devising sketches for himself and Babe, not in a morbid sense, but in a tributary one. His apartment was open to everybody from famous comedians to teenagers who had fallen in love with him and his rotund friend. His desk was filled with fan mail from all over the world. Stan determinedly tried to answer each one personally, enclosing a portrait of himself and Babe. Those fortunate enough to sit with Stan and view his films with him on television always noted that Stan was fascinated by Ollie.* He would observe his antics carefully, commenting, "He really is a funny, funny fellow, isn't he?"

Stan received a special 1960 Oscar statuette "for his creative pioneering in the field of cinema comedy." But he was too ill to accept it personally (Danny Kaye went to collect it instead), and bittersweetly remarked, "You know, it's a great honor. I really appreciate it, but why couldn't it have happened while Babe was still alive? Why now?" Though mellowed in his last years, he was still proud. He returned every penny he received from fans who believed the exaggerated reports that he was nearly destitute. He refused a lucrative offer from Stanley

Kramer to appear in *It's a Mad, Mad, Mad, Mad World* (1963) because "the way I look would disappoint the kids." Following bouts with diabetes and heart trouble, Stan Laurel died on February 23, 1965, at the age of 74.

Stan Laurel's funeral was an event. Some 350 mourners, including Buster Keaton, Alan Mowbray, Andy Clyde, and Patsy Kelly, filled Forest Lawn's Church of the Hills, where Laurel lay in a plain wooden coffin and the organ played "The Cuckoo Song" almost as a dirge. His body was buried in the Court of Liberty of Forest Lawn. Dick Van Dyke delivered the eulogy, reading a poem ("God Bless All Clowns") Stan loved.

The oft-repeated statement that "Laurel and Hardy died broke" is not exactly true and certainly irrelevant to the legacy of humor they bequeathed the world. The Sons of the Desert, a Manhattan-based club devoted to the team with "tents" all over the world, reports interest in the comedians to be at an all-time high. In late 1975 the pair's duet from *Way Out West* (1937), "The Trail of the Lonesome Pine," became a smash bestselling single, reaping over 500,000 sales within weeks of its "debut" in London.* And, of course, their films constantly win great popularity on television and in home sales and rental.

In fact, the commercial appeal of Laurel and Hardy is so high that Larry Harmon, original portrayer and promoter of Bozo the Clown, recently won a five-year legal bout to ensure royalties for the widows of both actors from the sale of novelties that bear the performers' likeness. On August 10, 1975, New York Judge Charles Stewart awarded Babe's widow (now Mrs. Lucille Price of the San Fernando Valley) and Stan's widow, Ida (still living in the Santa Monica apartment she shared with her spouse), $1,000,000 in

* The cutting and the commercials inserted into the Laurel and Hardy films tortured Stan. He once wrote to a distributor of their pictures, offering to reedit them for free, but never received a reply.

* In the early Seventies there was a proliferation of LP albums devoted to the soundtrack routines performed by Laurel and Hardy. In England "In The Blue Ridge Mountains of Virginia" (from *Way Out West*) became a hit single, no one seeming to mind that the soundtrack selection had Chill Wills dubbing in the vocal tones of Stan.
On November 16, 1977, a musical play entitled *Mr. Laurel and Mr. Hardy* opened at the Mayfair Theatre in London. Written by Tom McGrath, it featured John Shedden as Stan and Ian Ireland as Oliver. The tribute was not well received. "[The] biographical treatment is too sketchy, and the concept of having the two comics meet in the hereafter to reminisce is so contrived that it seems corny" (*Variety*).

their suit against Hal Roach Studios for unauthorized selling of their husbands' likenesses and names.

Although Harmon is currently marketing everything from Laurel and Hardy wristwatches to food outlets bearing the team's likeness, gimmicks are unnecessary to keep alive the love for the magical screen pair.

Fortunately, both men realized it in their final years. Stan Laurel once smiled, "Maybe people loved us and our pictures so much because we put so much love in them." Oliver Hardy, the quiet partner, expressed it even more eloquently: "Those two fellows we created—they were nice, very nice people."

FEATURE FILMS

The Hollywood Revue of 1929 (*MGM 1929*)
The Rogue Song (*MGM 1930*)
Pardon Us (*MGM 1931*)
Pack Up Your Troubles (*MGM 1932*)
The Devil's Brother [Fra Diavolo] (*MGM 1933*)
Sons of the Desert (*MGM 1933*)
Hollywood Party (*MGM 1934*)
Babes in Toyland (*MGM 1934*)
Bonnie Scotland (*MGM 1935*)
The Bohemian Girl (*MGM 1936*)
Our Relations (*MGM 1936*)
Way Out West (*MGM 1937*)
Pick a Star (*MGM 1937*)
Swiss Miss (*MGM 1938*)
Blockheads (*MGM 1938*)
The Flying Deuces (*RKO 1939*)
A Chump at Oxford (*United Artists 1940*)
Saps at Sea (*United Artists 1940*)
Great Guns (*20th Century-Fox 1941*)
A-Haunting We Will Go (*20th Century-Fox 1942*)
Air Raid Wardens (*MGM 1943*)
Jitterbugs (*20th Century-Fox 1943*)

The Dancing Masters (*20th Century-Fox 1943*)
The Big Noise (*20th Century-Fox 1944*)
Nothing but Trouble (*MGM 1944*)
The Bull Fighters (*20th Century-Fox 1945*)
Atoll K (*Utopia-Fortezza 1951*)

Oliver Hardy alone:

Fortune's Mask (*Vitagraph 1922*)
Little Wildcat (*Vitagraph 1922*)
One Stolen Night (*Vitagraph 1923*)
Three Ages (*Metro 1923*)
The Girl in the Limousine (*Associated First National 1924*)
The Wizard of Oz (*Chadwick 1925*)
The Perfect Clown (*Chadwick 1925*)
The Gentle Cyclone (*Fox 1926*)
Stop, Look, and Listen (*Pathé 1926*)
No Man's Law (*Pathé 1927*)
Zenobia (*United Artists 1939*)
The Fighting Kentuckian (*Republic 1949*)
Riding High (*Paramount 1950*)

Jack Lemmon

Jack Lemmon was once described by Billy Wilder, his mentor of *Some Like It Hot, The Apartment, Irma la Douce,* etc., as "the actor's actor, the divine clown, who could come out and just *do it* and look natural." Indeed, Lemmon has supplied film audiences with many unforgettable comic vignettes: his bobbing in the rampaging soapsuds of the U.S.S. *Reluctant* in *Mister Roberts* (1955), his hysterical sashaying in drag in *Some Like It Hot* (1959), his straining spaghetti through a tennis racket in *The Apartment* (1960), his dismally timed crying jag over his divorce before the amorous Pigeon sisters in *The Odd Couple* (1968), and many more.

Lemmon, moreover, occupies a rare niche in American cinema history. He is one of the first actors to superbly mix comic *and* dramatic skills on a continuing basis. His screen credits include such outstanding dramatic performances as *Days of Wine and Roses* (1962) and the 1976 television special *The Entertainer.* His versatility is reflected in cinema reference books, which have footnoted his status as the only male performer to date to own a Best Actor and Best Supporting Actor statuette (respectively for the pathetically conniving businessman of *Save the Tiger* [1973] and the raucous Ensign Pulver of *Mister Roberts*). As *Films in Review* astutely noted in its 1970s career study of the star, Lemmon "has the potential to succeed Bob Hope or Fredric March." Indeed, he is one of the sterling, if misused, assets in the declining film scene of today.

He was born John Uhler Lemmon III (prematurely in an elevator) in Newton, Massachusetts, on Sunday, February 8, 1925. His father was a salesman of the Doughnut Corporation of America, eventually becoming its president. His mother, Mildred (LaRue Noel) Lemmon, was a housewife. As a child, the boy was quite frail and sickly ("They called me the yellow Lemmon"), and while he attended the Rivers Country Day School and the Philips Andover Academy, he was given extensive physical workouts on his dad's orders to build up his physical endurance. Jack would say later, "Whatever balance and

With Anne Bancroft in The Prisoner of Second Avenue *(1975).*

good sense I bring to my life I owe to my father. He was a very simple, honorable man. He saw life clearly and didn't try to complicate it."

Jack's intelligence launched him into Harvard in 1943 where he enrolled in the Navy V-12 Officer Training Program. While at college he acted with the Harvard Dramatic Club, the Hasty Pudding, playing the lead in *The Playboy of the Western World.* Upon graduation he joined the navy as an ensign-communications officer aboard the aircraft carrier U.S.S. *Lake Champlain.* After his discharge he hastened to New York City to transform his love of the theatre into a career.

Jack experienced all the humble beginnings facing an ambitious, stagestruck young man. His first real stint was at the old Knicker-bocker Music Hall on Second Avenue and 54th Street. There Darren McGavin, Jack Cassidy, Cliff Robertson, and Gene Barry were among his apprenticing cohorts. Lemmon began as a pianist, accompanying the silent-screen comedies shown the customers. He remembers, "I made practically no money, but watching Chaplin and Keaton night after night was like a Harvard education in comedy technique." Soon Lemmon's talents were applied to other activities there. "We did everything from old-time melodrama to waiting on tables to community sings to M.C. bits to oleo bits [everything in one]." At times he aided visiting celebrities who played the Music Hall (for example, playing straight man for Jack Albertson).

For a Harvard graduate, this lifestyle was hardly attractive. Lemmon enjoys recalling how he and a friend, lacking funds for a rooming-house bed, once slept in a condemned building and were awakened by a crane swinging a destruction ball into the walls. "Those were the days. Nothing bothered you, because you didn't give a damn about physical comfort. I've forgotten where we slept the next night. We were just nomads, scrounging whatever we could—anything, anywhere."

In 1948 Jack won his first stage role. It was an off-off-off-Broadway production of Tolstoy's *The Power of Darkness,* performed upstairs in the old Ethnological Dance Studio way downtown. Uta Hagen was the director. When Jack made his entrance in the poorly ventilated hall, the first sight he saw was two elderly people collapsing in the first row from heat prostration. In the cast was a blonde model and radio player named Cynthia Stone, with whom Jack began a serious romance. He also played summer stock in 1948 with the Hayloft Theatre of Allentown, Pennsylvania, landed radio jobs on NBC's science-fiction program "Dimension X" and soap opera "The Brighter Day," and managed to break into the hectic but exciting world of live television.

Jack estimates that he appeared on some 500 video shows during the late Forties and early Fifties. From late 1949 to early 1950 he appeared with Cynthia Stone on the CBS-TV series "That Wonderful Guy," and, with Cynthia as a partner, he was a regular lead on the program "The Ad-Libbers" (a CBS audience-participation game show). In 1951 he performed in the ABC-TV daytime soap opera "The Couple Next Door" and the next year in CBS-TV's "Heavens to Betsy," which began its run on September 30, 1952. In the meantime, Jack wed his co-star Cynthia in her hometown of Peoria, Illinois, on May 7, 1950. They had a child, Christopher, born on June 22, 1954.

The real break for Jack occurred on April 6, 1953, when he starred as Leo Davis with Everett Sloane and John Randolph in the revival of *Room Service* (48th Street Playhouse). The comedy ran for only 18 performances, but the young performer was spotted by Max Arnow, a Columbia Pictures talent scout. Arnow interested Jack in the idea of motion pictures. After the play flopped, Lemmon left New York for the West Coast where he signed a contract with Columbia, then the domain of the brutally efficient mogul Harry Cohn.

Jack's first screen work was a test for the lead in *The Long Gray Line.* Lemmon was impressive but he lost the role when Tyrone Power became interested in the meaty part. Jack's initial picture proved to be *It Should Happen to You* (1954). The comedy was directed by George Cukor, with a scenario by Garson Kanin, and the star was Judy Holliday. (All three major talents had collaborated on the 1950 smash hit *Born Yesterday.*) While many screen newcomers have been upset by the vanity and inhumanity of the celluloid stars they encountered, Jack was fortunate to work with the docile perfectionist Judy Holliday. "She didn't give a damn where the camera was placed, how she was made to look, or about being a star. She just played the scene—acted with, not at. She was also one of the nicest people I've ever met." Columbia's publicity campaign for *It Should Happen to You* summed up Jack—playing the ever pleasant boyfriend of ambitious model Judy—as "a guy you're gonna like."

Neither Judy nor Jack had much to like in *Phffft!* (1954), a comedy of divorce directed by Mark Robson and featuring Columbia's apprentice screen goddess Kim Novak. Lemmon wholeheartedly disliked his next entry, *Three for the Show* (1955), a musicalized remake of *Too Many Husbands* (1940). It was a dismal song-and-dance offering in which he played a veteran who returns after years of being missing in action to find that Gower Champion has wed his wife (played by aging, sung-out Betty Grable).

But Lemmon's next film was a boost upward. It is still one of his best-remembered movie credits—*Mister Roberts.* Columbia lent Jack's services to Warner Bros. for the cinema version of the smash hit Broadway play. The young actor won the plum part of wacky, lecherous, epically unreliable Ensign Pulver (a part played on stage by David Wayne). With Henry Fonda repeating his stage role, James Cagney as the irascible captain, William Powell as "Doc," and John Ford the director, the company filmed the picture on location in Hawaii and on Midway Island, as well as back at the Burbank lot. Jack was delighted by veteran Ford. However, star Henry Fonda was less impressed with his old mentor and there were physical clashes between the two over the slant of the film. Eventually Ford left the film and Mervyn LeRoy completed the project, with some assists from Joshua Logan.

But Fonda had no complaints with Lemmon's interpretation of the junior officer: "I had never been more impressed. Lemmon gave Pulver another dimension, something more." Jack regarded his role thus: "Pulver's frenetic behavior, as I saw it, came out of this tremendous drive to prove himself to Roberts, and, secondarily, to everyone else—to be accepted. It's that simple. A lot of acting is sheer instinct." Millions of viewers recall delightedly how Pulver blew up the ship's

laundry, and his persistent habit of humming "If I Could Be with You." (Interestingly, this touch was added after the film was completed; the humming was dubbed onto the soundtrack to pad some long shots.)

When the 1955 Oscar nominees for Best Supporting Actor were announced, Jack was in competition with Arthur Kennedy (*Trial*), Joe Mantell (*Marty*), Sal Mineo (*Rebel Without a Cause*), and Arthur O'Connell (*Picnic*). Despite the anguish of forgetting his Oscar ceremony admission tickets and leaning against wet paint in his tuxedo, the evening ended on a high note for Lemmon. He won the statuette.

However, he faced a dry professional spell when he returned to Columbia. In *My Sister Eileen* (1955) he had the throwaway role of being Betty Garrett's amiable suitor. Then Lemmon had the misfortune of playing the Clark Gable role in the anemic musicalized version of *It Happened One Night*, entitled *You Can't Run Away from It* (1956). June Allyson was cast in Claudette Colbert's original part. *Fire Down Below* (1957) was a ridiculous melodrama in which he was involved with taciturn Robert Mitchum and a burnt-out Rita Hayworth in smuggling. (Lemmon composed the tune "Harmonica There" which he played in the film.)* The same year Lemmon was among the cast of *Operation Mad Ball.* Though the comedy was a Lemmon favorite (it co-starred him with Ernie Kovacs, whom Jack recalls as "a man of immense talent"), the film, compared with the service comedies *Mister Roberts* and *No Time for Sergeants,* was a washout.

It was Glenn Ford who bullied Jack into doing *Cowboy* (1958), an excellent offbeat Western based on Frank Harris' *My Reminiscences as a Cowboy,* directed with beautiful New Mexico location footage by Delmer Daves. Jack's performance as Frank Harris, the tenderfoot who learns firsthand the unglamorous facts of cowboy life, is one of his best. He was in the cast of the highly promoted *Bell, Book and Candle* (1958), well summed up by Joe Baltake in his *Films in Review* piece on Lemmon, "He was too gen-

* Lemmon's LP album "A Twist of Lemmon" which has the performer vocalizing and playing the piano also offers Lemmon's own song, "With All My Love." His other albums are "Some Like It Hot" (1959) and "Irma la Douce" (1960).

tlemanly to compete in the scene stealing perpetrated by such masters thereof as Kim Novak, Hermione Gingold, Elsa Lanchester, and Ernie Kovacs."

During this period Lemmon continued to work in television. One especially fine credit is his portrayal of John Wilkes Booth in *The Day Lincoln Was Shot* on "Ford Star Jubilee" (NBC-TV: February 11, 1956). While his film output was basically disappointing, also perplexing was his salary, still only about $15,000 per picture, a fact the actor felt was irrelevant to his growing industry status.

"When I read it, I fell off the couch in hysterics. It was just bloody brilliant." In these words, Jack described his initial reaction to Billy Wilder-I. A. L. Diamond's *Some Like It Hot,* the screen comedy which would gross some $8 million in U.S. and Canadian distributors' rentals. (It was the most successful cinema comedy to that time.) As Jerry/Daphne, the bass player who goes drag (with Tony Curtis, of course) to escape the perpetrators of the St. Valentine's Day Massacre, Jack starred in one of the great classics of the U.S. cinema. Lemmon and Curtis were extremely amusing in their female attire; Wilder had them coached by a noted female impersonator. The performers tested their skill by visiting (successfully) a ladies' rest room. George Raft, Pat O'Brien, and Joe E. Brown (as Jack's millionaire pursuer who mouths the famous tag line "Nobody's perfect!") headed the supporting ranks. Top-starred in the proceedings was a definitely plump Marilyn Monroe as Sugar, the lead singer of the all-girl band which the boys join on the romp to Florida. *Saturday Review* called *Some Like It Hot* "hilarious," *Variety* dubbed it "probably the funniest picture of recent memory," and critic Stanley Kauffmann wrote of Jack, "Easily one of the most expert American actors of his generation. . . . His deft, hilariously agonized performance here sets the tone." Jack was nominated for a Best Actor Oscar, but lost to Charlton Heston (of *Ben-Hur*).

Jack was more than professionally generous in his next picture, *It Happened to Jane* (1959), allowing Ernie Kovacs (as the meanest man in the world) and star Doris Day to collect the best screen moments. But the film was a box-office dud, and was re-released by Columbia in 1960 as *Twinkle and Shine* to no

better financial results. But *The Apartment* (1960), another Wilder-Diamond script directed by Wilder (as was *Some Like It Hot*), was hailed by *Time* magazine as "the funniest movie made in Hollywood since *Some Like It Hot*. . . . It is actor Lemmon, surely the most sensitive and tasteful young comedian now at work in Hollywood, who really cuts the mustard and carries the show." The story focuses on a young executive, C. C. Baxter (Jack), who works his way to the business top by lending his apartment to his superiors for their extramarital exploits. Shirley MacLaine was a fine romantic partner for Jack as the girl who falls in love with him after being sexually exploited by Jack's top-level boss, Fred MacMurray. *The Apartment* won a Best Picture Oscar, with Jack again nominated for Best Actor. (This time he was defeated by Burt Lancaster of *Elmer Gantry*.) *The Apartment* grossed over $9 million in distributors' domestic rentals.

A string of less than top films followed for Jack: a guest bit in *Pepe* (1960), repeating his drag routine; a co-starring stint opposite Rick Nelson in *The Wackiest Ship in the Army* (1961); a role with Kim Novak, Fred Astaire, and Estelle Winwood in *The Notorious Landlady* (1962—Lemmon's dad has a silent cameo in the tongue-in-cheek thriller); and the narrator of the French fantasy *Stowaway in the Sky* (1962). It was also during this period that Lemmon made an ill-advised return to Broadway playing in the heavy-handed drama *Face of a Hero* (Eugene O'Neill Theatre: October 20, 1960, 36 performances).*

While in these mild offerings, Jack had been pestering Columbia (under the fluctuating control of a string of executives since the death of Harry Cohn in 1958) to star him in *Days of Wine and Roses* (1962). It was

---

* Lemmon had starred on "Playhouse 90" in *Face of a Hero* (CBS-TV, January 1, 1959) and was convinced that the teledrama could be translated to the stage. Lemmon was wrong. He would admit later, "It was a lesson for me. I learned that failure isn't important because even while you're failing you are learning—and you often learn more from your failures than from your successes; I'm convinced of that. *Face of a Hero* didn't harm me professionally, although a lot of people thought it would. The next morning after we opened there were nine reviews, eight of them stinking! Yet when I came out of my hotel room that day, there were three scripts propped against the door from producers who'd heard we'd flopped and figured I would be available soon. *That's* how much I got hurt."

With Doris Day, Teddy Rooney, Ernie Kovacs, and Walter Greaza in It Happened to Jane *(1959).*

based on a script by J. P. Miller, in turn based on Miller's 1958 teleplay which had starred Cliff Robertson and Piper Laurie. Lemmon finally tried Warner Bros., and studio head Jack L. Warner gambled on Jack's pet project. As Joe Clay, the alcoholic who struggles to reform even if it costs him his marriage to a hopeless drinker (Lee Remick), he gave a powerful dramatic account nicely modulated by director Blake Edwards. Wrote Arthur Knight in *Saturday Review,* "*Days of Wine and Roses* forces recognition of the fact that Jack Lemmon is not only one of our ablest young comedians, but actually one of the screen's finest all-around performers." Jack received his third Best Actor nomination; this time he lost to Gregory Peck (*To Kill a Mockingbird*).

United Artists' *Irma la Douce* (1963), a Billy Wilder-I. A. L. Diamond straight comedy version of the musical play that had been a Broadway hit), is a fondly remembered naughty—in fact, crude—comedy. As Shirley

MacLaine's policeman protector, Jack did *not* win critical kudos. The *New York Herald-Tribune* noted, "Our adored Lemmon has become a mere mugger." Jack was not thrilled with his role or his interpretation of it: "The character I played came out as an unpleasant nasty voyeur . . . it'll never happen again with Lemmon, I'll tell you." While in Paris on location, the divorced Lemmon wed actress Felicia Farr on August 15, 1962.* She had a daughter (born in 1950) by her first marriage to musician Lee Farr. Lemmon and Felicia have a daughter, Courtney Noel, born January 7, 1966. The Lemmon-Farr union has supplied Hollywood with much gossip. Says a friend, "They're like a madcap couple in a 30s movie. They spar all day and then make up in bed."

It took some time before there was another Lemmon screen hit. *Under the Yum Yum Tree*

* Jack and Cynthia Stone Lemmon were divorced in December 1956. She then married Cliff Robertson; they later divorced.

(1963), with Carol Lynley and Dean Jones, was not top-drawer fluff. *Good Neighbor Sam* (1964), with Romy Schneider, Dorothy Provine, and Edward G. Robinson, concluded his memorable (if amazingly nonlucrative) Columbia pact. Forming his own production company, Jalem, which has (co-) produced all his own films since (including some others, such as *Cool Hand Luke,* 1967), Jack starred in *How to Murder Your Wife* (1965), wherein supporting players Mary Wickes, Eddie Mayehoff, and Terry-Thomas glittered. Also in 1965 he played the villain (and a hilariously mad duke) in Warner Bros.' "epic" comedy *The Great Race,* co-starring Tony Curtis as the hero, Natalie Wood as the heroine, and a hugely publicized (and rather disappointing) Technicolor pie fight. In *The Fortune Cookie* (1966), another Wilder-Diamond concoction, Jack made his first screen vehicle with Walter Matthau. When they first read the script, Matthau protested, "But I'll get all the laughs!" to which Lemmon

replied, "Isn't it about time?" (Matthau won a Best Supporting Actor Oscar for his work in the film.)

After a complete misfire in *Luv* (1967), with Peter Falk and Elaine May (". . . goes on endlessly with Jack Lemmon doing a very heavy-handed impersonation of a young Sam Levene," wrote Judith Crist), Jack starred in the Gene Saks–directed movie version of *The Odd Couple* (1968) for Paramount. Based on Neil Simon's Broadway play, which featured Art Carney in the Lemmon role of fussy Felix Unger, the hilarious screen fling ideally paired Jack as the neurotic New Yorker and Matthau as militantly sloppy Oscar Madison. *The Odd Couple,* if a bit stagy, emerged a comedy classic, making a fortune for Jack (his contract called for $1,000,000 against 10 percent of the gross—the picture grossed some $20,000,000). Lemmon was a delight in his part, but there were many who lamented that he allowed too many of the scenes to be dominated by Matthau (already skilled in the

In Days of Wine and Roses *(1963).*

With Michael Connors and Romy Schneider in Good Neighbor Sam *(1964).*

part, having won a Tony for his work in the New York original cast). Matthau was dubbed "America's finest comic actor" by *Time,* a publication that a few years before had conferred that title on Jack. (The stars later appeared on television on "The David Frost Show" and exchanged roles for a few scenes.)

The Odd Couple served to boost Jack back into the top 10 box-office list. There followed *The April Fools* (1969) with Catherine Deneuve, Myrna Loy, and Charles Boyer; *The Out of Towners* (1970) with Sandy Dennis and a Neil Simon script; *Kotch* (1971), which he directed only—the cast included Matthau, who received an Oscar nomination, and Felicia Farr; and *The War Between Men and Women* (1972), based on James Thurber short stories.

Then Lemmon realized another pet project, *Save the Tiger* (1973). It was the depressing tale of a Beverly Hills businessman, Harry Stoner, a none too charming heel who yearns

for the good old days. As with *Days of Wine and Roses,* producers were reluctant to aid in developing the picture project. Jack had to work for $165 per week (base scale) and a percentage to make his film materialize. The result is probably Jack's most skillful screen interpretation. The *New York Daily News* called his work "Lemmon's finest performance in years. . . . He creates a full-bodied man, an angry and pathetic victim of future shock." Jack was Oscar-nominated, facing the toughest competition from Marlon Brando (of *Last Tango in Paris*). Lemmon emerged the victor, hailing his win as "one hell of an honor."

Since his Oscar, Jack has appeared in *Avanti!* (1973), a disappointing Wilder-Diamond project filmed in Italy; *The Prisoner of Second Avenue* (1974) with Anne Bancroft—Jack is the displaced advertising man, a part created on Broadway by Peter Falk; *The Front Page* (1974), an overly broad Wilder-Diamond version of the famed newspaper stage hit, with Matthau as editor Walter Burns and Jack as ace reporter Hildy Johnson; and 1976's box-office dud, *Alex and the Gypsy* ("one of those virtually plotless movies that leaves you wondering who in the world would want to see it" insisted the *Hollywood Reporter*). When Lemmon appeared in *Airport '77* (1977), *Variety* quipped, "Charlton Heston either busy elsewhere or exhausted from earthquakes, World War II, and previous aerial disasters, Jack Lemmon assumes the Noah lead. . . ." Despite an expensive cast which included Olivia de Havilland, Lee Grant, Brenda Vaccaro, Joseph Cotten, Darren McGavin, and James Stewart, the film was met with disgust by the critics. ". . . [it] is a disaster movie that suffers from arrested development: it is a disaster all right, but it never quite makes it to being a movie. . . . After all, even if Jack Lemmon [as the stalwart pilot of the 747 craft] died horribly [within the picture] . . . the film would still be a farce, because there

is something deeply farcical about Lemmon's every expression and intonation, indeed about his very face, however much he may wrinkle it up in heroic self-abnegation" (*New York* magazine).

Lemmon continues to sail through movie roles, but in recent times has explored some fresh territory. On stage he appeared as Harry Van in *Idiot's Delight* at Los Angeles' Ahmanson Theatre in March 1971 playing opposite Rosemary Harris in the revival of Robert Sherwood's anti-war drama. In the winter of 1974 Jack joined with Matthau and Maureen Stapleton to offer Sean O'Casey's *Juno and the Paycock,* presented at the Mark Taper Forum in Los Angeles. Lemmon gave a curiously pallid performance in this revival directed by George Seaton.* In the late spring of 1978 Jack returned to the New York stage to star in *Tribute* by Bernard Slade, the

* Lemmon had been scheduled in 1968 to star in Seaton's *What's So Bad About Feeling Good?* but it was George Peppard who played the lead in the screen comedy.

With Elaine May in Luv *(1967).*

With Sandy Dennis in The Out of Towners *(1970).*

author of *Same Time, Next Year.* When asked why he returned to Broadway, Lemmon confided, "I'm an actor, and there really is nothing complete for an actor unless he can do a job in New York. Everyone says Broadway isn't what it was. That's not true. Besides, this is a good play." (Lemmon was paid $13,000-$15,000 weekly—a lot by stage standards, but not much in Hollywood circles.)

When *Tribute* bowed at the Brooks Atkinson Theatre (June 1, 1978), the critics were unenthused about Slade's script but were extremely impressed with Lemmon. Extolled Clive Barnes (*New York Post*): ". . . [his] performance [is] of such style and grace that he leapt headlong with a clown's panache into the realms of the Broadway greats. . . . It was beautiful. I can only compare it with Laurence Olivier as Archie Rice in John Osborne's *The Entertainer,* and I think Lemmon was the better." Walter Kerr (*New York Times*) observed, "One of the remarkable things about Jack Lemmon is

that, as an actor, he seems to think with his entire body. Merely cocking his head and looking reflective as he spins an idea into the air isn't enough for him. The idea must *be* in the air, weaving its patterns through his restless, nimble, shapely fingers, fingers that play over the face of a telephone dial as though he hadn't quite finished doodling at the piano, fingers that speculatively toy with a brandy glass as though he just considered challenging it to a duel, fingers that probe the corners of his eyes in a busy but vain effort to improve the landscape." Thanks to top business in pre-New York engagements, the show's producer was able to repay the investors in full the day *Tribute* opened on Broadway; sixteen weeks after the Manhattan opening the show had amassed a $418,758 income. When the production closed on Broadway on December 2, 1978, it had earned a 58.3% profit for the investors, and there were still the proceeds from film rights and the West Coast tour (with Lemmon) to consider.

Before *Tribute* became a way of life for Lemmon, he found time to join Walter Matthau and Laurence Olivier in the narration for *The Gentleman Tramp* (1978), a documentary about Charlie Chaplin; to appear in *Oscar's First Fifty Years,* a seven-minute featurette for theatrical release in 1978; to join with Jane Fonda, Bob Hope, et al., in *50 Fabulous Years* (syndicated TV, April 2, 1978), dealing with the Oscars; and to star with Jane Fonda and Michael Douglas in Columbia's feature film *The China Syndrome* (1979), directed by James Bridges. After becoming involved with *Tribute,* Lemmon was seen on the annual Tony Awards (CBS-TV, June 4, 1978).

On television Jack made a bold move when he played Archie Rice, a role supposedly owned by Sir Laurence Olivier, in John Osborne's *The Entertainer.* The tale of the seedy song-and-dance man, who tarnishes the lives of all he comes in contact with as he pathetically hams it up at a cheap burlesque house, was transferred from a British setting to Santa Cruz, California, of 1944, and given a Marvin Hamlisch score. Presented by NBC-TV on March 10, 1976, *The Entertainer* was rejected by many critics, who refused to forgive Lemmon for playing "Olivier's part." Critiques dismissed Lemmon with, "An actor must have no fear of failure." (Actually his performance rated more sympathetic attention, as did those of supporting players Sada Thompson and Ray Bolger.) Lemmon has also found time in recent seasons to participate in some diverse Emmy Award-winning television fare. In 1969, for KNBC-TV in Los Angeles, Jack narrated a controversial documentary, *The Slow Guillotine,* dealing with environmental pollution. On January 17, 1972, on NBC-TV, Jack joined with the likes of Fred Astaire, Ethel Merman, Larry Kert, Leslie Uggams, and Peter Nero in *'S Wonderful 'S Marvelous 'S Gershwin,* an elegant salute to the late composer. Other ventures on the video scene have included hosting the 10-segment "The Best of Ernie Kovacs" series (1976), assorted public service commercials, and reading verse on the PBS-TV poetry series "Anyone for Tennyson?"

Jack Lemmon, who has been undergoing his own public and private battles with temperance over the years, divides his time between a $400,000 Beverly Hills house and a $170,000 retreat at Trancas Beach. He remains fascinated with acting, recently commenting, "Acting for me is what analysis must be for some people. It's such a terrible self-exposure, such a delicious hell."

His pal and long-time associate Billy Wilder sums it up even better. Lemmon "had to be an actor. I doubt he could have done anything else except play a piano in a whorehouse."

FEATURE FILMS

It Should Happen to You (*Columbia 1954*)
Phffft! (*Columbia 1954*)
Three for the Show (*Columbia 1955*)
Mister Roberts (*Warner Bros. 1955*)
My Sister Eileen (*Columbia 1955*)
You Can't Run Away from It (*Columbia 1956*)
Fire Down Below (*Columbia 1957*)
Operation Mad Ball (*Columbia 1957*)
Cowboy (*Columbia 1958*)
Bell, Book and Candle (*Columbia 1958*)
Some Like It Hot (*United Artists 1959*)
It Happened to Jane [a.k.a. Twinkle and Shine] (*Columbia 1959*)
The Apartment (*United Artists 1960*)

Pepe (*Columbia 1960*)
The Wackiest Ship in the Army (*Columbia 1961*)
The Notorious Landlady (*Columbia 1962*)
Stowaway in the Sky (*United Artists 1962*) [narrator only]
Days of Wine and Roses (*Warner Bros. 1962*)
Irma la Douce (*United Artists 1963*)
Under the Yum Yum Tree (*Columbia 1963*)
Good Neighbor Sam (*Columbia 1964*)
How to Murder Your Wife (*United Artists 1965*)
The Great Race (*Warner Bros. 1965*)
The Fortune Cookie (*United Artists 1966*)

Luv (*Columbia 1967*)
The Odd Couple (*Paramount 1968*)
The April Fools (*National General 1969*)
The Out of Towners (*Paramount 1970*)
Kotch (*Cinerama 1971*) [director only]
The War Between Men and Women (*National General Pictures 1972*)
Save the Tiger (*Paramount 1973*)
Avanti! (*United Artists 1973*)

The Prisoner of Second Avenue (*Warner Bros. 1974*)
The Front Page (*Universal 1974*)
Alex and the Gypsy (*20th Century-Fox 1976*)
Airport '77 (*Universal 1977*)
The Gentleman Tramp (*Marvin Films 1978*) [narration only]
The China Syndrome (*Columbia 1979*)

Harold Lloyd

In the silent era, Hollywood's trinity of screen comedians in order of popularity, box-office receipts, and general critical evaluation was: Chaplin, Lloyd, and Keaton. Today Lloyd is generally assigned third place in the succession. Although he lacked the multi-talented artistry of Chaplin and the genius of Keaton, his considerable contributions to the history of screen comedy cannot be minimized.

Lloyd's films were funny. He was forever playing the bespectacled, strawhatted, bound-to-succeed American boy, garbed in bargain-basement suit. He was the average everyday man confronted with life's struggle in the never-ending pursuit of happiness. Within the framework of the deceptively shy, hesitantly smiling go-getter, Harold devised some of the most thrilling sight gags put on film. His character was always coping with a less than friendly world and combatting the recurring animosity of inanimate objects. But no matter what, his goals were clear—he was seeking career success and the affection of the girl of his dreams.

Harold Clayton Lloyd was born on Thursday, April 20, 1893, in Burchard, Nebraska, to James Darsie Lloyd and his wife, Sarah Elizabeth Fraser Lloyd. Restless Mr. Lloyd was constantly on the move and the family relocated frequently. Harold's schooling continued in various towns. It was in Omaha that he made his stage debut with John Lane Connor's Burwood Stock Company, eventually playing Abraham in *Tess of the D'Urbervilles*. In 1911 he completed high school in San Diego, California. He then rejoined Connor's stock company touring California in repertory. A year later he made his film debut as an Indian in an Edison Company short film. Rejoining his father in Los Angeles, he found work with the Morosco Stock Company, but he soon left the stage to concentrate on the fledgling flickers where three to five dollars a day could be made as an "extra."

At Universal Studios Harold found extra work in a series of Westerns directed by J. Farrell MacDonald and starring J. Warren Kerrigan. For the director/star's epic, six-reel feature *Samson* (1914) Harold doubled as

With Anna Townsend in Grandma's Boy (1922).

makeup man and Philistine. While working in a series of pictures based on L. Frank Baum's *Oz* stories, Lloyd met another extra, Hal Roach. When the latter suddenly inherited a few thousand dollars he decided to produce his own pictures. He hired Lloyd as his leading man at $5 daily. After having played lurking villains and background characters, Lloyd was suddenly a movie comedian playing an uninspired Willie Work screen character. He also supplied comedy relief for Roach's two-reel mini-dramas featuring Jane Novak and Roy Stewart, dramas like *From Italy's Shores.* The Lloyd-Roach films were successful, but Harold's request for a larger weekly salary was not. He therefore left Roach for the bedlam of Mack Sennett's Keystone film factory.

Lloyd's career with Sennett was brief and he returned to Roach to begin a new screen character blatantly founded on Chaplin's "Tramp." Lloyd and Roach called their creation "Lonesome Luke." Lloyd as "Luke de Fluke" remodeled Chaplin's image of the oversized baggy pants to one of extremely tight, too-short pants, accentuated with an undersized vest over a vertically striped shirt and abetted by a woman's tailored coat. Darkened arched eyebrows and a black waxed moustache increased the Chaplin-derived image. Strangely, the Lonesome Luke one-reelers were successful. The shorts were helped no end by the addition of a dark-eyed 15-year-old beauty, Bebe Daniels, who played the leading lady.

The Luke series earned Harold mild acclaim as a resilient slapstick comic and the tag "The Human Rubber Ball." After making nearly 60 one-reelers the series graduated to two-reel farces in 1917. With the Luke character embellished with many of Chaplin's mannerisms, the two-reelers extended the duplicity by closely approximating plots and themes from the Chaplin films. Lloyd was not happy with this approach and reasoned, "I didn't want to go on forever being a third-rate imitator of anybody—even a genius like Chaplin." The situation encouraged him to seek a new screen image. He hit on the idea of a comic Frank Merriwell.

"The Boy," shy, alternating nervousness with untapped inner courage, and romantically inclined, emerged in the one-reeler *Over the Fence* (1917). The new guise fit well;

the public approved and identified with it. With little variation, it would remain Harold's screen persona through almost all of his remaining screen career. His "glass character" became world famous. When his first treasured pair of horn-rimmed glasses (the glass had been hammered from the frame to avoid reflection of light in the camera) were almost beyond repair, he sent them to an eastern optical company to replace them. The firm returned his prize glasses, his check, and added to the package 20 pairs of tortoise shell rims. It was the firm's appreciation for the upsurge in business in horn-rimmed glasses since his introduction of the celebrated screen character. (Interestingly, off screen and without the phony glasses, Lloyd would seldom be recognized as the great clown.)

Bebe Daniels left Lloyd in 1919 to join Cecil B. DeMille at Paramount. To succeed her as the comedian's leading lady, a 5'2" blue-eyed blonde named Mildred Davis was hired. The Philadelphia-born Miss Davis had some prior screen experience and proved to be adequately pleasant as the new heroine. Her quiet, unobtrusive playing opposite Harold began with *From Hand to Mouth,* and she would remain with Lloyd on camera through his first four features.

Away from the studio, Miss Davis and Lloyd began a romance that culminated in their marriage at St. John's Episcopal Church in Los Angeles on February 10, 1923. Harold's five-year-older brother, Gaylord, was best man. After playing a role in Principal Pictures' *Temporary Marriage* (1923) Mrs. Lloyd retired from the screen. She returned once again in 1927 for Harold's onetime director Fred Newmeyer to play the lead in Paramount's *Too Many Crooks.* On May 22, 1924, the Lloyds' daughter Gloria was born. In 1929 the couple adopted five-year-old orphan Gloria Freeman and renamed her Marjorie Elizabeth (Peggy) Lloyd. In January 1931 Harold Lloyd Jr., nicknamed Duke, was born.

Lloyd's screen career nearly ended on August 24, 1919, when a round black "gag" bomb he was using to light a cigarette while posing for publicity stills exploded in his hand. The incident nearly blinded him and blew off the thumb and forefinger of his right hand. A prosthetic device was designed for his hand, replacing the missing fingers. He wore it to

the end of his career before the camera. It made all the more remarkable the strenuous and often-dangerous stunts he recorded on film. Released from the hospital in March 1920, Harold returned to complete the two-reel *Haunted Spooks* he had started at the time of the accident.

The prolific releases of Lloyd's two-reelers exceeded the output of Chaplin and Keaton. When his two closest competitors entered the feature-length comedy field, Harold followed suit. A planned short film, *A Sailor-Made Man* (December 25, 1921), was extended to a qualifying feature of four reels.

Grandma's Boy was a painstakingly constructed comedy on which Lloyd spent an unbelievable six months filming. When it was released in May 1922, the five-reel comedy was a rousing success. It traced the courage of a small-town coward given his heroic Civil War grandfather's lucky talisman (an umbrella handle) by his sagacious grandma. It propels him to heroics and to winning the girl (Miss Davis). With *Grandma's Boy* doing so well at the box office, Pathé gave Harold a contract for six features

that it would finance. It was agreed that 80 percent of the profits would be split between them, with the remaining 20 percent going to Hal Roach and the distributor. By now Lloyd was firmly entrenched as one of the leading screen comedians and advancing toward his later affluence as a multimillionaire.

In November 1922 when *Dr. Jack* was released, Lloyd's obvious attempt to extend his comedy to moralistic overtones gave pause to several reviewers. *Photoplay* thought he had conceived the picture as a comedy with a mission: "The old fast tempo and adroit ingenuity are only apparent now and then. Lloyd is striving too obviously to be legitimate at any cost."

While Keaton's features *Three Ages* and *Our Hospitality* glowed with Buster's cinematic gifts, Lloyd's classic *Safety Last* (1923) burst upon the screen. It contains his most memorable and virtually immortalized film sequence as "the human fly." He scales a skyscraper to win, naturally, a thousand-dollar prize so he can marry "the girl." The film was tremendously enhanced by the 12-floor scaling sequence and Harold's desperately agonizing clinging to the building clock as the face of the clock pops out. It remains as one of the greatest, meticulously constructed and filmed sequences in the entire comedy genre.

Lloyd's fascination with height was evident in the earlier, three-reel *Never Weaken*, in which a steel girder, being placed on another skyscraper opposite his office, swings into the window lifting Harold and his chair into space. Later, in the sound feature, *Feet First* (1930), he would repeat the exciting climbing stint. Harold's thrill gags were carefully blueprinted, developed, executed, and heightened by expert editing. If they were not always relevant to the story, they remain some of the most exciting exploits devised by any screen comedian. Like Chaplin in *Modern Times* and Keaton in his constant war against inanimates, Lloyd sensed the comic value of the insignificance of humanity confronted with the juggernaut of progress.

Why Worry? (1923) was a South American revolution romp in which Lloyd, as a wealthy hypochondriac, was mistaken for a spy. He escapes a firing squad by befriending a giant (Colosse). With *Why Worry?* Harold acquired a new leading lady, pert and pretty Jobyna Ralston. She would remain his vis-à-vis for the next four years and was a marked improvement over Mildred Davis Lloyd. When *Why Worry?* was completed, Lloyd severed his ties with Hal Roach, established his own studio, and maintained control of all of his films. He also purchased 16 acres of land in Benedict Canyon in Beverly Hills.

If Douglas Fairbanks and Mary Pickford's Pickfair Estate was regarded as Hollywood's royal domain, Lloyd's Italian renaissance 44-room mansion was a close rival. It was constructed at a cost of some $2.5 million over a period of four years. It boasted an Olympic-size swimming pool, a 9-hole golf course, an 11-foot waterfall cascading to the canyon floor, and exquisite formal gardens. Kennels that would later house some 60 to 70 Great Danes were added. King Alfonso of Spain presented Harold with a bell that was tolled vigorously on the day of Harold Jr.'s birth from the courtyard tower. The opulence of Greenacres, as Lloyd named the baronial estate, was staggering.

The Harold Lloyd Corporation utilized a stable of gag writers, cameramen, and directors with whom he had worked at Hal Roach's plant.* But it was Lloyd's influence that ultimately put the comedy on the screen despite his haphazard ways and his admitted lack of "method." His first production was *Girl Shy* (1924). As in many of Lloyd's films, while the expository reels held interest and provided laughs, it was the movie's climax that was outstandingly memorable. As a tailor's apprentice trying to prevent "his girl" from marrying the villain, Harold pulled out all the stops. He filmed one of the greatest chase sequences ever put on film.

Using automobiles, fire engines, streetcars, motorcycles, and, finally, a pair of horses and a dump cart, Harold's hero ends his perilous ride on horseback. He reaches the wedding in time to carry off the bride. The sheer mania, force, and pace of the segment were breathtakingly thrilling and funny. *Time* thought it "not only the funniest picture that Harold Lloyd has done, but pretty nearly the funniest that anybody anywhere has done including all of California."

Hot Water (1924) found wide appeal because of Harold's persistence in coping with an array of mundane crises (for instance, boarding a streetcar with a stack of unmanageable bundles and a ridiculous live turkey he won at a raffle). Another lengthy, laugh-provoking sequence was a family outing in Harold's new car which is eventually demolished by unlikely hazards.

Chaplin's *The Gold Rush* was earning world acclaim when *The Freshman* (1925), Lloyd's best feature picture, was released. With it Harold hit the top of his motion picture career. The film had sight gags, like a quickly basted tuxedo falling apart at a dinner dance; Lloyd's misadventures as an ineffectual campus cavalier; and his football team's water boy entering the big game to win it for the college. The *New York Times* recorded, "If laughter really is a panacea for some ills, one might hazard that a host of healthy persons were sent away from the Colony [Theatre] yesterday after regaling themselves in wild and rollicking explosions of mirth over Harold Lloyd's comic antics in

* Sam Taylor, Ted Wilde, Frank Terry, Tim Whelan, and Tommy Gray functioned as gagsters, with Fred Newmeyer and Sam Taylor assisting Lloyd in the direction.

In Hot Water *(1924).*

In The Freshman
(1925).

his latest effusion, *The Freshman*." But a few scribes thought it less funny than some of the star's past efforts.

The Freshman started Harold on a one-picture-a-year schedule. It also involved him in an unsettling law suit. H. C. Witwer sued Lloyd for copyright infringement. He asserted that *The Freshman* was taken from his story "The Emancipation of Rodney." After Witwer's death in August 1929 his widow continued the legal action. She was awarded a share of the film's profits for the period 1926-31. However, in 1933 the U.S. Circuit Court of Appeals in San Francisco set aside the Witwer claim.

His 1926 feature, *For Heaven's Sake,* was the first Lloyd-Paramount release. The studio rather grandly advertised the initial such entry: "It is fitting that the leading individual exponent of clean, wholesome screen comedy should be allied with the world's foremost screen organization."

Robert E. Sherwood, writing in the *New Yorker* magazine, announced, "Harold Lloyd has his own company now; he selects his own collaborators, spends his own money and takes his own time. He works on his pictures until he feels that they are right, and then he turns them over to Famous Players to be handed on to the public. Lloyd is a painstaking, conscientious craftsman." Yet Sherwood acknowledged, "Harold Lloyd himself is not a great comedian—not to be compared, individually, with Charlie Chaplin, Buster Keaton, Harry Langdon, W. C. Fields, Raymond Griffith, or Leon Errol. He has no genius for pantomimic clowning; his humor is reliant, at all times, upon the surrounding situations. But he has something that all these others lack—and that is a shrewd, selective intelligence which enables him to distinguish between the funny and the unfunny. He also possesses an uncanny mastery of pace; whatever else his comedies are or are not, they are always fast on their feet. They start moving toward a definite objective and they gather momentum as they progress."

While *For Heaven's Sake* engaged Harold in the risky element of religion for comedic effect and background, *The Kid Brother* (1927) returned him to the country-bumpkin genre (a specialty played better by silent star Charles Ray). Jobyna Ralston left Lloyd after

this film to pursue a less notable career. For his last silent picture in 1928, *Speedy,* Ann Christy supplied the love interest. Baseball's home-run king, Babe Ruth, made an appearance and Harold gave him a wild ride in a horse-drawn streetcar to Yankee Stadium.

Welcome Danger (1929) was completed as a silent picture. However, Lloyd scrapped much of the footage, added sound effects to the remaining reels, and refilmed the cut segments with dialogue. Despite all of Harold's efforts, his first talkie was a cumbersome affair. Although he read dialogue convincingly, his voice was rather colorless. His second talking picture, *Feet First* (1930), succeeded because he returned to what he did best. He devised thrilling visual comedy. He kept the audience in awe with such stunts as teetering on a scaffold and clinging dearly to a building and, finally, screaming for help—all from a window just inches above the ground.

Harold's wavering talking films improved with *Movie Crazy* (1932), one of the better comedies on Hollywood. *Theatre Arts* magazine, after commenting on Lloyd's first unfortunate sound-film encounters, felt he had properly returned to the Lloyd of old who could "send us into convulsions one minute and frighten us out of our seats by some hair-raising exploit the next." A fun bit with a magician's coat sparked the film and it was further highlighted by an exceptionally good performance from lovely Constance Cummings as a glittery movie star.

Lloyd devoted nearly two years to *The Cat's Paw* (1934), released by Fox. It was based on a Clarence Budington Kelland story, which Lloyd adapted for the screen with Samuel Taylor. It was Harold who decided that the story should be told without his usual, and familiar, sight gags. Here was Ezekial Cobb, a missionary's son caught up in a Chinatown crime wave. It proved to be the worst feature that Lloyd would make. (According to Richard Schickel in his book, *Harold Lloyd, The Shape of Laughter,* 1974, "What one can't help thinking is that Lloyd was attempting, in this film, to make a transition from comedies to straight actor, sensing correctly that his vogue as a comic had nearly passed. . . . Without gags to fall back upon, he was simply too colorless to carry the picture."

In 1936 Harold signed with Paramount for its screen version of the Broadway comedy hit *The Milky Way,* briskly directed by Leo McCarey. As a diffident milkman who becomes a prizefighter, Lloyd gave a straight comedy character portrayal and did it extremely well. Adolphe Menjou and Veree Teasdale, however, garnered most of the critical applause for their comedy interplay. Two years later, a committee-written script, *Professor Beware!* (1938), was roughly dismissed by press and public. The *New York Times'* comment, "Even a fair Lloyd, of course, is better than no Lloyd at all," could not have eased Lloyd's decision to retire.

Harold withdrew from filmmaking and retired to Greenacres. He briefly hosted the "Old Gold Comedy Hour" on radio in 1940 and the following year he produced two undistinguished programmers at RKO: *A Girl, a Guy and a Gob* (with Lucille Ball and George Murphy) and *My Favorite Spy* (with Kay Kyser and Jane Wyman). Then, in one of the strangest alliances in the history of Hollywood, Lloyd returned to the screen.

Preston Sturges, who had brought to the screen several of the most original and offbeat comedies of the era, joined with billionaire Howard Hughes, who had not, to form a producing company—California Pictures. For their first venture, Sturges scripted, Harold Lloyd agreed to star, and the team utilized the last reel of *The Freshman.* The hodgepodge venture was called *The Sin of Harold Diddlebock* (1947). It should have been entitled "The Sin of Sturges, Hughes, and Lloyd."

When the last reel of *The Freshman* ran out, Sturges' script ran steadily downhill and the picture was justifiably panned following its April 1947 release. Hughes withdrew the Diddlebock fiasco and supervised the re-editing of the picture with his usual meddling and disastrous results. In 1950 Hughes re-released the picture through RKO as *Mad Wednesday.** Under any name it was "A Sin."

But there was a resurgence of interest in Harold's career. A *Time* cover story, when he was elected Imperial Potentate of the Order of Nobles of the Mystic Shrine, furthered it.

Unfortunately, committed to the Sturges-Hughes charade, Harold had turned down a bid to star on Broadway in a new Mary Chase comedy about a rabbit called *Harvey.*

In 1952 Chaplin started his controversial exile in Europe and Keaton was adding considerable brightness in a small part in Chaplin's new movie, *Limelight.* At the Academy Award ceremonies in 1952, Harold Lloyd received an honorary Oscar for being a master comedian and good citizen. At least he had been finally recognized by the industry.

Greenacres occupied his various hobbies until 1961,* when he assembled a compilation of his old films under the title *Harold Lloyd's World of Comedy* (1962). It contained gems from his silent pictures: the football sequence from *The Freshman; Hot Water's* trolley-car-turkey and wrecked-car segments; the revolution from *Why Worry?; Girl Shy's* frenetic chase; clips from his talkies, *Feet First, Movie Crazy,* and *Professor Beware;* and, above all, the thrilling clock sequence from *Safety Last. Lloyd's World* was well received. To a generation to whom he was but another name in Hollywood's history, it was a revelation and a source of abundant laughter.

Lloyd's life at Greenacres was beset with family problems that resembled an O'Neill tragedy played out against a background of faded but still opulent grandeur. Mildred had become an alcoholic; his daughters had married and divorced; his son, trying to escape the shadow of a famous father, wound up in show business. He made his screen debut in *Our Very Own* (1950), and then sought a career as a singer. However, his path was plagued by alcoholism, sexual confusion, and failure. Harold sought refuge from the mounting traumas and family disintegration by absorbing himself in painting, collecting slides, and objets d'art. He devoted a good deal of energy to enlarging his collection of ornaments for his Christmas tree, which stood choked with decorations all year in the garden room. And he compiled another selection of his silent-film highlights under the title of *The Funny Side of Life* (1963), which enjoyed better success in Europe than in the

* In mid-June 1950 Lloyd sued RKO for $750,000 damages to his professional reputation when Hughes released the picture without giving Harold star billing.

* On January 29, 1956, Lloyd appeared on television with a clutch of other screen personalities in a filmed-in-color special, *Inside Beverly Hills.* He was interviewed by master of ceremonies Art Linkletter.

With Barbara Kent in Welcome Danger *(1929).*

States. In 1964 William Cahn wrote a biography of the comedian entitled *Harold Lloyd's World of Laughter.*

The two re-edited reissues of his career renewed Lloyd's status as a major screen comedy talent. It brought much the same appraisal of his work as had been pronounced decades before. "Although his characterizations are less individual than those of Keaton and Chaplin, he veered successfully between playing the resilient booby and a bland, sophisticated man-about-town and proved delightfully accident-prone in both. The criticism often leveled at Lloyd is that he requires more mechanical props than his colleagues, which tended to restrict his work to a series of highly wrought disaster gags with little in-between" (British *Monthly Film Bulletin*).

On August 18, 1969, Mildred died of a coronary in St. John's Hospital in Santa Monica. She had recovered from a stroke earlier that year. A year later Lloyd was informed that he had incurable cancer. He died at the age of 77 on March 8, 1971. Funeral services were held at the Scottish Rite Temple on Wilshire Boulevard in Los Angeles and he was entombed at Forest Lawn Memorial Park in Glendale. The following week, in London, his former leading lady Bebe Daniels passed away. Three months later to the day, his son Harold Jr., physically impaired since experiencing a brain hemorrhage in 1965, expired in a North Hollywood sanatorium.

Greenacres, Harold's sumptuous palace that housed his many hobbies and whims, has withstood the passing years better than his slowly disintegrating family. When daughter Gloria became emotionally disabled and later was confined to a Swiss sanatorium, the Lloyds were responsible for raising their granddaughter, Suzanne Lloyd Guasti. The girl brought the star great joy in his final years.

After his death Greenacres was turned over to the Harold Lloyd Foundation, which endeavored to follow his instruc-

With Dorothy Wilson in The Milky Way (1936).

tions that the estate be used as a museum by the film industry.* That effort failed and mounting debts forced the foundation to put Hollywood's most lavish remaining memory of an age long gone on the auction block.

On July 27, 1975, Iranian Nasrollah Afshani bid $1.6 million for the estate. Later the furnishings of the mansion were auctioned off separately. In November 1975

Afshani put Greenacres back on the market, asking $4.5 million for the package, which included the life-size playhouse, the first structure built on the estate for Lloyd's daughter Gloria.

While the fate of Greenacres was unpleasant, Lloyd's screen personality has come back in vogue. In the early Seventies, there was an ABC-TV special entitled *Harold Lloyd's World of Comedy* hosted by Dick Van Dyke, and in 1976 Time-Life Films reissued 14 of Lloyd's screen features as well as pruning footage from the comedian's screen work for a 26-part, half-hour TV series. It demonstrates that his best celluloid contributions possess a timelessness.

* Several television series (including "Cannon" and "Columbo") have filmed segments for their telecast on the Lloyd estate. ABC-TV filmed its telefeature *Death at Lovehouse*, with Robert Wagner, Joan Blondell, Sylvia Sidney, and Dorothy Lamour, at Greenacres in 1976.

FEATURE FILMS

A Sailor-Made Man (*Associated Exhibitors 1921*)

Grandma's Boy (*Associated Exhibitors 1922*)

Dr. Jack (*Pathé 1923*)

Safety Last (*Pathé 1923*)

Why Worry? (*Pathé 1923*)

Girl Shy (*Pathé 1924*)

Hot Water (*Pathé 1924*)

The Freshman (*Pathé 1925*)

For Heaven's Sake (*Paramount 1926*)

The Kid Brother (*Paramount 1927*)

Speedy (*Paramount 1928*)

Welcome Danger (*Paramount 1929*)

Feet First (*Paramount 1930*)

Movie Crazy (*Paramount 1932*)

The Cat's Paw (*Fox 1934*)

The Milky Way (*Paramount 1936*)

Professor Beware! (*Paramount 1938*)

The Sin of Harold Diddlebock [a.k.a. Mad Wednesday] (*United Artists 1947*)

Harold Lloyd's World of Comedy (*Continental Distributors 1962*)

The Funny Side of Life (*Harold Lloyd 1963*)

With Wallace Beery in The Bugle Sounds (1941).

442

Marjorie Main

"It's difficult to reconcile the name Marjorie with Marjorie Main's appearance, and her manner. She has a dead pan, square shoulders, a stocky build, a voice like a file, and an uncurried aspect. She has a stride like a section boss. She has bright, squinty eyes. She generally starts off looking as if she never smiled in her life, then suddenly she smiles from her eyes out."

These words were penned by Damon Runyon, who, along with most of the moviegoing public of the Forties and Fifties, was keenly aware and appreciative of the comic abilities of Marjorie Main. A conscientious, very professional actress, Marjorie was a graduate of stock, vaudeville, and Broadway. She was a versatile performer who gave a gallery of splendid performances: the bitter gangster's mother of *Dead End* (1937), the cathouse madam of *Johnny Come Lately* (1943), her many co-starring vehicles with Wallace Beery, and her definitive characterization of the cantankerous Ma Kettle in the Universal comedy series. From 1940 to 1954 she was one of the most skilled members of the MGM Stock Company.

She was born Mary Tomlinson in Acton, Indiana, on Monday, February 24, 1890, the daughter of the Reverend Samuel J. Tomlinson and Mary (McGaughey) Tomlinson. The girl attended public schools in Elkhart, Indiana, and later enrolled at Franklin College in Franklin, Indiana, and then at Hamilton College in Lexington, Kentucky. It was there that she developed her love for and skill at drama. After graduation she studied dramatic art in Chicago and New York.

Marjorie first practiced her craft as an instructor on the faculty of Bourbon College in Paris, Kentucky. At the end of her first year there she had the audacity to request a raise—and was promptly fired. She then turned to the Chautauqua lecture circuit, offering readings from Dickens and Shakespeare for $18 weekly. Eventually she was promoted to a $25 a week actress in repertory groups on the circuit. This was followed by stock work in Fargo, North Dakota, and vaudeville jobs. At this time she changed her name to Marjorie Main. She explained, "I didn't want to use my family's name on the stage because I knew they disapproved. The name I chose was my idea of a name easy to remember."

Marjorie accumulated a good deal of show-business experience in rather short order. In 1916 she toured in some fluff called *Cheating Cheaters* and then was selected by W. C. Fields to co-star with him in "The Family Ford," a vaudeville sketch favorite that brought Marjorie to the Palace Theatre in New York several times in the late Teens.

Just as Marjorie's career was ripening, she abandoned it temporarily—for love and marriage. Her groom was Dr. Stanley LeFeire Krebs, a 57-year-old lecturer of the Chautauqua circuit who had created the curriculum of the American University of Washington, D.C. The couple wed on November 2, 1921. Thereafter the 31-year-old bride worked with her husband in the capacity of secretary and booking agent. "Doctor was a creative man, always writing. We didn't need anyone else. We had each other."

The Krebs family resided in Manhattan between tours. In 1923 Marjorie decided to seek theatrical work once again. She appeared in a variety of shows: *House Divided* (Punch and Judy Theatre: November 11, 1923), *The Wicked Age* (Daly's 63rd Street Theatre: November 4, 1927—she played Mae West's burlesque queen mother!), and *Salvation* (Empire Theatre: January 31, 1928). In 1929 Marjorie toured with Barbara Stanwyck in *Burlesque* and on November 8, 1932, she opened at the Alvin Theatre as part of the huge cast of the Jerome Kern–Oscar Hammerstein II musical *Music in the Air*.

Meanwhile, Marjorie had entered the world of moviemaking. Her debut was in Universal's film version of *A House Divided* (1931), directed by William Wyler. She played a bit as a townswoman. At Paramount she was on screen briefly as a gossip in *Hot Saturday* (1932), starring Nancy Carroll, Cary Grant, and Randolph Scott. She had another minute part in *Take a Chance* (1933), starring James Dunn, Cliff Edwards, and Lillian Roth. In 1934 she made another entry that was filmed in New York, *Crime Without Passion*, starring Claude Rains and Margo. It was not until Fox decided to film *Music in the Air*, a 1934 release packaged as a comeback vehicle for Gloria Swanson, that Marjorie first went to California. She repeated her stage role of Anna the maid.

Main interrupted her cinema sojourn to return to New York when her husband became cancer-stricken. On September 27, 1935, Dr. Krebs died at St. Luke's Hospital at the age of 71. Marjorie was crushed and recalled the bereavement as "the low point of my life. I was brokenhearted and desperately needed work as much to occupy my mind as well as to make a living."

The vulnerable woman soon found a perfect outlet for her sorrow, the role of Mrs. Martin, the slum-dwelling mother of an infamous gangster in Sidney Kingsley's *Dead End* (Belasco Theatre: October 28, 1935). "When he died," Marjorie once said of her husband, "I used to pour my sorrow on the audience night after night as the mother in *Dead End* here on Broadway." Her big scene took place when her killer son (Joseph Dowling) visits his old neighborhood and rushes joyfully to his mother—who slaps him in the face and calls him "Ya' dirty yellow dog." The *New York World-Telegram* reported that, of the cast, "none rises to quite the smoldering intensity of Marjorie Main's Mrs. Martin, the mother of a gunman and a soul in torment." While giving 460 performances as Mrs. Martin, Marjorie kept to herself, avoiding confrontations backstage with the frequently abrasive "Dead End Kids" (Leo Gorcey, Huntz Hall, Bill Halop, et al.), who came to the fore in this production.

It was on December 26, 1936, that Marjorie opened in *The Women* at the Ethel Barrymore Theatre. In Clare Boothe's spicy comedy of civilized bitchery, Marjorie played Lucy, a Reno hotel keeper. The all-women cast starred Ilka Chase, Margalo Gilmore, and Betty Lawford. (Marjorie, along with Phyllis Povah and Mary Cecil, would be the only members of the Broadway cast to repeat their roles when MGM filmed the property some three years later.)

Meanwhile, Samuel Goldwyn bought the screen rights to *Dead End* and signed Marjorie to re-create her dramatic part of Mrs. Martin on screen. Marjorie arrived in Hollywood, where the "older ladies" of the screen who found steady character work included Edna May Oliver, May Robson, and Jessie Ralph; their peer, Marie Dressler, had died of cancer in 1934. Since *Dead End* had a delayed starting date at the Goldwyn lot, Main visited Universal to support Nan Grey and

Kent Taylor in *Love in a Bungalow* (1937), an assembly-line confection that typified the studio's innocuous product of this period.

When the prestigious *Dead End* was finally ready to roll, Marjorie joined a solid cast boasting Joel McCrea, Sylvia Sidney, Wendy Barrie, Humphrey Bogart, Claire Trevor, Allen Jenkins, and, of course, the rambunctious Dead End Kids. Director Wyler, with his usual penchant for extensive rehearsals, allowed Marjorie ample time to practice her big scene with Bogart (as her son Baby Face Martin). The result was that she, as Bogart would recall, "had slugged me raw-faced" by the time the final take was filmed. After film industry figures witnessed Marjorie's extremely dramatic work in this class production, she was the recipient of many offers from the major studios.

Throughout the late Thirties, Marjorie was a very busy performer, but worked on a freelance basis, believing it would allow her full choice of offered roles. She had a variety of parts in major and minor productions. She was Barbara Stanwyck's mother in *Stella Dallas* (1937), the heartless prison matron in *Prison Farm* (1938), Bernard Punsley's mama in *Angels Wash Their Faces* (1939), a nasty aunt in *Two Thoroughbreds* (1939), and Walter Pidgeon's mother in Republic's rowdy Western *Dark Command* (1940). In the last film she had a telling death scene.

In the meantime she worked steadily in the radio medium, guesting on such programs as those starring Fred Allen, Rudy Vallee, and Edgar Bergen–Charlie McCarthy. However, Marjorie appeared to face her most promising future on the glorious MGM Culver City lot where between 1938 and 1940 she played in some of the studio's finest productions. She was Walter Connolly's ever so wise secretary in the Clark Gable–Myrna Loy–Walter Pidgeon adventure *Too Hot to Handle* (1938), and an old woman in *Three Comrades* (1938), a film version of Erich Remarque's novel of pre–World War II Germany. In 1939 she repeated her stage role of horsey Lucy in the plush, all-female screen version of *The Women*, starring Norma Shearer, Joan Crawford, Rosalind Russell, Paulette Goddard, et al. Many thought that Marjorie gave the most delightful and consistent performance in the show. The same year Main was a boarding-house matron in *Another Thin Man*, which

rematched William Powell and Myrna Loy. In 1940 she joined the supporting ranks of *I Take This Woman*, the notoriously long-in-filming Spencer Tracy–Hedy Lamarr romance drama; appeared in Joan Crawford and Fredric March's *Susan and God*; and enlivened the flavorful *The Captain Is a Lady*, which starred fellow character players Charles Coburn and Beulah Bondi.

Then came Marjorie's chance for screen stardom. Louis B. Mayer, as well as a majority of the American public, had been enchanted by the on-screen chemistry of Marie Dressler and Wallace Beery in such classics as *Min and Bill* (1930) and *Tugboat Annie* (1931). Since Dressler's demise no actress had been able to fill her void as a proper cinema mate for the scene-stealing Beery. Actually, few actresses wanted to attempt the feat. Beery had perhaps the worst reputation in the movie colony for crassness and temperament. His output at Metro by the early Forties was confined largely to stock characterizations that allowed him to be his slovenly self and permitted the studio to accrue a tidy profit. In her last release of 1940, *Wyoming*, Marjorie found herself professionally in tandem with Beery. In this Western potboiler, directed by Richard Thorpe, she played Mehitabel, a local blacksmith. Though seventh-billed, she emerged the star with the critics and the audience. The *New York Daily News* detailed, "Beery takes advantage of a lot of footage but he isn't the whole show, not when Marjorie Main is around. . . . To me, she is the first picture stealer and the greatest picture saver in Hollywood. Here, she is as tough as a Cornell linesman. I've been waiting all these years to see her whack Beery in the seat of the pants with a shovel."

A delighted Louis B. Mayer offered the 50-year-old actress a seven-year MGM contract, which she signed happily. As she commented later, "Guess I'd still be doing *Dead End* out in Hollywood if MGM hadn't been looking for a new gal friend for Wally Beery."

The Beery-Main team went on to star in five more features. *Barnacle Bill* (1941) was another variation of *Min and Bill* and caused the *New York Times* to report, "Wallace Beery has found the perfect foil in Marjorie Main, all right. And, perhaps more than either he or his Metro bosses bargained for,

Posing with Peter Whitney, Helen Walker, Fred MacMurray, Jean Heather, Porter Hall, and Mabel Paige in Murder, He Says *(1945).*

as competition who comes close to stealing some of his best scenes." *The Bugle Sounds* (1941) was amusing pre-war propaganda. *Jackass Mail* (1942) was a circa 1850s oater. *Rationing* (1944) spoofed that wartime fact of life. *Bad Bascomb* (1946) found little Margaret O'Brien giving established scene-swipers Beery, Marjorie, and J. Carroll Naish a healthy run for their money. *Big Jack* (1949) was an 1890s melodrama in which Beery was ill during most of the shooting. (He died of a heart attack on April 1, 1949, shortly after completing his scenes.)

Like so many screen teamings, the Beery-Main relationship was not a particularly pleasant one. "Working with Wally wasn't always easy," she later admitted. "He'd never rehearse his lines or bits of 'business,' but he'd want me to rehearse mine. I've always been extremely conscientious in my work and his behavior sometimes unnerved me."

Marjorie received ample opportunity to act in other glossy MGM products. In 1941 she worked with Joan Crawford, playing an austere housekeeper in *A Woman's Face,* and with Clark Gable and Lana Turner in *Honky Tonk,* enacting a sagebrush crusader who quips of Gable's charm, "I'm young enough to like it, and too old to believe it." Main played in Norma Shearer's forgettable last picture, *We Were Dancing* (1942) and years later would speak unkindly of the demanding Metro star. Ever busy Main was Katie the maid in *Meet Me in St. Louis* (1944), tending that very glamorous household of Leon Ames, Mary Astor, Judy Garland, Margaret O'Brien, Lucille Bremer, et al.

From time to time, Metro—at a nice profit—loaned Marjorie to other studios. She was especially impressive in Ernst Lubitsch's *Heaven Can Wait* (1943), playing Gene Tierney's wealthy, beautifully gowned mother in that Technicolor fantasy. The character actress was seen later that year as "Gashouse Mary" in *Johnny Come Lately,* starring James Cagney.

Off screen and in contrast to her usual screen image, Marjorie was noted as a chic and tasteful dresser. She was a very quiet and professional lady who mixed very little with the Hollywood crowd. She visited a Los Angeles nightclub, the Hollywood Trocadero, for the first time in 1946, to see herself imitated by female impersonator Arthur Blake. During her California years she acquired no notably steady beaus and remained single throughout the rest of her life.

As her original Metro contract neared completion, the lot supplied the popular actress with a new seven-year pact, assuring her $1,000 weekly. It also provided for a dressing-room trailer on the lot. But it was not MGM where Marjorie would achieve her greatest screen success. It was over at Universal, the home of Abbott and Costello, where fame awaited. In 1947 the lot retained her to support Claudette Colbert and Fred MacMurray in *The Egg and I*, based on Betty MacDonald's bestselling novel. Memorably, veteran performer Percy Kilbride and Marjorie created the characters of Ma and Pa

Kettle, Pacific Northwest farmers who are neighbors to the chicken-farming newlyweds (Colbert and MacMurray) from the city. With their squad of children (13 in this entry) and hilariously bucolic manner, the Kettles were great hits (despite being quite toned down from the book's counterparts). James Agee wrote in *The Nation*, "Marjorie Main, in an occasional fit of fine, wild comedy, picks the show up and brandishes it as if she were wringing its neck. I wish to God she had." If some critics had reservation about the contrived urban versus rural comedy, the public had none. *The Egg and I* reaped $5.5 million in U.S. and Canadian film rentals.

In addition, Marjorie won an Oscar nomination for Best Supporting Actress of 1947. Her competition included Ethel Barrymore (*The Paradine Case*), Gloria Grahame (*Crossfire*), Anne Revere (*Gentleman's Agreement*), and Celeste Holm (*Gentleman's Agreement*). Miss Holm won.

Also in 1947 Universal used Marjorie to play the title role in *The Wistful Widow of Wagon Gap*, starring Abbott and Costello. It

With Wallace Beery and Vanessa Brown in Big Jack *(1949).*

447

was not long before Universal decided to spin off the Kettles as a series of their own, the first being *Ma and Pa Kettle* (1949). Along with the declining Abbott and Costello and Donald O'Connor-Francis the Talking Mule, they kept Universal solvent.

Marjorie had a good deal to do with the creation and continued freshness of the Ma Kettle characterization. "I have a feeling for costumes. I read a script, confer with the producer or director about what kind of woman it is, and then usually ask for the right to work out my own wardrobe. On the majority of my films I've done my own costumes, and for the Kettle series my motto was 'If it's wrong, it's right.'" She got along well with Kilbride. He once commented, "Marjorie's too busy for temperament; her gusto and versatility are fascinating." As for Marjorie, she said she deemed "Percy the best deadpan actor in the business, and a complete gentleman."

After 1955's *Ma and Pa Kettle at Waikiki* (the title illustrates just how desperate the writers were getting for formats), Kilbride refused to extend his contract.

Thereafter the series hobbled on without him. *The Kettles in the Ozarks* (1956) featured Arthur Hunnicutt as cousin Sedge and *The Kettles on Old MacDonald's Farm* (1957) volleyed the Pa role to Parker Fennelly. All in all, the Kettle characters appeared in 10 Universal pictures and the studio later credited them with supplying the lot with $35,000,000.

While laboring in the Kettle series, Marjorie displayed her ample talents elsewhere. At MGM she continued appearing in such fare as Judy Garland's *Summer Stock* (1950) and Lana Turner's *Mr. Imperium* (1951). The detective mystery-comedy *Mrs. O'Malley and Mr. Malone* (1950) was projected as a Metro series for Marjorie and James Whitmore, but the concept was abandoned after the initial picture. Main bolstered such other MGM fare as *The Long, Long Trailer* (1954), starring Lucille Ball and Desi Arnaz, and teamed with Bert Lahr in comedy relief roles for an overdrawn remake of *Rose-Marie* (1954). It proved to be her final MGM film, and, like many other contract players, she departed the lot.

With Percy Kilbride in Ma and Pa Kettle on Vacation *(1953).*

With Arthur Hunnicutt and Una Merkel in The Kettles in the Ozarks *(1956).*

In 1956 she appeared as the zealous Widow Hudspeth in Allied Artists' *Friendly Persuasion*, third-billed under Gary Cooper and Dorothy McGuire. The affectionate bit of Americana was directed by her favorite mentor, William Wyler. Thereafter Marjorie did a bit of television work. She appeared in a 1957 episode of "December Bride," and guested (with Linda Darnell and Margaret O'Brien) on a 1958 segment of "Wagon Train." But Main did not care for the helter-skelter pace of the TV medium, and soon disappeared from the Hollywood scene. She preferred to relax at her homes in Los Angeles and Palm Springs, secure with the money she had invested shrewdly.

During the final 17 years of her life, Marjorie was rarely seen in show-business circles, though she participated each year in the annual Santa Claus Lane Parade in Los Angeles. She devoted her time to relaxation and to the Moral Re-Armament Movement, which she believed was "the one hope for the world."

Little news was made by Marjorie until April 3, 1975, when she entered Los Angeles' St. Vincent's Hospital; she had long been battling cancer. She died a week later, on April 10. She left no known survivors—she had lived alone for nearly 40 years. The funeral was held on April 14 at the Church of the Hills at Forest Lawn in Hollywood Hills.

As could be expected, most of the obituaries identified Marjorie as the actress who played the energetic but lovable Ma Kettle. Perhaps this was an inequity to an actress who played so many diverse roles so very well. But Marjorie would not have minded. As she herself admitted, Ma Kettle was "good for a lot of laughs—and I would rather make people laugh than anything else."

FEATURE FILMS

A House Divided (*Universal 1931*)
Hot Saturday (*Paramount 1932*)
Take a Chance (*Paramount 1933*)
Crime Without Passion (*Paramount 1934*)
Music in the Air (*Fox 1934*)
Love in a Bungalow (*Universal 1937*)
Dead End (*United Artists 1937*)
Stella Dallas (*United Artists 1937*)
The Man Who Cried Wolf (*Universal 1937*)
The Wrong Road (*Republic 1937*)
The Shadow (*Columbia 1937*)
Boy of the Streets (*Monogram 1937*)
City Girl (*20th Century-Fox 1937*)
Penitentiary (*Columbia 1938*)
King of the Newsboys (*Republic 1938*)
Test Pilot (*MGM 1938*)
Prison Farm (*Paramount 1938*)
Romance of the Limberlost [a.k.a. In Old Indiana] (*Monogram 1938*)
Little Tough Guy (*Universal 1938*)
Under the Big Top (*Monogram 1938*)
Too Hot to Handle (*MGM 1938*)
Girls' School (*Columbia 1938*)
There Goes My Heart (*United Artists 1938*)
Three Comrades (*MGM 1938*)
Lucky Night (*MGM 1939*)
They Shall Have Music (*United Artists 1939*)
Angels Wash Their Faces (*Warner Bros. 1939*)
The Women (*MGM 1939*)
Another Thin Man (*MGM 1939*)
Two Thoroughbreds (*RKO 1939*)
I Take This Woman (*MGM 1940*)
Women Without Names (*Paramount 1940*)
Dark Command (*Republic 1940*)
Turnabout (*United Artists 1940*)
Susan and God (*MGM 1940*)
The Captain Is a Lady (*MGM 1940*)
Wyoming (*MGM 1940*)
Wild Man of Borneo (*MGM 1941*)
The Trial of Mary Dugan (*MGM 1941*)
A Woman's Face (*MGM 1941*)
Barnacle Bill (*MGM 1941*)
The Shepherd of the Hills (*Paramount 1941*)
Honky Tonk (*MGM 1941*)
The Bugle Sounds (*MGM 1941*)

We Were Dancing (*MGM 1942*)
The Affairs of Martha (*MGM 1942*)
Jackass Mail (*MGM 1942*)
Tish (*MGM 1942*)
Tennessee Johnson (*MGM 1942*)
Heaven Can Wait (*20th Century-Fox 1943*)
Johnny Come Lately (*United Artists 1943*)
Rationing (*MGM 1944*)
Gentle Annie (*MGM 1944*)
Meet Me in St. Louis (*MGM 1944*)
Murder, He Says (*Paramount 1945*)
The Harvey Girls (*MGM 1946*)
Bad Bascomb (*MGM 1946*)
Undercurrent (*MGM 1946*)
The Show-Off (*MGM 1946*)
The Egg and I (*Universal 1947*)
The Wistful Widow of Wagon Gap (*Universal 1947*)
Feudin', Fussin' and Fightin' (*Universal 1948*)
Ma and Pa Kettle (*Universal 1949*)
Big Jack (*MGM 1949*)
Ma and Pa Kettle Go to Town (*Universal 1950*)
Summer Stock (*MGM 1950*)
Mrs. O'Malley and Mr. Malone (*MGM 1950*)
Ma and Pa Kettle Back on the Farm (*Universal 1951*)
The Law and the Lady (*MGM 1951*)
Mr. Imperium (*MGM 1951*)
It's a Big Country (*MGM 1951*)
The Belle of New York (*MGM 1952*)
Ma and Pa Kettle at the Fair (*Universal 1952*)
Ma and Pa Kettle on Vacation (*Universal 1953*)
Fast Company (*MGM 1953*)
The Long, Long Trailer (*MGM 1954*)
Ma and Pa Kettle at Home (*Universal 1954*)
Ricochet Romance (*Universal 1954*)
Rose-Marie (*MGM 1954*)
Ma and Pa Kettle at Waikiki (*Universal 1955*)
The Kettles in the Ozarks (*Universal 1956*)
Friendly Persuasion (*Allied Artists 1956*)
The Kettles on Old MacDonald's Farm (*Universal 1957*)

Martin & Lewis

Show-business followers enjoy glimpses into the personal lives of celebrities, particularly glances that scan an unhappy, even ugly, area. Especially have personal relationships between artists in the often seamy, frighteningly unpredictable world of entertainment always fascinated the public. From the inadequacies and pettiness of many of these working relationships many of Hollywood's most touching tragedies have occurred.

In the supposedly happy-go-lucky world of comedians such behind-the-scenes glimpses are especially alluring. There is perverse joy in discovering that performers who can jointly fill an audience with laughter can simultaneously fill one another with disgust. (It was a theme exploited shrewdly by Neil Simon in the play/movie *The Sunshine Boys.*) For example, Hollywood insiders knew quite well that Oliver Hardy was often upset by the egotism of Stan Laurel; the world learned slowly and over many episodes that Bud Abbott and Lou Costello waged private differences with the same

ebullience that trademarked their dog-eared routines.

However, no set of personal differences won so much notoriety as those of Jerry Lewis and Dean Martin. The assorted problems of the wildly slapstick clown and the relaxed crooner were so dramatically amplified that even today the mention of their names evokes images of personality conflict long before it draws forth memories of their joint movies, TV shows, radio performances, and nightclub acts.

Thus it was something of a milestone when over Labor Day weekend 1976 Martin and Lewis ended two decades of professional feuding when Dean dropped by Jerry's muscular dystrophy telethon in Las Vegas for a surprise visit. As the comedians greeted one another, many viewers undoubtedly recalled their madcap performing relationship only after the personal drama's effect subsided.

Dean Martin was born Dino Paul Crocetti in Steubenville, Ohio, on Sunday, June 17, 1917, son of barber Guy Crocetti and his wife Angela. (He had a brother Bill—born in

With Corinne Calvet and John Lund in My Friend Irma Goes West *(1950).*

1914—who would later manage Dean's business affairs until the former's death in 1963.) With the aid of morally demanding parents, Dean managed to avoid most of the temptations present in Steubenville (known as "Little Chicago") and to pass through Grant Jr. High School and through the 10th grade of Wells High School. At that point the unacademically inclined youth dropped out of scholastics. A stretch of odd jobs (milkman, steel mill laborer, amateur boxer) preceded his entry into the Rex Cigar Store. The store was one of Steubenville's more popular gambling fronts, where he worked the chips-and-dice tables for $8 per diem. With tips and some pilfering ("During the course of a day, I could steal maybe as many as five silver dollars"), he was doing quite well—well enough at least initially to refuse bandleader Ernie McKay's offer to sing with his group. McKay, who had heard Dean singing for friends at the store, was only offering $50 per week—Dean was making about $125—but his employers encouraged him to accept the offer and with it a potentially lucrative career. Thus Dean became McKay's lead singer.

From there, Dean joined the Sammy Watkins Band, a group very "big" in Cleveland. It was during this period that Martin met Elizabeth MacDonald, whom he wed at Cleveland's St. Anne Church on October 2, 1940. While children were arriving at frequent intervals (Craig, 1942; Claudia, 1944; Gail, 1945; Deana, 1948), Dean worked with a succession of bands. He also had his oversized, squat nose reshaped by plastic surgery, hoping to consolidate his chances as a swoon-inspiring crooner. He worked quite steadily throughout the Forties—many of his competitors were on active duty during World War II—but his performing notices were never raves and sometimes the critics were insulting. *Variety*, for example, noted of his 1943 engagement at New York City's Riobamba Club, "He's lacking in personality, looks ill-fitting in that dinner jacket, and, at best, has just a fair voice that suggests it would have little resonance without the P.A. system." (At one point, an MGM talent scout became interested in the crooner and Dean was screen-tested, specifically for a role in 1946's *Till the Clouds Roll By*. The contract was vetoed by Metro executives who telegrammed, "We already have Tony Martin

under contract. Why do we want another Italian singer?" [Tony Martin is Jewish].)

About the time of the futile screen test, Dean was residing with his family at Manhattan's Belmont Plaza Hotel and singing at the Glass Hat Club. Also residing in the Belmont and also performing at the Glass Hat that summer of 1945 (as well as playing babysitter for the Martins) was 19-year-old Jerry Lewis.

Lewis was born Joseph Levitch in Newark, New Jersey, on Friday, March 16, 1926. He was the son of Anny and Rea Levitch, entertainers whose playdates centered largely in the Catskill burlesque houses. As a small boy, Jerry was singing "Brother, Can You Spare a Dime?" in his parents' act, but more often was farmed out to relatives—especially his grandmother—while his mom and dad accepted playdates on the road. His education was spotty and classmates somehow always arrived at nicknaming the gangly extrovert "Idiot." As a teenager, Jerry labored as an usher at New York City's Paramount Theatre and later was a busboy at Brown's Hotel and Hotel Southern. His show-business debut took place at the lowercase Palace Theatre in Buffalo, New York. There, in fright wig and bizarre clothing, Jerry mouthed and mugged to the lyrics of Igor Gorin's operatic recordings. From all reports the newcomer was unengaging and the customers shouted "Bring back the babes!"

During one of his infrequent performing stints, Jerry met Patti Palmer (née Esther Calonika), a singer with the Ted Fio Rito Orchestra. They fell in love and eloped to New York City, marrying on October 3, 1944. (They are still married today, have a son Gary*—born in 1945—plus five adopted sons: Ronald, Scott, Christopher, Anthony, and Joseph.)

While the two entertainers played the Glass Hat that summer of 1945, 28-year-old Martin became something of a "big brother"

---

* Gary Lewis would become the lead singer and drummer of the pop group "Gary Lewis and the Playboys," which enjoyed a vogue in the mid-Sixties. After Gary was drafted and served in Vietnam (where two of his best buddies were killed), he returned to the States a changed person, unable to pick up the pieces of his performing career. He has a wife and child. Of his dad he has said, "Having Jerry Lewis for a father is like being the son of the *Encyclopaedia Britannica*. . . . It's not that he knows everything, but he takes the time."

to 19-year-old Lewis, the latter a prized target of hecklers. Ever relaxed Dean often came to the aid of Jerry when bored audiences became excessively rude. Soon Jerry began "butting into" Dean's act, like posing as a busboy who drops dishes and wreaks havoc while Martin tries to sing. Dean enjoyed the interruptions and went along with it all. After the Glass Hat engagement, the entertainers often left notes and jokes for each other at the various theatres where they performed.

The official union of Martin and Lewis occurred during the week of July 20, 1946. Jerry was performing his lip-synching record routine at Atlantic City's Club 500 where he was greeted with audience hostility. The manager hated his work and threatened to fire him. Almost hysterical—he badly needed the job—Jerry phoned Lou Perry, Dean's agent, to ask advice. (The Club 500 entrepreneur had informed Jerry that his own agent, Abby Greshler, was persona non grata at the club.)* Perry, a bighearted soul who had allowed ever insolvent Dean to share his apartment during tough times, agreed to send Dean to Atlantic City to help out.

On July 25, 1946, Martin and Lewis began their joint act to apathetic response. As Dean tried to sing, Jerry would scream and bray. When a customer would order a drink, Dean would pour it in his face. As things became more raucous, Dean would chase Jerry around the audience. Martin would usually be brandishing a bottle of seltzer, with which he would soak the customers. Somehow the mayhem caused the patrons to yell for more. The Club 500 held the "team" over for six weeks and escalated the act's salary to $750 weekly.

Thus began the decade of Martin and Lewis. Abby Greshler, Jerry's agent, rushed to Atlantic City and signed Martin and his client as a team. (Dean abandoned his association with Lou Perry, eventually settling the contract for about $3,500.)** The pair began a tour of nightclubs—the Chez Paree in Chicago, the Latin Casino of Camden, New

* Lewis insists today that he contacted Martin because an opening evolved on the Club 500's bill and he wanted to do his pal a favor.

** Ironically, Lewis would later dismiss Greshler over financial differences.

Jersey, etc.—and entertainment houses such as Loew's State in New York. Their introduction to the big time came on April 8, 1948, when they appeared at the plush Copacabana Club where they were signed as a backup act to Vivian Blaine, the ex-Twentieth Century-Fox player. That night, after they performed their wild routine (squirting seltzer bottles, tackling the bandleader, Dean singing "Slow Boat to China," etc.), the audience was in hysteria and screamed, "Bring back Martin and Lewis" throughout Miss Blaine's introduction. The club's management quickly decided to reverse the stars' billing and place the chanteuse as a warm-up for the comedians. Miss Blaine, a few seasons away from her triumph as Adelaide in Broadway's *Guys and Dolls*, tearfully refused. The situation allowed for Martin and Lewis to hold sway all by themselves at the Copacabana for 18 weeks. During this period they also performed at the Roxy Theatre for three weeks of personal appearances, and all told were earning an outstanding $15,000 weekly.

In the following months, Martin and Lewis were to conquer every medium of show business. In the summer of 1948 they played at Slapsie Maxie's Club in Hollywood where all the studios heeded the advance publicity and sent talent representatives to watch the act. Producer Hal B. Wallis, then berthed at Paramount Pictures, placed the winning bid, signing the team to a seven-picture, five-year contract at $50,000 per picture—later elevated to $75,000 per film. The team was also permitted to produce its own pictures via its own York Productions.

In April 1949 NBC premiered "The Martin and Lewis Show" on Monday night radio at 10:00 (later broadcast Friday night at 8:30). In 1950, after they ran wild as guests on Milton Berle's Texaco TV show, Martin and Lewis joined Eddie Cantor, Donald O'Connor, and Abbott and Costello as the rotating (once monthly) hosts of NBC-TV's "The Colgate Comedy Hour." Their initial appearance earned them $25,000, but response was so great that the pair demanded and received $75,000 per program thereafter.

Adding to their hectic schedule, the "hot" act appeared at nightclubs throughout the country, and seemed unhurt by the threat of overexposure. America simply could not get enough of the madcap twosome. Lewis recently analyzed that their popularity back then was due to their affection and rapport for each other. "Any other two guys could have done the same act and they wouldn't have made a dollar." Dean stated not long ago that "meeting Jerry was the greatest thing that ever happened in my life. He'd break me up, I'd break him up. We hardly ever looked at the audience."

If the country could not get enough of Martin and Lewis and Martin and Lewis (initially) could not get enough of each other, there was another vital reason why they worked so diligently. Their creditors could not get enough of their paychecks. Martin, in particular, was immersed in a variety of financial dilemmas. Even after he achieved stardom, all shades of underworld figures appeared on the scene waving contracts they insisted entitled them to a share of his good fortune.* So numerous were Dean's bills that in January 1949 he actually had to declare bankruptcy. The singer also proved weak to temptation by shapely ladies while wife Betty was at home supervising the children. It was a human flaw exploited by a Florida beauty queen named Jeanne Beiggers, who determinedly pursued Dean until Betty Martin sued for divorce. When the court granted the suit on August 24, 1949, a huge settlement went along with it. Dean married his new love on September 1, 1949, in Beverly Hills. (The offspring were Dean "Dino" Jr., born 1951; Ricci, 1953; and Gina, 1956.) In the meantime, Jerry was engaged in some high spending, ranging from lavish gifts for friends to producing opulent home movies.

The Martin and Lewis team was something of a social phenomenon: the good-looking, suave straight man who sang popular songs and the spastic goof whose slapstick antics and outrageous mugging fractured audiences. The chemistry of their brand of performance appealed tremendously to audi-

ences of the time. However, when their performing, especially their film work, is viewed today, it leaves much to be desired. Neither was a true comic artist, although Jerry has admirers who still insist that he is "another Chaplin." Their undisciplined romping through their pictures (often reworking of earlier Paramount vehicles for the likes of Bob Hope and Bing Crosby) provides no canon of celluloid comedy greatness.

Nevertheless, Martin and Lewis were fun and irresistible (to some) when at their best, inoffensive if silly at their worst. They certainly made themselves known on the Paramount lot. (Vice president in charge of production Y. Frank Freeman reputedly offered the men bribes on numerous occasions if they would promise to resist creating mayhem in the studio commissary.) Veteran director Norman Taurog, who helmed six of their joint Paramount films, remembers, "In their early days, we had a lot of fun on the set during the pictures. We all liked to come to work in the morning. There'd be lots of gags. Jerry once sneaked up into the catwalks and tied and gagged our head electrician. If he and Dean were good and didn't fool around, I'd give them lollipops as a gag bribe."

The first Paramount release was *My Friend Irma* (1949).* The feature was almost never produced because of a major problem. Screen tests strongly suggested that Jerry could not act. The result was that the scenarists had to invent a part for him, that of Seymour the hopeless assistant to Dean's straight man, which allowed him to mug and cavort in his usual, unbridled fashion. The studio, with no illusions of originality in marketing the team, shot *My Friend Irma Goes West* (1950) as a follow-up, employing the same leads (John Lund, Diana Lynn, and Marie Wilson), with luscious Corinne Calvet tossed into the juvenile proceedings. The team made monkeys of the military in *At War with the Army* (1950), in which Jerry waged his famous war with the coke machine that kept issuing bottles. They continued their zany encounters with the service in *Sailor Beware* (1951) and *Jumping Jacks* (1952), and then resurrected the Bob Hope-Paulette Goddard *Ghost Breakers* as *Scared*

* Another creditor was comic Lou Costello who sued Dean for $100,000, claiming that in 1946 Martin had signed a contract in which he would be managed by Costello. Although the relationship was short-lived, Lou paid for the crooner's nose surgery and assorted other expenses. Dean had to borrow $20,000 from film producer Hal B. Wallis to settle the claim. Later Martin and Costello smoothed over their feud; in fact Martin and Lewis appeared at one of the benefits for the Lou Costello Jr. Youth Foundation. Dean played straight man to Lou, while Bud Abbott performed the classic "Who's on First" routine with Jerry.

* Irma being Irma Peterson, played by "dumb blonde" Marie Wilson on the CBS radio series "My Friend Irma." Wilson played Irma on radio, in films, and later on TV.

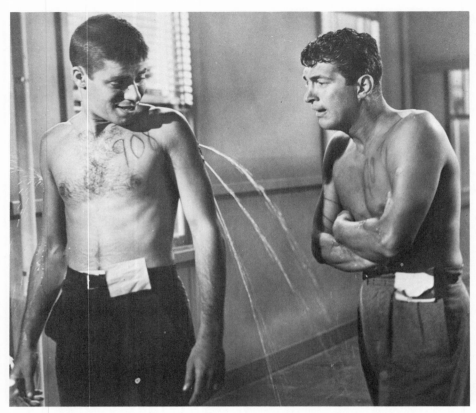

In Sailor Beware
(1951).

Stiff (1953), with Lizabeth Scott and Carmen Miranda. It was a foregone conclusion that Lewis would do an on-camera imitation of the Brazilian bombshell, providing a sequence which delighted his huge following. *Money from Home* (1953) was a Damon Runyonesque tale shot in 3-D, and *Three-Ring Circus* (1954) was filmed in VistaVision and color, distracting from the somewhat tepid story situation. To provide the basis of *Living It Up* (1954), the classic *Nothing Sacred* was revamped for the top-attraction team, and Janet Leigh and Sheree North (in a wild dance) provided feminine allure. A year earlier when the team made *The Caddy* (1953), with Donna Reed and Fred Clark, Martin had an interlude in which he sang "That's Amore." The song became a best-selling record and led Dean's pals to start whispering, "Get rid of the kid." It was the start of another facet of disharmony between the hugely successful performing team.

It became clear early in the screen game that Dean did not have the easiest of jobs in his position as the good-looking singing half of the comedy team. In reviewing the Martin-Lewis entry *That's My Boy* (1951—which benefited greatly from the performance of Eddie Mayehoff as Lewis' domineering dad), the *Los Angeles Examiner* typified most critiques: "Dean Martin has a few moments as the personable football hero. . . . He sings a couple of numbers and carries on a romance with Marion Marshall, the campus cutie. But as always most of the laughs come from the antics of Jerry Lewis, who can fracture an audience by the mere lift of an eyebrow." Jerry, in the course of their films, not only would butt into Dean's singing (with complete audience approval) but at times would even swipe Dean's prerehearsed ad-libs.

The first widely publicized flare-up of the Martin-Lewis tandem came via the shooting of *Three-Ring Circus*. While on location in Phoenix, Arizona (where Clyde Beatty's troupe had winter headquarters), Dean was taunted by local extras who queried, "Are you still Jerry Lewis' partner?" and beleaguered by children who asked him where Lewis was so they could obtain his autograph. Feelings became very strained and both men were quoted as having strong words on the subject.

456

DEAN: I'm sick of playing stooge to that crazy mixed-up character.

JERRY: I'm fed up with my partner's sensitivity. Everything I do is wrong. Anything happens to me he don't like, he blames it on me. He hates me. He's always got a chip on his shoulder.

Three-Ring Circus was completed and released at Christmas time 1954 and the differences of Jerry and Dean turned out to be irrelevant—Elsa Lanchester stole the picture as a bearded lady. But show-business insiders gave little hope that the Martin-Lewis unity could continue much longer.

As the mid-Fifties progressed, Martin and Lewis provided the gossipers with plenty of fuel, for there was little joy on the sets of the later Martin-Lewis pictures. Jerry would prolong rehearsals with his leviathan bursts of whimsy and Dean would leave early to rush to the golf course. *You're Never Too Young* (1955) was a remake of the well-remembered *The Major and the Minor* with Dean in the Ray Milland part and Jerry

uncharmingly tackling the 12-year-old masquerade so winningly played by Ginger Rogers. On the other hand, *Artists and Models* (1955) was a decent comedy; Jerry was well cast as a comic-book addict and the film was bolstered by the lovely presence of Dorothy Malone, Eva Gabor, a trim Anita Ekberg, and 19-year-old Shirley MacLaine (in her film debut for producer Hal B. Wallis). *Pardners* (1956) was a tepid remake of Bing Crosby-Martha Raye's *Rhythm on the Range*. *Hollywood or Bust* (1956), which proved to be their last joint effort, ironically cast them as partners intent on crashing the movies.

When Martin learned he was to play a cop in the next Martin-Lewis project, *The Delicate Delinquent* (1957), he flatly refused. Jerry said, "Then we'll have to get somebody else." Dean's reply, "Start looking, boy." An emergency conference was called in the office of Paramount's Y. Frank Freeman, and after listening to arguments, sermons, and statistics as to why he and Jerry should remain a team, Dean issued a one-word response, "Bulls--t." (Darren McGavin was assigned to

Posing with Marjie Millar and Pat Crowley for Money from Home *(1953)*.

With Donna Reed and Marshall Thompson in The Caddy *(1953).*

play the policeman role in *The Delicate Delinquent*.) The following summer Dean and Jerry fulfilled a contract to play the Copacabana Club in New York. Their final show was performed on July 25, 1956, exactly 10 years after their opening at the Club 500 of Atlantic City. The following April Dean sold his interest in the team's York Productions, officially ending the Martin-Lewis partnership.*

"It took a lot of guts to leave Jerry," Dean said recently to *TV Guide*. "All those guys

* Dean would say years later, "I know that 90 percent of the audience was watching Jerry. He was a funny guy. But lemme tell you something: I knew in my guts that I was funnier 'n he was." Lewis would recall on another occasion, "He was my brother, my father. He was everything I wanted to be and then, at 26, eight years later, you find none of these things are valid."

On September 30, 1958, Lewis was a guest of Eddie Fisher's TV program. He was about to sing when Dean and Bing Crosby appeared from the wings and Dean shouted, "Don't sing!" Jerry and Dean chased one another around the stage and then Dean left. The gag was supposedly spontaneous and caused speculation that a reteaming would occur. Of course, nothing more came of it.

crying, 'Poor Dino, without Jer' he's goin' to fall right on his butt!' Know what? I thought so too." Certainly Dean had cause for remorse in the months directly following the split. Jerry recorded a gold record ("Rock-a-Bye Your Baby"), finished *The Delicate Delinquent*, and juggled more work than he could handle. Dean turned to his ambition of becoming a straight actor. He almost demolished his hopes with his first "solo" effort, MGM's *Ten Thousand Bedrooms* with Anna Maria Alberghetti. Martin was cast as a playboy on the prowl in Rome. "That picture stunk up the place so bad even my best friends wouldn't talk to me. I was in Pittsburgh in 1957 with no prospects, seven kids, and enough alimony and child support to start a foundation. Jeannie and me was just wondering what bar I could make a deal with when the phone rang. My agent wanted to know if I'd like to take a $230,000 cut in salary. MGM was offering $20,000 (I got $250,000 for *Bedrooms*) to play the draft dodger in *The Young Lions* with Brando and

Monty Clift. Seems after hirin' all that high-priced talent, they just plum ran outa money."

The 1958 Twentieth Century-Fox release, based on the Irwin Shaw novel and directed by Edward Dmytryk, started Dean on a positive career direction that has prospered to this day. He has triumphed in motion pictures,* proving himself a surprisingly effective actor in a variety of genres: musicals (like *Bells Are Ringing*, 1960, with Judy Holliday), comedies (especially with his carefree Rat Pack cronies, Sinatra, Davis, Lawford, et al., in *Ocean's 11*, 1960, *Sergeants 3*, 1962, *Robin and the 7 Hoods*, 1964, etc.), sex melodrama spoofs (his "Matt Helm" superspy characterization in the Columbia Pictures series, *The Silencers*, 1966, *Murderers' Row*, 1966, *The Ambushers*, 1967, and *The Wrecking Crew*, 1968), top-budget audience pictures (for *Airport*, 1970, he received a salary plus 10 percent of the profits after the break-even point), and even Westerns, a film type seemingly alien to Martin's sleepy-eyed, hard-drinking nightclub image. Among his appearances in the last genre are *The Sons of Katie Elder* (1965) with John Wayne; *Rough Night in Jericho* (1967), in which he played the heavy; *Bandolero!* (1968), a sagebrush spoof with James Stewart and Raquel Welch; and the disappointing *Showdown* (1973) with an equally bored-looking Rock Hudson.

As a recording artist Dean has accumulated (at last count) three platinum and eighteen gold records. His NBC-TV network show has stood strong through several formats since its September 16, 1965 premiere. He now enjoys an MGM contract that calls for six weeks of club performing per year in Las Vegas (at its Grand Hotel, where he tapes his NBC-TV "Roasts") at $150,000 per week plus a movie option (which led to the dullish *Mr. Ricco* detective film in 1975). Occasionally, Martin will make a guest appearance in a teleseries, such as his role as a Las Vegas casino owner in "Charlie's Angels" (ABC-TV, September 13, 1978). When Martin and Jeannie underwent a costly, lengthy divorce in

1972, Dean's worth was then estimated at about $26 million, including property, cash, picture-recordings income, and numerous other assets.*

Jerry Lewis' years as a solo performer took a far different turn. Initially, his career after the split appeared promising enough. He both directed and starred in a procession of comedies for Paramount: *The Errand Boy* (1961), *The Nutty Professor* (1963), *The Patsy* (1964). And he starred in many others which he did not direct: *Don't Give Up the Ship* (1959), *Visit to a Small Planet* (1960), *It's Only Money* (1962), etc. These profitable film ventures endeared him more to the Saturday matinee kiddie crowd than to the connoisseurs of cinema comedy. (Abroad, especially in France, Lewis saw to it that he came to the attention of the new-breed critics and he was soon being proclaimed a cinema genius.) Like many another funnyman, Jerry hankered to prove that he could be a serious performer in a nonslapstick role. He chose as his vehicle *Boeing-Boeing* (1965), a sex farce that had done well on European stages but had flopped on Broadway. However, Lewis proved unmemorable as a "funny" romantic lead, and neither the presence of Tony Curtis nor that of Thelma Ritter (nor even a bevy of shapely girls) could bolster the sagging film.

In the fall of 1963 Jerry embarked upon a lavish ABC-TV Saturday night show ("People are gonna break dates to watch my show") that turned into an entirely offensive case of egomania-run-amok as Jerry did everything from bursting into guests' routines to conducting the orchestra to singing. The expensively mounted variety show was a dismal failure. From 1967 to 1969 he headed "The Jerry Lewis Show" on NBC-TV. Before Lewis' new-format TV program debuted, Dean signed off his back-on-the-air hit video show by saying to the audience, "Y'all watch 'The Jerry Lewis Show' this Tuesday night,

---

* Martin was Marilyn Monroe's co-star in the abortive *Something's Got to Give*, which was halted two months before Monroe committed suicide in August 1962. When the project was revamped for Doris Day as *Move Over Darling* (1963), Martin had dropped out of the comedy and James Garner had replaced him.

* On April 24, 1973, Dean wed Catherine Mae Hawn, a young Hollywood beautician. Dean adopted her daughter Sasha by a previous marriage. The Martin-Hawn wedding in Dean's Bel Air home came close to setting a new high in Hollywood opulence. However the couple were soon engaged in a series of separations and reconciliations, ending in divorce proceedings in mid-1976 which became final on February 24, 1977. Although Dean's three marriages have cost him an estimated $10 million, he still continues to be the man-about-town, seemingly always involved with a new girlfriend, usually women 30 or more years younger than he.

'cause I will." He was entirely sincere. Unfortunately, the show merited no great ratings. Starting on September 12, 1970, and running for two seasons, Jerry was represented on TV by the series "Will the Real Jerry Lewis Please Sit Down," an ABC-TV animated cartoon program dealing with the misadventures of Lewis, a fumbling janitor for the Odd Job Employment Agency. The format allowed for the incorporation of many of Jerry's movie creations, including The Playboy, The Errand Boy, and The Nutty Professor. Over the years, Lewis would turn up as guest host on Johnny Carson's "Tonight Show," demonstrating that he could be an effective talk program host when he so chose.

Meanwhile, Jerry's films were meeting more and more apathy at the box office.* Columbia distributed *Three on a Couch* (1966), *The Big Mouth* (1967), *Don't Raise the Bridge, Lower the River* (1968), and *Hook, Line and Sinker* (1969), and then the studio and performer went their separate ways. *Which Way to the Front?* (1970) was a terribly unfunny World War II-set comedy which earned little artistic credit or revenue for Warner Bros. Lewis made a career switch when he directed (but did not appear with) Peter Lawford and Sammy Davis Jr. in *One More Time* (1971), a poorly received sequel to the actors' *Salt and Pepper*. Lewis' next feature, a European-lensed study of a circus clown, was never completed for release. More recently, in early 1979, Lewis directed and starred in *Hardly Working*, produced by Gold Coast Productions. The episodic comedy, co-starring Susan Oliver and Jerry Lester, was shot on location in Palm Beach, Florida.

No one was quite prepared for the chaos that ensued when Jerry agreed to star in his first "legitimate" show, *Hellzapoppin*, a lunatic revue format rendered so delicious in the late Thirties by the comedy team of Olsen and Johnson. With Lynn Redgrave co-starred, Alexander H. Cohen supplying a lavish production, Jerry Adler staging (replacing chief writer Abe Burrows), and Donald Saddler contributing the choreography, the oversized production opened at the Morris Mechanic Theatre in Baltimore on

November 22, 1976, the first stop on its pre-Broadway tour. The reviews were disastrous. *Variety's* reporter on the scene judged, "What *Hellzapoppin* needs at this stage in its development is work, tons of it, before it lands on Broadway." On January 15, 1977, the million dollar "musical circus" was closed in Boston by producer Cohen at a loss of $1.25 million. One of the major complaints issued by those behind the scenes was that Lewis had apparently refused to do any numbers with Miss Redgrave, who was winning plaudits for her solo routines. There had been drastic, frantic changes along the way, and in Boston Lewis kept complaining that the show had to be "frozen" into shape, if the scheduled February 13 opening at the Minskoff Theatre on Broadway was ever to occur. (NBC-TV had planned to telecast a large segment of the show's first act live for one of its "Big Event" programs.)

In the aftermath of the closing, there were accusations by both camps, as sides formulated in the pending suit by Cohen against Lewis. (Cohen was also being sued by the Minskoff Theatre Corporation.) There were those who insisted that Lewis' interest in 27-year-old performer Jill Choder beclouded his judgment and diverted his energy, as he sought to have her part in the on-stage proceedings expanded. There were rumors that *Hellzapoppin* might be refinanced and open in New York at a later date under a new management, but that never occurred.

In a blow-by-blow rendering of the making and closing of *Hellzapoppin*, Cliff Jahr wrote in *New York* magazine,

> [Jerry] Lewis could have used a Broadway hit. When demand for him as a performer and film director dipped in the late sixties, he rechanneled some of his driving energy into other areas like overseas concertizing and playing the visiting elder statesman at film schools. Oddly enough, his popularity today in parts of Europe may rival the frenzy he and ex-partner Dean Martin whipped up in the fifties. There is still his annual Labor Day telethon, of course, which now rivals the Miss America contest as institutionalized kitsch. It is probably watched as much for all those Vegas

* Another Lewis project that fell apart was the Jerry Lewis (Mini) Cinemas, a corporation that was devoted to family style films. It was one of the industry fiascos of the Sixties still talked about years later.

types caught in naked moments as it is for its tour-de-force bad taste.

Lewis could have used a Broadway hit. But *Hellzapoppin* proved to be aptly named. . . .

It was a sad obituary to Jerry's great show-business comeback attempt.

In recent years most of Lewis' publicity and continued industry standing has been garnered not from his club dates, TV appearances, or European tours, but from his herculean tasks in overseeing and hosting the annual Muscular Dystrophy-Labor Day Telethon, for which he has raised many, many millions of dollars. (Despite much speculation and investigation over the years, the origin of Lewis' pervading interest in this particular charity has not come to light, nor will he give any concrete clues to the matter.)

It was at the 1976 Labor Day telethon, aired from Las Vegas, that Martin and Lewis finally reconciled publicly. Frank Sinatra came onto the Vegas stage, and after singing told Jerry, "I have an old friend of yours backstage." Out came Dean. While the audience cheered, Dean and Jerry hugged and kissed one another, ending an alienation that had existed professionally for two decades. Since then, however, there have been no hints that a reprise of their teaming might be in the offing. (After Dean performed on the telethon, and the question was voiced if they might work together again, Jerry cracked, "Who wants to work with that drunk?" though his aides on the show insist that he was deeply touched by Dean's surprise appearance.) For industry observers a highlight of the 1977 telethon, which raised nearly $27 million, was a telegram of congratulations to Lewis from producer Alexander H. Cohen (then still in arbitration regarding the *Hellzapoppin* shut-down). Lewis' 1978 Telethon earned over $29 million and saw him refuting a charge that he made a personal profit from the charity event.

Despite their establishment today as separate celebrities, neither Dean Martin nor Jerry Lewis enjoys talking of the highly publicized split. As Lewis assessed, "You don't live and work with a guy as long as I did without the divorce being painful. How do you tell your audience you loved the guy? To kid what was and still is painful because it might be salable today would be beneath my dignity. I'm still too sensitive about it. Dean can do it because the character he plays lets him do it. I can't."

However, Martin, today the more successful of the most popular comedy team of the post-World War II years, speaks openly and sincerely about his partner, who has never realized his full potential: "Too bad about Jer'. The guy just didn't grow with the times. You can't do that. You gotta change."

FEATURE FILMS

With Dean Martin and Jerry Lewis:
My Friend Irma (*Paramount 1949*)
My Friend Irma Goes West (*Paramount 1950*)
At War with the Army (*Paramount 1950*)
That's My Boy (*Paramount 1951*)
Sailor Beware (*Paramount 1951*)
Jumping Jacks (*Paramount 1952*)
Road to Bali (*Paramount 1952*)*
The Stooge (*Paramount 1953*)
Scared Stiff (*Paramount 1953*)
The Caddy (*Paramount 1953*)
Money from Home (*Paramount 1953*)
Living It Up (*Paramount 1954*)

Three-Ring Circus (*Paramount 1954*)
You're Never Too Young (*Paramount 1955*)
Artists and Models (*Paramount 1955*)
Pardners (*Paramount 1956*)
Hollywood or Bust (*Paramount 1956*)

Dean Martin alone:
Ten Thousand Bedrooms (*MGM 1957*)
The Young Lions (*20th Century-Fox 1958*)
Some Came Running (*MGM 1958*)
Rio Bravo (*Warner Bros. 1959*)
Career (*Paramount 1959*)
Who Was That Lady? (*Columbia 1960*)

Bells Are Ringing (*MGM 1960*)
Ocean's 11 (*Warner Bros. 1960*)
Pepe (*Columbia 1960*)*
All in a Night's Work (*Paramount 1961*)
Ada (*MGM 1961*)
Sergeants 3 (*United Artists 1962*)
The Road to Hong Kong (*United Artists 1962*)*
Who's Got the Action? (*Paramount 1962*)
Come Blow Your Horn (*Paramount 1963*)*
Toys in the Attic (*United Artists 1963*)
Who's Been Sleeping in My Bed? (*Paramount 1963*)
4 for Texas (*Warner Bros. 1963*)
What a Way to Go! (*20th Century-Fox 1964*)
Robin and the 7 Hoods (*Warner Bros. 1964*)
Kiss Me, Stupid (*Lopert 1964*)
The Sons of Katie Elder (*Paramount 1965*)
Marriage on the Rocks (*Warner Bros. 1965*)
The Silencers (*Columbia 1966*)
Texas Across the River (*Universal 1966*)
Murderer's Row (*Columbia 1966*)
Rough Night in Jericho (*Universal 1967*)
The Ambushers (*Columbia 1967*)
Bandolero! (*20th Century-Fox 1968*)
How to Save a Marriage—And Ruin Your Life (*Columbia 1968*)
Five Card Stud (*Paramount 1968*)
The Wrecking Crew (*Columbia 1968*)
Airport (*Universal 1970*)
Something Big (*National General 1971*)
Showdown (*Universal 1973*)
Mr. Ricco (*MGM/United Artists 1975*)

Jerry Lewis alone:
The Delicate Delinquent (*Paramount 1957*)
The Sad Sack (*Paramount 1958*)
Rock-a-Bye Baby (*Paramount 1958*)
The Geisha Boy (*Paramount 1958*)
Don't Give Up the Ship (*Paramount 1959*)
Li'l Abner (*Paramount 1959*)*
Visit to a Small Planet (*Paramount 1960*)
The Bellboy (*Paramount 1960*)
Cinderfella (*Paramount 1960*)
The Ladies' Man (*Paramount 1961*)
The Errand Boy (*Paramount 1961*)
It's Only Money (*Paramount 1962*)
It's a Mad, Mad, Mad, Mad World (*United Artists 1963*)*
The Nutty Professor (*Paramount 1963*)
Who's Minding the Store? (*Paramount 1964*)
The Patsy (*Paramount 1964*)
The Disorderly Orderly (*Paramount 1964*)
The Family Jewels (*Paramount 1965*)
Boeing-Boeing (*Paramount 1965*)
Three on a Couch (*Columbia 1966*)
Way, Way Out! (*20th Century-Fox 1966*)
The Big Mouth (*Columbia 1967*)
Don't Raise the Bridge, Lower the River (*Columbia 1968*)
Hook, Line and Sinker (*Columbia 1969*)
Which Way to the Front? (*Warner Bros. 1970*)
One More Time (*United Artists 1971*) [director only]
Hardly Working (*Gold Coast 1979*)

* Unbilled guest appearance.

The Marx Brothers

It is a fitting episode of show-business legend that the internationally accoladed zaniness of the Marx Brothers was inspired by a jackass. The year was about 1911, the locale a grimy Nacogdoches, Texas, vaudeville house. Inside playing a sweltering matinee were Julius, Adolph, Leonard, and Milton Marx, a singing team promoted and encouraged by their ambitious mother, Minnie. The lads were doing their best to keep on key with the usual mixed results. Suddenly, outside the theatre a mule went insane and began attacking a cart. The crowd rushed from the theatre to witness the ass' antics, leaving the songsters stranded with the attention of nobody but a desperately glaring stage manager. Faced with the challenge of wooing the crowd away from the kicks, butts, and brays of the intense donkey, the Marx boys began trying to be funny. The audience came back laughing. A comedy act was born.

About two decades later, George Bernard Shaw remarked, "Cedric Hardwicke is my fifth favorite actor, the first four being the Marx Brothers." Almost the entire world shared his enthusiasm. Indeed, the Marx Brothers—rolling-eyed, moustached Groucho; Italian-accented, crafty, piano-playing Chico; top-hatted, red-wigged, horn-honking Harpo; and, for a time, dreadfully wooden straight man Zeppo—became the most universally successful comedy team in show-business history.

Samuel Marx, a Jewish immigrant from Alsace whose imperfections as a tailor earned him the nickname of "Misfit Sam," met Minna (later "Minnie") Palmer Schoenberg (born in a tiny German village) on the Staten Island ferry. They fell in love, married, and produced five sons: Leonard Marx, born Tuesday, March 22, 1887; Adolph Arthur Marx, born Friday, November 23, 1888; Julius Henry Marx, born Thursday, October 2, 1890; Milton Marx, born in 1897; and Herbert Marx, born Monday, February 25, 1901. They would become known to the world, respectively, as Chico, Harpo, Groucho, Gummo, and Zeppo.*

* The brothers earned their professional names thus: Groucho—because of his serious expression and moody character off stage; Harpo—obvious reason: his musical ability on the harp; Chico—he was a girl or "chick" chaser and his nickname was to be pronounced "Chicko"; Zeppo—was born when the zeppelin arrived in Lakehurst, New Jersey; and Gummo—called "Gumshoes" by his brothers because he was given a pair of rubbers.

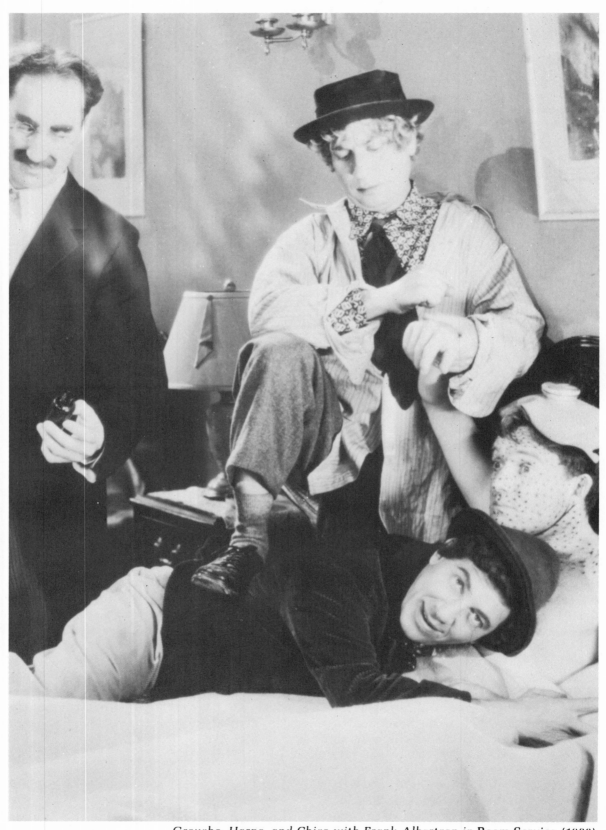

Groucho, Harpo, and Chico with Frank Albertson in Room Service *(1938).*

Mother Minnie's brother was the great vaudevillian Al Shean and his affluence occasioned in her show-business aspirations for her children. Her third son, Julius, after some uninspiring academics at Yorkville, Manhattan's P.S. 86, was willing to undertake such a course. In 1905 he answered an ad in the *New York World* for a boy singer for the Larong Trio. Groucho had no fond memories of his first theatre employer, for, among other things, he left the boy stranded in Cripple Creek, Colorado.

Before long Minnie managed to send money to return her son to New York. Undaunted by Groucho's adventure out West, she began seeking bookings for her offspring. "She used to book us herself," Groucho recalled. "She thought she ought to look young, so she wore a corset and a blonde wig when she went to see agents. She was probably around 50 then, and everybody knew it was a wig. When she was at somebody's house playing cards, she'd get tired of wearing the corset, take it off and wrap it up in a newspaper with the strings hanging out." Unsophisticated though she may have been, Minnie managed to find bookings for Groucho, Gummo, and a homely girl singer with a glass eye named Mabel O'Donnell, billing her hopefuls as "The Three Nightingales." Gummo would relate of Miss O'Donnell, "She had a beautiful voice and mother bought her a wig which covered the one eye so no one could tell she was cockeyed or had a glass eye." Still, Minnie soon replaced Mabel with a boy tenor and added Harpo to the act. "The Four Nightingales" opened at Coney Island, and Groucho remembered of the nervous Harpo, "At the opening performance he . . . [defecated] in his pants."

For all their problems, the Marx troupe managed to obtain work. The restructured group soon consisted of Chico (an excellent pianist), Harpo (an excellent harpist), Zeppo (a really rather bad, bland performer all-around and he realized it), and Groucho. In 1910 their Aunt Hannah and Minnie herself briefly joined the act. Their name was "The Six Mascots." Gummo later replaced Zeppo on the tours, and still later, when Gummo was called into the army during World War I, Zeppo returned to the fold. (Gummo later developed a business career and for a time was partnered with Zeppo in a Hollywood talent agency.)

As mentioned, it was a violent mule, plus puberty, that led the Marx clan to discover that their future might very well rest in comedy. They developed the sketch "Fun in High Skool," which was booked into numerous small-town theatres all over the country. Exhaustive vaudeville sojourns, monitored by pep-talking Minnie,* finally led to a 1919 hit in Chicago—a sketch entitled "Home Again," written by Uncle Al Shean. This hit led to an engagement at the famed New York City Palace Theatre. While there a footnote to theatrical history was written when Groucho, late to work one night, lacked the time to paste on his false moustache. Instead he smeared one on with greasepaint. The painted moustache would remain a trademark with him for a goodly portion of his show-business career.

In 1922 the brothers scored again, this time with the skit "On the Mezzanine." It led to an engagement at the Coliseum in London. Unfortunately, "On the Mezzanine" failed to amuse the British, so the Marxes hastily reprised "Home Again" and were judged a hit.

The Marx Brothers won more and more vaudeville popularity until finally Groucho and Harpo became the headliner comedians of a Broadway-bound revue entitled *I'll Say She Is.* The show played for 18 months on the road. When it opened on Broadway at the Casino Theatre (May 19, 1924), Chico was on tap as a pianist on a late bill of the program. *I'll Say She Is* ran for 313 performances. However, Groucho dismissed this production as "a real stinker." Yet the show was a major factor in winning the Marxes the approval of the "legitimate" audiences of Broadway. The *New York Times* reported, "Such shouts of merriment have not been heard in the Casino these many years." Top Broadway critic Alexander Woollcott raved about the show and described himself as "one who, at its conclusion, had to be picked up out of the aisle and placed gently back in his seat."

* These early antics of the Marxes were the subject of a flop Broadway musical, *Minnie's Boys* (Imperial Theatre: March 26, 1970). The book was by Arthur Marx (son of Groucho) and Robert Fisher, with music by Larry Grossman, and the lyrics by Hal Hackady. Shelley Winters was Minnie, with Lewis J. Stadlen as Groucho, Irwin Pearl as Chico, Daniel Fortus as Harpo, Alvin Kupperman as Zeppo, and Gary Raucher as Gummo. The show underwent 64 Broadway previews before it finally opened to bad notices; it closed after 80 performances.

Thereafter the Marx Brothers were much in demand, and they made an auspicious return to Broadway in *The Cocoanuts* (Lyric Theatre: December 8, 1925).* The show contained four of the brothers: Groucho as Henry W. Schlemmer, Chico as Willie the Wop, Harpo as Silent Sam, and Zeppo as Jamison. The book was by George S. Kaufman and Morrie Ryskind, the music by Irving Berlin. "Sam Harris had hired Kaufman and Ryskind," remembered Groucho in *The Marx Brothers Scrapbook* (1973). "They wrote the script because the Florida land boom was on at the time. By the time we saw the script it was finished. And it was goddamn funny!" Indeed it was. "One must not forget the brilliance of the patter and joking; it is never commonplace," wrote the *New York Times*. The show played for 375 performances at the Lyric Theatre, later reopening at the Century Theatre (May 16, 1927) for 16 additional performances. When the production went on the road for an extensive tour, the brothers were joined by their Broadway co-star, Margaret Dumont (1889-1965), the regal, matronly society type who turned out to be the greatest foil Groucho ever had. Groucho would later tell *Playboy* magazine, "She was a wonderful woman. She was the same off the stage as she was on it—always the stuffy, dignified matron. And the funny thing about her was she never understood the jokes. Seriously, she never knew what was going on. At the end of *Duck Soup*, we're alone in a small cottage and there's a war going on outside and Margaret says to me, 'What are you doing, Rufus?' and I say, 'I'm fighting for your honor, which is more than you ever did.' Later she asked me what I meant by that."**

It was the ace writing team of George S. Kaufman and Morrie Ryskind who created (with music and lyrics by Harry Ruby and Bert Kalmar) the next Broadway hit for the brothers—*Animal Crackers* (44th Street Theatre: October 23, 1928, 213 performances). As usual, the show had a rugged pre-Broadway shakedown tour to smooth out the constantly-being-refined routines. Groucho cavorted as the infamous Captain Spaulding (this, of course, was the show that provided Groucho's theme music, "Hooray for Captain Spaulding"), Chico as Emmanuel Ravelli, Harpo as the professor, and Zeppo, once again, as the straight man Jamison.* "If anything is more remarkable than the outrageous buffoonery of this team of cutups," wrote the *New York Times*, "it is their fabulous popularity. . . . They are nihilists, these Marx Boys, and the virtue of their vulgar mountebankery is its bewildering, passing, stinging thrusts at everybody in general, including themselves." In *Animal Crackers*, the ad-libbing team was free to be insane to their hearts' delight.

SPAULDING: How much do you want to run into an open manhole?
RAVELLI: Just the cover charge.
SPAULDING: Well, if you're ever in the neighborhood, drop in.
RAVELLI: Sewer. Looks like he's got me in a hole. Now let's see how we stand. . . .

While *Animal Crackers* was playing to capacity audiences in New York, Paramount Pictures became interested in the possibilities of using the zany comedy team in talkies to be filmed at the company's Astoria, Long Island, studio. Paramount obtained the screen rights to *The Cocoanuts* (1929).** The directors were Robert Florey and Joseph Santley (the latter on hand because his young co-director, a Frenchman, could speak little

* It was during this period that the Marx Brothers made inauspicious motion picture debuts. In 1925 Harpo appeared in the feature *Too Many Kisses*, a Paramount release starring Richard Dix. Harpo's role was almost entirely cut from the release prints. In 1926 the four performing Marx Brothers starred in a picture they helped to finance. *Humorisk* was never released.

** Groucho's respect for Miss Dumont hardly made things easier for her as part of a Marx Brothers tour. Groucho remembers, "Once we took off all her clothes on a train we were all traveling on. You could hear her screaming all the way from the drawing room where she was to where the engineer was blowing the train's whistle." Groucho would perform a routine with Miss Dumont on ABC-TV's "The Hollywood Palace" in 1965 only weeks before her death from a heart attack.

* While rehearsing *Animal Crackers*, Zeppo was asked by the producer if he could not work a little more "variety" into his woefully bland part. Snapped Zeppo, "How many different ways are there to say 'Yes'?"

** It was during this period that Groucho nearly suffered a nervous breakdown. Besides performing on stage at night, and then arising early to be on the soundstage at day, he was coping with the repercussions of the stock market crash (he lost all his savings—$240,000). As a result of personal and professional problems, Groucho developed severe insomnia which remained with him throughout the rest of his life.

Zeppo, Groucho, Chico, and Harpo Marx in The Cocoanuts (1929).

English). Despite the presence of Miss Dumont, Broadway's Mary Eaton, and a new, vampy Paramount contractee named Kay Francis as a jewel thief, *The Cocoanuts* resulted in a rather stagy effort. Robert Florey would recall the on-set problems:

> They really weren't disciplined. One of them was always missing. This was during Prohibition and Chico found an Italian restaurant whose owner produced homemade wine. And that's where we'd find Chico most of the time. Zeppo would also frequently be missing. Actually they seemed to take turns and I'd always have to send assistants all over the place to look for the missing member.

Nevertheless, *The Cocoanuts* was impressive enough to start the brothers on their Paramount film career. There, in a matter of a few years and four more films, they almost destroyed their future screen potential. The Marxes were amusing enough in *Animal Crackers* to be shipped out to Hollywood for exclusive movie purposes.

Once out on the West Coast, Paramount decided to star the Marxes in one motion picture per year. In 1931 it was *Monkey Business*, directed by Norman McLeod and co-starring Thelma Todd.

TODD: I didn't know you were a lawyer. You're awfully shy for a lawyer.
GROUCHO: You bet I'm shy. I'm a shyster lawyer.

Monkey Business placed the brothers on a luxury liner, with a comic highlight having the quartet trying to escape the heavies by disguising themselves as Maurice Chevalier. *Time* judged, "*Monkey Business* makes as little sense as possible. For this and other reasons, admirers of the Marx Brothers will find it marvelously funny." (The film later became one of the favorite pictures of Winston Churchill, who was known to run the feature in his home during times of crisis.)

Paramount's *Horse Feathers* (1932) reunited the brothers with charming Thelma Todd and director Norman McLeod. Here Groucho was a college dean. The film contains one especially memorable vignette wherein a bum approaches Harpo on the

467

street and asks, "Say, buddy, could you help me out? I'd like to get a cup of coffee." At which Harpo reaches into his trousers—and pulls out a cup of coffee. In 1933 the Marx Brothers made *Duck Soup*, their last film for Paramount and their last picture with Zeppo (who retired from the screen to open a Hollywood talent agency). It was directed by Leo McCarey ("the only first-class director we ever had," said Groucho) and returned Margaret Dumont to the proceedings.

DUMONT [regarding her late husband]: I was with him till the very end.
GROUCHO: Huh! No wonder he passed away.
DUMONT: I held him in my arms and kissed him.
GROUCHO: Oh, I see. Then it was murder. . . .

Duck Soup, a particular favorite of Groucho and Marx Brothers aficionados (it pokes outrageous fun at politics and satirizes war), was hilarious stuff. But Paramount executives realized a serious problem. The studio had allowed the team to "shoot the works," using up much of their repertoire of routines in the five films they had done for the lot. In addition, depression-numbed audiences could not identify with the zany characters (as they could with Laurel and Hardy who invested their work with nice quantities of sympathy). The Marxes had remained amusing curiosities to moviegoers. Paramount allowed their option to lapse, and the brothers found themselves at liberty.*

* Despite their hectic work life, the brothers found ample opportunity for domesticity.
   Groucho married Ruth Johnson on February 4, 1920; their children were Arthur (July 21, 1921) and Miriam (May 20, 1927); the couple divorced on July 15, 1942. He wed Catherine Marvis Gorcey (ex-wife of actor Leo Gorcey) on July 21, 1945; their one child was Melinda (August 16, 1946); they divorced on May 15, 1951. He next wed Eden Marie Hartford on January 17, 1954; they were divorced on December 4, 1969.
   Chico married Betty Carp; they had one child, Maxine; they divorced. He next wed Mary DeVithas on August 22, 1958.
   Zeppo married Marion Benda on April 12, 1927; they had one child, Tim; the couple later divorced. He then wed Barbara Blakely on September 15, 1959; they were divorced on December 26, 1972. (She more recently wed Frank Sinatra).
   Harpo married Susan Fleming on September 28, 1936; they had four adopted children: William, Alexander, Minny, and James.
   Gummo married Helen von Tilzer (widow of composer Russell von Tilzer) on March 16, 1929; they had two children: Robert and Kay.

Metro-Goldwyn-Mayer was the top studio in Hollywood in the Thirties, but its stable of players was rather weak in the comedy field. In 1935 36-year-old producer Irving G. Thalberg determined to remedy this situation and recognized the Marx Brothers as his panacea. Groucho hurried back from Skowhegan, Maine, where he was performing *Twentieth Century* in stock, to join his brothers in conferring with Thalberg.* The collaboration between the comedy team and the overworked genius of a producer was initially fraught with problems: Thalberg's notorious habit of keeping artists waiting hours in his office foyer and leaving conferences on long emergency consultations incensed the Marxes. They finally solved the problem by greeting Thalberg's return from such an emergency meeting by standing stark naked in front of his office fireplace, roasting Metro commissary potatoes. The executive got the message.

To ensure success with the forthcoming Marx Brothers-MGM film, Thalberg shrewdly approved the idea of writer James K. McGuiness, namely, that of turning the dignity-scorning Marxes loose in America's most decorous bastion of dignity, the Metropolitan Opera. George S. Kaufman and Morrie Ryskind reported to Culver City to fashion the script. The creative forces all heeded Groucho's theory, "The reason our first two pictures were so good was because we played the gags hundreds of times in the theatre. The other three pictures turned out not as good because we never knew whether the gags were going to work or not." Hence the Marx Brothers toured the Northwest before shooting *A Night at the Opera* (1935), perfecting comic highlights that would make their debut Metro film their greatest cinema success. As Harpo, in his autobiography, *Harpo Speaks* (1961), recalled:

So we hit the road with *A Night at the Opera*. Thalberg was so right. Some of the writers' favorite bits didn't get a snicker. They were cut. On the other hand, stuff that we ad-libbed on the stage, as in the "stateroom scene," went

* During their filmmaking hiatus, Groucho and Chico began, among other ventures, a short-lived radio show in February 1934. It was entitled "Flywheel, Shyster, and Flywheel."

Groucho and Chico Marx with David Landau in Horse Feathers *(1932).*

into the shooting script. As written—a bunch of guys jamming into a stateroom for no very good reason—this bit failed to get a laugh on stage. The writers got very depressed over it and decided to cut it. We decided, however, to give it one more chance.

So this night we did it our way. Groucho, ordering a meal from a steward while being jostled into the corner of the jammed-up stateroom, said, "And a hard-boiled egg. . . ." I honked my horn, "Make it two hard-boiled eggs," said Groucho.

The audience broke up, and as simply as that, a dud became a classic. The stateroom scene is still the best remembered of any bit the Marx Brothers ever performed.

A Night at the Opera would emerge as the most accoladed of the Marx Brothers pictures; indeed, some of their greatest screen moments emerge as Otis B. Driftwood

(Groucho), Fiorello (Chico), and Tomasso (Harpo) run amok through the Margaret Dumont-sponsored production of *Il Trovatore.* Besides the classic stateroom fracas, there is the famous wrangling over contracts between Groucho and Chico.

GROUCHO: That's what they call a sanity clause.

CHICO: You can't fool me. There ain't no Sanity Claus.

The raucous climax finds Chico and Harpo kidnapping hammy tenor Walter Woolf King so that young lovers Allan Jones and Kitty Carlisle can operatically clinch their on-screen romance.* All the zaniness worked

---

* In his book *The Wit and Wisdom of Hollywood* (1971), Max Wilk records an anecdote in which Mike Nichols met Groucho at a cinema colony party.

"'Groucho,' said Nichols, 'I must tell—I've seen *A Night at the Opera* seventeen times.'

"Very touched, all Groucho could manage was a 'Really?'

"'Yes,' said Nichols, 'I just couldn't get over that love story between Allan Jones and Kitty Carlisle!'"

especially well with the mixture of straight scenes, sympathetic episodes (as when Harpo is fired as Walter Woolf King's valet), and song (Jones and Carlisle sing Nacio Herb Brown's "Alone"), and the Marx Brothers moved into Metro in triumph.

The Marxes enjoyed themselves at Metro, where Groucho soon developed a strong desire, "I'd have liked to have gone to bed with Jean Harlow. She was a beautiful broad." He never got his wish, but Thalberg indulged his comedians with care and tolerated their sometimes bizarre, antiestablishment behavior. Concerning this brand of high spirits, Groucho's favorite memory was of the time he and Harpo* were on an elevator at MGM and Greta Garbo entered the elevator, semi-disguised under a floppy hat. Though the other passengers all recognized the famed star and hushingly backed away, Groucho and Harpo, wondering who this revered personage was, lifted up the back of her chapeau. Garbo swiveled with a frigid stare. "I'm terribly sorry," quipped Groucho to the austere actress. "I thought you were a fella I knew from Kansas City!"

Thalberg proceeded with another film for the Marxes, *A Day at the Races* (1937), scenes from which were also pre-tested on the road. Sam Wood directed, as he had *A Night at the Opera.* (Groucho disliked him, and Thalberg harbored little respect for the veteran. Notwithstanding, as John Baxter writes in *Hollywood in the Thirties* [1968], "Under Wood's direction, the Marx set-pieces do not come as high points in a dull landscape but arise naturally from the smooth fabric of the film.") Maureen O'Sullivan and Allan Jones took the romantic leads, Margaret Dumont was her usual priceless self as Mrs. Upjohn, and Douglass Dumbrille was an expertly smooth villain. The comedy highlights were great fun, especially the fleecing of Groucho's Dr. Hackenbush by Chico's Tony ("Tootsie-fruitsie ice cream!") at the racetrack.

CHICO: One dollar and you remember me all your life.

GROUCHO: That's the most nauseating proposition I've ever had!

Tragically, on September 14, 1936, in the midst of production, Thalberg died of pneumonia. Sam Wood announced tearfully to the cast and crew on the soundstage. "The little brown fella just died." Groucho commented bitterly, "Why is it the great men always go early? The schlemiels live to be a hundred."

The three Marxes remained at Metro after Thalberg's death, but they missed the cultured producer very much and could not adapt happily to the direct supervision of tyrannical, crude Louis B. Mayer. "Mayer took things too seriously," says Groucho. "Nobody else took us seriously in Hollywood—just Mayer. One day he was having a conference with the censor about Lana Turner showing too much cleavage in her last film and Mayer was trying to convince the censor that MGM was a highly moral studio. So Harpo hired a stripper for the afternoon and chased her around the room while Mayer was talking to the censor. Another time we were sitting in Mayer's waiting room and after hours of waiting, we started a bonfire in his outer office. We'd done that to Thalberg years before. But Mayer didn't think it was funny. . . . I think he wanted us to bomb. He didn't want us to take road tours and he refused to hire the best directors and writers. . . . Mayer was cutting off his nose to spite his face. Now that I think about his nose, his face would have been better off without it." (Plans for the Marxes to star in the Broadway hit *Of Thee I Sing* were abandoned by MGM.)

While the Marxes adjusted to Mayer, RKO borrowed them for *Room Service* (1938),* a Broadway comedy that could *not* be invigorated by the Marxes or, for that matter, by zesty young RKO ingenues Lucille Ball and Ann Miller. "It was the first time we tried doing a play we hadn't created ourselves," says Groucho. "And we were no good. We can't do that. We've got to originate the characters and the situations ourselves."

---

* During the Twenties Harpo became part and parcel of the Algonquin Hotel intellectual set (Dorothy Parker, Woollcott, et al.). When asked how he, a performer who never spoke in public, became close to that "round table" of wits, he replied, "Very simple. They had to have someone to listen."

* When they signed with RKO in October 1937 to make *Room Service* (at a fee of $250,000), it was agreed that thereafter they would make a second film, *Of Thee I Sing*, for the studio at a salary of $350,000. The second picture was not made after the unfortuitous experience with *Room Service*.

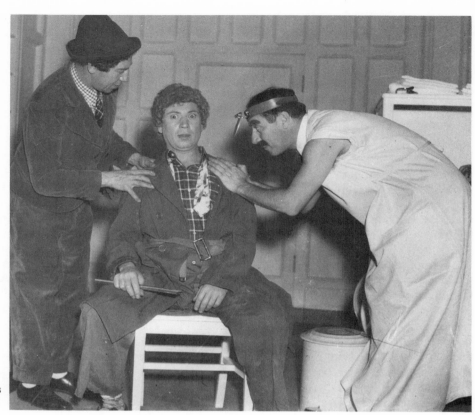

In A Day at the Races
(1937).

*With Diana Lewis and
John Carroll in* Go
West *(1940).*

Returning to MGM, the trio completed their contract with restrained enthusiasm. *At the Circus* (1939)—with Margaret Dumont, tenor Kenny Baker, and Eve Arden—had its moments and featured Groucho's singing of "Lydia the Tattooed Lady." The otherwise dreary *Go West* (1940), festooned with John Carroll and Diana Lewis as the romantic leads, was saved in the last reel by the famous train chase with the Marxes tearing the train apart for fuel. Both this and *At the Circus* were directed in helter-skelter fashion by Edward Buzzell. The team's Metro stay terminated with *The Big Store* (1941), which, aside from the tedious specialty spots of Tony Martin (singing his endless "Tenement Symphony") and stone-faced Virginia O'Brien, featured dastardly Douglass Dumbrille, ever welcome Margaret Dumont, and a long, luscious climactic chase through the store. This feature was, in many ways, the real end to the Marx Brothers' screen career. The few subsequent efforts are almost better left forgotten.

Free from Metro the brothers went separate ways for a time. On July 28, 1941, Harpo played the speaking role of Banjo (interpreted on screen by Jimmy Durante) in *The Man Who Came to Dinner* at the Bucks County Playhouse in New Hope, Pennsylvania. He later had a bit in the all-star film *Stage Door Canteen* (1943). Chico headed a Broadway revue, *Take a Bow* (Broadhurst Theatre: June 15, 1944, 12 performances). The vaudeville format featured Jay C. Flippen, Pat Rooney, the dance team of Mary Raye and Naldi, and Gene Sheldon (who did an imitation of Harpo in a comic turn with Chico). Groucho turned to radio, starring in the comedy-variety series "Blue Ribbon Town," which premiered on CBS on March 27, 1943. Regulars included Virginia O'Brien and Kenny Baker. CBS replaced Groucho with Danny Kaye in March 1944.

In 1946, almost solely because of the financial plight of Chico, whose money was ever evaporating to pay gambling debts, the Marx Brothers starred in United Artists' *A Night in Casablanca*. Directed by Archie Mayo, it was erroneously billed as "The Howl Raiser of 1946." The three stars looked a bit aged and at times somewhat bored. The following year Groucho starred with Carmen Miranda, Andy Russell, and Steve Cochran in the dud

musical comedy *Copacabana*. In 1949 the three brothers got together again professionally at United Artists for *Love Happy*. Directed by David Miller, it co-starred Ilona Massey and Vera-Ellen, and was mainly memorable because it supplied an early glimpse of Marilyn Monroe in a bit part.

In 1947 Groucho earned a new lease on his career when, under the sponsorship of the Elgin-American Compact Company, he began hosting "You Bet Your Life" on ABC network radio. With the Billy May Orchestra delivering the theme song of "Hooray for Captain Spaulding," and able announcer George Fenneman assisting, "You Bet Your Life" became a radio institution. It won the Peabody Award in 1948 and became one of the very few radio shows to play on all three networks. (CBS lured Groucho away from ABC and NBC later bought the show from CBS in 1950.) On October 5, 1950, "You Bet Your Life" began an 11-year run on NBC-TV. Groucho was assisted by announcer George Fenneman, the Jack Meakin Orchestra, and a duck who listened for the secret word. (The show would be later syndicated as "The Best of Groucho.") "It was some of the best stuff I ever did," says Groucho of his show. "I really had to think. I never worked so hard." "You Bet Your Life" won an Emmy in 1951 and the *Motion Picture Daily* Annual TV Poll from 1951 to 1954. A subsequent TV quiz show on CBS, "Tell It to Groucho," with announcer Fenneman and Jerry Fielding's Orchestra, failed to win ratings in 1962 and was a dismal memory for Groucho and viewers.

While participating in "You Bet Your Life," Groucho continued doing some film work. He performed roles in *Double Dynamite* (1951—with Frank Sinatra and Jane Russell) and *A Girl in Every Port* (1952—with William Bendix and Marie Wilson). He made cameo appearances in Bing Crosby's *Mr. Music* (1950) and Jayne Mansfield-Tony Randall's *Will Success Spoil Rock Hunter?* (1957—replacing Jack Benny). Meanwhile, Harpo and Chico worked sporadically. Harpo guested on such shows as "I Love Lucy" (CBS-TV, May 9, 1955) and Chico was seen, among other appearances, on the *Papa Romani* episode of "Silver Theatre" (CBS-TV, January 9, 1950). In the dismal *The Story of Mankind* (1957), made at Warner Bros., Groucho, Chico, and Harpo appeared together for the last time in a

Gummo, Zeppo, Chico, Groucho, and Harpo Marx in 1957.

feature film. Grotesque as it may seem, the historical survey film cast all three in *separate* segments: Groucho was Peter Minuit, Chico was a monk, and Harpo was Sir Isaac Newton. (Eden Hartford, then Mrs. Groucho Marx, played Laughing Water and Groucho's daughter Melinda was seen as an early-Christian child.) The performing trio worked together for the final time on the March 8, 1959, episode of CBS-TV's "G. E. Theatre." *The Incredible Jewel Robbery* starred Chico and Harpo with Groucho in a cameo. In the late Fifties, Groucho and Chico made a few appearances together on the Las Vegas club circuit.

On October 11, 1961, a financially insolvent Chico Marx died of a heart attack in his Hollywood home. He was buried in the Freedom Mausoleum at Forest Lawn.* Harpo,

who spent many of his later years enjoying the plush life of Palm Springs, died on September 28, 1964, of a heart attack at Mt. Sinai Hospital in Hollywood, having undergone open heart surgery. He was 75 and quite wealthy. He was buried at Forest Lawn also.

This left Groucho in the spotlight wherein he apparently basked.* He appeared in the Otto Preminger-directed *Skidoo* (1968), playing a gangland boss called "God." The would-be comedy was an outrageous misfire and received only limited bookings.

Groucho made no motion pictures after 1968, but he did stay in the limelight, mainly as the recipient of a wide variety of accolades, embracing the work of the great com-

---

* It is reported that when Groucho and Harpo were returning from Chico's funeral services, they agreed that the ceremony had been too sugary and that Groucho should have delivered the eulogy. Groucho said, "At least I wouldn't have been hypocritical. They'd have known what Chico was really like when I got through with him."

* Groucho's son Arthur Marx wrote *Life with Groucho* (1954), a biography of his father, and later turned out *Son of Groucho* (1972), an autobiography in which he admits he had many problems having so famous a father. "A giant's shadow," said Arthur, "often falls a great distance." He is also the author of *Everybody Loves Somebody Sometime (Especially Himself)* (1974), an account of Dean Martin and Jerry Lewis; and of the Broadway hit *The Impossible Years.*

473

edy team.* In May 1972 Groucho was the guest of honor at the Cannes Film Festival, where he was made a commander of the French Order of Arts and Letters. A few days before (May 6, 1972) he performed a one-man show at Carnegie Hall, playing to a sold-out crowd. (A two-record set LP album was released in late 1972 documenting the evening.) In 1974 Groucho received a Special Oscar. He told the audience how proud he was of his brothers, adding, "I wish they were here. . . . I wish Margaret Dumont was here."

As he closed in on 90, Groucho was frequently indisposed and sometimes his public performances turned out unfortunately, such as a 1976 appearance on a Merv Griffin TV talk-show salute to Ernie Kovacs. (Groucho seemed completely lost as to where he was and why he was there.) One person who spoke out against Groucho's limelight-seeking was Harpo's widow, Susan Marx, who felt such appearances by the aged wit were a disservice to the memory of the team at its professional peak. In October 1976 Groucho bowed out of a scheduled appearance at the Smithsonian Institution where he was to receive several honors. It seemed his comely secretary-companion Erin Fleming was ill with the flu in Los Angeles, and Marx refused to travel anywhere without her.**

The attractive Miss Fleming was much in the news in 1977, the last year of Groucho's life. While the elderly comedian was combatting a series of ailments (hip surgery, pneumonia, etc.) which found him hospitalized at Cedars-Sinai Medical Center for lengthy periods, Erin was the subject of a lawsuit by Groucho's son Arthur. The younger Marx was seeking to remove his father's long-time woman companion as overseer of his assets. It was Arthur's contention that she was a threat to Groucho's life. The Los Angeles court removed Miss Fleming as his temporary conservator and replaced her with Nat Perrin, a long-time friend of Groucho (he collaborated on *Horse Feathers* and *Monkey Business*). Later Perrin, who was serving jointly with the Bank of America in handling Groucho's estimated $2.5 million assets, asked to be removed from his post. In July Groucho's grandson Andrew was named conservator, a position confirmed in a bedside session at Cedars-Sinai Hospital. Said son Arthur of Groucho's reaction to the termination of the lengthy hassle, "He seemed just relieved to close his eyes and forget about it."

Meanwhile Groucho had been too ill to be informed of Gummo's death on April 21, 1977. The actor-turned-agent passed away of natural causes at the Eisenhower Medical Center in Palm Desert and was buried at Forest Lawn Cemetery.

Then on Friday night, August 19, 1977, Groucho died. Private services were held on August 21 and his body was then cremated.* The flow of tributes for the late comedian were staggering. The *New York Times* recorded,

> Effrontery, of the most lunatic, unsquelchable sort, was the chief stock in trade of Groucho Marx. As the key man in the most celebrated brother act in motion pictures, he developed the insult into an art form. And he used the insult, delivered with maniacal glee, to shatter the egos of the pompous—and to plunge his audiences into helpless laughter.

* * *

The private world of Groucho Marx was not far removed from his public

---

* Groucho wrote several books on his career and private life: *Beds* (1930; republished in 1976); *Many Happy Returns: An Unofficial Guide to Your Income Tax Problems* (1942); *Groucho and Me* (1959); *Memoirs of a Mangy Lover* (1963); *The Groucho Letters* (1967); *The Marx Brothers Scrapbook* (1974—with Richard Anobile); *The Groucho Phile: An Illustrated Life* (1976); and *The Secret Word Is Groucho* (1976—with Hector Arce).

During this period Groucho was a guest on several TV series ("I Dream of Jeannie," 1967, "Julia," 1968), appeared on many video talk shows, and was an occasional guest performer in a TV special (*Joys*, NBC-TV, March 5, 1976).

** In January 1977 Groucho, Harpo, Zeppo, and Chico were inducted into the Hollywood Hall of Fame. George Fenneman, the announcer on Groucho's "You Bet Your Life" show, represented his former boss and stated that a recent college poll among freshmen listed as the three most admired men, Christ, Albert Schweitzer, and Marx. Said Fenneman, "I'm sure Groucho didn't mind taking third billing."

---

* Per Groucho's will of September 24, 1974, the bulk of his estimated $2 million estate went to his three children; Erin Fleming received $150,000; Zeppo $50,000; Groucho's ex-wife Catherine received $25,000; four grandchildren were bequeathed $5,000 each; most of the comedian's trophies and memorabilia were donated to the Smithsonian Institution.

image. He was the kind of man who could, during his wedding ceremony, fling insults at the minister and, 21 years later, when his wife was leaving him for good, shake hands with her and say, "Well it's been nice knowing you; if you're ever in the neighborhood again, drop in."

Groucho was larger and more antic than life. He was the gruesomely stooped man in the swallowtail coat who took great loping steps across the stage or screen, holding a long, plump cigar behind him. His seemingly depraved eyes rolled and leered from behind steel-rimmed glasses. Below his large nose a smudge of black greasepaint passed for a mustache.

* * *

... Groucho's expertly delivered, rapid-fire insults were more mad than maddening; they really weren't unkind, for they evolved from his interest in humor that deflated rather than annihilated. This quality was, in fact, the distinguishing mark of the comedy so richly dispensed by Groucho Marx, his brothers and their great contemporaries, such as Charles Chaplin, W. C. Fields, and Buster Keaton.

Once asked as to the formula for the team's success in working together for so many years, Groucho replied, "I think we were the only group that never fought. . . . Four-a-day on edge, tired, fighting the audience, we never fought."

In *The Marx Brothers* (1975) author William Wolf writes, "The effects of Marx Brothers film comedy are so far-reaching that a full measurement may not be possible. . . . Their films have achieved a durability in themselves, but also a longevity through their influence on the art of others." Wolf cites such qualities as "universality," "anarchy," and "rebellion" as elements contributing to the team's durability. He sums up, "Their superb slapstick and horseplay are delivered in a free form, with multiple levels from which diverse audiences can find amusement on individual terms. The range is from simple slapstick to satirical demolition of the social order. There has been no other combination remotely like them, and, because their training ground no longer exists, there are not likely to be any comedians like them in the future."

FEATURE FILMS

With Groucho, Harpo, Chico, and Zeppo:
Humorisk (1926) [unreleased]
The Cocoanuts (*Paramount 1929*)
Animal Crackers (*Paramount 1930*)
Monkey Business (*Paramount 1931*)
Horse Feathers (*Paramount 1932*)
Duck Soup (*Paramount 1933*)

With Groucho, Harpo, and Chico:
A Night at the Opera (*MGM 1935*)
A Day at the Races (*MGM 1937*)
Room Service (*RKO 1938*)
At the Circus (*MGM 1939*)
Go West (*MGM 1940*)
The Big Store (*MGM 1941*)
A Night in Casablanca (*United Artists 1946*)

Love Happy (*United Artists 1949*)
The Story of Mankind (*Warner Bros. 1957*)

Groucho alone:
Copacabana (*United Artists 1947*)
Mr. Music (*Paramount 1950*)*
Double Dynamite (*RKO 1951*)
A Girl in Every Port (*RKO 1952*)
Will Success Spoil Rock Hunter? (*20th Century-Fox 1957*)*
Skidoo (*Paramount 1968*)

Harpo alone:
Too Many Kisses (*Paramount 1925*)
Stage Door Canteen (*United Artists 1943*)

* Unbilled guest appearance.

With Alison Skipworth in Two Wise Maids *(1937).*

Polly Moran

She was 5'4", with a long face, beady blue eyes, and mousy brown hair. Essentially a low comic, she had a motion picture career that spanned several decades encompassing stardom, comic relief roles, bits, and being one of Mack Sennett's top female clowns. Teamed with lovable Marie Dressler, Polly attained her greatest recognition and success on the screen. Neither actress was in even the last blush of youth when she became part of the screen's most notably successful female comedy duo. Polly was nearing the half-century mark and Miss Dressler had passed 60.

Unlike her co-starring sparring partner, Marie Dressler, whose versatile, massive talent gained her a niche in screen history as one of the cinema's greatest character actresses, the irrepressible and uninhibited Polly remained basically a roughhewn primitive. She was never far removed from earlier slapstick or outrageous farce.

Polly's sharp-featured expressive face would frequently burst into a smile that exposed an astonishing collection of teeth. She once verified her credo of anything-for-a-laugh: "I don't mind getting slapped in the face by a swinging door if I know that it's going to make a million or so people laugh and forget their troubles. I didn't even mind when everybody fiddled me about my broken nose. Wounds are just badges of honor to soldiers and comediennes!"

Pauline Therese Moran was born on Thursday, June 28, 1883, in Chicago. She first appeared on the stage in a school production of Gilbert and Sullivan's *H.M.S. Pinafore.* While playing a torch-carrying page in *Hamlet,* trouble-prone Polly accidentally set her hair on fire. At 15 she became a vaudeville performer and within five years was touring the music halls of Europe and South Africa. Filmmaker Mack Sennett witnessed her act at Los Angeles' Orpheum Theatre and signed her for his Keystone comedies. She made her screen debut as Charlie Murray's broom-brandishing wife in Sennett's short subject *The Janitor* (1914), and was with Murray, Mabel Normand, and Slim Summerville in the April 26, 1915, release, *Their Social Splash.*

In the two-reeler *A Favorite Fool* (1915), starring Eddie Foy, Polly was a widowed trapeze performer with seven children (the Seven Little Foys) whom the reluctant Eddie marries. With Hale Hamilton and Charlie Murray she played in *Her Painted Hero* (1915). For one of Sennett's rare blackface comedies, Polly was a dusky bride in gleaming white in *The Hunt* (1915), co-starring Ford Sterling. In 1916 she appeared as "the Sweetheart" of *The Village Blacksmith* (Tom Kennedy) and was with Joe Jackson and Mae Busch in *A Bath House Blunder*. The following year she transferred a character she had used in vaudeville to the screen when Sennett featured her as *Cactus Nell* in the short subject with Wallace Beery. Polly romped through several riotous screen adventures as "Sheriff Nell," proving herself a fine equestrienne and expert clown.

Although ignored by Sennett in his autobiography, Polly was to his Paramount comedy releases what Mabel Normand had been to Keystone. However, Miss Moran had neither Mabel's extreme wealth of talent nor her popularity: nor did she threaten Louise Fazenda's burlesquing buoyancy. But her "Sheriff Nell" characterization made her name known to the moviegoing public and it probably delighted Polly to have *Photoplay* enlighten her fans that she was actually born in Death Valley.

According to the 1916 *Photoplay* piece, entitled "Polly of the Laughs," the magazine insisted that she was not English-born but an "American of the Americans." According to the fan journal, "Her mother's arm cradled her first on the ovenish brink of Death Valley, that deep basin of heat that lies like a curse between the Panamints and the Funerals; and there is something of the wideness of the Desert in her eyes, and of the Wastes' inscrutable calm." By 1923 *Photoplay* was still tabbing her as the wanderer of the wasteland and suggesting that the Death Valley chamber of commerce was considering changing the town name to Moran, since Polly had brought it immortality. The magazine further noted that Polly's playing of the blustering, eccentric Nell "went through the wildest series of adventures ever recorded by a comedy camera, brought fame to her creator and added to Sennett's lustre."

Polly's fondness over the years for mimicking an exaggerated English accent and her proclivity for deliberate, outrageous overstatement of fact, coupled with her notorious practical joking, probably instigated the fiction of her background.

Mack Sennett's inability to retain his comedians in his studio stable resulted as much as anything else from his reluctance to pay them an appropriate salary. Polly left the Keystone fold to make a series of over two dozen two-reel comedies for National Film Corporation of America in 1920. The following year she signed for another group of comedy shorts with "Smiling Bill" Jones, released by CBC Film Corporation. Also in 1921 Polly made her first five-reel feature, a zany circus farce. The Fox film *Skirts* was directed by Hampton Del Ruth and co-starred Clyde Cook, Chester Conklin, and Slim Summerville. She was then seen on the screen as a chambermaid in Bebe Daniels' *Two Weeks with Pay* (1921) and was a cabaret entertainer in Cecil B. DeMille's multistar *The Affairs of Anatol* (1921).

Escorted by film industry executive Marcus Loew, a caravan of 25 Hollywood stars arrived in the East in late October 1922 on the "Metro Star Express" to parade and appear in person at prime opening dates of *The Prisoner of Zenda*. Polly was part of the contingent—one of the first of many later "star junkets"—which also included Buster Keaton, Anita Stewart, Johnny Hines, Leatrice Joy, and Nita Naldi. After a bit as a prizefight fan in the feature *Luck* (1923), Polly returned to vaudeville wearing a frightful wig, singing an awful song, "I'm Polly with a Fractured Past," and kidding the tinsel off Hollywood, its nouveau riche stars, and her past photoplays. She remained on the two-a-day circuit for the next three years. Then MGM signed her to a term contract and cast her in another bit, as a gal buying shoes in *The Auction Block* (1926).

Hoping to solve the plight of Marie Dressler's diminishing career, screen writer Frances Marion unearthed a story by Kathleen Norris in Metro's fertile story department. The scenarist imaginatively lengthened the short novel into a five-reel comedy script. She told MGM executive Irving Thalberg that the lead roles would be perfect for their own contractee Polly Moran and for the nearly forgotten onetime star Marie Dressler.

The Callahans and the Murphys (1927) was a rollicking comedy that Polly (as Mrs. Murphy) and Marie (as Mrs. Callahan) played with all stops out. Their romping as two blowsy, boozing Irish biddies, with a subplot on young love between Polly's son and Marie's daughter, made for a delightfully funny picture. It was anticipated that the Irish of America would lovingly embrace the comedy. However, after the picture's opening in early July 1927 at Broadway's Capitol Theater, the descendants of the Emerald Isle lost their Irish wit and arose in loud outcry. They cited Polly's and Marie's beer-guzzling, tenement-fighting dames as an insult to Irish womanhood.

Strenuous objections from the Roman Catholic church were underscored with demands by the Knights of Columbus, headed by Fathers Rudin and Fay of Boundbrook, to stop the showing of the film. Theaters were picketed by various Irish factions and several incidents of cinemas being stinkbombed were reported. In August MGM conceded to Irish demands and cut several objectionable scenes from the picture. But the hue and cry continued and the studio finally withdrew the picture from distribution. Despite the unwarranted failure of *The Callahans and the Murphys*, Polly was given a long-term contract with MGM as a result of her performance in the picture.

Having a contract with the glittering star-studded studio did not assure one's success. Polly was assigned a comic relief role in Lillian Gish's *The Enemy* (1927), and she lightened the suspense of Lon Chaney's *London After Midnight* (1927). As Lars Hanson's friend, Polly gave a fine performance as a laundress befriending seductive Greta Garbo in *The Divine Woman* (1928).*

Polly played a saloonkeeper—Lady Jane Dunstock—in Joan Crawford's silent version of *Rose-Marie* (1928) and was reunited with Dressler for *Bringing Up Father* (1928). As the landlady in *Telling the World* (1928) Moran was joined with a kindred spirit, William Haines. With him she could frolic, lampoon the pompous, and deflate pretentiousness. Off screen she became a great companion to the MGM star. For the next four years the irrepressible Haines-Moran combination would frequently announce their engagement to marry. The wild-eyed, frequently gullible press often believed the jokesters.

Meanwhile, on screen Polly continued to play an assortment of supporting roles. She was in Lon Chaney's *While the City Sleeps* (1928). In *Show People* (1928) she had two roles. She was showy and funny as Marion Davies' droll and snobbish maid, and then doubled as herself in a long, panning sequence in the MGM commissary as one of many stars at a banquet table. In a minor comedy, *Honeymoon* (1928), Polly played the lead opposite former Sennett comic Harry Gribbon.

While her screen partner Marie Dressler was finding little employment in the dream factories, Polly was playing Josephine Dunn's maid in the George K. Arthur-Karl Dane comedy *China Bound* (1929). When Dressler joined the MGM factory line, Polly and Marie were reunited joyously in Metro's all-star *The Hollywood Revue of 1929*. Together they had a musical number ("Strolling Through the Park One Day") and a comedy sketch ("For I'm the Queen"). Polly reverted again to playing maids, waitresses, or comedy relief in *The Unholy Night* (1929), *Speedway* (1929), *So This Is College* (1929), and, on loan-out to Fox and with El Brendel, in *Hot for Paris* (1929).

Metro cast Bessie Love and Charles King, stars of its Award-winning *The Broadway Melody*, in a highly touted film, *Chasing Rainbows* (1930). It featured Jack Benny, George K. Arthur, and the team of Dressler and Moran. The picture afforded the two middle-aged comediennes with another low-comedy drunk bit. The film itself was hardly a success.

Eddie Cantor's amusing book on the stock market became the basis for MGM's first box-office Dressler-Moran hit, *Caught Short* (1930). Most of the major critics dismissed

---

* Her casual acquaintance with the great Swedish actress lost its presumption when in 1932 at the premiere of *Grand Hotel*, celebrity Polly stepped to the microphone and announced, "Hello, everybody; you too, Greta Garbo. I hope you're here, for my shoes are pinching so horribly. I wish I had your boats!" The furious MGM management reprimanded its ebullient Polly to be more discreet in her revelations about studio stars, but it was futile to attempt to curb the woman's spontaneous brashness.

the vehicle as unworthy of the two laugh-makers.* But *Photoplay*, although finding some of the comedy feeble, thought it also contained some wildly hilarious moments provided by "that incomparable pair of funsters, Marie Dressler and Polly Moran." In the fast-paced feature Polly was a delight as pretentiously elegant Polly Smith who inveigles Marie to invest in the stock market. Her role called for her to be a road company Mrs. Malaprop by staggering and struggling over three-syllable words.

While Dressler was deservedly winning an Academy Award for Best Actress of the Year in *Min and Bill* (1930), Polly was adding her rough humor to a couple of William Haines' starrers—she had a brief stint in John Gilbert's *Way for a Sailor* (1930), and took a crack at a dramatic moment in Joan Crawford's *Paid* (1930). *Reducing* (1931) was critically dismissed as "slapstick," "a hodgepodge," and a waste of Dressler-Moran's time. But the public loved it. Here Polly was a pseudosophisticated beauty specialist shoved into a mud bath by Marie. The *New York Times* insisted, "The assumption throughout is that the spectacle of two unattractive women of advanced years fighting about matters of a personal nature constitutes a good basis for comedy." It did!

Polly had a bit (as a housekeeper) in the all-star short subject *The Stolen Jools* (1931), and it was announced that she would be teamed with comedian Karl Dane. But she returned to being the comedy foil for Miss Dressler. The team's next co-starring feature, *Politics* (1931), offered Marie greater depth of character. In a role less demanding and showy, Polly was Ivy Higgins, who believes Dressler's acclaimed nomination for mayor of the town was really intended for her.

Following *Politics*, Polly was signed for an "in-person" tour headlining Loew's vaudeville presentation houses. After all her years in vaudeville she had never played Broadway. She came close when she opened (October 23, 1931) at Loew's Paradise Theatre in New York, headlining a gala "Birthday Party Revue."

* In 1929 Moran and Dressler teamed in Al Christie's Paramount two-reel comedy *Dangerous Females*. The girls played sisters in a merry, very funny misidentification mixup, and should have convinced the Metro menage then and there of the public acceptance of the two funsters.

Back in Hollywood Polly and Marie were reunited for *Prosperity* (1932), which fared modestly well with the press and at the box office. This time around, Polly was Lizzie Praskins, comedy foil for Marie's bank president who is battling to save her bank and protect her depositors during the depression. *Photoplay* reported, "Not bad, but not good enough for the Dressler-Moran team." After an appearance in MGM's one-reel short *Jackie Cooper's Christmas* (1932), the team of Dressler and Moran would be no more. If Metro had never devised a comedy worthy of their considerable talents, the screen was at least enriched by laughter for the few pictures they did make together.

Polly was Paramount's Dodo Bird in its all-celebrity screen version of *Alice in Wonderland* (1933). On October 19, 1933, she announced her engagement to Los Angeles attorney Martin T. Malone, a friend of her legal adviser, Pat Cooney. (Polly's first, brief marriage had disappeared in divorce in 1917 and she had lived with her mother while raising her adopted son, John Michael Moran, whom she legally adopted when he was nine months old.) On Saturday, October 21, 1933, Polly became the wife of Malone, a former Pacific Coast collegiate welterweight boxing champion who was then practicing law in Los Angeles, They were wed in Las Vegas. Nelson Eddy gave the newlyweds a cocktail party. Polly returned to work, and after brief roles in two terrible pictures, a Metro bomb, *Hollywood Party* (1934),* and RKO's deplorably unfunny *Down to Their Last Yacht* (1934), Polly retired from the screen.

On July 15, 1936, Polly made the headlines. It seemed that during a local Elks' convention, her attorney husband had been called "Mr. Moran." He rose in a rage and aimed a revolver at his wife. Mr. Malone was arraigned before Justice Cecil Holland in Beverly Hills, who told Polly she was a lucky woman—the gun had jammed. Malone was charged with assault with a deadly weapon and freed on $500 bail.

Republic Pictures, well aware of the commercially successful teaming of Dressler and Moran, attempted to duplicate it. They

* Moran and co-star Jimmy Durante would headline the Capitol Theatre's stage show in New York after completing work on *Hollywood Party*. Their March 13, 1934, stage romp was an exercise in zaniness.

With Anita Page and Marie Dressler in Prosperity (1932).

With Ruth Donnelly
in Petticoat Politics
(1941).

481

paired rotund Alison Skipworth and Polly as grade-school teachers in *Two Wise Maids* (1937).* Both veteran performers gave professional interpretations in equally balanced parts. Republic teamed them again in what was called "a roundelay of good fun" in *Ladies in Distress* (1938). Here Polly was the sister-secretary of the town mayor (Skipworth).

Following brief bits in a few unimportant programmers, Polly retired to Laguna Beach in 1944 but maintained her close friendships in Hollywood. She frequently visited her dear friend Fanny Brice. She would often astound Fanny's elegant dinner guests by doubling as an unlikely maid. Without her dentures, mouth ablaze with lipstick, and her apple-round cheeks aflame with rouge, she would casually serve soup. On one such occasion she spilled a bit of the broth on debonair, sophisticated, but deadly serious Lionel Atwill and brushed off the startled diner with, "Helluva night, ain't it?" By the time Fanny would have secured her guests in another room for coffee, Polly would appear with dustpan, broom, and sarcastic comments to Fanny's unknowing guests. She would top her domestic performance with a horrendous rendition of "God Bless America."

In 1946 Polly actively campaigned for councilwoman on the Laguna Beach city council running on a "Pro-Dogs" platform. Raucously she would address her gathered voters: "I'm for Dogs!" She was defeated by a landslide.

The late Forties saw Polly make a brief return to show business. She appeared as the "Prize Maid" in an unfunny RKO two-reel comedy *Newlyweds* series in 1948. For

* Moran made a pair of two-reel comedies at Columbia: *Oh, Duchess* (1936) and *Sailor Maid* (1937).

Garson Kanin's great Katharine Hepburn-Spencer Tracy comedy *Adam's Rib* (1949), Polly returned to MGM to play the housekeeper Mrs. McGrath, who is cross-examined by attorney Hepburn. Directed by her acquaintance George Cukor, Polly's bewildered, obtuse mien on the witness stand made for a delightful vignette. Her last screen appearance was in MGM's *The Yellow Cab Man* (1950). In this Red Skelton comedy she played an overdressed, well-coiffed, corsage-dripping mother of the bride. It was a brief bit that gave her an opportunity to parlay her pseudoelegance once more for the camera.

As the years progressed, Polly's health continued to fail and she was dependent on nitroglycerin for survival. But her Laguna Beach parties continued. She welcomed guests in her modest wooden bungalow and retained her outrageous sense of humor and racy commentary. Her long battle against heart trouble ended at the Cedars of Lebanon Hospital in Hollywood on January 25, 1952, shortly after midnight. She was survived by her husband and son.

Polly's buxom slapstick had delighted audiences for several decades. But as the talkies progressed, other theatre-trained, more adept, sophisticated comediennes gained prominence on the screen. Most of these "newcomers" were more skilled than Polly at alternating their mirthmaking with telling dramatic roles. Miss Moran never attained the screen prominence of her frequent co-star, Marie Dressler, or that of other middle-aged actresses like Mary Boland, Edna May Oliver, Alice Brady, and Laura Hope Crews. In a way, Marjorie Main's later-day screen roles could have been grist for the Moran mill. But by that time Polly's filmmaking day was nearing its end. The party was almost over.

FEATURE FILMS

Skirts (*Fox 1921*)
Two Weeks with Pay (*Paramount 1921*)
The Affairs of Anatol (*Paramount 1921*)
Luck (*C. C. Burr 1923*)
The Auction Block (*MGM 1926*)
The Blackbird (*MGM 1926*)

Twinkletoes (*First National 1926*)
The Callahans and the Murphys (*MGM 1927*)
The Enemy (*MGM 1927*)
The Thirteenth Hour (*MGM 1927*)
Buttons (*MGM 1927*)
London After Midnight (*MGM 1927*)

With Katharine Hepburn in Adam's Rib *(1949).*

The Divine Woman (*MGM 1928*)
Rose-Marie (*MGM 1928*)
Detectives (*MGM 1928*)
Bringing Up Father (*MGM 1928*)
Telling the World (*MGM 1928*)
While the City Sleeps (*MGM 1928*)
Beyond the Sierras (*MGM 1928*)
Shadows of the Night (*MGM 1928*)
Show People (*MGM 1928*)
Honeymoon (*MGM 1928*)
The Trail of '98 (*MGM 1928*)
China Bound (*MGM 1929*)
The Hollywood Revue of 1929 (*MGM 1929*)
The Unholy Night (*MGM 1929*)
Speedway (*MGM 1929*)
So This Is College (*MGM 1929*)
Hot for Paris (*Fox 1929*)
Chasing Rainbows (*MGM 1930*)
The Girl Said No (*MGM 1930*)
Caught Short (*MGM 1930*)
Three French Girls (*MGM 1930*)

Way Out West (*MGM 1930*)
Way for a Sailor (*MGM 1930*)
Remote Control (*MGM 1930*)
Paid (*MGM 1930*)
Reducing (*MGM 1931*)
Guilty Hands (*MGM 1931*)
It's A Wise Child (*MGM 1931*)
Politics (*MGM 1931*)
The Passionate Plumber (*MGM 1932*)
Prosperity (*MGM 1932*)
Alice in Wonderland (*Paramount 1933*)
Down to Their Last Yacht (*RKO 1934*)
Hollywood Party (*MGM 1934*)
Two Wise Maids (*Republic 1937*)
Ladies in Distress (*Republic 1938*)
Ambush (*Paramount 1939*)
Tom Brown's School Days (*RKO 1940*)
Meet the Missus (*Republic 1940*)
Petticoat Politics (*Republic 1941*)
Adam's Rib (*MGM 1949*)
The Yellow Cab Man (*MGM 1950*)

Mabel Normand

Mabel Normand is essaying the greatest adventure of her surprising career. Firmly established as the Queen of Slapstick, she abdicated her throne and is now bending her talent toward comedy-drama. A daring move, but Mabel is capable of anything.

The star.

Mabel Normand

She was the first, greatest, and foremost comedienne of the American silent screen. Vivacious, fey, and adventurous, Mabel's existence was a whirl of fantasy, whimsy, and laughter. Both on and off screen her life burned brightly at both ends. It did not last the night of her life.

Probably Mabel's pixie nature and zestful immaturity were partially responsible for the innumerable fictions and inaccuracies recorded, published, and perpetuated about her birth. Only the month of November seems accurate regarding her birth. The day and the year of the event vary and her birthplace has been designated from Quebec, Canada, to Atlanta, Georgia. Her grandnephew, Stephen Normand, says that family records indicate Mabel was born on Wednesday, November 9, 1892, on Tysen Street, Stapleton, Staten Island, New York. Mabel's father, Claude George Normand, was born in Providence, Rhode Island, of French-Canadian parents who had moved to the States from Quebec. Itinerant piano player Claude George married a Providence-born Irish lass, Mary Drury. Their first three children died in infancy. Gladys, Claude Drury, and Mabel Ethelreid Normand survived.

Dainty, feminine Mabel was an incurable cutup. She was a natural athlete, tomboy, and devil-may-care beauty. By the time she was in her late teens she was modeling. In her teens she had a dreary job with the Butterick Company, a dress-pattern printer. But Mabel wanted a more glamorous job. Being a breath over five feet tall, petite Miss Normand, with jet-black hair and huge, expressive black eyes, sought a modeling career. Soon she was posing for the era's leading artists, including Charles Dana Gibson, Penrhyn Stanlaws, Orson Lowell, James Montgomery Flagg, and F. X. Leyendecker. For the last she was "The Girl at the Spinning Wheel" on a *Saturday Evening Post* magazine cover.

When fellow model Alice Joyce, later to become a star of the silent screen, mentioned that "posing" for moving pictures paid well, Mabel found work as an extra. In 1910 she was seen with Maurice Costello in Vitagraph's *Over the Garden Wall*. By midsummer 1911 she had worked at Vitagraph's Brooklyn studio in *Picciola, Betty Becomes a*

Maid, The Maid's Night Out, The Troublesome Secretaries (with John Bunny), and The Subduing of Mrs. Nag with Flora Finch. With her Vitagraph experience she applied for work at Biograph's Manhattan studio and was given a bit as a page in a Griffith costume one-reeler.

Also for Griffith she appeared in The Squaw's Love (September 14, 1911). Therein, because she was an excellent swimmer, she was able to execute a back dive into a river. In A Dash Through the Clouds she became one of the first screen actresses photographed in an early biplane. At Biograph she met Canadian-born Michael Sinnott who was working for D. W. Griffith under his stage name, Mack Sennett.* As their professional relationship developed, so did the off-camera romance of Mack and Mabel.

Normand made several Biograph comedies with Mack Sennett: A Spanish Dilemma, The Brave Hunter, Tomboy Bessie, The Tourists, and others. She appeared with Mary Pickford in The Mender of the Nets and with Blanche Sweet in The Eternal Mother.

As with her time at Vitagraph, the Biograph stay was more of a training period than anything else for Mabel. When Sennett, backed by bookmakers Charles O. Bauman and Adam Kessel, formed the Keystone Company, Mabel left Biograph for the new firm, which was to be geared to the comic muse. For Mabel, the changeover was mere whimsy and a chance to be the leading light of Sennett's new comedy company. In this venture she joined such personalities as Sennett, Fred Mace, Ford Sterling, and a vacillating, ersatz, troublemaking Frenchman, Henry "Pathe" Lehrman.

Keystone's The Water Nymph (1912) featured Mabel in a bathing suit—a bit of wardrobe Sennett later extended to clothe his famous "Sennett Bathing Girls." Many of the Keystone short comedies were shot on an improvisational basis against backgrounds of events of the day, like Shriners' parades, other directors' crowd scenes, or local municipal affairs. This setup provided Sennett at no cost with casts of thousands and unusual, unanticipated settings for his uninhibited, manic farces. When the Keystone Company transferred to California in 1912, the output of split reels gradually increased to one-reelers, and later to two reels. To the Edendale, California, ramshackled studio came a cluster of the screen's greatest clowns, including a personable, funny fat boy, Roscoe Arbuckle.

Mabel and Arbuckle were first teamed in The Waiter's Picnic (June 13, 1913) and continued for the next three years to turn out a series of exceptionally funny films that became popular with the moviegoing public. The huge, overweight "Fatty" and the diminutive (100 pounds) Mabel became so well known that their pictures were promoted with their names in the titles: Fatty and Mabel's Married Life, Fatty and Mabel at the San Diego Exposition, Fatty and Mabel Viewing the World's Fair at San Francisco, and a hilarious three-reeler, Fatty and Mabel Adrift. (The last entry was included in the 1960 compilation feature When Comedy Was King and engendered great laughter.)

By 1914 a new clown had joined the Sennett ranks. Mabel had badgered Sennett into hiring Charles Chaplin, the English comic, and, as she had done with Arbuckle, persuaded Mack into giving him more opportunity on the screen. Chaplin and Normand first appeared together in a February 9, 1914, release, Mabel's Strange Predicament. Although the future Comedy King of Hollywood admired Mabel (if not her sporadic experiments in directing that Sennett permitted), he did not acknowledge her contribution to his filmdom success. Many agree that Chaplin took stock of Mabel's gestures, facial expressions, and nuances, and then adopted and refined them for his own screen characterization.

The first feature-length comedy made in the U.S. was Sennett's Tillie's Punctured Romance (1914) and it starred the great Marie Dressler. Chaplin was cast as her larcenous lover, with Mabel as his accomplice, the Other Woman. During the long filming of Tillie, Marie Dressler learned to love and respect Mabel and later wrote, "She had courage, and courage, perhaps, is the quality I admire most. Dark, little, vivaciously pretty, as active and as mischievous as a

* David Merrick's musical Mack and Mabel opened on Broadway on October 6, 1974, after a West Coast break-in. Despite the illustrious talents of Robert Preston (as Mack) and Bernadette Peters (as Mabel) the attempt to reconstruct the lives and aura of past Hollywood greats failed—as most such efforts have failed.

In the short subject Fatty and Mabel Adrift (1916) with Roscoe "Fatty" Arbuckle.

monkey, she was the first great comedienne of the screen. Always willing to risk life and limb to give her fans a thrill." Linda Arvidson, D. W. Griffith's wife, thought Mabel was "the most wonderful girl in the world, the most beautiful and the best sport. Daring, reckless, and generous to a fault, she was like a frisky colt that would brook no bridle."

During these important career years, Mabel's romance with Sennett had a seesawing status that was always supposed to culminate in marriage, but never did. Despite their mutual love, extravagant senses of humor, and professional pairing, they just could never make the commitment of matrimony. At one point, a July 4, 1915, date was announced for the long-discussed nuptials. But then Mabel unwittingly intruded on Mack's tête-à-tête with actress Mae Busch. This revelation ended her plans to become Mrs. Sennett and thereafter she vigorously pursued her career.

Mabel started another standard for the wild Keystone film circus when in *A Noise from the Deep* (1913), in a moment of her usual skittish improvisation, she tossed with

deadly accuracy a pie into Roscoe "Fatty" Arbuckle's moon face. In later years Mabel would say, "I had nobody to tell me what to do." She added, "I had to cleave a new path to laughter through the wilderness of the industry's ignorance and inexperience. I created my own standard of fun, simply letting spontaneity and my inborn sense of what is mirth-provoking guide me, for no director ever taught me a thing."

For the inaugural program of Triangle Films (composed of filmmakers D. W. Griffith, Thomas Ince, and Sennett), on Thursday, September 23, 1915, Keystone's contribution was a four-reel comedy, *My Valet*, featuring Broadway star Raymond Hitchcock with Mabel as "The Affianced Girl." The farce was tagged as "excellent" and "rip-roaring." And high praise was tendered Mabel: "Besides being very pretty and possessing a figure that calls forth admiration, she is a comedian of the first class. Irrespective of the pulchritudinous admiration she inspires, it is also an extreme pleasure to watch her other work of a purely comical nature." As undisputed Queen of Keystone, Mabel could be demanding, leaping into tantrums, and insisting upon a say in all aspects of her filmmaking. In the spring of 1916 she inveigled Sennett to star her in a full-length comedy, *Mickey*.

The Mabel Normand Feature Film Company was established and production on *Mickey* began in August 1916. From the onset the picture was besieged by troubles. Not only did Mack permit her to manage the entire enterprise, but she was plagued by erratic health. She was given to spasms of coughing and sinus infections—harbingers of the tuberculosis that eventually consumed her. James Young and J. Farrell MacDonald were replaced as directors by young F. Richard Jones. The simple tale of a nouveau riche western Cinderella pursued in New York City by a socialite villain took over seven months to shoot. When Sennett screened the finished product for New York distributors, they were mightily displeased. No one wanted *Mickey*.

Originally it had been announced that Mabel's next feature with Sennett would be Sir James Barrie's *The Little Minister*. It would have been a great role for the mercurial, effervescent Mabel. But the combination of her disappointment over *Mickey* and her heartache over Sennett's amorous flings caused her to sign a long-term contract to make feature pictures for Samuel Goldwyn. The new setup would allow Mabel to prove that Sennett and his Keystone factory were not supporting her. She did just that. Her Goldwyn pictures were great hits and merry comedy films.

Normand's first Goldwyn release was *Dodging a Million* (1918), a comedy of errors brightly directed by George Loane Tucker. Her "very charming" portrayal brought comment: "Mabel Normand in many respects is a surprise. She has the ease and repose of a screen actress long trained to the requirements of the photoplay, and she seems to have evolved a new personality besides, but she is the same bubbling Mabel as a rule and, as such, she is very acceptable, a veritable artist at times, unafraid to give her feelings free expression at all times." In *The Floor Below"* (1918) she was directed by Clarence Badger. Her co-star was Tom Moore and she played a clowning, irrepressible newspaper copygirl getting the big scoop and wedding a millionaire.

Joan of Plattsburg (1918) proved to be a big turgid, pretentious, patriotic pastiche. Mabel nearly sank in the murky emotional waters of the plot. Her stab at spirituality as a modern-day Joan of Arc was dismissed: "To expect an actress who has scored her biggest success in broad farce to illuminate the face of a modern Joan with the divine fire of the Maid of Orleans is to look for a miracle." Mabel returned to comedy in *The Venus Model* (1918) with Rod LaRocque. Her striking talent saved the insipidly scripted *Back to the Woods* (1918). Also for Goldwyn, she appeared as an Italian girl in his Liberty Loan film *Stake Uncle Sam to Play Your Hand* (1918).

Mabel's madcap, unpredictable behavior plagued the Goldwyn lot. She arrived inexcusably late, took off for Paris in the midst of a picture, and, although a woman of outstanding beauty and wit, continued her childish pranks. That Sam Goldwyn was a victim of unrequited love for Mabel probably saved her professional standing there.

In the summer of 1918 fortune was kind to Mack Sennett. At an unscheduled showing on Long Island, *Mickey* was substituted for a missing feature and proved to be a raging, roaring success. The picture's theme song, "Mickey," became a national song hit and, eventually, a standard. The seven-reel picture ran over an hour, and P. S. Harrison reported, "We have all been waiting for this offering for quite a long time, but I'm sure you will be rewarded for the extended wait." *Billboard* enthused, "As a box-office balahoo, *Mickey* will shriek louder than our long-distance guns over No Man's Land." *Exhibitor's Trade Review* lauded, "*Mickey* is a remarkable feature in many ways and not the least of these is the rare dramatic ability displayed by the star, Mabel Normand. She brings tears to the eyes at one moment, and at the very next has her audience roaring with laughter."

Mabel was superb as tomboy *Mickey*. She is the one who is raised by a miner and nurtured by an Indian squaw. Later in the story she jockeys a horse in a thrilling scene. The hero of the piece was Wheeler Oakman; the suave villain was Lew Cody. *Mickey* would earn substantial grosses at the box office.

In *Peck's Bad Girl* (1918) Mabel helps to round up a gang of bank robbers. As a boardinghouse slavey who becomes a shirt-waist salesgirl, Mabel was back in a bathing suit doing clever diving stunts in *A Perfect 36* (1918). The stage hit *Sis Hopkins* (1919) was a natural role for Mabel.* *Motion Picture World* reported, "She is not quiet for a moment and she is able to reveal something amusing as well by the mobility of her expressive face and an inexhaustible source of energy, inured to the roughest kind of farce. The character does not exactly fit her, though she manages to make it the more amusing on that account for Mabel has not yet found her best role. What it is going to be no one can guess, but it will not be far removed from her own happy temperament. Her entire attitude is that 'I should worry' and she rarely fails to express this to her audience."

William Christy Cabanne directed Mabel in a plot of mistaken birthright called *The Pest* (1919) in which she was a rural slavey/flatboat-ferry pilot. Victor Schertzinger directed her last seven Goldwyn features. "She's a gawky hoyden; she's a spoiled child; she's Mary Pickford; she's Charlie Chaplin," reported the critics of her playing in *When Doctors Disagree* (1919). In *The Jinx* (1919) Mabel was back in overalls getting high praise for her playing of a rough-and-ready circus drudge pedicuring elephants with lampblack.

In *Pinto* (1920) Mabel demonstrated expert riding and stunts that were called close to professional. In August 1920, as Kalora, Princess of Morevania, she was an exotic Oriental, clad in an inflated rubber suit that gave her a voluptuous figure until she backed into a cactus in Goldwyn's remake of *The Slim Princess* (1920). Her freewheeling performance was pure Normand and "she romped at will among sedate dignitaries, scattering self-importance to the four winds."

In the early fall of 1920 Mabel played hopelessly romantic salesgirl Mayme Ladd, masquerading as a seductive senorita in *What Happened to Rosa*. In the course of the proceedings, Mabel's heroine falls down a coal chute, is run down by a pushcart, and

swims ashore from a yachting port. Her final Goldwyn picture, completed at the end of 1920, would be held back from release until May 1922.* *Head Over Heels* was received with great lack of enthusiasm by the public and the critics.

With her Goldwyn days finished and being at loose ends, Mabel returned to her former employer and lover, Mack Sennett. In 1921 he had issued through States Rights a film entitled *Oh, Mabel, Behave!*, a five-reeler set in colonial times. It had Ford Sterling as a miserly country squire, Mack Sennett as the boob valet, Owen Moore as the hero, and Mabel as the beleaguered innkeeper's daughter. The film was advertised as *not* a reissue, but it very closely resembled, in construction, filming, and cast, something that Sennett had put together during the Triangle days.

If the vintage slapstick burlesque of *Oh, Mabel, Behave!* was dubious, there was nothing questionable about Sennett's expensive production of *Molly O'*. Mabel was lovely in the title role of Molly O'Dair and Sennett anticipated another multi-million-dollar grosser like *Mickey*. The *New York Times* called it "good old-fashioned hokum and high jinks, and high jinks it is without pretense of anything else." The picture opened at Los Angeles' Mission Theatre in January 1922 on a reserved-seat basis. The King of Comedy's dream of another box-office bonanza exploded in a murder.

The front page of the *New York Times* for Friday, February 3, 1922, headlined, "Movie Director Found Murdered in Los Angeles. Jealousy May Be Motive. Mabel Normand Tells of Leaving Him Alive at 9 o'clock After Conference on New Production. Rumors of Their Engagement."

William Desmond Taylor was a handsome six-foot tall, blue-eyed Irishman. He was a onetime stage and screen actor and a top Paramount director. He was sophisticated, charming, erudite, and greatly admired by the female sex. On the morning of February 2 in the living room of his home at 404¼ South Alvarado Street, his butler, Henry Peavey, found him dead. He had been shot very accurately through the chest.

---

* In 1941 Judy Canova remade *Sis Hopkins* for Republic. The Canova *Sis* was the first picture made on the studio's $250,000 sound stage dedicated to the memory of Mabel Normand.

* An announced picture, called *The Last Chance*, which was to star Mabel with two of her former leading men, Tom Moore and Herbert Rawlinson, was not made.

"It's a Goldwyn Picture"

SAMUEL GOLDWYN PRESENTS

MABEL NORMAND IN "SIS HOPKINS"

From The World-Famed Stage Success

By Rose Melville

Goldwyn Pictures

DIRECTED BY CLARENCE G. BADGER

Advertisement for Sis Hopkins *(1919).*

The ensuing investigation was quixotic. Obvious clues and pertinent facts were ignored, but steaming segments of Taylor's past life were unearthed. There were such tidbits as a mysterious vanished brother, Dennis Deane-Tanner, alleged to have been Taylor's former butler, Edward F. Sands. In his home a luridly erotic cache of selective, seductive ladies' lingerie was discovered. More damaging was a collection of letters from various actresses, including Mabel. The most publicized group of notes was from the screen's pristine, golden-haired embodiment of virginity, Mary Miles Minter, whose 10-year screen career would come to an abrupt end.

As the "facts" were pieced together, it seemed that fun-loving Mabel, like so many others, had been enchanted with Taylor's mundane manner and erudition. He guided her voracious, undisciplined reading. On the night of his death Taylor had lent Mabel a copy of Freud when she stopped by. She read it with the same interest that she devoted to *True Confessions* and the *Police Gazette.* Less than a half-hour after Mabel and her chauffeur had driven away from South Alvarado Street, Taylor was killed.

In San Francisco, the jury for Roscoe "Fatty" Arbuckle's second trial was still out—a third jury would acquit him of any responsibility in the death of Virginia Rappe—when the Taylor case hit the headlines.

Mabel offered a cash reward for the apprehension of Taylor's killer. She gave a long, published statement to the Los Angeles district attorney that closed with a plea to her public to realize that she and Taylor were not lovers, that they had not quarreled, that she was in no way connected with the crime, and that she knew absolutely nothing about it. While the Taylor case wallowed in a swamp of conjecture and theory, which included outraged mother-love, homosexuality, and blackmail, Mabel completed another picture for Sennett.

Unlike Arbuckle and Mary Miles Minter, whose pictures were withdrawn from circulation and their careers finished, Mabel survived the Taylor scandal.* She continued on the screen in Sennett's *Suzanna* (1923), another tale of mixed birthright, set in old Mexico. The *Motion Picture World* declared, "Mabel Normand has never appeared so beautiful nor given us such splendid dramatic work. Her work probably surpasses anything she has ever done. Her transitions and moods are exquisitely well done as the daughter of an old family servant who is in reality an heiress."

With *Molly O'* and *Suzanna* well received and supported at the box office, Mabel left for Europe where her wildly extravagant spending of money and energy and her touring the Continent with Prince Ibrahim of Egypt made headlines. When she returned, Sennett had another picture set for her, *The Extra Girl,* scheduled for a Christmas release, But, by New Year's 1923 Mabel was back in the headlines.

Courtland S. Dines, a romantic accruement of Charlie Chaplin's leading lady Edna Purviance, was shot with Mabel's .25-caliber, pearl-handle pistol by Normand's new chauffeur, Kelly. Colorado millionaire Dines was seriously wounded but did not press charges. However, the investigation disclosed that Kelly was an ex-convict and drug user. Again Mabel remarkably escaped damnation by association.

Then on January 18, 1923, came the death of screen idol, all-American boy Wallace Reid, who died of agonizing drug addiction. Hollywood once again came under attack as a veritable den of iniquity. Rumors of Mabel's drug addiction were rife, and the unfounded, tendentious gossip has persisted through the years.

* The case to this day remains officially unsolved.

In Upstairs *(1919).*

491

With Cullen Landis in Pinto
(1920).

In Suzanna (1923).

492

With all the scandal surrounding Mabel, Sennett was forced to delay the release of *The Extra Girl* for nearly a year. As with *Suzanna*, Mabel made personal appearances to promote the picture. The highlight of the story about a movie extra focused on Mabel's pulling a huge lion about a movie set, she thinking the beast is a disguised dog. The *New York Times* thought the lion was the whole show. In actuality, Mabel gave a delightful performance and the film is still shown on television today.

But by this point in her career, the public had lost faith in Mabel's screen ways and she, having lived a much too full life in such a short time, was too exhausted to disprove their lack of enthusiasm for her. She tried to recapture her dwindling popularity on the stage. Producer Al Woods signed her for the lead in *The Little Mouse*. The farce tried out in New Jersey and then tottered to Washington, D.C., opening there on September 7, 1925. Mabel's legitimate stage debut was notable only for the lack of critical and public response and her weak voice, which could barely be heard beyond the third row of the orchestra. The show closed in Providence, Rhode Island, on September 26, 1925.

Filmmaker Hal Roach brought Mabel back to the screen in a brief series of short comedies. (Other major producers, including Sennett, had been reluctant to sign her for screen work.) A few of her old friends remained faithful. In the spring of 1926 Mary Pickford, with whom she had worked so long ago at Biograph, wrote an open letter welcoming Mabel back to the screen. It was published in Los Angeles newspapers.

Mabel's first Roach comedy was a three-reeler, *Raggedy Rose* (November 13, 1926), followed by *The Nickel Hopper*, in which she was a five-cents-a-dance girl pursuing Theodore von Eltz. In January 1927 von Eltz, Gustav von Seyffertitz, and Max Davidson supported her in another three-reeler, *Anything Once*. Her last screen appearance was in Roach's February 5, 1927, two-reeler, *Should Men Walk Home?* with Oliver Hardy, Creighton Hale, and Eugene Pallette.

At this juncture, Mabel, in one of her outlandishly prankish moods, got married.

In the wee hours of the morning of September 16, 1926, following a party at her home, actor Lew Cody suggested that Mabel and he get married. They did, in Ventura County, but the hilarity of the impromptu nuptials blurred with the dawn. Mabel returned to her home in Beverly Hills at 526 North Camden Drive and Cody retired to his 609 North Maple address.

Mabel faded from public view. In September 1929 she was taken to Dr. Francis Pottenger's sanatorium in Monrovia, California, accompanied by her close companion, registered nurse Julia Benson. (In recent years Miss Benson, who had been with Mabel since the 1918 flu epidemic, has vigorously denied the lurid tales of Mabel's drug addiction.) For the next six months Mabel was treated for advanced tuberculosis. She died at 2:30 A.M. on February 23, 1930, three weeks after her father had succumbed to pneumonia.*

Even in death controversy persisted. There was a crisis about her being buried in consecrated ground because of her marriage to twice-divorced (both by actress Dorothy Dalton) Lew Cody. A final determination that the marriage had never been consummated permitted Mabel to be buried in the Calvary Roman Catholic Cemetery in Los Angeles.

It is ironic that Mabel's career—and those of other Twenties luminaries—was so badly damaged by standards of mores that have so drastically changed. Ironic too that both of Sennett's foremost comedians, Fatty and Mabel, faded out in scandalous headlines, whereas Chaplin, whose entire career was plagued by lurid publicity, survived so well.

During her years on screen, Mabel established a precedent for uninhibited screen comedy that, in recent years, has been carried on by the expert clowning of Lucille Ball and Carol Burnett. But childlike Mabel was the screen's first and greatest comedienne. The *true* like of the beloved little clown has not been seen since and probably will not be seen again.

* Mrs. Normand died in February 1932 and in 1945 Mabel's brother Claude hanged himself in the basement of the Normand home Mabel had given her family in Staten Island, New York.

FEATURE FILMS

Tillie's Punctured Romance (*Keystone 1914*)
  [TV title: Charlie's Big Romance]
My Valet (*Keystone 1915*)
Dodging a Million (*Goldwyn 1918*)
The Floor Below (*Goldwyn 1918*)
Joan of Plattsburg (*Goldwyn 1918*)
The Venus Model (*Goldwyn 1918*)
Back to the Woods (*Goldwyn 1918*)
Mickey (*Sennett-Western 1918*)
Peck's Bad Girl (*Goldwyn 1918*)
A Perfect 36 (*Goldwyn 1918*)
Sis Hopkins (*Goldwyn 1919*)
The Pest (*Goldwyn 1919*)
When Doctors Disagree (*Goldwyn 1919*)

Upstairs (*Goldwyn 1919*)
The Jinx (*Goldwyn 1919*)
Pinto (*Goldwyn 1920*)
The Slim Princess (*Goldwyn 1920*)
What Happened to Rosa (*Goldwyn 1921*)
Oh, Mabel, Behave! (*Triangle-Photocraft-States Rights 1921*)
Molly O' (*Sennett-Associated Producers 1921*)
Head Over Heels (*Goldwyn 1922*)
Suzanna (*Sennett-Allied Producers and Distributors 1923*)
The Extra Girl (*Sennett-Associated Exhibitors 1923*)

Edna May Oliver

For many laughmakers, unique physical appearance has great value. Many of the greatest clowns could be classified as losers in the world of beauty. But utilization of their enormous talents despite a lack of physical attractiveness has brought many of them fame and lasting memory.

Edna May Oliver exemplified just such a comedienne. A tall, handsome woman in repose, she utilized her body for comedic effect. Like Chaplin, she knew that the essence of comedy was gained by outrageous footwork. One of her stock-in-trade bits was to manipulate her seemingly large feet (she wore an ordinary 6½) by crooking her foot, sliding on her heels, or walking on the edge of her shoes. Miss Oliver's most remembered gesture, however, was her constant, exemplary sniff, accomplished by twitching her nose to the left, lifting the left side of her lips, and sniffing audibly.* All told, she was a fine comedienne and a very accomplished character actress.

She also became resigned to the fact that she was known whisperingly in Hollywood as "hoss-faced Oliver." It had once come as a great shock when an unkind drama critic wrote, "Edna May Oliver looked her usual self—as though she'd just been taken out of harness." However, as the years passed, she grew more tolerant of her appearance. "I

* The trademark sniff was accidental. Supposedly it originated at her annoyance with comics Wheeler and Woolsey after she assumed a scene in one of their joint RKO efforts had been completed. But the camera captured the Oliver sniff. After years of being identified with it, Edna May would say, "Yes, I know I do it a great deal, I know that people are beginning to expect it when they see me walk into a scene. But I don't want them to. I'm trying to get away from that sniff. It'll be fatal if I don't. When people know what to expect from you, it's fatal."

With Ann Harding and Richard Dix in The Conquerors *(1932).*

don't mind making myself grotesque," she once said. "Women who look beautiful on the stage don't make a lasting impression. I get great joy out of making people laugh. People need laughter very, very much. It is proven every day. I'm so grateful I've found my forte in life. Regret that I'm not a beauty? None, whatever. When I decided to go on the stage, I remember my uncle telling me, 'Edna, there's no place for you on the stage. You are not the build physically. You are all bones. You'll never be successful.'" Her uncle was Freeman A. Oliver, first violinist of the Boston Handel and Haydn Symphony. He was her father's half-brother. She fortunately did not take his advice but did assume his last name, becoming Edna May Oliver and going on the stage.

Edna May was born on Friday, November 9, 1883,* on Charlotte Avenue in Boston, to Ida May Cox and Charles Edward Nutter. When she was 14 her plumber father died and she left school to work in a milliner's shop. Besides becoming an expert pianist, she possessed a fine mezzo-soprano voice and sang in a quartet at the Arlington Street Unitarian Church. Chorus work in summer opera followed, but as Edna would later remark, "For $18 a week I toured New England with an open-air opera company and I ruined my singing voice." She later toured as pianist with an all-female orchestra. In 1900 she joined Lindsay Morrison's Boston Stock Company at $25 weekly playing Miss Hazy in *Mrs. Wiggs of the Cabbage Patch.* After several years with Morrison's stock company, Edna joined professional touring shows, appearing with Fannie Ward in *The New Lady Bantock.* By 1915 she joined Jefferson DeAngelis and Ivan Simpson for a road tour as Alvina Smythe in *Some Baby.*

Edna made her Broadway debut in *The Master* (December 16, 1916). The play lasted 47 performances and she was then offered a fine chance in a new musical comedy. In Jerome Kern's *Oh, Boy!* (1917) she was the eccentric Quaker aunt, Miss Penelope. Included in the cast were Marion Davies, Lynne Overman, and Justine Johnstone. After 465 performances in New York, Edna remained

with the show for an extensive road tour. She was back on Broadway in *Rose of China* (1919), was in Victor Herbert's *The Golden Girl* (1920), and on November 1, 1920, *The Half Moon* opened at the Liberty Theatre with Edna May as Mrs. Frances Adams Jarvis.

Leaving musical comedy she played in *Wait Till We're Married* (1921) and that November was involved in the short-lived *Her Salary Man.* In July 1922 she was in Atlantic City, New Jersey, trying out a new show, *Wild Oats Lane,* having played for four months in *The Rubicon.* The new show moved to New York on September 6, 1922, for a long run of 451 performances. One of her greatest hits was as the awkward and tragic factotum in Owen Davis' Pulitzer Prize-winning play *Icebound* (1923). During the show's successful run she made her film debut as Tyrone Power Sr.'s wife in *Wife in Name Only* (1923). Then for C. C. Burr Pictures she played Hetty in Constance Binney's *Three O'Clock in the Morning* (1923) and remained with the Burr Company to play James Rennie's secretary in *Restless Wives* (1924).

Edna May enjoyed the motion picture medium and was pleased with the arrangement of making films during the day and continuing to perform on stage at night. Paramount's Astoria, Long Island, studios were active in the mid-Twenties and Edna May signed for its William C. De Mille-directed screen version of *Icebound* (1924), repeating her role of Hannah. While on stage with Cornelia Otis Skinner and Effie Shannon in *In His Arms* she supported Richard Dix in Paramount's *Manhattan* (1924).

On January 13, 1925, she was in the short-lived Leslie Howard play *Isabel,* her first attempt at playing a sedately intoxicated grande dame. She was hilariously funny in the assignment. While in *Isabel* producer George Tyler offered her stardom in Owen Davis' new play, *Ma Pettengill,* based on Harry Leon Wilson's *Red Gap* stories. Her first bid for stardom opened in Chicago in March 1925 and closed two weeks later there. She returned to Broadway via Paramount's *Lucky Devil* (1925), as Esther Ralston's aunt. In *Lovers in Quarantine* (1925) Oliver was the spinsterish chaperone of Bebe Daniels.

---

* Miss Oliver would tell biographers she was born on January 12, 1885, in New York City. Other sources indicate she might have been born on November 9, 1883, in Malden, Massachusetts.

Edna May admitted, "I always stood out," referring to her stage roles. She shone brightly indeed in the stage farce *Cradle Snatchers*. From its first tryout in July 1925 through over three hundred performances on Broadway, the comedy was a huge success. The show featured Edna May, Mary Boland, and Margaret Dale as three lonely wives pursuing three youths in hope of agitating their preoccupied husbands. One critic lauded Edna for her smart interpretation of predatory Ethel Drake: "The character she plays is quite as unedifying as the other two middle-aged women in the cast, but somehow she contrives to give it the aspect of a regrettable lapse on the part of a beloved aunt instead of the habitual mode of amusement of the lacquered ladies in a Broadway deluxe apartment. And with the severe and melancholy hilarity of her interpretation she contributes the one human touch of realism to this uproarious and incredible farce." The critic could have mentioned the impeccable Oliver timing that could turn an ordinary line into a laugh-getter. (Later-day critics would find in Eve Arden's performing much of Edna May's qualities, especially the astute, terse delivery of lines.)

In 1926 Edna made two Paramount, Astoria-filmed movies. *The American Venus* (made with Technicolor sequences and Atlantic City location shots) found her as Ford Sterling's wife. In *Let's Get Married* Edna was amusing as an alcoholic hymnal saleswoman, getting Richard Dix arrested in a cabaret brawl. *Photoplay* awarded her its citation for one of the best performances of the month.

In the summer of 1927 Edna was engaged by producer Edgar Selwyn for a new Gershwin musical, *Strike Up the Band*. The role of Mrs. Draper never materialized for the frenetic-footed Miss Oliver. She left the production during the pre-Broadway tryout and was replaced by Blanche Ring. (The show would later close in Philadelphia, only to be revamped, recast, and revived three years later; it made a modest splash on Broadway.)

From its opening in Washington, D.C., in November 1927 to its Broadway bow on December 27, 1927, word spread that the Jerome Kern–Oscar Hammerstein II version of Edna Ferber's *Show Boat* was creating show-business history. It did. Edna May was

Cap'n Andy's bossy, nagging wife, Parthy Ann Hawks. It was to become one of her most memorable (and longest-running) stage roles. During the second month of *Show Boat's* run, Edna May attempted a new, untried part. She wed.

On Tuesday afternoon, January 24, 1928, Edna May Nutter,* age 44, married David Welford Pratt, a Newark, New Jersey, broker from Norfolk, Virginia. They were married at New York City's municipal building in a civil ceremony. The guests included Florenz Ziegfeld, Helen Morgan, Charles Winninger, Norma Terris—all from her *Show Boat* family—and George Jessel. A wedding dinner was held at Edna's home at the Hotel Warwick, where the newlyweds announced they would maintain separate residences. The 37-year-old Mr. Pratt would retain his West 52nd Street apartment, and the new Mrs. Pratt would remain at the Hotel Warwick. The marriage lasted five years; the Pratts were divorced in 1933. Edna May never remarried.

On October 1, 1929, *Show Boat* was brought to Chicago, retaining most of the New York company with some reassignments. Irene Dunne was now featured as Magnolia while Edna May continued bossing Cap'n Andy (Charles Winninger) and his boat. At this time both Miss Dunne and Miss Oliver were sought as contract players for RKO. Edna's reply to William LeBaron's offer of salary to join the RKO ranks was a "no" and she continued playing Parthy Ann. By the closing of *Show Boat* in Chicago in mid-January 1930, Oliver and LeBaron had come to mutual financial terms. She left for Hollywood.**

RKO tossed Edna into the first Wheeler and Woolsey starring feature, *Half Shot at Sunrise* (1930). She played a colonel's wife whose daughter is pursued in a wild World War I romp by the two clowns. In Wesley Ruggles' Academy Award–winning prestige film *Cimarron* (1931), Edna was splendidly cast as the

---

* At one point in reflecting on her professional name changing, Edna commented, "No woman named 'Nutter' would ever get anywhere in the theatre." In 1931 her name was legally changed to Oliver.

** Her last picture made for Paramount before leaving New York had been Clara Bow's *The Saturday Night Kid* (1929), in which she played a fussy department-store forewoman. It was her first talkie film.

town busybody. With Wheeler and Woolsey she provided the funniest performance in a dud entitled *Cracked Nuts* (1931). Then RKO decided to team flibbertigibbety Hugh Herbert with Edna, announcing that "America takes them to heart," and assigned them to Gregory LaCava's *Laugh and Get Rich* (1931). Although the two funsters provided some raucous fun as boardinghouse keepers, America did not take them to heart as a team. Future projects for the pair were abandoned. Edna May was also announced for RKO's reuniting of the *Cimarron* leads, Richard Dix and Irene Dunne, in another historical epic, *Frontier*. That project was delayed and would finally appear as *The Conquerors* in 1932 with Oliver and Dix, but with Ann Harding replacing Dunne. As for the studio's proposed production of Victor Herbert's *Babes in Toyland* to headline Irene Dunne, Wheeler and Woolsey, Edna, and a cast of thousands, it was dropped from RKO's ambitious filming schedule.

The studio loaned her to Paramount to play Mitzi Green's stage mother in *Newly Rich* (1931). When she returned to RKO she would be starred in her next film. *Fanny Foley Herself* (1931) was lensed in not very successful Technicolor. Oliver played a $1,000-a-week vaudeville performer who does a low-comedy act to support two daughters in finishing school. Edna was far better than the material warranted. RKO gave her Mrs. Fiske's plum stage role of the woman arriving with her maid and chauffeur to serve on a jury in *Ladies of the Jury* (1932). As the fluttering, gaunt, dour-faced matron,* Mrs. Livingston Baldwin Crane, stubbornly holding out for an acquittal against all the other jurors, Edna was in good form. *Time* enthused, "Like Marie Dressler and Polly Moran, Edna May Oliver is an old-time actress who, with the disappearance of exterior attractions, has had ample time to perfect her comedy technique." Mordaunt Hall (*New York Times*) decided, "Miss Oliver is one of the most talented comediennes

on the screen, who makes the most of her lines and whose diction is excellent."

Again she was back with Wheeler and Woolsey playing Edgar Kennedy's sister in *Hold 'Em Jail* (1932). She contributed a broadly funny scene vocalizing at a piano in a manner defying any resemblance to her once fine mezzo voice. When she finished her chore in this film she received RKO's permission to return to New York for a revival of *Show Boat*, which boasted many members of the original cast. New additions included Dennis King as Gaylord Ravenal and the marvelous Paul Robeson as Joe. The successful revival opened on May 19, 1932, at the Casino Theatre and played through 180 performances. Edna discovered that she "liked the movies more than the stage. Perhaps it's just the California sunshine, but the working hours are easier than the night work in the theatre, in spite of the fact that I get up at five o'clock in the morning. I've grown entirely away from the East; I'm afraid for now I've become so attached to California, I should hate to live anywhere else. I have a home in Beverly Hills and a small group of friends I can play around with. Then, too, after you finish a picture you get two, and sometimes three or four, weeks' vacation. I take my car to Santa Barbara where I can lie on the beach all day between swims. I live by myself. I neither cook nor sew but I have an excellent housekeeper who does these things for me." On the set her cook prepared her food in bags. Edna May considered food contaminated if tossed into pans or even water.

When she returned to Hollywood, RKO assigned her the role of a middle-aged schoolteacher sleuth, Hildegard Withers. *The Penguin Pool Murder* (1932) was the first of three Stuart Palmer mysteries she would solve on camera. Teamed with explosive, and fine actor, James Gleason, who played Inspector Piper, Edna's Hildegard went on to unravel *Murder on the Blackboard* (1934) and *Murder on a Honeymoon* (1935).* In 1933 Edna gave a showy performance as fortune-teller Madame Talma in Richard Dix's *The Great Jasper.* (In a decade she had been in seven of Dix's pictures.)

Sinclair Lewis' turgid novel of a noble social worker, *Ann Vickers* (1933), was

---

* There was always an ambiguity within Edna about her looks. At one point in her career she said, "It was not until I was getting in my late twenties that my face and figure began to grow long and angular." On another occasion she allowed, "I never like to see myself on the screen. It hurts my vanity. So I stay away from my own pictures. If other people enjoy seeing me, that's all right and I'm glad, but I certainly don't enjoy seeing myself."

* Miss Hildegard was later played on the screen by Helen Broderick and ZaSu Pitts.

*With Hobart
Bosworth in* Fanny
Foley Herself *(1931).*

*With Sid Miller
(hidden), James
Donlan, and Edgar
Kennedy in* The
Penguin Pool Murder
(1932).

With Donald Cook and James Gleason in The Penguin Pool Murder.

brought to the screen as a starring vehicle for Irene Dunne. As her friend, Dr. Malvina Wormser, Edna summed up the whole picture, "Ann has a passion for helping. She's going to make the world over if it takes her all winter." RKO loaned Edna May to Fox for a nonsensical piece of fluff, *It's Great to Be Alive* (1933), and to Metro for completing a cast of inspired zanies (Frank Morgan, Alice Brady, Jimmy Durante, ZaSu Pitts, and Ted Healy with his Three Stooges) in *Meet the Baron* (1933).

George Cukor's excellent screen version of *Little Women* was enormously successful from its premiere at Radio City Music Hall on November 16, 1933. Edna May was happily cast as Aunt March. The *New York Times* exuded, "This crabbed old lady is cleverly acted by Edna May Oliver. Aunt March is an ogre who has a good-natured side." The type of role became one in which Miss Oliver excelled. She played Leona in Margaret Sullavan's *Only Yesterday* (1933) and was the wretched Red Queen for Paramount's all-star *Alice in Wonderland* (1933).

In 1934 the constantly busy Edna played in *The Poor Rich* with Edward Everett Horton. It was a very mild comedy. Over at United Artists she was aged George Arliss' daughter Augusta in *The Last Gentleman* (1934). She was back into broad comedy as a polo-playing grandmother, the family matriarch, in *We're Rich Again* (1934). In 1935 she left RKO and signed with the studio of stars, Metro-Goldwyn-Mayer, where she would create several memorable screen portrayals and be touted as the "second" Marie Dressler. It is not impossible to believe Edna might have inherited several plum roles at Metro that might have been played by Dressler. But the two actresses were not that similar in their interpretations. About Edna's portrayal of the memorable Aunt Betsy Trotwood in Metro's *David Copperfield* (1935), writer Jim Tully enthused, "It was long an axiom in Hollywood that only the great Charlie Chaplin himself could prevent W. C. Fields from 'stealing' a scene. Edna May Oliver held her own with the renowned juggler, and by so doing she moved with a magnificent gesture into the cinema Hall of Fame."

Edna was a masterful scene stealer, able to ferret away an entire picture. About MGM's *No More Ladies* (1935) its star Joan Crawford has written, "*No More Ladies* wasn't my pic-

With Frances Dee in
Little Women (1933).

With Donald Woods
and Elizabeth Allan in
A Tale of Two Cities
(1935).

502

*With Madge Evans
and Frank Lawton in
David Copperfield
(1935).*

ture. It went strictly to Edna May Oliver as a highball-drinking grandmother, a grande dame who wore trains and said, 'Scram!'" And that year Edna gave a glowing portrayal of Miss Pross in *A Tale of Two Cities.* She played her role without sniffs and in the course of the action killed French Revolution firebrand Madame DeFarge (Blanche Yurka) in an acrobatic, rough-and-tumble struggle for a gun.

Her only release in 1936 was *Romeo and Juliet,* in which she was superb as Juliet's nurse. Frank S. Nugent of the *New York Times* wrote, "And Edna May Oliver, the very nurse of the Bard's imagination; droll, wise, impish in her humor and such a practical romanticist at that. She is grand." Her playing of Shakespeare's nurse was followed by a dull role of the aunt in a picture Metro would like to have forgotten, *Parnell* (1937). The lanky character star, as Mrs. Atherton, provided the only source of vitality and amusement in *My Dear Miss Aldrich,* and was the queen (opposite Frank Morgan's king) in MGM's Cole Porter musical *Rosalie* (1937), starring Eleanor Powell and Nelson Eddy.

Edna played nosy Mrs. Kunkel in Metro's *Paradise for Three* (1938) which ended her MGM contract. (The studio was undergoing an "economy" wave and one of those chopped off the payroll was Edna.) She went to Twentieth Century-Fox for *Little Miss Broadway* (1938). In the latter film she was the wretched owner of a hotel for down-and-out vaudevillians, and the one who sends Shirley Temple back to the orphanage. She remained at Fox for a comedy relief role in Sonja Henie's *Second Fiddle* (1939). Then she went over to RKO sympathetically to play the Comtesse de Mavon in *Nurse Edith Cavell* (1939). For RKO's last Fred Astaire-Ginger Rogers musical, *The Story of Vernon and Irene Castle,* Edna gave an excellent performance as crusty, efficient Maggie Sutton, business manager and confidante of the dancing, romancing Castles.

After sixteen years in pictures Edna finally received an Academy Award nomination for her next role. As Mrs. Sarah McKlennar in John Ford's *Drums Along the Mohawk* (1939), she gave a lusty, gutsy portrayal of a self-sufficient pioneer woman. Her characterization (which allowed her a touching death scene) was one of the color film's best performances. It overshadowed the playing of stars Claudette Colbert and Henry Fonda. But 1939 was the year of *Gone with the Wind* and the Oscar for Best Supporting Actress went, justifiably, to Hattie McDaniel for her devoted Mammy.

In 1940 Edna went back to Metro-Goldwyn-Mayer to play Lady Catherine De-Bourgh in Jane Austen's *Pride and Prejudice.* (RKO had planned to make the project with its 1933 *Little Women* cast after the enormous success of that picture.) In a perfectly cast film, Edna's characterization was handsomely executed. She returned, pictorially, to her native Boston in 1941, playing Merle Oberon's perky grandmother, a widow of a Back Bay sea captain, in *Lydia.* On September 22, 1941, Edna May repeated her Granny role for "Lux Radio Theatre" with Miss Oberon and Alan Marshal. It proved to be her

last professional chore. She attended concerts and the theatre in the Los Angeles area, often accompanied by comedian Franklin Pangborn. But in August 1942 she began an illness that became terminal. She had been suffering from severe arthritis for some time, and had no idea that the cause of her latest infirmity was an advanced case of intestinal infection.

Actress Virginia Hammond, her close friend, was with Edna when she died on her 59th birthday, Tuesday, November 9, 1942, at the Cedars of Lebanon Hospital in Los Angeles. It was Edna May's wish to be cremated (with the ashes shipped to Massachusetts). Private funeral services were held on November 12 at Forest Lawn Memorial Park where her friend, playwright Lynn Starling, read from Kahlil Gibran's *The Prophet,* "And let today embrace the past with remembrance and the future with longing."

With Greer Garson in
Pride and Prejudice
(1940).

FEATURE FILMS

Wife in Name Only (*Pyramid Pictures 1923*)

Three O'Clock in the Morning (*C. C. Burr 1923*)

Restless Wives (*C. C. Burr 1924*)

Icebound (*Paramount 1924*)

Manhattan (*Paramount 1924*)

Lucky Devil (*Paramount 1925*)

Lovers in Quarantine (*Paramount 1925*)

The American Venus (*Paramount 1926*)

Let's Get Married (*Paramount 1926*)

The Saturday Night Kid (*Paramount 1929*)

Half Shot at Sunrise (*RKO 1930*)

Cimarron (*RKO 1931*)

Cracked Nuts (*RKO 1931*)

Laugh and Get Rich (*RKO 1931*)

Newly Rich (*Paramount 1931*)

Fanny Foley Herself (*RKO 1931*)

Ladies of the Jury (*RKO 1932*)

Hold 'Em Jail (*RKO 1932*)

The Conquerors (*RKO 1932*)

The Penguin Pool Murder (*RKO 1932*)

Ann Vickers (*RKO 1933*)

Meet the Baron (*MGM 1933*)

The Great Jasper (*RKO 1933*)

It's Great to Be Alive (*Fox 1933*)

Only Yesterday (*Universal 1933*)

Little Women (*RKO 1933*)

Alice in Wonderland (*Paramount 1933*)

The Poor Rich (*Universal 1934*)

The Last Gentleman (*United Artists 1934*)

Murder on the Blackboard (*RKO 1934*)

We're Rich Again (*RKO 1934*)

David Copperfield (*MGM 1935*)

Murder on a Honeymoon (*RKO 1935*)

No More Ladies (*MGM 1935*)

A Tale of Two Cities (*MGM 1935*)

Romeo and Juliet (*MGM 1936*)

Parnell (*MGM 1937*)

My Dear Miss Aldrich (*MGM 1937*)

Rosalie (*MGM 1937*)

Paradise for Three (*MGM 1938*)

Little Miss Broadway (*20th Century-Fox 1938*)

Second Fiddle (*20th Century-Fox 1939*)

Nurse Edith Cavell (*RKO 1939*)

The Story of Vernon and Irene Castle (*RKO 1939*)

Drums Along the Mohawk (*20th Century-Fox 1939*)

Pride and Prejudice (*MGM 1940*)

Lydia (*United Artists 1941*)

With Lucien Littlefield in She Gets Her Man *(1935).*

ZaSu Pitts

For six decades the moviegoing public warmly smiled and guffawed at and embraced a deceptively frail, 5'6", thin woman. Her woebegone face with drooping mouth was accentuated with pensive, sad, blue eyes. There was always something about her screen characters that reflected a perpetual air of helplessness, bewilderment, and confusion. This image was further orchestrated by a whimpering Midwest drawl and enriched by the most expressive pair of hands in show business, which she used in a flux of fluttering.

Even her name evoked spontaneous chuckles: ZaSu Pitts.

She was born on Monday, January 3, 1898, in Parsons, Kansas. Her mother, Nellie Shay Pitts, reluctant to offend her two sisters, Eliza and Susan, lopped off the last two letters of Eliza and added the first two letters of Susan, christening her daughter ZaSu. When she was still a youngster, the Pittses relocated to Santa Cruz, California.

At 19, fired with the conviction that she could succeed in motion pictures, young ZaSu left Santa Cruz for Los Angeles. A constant round of casting offices won her extra work in one-reel comedies and stunt work for producer Al Christie. After a successful test at Universal, she earned featured parts in a series of one-reel comedies with William Franey and Bobbie Mack, four of which were: *He Had 'Em Buffaloed, The Battlin' Bell Boy, O' My the Tent Mover,* and *Uneasy Money.* At Mack Sennett's studio she was told she did not have a chance in the world to succeed on the screen, but ZaSu was persistent. She won small bits in Douglas Fairbanks' *A Modern Musketeer* (1917) and Mary Pickford's *Rebecca of Sunnybrook Farm* (1917).

ZaSu's first opportunity for screen recognition in a major production occurred when *Rebecca*'s director, Marshall Neilan, cast her as the slavey Becky (doing a comedy routine as a grand lady) in Paramount's *The Little Princess* (1917). D. W. Griffith rehearsed ZaSu for his *The Greatest Thing in Life,* but decided she too closely resembled his star, Lillian Gish. "Of course," said ZaSu, "I felt terribly flattered but I was out of a job again." Prior to the Griffith experiment she had played the lovesick sweetheart in Mary Pickford's *How Could You, Jean?* (1918). She had also languished for six months—unnoticed and never filming a scene—in the employ of Charles Chaplin, to whom she had been recommended by Neilan.

Universal's *A Society Sensation* (1918) featured alluring Carmel Myers and young Rudolph Valentino—and the comic relief of ZaSu Pitts. Supporting roles in Edith Storey's *As the Sun Went Down* (1918) and Constance Talmadge's *A Lady's Name* (1919) led to a series of domestic comedy-dramas directed by King Vidor. She was impressive in the lead in Vidor's *Better Times* (1919) and was effective in support of his wife, Florence, in *The Other Half* (1919) and *Poor Relations* (1919). For Brentwood Pictures and Robertson-Cole release, ZaSu made a series of small-town comedy-dramas: *Seeing It Through* (1920), *Bright Skies* (1920), and *The Heart of Twenty* (1920). In the two last features her leading man was a personable, handsome actor, Tom Gallery. ZaSu became Mrs. Thomas S. Gallery on July 23, 1920, when they wed in Santa Ana, California.

The newlyweds appeared in a quickie called *Patsy* (1921) and ZaSu cleverly portrayed murderess Jennie Dunn in Paramount's *For the Defense* (1922). In *A Daughter of Luxury* (1922), Pitts was an heiress, while Tom Gallery was the romantic lead of star Agnes Ayres. *Poor Men's Wives* (1923) found her cast with her dear friend, Barbara LaMarr, the almost "too beautiful" actress. In 1923 Miss LaMarr adopted a baby boy about the same time ZaSu was giving birth to her daughter Ann Gallery. When Barbara became ill late in 1925, ZaSu cared for her son "Sonny." Following Miss LaMarr's tragic death on January 30, 1926, ZaSu and Tom Gallery adopted the boy, who legally became Donald Michael Gallery.

In the Twenties ZaSu was in constant demand by the studios and her popularity increased with such films as *The Girl Who Came Back* (1923), *Three Wise Fools* (1923), and *Tea—With a Kick* (1923). In *Souls for Sale* (1923) she shot a scene for Metro-Goldwyn's *Greed* which would not be released until the following year. When Gallery's film activities diminished, he accepted in 1925 the position of manager of the American Legion Stadium in Hollywood, promot-

ing boxing bouts until they became a weekly social event in the film colony.

Through 1924 and 1925 ZaSu's screen portrayals ranged from the lead of movie-struck Mary Brown in the dramatic *The Legend of Hollywood*, to a supporting role in Metro's *Wine of Youth*, to playing a streetwalker in *The Fast Set*, to her bravura performance as Trina in *Greed* (1924).

Basically, all her career ZaSu had been (and would be) a comedienne. It was Erich von Stroheim, confirming his belief that comedians were better trained for the demands of acting than straight actors, who recognized ZaSu's dramatic potential. He cast her in his masterpiece *Greed*, the misguided dramatic epic which shot for nine months and then went through the chaos of editing for a year. According to reports, the extravagantly meticulous von Stroheim filmed at a cost of $470,000 some 200,000 feet of scenes, which footage was reduced to 24,000 by him. It was further chopped by studio demands to 10,067 feet, ruining, according to the genius filmmaker, his great photoplay of Frank Norris' novel.

In the course of the oversized drama, ZaSu is the thrifty San Francisco woman who has won a $5,000 lottery prize. She later weds dentist McTeague (Gibson Gowland) and continues through the years to hoard her money, despite her husband's need for help. Eventually he kills her and escapes to Death Valley, where he is followed by Trina's frustrated suitor (Jean Hersholt). Both men die in the desert.

When the film opened at the Cosmopolitan Theatre in New York City on December 4, 1924, the *New York Times* reported that the picture was greeted with mixed audience reaction. But, stated the journal, "The three principals . . . deliver splendid performances. . . . ZaSu Pitts portrays the role of Trina, into which she throws herself with vehemence. She is natural as the woman counting her golden hoard, and makes the character live when she robs her husband of trifling amounts."

Miss Pitts would remain the filmmaker's favorite actress. Von Stroheim later said, "It is difficult to explain why I consider ZaSu Pitts a great emotional actress. There is an elusive something that is the secret of her personality and therein lies her greatness.

Mystery—she breathes it. A woman of sweet, gentle moods, capable of tenderness. A woman of fire, capable of conflicting emotions smoldering within her. One looks at ZaSu Pitts and sees pathos, even tragedy, and a wistfulness that craves for something she has never had or hopes to have. Yet she is one of the happiest and most contented women I have ever known."

Later appraisals of ZaSu's performance in *Greed* reinforce von Stroheim's belief that she was "the greatest tragedienne of the screen." Herman G. Weinberg in his *The Complete Greed* (1972) offered a final word on her performance as Trina: she gave "the greatest performance with the widest range any actress ever was called on to give on the screen. There is only one to match it, and that came four years later, in 1928, Falconetti's in the title role of Carl Dreyer's *The Passion of Joan of Arc*. But Stroheim did it first, as he did so many things first."

Metro cast ZaSu in the leading role of the Follies star-comedienne in *Pretty Ladies* (1925) and she gave an impressive performance that ranged from comedy to drama. She was a suicidal miss in Fox's *Lazybones* (1925) and struck out for women's rights with screen sister Jacqueline Logan in *Wages for Wives* (1925). In *Mannequin* (1926) she was a dull-witted nursemaid who raises a child (Dolores Costello) she kidnaps and later performs an impressive death scene.

On November 24, 1926, ZaSu separated from Tom Gallery charging the philandering sports promoter, sometime actor, with desertion. In 1927 she was seen as the sweetheart of the mighty Casey (Wallace Beery) in *Casey at the Bat* (1927). She was back with Beery again in *Wife Savers* (1928), Paramount's screen version of Leon Errol's Broadway musical, *Louie the 14th*. She played the lead in a two-reel drama, *Sunlight*, and was Eddie Gribbon's substitute bride in *Buck Privates* (1928). After an intelligent character study in *Thirteen Washington Square* (1928), ZaSu was excellent as the sickly, overworked, loyal, and deceived wife of Emil Jannings in *Sins of the Fathers* (1928).

In the meantime, she had been working again for von Stroheim. His *The Wedding March* began shooting in June 1926 and the final scenes were filmed in February 1927. ZaSu was the pathetic magnate's daughter caught in a loveless marriage with the arrogant, amoral Prince "Nicki" (forcefully played by von Stroheim) in 1914 Vienna. The first part of von Stroheim's massive sexual adventure, *The Wedding March*, had its world premiere on Broadway at the Rivoli Theatre on October 12, 1928. The aborted second part of the project, *The Honeymoon*, was released in Europe as *Mariage de Prince*. Even with the typical problems on this von Stroheim production, it was not the final time ZaSu would work with the maestro.

Despite ZaSu's forays into heavy drama—where she proved her mettle—audiences associated her with comedy. This led her more and more into typecasting. After her talkie debut in Paramount's *The Dummy* (1929) she was acceptable on the screen only as a celebrated funster. She generated laughter as the waitress pursued by James Gleason in *Oh, Yeah!* (1930) and as the overworked, irritated maid in Warner Bros.' first Technicolor screening of the musical *No, No, Nanette* (1930),* and she brightened *Honey* (1930).

Universal's still-brilliant *All Quiet on the Western Front* (1930) was previewed following a showing of *Honey*. When ZaSu, as Lew Ayres' sick German mother, appeared on the screen, the audience roared at what was a touching, homecoming scene. The studio panicked, withdrew Remarque's World War I epic, and reshot the scenes with mother-figure Beryl Mercer in ZaSu's original role. *All Quiet* would win Academy Awards for Best Picture of the Year and for its director, Lewis Milestone. ZaSu's contributions to the project remained on the cutting-room floor in the sound version (although her scenes as the dying Mrs. Baumer were retained in the silent edition).

Alfred E. Green, a noted Hollywood director, would later observe, "ZaSu Pitts' face has been on more cutting-room floors than any other actress.** Every director is carried away with her responsiveness and invariably gives her more space than her role demands and she steals the scene. The result

* She repeated the same role for RKO's 1940 *No, No, Nanette*.

** After rigorously learning to ice skate for a minor role as Greta Garbo's skating partner in Metro's *Love* (1927), a version of *Anna Karenina*, ZaSu's efforts were deleted from the release print.

"Five more minutes and I would have been married." 1264-8

With Jeanette MacDonald in Monte Carlo (1930).

is that the part is cut and trimmed until she no longer overshadows the star—that is, in footage!" ZaSu could still take heart in von Stroheim's continual praise for her work. "The average person thinks she is funny looking. I think she is beautiful, more beautiful than the famous beauties of the screen, for I have seen in her eyes all the vital forces of the universe and I have seen in her sensitive mouth all of the suppressions of human-kind. I've seen her lifted to the heights of great acting. Art must weep when ZaSu Pitts plays a comedy role."

ZaSu continued enacting the comedienne on camera. Her supporting roles included playing Nurse Monica, who offers marriage to a surprised, unmarried father (Douglas Fairbanks Jr.), in The Little Accident (1930); a Norwegian cafe owner in Jeanette MacDonald's The Lottery Bride (1930); and another nurse in MGM's War Nurse (1930). Teamed with Leon Errol, ZaSu, as Hattie Haddock, struggled for recognition in Finn and Hattie (1931), in which Mitzi Green, as their brattish daughter, romped off with the picture. In Alfred Lunt and Lynn Fontanne's sole talkie, The Guards-

man (1931), ZaSu was their maladroit maid. The film did not lure audiences into theatres.

Despite poor appraisal of several of the features in which she played minor, but showy parts (stagecoach passenger in Tom Mix's Destry Rides Again, 1932), critics agreed that "ZaSu Pitts gets a laugh whenever she talks or moves those long, expressive hands."

In 1932 Universal teamed her with long, lanky, dour-faced comedian Slim Summerville in Unexpected Father. A more unlikely "love team" would be difficult to arrange but their co-starring comedies delighted audiences. They were not as well made and popular as Paramount's domestic comedy series with Mary Boland and Charlie Ruggles, or as the late Forties Ma and Pa Kettle series with Marjorie Main and Percy Kilbride, but they made money. The Pitts-Summerville entries included: They Just Had to Get Married (1933), Out All Night (1933), Her First Mate (1933), Love, Honor and Oh, Baby! (1933), and Love Birds (1934). In 1934 RKO would borrow them for a misadventure called Their Big Moment and in 1941 United

Artists would pair them in *Niagara Falls* and *Miss Polly.*

On January 14, 1932, ZaSu finally filed for divorce from Tom Gallery. On April 26, 1932, she received her final decree and custody of her nine-year-old children, Ann and Mike. On screen she was the incredibly stupid movie studio receptionist Miss Leighton in *Once in a Lifetime. Time* said that she "utters genteel moans so sad that they are almost yodels."

Between enlivening features with her comic vignettes, ZaSu was teamed with the beauteous (and clever comedienne) Thelma Todd in a series of two-reel comedies for Hal Roach. The Pitts-Todd combination made for a good comedy team, even if they fell short of Roach's premise that they were the distaff Laurel and Hardy. From *Let's Do Things* (1931) through 1933's *One Track Minds,* the girls romped through 17 shorts, often radiating weak and improbable scripts through the force and enthusiasm of their performing. When ZaSu left Roach to further (she hoped)

her career in features, Patsy Kelly was teamed with Thelma Todd.

The last von Stroheim–Pitts venture was in 1932, when he was asked to direct Fox's *Walking Down Broadway.* It would be the director's first handling of a sound feature and the last he would direct in Hollywood. He collaborated with writer Leonard Spigelgass, but the script emerged with recognizable von Stroheim overtones of subtle depravity and psychological sadism mingled with a latent theme of lesbianism. For the role of the excessively jealous, suicidal lead, von Stroheim cast ZaSu. He described her part as "a very complicated and interesting character, in love with love, an introvert, an accident chaser—who goes to funeral parlors on Saturday afternoons to have a good cry at some stranger's last rites. In short, a psychopathic case." Fox officials thought the "in short" amply described von Stroheim and fired him before the picture was completed.

Sol Wurtzel, a producer of cheap, commercially profitable films, ordered much of von

With Lucien Littlefield and Barbara Stanwyck in Shopworn *(1932).*

With Carole Lombard in The Gay Bride *(1934).*

Stroheim's footage (done in conjunction with uncredited Raoul Walsh) scrapped and new scenes filmed by journeyman directors Alfred Werker and Edwin Burke. The end result was a calamity, which was finally released in May 1933 as *Hello, Sister.* Thereafter ZaSu returned to comedy.

ZaSu quietly married tennis pro John E. Woodall at Minden, Nevada, on October 8, 1933, but the marriage was not revealed until February 12, 1934, when the Woodalls entrained for a New York City honeymoon. On the screen ZaSu was Will Rogers' wife in *Mr. Skitch* (1933). In *Mrs. Wiggs of the Cabbage Patch* (1934) Pauline Lord was busily seeking a husband for ZaSu (as Miss Hazy) in the unlikely person of W. C. Fields. The *New York Times* noted, "The patient and doleful Miss Hazy has become the fluttering ZaSu Pitts and, for no more pious reason than to make you roar, she has been provided with a suitor in the outlandishly funny person of W. C. Fields."

Ruggles of Red Gap (1935) was distinguished by Charles Laughton's superb performing. Keeping apace of the English actor,

ZaSu was the Widow Judson, the butler's romantic interest in the crude, old West. (They would repeat their performances on "Lux Radio Theatre" in 1939.) Stuart Palmer's spinster sleuth, Hildegarde Withers was originated on the screen by Edna May Oliver, who was succeeded by Helen Broderick. For RKO's 1936 snooping schoolmarm adventure, *The Plot Thickens,* ZaSu was teamed with the series' scatterbrained detective, James Gleason. In 1937 Pitts made her English-film debut in a tale of mistaken identity, *Wanted. Nurse Edith Cavell* (1939) proved that ZaSu had lost none of her talent for playing a straight, dramatic role. In this World War I account of espionage and bravery, she is the canal-boat drudge who helps Allied soldiers escape.

In the summer of 1938 ZaSu was dazzled by live audiences that encouraged her during a vaudeville tour. Her act included her impression of an impersonator doing a devastating impersonation of ZaSu Pitts with flailing, fluttering hands, and a wrenching moan of "Oh, Myyyyy." In the early Forties she ventured onto the legitimate stage with a brief appearance for the British War Relief in Noël Coward's *Tonight at 8:30*. In late autumn of 1942 she made a midwestern tour of the farce *Her First Murder*. It opened in Chicago in January 1943 and mercifully disappeared thereafter, although that summer she would tour in it on the strawhat circuit. She opened on Broadway on January 5, 1944, in George Batson's *Ramshackle Inn*, a melodramatic farce that pleased not the critics. But the show lasted for 216 performances, then moved on to Chicago for 11 more weeks and onward to the West Coast. Batson would write another comedy for ZaSu. But *Cordelia*, a tale of an early 1900s New England fishing village spinster raising two children, died on the road in the summer-autumn of 1946.

Compared with the previous decade, ZaSu's screen activities were slight in the Forties. She played Irene Dunne's Cousin Cora in *Life with Father* (1947). Then she returned to the theatre, which offered her far more challenges. In the summer of 1947 she starred as Abby in *The Late Christopher Bean*. When the revival reached Chicago in October, noted critic Ashton Stevens pre-

ferred ZaSu's performance to the original portrayal by Pauline Lord. He proclaimed Miss Pitts "The American Duse" and wrote, "I think Miss Pitts' evocation of the unsung guide, philosopher and lover and her kitch-ened youth marks the best felt and the best projected characterization of her too limited stage career. The sum of my story is that I still love ZaSu Pitts as an actress as well as a woman." ZaSu played Abby again on a sum-mer theatre tour in 1949 and returned to Hollywood to lend support to Donald O'Con-nor's film *Francis*, a role she reprised in Universal's *Francis Joins the Wacs* (1954).

During the summer of 1950 ZaSu played in *Post Road*, a part which Lucile Watson did first on Broadway and then was reworked for the inestimable talents of Charlotte Green-wood in her huge success, *Leaning on Letty*. For the strawhat season of 1952 ZaSu was playing the East Coast summer stages in *Ramshackle Inn*.

Mary Roberts Rinehart and Avery Hop-wood's creaky mystery play *The Bat* had weathered many revivals and several screen treatments. In January 1953 a new stage

With Charles Laughton, Charlie Ruggles, and Maude Eburne in Ruggles of Red Gap *(1935).*

With Raymond Walburn, Billie Burke, Tom Breneman, Beulah Bondi, Bonita Granville, and Edward Ryan in a publicity pose for Breakfast in Hollywood *(1945).*

production was mounted with ZaSu (as the terrified maid) co-starred with grand, aging Lucile Watson. *The Bat* opened at Broadway's National Theatre on January 20, 1953. But unlike the original production that had scored 867 performances, it closed after 23. Six years later ZaSu again played Lizzie in *The Bat*, but on the summer circuit.*

Television, among other factors, reduced the demand for players and decreased production in Hollywood. In 1954 ZaSu joined the new medium on "G. E. Theatre" in its telecast of *Pardon My Aunt*. In August 1954 she was seen in *The Happy Touch* episode of "Kraft Theatre" and that October was prissy Nurse Preen on a TV version of *The Man Who Came to Dinner*. ZaSu was teamed in September 1956 with Gale Storm in a successful TV series, "Oh, Susanna." For the next two years she played Gale's chum, Nugey, the addled beautician aboard the S.S.

* ZaSu had originally played Lizzie in *The Bat* in the spring of 1943, with Jane Darwell, for a brief midwestern tour.

Ocean Queen. From June to September 12, 1958, the cheerfully mated Pitts-Storm team filmed 15 half-hour segments of what was then called "The Gale Storm Show." The soundstages of the Hal Roach studios were used to depict the setting aboard the Pacific liner S.S. *President Wilson.*

Infrequent, and dismally minor, bits marked ZaSu's last screen efforts. Hers was a bottom-of-the-cast listing as Mrs. MacGruder in MGM's *The Gazebo* (1959), for which Erich von Stroheim Jr. worked as an assistant director. ZaSu had a thankless task in Doris Day's *The Thrill of It All* (1963). Her final picture justifiably united her with most of Hollywood and television's top comics. In Stanley Kramer's *It's a Mad, Mad, Mad, Mad World* (1963) she played a harassed telephone switchboard operator. She was still waving her wonderfully expressive hands, clutching misdirected telephone cords, and, as ever, plunging audiences into gales of laughter. Her last television exposure was on the series

"Burke's Law," in the segment *Who Killed Holly Howard?* (September 20, 1963). Both the film and the telecast would be shown after her death.

On the morning of June 7, 1963, ZaSu Pitts died of cancer at Hollywood's Good Samaritan Hospital. She had suffered from the disease for a long time and entered the hospital the day prior to her death. She had been living at her home in Pasadena with her husband of 30 years, John Woodall, then a real-estate broker.

As one of Hollywood's foremost female funsters, ZaSu probably established a record for screen appearances during her long, active, and pleasurable 46-year career. As she once told a reporter, "I was what they called a feature player, never a star. They say I was in 500 films, everything but the newsreels."

But her film credits are impressive. She was distressed that producers and the public never accepted her as a serious dramatic actress and she yearned to do a musical comedy on Broadway. And in 1938 she was disappointed, if undismayed, by her failure to land the role of the amateurish would-be ballet dancer in the film *You Can't Take It with You.* "It was a perfect part for me," ZaSu later recalled, "except that I had never danced ballet. So I went to a ballet professor and said that I wanted to be able to whirl on my toes in a week. So we started to work and at the end of the week my screen test for the role was arranged. I could get up on my toes all right, but the only way I could get off them was to fall flat on my face and, oh, dear, I usually did. So they gave the role to Ann Miller, that Texas girl who is such a good dancer, and has glamour too."

With Donald O'Connor and Olan Soule in Francis Joins the Wacs *(1954).*

FEATURE FILMS

A Modern Musketeer (*Paramount 1917*)
The Little Princess (*Paramount 1917*)
Rebecca of Sunnybrook Farm (*Paramount 1917*)
How Could You, Jean? (*Paramount 1918*)
A Society Sensation (*Universal 1918*)
As the Sun Went Down (*Metro 1918*)
A Lady's Name (*Select 1919*)
Better Times (*Brentwood-Mutual 1919*)
Men, Women and Money (*Paramount 1919*)
The Other Half (*Robertson-Cole 1919*)
Poor Relations (*Robertson-Cole 1919*)
Seeing It Through (*Robertson-Cole 1920*)
Bright Skies (*Robertson-Cole 1920*)
The Heart of Twenty (*Robertson-Cole 1920*)
Patsy (*Truart 1921*)
Is Matrimony a Failure? (*Paramount 1922*)
For the Defense (*Paramount 1922*)
Youth to Youth (*Metro 1922*)
A Daughter of Luxury (*Paramount 1922*)
Poor Men's Wives (*Preferred 1923*)
Mary of the Movies (*FBO 1923*)
Souls for Sale (*Goldwyn 1923*)
The Girl Who Came Back (*Goldwyn 1923*)
Three Wise Fools (*Goldwyn 1923*)
Tea—With a Kick (*Associated Exhibitors 1923*)
Hollywood (*Paramount 1923*)
West of the Water Tower (*Paramount 1924*)
Triumph (*Paramount 1924*)
Daughters of Today (*Selznick 1924*)
The Goldfish (*Associated First National 1924*)
The Legend of Hollywood (*Producers Distributing Corporation 1924*)
Changing Husbands (*Paramount 1924*)
Wine of Youth (*Metro-Goldwyn 1924*)
The Fast Set (*Paramount 1924*)
Greed (*Metro-Goldwyn 1924*)
Secrets of the Night (*Universal 1925*)
The Great Divide (*Metro-Goldwyn 1925*)
Old Shoes (*Hollywood Pictures 1925*)
The Re-Creation of Brian Kent (*Principal 1925*)
Thunder Mountain (*Fox 1925*)
A Woman's Faith (*Universal 1925*)
The Business of Love (*Astor 1925*)
Pretty Ladies (*Metro-Goldwyn 1925*)
Lazybones (*Fox 1925*)

Wages for Wives (*Fox 1925*)
The Great Love (*MGM 1925*)
Mannequin (*Paramount 1926*)
What Happened to Jones (*Universal 1926*)
Monte Carlo (*MGM 1926*)
Early to Wed (*Fox 1926*)
Her Big Night (*Universal 1926*)
Sunny Side Up (*Producers Distributing Corporation 1926*)
Risky Business (*Producers Distributing Corporation 1926*)
Casey at the Bat (*Paramount 1927*)
Wife Savers (*Paramount 1928*)
Buck Privates (*Universal 1928*)
Thirteen Washington Square (*Universal 1928*)
Sins of the Fathers (*Paramount 1928*)
The Wedding March (*Paramount 1928*)
The Dummy (*Paramount 1929*)
The Squall (*Warner Bros. 1929*)
Twin Beds (*Warner Bros. 1929*)
The Argyle Case (*Warner Bros. 1929*)
This Thing Called Love (*Pathé 1929*)
Her Private Life (*Warner Bros. 1929*)
Paris (*Warner Bros. 1929*)
The Locked Door (*United Artists 1929*)
Oh, Yeah! (*RKO 1930*)
No, No, Nanette (*Warner Bros. 1930*)
Honey (*Paramount 1930*)
The Devil's Holiday (*Paramount 1930*)
Monte Carlo (*Paramount 1930*)
All Quiet on the Western Front (*Universal 1930*) [deleted from revised, sound version]
The Little Accident (*Universal 1930*)
The Lottery Bride (*United Artists 1930*)
The Squealer (*Columbia 1930*)
Passion Flower (*MGM 1930*)
War Nurse (*MGM 1930*)
Free Love (*Universal 1930*)
Sin Takes a Holiday (*RKO 1930*)
Finn and Hattie (*Paramount 1931*)
Bad Sister (*Universal 1931*)
River's End (*Warner Bros. 1931*)
Beyond Victory (*RKO 1931*)
Seed (*Universal 1931*)
A Woman of Experience (*RKO 1931*)
The Guardsman (*MGM 1931*)
Their Mad Moment (*Fox 1931*)

Big Gamble (*Pathé 1931*)
Penrod and Sam (*Warner Bros. 1931*)
Secret Witness (*Columbia 1931*)
The Man I Killed [Broken Lullaby] (*Paramount 1932*)
Destry Rides Again (*Universal 1932*)
Unexpected Father (*Universal 1932*)
Steady Company (*Universal 1932*)
Shopworn (*Columbia 1932*)
The Trial of Vivienne Ware (*Fox 1932*)
Strangers of the Evening (*Tiffany 1932*)
Westward Passage (*RKO 1932*)
Is My Face Red? (*RKO 1932*)
Blondie of the Follies (*MGM 1932*)
Roar of the Dragon (*RKO 1932*)
Make Me a Star (*Paramount 1932*)
Vanishing Frontier (*Paramount 1932*)
The Crooked Circle (*Sono Art–World Wide 1932*)
Madison Square Garden (*Paramount 1932*)
Once in a Lifetime (*Universal 1932*)
Back Street (*Universal 1932*)
They Just Had to Get Married (*Universal 1933*)
Out All Night (*Universal 1933*)
Hello, Sister (*Fox 1933*) [revised version of Walking Down Broadway]
Professional Sweetheart (*RKO 1933*)
Her First Mate (*Universal 1933*)
Aggie Appleby, Maker of Men (*RKO 1933*)
Meet the Baron (*MGM 1933*)
Love, Honor and Oh, Baby! (*Universal 1933*)
Mr. Skitch (*Fox 1933*)
The Meanest Gal in Town (*RKO 1934*)
Sing and Like It (*RKO 1934*)
Two Alone (*RKO 1934*)
Love Birds (*Universal 1934*)
Three on a Honeymoon (*Fox 1934*)
Private Scandal (*Paramount 1934*)
Mrs. Wiggs of the Cabbage Patch (*Paramount 1934*)
The Gay Bride (*MGM 1934*)
Their Big Moment (*RKO 1934*)
Dames (*Warner Bros. 1934*)
Ruggles of Red Gap (*Paramount 1935*)

Going Highbrow (*Warner Bros. 1935*)
Hot Tip (*RKO 1935*)
She Gets Her Man (*Universal 1935*)
The Affairs of Susan (*Universal 1935*)
Spring Tonic (*Fox 1935*)
13 Hours by Air (*Paramount 1936*)
Mad Holiday (*MGM 1936*)
The Plot Thickens (*RKO 1936*)
Sing Me a Love Song (*Warner Bros. 1936*)
Forty Naughty Girls (*RKO 1937*)
52nd Street (*United Artists 1937*)
Wanted (*British 1937*)
Merry Comes to Town (*British 1937*)
The Lady's from Kentucky (*Paramount 1939*)
Mickey the Kid (*Republic 1939*)
Naughty but Nice (*Warner Bros. 1939*)
Nurse Edith Cavell (*RKO 1939*)
Eternally Yours (*United Artists 1939*)
It All Came True (*Warner Bros. 1940*)
No, No, Nanette (*RKO 1940*)
Broadway Limited (*United Artists 1941*)
Mexican Spitfire's Baby (*RKO 1941*)
Niagara Falls (*United Artists 1941*)
Weekend for Three (*RKO 1941*)
Miss Polly (*United Artists 1941*)
Mexican Spitfire at Sea (*RKO 1942*)
The Bashful Bachelor (*RKO 1942*)
Tish (*MGM 1942*)
Meet the Mob (*Monogram 1942*)
So's Your Aunt Emma (*Monogram 1942*)
Let's Face It (*Paramount 1943*)
Breakfast in Hollywood (*United Artists 1946*)
The Perfect Marriage (*Paramount 1946*)
Life with Father (*Warner Bros. 1947*)
Francis (*Universal 1949*)
The Denver and Rio Grande (*Paramount 1952*)
Francis Joins the WACs (*Universal 1954*)
This Could Be the Night (*MGM 1957*)
The Gazebo (*MGM 1959*)
Teen-Age Millionaire (*United Artists 1961*)
The Thrill of It All (*Universal 1963*)
It's a Mad, Mad, Mad, Mad World (*United Artists 1963*)

With Ben Blue in The Big Broadcast of 1938 *(1937).*

Martha Raye

Perhaps the least flamboyant adjective to describe freewheeling Martha Raye is bombastic. Possessor, reputedly, of the biggest mouth and best legs in Hollywood, Olympian tonsils, an enviable bust (at least a "38"), and a six-time marital record, Martha has practiced her oversized clowning in motion pictures, several Broadway plays and nightclubs, and on radio, television, and recordings.

Usually Martha has had opportunity to do little more than be a shallow, but highly diverting, whirlwind in light cinema escapism. However, a few performances, especially her portrayal of Annabella Bonheur in Charles Chaplin's *Monsieur Verdoux* (1947), have revealed an actress who has the ability and potential—if not the show business breaks and discipline—to become a brilliant comedienne. But earthy, fun-loving Martha has never had pretensions. Like confrere Red Skelton she describes herself simply as "a clown."

She was born Margaret Theresa Yvonne Reed in Butte, Montana, on Sunday, August 27, 1916, to Irish-born parents: singer Pete Reed and singer Peggy Hooper. Her parents were performing in a remote vaudeville theatre at the time, and the birth took place backstage. When she was old enough to walk, "Maggie" was shoved into the spotlight by her parents. She did not need much prompting and was soon belting out "I Wish That I Could Shimmy Like My Sister Kate" with obvious glee. In 1975 she told Doug McClelland in an *After Dark* magazine interview, "As a child, there was no city, no town, no house I could ever call home. My mother taught me how to read and write, and after that, whatever education I picked up I just got on the fly. I learned a lot about life in the backstage of theaters, and I can tell you that's not the easiest or most dignified way of getting an education. Maybe if I'd gone to school with other children I would have become more perceptive about judging people or human relationships."

After touring as a twosome with her brother Bud,* Martha aimed for Broadway.

* Bud was born in 1918; sister Melodye in 1920.

She allegedly plucked the name Martha Raye out of a telephone book, and soon after appeared in the revue *Calling All Stars* (Hollywood Theatre: December 13, 1934, 36 performances), singing "So This Is Hollywood"—as a drunk. Earlier in 1934 Martha had made her attempt at crashing Hollywood, but only managed to earn a singer's spot in a musical short subject, *A Night in a Nightclub.*

When her initial flings with Hollywood and Broadway did not lead to bigger professional jobs, Martha attacked the nightclub circuit, displaying a belting style made so popular by Ethel Merman. The trek led her back to Hollywood and an engagement at the popular boiterie, the Trocadero. Director Norman Taurog saw her perform and brought her to Paramount to play Emma Mazda, the garish aficionado of Lucille Gleason's dude ranch, in the Bing Crosby vehicle, *Rhythm on the Range* (1936). In the course of the 87 minutes, Martha on screen got drunk, performed double takes and face falls, and sang

a Sam Coslow specialty number that would become her trademark—"Mr. Paganini." The *New York Times* was enthusiastic: "Martha Raye is a stridently funny comedienne with a mammoth cave, or early Joe E. Brown mouth, a dental supply vaguely reminiscent of those frightening uppers and lowers they used to hang over the portals of painless extraction emporiums, and a chest which, in moments of burlesque aggressiveness, appears to expand fully 10 inches. . . . Hollywood has found a truly remarkable pantomimist and actress who can glare in several languages, become lovelorn in Esperanto and register beatific delight in facial pothooks and flourishes. She sings too, swing music in a voice with saxophone overtones and an occasional trace of pure foghorn."

Martha soon discovered that she had won fame. Paramount, which maintained an impressive roster of comic performers (ranging from Burns and Allen to W. C. Fields, Charles Ruggles, Mary Boland, Bob Burns, and the satiric Mae West), signed her to a seven-year

With Bob Burns in Rhythm on the Range *(1936).*

520

contract. Al Jolson, a regular host of the CBS network "Shell Chateau" radio show, contracted Martha to support his stardom over the Tuesday night airwaves.

Paramount never really packaged Martha to fully effective advantage. (Forgetting her trademark wide-mouth image, Martha is actually a very attractive woman and her singing voice could always be pure joy.) She bounced and yodeled through a dozen features, sharing billing with such personalities as Crosby, Jack Benny, and Bob Hope. In *The Big Broadcast of 1937* (1936) she was Benny's trouble-prone secretary; in *College Holiday* (1936), a boy-mad coed; *Hideaway Girl* (1937) cast her as a socialite crooner; *Waikiki Wedding* (1937) saw her explode in a hula shirt as another "different" secretary in another frothy Crosby vehicle; *Mountain Music* (1937) teamed her with raucously rustic Bob Burns; in *Double or Nothing* (1937), Martha had trouble refraining from stripping whenever she heard "It's Off, It's On." In Jack Benny's *Artists and Models* (1937) she performed a specialty number ("Public Melody No. 1") in dark face with Louis Armstrong. She was W. C. Fields' tomboyish daughter in *The Big Broadcast of 1938* (which was the feature film debut of Bob Hope), and in *College Swing* (1938) she was "Professor of Applied Romance" on Paramount's collegiate lot. Obviously, all these tasks were designed by the studio to showcase Martha as a loud, garish, and irresistible specialty player. Her enthusiastic film appearances caused the *New York Post* to dub her "the hot-lipped, jazz-swinging Raye of Hollywood sunshine" and "the 1937 Polly Moran—only younger and possessed of a weird and wicked coon-shouting voice." Audiences, especially the younger set, adored the slapstick-bent prankster.

Despite Martha's popularity in this mold, Paramount, studying her quite incredible figure and potential attactiveness,* decided to revamp her celluloid image and switch her brand from klutz to glamour girl. The tran-

sitional vehicle was *Give Me a Sailor* (1938), in which as "Legs Larkin" she defeated no less than Betty Grable (herself then a Paramount contractee) in a beautiful legs contest. She sang "Little Kiss at Twilight," and after some typical Rayesian shenanigans (for old times' sake) won leading man Bob Hope. But the metamorphosis was a professional mistake. Audiences and critics did not care for the new packaging. Paramount failed to comprehend this fact and offered a subdued Martha as a too conventional screen heroine in *Tropic Holiday* (1939), *Never Say Die* (1939), *$1,000 a Touchdown* (1939—teamed with equally floundering Joe E. Brown), and *The Farmer's Daughter* (1940). Despite the presence of increasingly popular Bob Hope in some of these pictures, Martha's screen status was fast declining. "Overexposure" was the verdict of some Hollywood observers.

On the last day of shooting of the low-budget *The Farmer's Daughter*, Paramount fired her. Martha has been quoted as saying, "They did it this morning with a yellow slip. They stuck it under my dressing room door. I picked it up and read that I was fired. There were no goodbyes and not one little bitty thank you. I packed my things and left."

After her traumatic rejection by Paramount, Martha accepted an offer from Universal, a studio which had picked up the screen services of such ex-Paramount stars as Marlene Dietrich, W. C. Fields, and Mae West. Raye was cast as the servant girl Luce in the screen version of Rodgers and Hart's musical *The Boys from Syracuse* (1940). To secure the role, she had to agree to a salary cut. Then former radio mentor Al Jolson received an offer to return to the Broadway stage and took Martha with him. The play was *Hold on to Your Hats* (Shubert Theatre: September 11, 1940). Martha dueted with Jolson "Would You Be So Kindly," performed the specialty number "She Came, She Saw, She Can-Canned," and won top approval from the critics and audiences. Only Jolson's illness caused the play to expire after 158 performances.

Hollywood again called and Martha returned.* She played in Warner Bros.' *Navy*

---

* Willy DeMond, who has made hosiery for Hollywood stars for 40 years, recently attested, "The best set of legs in Hollywood belong to Martha Raye! I'll bet I've measured the legs of 5,000 of the world's most beautiful women. And Martha Raye's are the best I've ever seen—and they're as beautiful today as they ever were." DeMond's runner-ups to Martha were: Marlene Dietrich, Raquel Welch, Mitzi Gaynor, and Ann-Margret.

* Martha and Milton Berle were the original choices to star in Cole Porter's musical *Let's Face it* (1941), but it was Danny Kaye and Eve Arden who starred in the hit Broadway show.

With Richard Denning in The Farmer's Daughter *(1940).*

Blues (1941), stealing the lackluster film from stars Ann Sheridan and Jack Oakie. "At least she's quit the glamour girl gig and gone back to her clowning," approved one critic of Martha's performance. Universal's Abbott and Costello box-office bonanza *Keep 'Em Flying* (1941) allowed Raye to cavort as the marvelous twin sisters, Barbara and Gloria Phelps. She remained at the studio to help another contract screen comedy team, Olsen and Johnson, romp through their nonsensical *Hellzapoppin* (1941) based on their Broadway hit. Martha was a man-hungry dame in pursuit of difficult Count Mischa Auer.

During World War II, Martha joined Kay Francis, Mitzi Mayfair, and Carole Landis on a North African USO tour, and stayed on to entertain the soldiers long after her three cohorts returned to Hollywood. Her efforts resulted in a serious bout with yellow fever. With the Misses Francis, Mayfair, and Landis, Martha appeared in *Four Jills in a Jeep* (1944), Twentieth Century–Fox's glamorized version of the book Carole Landis "prepared" on the North African sojourn. Raye's material was perfect for her. In one scene she asks where she is to dine:

SOLDIER: You mess with the men.
RAYE: I know, but where do we eat?

The *New York Post* saluted, saying that Martha's comedy "has never been more raucous, rough, and pleasing."

After a supporting role in Fox's *Pin-up Girl* (1944), in which Betty Grable was the star and Joe E. Brown was also a subordinate player, Martha was off screen for two years. But her return was auspicious. She recalls, "Charles Chaplin called me when I was playing the Latin Quarter in Chicago and asked me to do *Monsieur Verdoux*. I thought somebody was kidding and hung up on him. It turned out it was on the level. The story is about a Bluebeard, and I played the part of the ex-tart wife he couldn't kill. I was extremely honored to work with him; I learned a great deal. I was a little nervous when I started, but he was marvelous. He told me he had written it for me, and said I should just relax until we had time to rehearse. Then I felt comfortable. On the set I had called him Chuck, and people around were aghast because everyone calls him Charles or Mr. Chaplin. When he was in

Hollywood recently, Walter Matthau gave a party for him, and I said, 'Hello, Charles.' His reply was, 'What's the matter with Chuck?'"

Released in 1947 *Monsieur Verdoux* was a critical triumph for Martha although the public and some censorial groups were astounded by Chaplin's black comedy. The *New York Herald-Tribune* evaluated Martha, "In her rough-and-tumble scenes with the star something of the gaiety of the early Chaplin masterpieces is recaptured." Had *Monsieur Verdoux* been a box-office success, Martha might have gone on to become one of the major Hollywood stars of the post–World War II era. There was talk of David O. Selznick producing *The Mabel Normand Story* with Martha starring, but nothing developed. As it was, *Monsieur Verdoux* was Raye's last film for 15 years.

In that gap between film roles, Martha never lacked for work. She played London's Palladium (in 1948), headlined in nightclubs, did plenty of television (including her own NBC network series, "The Martha Raye Show," from 1953 to 1956), and toured in stock productions of such Broadway shows as *The Solid Gold Cadillac, Wildcat,* and *Calamity Jane.* An NBC-TV pilot of "Baby Snooks" (the old Fanny Brice property) made in 1957 never sold.

If Martha remained familiar in the show-business media, she also maintained a top status in the headlines for her (mis)adventures in matrimony. There have been six official mates. The first was Paramount makeup artist Buddy Westmore, whom she wed in 1937; they divorced in 1938. That year she wed David Rose, the musician who then was her music director at Paramount and on radio. The extremely romantic Martha later called him "the first great love I had," but she later discovered him at a Hollywood party romancing Judy Garland. She and Rose divorced in 1941. Husband number three was Neal Lang, hotel executive, and that union lasted only a few months in 1941. A happier memory came in the form of talented dancer Nick Condos (of the Condos Brothers), whom Martha married in 1942. He fathered her daughter Melodye Athenia (born February

With Frank Penny, Princess Luana, and Lou Costello in Keep 'Em Flying *(1941).*

In Hellzapoppin *(1941).*

22, 1943) and today is still Martha's manager, although they divorced in 1953. Martha reviews Condos (who was also in the film *Pinup Girl* with her) as "the best for *me*" of her husbands. In 1954 she married dancer Edward Begley; they divorced in 1956, the year Martha made headlines for taking a very nearly fatal overdose of sleeping pills. Her last spouse, to date, was Robert O'Shea, a patrolman who was bodyguard to Martha following crank threats in the mid-Fifties. When they fell in love, Martha received "the worst publicity of my career." Mrs. O'Shea sued Martha for $50,000 worth of alienated affections. Martha settled out of court for $20,000, wedding O'Shea in 1958 and divorcing him in 1962. Martha laughs that "when we were divorced, several of my husbands collected small fortunes" (only Lang and Condos did not). She insists, "I don't think I could ever become marriage shy. Only cowards give up the search for happiness because they're afraid of getting hurt."

In the year of her last divorce, 1962, Martha returned to feature films in MGM's plush

Billy Rose's Jumbo, filling out a star quadrangle sporting Doris Day, Stephen Boyd, and Jimmy Durante. As Lulu, Durante's fiancée of 14 years, Martha dueted with Day "Why Can't I?" and joined her three co-stars in the number "Sawdust, Spangles, and Dreams." With Busby Berkeley directing the opulent circus sequences, *Time* called *Jumbo* "a great big blubbery amiable polkadotted elephant of a show," and rated Martha "hilarious."

The comedienne enjoyed the comeback production and shortly after *Jumbo's* release told columnist Louella Parsons, "No more nightclubs for me. I'm definitely through competing with noisy drunks and the clatter of crockery. I've bought a home in Bel Air and I'm here to stay—I hope, I hope." Indeed, in 1963 Martha played on such television shows as "Dr. Kildare" and "The Red Skelton Show." But when the Vietnam conflict worsened, Martha left her cozy Bel Air habitat for exhaustive USO tours of Southeast Asia, where she was wounded twice ("Once in the foot, once in the ribs. I've had worse hangovers"). The delighted troops nicknamed her "Boondock Maggie." She won many honorary citations, including one as an honorary marine colonel (July 18, 1969). President Lyndon Johnson designated the actress "the only person outside the elite corps [Green Berets] to wear their proud symbol."

From February 27, 1967, to June 10, 1967, Martha played the celebrated title role of *Hello, Dolly!* at Broadway's St. James Theatre, following Carol Channing and Ginger Rogers and preceding Betty Grable, Phyllis Diller, Pearl Bailey, and Ethel Merman. The *New York Times* reviewed Martha's stage return affectionately but stated, "Martha belongs on Broadway, but in a different kind of show than *Hello, Dolly!*" Still, Martha proved to be a big drawing attraction for the musical, clowning with the audience after the curtain calls. She would headline an abridged version of the show in Vietnam following her Broadway stint. At the 41st Annual Academy Awards in April 1969, Martha was awarded the Jean Hersholt Humanitarian Award for "her devoted and often-dangerous work in entertaining troops in combat areas almost constantly since World War II." The crowd approved the honor with a standing ovation, and Martha tearfully accepted with the vow to devote her remaining years "to deserving this."

After receiving the Hersholt Award, Martha tried to step up her Hollywood activity. But she found that her involvement with the Vietnam situation had been professionally costly. "It was hard to get guest shots or do any TV shows. People would say, 'Oh, she's a warmonger.' Which is ridiculous, but some narrow-minded people thought that way. That hurt. I was just helping the men who were there. They didn't want a war any more than anyone else in the world. Yes, it hurt."

Raye resorted to some slim pickings to keep busy. She appeared as a regular on the NBC-TV children's show "The Bugaloos" as witch Benita Bizarre, and in two quickly dismissed features: *The Phynx* (1970), which was stocked with old-timers Butterfly McQueen, Cass Daley, Patsy Kelly, Edgar Bergen, et al.; and *Pufnstuff* (1970), in which Martha was "Boss Witch."

In 1971 Martha returned to Broadway, replacing Patsy Kelly in *No, No, Nanette.* Martha commented, "I think it was silly of Patsy Kelly to leave *No, No, Nanette* for *Irene.* Of course, it's a good break for me—I'm glad to get her part, but I still think Patsy should have stayed in. You don't back away from a winner." Ruby Keeler was also leaving *Nanette* after 751 performances. Therefore, in addition to succeeding Miss Kelly in her maid's role (and equipped with a new song, "Don't Turn Your Back on a Bluebird"), Martha performed the famous tap-dancing number that had been Keeler's specialty spot in the musical.

A follow-up pre-Broadway tour of *Hello Sucker,* based on the life of stage, club, and film personality Texas Guinan, and with Martha in the stellar spot, never made it into New York. But Martha found popularity on the dinner theatre circuit in the comedy *Everybody Loves Opal.* Martha recalls of this stint, "There's a part in it for a cat and in every town we went to I insisted they get a cat from the animal shelter, one that was due to be put to sleep. It was in my contract. After the show closed, the cat would be up for adoption. Everybody wanted a famous cat. Somewhere there are more than 200 cats that have happy homes because of *Opal.*"

When work in the mid-Seventies became scarce for Martha, an old friend came to her rescue. Leonard Stern, the one-time head writer of the "Steve Allen Show" and the creator of many of Martha's best TV skits, had become the executive producer of the Rock Hudson teleseries, "McMillan and Wife." She implored him, "Can't you use me? I'm available." Stern and producer Jon Epstein created the character of Nancy Walker's rambunctious sister. It was suggested that if everything worked out, Martha would replace Walker (who was getting her own TV series) as Hudson's new housekeeper.

Producer Epstein recollects of that February 15, 1976, episode *(Greed),* "Everybody had a lot of doubts. Martha hadn't worked in Hollywood for years. People wondered whether she could remember her lines, whether she was physically up to it. And let's face it, some thought she was a political nut. . . . It was a tremendously taxing part. She had to spend most of one day on the ocean and she can't swim. It turned out she had the energy of a 25-year-old. Never muffed a line or missed a cue. She and Rock and Nancy hit it off from the start."

*With Mike Kellin in
The Phynx (1970).*

Although Martha proved a delight in the entry (and was Emmy-nominated for her performance), she almost did not get signed to the series. According to Epstein, "There were people, top people, who didn't want her. Everything in Hollywood is run by committee. A big part of this committee said no to Martha Raye." However, Hudson, who had cast approval for his detective show, insisted on Martha and she was finally hired. After that, Raye received first-class treatment. She was given a three-room dressing suite on the lot and a limousine. "They asked what kind of decor I wanted. I thought they were kidding. I said if there's a door that closes and a nail to hang my clothes on, that'll be great decor. They kept asking. I said Early American because it was all I could think of. I came in the next day and, by God, the place is Early American." Of her role, Martha described, "She is a warmhearted busybody who means well but is a little dingy. In other words, I'm playing my normal self." The sixth season of "McMillan" (the title shortened after Susan St. James left the series) began on December 5, 1976, with the episode *All Bets Off.* Martha was in fine form as the doting new house-

keeper, a part she played to the hilt in subsequent episodes throughout the season. The series, however, was cancelled in the spring of 1977. She then returned to touring in her favorite stage show, *Everybody Loves Opal*; projected plans to star on Broadway in a musical based on the life of Marie Dressler; and joined Alain Delon, Robert Wagner, George Kennedy, and Eddie Albert in *Airport '79 Concorde* (1979), the fourth entry in *that* airborne series.

Despite her pace (she also guest-stars on assorted TV variety shows),* Martha does manage to relax, mainly by "getting drunk with my friends." She sums up her lifestyle. "I get away at home in Bel Air, California, where I live in a converted carriage house decorated in early-American style. I cook

---

* On December 7, 1977, she joined with Paul Lynde, Alice Ghostley, and George Gobel in the TV special *'Twas the Night Before Christmas*, an ABC-TV lark based on Clement Moore's Christmas verse. On *Just for Laughs* (NBC-TV, February 7, 1978), she joined with Milton Berle, Red Buttons, and Rose Marie for a series of sketches. Martha's recordings, especially her LP albums "Together Again for the First Time" (with Carol Burnett) and "Here's Martha Raye," remain collectors' items. This suggests that TV producers should utilize the funster's capacity for vocalizing more frequently.

every day—Mulligan stew is one of my favorites." She shares her home with secretary-companion, Ann Boddington, and five small dogs. Socially, she still sees a good deal of her manager-ex-husband, but rarely encounters her daughter Melodye (who became the mother of Nick in 1967, and who maintains an off-again-on-again singing career). A recent *TV Guide* interview described the situation between mother and daughter: "[Melodye] and Martha have long found they get along best when they see each other least."

Martha obviously thrives on performing ("I'll retire when I'm dead") but recently reflected, "If I hadn't become an entertainer, I would like to have been a doctor or a nurse. I feel that the American nurse has never been sufficiently honored or even acknowledged for her services overseas. And I've known too many who lost limbs or were killed. I'll be happy when I see a ticker-tape parade honoring the American nurses. Even the military brass and government have never given these women the recognition they deserve." (Martha herself is an accredited nurse.)

Martha is realistic about her career and her life. Of her cinema excursions she admits, "I think I was *used*...except for *Rhythm on the Range* and *Monsieur Verdoux*....But in those days actors didn't fight the system—then we thought we were lucky to be under contract." Of her very publicized romances and sleeping-pill episodes Martha shrugs, "That happened a long time ago. That was rather infantile on my part. I'm very content with my life. I'm very happy." Whenever asked if she really minds the jokes about the size of her famous mouth, Raye replies sincerely, "No...I'm a clown. Clowns are singular. To be a clown is a gift. There are no schools for clowns. Take Chaplin, Keaton, W. C. Fields. Do you think any of them minded making fun of himself?"

Why does Martha continue working? "My husbands cost me a fortune, and I'm not getting residuals from my old movies, but that's not why I'm working. I'm working because I'd die if I didn't. You know, in this business, you have to keep on your toes. There's always someone to replace you, someone better or someone just as good.... I'm just lucky that nostalgia is in. I intend to stay on the boards as long as I can. I'm staying because I love it." On another occasion she added, "I want security. I want money. I want my own TV series—and I'm going to do everything I can to get it." In short, "Martha the mouth" intends to remain a focal part of the show-business scene.

FEATURE FILMS

Rhythm on the Range (*Paramount 1936*)
The Big Broadcast of 1937 (*Paramount 1936*)
College Holiday (*Paramount 1936*)
Hideaway Girl (*Paramount 1937*)
Waikiki Wedding (*Paramount 1937*)
Mountain Music (*Paramount 1937*)
Double or Nothing (*Paramount 1937*)
Artists and Models (*Paramount 1937*)
The Big Broadcast of 1938 (Paramount 1938)
College Swing (*Paramount 1938*)
Give Me a Sailor (*Paramount 1938*)
Tropic Holiday (*Paramount 1938*)
Never Say Die (*Paramount 1939*)

$1,000 a Touchdown (*Paramount 1939*)
The Farmer's Daughter (*Paramount 1940*)
The Boys from Syracuse (*Universal 1940*)
Navy Blues (*Warner Bros. 1941*)
Keep 'Em Flying (*Universal 1941*)
Hellzapoppin (*Universal 1941*)
Four Jills in a Jeep (*20th Century-Fox 1944*)
Pin-Up Girl (*20th Century-Fox 1944*)
Monsieur Verdoux (*United Artists 1947*)
Billy Rose's Jumbo (*MGM 1962*)
The Phynx (*Warner Bros. 1970*)
Pufnstuf (*Universal 1970*)
Airport '79 Concorde (*Universal 1979*)

Nat Pendleton, Harry Ritz, Jimmy Ritz, and Al Ritz in *Life Begins in College* (1937).

The Ritz Brothers

Some years ago I attended an evening of mime by Marcel Marceau, an elaborate exercise in aesthetic purification during which the audience kept applauding its own appreciation of culture and beauty.... Afterward, when friends were acclaiming Marceau's artistry, it just wouldn't do to say something like "I prefer the Ritz Brothers" though I do, I passionately do). They would think I was being deliberately lowbrow, and if I tried to talk in terms of Marceau's artistry versus Harry Ritz's artistry, it would be "stupid," because "artist" is already too pretentious a term for Harry Ritz, and so I would be falsifying what I love him for.

—Pauline Kael

A review of Michelangelo Antonioni's *Blow-Up* (1966) is one heck of a place to find a tribute to the Ritz Brothers, but the great charm of Ritzian comedy is that it has been turning up in the most unlikely places for nearly 50 years now: be it in an adaptation of Dumas' *The Three Musketeers* (1939), or in the cleaning women in the lethargic *Won Ton Ton, the Dog Who Saved Hollywood* (1976), at a point in the film when it desperately needed some good knockabout humor.

The very point of Ritz Brothers comedy is that it has no logical point, that it defies plot, consistency, or motive. This is perhaps why most of their film material has rarely been revived. When the brother trio went to Universal Studios in 1940 to make four films, it might have seemed the ideal place for them. After all, coherence and motive never intruded on the W. C. Fields films then being made there. But oddly enought, the Ritzes—for all the ego indicated in their sundry negotiations with Darryl F. Zanuck at Twentieth Century-Fox—never took the time or energy to steal away the Universal limelight from the insipid romantic leads in their films there.

With one or two exceptions, the movies never quite knew what to do with the Ritz Brothers and in return the freres never quite knew what to do with the movies.

All three were born in Newark, New Jersey: Al Joachim on Thursday, August 27, 1903; Jimmy Joachim on Thursday, October 5, 1905; and Harry Joachim on Friday, May 22, 1908. Their father, Max Joachim, was a good-humored Austrian Jewish immigrant who after failing at various trades (including a brewery) became a success as a haberdasher. He moved the family business to Brooklyn with a retail outlet shop on Broadway. Unlike many fathers of comics, he was very sympathetic to his sons' desire to enter show business, and much of their comedic point of view may have derived from him. He did, however, insist that all three complete their high school education.

Similar to so many New Yorkers growing up in the Teens and Twenties, the Ritz Brothers had a salty youth, taking more than full advantage of the sights and attractions of the urban center. It was Al who first entered show business. He had tried his luck in several dance contests with pal George Raft and later not only would perform professionally as a ballroom dancer (he would marry his partner Annette Nelson) but also would run a dance school. By the early Twenties, Al, Jimmy, and Harry were all involved in vaudeville.

However, it was the fourth brother, George—there was also a sister named Gertrude—who persuaded the boys to join together as a professional trio. George acted as their agent, and reportedly it was at his urging that the team changed their surname from Joachim to Ritz.* It is on record, though, that under the name "Ritz Brothers" they made their joint professional bows at Coney Island's College Inn in 1925, where on occasion Jimmy Durante was their pianist. This was followed by a stint at Fox's Folly Theatre in Brooklyn. The trio's lowbrow zaniness had an instant appeal, and they toured all the top vaudeville houses earning as much as $400 weekly, in a package called "South Sea Cruise."

In an act called "The Collegians," they cavorted in wild costumes a la the Marx Brothers' *Horse Feathers,* as a backup skit for

exotic dancer Gilda Gray, at New York's Palace Theatre in March 1929. The *New York Times* reported, "Then there were contributions by the Ritz Brothers, whose efforts to be collegiate indicate they look with marked disfavor upon higher education." Showman Earl Carroll witnessed their orchestrated mayhem and signed them for his 1932 *Vanities,* which played at the Broadway Theatre for 87 performances. (The trio had been in Carroll's 1925 book show, *The Florida Girl,* billed as Al Socrates, Jimmy Plato, and Harry Aristotle.) Along the way the Ritz Brothers appeared briefly in *Everybody's Welcome* (Shubert Theatre: October 13, 1931). During the out-of-town tryouts on that production, which starred Frances Williams and Oscar Shaw, there were problems between the brothers and the Shuberts. Before the Broadway opening, Harry's part was reassigned to Jack Sheehan, Al's to Cecil Lean, and Jimmy's part was dropped. The brothers were brought before Actors Equity Association and Equity insisted they remain with the show and do their speciality "Putting on the Ritz." They soon departed the musical.

It was in the *Continental Varieties* that the brothers' career took a turn for the better. The show opened at the Little Theatre on October 23, 1934, for a 78-performance run. In the audience one night was an agent from Educational Pictures, a small company that was attempting with modest success to revive the two-reel film comedy. The representative signed the Ritzes for *Hotel Anchovy* (1934), an 18-minute romp in which the boys starred as hotel employees who cause (predictable) mayhem. Even when viewed today (the short was part of the 1963 film anthology *Sound of Laughter*), the Ritzes prove very funny screen newcomers.

In turn *Hotel Anchovy* led to bigger and better career offers. After the Brothers had appeared out of town in Earl Carroll's *Sketch Book* (1935), they were fired by the producer and engaged in lengthy litigation. Later they emerged in Hollywood appearing at the Clover Club for a very successful four week engagement. It was at this point that director Sidney Lansfield at the newly formed Twentieth Century-Fox screened *Hotel Anchovy.* He was seeking a comedy backup for the company's new string of musicals. Studio head Darryl F. Zanuck shared Lansfield's enthu-

---

* Legend has it that the name "Ritz" was derived from a passing laundry truck, although as early as 1918, Al used the name "Ritz" for his extra work in the movie *The Avenging Trail,* a Harold Lockwood Western filmed on Long Island.

siasm for the trio, and they were signed for their first feature, *Sing, Baby, Sing* (1936). It was a spoof on the John Barrymore-Elaine Barrie romance and starred Alice Faye and Adolphe Menjou in thinly disguised characterizations. Like those of so many comics making their *feature*-film debuts in the Thirties (Laurel and Hardy, Wheeler and Woolsey), the Ritzes' contribution to the main plot was totally extraneous. As if to justify their obvious irrelevance, Zanuck devised a unique curtain-call epilogue in which the brothers were formally introduced to film audiences. In reviewing their feature bow, the *New York Times* reported, "They dash on and off the screen without any real justification, but excuse their presence so cheerfully that we rather welcomed their escapes from their keepers. Conspicuous in their repertoire this time is the Jekyll-Hyde-Frankenstein number and an acrobatic-operatic aria in the film's beginning."

Sing, Baby, Sing was greeted enthusiastically by the public and Fox signed the brothers to a long-term contract. The popularity of the movie (and the increased publicity on the team) did a good deal to raise their status on the vaudeville circuit. Prior to the film they were earning $2,250 weekly, but now they could (and did) command $5,500 per week.

Just as Fox was using (some insisted overexposing) Joan Davis for comedy relief in its array of features, so the Ritzes were tossed into a wild medley of studio products. Usually they were assigned to musical entertainments in which their inspired lunacy could be easily integrated into the plot (as "specialty" performers) without too much tampering with the scenario structure. In 1937 they ran amok through four Fox releases. In *One in a Million*, starring Scandinavian ice-skating beauty Sonja Henie, the boys took to skates and did impersonations of Peter Lorre, Boris Karloff, and Charles Laughton. *On the Avenue*, top-lining Dick Powell, Madeleine Carroll, and Alice Faye and boasting an Irving Berlin score, saw the Ritz Brothers performing "Slumming on Park Avenue," with Harry doing a drag act for his first time on screen.* *You Can't Have Everything* was

their third and final appearance with Miss Faye, and was set in a nightclub. It featured the brothers' rendition of "Long Underwear." For their final release of the year, the Ritzes were at last permitted to "carry" a film as the stars. But *Life Begins in College* was no gem. The team appeared as the proprietors of Kampas Klassy Klothes who attend Lombardy College and become intertwined in slapstick galore. It was just another of the seemingly endless variations on Fox's *Pigskin Parade* (1936) and was *not* a prestige vehicle by any means.

On loan-out to Samuel Goldwyn, the Ritz Brothers must have been greatly honored when they were invited to appear with Vera Zorina, Kenny Baker, Edgar Bergen & Charlie McCarthy, and Charles Kullman and Helen Jepson and the American Ballet of the Metropolitan Opera. But the 120-minute color *Goldwyn Follies* (1938) lived up to its title too literally. The Ritzes' big showcase number, "Serenade to a Fish," seemed to be the only honest bit of entertainment in the overblown opus.

Ironically, when *Goldwyn Follies* was released, and failed at the box office, it did a good deal of damage to the brothers' screen reputation. When they returned to Fox they were assigned to two grade B productions for 1938: *Kentucky Moonshine* (a hillbilly farce with Tony Martin) and *Straight, Place, and Show* (a Damon Runyon comedy in which their leading lady was Ethel Merman). The brothers, intensely loyal among themselves, vented their anger on the front office and demanded that the studio assign them projects of better quality. It was a "squeeze" play that caused raised eyebrows on the lot and across Hollywood. However, Zanuck, surprisingly, honored their demands. The result was a musical comedy version of *The Three Musketeers*, easily their best film.

Directed by veteran Allan Dwan* (who had helmed Douglas Fairbanks Sr.'s *The Iron*

---

* At one point, Zanuck wanted to use Jimmy Ritz—without his brothers—in *On the Avenue.* When the team, then appearing on stage in Boston, learned of this, they balked. The studio mogul had the part enlarged to accommodate all three brothers.

* Years later Dwan would recall, "Harry [Ritz] was a hard worker. I remember the other two wanted to get off early one day to go to the racetrack, and it was always hard to get them on, so finally I got impatient and said, 'Go ahead—go to the track—I'd rather work here alone with Harry. And by the way, you don't need to come back tomorrow either because this sequence I'm starting will run on. So take tomorrow off at the track too and let Harry do it alone—he can do a hundred percent better—you two fellows get in his way. Glad to have you go.' They didn't go to the track. That was the only way I could handle them."

With Gloria Stuart in a pose for Life Begins in College.

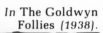

In The Goldwyn Follies *(1938).*

Jimmy Ritz, Al Ritz, and Harry Ritz with Vera Zorina in The Goldwyn Follies.

Mask, 1929) it was an A production in all aspects. There was a singing Don Ameche as D'Artagnan, such splendid villains as Lionel Atwill, John Carradine, Joseph Schildkraut, and Douglass Dumbrille, and the beauty of Gloria Stuart, Pauline Moore, and Binnie Barnes. The last, in the course of the picture, was turned upside down by the frantic Ritzes in order to dump some secret documents out of her bodice. Recalled Binnie in 1973, "They taught me a lot about comedy. I never took my eyes off those three all the time they were working; their timing was so perfect, and I wondered how they came to get a laugh where I couldn't. It was all timing, and I watched them a lot."

Surprisingly, the film is very reverent toward the Dumas novel. This literary re-spect does not prevent some pretty ghastly puns like "No noose is good noose" or, when Ameche introduces himself, "My name's D'Artagnan. What's yours?" and Harry retorts, "Scotch and water." The critics of the time, however, may have become a little bored by the frenetic brothers. The *New York Times,* not above a ghastly pun itself, opined, "The Three Musketeers is too Ritz a mixture for our taste."

The Gorilla (1939) was a chestnut that First National had previously filmed in silent and sound versions. Fox, deciding it had paid its debts to the brothers in *The Three Mus-keteers,* purchased the screen rights and revamped it for the brothers. But on the eve of production, the team staged a walkout. Zanuck angrily placed the team on suspen-

In The Three Musketeers
(1939).

sion on January 30, 1939, and filed suits against the performers in the amount of $150,000 for damages in delaying the picture's start. Within a matter of weeks, the trio was back on the lot ready to start production. Harry, the spokesman for the group, told reporters, "Want to tell you this is a great corporation we're working for. They're right and we're right. You know what I mean?" As it turned out, the brothers were more right about the property than their studio bosses. Despite a cast that included Anita Louise, Patsy Kelly, Lionel Atwill, Bela Lugosi, and Joseph Calleia, the 66-minute haunted-house comedy was no hit.

What proved to be their final contractual entry at Fox was *Pack Up Your Troubles* (1939), a minor entry starring fast-maturing Jane Withers. As the *New York Times* snidely remarked, the film "reminds us that Miss Withers is growing, even if the art of the Ritzes is not."

It is possible that had the team been more agreeable to appearing in programmers they might have continued on at Fox. But ever mindful of how much better the Marx Brothers were being treated at MGM, they left the lot. Part of the wrap-up of their contract was that Fox sometime in the future might produce a film called *Three Blind Dates* starring the trio (it never did) and that Republic Pictures, for a fee, had the rights to use the Ritz Brothers in one upcoming film. Republic planned to use the boys in *Hit Parade of 1940*, but that venture never came to pass in the proposed format that would have included them.

Meanwhile, while waiting for other film offers to materialize, the trio returned to the stage, appearing at the Paramount Theatre in Los Angeles in November 1939.

It proved to be Universal, the new home of so many cast-off onetime major stars (W. C. Fields, Mae West, Marlene Dietrich, Martha

534

Raye, Constance Bennett), that offered the Ritzes a one-film deal. It was mentioned that the recently acquired screen rights to the stage hit *The Boys from Syracuse* would be turned into a vehicle for the comedians. But when it was produced in 1940, the trio was not among the cast. Instead they appeared in *Argentine Nights* (1940), a hastily concocted musical potpourri. It retains a spot in cinema history as providing the motion picture debut of the Andrews Sisters, the latter having recently signed a Universal pact. The celluloid nonsense was not an apt testing ground for the veteran funsters. In the course of the proceedings, which seemed to reach desperately for any bits of levity, the boys walked off a bridge, did their giant sandwich-eating routine, performed a lockstep, and for their highlight scene did an imitation of the Andrews Sisters singing "Rhumboogie." As in the Alice Faye musicals at Fox, the Ritz Brothers were conveniently divorced from the main thrust of the "story line." Just how far and fast the team had fallen in public estimation was indicated by Leo Mishkin's review of this film for the *New York Morning Telegraph*, "Rolling their eyes, going into high jinks, and spreading good will far and wide, the Ritz Brothers—remember the Ritz Brothers?—are up to their old tricks again."

When the Ritzes realized that Universal was going to continue building up the team of Abbott and Costello at the boys' expense, they decided to forgo further films at the lot. They moved back East to accept stage and nightclub engagements. In 1941 they performed at Loew's State Theatre, their first time there in five years. Ruth Terry, "also" of the movies, was on the bill with them.

In 1942 Universal, wanting further to enhance its reputation as the comedy studio, lured the Ritz Brothers back with a three-picture package that provided them with some of the weakest material of their careers. The first, *Behind the Eight Ball,* was the best of the worst. Reported Don Miller in his book *B Movies* (1974), "*Behind the Eight Ball* (1942) has its moments, garnished by a whodunit plot for a change, and its 60 minutes provide enough room for the Ritz brand of clowning and some song numbers by Carol Bruce, Johnny Downs, and Grace McDonald,

With Patsy Kelly in
The Gorilla (1939).

535

Posing for Behind the Eight Ball *(1942).*

directed by Eddie Cline in lively style. A devilish impersonation of Ted Lewis by Harry Ritz got special attention in the film and served as a suspenseful conclusion in unmasking the mysterious murderer (mysterious to the cast, not the audience)."

One has only to *try* to sit through *Hi' Ya, Chum* (1943) with Jane Frazee and Robert Paige to know what tedium can be. Wanda Hale reported in her one and a half star *New York Daily News* review of the Ritzes, "Their lines and gags are as stale and dull as their brand of comedy is repetitious and boring." *Never a Dull Moment* (1943) with the Ritzes and Frances Langford was enough to convince even the eternally optimistic brothers that their Hollywood days were done. They did appear in *Screen Snapshots No. 5*, a short subject which surveyed their extensive USO activities during World War II, and the later all-star *Screen Snapshots No. 8*. But as feature film performers, the trio would never work again. They left Hollywood to honor club and stage appearances.

Unlike a good many other washed-up Hollywood name attractions, the Ritz Brothers continued to command solid sala-

ries in their stage outings.* The critics were continuing to find it hard to justify the team's endurance in public favor, but had to admit that the boys usually won audience enthusiasm. Analyzing their rapport with the paying public, Al Ritz would later say, "Nobody knows what the public expects of funnymen. But we're pretty close to the public in our nightclub appearances. We never listen to the experts, just the people who see us perform. . . . From their reaction we've learned that they like what we're doing—fresh ideas, but the same old Ritz Brothers."

Perhaps the most frequent question put to the trio was how and why they remained a professional team. "We're just like one person," Al explained, "one for all and three for one. We talk things out and don't keep business secrets from each other. Something bothers us and we get it out in the open. There's no going behind the other's back. No secrets." Al also reconfirmed, "We're all

* They received $7,500 weekly for appearing at the El Rancho club in Las Vegas, the only nightspot on the strip in those days. (In later years they would perform at the Flamingo and then at the Dunes and still later at the Sands in the gaming center.) In 1946, they earned $12,000 weekly for stage-vaudeville work.

hams, but Harry is the hammiest. That's why Jimmy and I put him in the center spot."

Despite their advancing age, the three performers remained very young at heart, and continued their athletic gymnastic slapstick skits. Then in May 1952 they tackled a new medium, television, appearing on NBC's "All-Star Revue." Jack Gould of the *New York Times* reviewed the important (to those with a memory) occasion: "In one of those minor ironies peculiar to show business, the three brothers no doubt will find themselves being compared by the TV generation to Dean Martin and Jerry Lewis, who were mere tots when the Ritz entourage was established on the two-a-day boards. . . . On the basis of their Saturday night showing, however, the Ritz Brothers need not fear the comparision because their bedlam has a style and subtlety quite its own and their first venture was one of the most smoothly produced programs of the year." But no regular TV employment was offered them, and they returned to the club circuit (New York, Miami Beach, and Las Vegas).

In 1958 they were guest performers on a Ginger Rogers TV special and this engendered renewed interest in the Ritz Brothers as video performers. The team formed a video company, hoping to produce a TV series. "Comedy is in pretty bad shape," Harry explained, "and TV could use a few laughs. We could use the dough, too. . . . It's going to be a series of fairy tales—like Shirley Temple does, only ours will be crazy. We're gonna do stuff like 'Hysterical History,' 'Hamlet and Eggs,' 'Sons of Dracula,' and like that." But nothing materialized from this proposed venture, largely because their all-out brand of humor would be difficult to sustain on a weekly basis. As one critic wrote of their nightclub act in 1961, "Subtle they're not. New they're not. But they're funny!"

On December 22, 1965, Al, the oldest of the trio, suffered a fatal heart attack and passed away at the Towns Infirmary while the brothers were fulfilling a Christmas engagement at the New Orleans Roosevelt Hotel. The funeral and burial were held in Los Angeles, where Al's widow Annette lived.*

* Al had wed dancing partner Annette Calmare Nelson in 1928. Jimmy married singer Ruth Hilliard at the Actor's Synagogue in New York on April 14, 1938. They were later divorced. Harry wed Charlotte Greenfield in 1936. Their son Phil, a bullfighter residing in Mexico City, has frequently mentioned plans to produce a motion picture based on the Ritz Brothers.

Jimmy Ritz, Harry Ritz, and Al Ritz in Hi' Ya Chum (1943).

Jimmy and Harry Ritz in Blazing Stewardesses *(1974).*

Harry and Jimmy, saddened by the tragedy, nevertheless restyled the act and in the late Sixties made a memorable comeback appearance on "The Joey Bishop Show," during which a spotlight replaced the missing Al during a dance routine. Harry and Jimmy also toured the nightclub circuit.

Curiously enough, the renaissance of their type of anything-goes humor in the current films of Woody Allen and Mel Brooks has even brought the two performing brothers back into the world of movies.* With veter-

ans Robert Livingston and Yvonne DeCarlo, they appeared in the "R"-rated *Blazing Stewardesses* (1975), performing some of their old routines. Harry has cameoed solo in Mel Brooks' *Silent Movie* (1976). After they had completed their 60-second turn in *Won Ton Ton* (which also featured in a separate segment their old Fox co-star Alice Faye), British director Michael Winner turned to the laughing, applauding cast and crew and beamed, "These chaps are quite good! Who are they?" In October 1977 Harry and Jimmy Ritz were guests on Dick Cavett's TV talk program reminiscing about their vaudeville days. It was a welcome sight for nostalgia-prone viewers.

* In *Silent Movie* Mel Brooks parodied two routines used by the Ritzes in *Never a Dull Moment*. One need only review the 1943 Ritz comedy to determine how Brooks formulated the toreador dance routine for himself, Dom DeLuise, and Marty Feldman.

FEATURE FILMS

With Al, Jimmy, and Harry Ritz:

Sing, Baby, Sing (*20th Century-Fox 1936*)

One in a Million (*20th Century-Fox 1937*)

On the Avenue (*20th Century-Fox 1937*)

You Can't Have Everything (*20th Century-Fox 1937*)

Life Begins in College (*20th Century-Fox 1937*)

Ali Baba Goes to Town (*20th Century-Fox 1937*)*

The Goldwyn Follies (*United Artists 1938*)

Kentucky Moonshine (*20th Century-Fox 1938*)

Straight, Place, and Show (*20th Century-Fox 1938*)

The Three Musketeers (*20th Century-Fox 1939*)

The Gorilla (*20th Century-Fox 1939*)

Pack Up Your Troubles (*20th Century-Fox 1939*)

Argentine Nights (*Universal 1940*)

Behind the Eight Ball (*Universal 1942*)

Hi' Ya, Chum (*Universal 1943*)

Never a Dull Moment (*Universal 1943*)

Harry and Jimmy Ritz alone:

Blazing Stewardesses (*Independent International 1975*)

Won Ton Ton, the Dog Who Saved Hollywood (*Paramount 1976*)

Harry Ritz alone:

Silent Movie (*20th Century-Fox 1976*)

* Guest appearance in footage of a movie premiere.

With Myrna Loy in A Connecticut Yankee (1931).

Will Rogers

Never before has there been, and very likely never will there be, a performer as beloved, respected, or singular as Will Rogers. His grassroots, homespun humor, philosophical quips, and witty commentary on the American scene persist today with much the same impact as when he delivered them. He was a joyous Mark Twain of the theatre; an ebullient American ambassador of goodwill to the world; a deceptively good actor; a sharp comedian; and, above all, an exemplary human being.

Seven children had been born to Clement Vann Rogers and his quarter-blood Cherokee Indian wife, Mary America Sehrimsher Rogers. Three children died in infancy. On Tuesday, November 4, 1879, Sallie, Maud, Mary, and Robert (he would die when two years old) were joined by an eighth and last child. The boy, christened William Penn Adair Rogers, was born on the Rogers' ranch between the Verdigris and Caney rivers in Indian Territory. (In 1907 the area would become the state of Oklahoma.) At the age of seven Will was registered on the Authenticated Rolls of the Cherokee Nation as No. 2340.

Young Will was sent to Drumgoole School and later to the Harrell International Institute. His mother died in May 1890 and after Mr. Rogers remarried the family resettled in the town of Claremore, some 12 miles north of the family ranch. The teenaged Will was entered at Halsell College and later was expelled from Scarritt Collegiate Institute. Clem then entered the young man in the Kemper Military School in Missouri. Later Will recalled, "I went to pretty nearly every school in the country for a little while, except West Point. I could have gone there, too, only I was too proud to talk to a congressman." Will's academic pursuits gave way to wanderlust. After a variety of jobs, he entered show business in the unlikely northern Natal province of Ladysmith in South Africa, joining Texas Jack's Wild West Circus as the Cherokee Kid, a "fancy lasso artist and Rough Rider."

Rogers made his New York City debut at Madison Square Garden on April 27, 1905. When he roped a crazed steer that was heading into the stands, he received a good deal of publicity which opened doors for him in vaudeville. His roping tricks and authentic cowboy aura made for instant success that was repeated in Berlin and London. He became a vaudeville headliner, billed as "The Oklahoma Cowboy, Will Rogers."

On November 25, 1908, Rogers married Betty Blake, with whom he had maintained a feverish correspondence since their meeting in 1899 in the Territory hamlet of Oologah. The marriage was one of show business' most laudable and Rogers stated, "The day I roped Betty, I did the star performance of my life." The year before Rogers had made his legitimate stage debut at Chicago's Auditorium in *The Girl Rangers,* a short-lived musical.

Will's headlining in vaudeville gleaned good critical notices. By the time his first son, William Vann (later known as Will Rogers Jr.), was born on October 20, 1911, he had added impromptu dialogue to his lariat twirling. Rogers made his legitimate Broadway stage debut on April 15, 1912, featured with Blanche Ring in a musical, *The Wall Street Girl.* On May 18, 1913, his daughter Mary Amelia was born and in the spring of 1914 he was featured on the London stage with Nora Bayes in *The Merry-Go-Round.* Three days after Will opened in a Shubert flop, *Hands Up,* his second son, James Blake, was born on July 25, 1915. By then the Rogers clan had settled down in a home at Amityville, Long Island, opposite their close friend, actor Fred Stone.

In the fall of 1915 Will had a brief run in a Broadway dud, *Town Topics,* played two weeks at vaudeville's Palace Theatre, and was signed for Ziegfeld's *Midnight Frolic.* It was Mrs. Rogers who suggested that Will's act could be revitalized by commenting on daily events and personalities publicized in the daily press. And as he spun his rope, he spun a lasting chronicle of commentary on America, the world, "sacred cows," and (but never with venom) the pretensions of bombastic bores and politicians. His statement that "all I know is what I read in the papers" withstood comment for years; and if he was in need of new jokes, he announced he would visit his joke factory—Congress. Other later comedians have taken up the Rogers format to some extent in zinging cracks at the government, as well as at fleeting political and show-business personalties. However, none has attained that brilliance of observation

Rogers reached. Bob Hope is expert at the Rogers-type commentary, but Will wrote his own copy, whereas Hope has had the advantage of a stable of gag writers.

From *Midnight Frolic* Will went into Ziegfeld's *The Follies* (of 1916). In the 1918 *Follies* Will continued his "Timely Topics" and appeared in an act two sketch, "The Lower Regions." He was Satan with W. C. Fields as a senator. During the summer of 1918 while appearing in the *Follies,* Will made his silent motion picture debut for Samuel Goldwyn in *Laughing Bill Hyde,* filmed at Fort Lee, New Jersey. The *New York Times* announced, "Those inclined to believe that all of the magnetic Rogers personality is in his conversation will realize their mistake if they see this picture. The real Will Rogers is on the reels. Whether Rogers can act or whether he can do anything before the camera except be himself is not the question." He did mold all of his screen characterizations to the Rogers personality, but virtually all of the great Hollywood stars used the same acting approach.

Mr. Goldwyn was delighted with Will's reception on film and signed him for a series of motion pictures to be made in Hollywood.

Will was a man of many media outlets. His first book was a compilation of many of his *Follies* routines. *The Cowboy Philosopher on the Peace Conference* was published in 1919 and in the same year Harper and Brothers released his second tome, *The Cowboy Philosopher on Prohibition.* Meanwhile, on the nation's screens he was appearing in his first California-made feature, *Almost a Husband* (1919), as a New England schoolteacher with Peggy Wood as his leading lady. Of the dozen pictures Will made for Samuel Goldwyn in the next two years he said, "When Goldwyn decided to make fewer and worse pictures, he sent for me." But the dozen films were most amusing and successful. Will's favorite of the Goldwyn comedies was Ben Ames William's story of a lovable tramp, *Jubilo* (1920),* shot scene for scene from the *Saturday Evening Post* story. When Goldwyn suggested changing the title of *Jubilo* Rogers wired Goldwyn nine silly alternate titles and asked, "What would you have called *The Birth of a Na-*

---

* In 1924 Rogers made a two-reel comedy, *Jubilo, Jr.,* with the Our Gang kids and in 1932 he remade the story for Fox as *Too Busy to Work,* an uninspired picture.

tion?" Later Will decided that if Hollywood filmed the Lord's Last Supper it would release it as *A Red Hot Meal* or *The Gastronomical Orgy.*

Water, Water Everywhere (1920) was made near the Mojave Desert and featured Will as the hero who turns Hell's Bells Saloon into a soda fountain and rescues heroine Irene Rich. The lovely Miss Rich was a close friend of the Rogers clan and was Will's vis-à-vis in *Jes' Call Me Jim* (1920), *The Strange Boarder* (1920—in which young Jimmy Rogers was featured), and *Boys Will Be Boys* (1921). Rogers' films for Goldwyn were all directed by Clarence Badger and one of the liveliest was *Doubling for Romeo* (1921). It was a satire on movies in which Will played a cowpoke involved in dream sequences as Shakespeare's Romeo.

After he played a professor of psychology in *A Poor Relation* (1921), his Goldwyn contract expired. The actor thereupon decided to write, direct, and produce a series of two-reel films for Pathé distribution. One of the group, *The Ropin' Fool* (1922),* is still an amusing film with Will's titles and admission that the 50 various rope tricks he performs could not be deemed art, but "there is 30 years of hard practice in it." *Fruits of Fate,* another of the shorts, received praise as being more genuine entertainment than many agonizing miles of many features. *One Day in 365* enlisted the camera services of the entire Rogers household. But, despite good critical reception, the short-subject series drove him to the brink of bankruptcy. He left his family in the Beverly Hills home "that jokes built" and returned to play three weeks at Broadway's Winter Garden Theatre.

In January 1922 he received top billing on the road in *Ziegfeld's Frolics.* On June 5, 1922, he opened in New York in the 1922 *Ziegfeld Follies.* He contributed the sketch "Disagreement Conference" co-written with Ralph Spence and featuring Gallagher and Shean, with Will as secretary of state. On the screen he was in James Cruze's Paramount release, *One Glorious Day* (1922), and then made a delightful Ichabod Crane in a version of *The Legend of Sleepy Hollow* retitled for the screen *The Headless Horseman* (1922).

At the end of 1922 Will became a newspaper writer as well. The first Rogers article was published in the entertainment section of the *New York Times* on December 24, 1922, and his freewheeling, philosophical rambling prose continued until his death. His column soon became nationally syndicated.

He also signed with Hal Roach at $3,000 weekly to make a series of two-reel comedies. Of the dozen Roach shorts, a movie satire, *Uncensored Movies* (in which he parodied frozen-faced Western star William S. Hart), and a satire on *The Covered Wagon,* called *Two Wagons—Both Covered,* were among the best.* Of the latter, the *New York Times* wrote, "It is as funny as anything we have ever seen on the films, especially when Will Rogers, made up as Ernest Torrence in *The Covered Wagon,* is introduced leaning forward on his horse. One of the best burlesques Mr. Rogers has made." Will played two parts in the two-reel comedy: Bill Bunion, a fancy-dressed cowboy modeled after J. Warren Kerrigan's hero, and Joe Jackson, the Torrence burlesque. Between the Roach shorts, Will was one of many stars in James Cruze's feature, *Hollywood* (1923).

In 1923 Will made a set of his monologues for Victor Records, including "A New Slant on War," "Timely Topics," and "Prohibition." He brightened the 1924 *Follies* and made his last appearance for Mr. Ziegfeld at the New Amsterdam Theatre on July 6, 1925, that carried over into a "fall edition." Over a 26-station hookup Will addressed the second annual Radio Industries Banquet. He discovered another outlet for his humor over the airwaves. By the end of 1925 he had made an 11-week tour of the lecture circuit, telling his audience in Boston, "Can you imagine me appearing at Symphony Hall in Boston? Me, with my repertoire of 150 words (most of them wrong) trying to enlighten the descendants of the Cod?"

Through 1926 he continued his lectures and writings, and then sailed for Europe to write for *The Saturday Evening Post* a series of articles called "Letters of a Self-Made Diplomat to His President." He met the heads of every government, parried conversation with royalty, playwrights, and the populace.

* The short subject was directed by Clarence Badger and featured Irene Rich and Will's good friend Guinn "Big Boy" Williams.

* In the compilation film *The Golden Age of Comedy* (1957) an excerpt was used from *Uncensored Movies* in which Will parodied Tom Mix and Douglas Fairbanks.

With Irene Rich in Jes'
Call Me Jim *(1920).*

and did a series of 12 two-reel travelogues for Pathé as "Our Unofficial Ambassador Abroad." From his Russian trip came a book, *There's Not a Bathing Suit in Russia.*

In London he did a brief stint in Charles Cochran's *Revue.* At the same time he worked at Paramount's British National studios in a screen version of the musical *Tip Toes* (1927), joined by Dorothy Gish and Nelson Keyes.

Upon returning to the States, he continued his lecture tour. When he arrived in California on December 21, 1926, he was greeted by two brass bands, town officials, the police corps, and members of the film colony, including Douglas Fairbanks and William S. Hart. Will had been proclaimed "The Hon. Will Rogers, Mayor of Beverly Hills." The honorary post was brief but Will acknowledged that he was not the first comedian mayor and stated, "I won't say I'll be exactly honest, but I'll agree to split 50-50 with you and give the town an even break." He had some reflections on the state of Hollywood, observing, "I'm sorry somebody referred to movies as an art. For since then everybody connected with them stopped doing something to make them better and they commenced getting worse."

In the summer of 1927 Will was hospitalized. Always one to turn a situation into a forum, he documented his surgery with such quips as, "I am in the California Hospital, where they are going to relieve me of surplus gall, much to the politicians' delight." He later published articles on his hospital safari in *The Saturday Evening Post* and compiled them in book form, *Ether and Me, or "Just Relax."*

In the fall of 1927 Will checked into First National studios to play the role of Maverick Brander in his last silent picture, *A Texas Steer* (1927), for which he wrote the screen titles. (The vehicle had been derived from an 1894 Charles Hoyt play.) Location filming in Washington, D.C., highlighted the amusing film, which the studio advertised with, "Will Rogers goes to Congress! Don't forget he's read by millions and heard by millions—and there are hundreds of millions who are dying for a chance to see him."

Robert E. Sherwood, then editor of *Life* magazine, was aware that politicians were a vital source of American humor. He was appalled at the usual deplorable selection of leadership in both parties and used *Life* to establish "The Anti-Bunk Party." He nominated Will Rogers for President, the first intentionally funny candidate and authentic American. (Will always said, "My ancestors didn't come on the *Mayflower,* but they met the boat.") Sherwood's editorial gag was reinforced with campaign buttons with Will's picture and a slogan "He chews to run." (Will was an inveterate gum chewer.) Eddie Cantor, Leon Errol, Robert Benchley, and aviatrix Amelia Earhart were heard on radio to promote Sherwood's presidential gag. Rogers, occupied with his career, kept a low profile.

Will's last Broadway appearance was in the musical *Three Cheers* (October 15, 1928). He was a last-minute replacement for Fred Stone, who had broken both ankles in a plane accident (both Stone and Rogers were early aviation-pioneering enthusiasts). Rogers rushed to New York to play King Pompanola of Itza opposite Fred's daughter, Dorothy. He declined billing but finally relented to star billing with the parenthetic notation, "Pinch hitting for Fred Stone." The musical remained for 210 performances on Broadway with Rogers ad-libbing a different performance nightly. (Featured in the cast was a young Patsy Kelly.)

George Jean Nathan wrote of Will's romp in *Three Cheers,* "Rogers single-handed takes one of the poorest librettos ever written, sticks it peremptorily into his back pants-pocket, manufactures a whole evening of wheezes in its stead and converts the session into a ribtickling affair." St. John Ervine was more lavish: "Not every day does one meet a comedian who can keep our interest incessantly engaged. To hear him discoursing on current politics is both illuminating and intensely funny. I now announce to the world that I have learned more about American politics from Mr. Rogers in one evening than I have learned from all the editorials and textbooks that I have read since I landed in New York."

Will's dissatisfaction with his silent-screen efforts was forever dismissed when his first talking picture, *They Had to See Paris,* was released in 1929. In the story of a newly rich Oklahoma millionaire taking his family to Paris, Will immediately established his screen image of the kindly common man given to homespun philosophy. He is the prototype of the man who quietly emerges as the victor over domestic and other encroaching daily crises of American life. The picture was selected as one of the year's ten best films; by 1932 Will Rogers would be the country's top box-office draw.

For Fox's all-star revue *Happy Days* (1929) Will was one of the stars of an elaborate minstrel show. *So This Is London?* (1930) gave Will a solid role as a wealthy cotton-mill owner who gets seasick on his first Atlantic crossing and riding to the hounds with an English lord. The *New York Times* noted, "Mr. Rogers' dry humor is wonderfully successful. His facial expressions are also extremely amusing." For the picture's hilarious final scene, Will dueted "My Country 'Tis of Thee" while an English lord (Lumsden Hare) sang "God Save the King." Irene Rich was again Will's screen wife (as she had been in *They Had to See Paris*) and she would repeat the assignment in 1932's *Down to Earth.*

The lead in the long-running stage hit *Lightnin'* (1930) was a natural and rewarding characterization for Rogers. Critics found his performance superior to anything he had done on the screen. As the whiskey-nipping, shiftless, easygoing philosopher, he gave a masterly portrayal.

Mark Twain's *A Connecticut Yankee at King Arthur's Court* had enjoyed translation into several media and in 1931 became a fine showcase for Rogers' wry comedy. *Time* reported of the movie, "Will Rogers' deliberate awkwardness, his shamble, mock shyness and ability on horseback, are all ideal for the role, and it does not matter that his drawl is Oklahoma instead of Connecticut. His personality and his multifarious activities have made him by this time, even to Americans, a figure symbolic of Americanism." Rogers gave a well-rounded, comic performance as Hank Martin or Sir Boss of Camelot. The film further benefited with the casting of old-time screen star William Farnum as King Arthur and an alluring Myrna Loy as Queen Morgan LeFay.

Frank Borzage's 1931 film *Young As You Feel* sparkled with Will dressed to the nines as a fashion plate and succumbing to vivacious Fifi D'Orsay's allure. As Bill Harper in *Ambassador Bill* (1931) Rogers had the opportunity again to record his expertise at rope twirling on the screen. As American razor manufacturer Earl Tinker he lifted *Business and Pleasure* (1932) into first-class entertainment.

Rogers' special rhythm in playing and remarkable ease in front of a camera made his role of farmer Abel Frake in *State Fair* (1933) one of his best. He is the one who spikes his wife's mince meat with brandy and wins a blue ribbon with his uncooperative giant hog, "Blue Boy." The Rogers magnetism pulled through such standard fare as *Doctor Bull* (1933) and *Mr. Skitch* (1933—with ZaSu Pitts as his wife). As banker and horse trader *David Harum* (1934) he played one of literature's most beloved characters. Peggy Wood, with whom he had made his first Hollywood picture in 1919, rejoined Will in *Handy Andy*. As druggist Andrew Yates, Rogers offered one of his tailor-made roles, and again he had a commercial success. *Liberty* magazine analyzed the typical Rogers part: "Rogers has been astutely shrewd in flattering the unsuccessful man and making him yearn for the good old days at the same time. Which is no mean trick. Then, too, Rogers, as many other favorites—Garbo, Chaplin, Crawford—adapts the role to himself and not himself to the role."

John Ford's *Judge Priest* (1934) was based on several Irvin S. Cobb stories and, like most of Ford's pictures, was laced with charming, well-wrought vignettes of character. The comic banter between Will, as the kindly judge, and loose-limbed Stepin Fetchit highlighted the film. The final sequence of the movie was dominated by one-time great silent actor, Henry B. Walthall. As on so many other occasions, Will, the star, submerged himself into the background and let the aging actor have the spotlight. Rogers' reputation for helping fellow players on his films is legend.

Between the 1934 films, Will was persuaded to make another stage appearance. On Monday night, April 30, 1934, he opened at the Curran Theatre in San Francisco in Eugene O'Neill's *Ah, Wilderness!* His playing of newspaperman Nat Miller drew raves from the press and public alike for three

weeks and continued when the show moved south to Los Angeles. An arrangement was made by MGM to borrow Rogers from Fox for its pending screen version of the stage comedy, to be made in the late summer of 1935. (Lionel Barrymore would eventually play Nat Miller in Metro's version.)

For *The County Chairman*, his first of five 1935 releases, Will went on location to the Mojave Desert. Louise Dresser played opposite Will and praised his kindness and consideration to all members of the company. Will was the small-town newspaper editor in *Life Begins at 40*, and *Photoplay* thought that "every recent Will Rogers picture seems to get better and better" and that Will was "perfect as the ink-stained tank-town crusader."

George Kelly's stage satire on the little-theatre movement, *The Torch Bearers*, was reshaped into Will's *Doubting Thomas*. Alison Skipworth was cast in her original stage role of the pretentious Mrs. Pampinelli with Billie Burke as the stage-struck wife and Will as her tolerant, if perplexed, husband. *In Old Kentucky* featured Rogers as horse trainer Steve Tapley.

In his *Autobiography* (1949), edited by Donald Day, Will relates his pleasure in *In Old Kentucky* and wrote, "Had a lot of awful fine people in it, and they sure were good. You know the old idea of one person trying to be the whole thing in a picture is all washed up. Pictures are like a ball team; the pitcher can't do it all. It's got to be the whole team. You just watch pictures close and see how well done are just small parts, or what they call 'Bits.' It's because they are done by real actors, . . . that anyone of them could go in and play the leading part."

Steamboat 'Round the Bend was an exuberant, inventive Mississippi River comedy directed by John Ford. Again Rogers stepped aside to give young actress Anne Shirley added screen exposure and interceded with Fox to hire his old friend Irvin S. Cobb to play rival steamboat captain Eli. Over the latter Will emerges victorious in a climactic riverboat race. The film would open at Radio City Music Hall on September 19, 1935. By that time Will Rogers was dead.

Aviation had long fascinated Rogers. Close friendships with Charles Lindbergh and Brigadier General William Mitchell extended

With Norman Foster, Janet Gaynor, and Louise Dresser in State Fair *(1933).*

With Louise Dresser in David Harum *(1934).*

to a fellow Oklahoman, Wiley Post. The famed aviator had broken the round-the-world flying speed record with navigator Harold Getty and later flew his craft, *Winnie Mae,* on a record-breaking solo flight in 1933. In 1935 Post had a plane assembled from parts of previously damaged aircraft, and added a pair of large pontoons. Prior to taking off to the north, he tested the hybrid plane in Seattle, Washington. Rogers was fascinated with Post's proposed flight. Deciding "I got to see that Alaska," Rogers underwrote the flight. On August 15, 1935, the plane carrying Post and Rogers crashed in a desolate tundra 16 miles from Point Barrow, Alaska. Arctic pilot Joe Crosson flew the bodies of Post and Rogers back to California.

A squadron of planes trailing long black streamers flew over New York City; radio networks maintained a half-hour silence; flags were flown at half-mast, and theatres were darkened. Singer John McCormack expressed a worldwide sentiment, "A smile has disappeared from the lips of America and her eyes are suffused with tears."

In a eulogy to Rogers, Lowell Thomas wrote,

The only pose in Will Rogers was the pretense that he was an ignorant and illiterate fellow. Actually he was nothing of the sort. As he once remarked, "We are all of us ignorant, but not about the same things." Though he made a bluff at concealing it, his writings from time to time betrayed an exceedingly wide knowledge. Whether he was conscious of it or not the system behind his humor was an exceedingly old one. It can be described in one word—Truth. It is one of the most ancient formulae of the Comic Spirit. As Max Eastman has remarked, "Truth is a chief source of joy motive in popular jokes—we are always hungry for the simple truth."

That, in the last anlaysis, is what Will Rogers gave.

On 20 acres of land donated by Betty Rogers, the Will Rogers Memorial was dedicated at Claremore, Oklahoma, on Will's 59th birthday, November 4, 1938. His daughter, Mary, unveiled a dark bronze statue created by Jo Davidson (a duplicate stands in the Capitol in Washington, D.C.) of Will. It bears his own epitaph, "I never met a man I didn't

548

like." From Hyde Park, New York, President Franklin Delano Roosevelt, in a radio broadcast, paid "grateful homage to the memory of a man who helped the nation to smile." He ended his tribute with, "The American nation, to whose heart he brought gladness, will hold him in everlasting remembrance."

On May 22, 1944, Rogers' body was transferred from California to a subscription-built crypt in the gardens of his Claremore Memorial. A month later his wife, Betty, died and, along with their infant son Freddie (who had died of diphtheria in 1919), was transferred to the Rogers County crypt. In 1944 Will's children donated his 300-acre Santa Monica ranch to the state of California for a state park.

Rogers was the first member of his profession to be commemorated on postage stamps, but that was but one of many honors bestowed upon the sagebrush sage and spokesman for America's conscience. In 1952 Warner Bros. filmed *The Story of Will Rogers* with Will Jr. impersonating his father. But the film recaptured none of Will's zest in its pedestrian unreeling. Recently various actors, including James Whitmore, have taken to the road in one-man shows spouting Will's wealth of pithy comments. In May 1976 the Franklin Mint released a limited edition of sculptured figures of gold and silver, representative of 10 of America's greatest, most beloved, legendary heroes. In company with Daniel Boone, Babe Ruth, Charles Lindbergh, Mark Twain, and Sergeant Alvin York was Will Rogers.

Perhaps the finest tribute to the showman-humanist came from Marie Dressler. In her book *My Own Story* (1934) she wrote:

> One of the most open-minded men I know is Will Rogers. He is my favorite philosopher and one of my favorite humans. His homespun wit, which is the window dressing for one of the keenest minds at large, and his native kindness are all essentially American. He is America at her best. That's why we like him so much—we see the best of ourselves in him. Will Rogers probably has more good deeds chalked up against his name than anybody you could mention offhand. He is practically the only public figure I know who has kept his hair, his wife and his sense of humor 25 years. And, I might add, he's kept his box-office appeal too; I'd be willing to stake my last dollar that if you took a poll of the five best-loved Americans today, you'd find Will Rogers' name heading the list.

FEATURE FILMS

Laughing Bill Hyde (*Goldwyn 1918*)
Almost a Husband (*Goldwyn 1919*)
Jubilo (*Goldwyn 1920*)
Water, Water Everywhere (*Goldwyn 1920*)
Jes' Call Me Jim (*Goldwyn 1920*)
The Strange Boarder (*Goldwyn 1920*)
Honest Hutch (*Goldwyn 1920*)
Cupid, the Cowpuncher (*Goldwyn 1920*)
The Guile of Women (*Goldwyn 1921*)
Boys Will Be Boys (*Goldwyn 1921*)
An Unwilling Hero (*Goldwyn 1921*)
Doubling for Romeo (*Goldwyn 1921*)
A Poor Relation (*Goldwyn 1921*)
One Glorious Day (*Paramount 1922*)
The Headless Horseman (*W.W. Hodkinson 1922*)
Hollywood (*Paramount 1923*)
Tip Toes (*British-National-Paramount 1927*)
A Texas Steer (*First National 1927*)
They Had to See Paris (*Fox 1929*)

Happy Days (*Fox 1929*)
So This Is London? (*Fox 1930*)
Lightnin' (*Fox 1930*)
A Connecticut Yankee (*Fox 1931*)
Young As You Feel (*Fox 1931*)
Ambassador Bill (*Fox 1931*)
Business and Pleasure (*Fox 1932*)
Down to Earth (*Fox 1932*)
Too Busy to Work (*Fox 1932*)
State Fair (*Fox 1933*)
Doctor Bull (*Fox 1933*)
Mr. Skitch (*Fox 1933*)
David Harum (*Fox 1934*)
Handy Andy (*Fox 1934*)
Judge Priest (*Fox 1934*)
The County Chairman (*Fox 1935*)
Life Begins at 40 (*Fox 1935*)
Doubting Thomas (*Fox 1935*)
In Old Kentucky (*Fox 1935*)
Steamboat 'Round the Bend (*Fox 1935*)

Posing with Mary Boland for If I Had a Million *(1932)*.

Charlie Ruggles

The denigration and ultimate retaliation of the underdog have long been a source of drama, comedy, and farce in show business. Generations of audiences have applauded the rebellion of the oppressed little man and cheered his rise to conquer, on stage, screen, and television. Brothers under the skin to the beleaguered little man pursued by all the furies were the timid souls, the Walter Mittys and Casper Milquetoasts of the world. Appearing to register zero on life's scale, these gentle people were usually harassed by wickedly harsh employers or in constant danger of imminent emasculation from a predatory female or a shrew of a wife. Of the various actors adept at portraying the underdog rising to triumph, few, if any, were better than Charlie Ruggles.

Ruggles created a screen character of diffident posture and self-belittling almost apologetic mien. He reinforced his characterization with an expressive face capable of registering thought without dialogue. Often he would display a sly, knowing smile, punctuated with quizzically raised eyebrows and a scene-stealing nervous cough. Charlie once said, "I'm not really so funny. I'm just the guy who laughs when he sees a man fall off the curb and the next minute runs to help him up. The art of nonsense is a necessary part of living and comedy is the most fascinating phase of the acting profession. But it is a serious business. A laugh sequence is a fragile thing and may topple into a heap with one false step that destroys the illusion being built up. Odd about comedy! It is always in demand, yet it hasn't the lasting qualities of drama."

He was born in Los Angeles on Monday, February 8, 1886, to wholesale druggist Charles Sherman Ruggles and his wife, Maria Theresa Heinsch Ruggles. Young Charles clerked in one of his father's drugstores, studied chemistry, and tried to adhere to his father's dictum that he would become a doctor. In 1905 he realized his life's dream by making his stage debut at San Francisco's Alcazar Theatre in a stock company production of *Nathan Hale*. His family took a dim view of his chosen profession but Charlie persevered, for the next three years touring the West Coast with Oliver Morosco's stock company based in Los Angeles. When *Soldiers of Fortune* played San Francisco, the Ruggles family* went to see the acting member of the family. Because of their disapproval he was then billed as Charles Sherman.

Many years later Charlie would recall, "Being informed that my father would be in the audience, although he had practically disowned me for being on the stage, was a jolt. In the last act when I came on the stage battered and torn and bleeding, waving an American flag and shouting at the top of my voice, 'Hooray! Hooray! The marines are here!' there was my dad clapping more lustily than the rest in hearty acclaim of his wayward son. But I had to wave the flag to do it!" Ruggles recalled playing character parts from little boys to old men in West Coast companies that featured such names as Laurette Taylor, Fritzi Scheff, Lewis Stone, Lenore Ulric, and Thomas Meighan. He had sharp memories of making his New York stage debut on February 11, 1914, in *Help Wanted*, which lasted 92 performances.

On March 14, 1914, Charlie married actress Adele Rowland.** Following the close of *Help Wanted*, the newlyweds left for Chicago where Charlie opened, and quickly closed, in a flop called *Our Children*. Then the actor made his motion picture debut for Oliver Morosco in a less than renowned screening of Ibsen's *Peer Gynt* (1915). The critics labeled Ruggles "unrecognizably sappy and unimpressive as the Button Moulder." For Bosworth Productions Charlie was Kent in the Julia Crawford-directed-and-written picture *The Majesty of the Law* (1915), featuring George Fawcett.

By the time both of these pictures were released, Charlie was back on Broadway in the comedy *Rolling Stones* (August 17, 1915). He played second lead to Harrison Ford and

critics were becoming conscious of the dimpled-cheeked comedian from the West. His droll performance and carefully rehearsed mannerisms delighted the boys from the press and the public. The show ran over a hundred performances.

After his stint in *Rolling Stones* he was back in front of the cameras as "Looney" Jim, dying with a dark, political secret in Frank Lloyd's Paramount Picture, *The Reform Candidate* (1915), starring Maclyn Arbuckle. After this, Charlie decided his future was on the stage.

For a year and a half Charlie played Jerry Summerfield in *Canary Cottage* with Trixie Friganza. Then on July 25, 1918, he joined Fred and Adele Astaire, the Howard Brothers (Willie and Eugene), Irene Franklin, and Nita Naldi at Broadway's Winter Garden Theatre for *The Passing Show of 1918*. A series of Broadway hits followed for him, with roles in Rudolf Friml's *Tumble In* (1919), *The Girl in the Limousine* (1919), *Ladies' Night* (1920), and the risqué (for 1921) *The Demi-Virgin* with Hazel Dawn.

Reminiscing about the notoriety generated by would-be moralists, Ruggles said, "Ah, what memories there are of it! We looked very much as though we'd just open and close. The front page screamed, 'Police Demand Script of *Demi-Virgin*'—our success was assured. We had two versions of the show. One clean and the other a bit off-color. Who was in the audience determined which version we'd play." The show, thanks to the New York police department and the moralistic mahatmas, ran a record 268 performances.

There followed a quick flop in *A Clean Town* in Washington, D.C., and then in October 1923 he was in the very successful musical comedy *Battling Butler*.* (Charlie had taken dancing lessons from teacher and vaudeville headliner Bothwell Brown, a female impersonator, so that he could provide proper footwork in the boxing scenes.) During the musical's run Charlie shuttled to Astoria, Long Island, to play insurance clerk Gaspard McMahon in *The Heart Raider* (1923), directed by brother Wesley.

After successfully playing in *White Collars* (1925) on the stage, Ruggles was given the lead in one of his most successful stage

* There was now a second son, Wesley, who would become one of Hollywood's top directors, helming such pictures as *Cimarron* (1931), *Are These Our Children?* (1931), *I'm No Angel* (1933), and *Too Many Husbands* (1940).

** The marriage was not enduring. Although he and Adele appeared together in Avery Hopwood's farce *Ladies' Night* (1920), they were divorced soon thereafter. It was not long afterward that Adele married actor Conway Tearle. Charlie did not remarry until May 4, 1942, when at the age of 56 he wed Marion Shields LaBarba. She was the former wife of cartoonist Billy DeGeck and Fidel LaBarba, former flyweight boxing champion.

* The vehicle became a 1926 feature for Buster Keaton.

552

ventures. The role was that of T. Boggs Johns, the junior partner of a garter business who because of losing a poker game must become his associate's butler for a year. The show was *Queen High* (1926) and he and Luella Gear sang "You'll Never Know," with Charlie reprising the show's hit song, "Cross Your Heart." (In 1930 Ruggles would repeat his stage role in Paramount's screen version of the musical with Frank Morgan as his senior partner and Ginger Rogers as the love interest.)

Rainbow had all the ingredients for a Broadway hit. It was billed as "a romantic musical play of California in the days of '49," with book by Laurence Stallings and Oscar Hammerstein II. The latter wrote lyrics to Vincent Youmans' music. After tryouts in Philadelphia and Baltimore the show arrived at the Gallo Theatre in New York on November 21, 1928. Charlie was "Nasty" Howell in a cast that included Libby Holman, Allan Prior, Brian Donlevy, and a temperamental female mule named Fannie. Ruggles was partnered with Fannie and came to hate her. "For I always admired, above all, a lady who acted like a lady. But up went the curtain. The show was packed with bright lyrics, good music, and magnificent girls. But Fannie's heart was bitter. Out she went with me into a gorgeous scene. But the instant she was to act, Fannie kicked up, knocked me down, distributed three other actors across the stage, scared the chorus girls into a panic, then calmly lay down before the footlights and refused to budge. She was largely responsible for a very poor opening night." *Rainbow* lasted only 29 performances. (When Warner Bros. filmed it as *Song of the West*, 1930, Joe E. Brown inherited Ruggles' role.)

Rodgers and Hart's *Spring Is Here* opened March 11, 1929, at Broadway's Alvin Theatre and Ruggles played an irate father. Brooks Atkinson reported in the *New York Times*, "Mr. Ruggles stamps and roars all evening, with a touch of personal pleasantness that belies the deadliness of his lines." Here was the crux of the Ruggles personality: a projected warmth that crossed to the audience despite his tirades, his stabs at sophisticated double entendre, or even his alcoholic interpretations. Through it all, there would always be the twinkle in Ruggles' eyes.

During the run of *Spring Is Here* producer Walter Wanger signed Charlie to a Paramount contract to play a drunken reporter in *Gentlemen of the Press* (1929). *Variety* observed, "He has the most effective part in the story, the strongest laugh lines, the best delivery and displays exceptional ability. He scores the heaviest return with the invitation he hands out to Snell's [Walter Huston] secretary, 'Come up to my apartment sometime and fight for your honor!'" Ruggles' expert playing here brought him a long-term Paramount agreement.

Charlie returned to Astoria to play in *The Lady Lies* (1929) and remained at the Long Island lot to play a French pickpocket opposite Gertrude Lawrence in *The Battle of Paris* (1929). The latter film was pretty much of a bomb and he returned to the stage, this time to the Palace Theatre and vaudeville.

He opened at the Palace on December 29, 1929, in a comedy sketch, "Wives, Etc.," which he had performed before and which he would repeat for a Vitaphone sound short subject. Back on Long Island he was in Paramount's *Roadhouse Nights* (1930) as a pie-eyed reporter. Praise for his tipsy newsmen did not impress Charlie, who said, "Frankly, there are times, when going through a drunk part, that I wish I had stayed in the chemical business!"

His screen work seemingly confined to Long Island, Charlie bought a home at Setauket and engaged a German couple to maintain the place, which included an overstocked aviary, four dogs, and a sizable vegetable garden. Charlie's love of animals would persist throughout his life. After settling in Hollywood he opened a dog shop in 1935.

Ruggles continued to brighten Paramount products. In *Young Man of Manhattan* (1930) he was chased by Ginger Rogers and in Clara Bow's *Her Wedding Night* (1930) his playing was thought "the funniest bit in the film. Mr. Ruggles shows how comic he can be." Ruggles also made two-reel shorts for Paramount at Astoria: *The Hot Air Merchant* (1930) and *The Family Next Door* (1931). He was announced for four additional shorts in 1931-32 that were not made.

Al Christie borrowed Ruggles in the summer of 1930 to film *Charley's Aunt* for Columbia release. Though Charlie was hilarious in

With Maurice
Chevalier in The
Smiling Lieutenant
(1931).

With Myrna Loy and
C. Aubrey Smith in
Love Me Tonight
(1932).

554

the title role of Brandon Thomas' enduring farce, he was happy to turn in his dress. "That costume spoiled my fun. We made it in summer, when Hollywood was good and hot. I had to wear everything that Charley's aunt from Brazil would wear, woolen underwear, corset, petticoats and all the rest. I was black and blue from it. But it's always good, that play."

For Paramount's *The Smiling Lieutenant* (1931), an Ernst Lubitsch production, he was Chevalier's soldier pal Max; then he returned to his reporter role as Ginger Rogers' beau in *Honor Among Lovers* (1931). The studio starred him in *The Girl Habit* (1931) and he, with Fredric March and his wife Florence Eldridge, attended the sneak preview at Great Neck, Long Island. Previews gave Charlie acute agony and he was miserable waiting for laughs that did not materialize. "So you see," Charlie reasoned, "you can't tell about comedy; what I think is funny, others don't and then something that does not seem to me at all comic will make 'em howl. That's how it is, and that's why I say being funny on the stage is just a business."

Returning to his native hearth, California, Ruggles made 11 films in 1932. The best of the lot was Lubitsch's musical remake of his fine silent film *The Marriage Circle.* The new version was entitled *One Hour with You* and starred Maurice Chevalier and Jeanette Mac-Donald. Rouben Mamoulian's *Love Me Tonight* glowed with a Rodgers and Hart score, good performances from Chevalier and Jeanette MacDonald, and a tandem race for laughing honors by two Charleses: Ruggles and Butterworth.

But Ruggles' most memorable screen role in 1932 was in Paramount's *If I Had a Million.* In the Norman McLeod–directed episode, he was a henpecked, beleaguered china-shop clerk. He gave a virtuoso performance of the mousy salesman who, receiving a million dollars, returns to his post at the shop. He is dressed to the nines, complete with derby and walking stick, which he uses virtually to demolish all the displayed merchandise. Told the scene would have to be made in one take, Charlie took the cane and "I let her fling and I took out all of the hate I had for everybody." The erratic feature contained several memorable vignettes, but the Ruggles–Mary Boland segment withstands the test of time along

with W. C. Fields' riotous scenes. The success of casting Charlie and Miss Boland in *If I Had a Million* led Paramount to team them in 14 features. They became the screen's most enduring husband-wife team.

For the next seven years Charlie was the on-camera butt of Mary Boland's bitchy if lovable wife and he played variations of the same browbeaten character. Between his stints as Boland's spouse he made a clutch of programmers; he spiced these "B"-type films with greatly needed humor. Paramount's all-star *Alice in Wonderland* (1933) had Ruggles as the March Hare. Warner Bros. borrowed him for the lead in *Friends of Mr. Sweeney* (1934), a dismal story that Charlie brought to life. The *New York Times* appraised, "Being no ordinary comic, Mr. Ruggles not only cartoons the feverish indecision and the mouselike timidity of his character, but inspires genuine affection for him. If he were not so amusing, if he allowed an enraptured audience to catch its breath, there would be misted eyes. When he rises to his might and casts off the cloak of futility, the audience is with him to the man."

Paramount had filmed Harry Leon Wilson's comedy *Ruggles of Red Gap* in 1923 and Leo McCarey assembled an inspired cast for his 1935 remake. As Egbert Floud, an undignified nouveau riche Western vulgarian given to loud suits, boots with spurs, and 10-gallon hats, Ruggles was the individual who wins an English valet (Charles Laughton) in a poker game. In this comedy classic Ruggles came close to overplaying and parodying the role. Some critics found Charlie's larger-than-life Egbert hilarious, but others felt his strained attempt to demonstrate the wild exuberance of the American West came perilously close to making this the worst performance of his career. He was flamboyant and possibly excessive but his drunken-spree scene with the valet was one of the film's highlights. (Charlie repeated his role of Egbert Floud on Cecil B. DeMille's "Lux Radio Theatre" on July 10, 1939, with Laughton and ZaSu Pitts.)

Charlie's work as Public Enemy No. 13, the Reverend Dr. Moon, in *Anything Goes* (1936) begged comparison with wistfully funny Victor Moore's performance. Many scribes thought that Ruggles as Moonface Martin failed to catch the touching, scowling nuances of Moore's stage performance in the Cole Porter hit.

Charlie's comedies with Mary Boland, *Mama Loves Papa* (1933), *Six of a Kind* (1934), *People Will Talk* (1935), and *Early to Bed* (1936) were sprightly and entertaining. In a complete change of pace, Ruggles played the tragic father of Frances Farmer in a dramatic newspaper saga, *Exclusive* (1937). As newspaperman Tod Swain battling yellow journalism he gave a surprisingly well drawn, straight dramatic performance. It was to be one of his few full-scaled dramatic roles and provided him with an effective death scene, his first since 1915's *The Reform Candidate*.* But he returned to and remained with comedy, giving one of his cleverest and most delightful characterizations as Major Horace Applegate, a big-game hunter, in RKO's wildly funny *Bringing Up Baby* (1938). It is in this picture that he is confronted with Katharine Hepburn's roaming leopard and is reduced to murmuring, "Here kitty, kitt. Puss, puss."

Like most of the comedians and superbly capable "supporting players," Ruggles injected life into many dreary reels of film, notably as eccentric millionaire Robinson in Constance Bennett's *Service De Luxe* (1938), a comedy salvaged by the star's supporting cast. Charlie worked for brother Wesley in *Invitation to Happiness* (1939) despite his brother's insistence that there was not a single laugh in the part and warning about introducing any "funny stuff." Charlie recalled, "Every now and then, during rehearsal, I'd try an innocuous little gag. Wes would call me aside and say 'No.' Finally I begged for just one comedy scene. Wes agreed and I was happy. I breezed through the rest of the picture. I went to the preview to see that one routine I'd devised in a boxing ring but Wes, or somebody, had left it on the cutting-room floor."

After over a decade with Paramount, Charlie started freelancing. In Warner Bros.' film version of S. N. Behrman's play *No Time for Comedy* (1940) Ruggles gave the best performance in the film as the husband of a patroness of the arts (Genevieve Tobin), resigned to her protégés and artistic pursuits.

* He also gave a powerful dramatic performance as Chuckawalla Bill Redfield defending *The Parson of Panamint* in 1941.

His twinkling, ever amused tolerance of his wife's dalliance with artists and the arts added to his playing of Philo Swift, investing the role with persuasive charm, wit, and intelligence.

A career of portraying drunks, henpecked timid souls, and buffoons, augmented by a few excursions into more sophisticated fare, gave way in the Forties for Ruggles to play fathers, friends, and more dignified, if humorous, gentlemen. His white hair and moustache added immeasurably to the dignified image. During the World War II years he visited both the European and Pacific theatres and was frequently active in bond drives and entertaining on the USO camp circuits. On radio he was heard as guest star on various top broadcasts and on his own series, "Barrel of Fun." On screen he was a memorable Otis Skinner in Paramount's well-paced hilarity *Our Hearts Were Young and Gay* (1944), and Cherokee Jim in Betty Hutton's *Incendiary Blonde* (1945). In 1947 he teamed with the master of the pathetic, downtrodden character, Victor Moore, in *It Happened on Fifth Avenue.*

In the late Forties, Ruggles did more stage work. During the Berlin airlift he appeared on Germany's stages with Constance Bennett in the play *Over Twenty-One.* In the later part of 1948 he starred with Mary Boland in a West Coast stage production of a new comedy *One Fine Day,* and the following summer took him back to the East Coast summer theatres in the play *Nothing but the Truth.* Charlie made his television debut for ABC in a half-hour series in 1949 called "The Ruggles," playing the program for 139 weeks. In the Fifties it became "The Charlie Ruggles Show." His film career meanwhile decreased to minor roles in *Give My Regards to Broadway* (1948) and playing June Haver's dad in *Look for the Silver Lining* (1949). In the summer of 1953 he was on *The Consul* episode of "Medallion Theatre" and remained on the East Coast for 36 weeks as Cicero P. Sweeney in *live* telecasts of the NBC-TV series, "The World of Mr. Sweeney."

On March 13, 1958, Ruggles as Dean Damon was fine with Andy Griffith and Ann Rutherford on "Playhouse 90" in the TV version of the hit comedy *The Male Animal.* Charlie returned to Broadway to great acclaim and his first award in *The Pleasure of*

With Ben Blue in Turn Off the
Moon *(1937).*

His Company. The drawing-room comedy, co-starring Cyril Ritchard and Cornelia Otis Skinner, opened at the Music Box Theatre on October 22, 1958. Before it closed in New York City on November 21, 1959, Charlie Ruggles received the Tony Award for the Best Supporting Actor of the season. Critic Robert Coleman wrote, "Charlie Ruggles, reclaimed from the films, gives the best performance of his lengthy career as a sage grandfather. Welcome back to Broadway, Charlie!" Charlie basked in his success, crediting his summer stock experience in such plays as *Heaven Can Wait* and *Jenny Kissed Me* for work that kept him happy and alert at the age of 72.

Before leaving Broadway to tour with the hit play, Charlie was seen on the TV special *The Bells of St. Mary's* (1959) starring Claudette Colbert and Robert Preston. He was the millionaire trying to turn a church into a parking lot. That same year he was heard as

the voice of Aesop on the animated cartoon series "Rocky and His Friends" on ABC-TV. In 1961 Ruggles made three feature pictures, including Paramount's version of *The Pleasure of His Company* and his first Walt Disney outing, as the grandfather of twin Hayley Mills, in *The Parent Trap.* Then he returned to the stage to portray the classical and patriotic puffing senator in *The Captain and the Kings.* Despite a cast that included Dana Andrews, Ruggles, Peter Graves, Conrad Nagel, and Lee Grant, the show lasted only seven performances after its January 2, 1962, Broadway opening.

The veteran performer spent most of the early Sixties doing a variety of television shows. He appeared on segments of such series as "Frontier Circus," "Ben Casey," "Destry," "The Man from U.N.C.L.E.," and several segments of "Burke's Law." He was a frequent guest star on Red Skelton's variety show and in 1963 was back in front of the

557

Hollywood cameras as Judge Murdock in Walt Disney's *Son of Flubber*. That same year he was the excessively generous grandpa in Jackie Gleason's comedy misfire, *Papa's Delicate Condition*. In the summer of 1963 he played the summer theatre circuit in an English mystery comedy, *Not in the Book*, and later was Cap'n Andy in a Dallas Musical Theatre version of *Show Boat*.

Hermione Gingold was the nurse, Charlie the doctor, and Maurice Chevalier the rich patient in Ross Hunter's *I'd Rather Be Rich* (1964). The comedy was a misfire all the way around. He was seen on the New York stage for the last time in a light inconsequential froth, *Roar Like a Dove* (1964), starring Betsy Palmer. Critic Walter Kerr welcomed him back to Manhattan: "With his silver hair and his silver smile and his gift for imitating a newly fooled Satyr, Mr. Ruggles is able to be amusing while declining a drink, while drinking the drink he has declined, and while scurrying across the floor on both knees to the feet of Jessie Royce Landis." The show had a very brief run.

After a warm, showy part as a veterinarian in Walt Disney's *The Ugly Dachshund* (1966), Charlie did a minor role in Disney's sentimental Boy Scout tribute, *Follow Me, Boys!* (1966). His screen career was over. In 1967 he was the wise, accommodating Starkeeper on the TV version of *Carousel* and he made one of his last media appearances the next year on the "Danny Thomas Show."

In September 1970 Ruggles was admitted to St. John's Hospital in Santa Monica for treatment of cancer. The disease claimed his life on December 23 of that year. One of his obituaries capsulized his film career: "Charles Ruggles Dies at 84, Famed for Milquetoast Role." A few years before, Charlie had informed a reporter who had asked what his future plans were, "Forest Lawn, I guess. After you've played everything I have, there ain't no more."

Charlie worried over the future of screen comedy and was concerned about the lack of comedian development in Hollywood. Shaking his white head he announced, "Comedy is a very serious business. There may be a lot of funny people in the world, but I'll defy any of 'em to be funny in front of a camera without working their heads off at it!" Mr. Ruggles was very funny and retained his handsome head.

FEATURE FILMS

Peer Gynt (*Paramount 1915*)
The Majesty of the Law (*Paramount 1915*)
The Reform Candidate (*Paramount 1915*)
The Heart Raider (*Paramount 1923*)
Gentlemen of the Press (*Paramount 1929*)
The Lady Lies (*Paramount 1929*)
The Battle of Paris (*Paramount 1929*)
Roadhouse Nights (*Paramount 1930*)
Young Man of Manhattan (*Paramount 1930*)
Queen High (*Paramount 1930*)
Her Wedding Night (*Paramount 1930*)
Charley's Aunt (*Columbia 1930*)
The Smiling Lieutenant (*Paramount 1931*)
Honor Among Lovers (*Paramount 1931*)
The Girl Habit (*Paramount 1931*)
The Beloved Bachelor (*Paramount 1931*)
Husband's Holiday (*Paramount 1931*)
This Reckless Age (*Paramount 1932*)

One Hour with You (*Paramount 1932*)
This Is the Night (*Paramount 1932*)
Make Me a Star (*Paramount 1932*)
Love Me Tonight (*Paramount 1932*)
70,000 Witnesses (*Paramount 1932*)
The Night of June 13 (*Paramount 1932*)
Trouble in Paradise (*Paramount 1932*)
Evenings for Sale (*Paramount 1932*)
If I Had a Million (*Paramount 1932*)
Madame Butterfly (*Paramount 1932*)
Murders in the Zoo (*Paramount 1933*)
Terror Aboard (*Paramount 1933*)
Melody Cruise (*RKO 1933*)
Mama Loves Papa (*Paramount 1933*)
Girl Without a Room (*Paramount 1933*)
Alice in Wonderland (*Paramount 1933*)
Six of a Kind (*Paramount 1934*)
Goodbye Love (*RKO 1934*)

Melody in Spring (*Paramount 1934*)
Murder in the Private Car (*MGM 1934*)
Friends of Mr. Sweeney (*Warner Bros. 1934*)
The Pursuit of Happiness (*Paramount 1934*)
Ruggles of Red Gap (*Paramount 1935*)
People Will Talk (*Paramount 1935*)
No More Ladies (*MGM 1935*)
The Big Broadcast of 1936 (*Paramount 1935*)
Anything Goes (*Paramount 1936*)
Early to Bed (*Paramount 1936*)
Hearts Divided (*Warner Bros. 1936*)
Wives Never Know (*Paramount 1936*)
Yours for the Asking (*Paramount 1936*)*
Mind Your Own Business (*Paramount 1936*)
Turn Off the Moon (*Paramount 1937*)
Exclusive (*Paramount 1937*)
Bringing Up Baby (*RKO 1938*)
Breaking the Ice (*RKO 1938*)
Service De Luxe (*Universal 1938*)
His Exciting Night (*Universal 1938*)
Boy Trouble (*Paramount 1939*)
Sudden Money (*Paramount 1939*)
Invitation to Happiness (*Paramount 1939*)
Night Work (*Paramount 1939*)
Balalaika (*MGM 1939*)
The Farmer's Daughter (*Paramount 1940*)
Opened by Mistake (*Paramount 1940*)
Maryland (*20th Century-Fox 1940*)
Public Deb No. 1 (*20th Century-Fox 1940*)
No Time for Comedy (*Warner Bros. 1940*)
The Invisible Woman (*Universal 1941*)
Honeymoon for Three (*Warner Bros. 1941*)
Model Wife (*Universal 1941*)

The Parson of Panamint (*Paramount 1941*)
Go West, Young Lady (*Columbia 1941*)
The Perfect Snob (*20th Century-Fox 1941*)
Friendly Enemies (*United Artists 1942*)
Dixie Dugan (*20th Century-Fox 1943*)
Our Hearts Were Young and Gay (*Paramount 1944*)
The Doughgirls (*Warner Bros. 1944*)
Three Is a Family (*United Artists 1944*)
Bedside Manner (*United Artists 1945*)
Incendiary Blonde (*Paramount 1945*)
A Stolen Life (*Warner Bros. 1946*)
Gallant Journey (*Columbia 1946*)
The Perfect Marriage (*Paramount 1946*)
My Brother Talks to Horses (*MGM 1946*)
It Happened on Fifth Avenue (*Allied Artists 1947*)
Ramrod (*United Artists 1947*)
Give My Regards to Broadway (*20th Century-Fox 1948*)
The Lovable Cheat (*Film Classics 1949*)
Look for the Silver Lining (*Warner Bros. 1949*)
All in a Night's Work (*Paramount 1961*)
The Pleasure of His Company (*Paramount 1961*)
The Parent Trap (*Buena Vista 1961*)
Son of Flubber (*Buena Vista 1963*)
Papa's Delicate Condition (*Paramount 1963*)
I'd Rather Be Rich (*Universal 1964*)
The Ugly Dachshund (*Buena Vista 1966*)
Follow Me, Boys! (*Buena Vista 1966*)

* Unbilled guest appearance.

With James Cagney and Richard Whorf in Yankee Doodle Dandy *(1942).*

S.Z. Sakall

From Shakespeare's Sir John Falstaff down through the centuries, the Fat Man has been frequently utilized for obtaining audience laughter. John Bunny, an abundantly obese man paired with scrawny, angular Flora Finch, was one of the screen's first great comedians. Later the coupling of thin, wispy Stan Laurel with oversized Oliver Hardy would create chuckles on sight. The corpulent complex has repeatedly been employed to evoke laughter on the premise that everyone loves a fat man and a fat man loves everybody. Roscoe "Fatty" Arbuckle exploited his hugeness to advantage (at least on the screen). In more recent memory, Jackie Gleason has garnered many guffaws by exaggerating his overweight. Infrequently, elephantine males have been used for villainy, as, for instance, Sydney Greenstreet, Laird Cregar, and Victor Buono.

S.Z. Sakall was a round, energetic man of medium height who employed his rotund figure and used his astonishing brace of chins to command waves of laughter. Slapping his chubby hands against his bubbled cheeks,

arching his expressive eyebrows, and shaking his wattles were the mainstays of his performing which few could resist without laughter.* He was also a good actor, an expert comedian, and one of Hollywood's most beloved characters.

He was born on Wednesday, February 2, 1887, in Budapest, Hungary, one of five children of Henrich Gero, a tombstone cutter and successful sculptor. He was named Eugene but his brother Julius and sisters Marishka, Freda, and Aranka nicknamed him "Yani"—and that variation was retained throughout his life. His mother died early and his father married her sister, adding two more daughters to the family. When Henrich later died, Yani's stepmother and aunt raised the seven children.

In his teens Yani started writing song lyrics and vaudeville sketches but discov-

* In his Hollywood years, Sakall would earn the jealousy of several of his character star co-workers, who were angered that a Hungarian could so "effortlessly" upstage them on camera. Among the latter group was Alan Hale, no novice at the art of scene stealing.

ered authorship won neither respect nor money, so he turned to acting. At age 18 he also discovered that a beard would add dignity to his appearance beyond his tender years. In Hungarian, blond is "szoeke" and beard "szakall" so he became known professionally as Szoeke Szakall, eventually anglicizing the nickname to S.Z. Sakall. Before this change he had made his first stage appearance in a charity performance of one of his one-act plays, *Girl Gymnasium*. Thereafter, in 1916, he made his first films in Budapest and married the sickly, invalid sister of his best friend.

During World War I, Yani was given an audience with Emperor Franz Joseph, who signed the actor's "Golden Book" of autographs. In 1918 his wife, Giza Grossner, died. After the war he joined the Royal Orpheum of Budapest and was becoming well known in the entertainment world through his writing, films, and vaudeville appearances. On August 1, 1920, he married the music hall's secretary, Anne Boezike Elizabeth Kardos. He called her "Bozi" for the next 35 years.

In the mid-Twenties, Yani and Bozi left for Vienna where he wrote and appeared in his play *String Quartet*. That led to an invitation to appear in Berlin where he acted in his play *Albert VIII* at the Nelson Theatre. He became a Berlin stage favorite. When in January 1927 he played at the Metropol Theatre in *Countess Maritza*, he was acclaimed by critics, who reported, "The real hero of the evening is a variety performer, one Szoeke Szakall in the role of the old waiter in the last act. He performs numerous magician's tricks of the clown order, but all with real humanity and characterization. One can't imagine the last act without him and the whole operetta without that last act would be nothing short of a tragedy." (In 1934, Sakall would make a German film version of the musical with Dorothea Wieck.)

The multitalented Sakall was offered a writer's contract with the German film studio UFA, but was soon used as an actor. In 1929 he appeared with Anna May Wong in *Crosstadt Schmetterling* [*The City Butterfly*] and with Francis Lederer and Kaethe von Nagy in *Ihre Majestaet die Liebe*. (Two years later First National Pictures would make an English-language version of the latter film, *Her Majesty, Love*, starring Marilyn Miller

with W. C. Fields in Sakall's old role of the leading lady's father.)

The rotund performer continued acting on the Berlin stage while making feature films, appearing with Albert Bassermann in *The Dictator* and in Max Reinhardt's *Phea*. After the release of the Robert Stolz film musical *Zwie Herzen im Drei-Viertel Takt* [*Two Hearts in Waltz Time*] (1930), critics applauded Sakall's performance, "Szoeke Szakall makes a natural and always interesting producer." This German musical film became an international success and Sakall was constantly at work in the German, Hungarian, and Austrian motion picture studios, soon becoming a box-office draw in Europe. Later, with Max Glass, former president of Terra Films, he established his own producing company, S. Z. Sakall Films, Ltd. With Otto Stransky he also became co-owner of Berlin's Boulevard Theatre and he worked constantly. "But," he later sighed, "I vas not happy. I vorked too hard!"

Along with millions of others, Sakall and his wife had been closely watching the beginnings of Adolf Hitler's brown-shirted frenetic followers. When the budding fuehrer ridiculed the actor in public after a showing of the German-made *Eine Stadt Steht Kopf* [*The Inspector General*] (1932), the Sakalls decided to relocate in Vienna. When not appearing on stage in *String Quartet* and later *Albert VIII*, Sakall continued to be active in the Continental film industry. He made a tremendous hit as Frosch, the comic jailer, a nonsinging role, in *Die Fledermaus* at Vienna's Famed Royal Opera House. He also found time to do a Viennese radio serial, "Herr Lampe," but when Hitler's swastika bearers began appearing in Vienna, the actor quickly accepted an offer for a stage tour of Holland.

When S.Z. accepted the role of Sandor in *The Lilac Domino* (1937), to be made in England with June Knight and Michael Bartlett, the battle of language began again. He learned to speak his lines in his first English-speaking film by rote, as he had done with the German language when he left Hungary to appear on the German-speaking stage and in German films.

It was fate that Sakall should have come to Hollywood. Many other Continental performers had fled German-dominated Europe to find asylum in the filmmaking capital of the world. But Sakall had a (distant) relative at court. His wife's brother, Leslie, had married producer Joe Pasternak's sister, Lenke. After completing the writing of a play with John Szekely, *The Man Who Couldn't Be Helped,* Sakall received an invitation from Pasternak to come to Hollywood to play Carl Ober in Deanna Durbin's starring vehicle, *It's a Date.* The Sakalls sailed from Rotterdam on May 13, 1939, and arrived on May 19 in Hoboken, New Jersey, where a telegram from Pasternak suggested S.Z. remain in Manhattan a few days to learn and improve his English. Sakall wired back, "Optimist!"

Sakall loved California and making films in assembly-line Hollywood. He soon became one of filmland's more notable scene stealers with his standard, energetic frustration giving way to dismay while deploring the situation with an almost set line "Nah! Nah! Nah!" He would alternate this perplexity with exaggerated excitement that usually culminated in slapping both pudgy cheeks to express further his agitation and amazement. His fractured English and true playing of supporting roles soon placed him in demand. He and Charles Winninger (another well-trained comedian in the art of attention getting) gave *My Love Came Back* (1940) its best performances. S.Z. again worked for producer Pasternak in Universal's charming, schmaltzy *Spring Parade* (1940). He had a custom-made role as a kindly, flour-covered baker monitoring a romance between country girl Deanna Durbin and soldier-composer Robert Cummings and delivering his baked goods to Emperor Franz Joseph (Henry Stephenson). What made this particular picture more than the usual joyous occasion for Sakall was that composer Robert Stolz, his old friend, had escaped Hitler's Europe, and had joined Universal to write the musical score for the picture.

Sakall's presence in a picture could add unexpected joy to an otherwise dull script. By the time he appeared as Paul in *The Man Who Lost Himself, Photoplay* magazine was calling him "the scene stealer of all time, the rascal." Yet even when surrounded by expert spotlight grabbers such as Charles Coburn, Edmund Gwenn, and Spring Byington in Jean Arthur's *The Devil and Miss Jones* (1941), Sakall managed to stand out. In Universal's remake of the hit play *Broadway* (1942), S.Z.

was cast as Nick Verdis, the proprietor of Paradise Nightclub. He was rather persuasive in a more serious role.

Yet Hollywood preferred to stereotype him in comedic parts. It hurt Sakall that his experience in semitragic roles was going almost untapped. He tried to instill a good deal of depth and honest characterization into his stock assignments, but he knew and understood the California situation. He was a realist and a diplomat and he accepted his fate, and was happy, at least, that he could ply his craft in such luxurious surroundings. Explaining the art of comedy in the performing arts, he once stated, "Humor is like religion. It cannot be explained, it has to be felt. It must be inside us, and if it isn't, the Devil can take it all!"

Sakall was delighted to be cast as Papa Van Masters, father of seven daughters, in MGM's *Seven Sweethearts* (1942). But the bulk of his acting assignments were at Warner Bros., which had signed him to a term contract. He joined the Burbank ranks of such fellow "character" performers as Sydney Greenstreet, Peter Lorre, Alan Hale, Gene Lockhart, and Jerome Cowan. Jack L. Warner's entertainment factory cast him in *Casablanca* (1942), a motion picture that became one of the year's 10 best films, won an Academy Award for the year's Best Picture, and has survived several decades to become a legend and cult. Directed by Michael Curtiz, S.Z.'s long-time friend from the Berlin days, *Casablanca* remains as a marvel of motion picture making. The stars of the wartime drama were Humphrey Bogart, Ingrid Bergman, Paul Henreid, and Claude Rains, and the supporting cast boasted such names as Greenstreet, Lorre, Conrad Veidt, and Sakall. S.Z. was cast as Carl, a humanistic, outgoing headwaiter and bookkeeper for Rick's place, an international saloon and gambling joint in the Moroccan city. One of his more delightful scenes in Casablanca was his send-off of a middle-aged German couple, the Leuchtags, to celebrate their departure for America. He brings them the house's best brandy and joins them in their jubilation. Basically the scene reflected Sakall's own personal joy of being in the United States and away from Hitler's madness.

Metro borrowed the in-demand Sakall for its production of William Saroyan's *The Hu-*

man *Comedy* (1943), a touching tale of an American family during wartime. He played a patriotic butcher and suggested a sight gag for his role to director Clarence Brown. The brief scene involved Sakall's reading the deplorable war news glaring from the morning newspaper as he was slicing a side of beef. The more he read, the angrier he became until he was stabbing the meat, eventually holding a large skewered piece over his head. Brown was enthusiastic about the sequence but when the overlong film was edited, that bit of business was left on the cutting-room floor. Warner Bros. then shuttled Sakall to Twentieth Century-Fox for Sonja Henie's *Wintertime*, in which he played Norwegian tycoon Hjalmar Ostgaard, the petite ice skater's uncle. At age 56 Sakall joined gleefully in an ice-skating roughhouse sequence with Miss Henie and Cesar Romero, although the producers were reluctant to ask him to do it. He thoroughly enjoyed the picture and the ice skating bit. He was also an excellent skater, but that he forgot to mention to the filmmakers.

Warner's *Shine On, Harvest Moon* (1944) featured Ann Sheridan and Dennis Morgan in a tepid musical biography of Nora Bayes and her husband Jack Norworth. Sakall was Poppa Karl and one critic said his portrayal was "easily the film's best comic performance with his quivering jowls." He played himself, with practically the entire Warner Bros. star roster, in *Hollywood Canteen* (1944). (Off screen S.Z. and his wife Bozi often served refreshments at the servicemen's retreat.) He was very funny as a frustrated potato-salad vendor in Danny Kaye's *Wonder Man* (1945), and in *Christmas in Connecticut* (1945) he enlivened the film as Felix Bassenak, a cafe owner posing as Barbara Stanwyck's uncle.

Loaned to Twentieth Century-Fox again, Sakall was the only real Hungarian in the whitewashed musical life story of the famous Hungarian sisters, *The Dolly Sisters* (1945). S.Z. played Uncle Latsie to nieces Betty Grable and June Haver. When he returned to the Warner Bros. lot he was cast as Sascha Bozic in Errol Flynn's *San Antonio* (1945) and Jack L. Warner dubbed him "Cuddles." *Photoplay*, reviewing the Flynn Western, commented, "S. Z. Sakall, who for some revolting reason is suddenly billed as 'Cuddles,' is a delicious old codger who proves he can do more than pat his fat little cheeks with his fat little hands."

Revolting or not, the nickname stuck, and when he published his autobiography, subtitled *My Life Under the Emperor Franz Joseph, Adolf Hitler and the Warner Brothers* (1954), he called his memoirs *The Story of Cuddles*. As for the screen, 1946 was undistinguished for a series of unmemorable quickies for Warners. But the newly christened Cuddles was enchanted with his personal life. He became a United States citizen, unsparing in praise for his new land. His only film release in 1947 was MGM's *Cynthia*. The film became notable for providing Elizabeth Taylor with her first screen kiss and her singing debut. Sakall "went through those typical and good Sakall motions" as Miss Taylor's music teacher. In one of the many excerpts from MGM musicals assembled for *That's Entertainment!* (1974), a clip of *Cynthia* was used. Miss Taylor is seen struggling with Strauss' "Melody of Spring" (as revised by Johnny Green and Ralph Freed) with Sakall as her bemused piano accompanist.

He endured minor parts in 1948. He was a hotel manager supplying greatly needed humor in an otherwise dreary vaudeville saga, *April Showers*. In *Romance on the High Seas* he was another uncle—Lazlo—tossed in for a few laughs. Acerb Oscar Levant cornered most of the picture's wit. Sakall's comedy relief work in two grim melodramas, *Embraceable You* and *Whiplash*, completed his year's work for the studio.

He was fine as Felix Hofer, a radio executive who hires singer Doris Day, in *My Dream Is Yours* (1949). He delighted audiences with his playing of the hotheaded, softhearted (now a near standard role for Cuddles) music-shop proprietor with Judy Garland and Van Johnson in Metro's *In the Good Old Summertime* (1949), produced by his in-law and good friend Joe Pasternak. Sakall appeared as himself with other guest stars in a backstage-at-Warner Bros. plot, *It's a Great Feeling* (1949), his third screen venture with Doris Day. *Look for the Silver Lining* (1949) was a purported musical biography of Marilyn Miller, starring June Haver and with Cuddles tossed into the melee for laughs. Miss Haver returned to Twentieth Century-

With Betty Grable and June Haver in The Dolly Sisters *(1945).*

With Spring Byington, Clinton Sundberg, Judy Garland, Buster Keaton, and Van Johnson in In the Good Old Summertime *(1949).*

Fox for *Oh, You Beautiful Doll* (1949) and S.Z. was loaned to that lot to play composer Fred Fisher. In the major role he was the creative soul who longed to compose classical music and found that his melodies became popular song hits. Unfortunately, the picture was uneven and witless.

Back at Warner Bros. he spruced up *Montana* (1950), a minor Errol Flynn Western, and among other screen chores that year was Doris Day's Uncle Max in *Tea for Two*, the third movie version of *No, No, Nanette*. In 1951 Miss Day and Sakall would reunite yet again, this time for *Lullaby of Broadway* in which rich S.Z. tries to perpetuate Day's illusion that her mother is a Broadway star instead of a cheap, lush, cabaret singer. Beset by a jealous wife (the great Florence Bates) and threatened with divorce, he continues to help Doris toward a happy ending by promoting her to Broadway stardom. In a post–Civil War Western, *Sugarfoot* (1951), Sakall was town merchant Don Miguel, who befriends hero Randolph Scott, in a picture that needed all the friends it could get. His last work at Warners was as Felix Hoff, owner of a Las Vegas motel and gambling joint, in an unhappy musical with the happy title *Painting the Clouds with Sunshine* (1951). As the owner of the Golden Egg, he was again the uncle, this time for Virginia Mayo and Lucille Norman.

Cuddles' last three features were made for Metro-Goldwyn-Mayer. The first was Dore Schary's massive flag-waving, overly sentimental, all-star, episodic (six scripters, six directors for six brief stories) *It's a Big Country* (1951). Sakall, oddly enough, played a Hungarian immigrant whose hatred of Greeks is mitigated and subdued when he discovers his daughter (Janet Leigh) has secretly married a Greek ice cream parlor proprietor (Gene Kelly). Cuddles was not seen on screen for two more years, and then he was in a musicalized version of Janet Gaynor's 1936 movie, *Small Town Girl*, reconstructed for the talents of Jane Powell. His final film proved to be *The Student Prince* (1954), which found Edmund Purdom in the title role mouthing the off-screen singing of Mario Lanza.

On April 8, 1954, Sakall made his video debut on Ford's "TV Theatre," playing Joanne Dru's boss in *Yours for a Dream*. With wife

With Phyllis Coates, Walter Catlett, and June Haver in Look for the Silver Lining (1949).

Bozi, he had settled into a peaceful life at Palm Springs, California. When his 67th birthday arrived on February 2, 1955, he was still reveling in the joys of life. Ten days later, on Saturday, February 12, he died of a heart attack at Hollywood's Cedars of Lebanon Hospital.*

Sakall's zest for living and contribution to screen comedy were considerable. His warm, excitable, often bombastic supporting roles rescued many films from oblivion. His ability to convey unspoken dialogue with his large, expressive eyes and bobbing chins was uniquely right for comedy. A year before his death he had penned these words, as an epilogue to his autobiography:

Dear Hollywood. Whoever is doing well in Montevideo sings the praises of Uruguay. If someone makes a lot of

money in London he enthuses about the thick pea-soup fog. From Greenland to Capetown, the most God-forsaken part of the world rivals the glitter of Paris for the man who finds in it his happiness. . . . All people love and respect the place that is kind to them.

Dear Hollywood, you are the only exception to the rule. It isn't *fashionable* to love you. . . . You must be abused and denounced. You must be reproached with being evil and bad-hearted . . . having too many orange and palm trees, too much sunshine and providing too much money. . . . They say that people are killed by boredom in your confines and only those can bear you who keep on drinking, gambling, taking dope, getting married and divorced.

I am sorry for you, my dear Hollywood . . . for I love you.

Yours,
S. Z. Sakall

* His widow died on February 25, 1977, at the age of 89.

FEATURE FILMS

As Szoeke Szakall:
Suszterherceg (*Hungarian 1916*)
Ujszulott Apa (*Hungarian 1916*)
Rutschbahn (*German-British 1928*)
Grosstadt Schmetterling (*German 1929*)
Ihre Majestaet die Liebe (*German 1929*)
Zwie Herzen im Drei-Viertel Takt (*German 1930*)
Kopfuber ins. Gluk (*German 1930*)
Die Faschingsfee (*German 1931*)
Der Schwebende Jungfrau (*German 1931*)
Der Zinker (*German 1931*)
Ihr Junge (*German 1931*)
Der Ubekannte Gast (*German 1931*)
Der Hamplemann (*German 1931*)
Susanne Macht Ordnung (*German 1931*)
Ich Heirate Meinen Mann (*German 1931*)
Rendez-Vous (*German 1931*)
Die Frau von der Man Spricht (*German 1931*)
Meine Cousine Aus Warschau (*German 1931*)
Gluk Uber Nacht (*German 1932*)
Eine Stadt Steht Kopf (*German 1932*)

Melodie der Liebe (*German 1932*)
Muss Man Sich Gleich Scheiden Lassen? (*German 1932*)
Pesti Szerelenn (*Hungarian 1932*)
Walzerparadies (*German 1932*)
Ich Will Nicht Wissen Wer du Bist (*German 1932*)
Pardon Tevedtem (*Hungarian 1933*)
Grossfurstin Alexandra (*German 1933*)
Mindent a Noert! (*Hungarian 1933*)
Az Ellopot Szerda (*Hungarian 1933*)
Ein Frau Wie du (*German 1933*)
Helyet az Oregeknek (*Hungarian 1934*)
Fruhlingsstimmen (*German 1934*)
Kaiserwaltzer (*German 1934*)
Graefin Maritza (*German 1934*)
Harom es Fel Musketas (*Hungarian 1934*)
Baratsagos Arcot Kerek (*Hungarian 1935*)
Das Tagebuch der Geliebten (*German 1935*)
4½ Musketiere (*German 1935*)
Jo as oreg a Haznal (*Hungarian 1935*)
Mircha (*Austrian 1936*)

The Lilac Domino (*British 1937*)

As S. Z. Sakall:
It's a Date (*Universal 1940*)
Florian (*MGM 1940*)
My Love Came Back (*Warner Bros. 1940*)
Spring Parade (*Universal 1940*)
The Man Who Lost Himself (*Universal 1941*)
That Night in Rio (*20th Century-Fox 1941*)
The Devil and Miss Jones (*RKO 1941*)
Ball of Fire (*RKO 1941*)
Broadway (*Universal 1942*)
Yankee Doodle Dandy (*Warner Bros. 1942*)
Seven Sweethearts (*MGM 1942*)
Casablanca (*Warner Bros. 1942*)
Thank Your Lucky Stars (*Warner Bros. 1943*)
The Human Comedy (*MGM 1943*)
Wintertime (*20th Century-Fox 1943*)
Shine On, Harvest Moon (*Warner Bros. 1944*)
Hollywood Canteen (*Warner Bros. 1944*)
Wonder Man (*RKO 1945*)
Christmas in Connecticut (*Warner Bros. 1945*)
The Dolly Sisters (*20th Century-Fox 1945*)
San Antonio (*Warner Bros. 1945*)
Cinderella Jones (*Warner Bros. 1946*)
Two Guys from Milwaukee (*Warner Bros. 1946*)

Never Say Goodbye (*Warner Bros. 1946*)
The Time, the Place and the Girl (*Warner Bros. 1946*)
Cynthia (*MGM 1947*)
April Showers (*Warner Bros. 1948*)
Romance on the High Seas (*Warner Bros. 1948*)
Embraceable You (*Warner Bros. 1948*)
Whiplash (*Warner Bros. 1948*)
My Dream Is Yours (*Warner Bros. 1949*)
In the Good Old Summertime (*MGM 1949*)
It's a Great Feeling (*Warner Bros. 1949*)
Look for the Silver Lining (*Warner Bros. 1949*)
Oh, You Beautiful Doll (*20th Century-Fox 1949*)
Montana (*Warner Bros. 1950*)
The Daughter of Rosie O'Grady (*Warner Bros. 1950*)
Tea for Two (*Warner Bros. 1950*)
The Lullaby of Broadway (*Warner Bros. 1951*)
Sugarfoot (*Warner Bros. 1951*)
Painting the Clouds with Sunshine (*Warner Bros. 1951*)
It's a Big Country (*MGM 1951*)
Small Town Girl (*MGM 1953*)
The Student Prince (*MGM 1954*)

George Sidney

Early on, America's polyglot population learned to laugh at themselves through burlesqued caricature stressing their ethnic background. During the 1800s, a century when minority pressure groups did not exist, all ethnic groups were grist for the comedian's mill. As time wore on, minstrels gained popularity and laughter from exaggerated and outlandish distortion of the blacks. The stage team of Harrigan and Hart provoked hilarity from all the ethnic groups, although Harrigan's plays were less harsh on the Irish. German-dialect comics became extremely popular, especially through the efforts of Weber and Fields, who had their own theatre company burlesquing hit plays and improvising a world of nonsense. Many of the early comedians were first- or second-generation Jews, but only a few of them relied on their origin for comedy routines. David Warfield, Barney Bernard, Louis Mann, Sam Bernard, and a few others played roles of native, if transplanted, Jewish origin.

George Sidney made a career of playing a warm human being, basically comic and distinctly Jewish. He created a comic Jewish character, Izzy Marks, that he played with great success for 14 years. He also became one of the first of these ethnic-based comedians to record the character on film; on September 24, 1915, Gaumont Mutual released a two-reel picture, *Busy Izzy*, starring the "World Famous Comedian in His World Famous Farce."

The Greenfield family migrated from Hungary, settled in lower Manhattan, and produced a large family. George, named Samuel Greenfield, was born on Friday, March 15, 1878. He grew up in and around Grand Street on the Lower East Side of Manhattan and attended the public schools. He worked in his father's shoemaker's shop until he found independence at $1.50 a week clerking in a pawnbroker's shop. When he was 12 he entered an amateur-night contest at Miner's Bowery Theatre. He won first prize (an order for a ton of coal). Return tryouts netted him a barrel of flour and more coal, but he decided the theatre was preferable to his odd jobs in a hat factory and a photographer's store.

With Charlie Murray (left) in 1930.

With another adventurous youth, Lou Heyman, Sidney made his first professional appearance at the Harlem Museum. When the stage manager asked them for their names they held to their surname initials and came up with "Hennessey and Gibbons." However, the following day they changed their billing to Lou Herbert and George Sidney. The new team toured awhile in various burlesque theatres on the Bowery and in Harlem until Sidney met and formed a team with tall Harry Von Tilzer. They debuted at the Harlem Music Hall, doing an unabashed Weber and Fields routine. Short, bandy-legged George played Weber. The team of Von Tilzer and Sidney continued for four years and then they were signed for a play, *His Nibs, the Baron*. Von Tilzer had the title role and George was cast as a "Dutch" butler. They were stranded six times on the show's tour, which finally collapsed in Dayton, Ohio. In Philadelphia's Arch Street Museum they did 12 performances a day in their old routine. When the team split, Von Tilzer went on to become one of the nation's top songwriters and George signed with one of A. H. Woods' first productions, *The Yellow Kid of Hogan Alley*, which lasted four weeks and folded in rural Pennsylvania.

George's development of the character of Izzy Marks came to life when he joined the Ward and Vokes organization in 1898. After three seasons with Ward and Vokes, the character of Izzy was well known to audiences. In 1901 George was starred for the first time in *Busy Izzy*. For the next 14 years he played the character throughout the United States and his humorous, warm, heavily bearded Jewish tramp continued in *Busy Izzy's Vacation, Busy Izzy's Boodle*, and *The Joy Riders*. The shows played the nation's cheaper houses, those priced 15 cents to a dollar. However, the *Izzy* shows never made it to New York City.

Toward the end of 1914 George was offered his first chance on Broadway by James Forbes, whose play *The Chorus Girl* had been a big hit. The Selwyns were producing Forbes' new play and having difficulty casting the role of a theatrical manager, Max Rosenbaum. Forbes sent for Sidney. George was apprehensive about the job and asked, "Well, how do you want me to play it—with a beard?" The answer was negative. "Dialect?"

asked Sidney. Again no. George bristled. "Well, then, you don't want me. You want a regular actor!" He had played nothing on the stage for nearly 15 years but a character with beard and dialect. When he decided to join the show he was warmly greeted by audiences in *The Show Shop*, which featured up-and-coming Douglas Fairbanks, with Ned A. Sparks, Patricia Collinge, and Zelda Sears in the cast. After 156 performances George and Zelda Sears went on the road as the featured players in *The Show Shop* that had been recast. One critic noted, "Mr. Sidney is at his best, playing a legitimate role that is absolutely different from the comedy Jewish characters ordinarily portrayed."

After a year on the road with *Show Shop* George was engaged for a new play by George M. Cohan, again for the part of a theatrical manager. Cohan had written *Honest John O'Brien* for Chauncey Olcott but the show never reached Broadway. Out of work, Sidney took *Busy Izzy* out of the storehouse while waiting for another Broadway offer.

Oh, Look! opened in New York on March 7, 1918. The musical, based on James Montgomery's play *Ready Money*, featured Sidney, Harry Fox, and Genevieve Tobin. It survived 67 performances. By July George was rehearsing the part of Felix Nobblestone in a three-act farce with Fanny Brice called *Why Worry?* The cast included the perennial comedy team of Smith and Dale and the fine Jewish actress Vera Gordon. (In later Hollywood years, she would frequently be Sidney's on-screen wife.) After tepid notices at its Atlantic City tryout in August 1918, *Why Worry* came to New York where it folded after 27 performances.

Ever anxious for work, Sidney conceived an idea for a play that would give him a chance to portray the Hebrew as he really was, without caricature or overemphasizing ghettoish aspects. After approaching several playwrights he met Aaron Hoffman who became very interested in Sidney's approach to the character. In May 1919 *Welcome Stranger* tried out in Atlantic City, was withdrawn for revision, reopened in Rochester, New York, and then went on to Chicago. On September 13, 1920, the play opened at the Cohan and Harris Theatre on Broadway and Sidney's portrayal of Isidor Solomon was lauded by both press and public. The hit ran for 309 performances and continued one more year on the road. George was delighted with his success as Isidor who finds himself unwelcome in a small New England town. The mayor explains to him, "It is not you to whom we object, but you are the nucleus." Isidor is astounded, "The what?" The mayor explains that by permitting him to remain in town he would be the nucleus of a ghetto. Eventually it is discovered that the mayor is of Jewish descent and Isidor is accepted in the community. George enthused about *Welcome Stranger*, "We ran for so many months in Chicago that we figured we had exhausted every Jew in the city. It will take longer than a few months to do that in New York." It did.*

To an interviewer Sidney said, "Everyone is going to like *Welcome Stranger* and I hope a few will learn a lesson from it. It deals with the faults of the Jew as well as with his virtues. For instance, it brings out that some of my people are prone to push in where they aren't wanted and to spend their money for the biggest diamonds they can buy and to let little Rachel and Isaac and Izzy and Esther play tag in the hotel corridors and annoy everyone. Also they love to proclaim in loud voices that they are rich and are spending their money prodigally." The interviewer interjected, "You know their failings, don't you, Mr. Sidney?" "I should," answered George. "I belong to them." He never forgot it and his future roles characterized the many facets of the Hebrew and most of the rest of contemporary humanity.

Aaron Hoffman's next play, *Give and Take*, provided George with a meaty role, that of Albert Kruger, foreman of a fruit cannery owned by his co-star Louis Mann. That show opened on January 15, 1923, on Broadway and ran for 172 performances. In the fall a cross-country road tour began. After playing 11 weeks in Chicago, Sidney was paged by Hollywood.

Samuel Goldwyn in 1923 had imported Alexander Carr and Barney Bernard from the New York stage to repeat their roles on the screen as *Potash and Perlmutter*. The success of the silent feature persuaded Goldwyn he

had the beginning of a profitable series. But Barney Bernard died on March 21, 1924, just as Goldwyn's sequel was about to start filming. No ethnic comedian could have replaced Bernard better than George Sidney or improved on the character of Abe Potash. Goldwyn had Frances Marion adapt the play *Business Before Pleasure* into a new adventure for the clothing manufacturers Potash and Perlmutter. The follow-up was called *In Hollywood with Potash and Perlmutter*. *Photoplay* glowed over Sidney's performance, naming it one of the month's six best performances. They judged, "George Sidney, Barney Bernard's successor as Abe, gives a finely pointed comedy performance." Norma and Constance Talmadge appeared as "vamps" in the film. The *New York Times* regarded the comedy as one of the funniest farces on the screen, and said the constant waves of laughter were "either caused by the expressions of the inimitable George Sidney, who has the role of Abe Potash, or elicited by the apt captions." And, for the first time, Vera Gordon was Sidney's screen wife.

While waiting for another Hollywood assignment, George starred in a revival of *Welcome Stranger* at San Francisco's Curran Theatre in December 1924. In his second Hollywood effort Sidney played the small role of Weinstein in Corinne Griffith's *Classified* (1925), and met for the first time a lanky comedic Irishman who played Miss Griffith's father in the picture. They were destined to become one of filmland's better known and most hilarious teams. Charlie Murray and Sidney would eventually make 14 more pictures together and bring abundant laughter to the land.

Back with Goldwyn, Sidney made the final Potash entry in *Partners Again—Potash and Perlmutter* (1926), directed by Henry King. The *New York Times* noted, "For fear that somebody might possibly overlook the fact that the two principal characters are 'Potash and Perlmutter,' these two names are added to the title." But the last entry in the film series was the least successful, although George boasted several hilarious sequences in the photoplay.

From Abe Potash, George went to Universal to start playing the first of many Jacob (or Nathan) Cohens in the studio's first teaming of Sidney and Murray. The picture was *The*

* David Belasco produced a film version of *Welcome Stranger* in 1924 while George was making his film debut for producer Samuel Goldwyn. Don Davidson inherited Sidney's role for the screen.

Vera Gordon, Nat Carr, Jane Winton, and George Sidney (right) in The Millionaires (1926).

Cohens and the Kellys (1926), based on the play *Two Blocks Away*. With Sidney as the owner of a dry-goods store and Murray a rugged Irish cop, they quarreled, battled, and reconciled through many trials and tribulations of the Irish and the Jew. And they were often extremely funny. Short, bandy-legged George was a perfect foil for rubber-faced, lean and lanky Murray and they played together with great success. Vera Gordon was usually Mrs. Cohen although there were occasionally different Kellys. For 1928's *The Cohens and Kellys in Paris*, the second in the series, J. Farrell MacDonald was Kelly. In 1929's *The Cohens and Kellys in Atlantic City*, Mack Swain became Kelly. The remaining battles of the Cohens and Kellys through 1933 retained George and Murray.

With the rousing worldwide success of Anne Nichols' *Abie's Irish Rose*, which ran for years on Broadway and throughout the nation, it was inevitable that Hollywood would produce similar themes just this side of plagiarism before Miss Nichols' play reached the screen in 1929. That which most resembled the Nichols opus was produced by the onetime United States ambassador to England and father of a United States President, Joseph P. Kennedy, while head of FBO Studios. Called *Clancy's Kosher Wedding* (1927), the picture starred George as Hyman Cohen whose daughter loves Clancy's son.

The *New York Times'* review of the first *The Cohens and the Kellys* expertly described Sidney's comedic gifts: "George Sidney displays a genius for such roles, and in many scenes in this picture his performance is worthy of a better vehicle. One instant he is ready to explode with fury and the next he is a pathetic wilted plump man desirous of sympathy." First National signed Sidney and Murray as a pair of unwitting bootleggers in *Sweet Daddies* (1926), which was more than slightly reminiscent of *Abie's Irish Rose*, with love blooming between George's daughter and Charlie's son. As Abie Finklebaum, George did the yeoman service and Vera Gordon was once again his wife. The on-screen marriage of Sidney and Vera Gordon was probably rivaled only by the later coupling of Mary Boland and Charlie Ruggles in film after film.

Without Murray, George made other screen appearances. He was seen as Hans Wagner in

With Gertrude Astor and J. Farrell MacDonald (right) in The Cohens and Kellys in Paris *(1928).*

The Prince of Pilsen (1926) with Anita Stewart as his daughter. The picture was a dreary affair. George and Vera Gordon were nouveau riche Mr. and Mrs. Meyer Rubens in Warner Bros.' *The Millionaires* (1926), and for Fox, George played a pawnbroker-auctioneer in *The Auctioneer* (1927). First National reunited Sidney with Murray in a rather funny comedy that previewed for the American Legion in New York City on June 6, 1927. In *Lost at the Front* the pair were in top form. George, as a German barkeeper, and Murray, as an Irish cop, join the Russian army. Disguised as women, they escape from the front. First National announced the two comedians would star in *Steve Brodie Took a Chance* as an immediate follow-up to their successful war adventure. But instead, George signed with producer Robert Kane for the role of Abraham Katz in *Hell's Kitchen*, to be filmed in New York City.

The project was to be directed by Frank Capra, who had recently resigned from developing Harry Langdon into a feature star. Given a good cast, four bright comedians, Sidney, Ford Sterling, Hugh Cameron, and

"Skeets" Gallagher, with Claudette Colbert and Ben Lyon as the romantic leads, Capra felt sure he had a potential hit in the picture. Now retitled *For the Love of Mike* (1927), it was shot at Hearst's old Cosmopolitan Studios at 125th and 2nd Avenue. But the finished product was a resounding flop. Miss Colbert, here making her film debut, vowed she would never make another movie and a decade later still growled about the wretched experience of shooting the film. Capra was never paid for his services but thought the venture worthwhile just to have met Colbert, George Sidney, and Leland Hayward, who was the production manager of the picture.

Back in Hollywood George teamed again with Murray, in *The Life of Riley* (1927), playing police chief Otto Meyer with Murray as the fire chief. After a brief role in Norma Shearer's *The Latest from Paris* (1928), Sidney returned to co-star with Murray in one of their wilder and funnier farces, *Flying Romeos* (1928). They played barbers trying to impress their manicurist by taking flying lessons, while she is off marrying a real airplane pilot. In Universal's well-conceived

We Americans (1928) George was cast as a pants presser with that marvelous actress Beryl Mercer as his wife. Both attend night school to learn to read and write the English language. The New York Times carefully reflected on his performance: "George Sidney is wonderfully effective as the middle-age Russian tailor. The various moods of this character, Morris Levine, are singularly well expressed. An exceptionally fine performance." Sidney, up from burlesque, had matured into a remarkably good actor and his comedic talents were great. Like most of the greater comedians, he could also play drama, whereas many of the most famous tragedians could not succeed in comedy. Motion Picture magazine raved about his We Americans performance, writing, "The first film to glorify the pants presser and as the pants presser is the rotund genius George Sidney. It's pretty hokumush but it will jerk tears from the eyes and dollars to the box office."

Before starting his first talking picture, Give and Take (1928), George did a summer vaudeville in-person tour, delighting audiences once again with his stage comedy in a clever monologue and relishing his return to a live audience. After filming The Cohens and Kellys in Atlantic City (1929), Sidney returned to the stage for eight weeks in Chicago in Edward G. Robinson and Jo Swerling's play The Kibitzer. (The part of The Kibitzer would have drawn a rich screen performance from Sidney or Robinson but it was comic Harry Green who had the lead in Paramount's 1930 talking version of the play.)

George returned to the tried and true. He was shuttled into another Cohen and Kelly misadventure, made Around the Corner (1930) with Murray for Columbia, and with his Irish teammate did a turn in Universal's all-star Technicolor musical The King of Jazz. He ended 1930 with The Cohens and Kellys in Africa.* It seemed that the addition of sound to the series had certainly extended the property's longevity. It was now possible to extend the contrasting ethnic antics far beyond pantomime and to allow the verbal contrast of mannerisms to amuse filmgoers.

Having finished a minor role in Warner Bros.' fast-paced High Pressure (1932), George was assigned the leading role in The Heart of New York. George played Mendel Maranta, a jovial plumber who invents a washing machine. It was a part played on Broadway by his former screen partner— Perlmutter, Alexander Carr. The rags to riches tale benefited from the appearance of Smith and Dale (repeating their stage roles) and Yiddish Theatre actress Anna Appel (as Mendel's wife); Aline MacMahon and Donald Cook also bolstered the exceptional cast. Sidney then returned to Universal for another Cohen and Kelly farce, this one in Hollywood (1932), and then left for another in-person tour, doing a vaudeville sketch in presentation houses.

The Jew and the Irishman finally came full cycle in parts they had played in variations on the theme for years when, in a Christmas matinee of 1932, George Sidney and Charlie Murray opened in Anne Nichols' Abie's Irish Rose at the Alcazar Theatre in San Francisco. George played Solomon Levy and Murray was Patrick Murphy. The theatre orchestra opened the performance playing the song "The Cohens and the Kellys." They had all got together at last. The two protagonists made one more Cohen and Kelly comedy in 1933, prophetically titled The Cohens and Kellys in Trouble. It was their final film together.

By 1933 new comedians were developing a following at the box office. The mad Marx Brothers had descended on Hollywood, RKO had a successful screen team in Wheeler and Woolsey, and at Hal Roach–MGM Laurel and Hardy started making features. Paramount was housing a stable of clowns from W. C. Fields to Burns and Allen and Mary Boland and Charlie Ruggles. The public was constantly discovering new favorites. Then too, the once-hilarious reservoir of ethnic humor was paling. Hollywood had entered an era of comedy more sophisticated than that of the Irish-Jewish combination of the Cohens and the Kellys, an era endorsed by the public.

In 1934, 56-year-old George Sidney played the small role of Max Eckbaum in a bottom-of-the-bill RKO flop with Ginger Rogers entitled Rafter Romance. He was then Papa Rosen in MGM's glossy feature Manhattan

---

* When not grinding out their feature Cohen and Kelly series, Universal kept George and Charlie Murray busy making a series of two-reel comedies: The Big Butter and Yegg Man, Discontented Cowboys, Divorce à la Carte, Go to Blazes, In Old Mazuma, The Love Punch, and others.

With Charlie Murray and June Clyde in The Cohens and Kellys in Hollywood *(1932).*

Melodrama (1934), with Clark Gable, Myrna Loy, and William Powell. In 1935 Sidney's only screen appearance was as the pawnbroker in Universal's expensive production of *Diamond Jim*. His last screen job was with gruff Wallace Beery in *Good Old Soak* (1937) at MGM. The following year he returned to Broadway.

Sidney starred in *Window Shopping* (December 23, 1938) with Gerta Rozan, a young Viennese actress making her first appearance on the English-speaking stage. Although there were expressions of gladness that the beloved character comedian had returned to Broadway, the joy was brief. It was an inconsequential comedy and folded after 11 performances. Two years later George's wife of many years, Carrie Weber Sidney, died. Of his remaining family, his brother, Louis K. Sidney, was a top executive at Metro-Goldwyn-Mayer and his nephew and namesake, George Sidney, became a director for Metro in 1941, eventually gaining recognition as one of Hollywood's best craftsmen.

But "Busy Izzy" made no more films. After a prolonged illness George Sidney died on Sunday, April 29, 1945. That he is not recognized by film historians as one of the screen's better comedians is odd. This lack of recognition could have nothing to do with his characterizations that had little variation. Most of the acknowledged "greats" rarely changed their format, and virtually no one could play the lovable, exasperated Jewish bungler more adroitly than Sidney. Additionally, like most good comedians, Sidney was also a good actor, who could turn laughter to tears with his astute and honest portrayals.

FEATURE FILMS

In Hollywood with Potash and Perlmutter (*Associated First National 1924*)

Classified (*First National 1925*)

Partners Again—Potash and Perlmutter (*United Artists 1926*)

The Cohens and the Kellys (*Universal 1926*)

Sweet Daddies (*First National 1926*)

The Prince of Pilsen (*Producers Distributing Corporation 1926*)

The Millionaires (*Warner Bros. 1926*)

The Auctioneer (*Fox 1927*)

Lost at the Front (*First National 1927*)

For the Love of Mike (*First National 1927*)

The Life of Riley (*First National 1927*)

Clancy's Kosher Wedding (*FBO 1927*)

The Cohens and Kellys in Paris (*Universal 1928*)

Flying Romeos (*First National 1928*)

The Latest from Paris (*MGM 1928*)

We Americans (*Universal 1928*)

Give and Take (*Universal 1928*)

The Cohens and Kellys in Atlantic City (*Universal 1929*)

The Cohens and Kellys in Scotland (*Universal 1930*)

Around the Corner (*Columbia 1930*)

The King of Jazz (*Universal 1930*)

The Cohens and Kellys in Africa (*Universal 1930*)

Caught Cheating (*Tiffany 1931*)

High Pressure (*Warner Bros. 1932*)

The Heart of New York (*Warner Bros. 1932*)

The Cohens and Kellys in Hollywood (*Universal 1932*)

The Cohens and Kellys in Trouble (*Universal 1933*)

Rafter Romance (*RKO 1934*)

Manhattan Melodrama (*MGM 1934*)

Diamond Jim (*Universal 1935*)

Good Old Soak (*MGM 1937*)

With Martha Raye in Four Jills in a Jeep (1944).

Phil Silvers

If any comedian should feel fulfillment today, it is Phil Silvers. The baldpated, bespectacled clown has made an enviable career for himself, becoming a true star in virtually every medium: burlesque, vaudeville, Broadway, motion pictures, and television. Phil won a special place in show-business annals (as well as several Emmy Awards) with his Sergeant Ernie Bilko, a conniving shyster whose toothy "Glad to see ya'!" weekly flashed on the television screens of 23,000,000 Americans. He owns two Antoinette Perry (Tony) Awards for his Broadway successes in *Top Banana* and the revival of *A Funny Thing Happened on the Way to the Forum*. He is affectionately remembered as one of the truly amusing funnymen of the madcap musicals of the Hollywood war years.

However, Phil Silvers is hardly a fulfilled individual. A veteran of two broken marriages and a lifelong gambling addiction (he only recently weaned himself away from the costly habit), Phil admits, "I only smile in public. When I'm alone, I just sort of stare."

Unfortunately, today there appears little hope that Silvers will learn to make peace with his image. A serious stroke (that terminated his triumph in a 1972 revival of *A Funny Thing*) has left him a proverbial shadow of his former comic self. As he admits, "There really isn't much to laugh at in the world today."

Phil Silvers was born on Thursday, May 11, 1911, in Brooklyn, New York, the eighth and youngest child of Russian immigrant Jews, Saul and Sarah Silvers. His father found work in New York as a sheet-metal worker, which hardly paid enough for the family to make ends meet in Brooklyn's Jewish ghetto, Brownsville.

"It was a stinking place to raise a family. Really rotten," recalls Phil. "Brownsville was electric chair country for sure. It was the home base of the gangsters who ran Murder Inc. Half the kids from my neighborhood wound up in prison or on the hot squat at Sing Sing." He began attending P.S. 149, but soon was in difficulty. A classmate knocked a monitor student down the steps. As the victim tumbled past, Phil cracked, "Hey, look, a human football!" The principal heard of the wisecrack and, to make an example, farmed Silvers out to P.S. 61, a reform school. There Phil mixed with the worst of the Brownsville juveniles. He says he was not harmfully indoctrinated into their habits. "It was that family love that kept me from turning into a punk."

Meanwhile, the extroverted Phil began singing in amateur kiddie shows, his first such session being in April 1922. The 11-year-old became a regular warbler at Willie Beecher's Brooklyn gymnasium, where local thugs worked out. He was recruited to entertain at testimonial dinners for "local politicians and crooks." In the course of all this, Phil developed such a fine tenor voice that one night at Coney Island as he partied with some friends on the beach, vaudeville impresario Gus Edwards heard him singing and tossed him a business card. The result was that Phil, now 13, quit school to join the Gus Edwards Revue as a featured juvenile singer. Since he was underage, his father had to accompany Phil to the signing of the contract. Mr. Silvers was flabbergasted to discover that his boy would be earning $40 a week; he himself earned only $27.50 weekly.

With Edwards, Phil made his professional debut at the Earle Theatre in Philadelphia. He was soon playing New York's famed Palace. But at 16, the inevitable occurred. "My voice changed. Just like that. In the middle of a song, it finally cracked." Edwards was kind, sending the boy home in hopes he would "recuperate," but the tenor splendor was gone forever. "Seems funny now," says Phil, "but you can imagine how I felt at the time. A has-been at 16!"

Soon Phil returned to the profession he had grown to accept. The vaudeville act of Joe Morris and Flo Campbell required a tall boy. Phil was recruited and toured with them from 1929 through 1934. He earned $150 weekly. "I loved the pay," Silvers would recall, "but I hated what I was doing. I was 21 years old, as big as a giraffe—and still wearing knee pants. I felt ridiculous." So he quit, and began a very educational and lengthy sojourn in burlesque. (In the early Thirties, Silvers had extra roles in several Vitaphone musical shorts, filmed in New York.)

He began working with Herbie Faye (later a regular on both of Phil Silvers' TV series) and Mildred Harris (Charles Chaplin's first wife) in an act that toured the borscht circuit of upstate New York. Then in 1934 Phil signed a contract with the Minsky Burlesque Troupe. For the next five years he spent most of his evenings at Broadway's Gaiety Theatre, honing the timing and style that later made him a major show-business attraction. Phil's remembrances of burlesque are candid and quite cavalier. "You hear a lot of guff these days about burlesque. About what a great school it was for comics. But who do they think they're kidding? Guys went to burlesque to see the strippers take their clothes off. When the comedians were on, most of the audience would read newspapers. A comic had to be real dirty to get them to stop reading."

Phil later graduated to another level of performing—Broadway. A musical comedy, *Yokel Boy*, was trying out in Boston. One of the stars, Jack Pearl, was unhappy with the production and quit. Hy Gardner, then a columnist for the *Brooklyn Daily Eagle*, was involved with *Yokel Boy* as a special materials contributor. He knew Phil Silvers from burlesque and recommended him to the producers as a replacement. Phil got the job and proceeded to add routines and gags from old burlesque routines, much to the delight of the producers. When the comedy opened at the Majestic Theatre on July 6, 1939, it was quickly declared a hit. In a cast that featured Judy Canova, Buddy Ebsen, and Dixie Dunbar Phil played "Punko" Parks. A comic highlight of this lampoon of Hollywood was Phil's routine of teaching Judy Canova how to sing. *Yokel Boy* ran for 208 performances and won Phil an MGM contract at $500 weekly.

Upon his arrival, Phil did nothing for six months. When he did get a call, it was to test for the role of a clergyman opposite Greer Garson in *Pride and Prejudice* (1940). The Jewish Brooklyn comic was naturally a fiasco as a bewigged, English clergyman. Phil later had Metro screen writer Harry Kurnitz move through the top ranks of the studio and have the test reel burned. Silvers learned later that he was the victim of a studio intrigue. Some MGM executives were waging war with Mayer and sought to discredit one of the mogul's discoveries by deliberate miscasting.

Throughout these shenanigans, Phil entertained at MGM and other Hollywood parties and played engagements at the Copa and Ciro clubs. Finally Silvers made his screen debut in Republic's *Hit Parade of 1941* (1940), an unpretentious grabbag that mingled such diverse talent as Kenny Baker, Frances Langford, Hugh Herbert, Mary Boland, Patsy Kelly, Ann Miller, and Phil. He followed this with a Metro film, *The Penalty* (1941), a minor mystery drama starring Edward Arnold, Lionel Barrymore, and Marsha Hunt, with Phil as a hobo.* But his next picture was a great career booster. It was *Tom, Dick, and Harry* (1941), the RKO comedy starring Ginger Rogers, George Murphy, Alan Mar-

shal, and Burgess Meredith. Phil was hilarious as the hatefully obnoxious ice cream man. The Garson Kanin-directed farce was popular enough for a wide number of filmgoers to observe Phil's splendid, frenetic characterization.

Thereafter Phil's roles fluctuated. He had specialty spots (as in MGM's *Lady Be Good*, 1941, with Eleanor Powell, Ann Sothern, and Red Skelton) and some character parts (as in Metro's Frank Morgan vehicle, *Wild Man of Borneo*, 1941). Metro also loaned Phil back to Republic for *Ice Capades Revue* (1941) before his option lapsed. As a freelancer, Phil was signed by Warner Bros. to star with Jimmy Durante and Jane Wyman in *You're in the Army Now* (1941), the sort of mindless drafttime comedy that amused some audiences on the eve of Pearl Harbor.

By this time Darryl F. Zanuck's Twentieth Century-Fox had taken notice of Phil and he was signed to a studio contract. Between

---

* Silvers claims he played a con artist trying to fleece Mickey Rooney in *Strike Up the Band* (1940), but that his scenes were deleted before the release of this Metro film. He also indicates he had more extensive footage—in tandem with Virginia O'Brien—in MGM's *Lady Be Good* (1941).

With Jimmy Durante in You're in the Army Now *(1941).*

1942 and 1946 he appeared in a dozen Fox releases, as well as four features on loan-out. Silvers would later dismiss all these films with, "I was always cast as Blinky, the hero's good friend, who told the girl, usually Betty Grable, in the last reel that the hero really loved her." Actually he made only four films which featured Miss Grable: *Footlight Serenade* (1942), *Coney Island* (1943), *Four Jills in a Jeep* (1944), and *Billy Rose's Diamond Horseshoe* (1945).

Phil's top cinema success of this time was scored on loan-out to Columbia for the sumptuous *Cover Girl* (1944). Starring Rita Hayworth, Gene Kelly, and Lee Bowman, Phil played "Genius" in this Jerome Kern-Ira Gershwin musical. Within the 107 minutes of superior escapism, Phil not only provided the humor, but demonstrated that he was a very fanciful dancer. Phil's favorite memory of the classic picture was the producer—the notoriously despised Harry Cohn. "You know, I'm the one guy in the world that misses Harry Cohn very much. That bestial man! He was a bastard, but at least he was honest, and man, he was a *picture maker*—as opposed to those college-educated men who say, 'You're too Jewish for pictures.' With him, I knew where I stood. I could reach him, I could get into his office."

Off screen Phil performed some impressive guest spots on major radio shows, and toured extensively with the USO in the Mediterranean. He also married—Jo-Carroll Dennison, Miss America of 1942. They wed in Los Angeles on March 12, 1945, and divorced in 1950. (She remains today a close friend and is the comedian's travel agent.)

Also, now in the big-money class, Phil luxuriated in his passion for gambling. He told the *New York Times* in 1972 (several years after he cured himself of the vice with a doctor's aid), "My gambling was comparable to an alcoholic's drinking. I couldn't bet a little amount and get a kick out of it. . . . I've always been able to pay my gambling debts because I was usually working and I had 10 percent of most of the shows I was in. I had good credit with the bookies, because everybody knew I was always good for my debts. They knew I would pay." Phil's great passion was betting on his favorite hobby, sports. "My biggest things were sports—football, basketball, baseball—and of course the track. I was a good analyst of sports. In fact, I was well respected in the sports field. I had a pass to every major league baseball park in the country."

Phil departed Twentieth Century-Fox after making *If I'm Lucky* (1946) with Perry Como, Carmen Miranda, and the Harry James Orchestra. He returned to New York and scored a major Broadway success that would revarnish his career. This was *High Button Shoes* (Century Theatre: October 9, 1947). With music and lyrics by Jule Styne and Sammy Cahn, and direction by George Abbott, the show starred Phil as schemer Harrison Floy, with a cast which included Nanette Fabray, Mark Dawson, and Helen Gallagher. The *New York Times* reported, "Phil Silvers is an uproarious comic. He has the speed, the drollery, and the shell game style of a honky-tonk buffoon." The hit ran for 727 performances.

When *High Button Shoes* closed, MGM called the star to Hollywood for a role in *Summer Stock* (1950), but once again he was cast as the wisecracking pal of Gene Kelly in this Judy Garland musical. Then it was back to New York, where he scored his greatest stage triumph, as Jerry Biff in *Top Banana* (Winter Garden Theatre: November 1, 1951). This wickedly pungent satire of an egotistical television comic (a thinly veiled Milton Berle), who attempts to save his program from cancellation by creating a romance between two of the show's regulars, was a streamlined volcano of comedy. It allowed Phil to overpower the show with a fleet of nasty wisecracks and to glide about the stage with a hilariously abusive air. The Johnny Mercer score included a well-remembered number, "A Dog Is a Man's Best Friend." The comedy derived pleasant support from cast members Rose Marie, Judy Lynn, Joey Faye, and Jack Albertson.

As a result of his performance in *Top Banana*, Phil won the Donaldson Award, the Tony Award, the *Variety* New York Drama Critics Poll, and a *Life* magazine cover story. The *New York Times* had warned the performer in its review, "Unless he is also Superman, he will be a physical wreck before *Top Banana* is a decade old and will lose what voice he has left at the moment . . . take plenty of vitamins this coming winter."

With Vivian Blaine and Carmen Miranda in **Something for the Boys** *(1944).*

With Philip Van Zandt, Dennis Hoey, Evelyn Keyes, and Cornel Wilde in **A Thousand and One Nights** *(1945).*

Indeed the exhaustive eight shows weekly soon wore on Phil. One night he made his entrance, looked down, and could see his heart pumping through his T-shirt. He staggered to the wings and collapsed. After an understudy went on, a doctor informed Silvers that he would recover, but required at least six weeks of rest. Out of loyalty to the company, Phil refused the advice and continued in the cast thereafter. But he spent the rest of the *Top Banana* run in terrible fear for his health. He lamented later, "People don't understand the special kind of hell a comic goes through. They think it's all one big happy yukkety-yuk. But every night I walked out on that stage, it was like being in the blitz, waiting for death to strike. I got through it by making a bet with myself that I could stay. And I did. But it used up everything I had."

Top Banana taxed Phil through 350 performances. After it closed he hastened to a rest home in Ojai, California. The high-powered performer endured the cure for a brief few days and then went to Hollywood. There United Artists contracted him to star in a color film version of *Top Banana*. When

the film was released in 1954 the *New York Times* reported, "It's the cheapest looking film we've ever seen. . . . But Mr. Silvers is in it, and so long as he is romping around, shouting his head off at people and prodigiously tossing out gags—which, we are happy to inform you, is just about all the time—there is gaiety and bounce in *Top Banana*. It is a very amusing mess of a film." Phil then accepted third billing (under Doris Day and Robert Cummings) in Warner Bros.' unexciting CinemaScope musical *Lucky Me* (1954). After that he entered a newer medium, where he would become a piece of Americana.

As Silvers recalls in his memoirs, *This Laugh Is on Me* (1973), "In October of '53, I had a golf date with Jack Benny which he canceled because of a cold. So I stopped in at his house. Jack looked sick and old. . . . That day he was reflecting on his life, and he wished he had been able to spend more time on the stage. 'They're going to be after you for television,' he warned. 'That's the wave of the future. But it's a drain. Stay in the theatre. It isn't the most fruitful in terms of money, but a

With Doris Day, Nancy Walker, and Eddie Foy, Jr. in Lucky Me *(1954).*

584

performer has dignity on the stage. People *pay* to see you.'"

In 1954 Phil played an engagement in Washington, D.C., at a radio-television correspondents-produced show for President Eisenhower. CBS-TV network vice president Hubbell Robinson Jr. was in the audience. Three days later CBS telephoned Phil with the proposal for a half-hour comedy series. It was to be scripted by Nat Hiken, veteran comedy writer for Fred Allen, Milton Berle, and Martha Raye. Together, Phil and Hiken concocted the idea of Sergeant Bilko. Thus was hatched the format for "You'll Never Get Rich."

With Nat Hiken as producer, director, and head writer, and Phil receiving $5,000 salary per week with 50 percent of the profits, the show began shooting at the DuMont Studios on New York's East 67th Street. Audiences sat on wooden bleachers, and each 25-minute program was shot in 50 minutes. Phil did the warm-up sessions and entertained the crowd between scene changes. Everything indicated that with Silvers as Master Sergeant Ernie Bilko, head of the motor pool at Fort Baxter in Roseville, Kansas, the show would be a hit.

Then Phil learned that the program was scheduled to run on Tuesday nights at 8:30 in direct competition with Milton Berle's hour on NBC-TV. Despair overtook the production. Even Berle called and, with genuine sympathy, told Phil, "Somebody's trying to destroy you." When "You'll Never Get Rich" premiered on September 20, 1955, Berle's show did overshadow Silvers' program in the ratings. When CBS moved the new comedy show from 8:30 to 8:00, Phil's program within a month was surpassing Berle's variety show in the rating battles. The Bilko outing soon grew so in popularity that the show was reaping a weekly audience of 23,000,000. "Bilko knocked Berle off the air," remembers Phil. "Milton phoned me: 'You rat, you had to go on Tuesday?'"

"You'll Never Get Rich," later retitled "The Phil Silvers Show," became one of the greatest comedy half-hours in television's history. The regulars included Elisabeth Fraser as Bilko's WAC girlfriend, Paul Ford as the easily harassed and hoodwinked Colonel Hall, and Maurice Gosfield as hopeless Private Doberman. Other cast members

were Harvey Lembeck, Allan Melvin, Herbie Faye, and Billy Sands. For Phil the series was the climax of his varied career. In 1956 he won three Emmy Awards as well as that year's Television Showman Award for Best Performer and Best Star. He won two additional Emmy Awards in 1957. The comedy ran for four seasons, until Phil's usual exhaustive devotion to his work forced him to ask CBS to halt production. "I'm turning in my chips," he commented in 1959. "If I don't, I'll be a babbling crazy man."

After the Bilko character faded from prime-time viewing, Silvers negotiated a deal with CBS-TV to appear in specials. This way he felt he would be free to spend more leisure time with his wife, Evelyn Patrick, "The Revlon Girl" from the old "$64,000 Question" show. They had married on October 21, 1956, and on June 27, 1957, had become the parents of a daughter whom they named Tracey Edythe. The couple have four more daughters, Nancey, Laury, and twins Candy and Cathy (the latter born on May 27, 1961). Describing himself as in "semi-retirement," Phil appeared on CBS-TV in the specials *The Ballad of Louie the Louse* (October 17, 1959) and *The Slowest Gun in the West* (May 7, 1960). He also made some nightclub appearances, notably at Manhattan's Copacabana.

However, the ambitious drive that trademarked Silvers' career could not stay dormant. On December 26, 1960, he returned to Broadway stardom in *Do Re Mi*, a musical comedy with music by Jule Styne and lyrics by Betty Comden and Adolph Green. The show cast Phil slightly against type, as a fall guy who discovers a singer (Nancy Dussault). Nancy Walker played his wife. The musical ran for 400 performances.

Thereafter, Phil worked at pell-mell pacing for some time. He returned to Hollywood to co-star with Tony Curtis and Suzanne Pleshette in *40 Pounds of Trouble* (1963); he played the fast-talking casino owner. Phil was riotous in Stanley Kramer's *It's a Mad, Mad, Mad, Mad World* (1963) as greedy Otto Meyer.

There followed a new teleseries. Phil had longed for a program over which he held total control and CBS-TV agreed. The result was "The New Phil Silvers Show," which premiered on September 28, 1963. Phil played Harry Grafton, a scheming factory employee

585

with a family. The show received apathetic public response and some barbed critical reaction. Despite attempts to alter the program's format into more of a Bilko mold, the show collapsed after a single season.

Phil relaxed his professional pace, but kept busy. In the early Sixties, *A Funny Thing Happened on the Way to the Forum*, a musical comedy based on the bawdy tales of Plautus, was conceived with Silvers in mind. But he refused it—"I didn't think it would go anywhere." Milton Berle was later contracted for the starring role but departed the production. Then Zero Mostel took over the leading role of Pseudolus and won a Tony Award and stardom as the hit ran for 966 performances. When United Artists filmed the property for 1966 release, Phil was signed for the second lead, as Lycus, a whoremaster (played on Broadway by John Carradine). The role was expanded and slightly revised to fit his style. Zero Mostel and Jack Gilford repeated their stage assignments.

Subsequently Phil alternated guest spots on various TV comedy series with film-making (although he admitted "making movies is not fun anymore"). He joined with Lucille Ball, Jack Benny, Art Carney, et al. in comedy cameos (at $10,000 for two days' work) for *A Guide for the Married Man* (1967) directed at Twentieth Century-Fox by his old acting cohort Gene Kelly. Then Phil went to England to film *Follow That Camel* (1968) and stayed in Europe for the hilarious *Buono Sera, Mrs. Campbell* (1968), playing the spouse of Shelley Winters.

On a personal level, the late Sixties were a sad period for Phil. A cataract on his left eye plunged him into a lengthy depression, despite successful surgery. "I started identifying with people who were in much worse shape than I was. I didn't want to do anything. . . . I thought I was suicidal." His marriage to Evelyn had already collapsed, although the 1966 divorce was quite amicable.

Except for a few TV guest spots and a potato chip commercial, Phil remained professionally withdrawn. Then in early 1971 he left his Los Angeles apartment to make another return to Broadway. *How the Other Half Loves* opened at the Royale Theatre on March 29, 1971. Phil played Frank Foster, with Sandy Dennis as his co-star. Reviews were favorable and the play lasted a moderate run of 104 performances.* Then, back in Los Angeles on October 12, 1971, Phil contracted to appear in a Los Angeles production of *A Funny Thing Happened on the Way to the Forum*, co-starred with Nancy Walker, Larry Blyden, and Reginald Owen. The revival found an enthusiastic audience.

At the last moment, money came through to finance a Broadway edition. Blyden, who played the part of Hysterium, was producer. The new version of *Forum* opened at Broadway's Lunt-Fontanne Theatre on March 30, 1972. The show was a rousing triumph for Phil, skyrocketing the 60-year-old performer back to the top of his profession. One critic huzzahed, "It's Sgt. Bilko in a toga!" On April 23, 1972, Phil won the Tony Award for Best Actor in a Musical. It was hoped that the show's box office would improve by the fall season.

But the show would be closed by the fall. Tragically, in early August of 1972, Phil suffered a serious stroke. His understudy, John Bentley, took over *Forum* while Tom Poston was rehearsed to replace Phil. But without its star, *Forum* could not survive and it folded on August 12, 1972.

After an elaborate, lengthy recuperative period, Phil partially recovered from his stroke.** With Robert Saffron, Phil wrote his autobiography, *This Laugh Is on Me: The Phil Silvers Story* (1973). One reviewer noted, "As a portrait of a comic who was more successful on stage than off, the book is interesting and entertaining. The underlying theme of sadness that permeates the book may dampen some reader appreciation, but

* The *New York Daily News* applauded Silvers' "superb gusto." According to the *Village Voice*, "He plays his role as though he were really an actor rather than a star comedian just concerned with getting a laugh. As a reward for his restraint, one wishes he were getting more laughs." And the *New York Times* endorsed Phil's portrayal as the cheated-upon husband as "remarkable." Clive Barnes of the *Times* elucidated, "He acts as if he has never heard of Sergeant Bilko, and his performance has style, pace and assurance."

** Silvers claims that the kindness of Cardinal Terence Cooke, head of the New York archdiocese, and Monsignor William McCormack, both of whom visited him weekly during his 10 weeks in the hospital following the stroke, helped to "rejuvenate" his lagging spirit. Silvers recalls telling the Cardinal, "I don't know if you know this about comedians, but if we're dying, we have to tell a joke. . . . If this is a sneaky way to convert me, it ain't gonna work."

In It's a Mad, Mad,
Mad, Mad World
(1963).

*With Buster Keaton,
Jack Gilford, and
Zero Mostel in
A Funny Thing
Happened on the
Way to the Forum
(1966).*

the mature audience that grew up with Blinky, Bilko, and Silvers will enjoy it anyway.... That he is essentially a sad man off stage is continually apparent although Silvers never labors this point or ever suggests reader sympathy." Since Phil was physically unable to promote the very readable book to the necessary degree, it was not the expected bestseller hoped for in the publishing trade.

As a warm-up for his show-business return, Silvers appeared in two features, looking very feeble in both: Walt Disney's *The Strongest Man in the World* (1975), as Krinkle the cereal king; and in *Won Ton Ton, the Dog Who Saved Hollywood* (1976), as a rather passive filmmaker. On radio he could be heard promoting a baking company's product.

With more stabilized health, Phil devoted himself to a more hectic performing schedule in succeeding seasons. On "The Ted Knight Musical Comedy Variety Special" (CBS-TV, November 30, 1976) Silvers was on tap as the hometown druggist staging a party for the returning celebrity, Knight. Others on the variety show were Fred MacMurray, Ethel Merman, Edward Asner, and Loretta Swit. In

a pilot episode of "The Love Boat" (ABC-TV, May 5, 1977) Silvers had a key role, portraying a dying man, a morose widower who develops great respect for life. In a later installment (November 26, 1977) of the series he would be cast as Captain Gavin MacLeod's father, an old salt who is driving his nautical son to the point of madness. Also during the year he was seen on the small screen in a two-hour segment of "Charlie's Angels" (ABC-TV, September 21, 1977) and as one of the distraught passengers aboard a hijacked plane in the telefeature, *The Night They Took Miss Beautiful* (NBC-TV, October 24, 1977).

Silvers has turned up in an unheralded youth-oriented feature, *The Chicken Chronicles* (1977), as the rambunctious owner of a greasy chicken takeout stand involved with the shenanigans of sex-oriented high schoolers. Geared to quick play-off engagements, the reviews were mixed on Silvers' participation in the low-jinks. *Variety* accused him of "playing his skimpy part with the aplomb of a dirty old man with foam flecks on the chin," while the *Hollywood Reporter* noted he "plays at top form as the

With Branscombe Richmond and Steve Guttenberg in The Chicken Chronicles *(1977).*

588

salacious owner of a ... stand where the youngsters work after school." Much more important to Phil's professional standing was his participation in Columbia Pictures' *The Cheap Detective* (1978) co-starring Peter Falk, Ann-Margret, Sid Caesar, James Coco, Dom DeLuise, Fernando Lamas, and Madeline Kahn. Directed by Robin Moore, it was scripted by Neil Simon who years before had been handed his first network writing job on Phil's "Sergeant Bilko" teleseries. For some strange reason, Silvers' role as Falk's side-kick Hoppy was almost totally excised from the release print. Silvers had a much healthier spot co-starring with Phil Harris on an episode (ABC-TV, December 2, 1978) of "Fantasy Island." The duo played ex-vaudevillians who want another crack at the big time.

One can only hope that Silvers' health allows him to continue being a familiar sight to audiences. It might help him to overcome his perpetual lament, "Why doesn't anyone understand me? I'm just a little baby at heart."

FEATURE FILMS

Hit Parade of 1941 (*Republic 1940*)

Strike Up the Band (*MGM 1940*) [cut from the release print according to Phil Silvers]

The Penalty (*MGM 1941*)

Tom, Dick, and Harry (*RKO 1941*)

Lady Be Good (*MGM 1941*)

Ice Capades Revue (*Republic 1941*)

The Wild Man of Borneo (*MGM 1941*)

You're in the Army Now (*Warner Bros. 1941*)

Roxie Hart (*20th Century-Fox 1942*)

My Gal Sal (*20th Century-Fox 1942*)

Footlight Serenade (*20th Century-Fox 1942*)

Just Off Broadway (*20th Century-Fox 1942*)

All Through the Night (*Warner Bros. 1942*)

Tales of Manhattan (*20th Century-Fox 1942*) [cut from release print]

Coney Island (*20th Century-Fox 1943*)

A Lady Takes a Chance (*RKO 1943*)

Cover Girl (*Columbia 1944*)

Four Jills in a Jeep (*20th Century-Fox 1944*)

Take It or Leave It (*20th Century-Fox 1944*)

Something for the Boys (*20th Century-Fox 1944*)

Billy Rose's Diamond Horseshoe (*20th Century-Fox 1945*)

A Thousand and One Nights (*Columbia 1945*)

Don Juan Quilligan (*20th Century-Fox 1945*)

Where Do We Go from Here? (*20th Century-Fox 1945*)

If I'm Lucky (*20th Century-Fox 1946*)

Summer Stock (*MGM 1950*)

Top Banana (*United Artists 1954*)

Lucky Me (*Warner Bros. 1954*)

40 Pounds of Trouble (*Universal 1962*)

It's a Mad, Mad, Mad, Mad World (*United Artists 1963*)

A Funny Thing Happened on the Way to the Forum (*United Artists 1966*)

A Guide for the Married Man (*20th Century-Fox 1967*)

Follow That Camel (*British 1968*)

Buona Sera, Mrs. Campbell (*United Artists 1968*)

The Boatniks (*Buena Vista 1970*)

The Strongest Man in the World (*Buena Vista 1975*)

Won Ton Ton, the Dog Who Saved Hollywood (*Paramount 1976*)

The Chicken Chronicles (*Avco Embassy 1977*)

The Cheap Detective (*Columbia 1978*)

In Ziegfeld Follies *(1946)*.

Red Skelton

All the world loves a clown. Through the centuries the ancient mask and posture of the clown have flourished from the *commedia dell'arte* of Renaissance time to the 20th-century's favorites at Ringling Brothers, and Barnum and Bailey's most famous funmakers.

Most comics and comedians have perfected a set image: Charlie Chaplin's tramp, W. C. Fields' misanthropic man of tarnished gentility, Buster Keaton's stoic, conquering genius, Harold Lloyd's bespectacled, shy persistent adventurer, Harry Langdon's embryonic lost aura, and Groucho Marx's crouching, would-be satyric zany. Clowns, however, are a different species of the comic world and the genre provides a wider scope of uninhibited expression. All funsters employ the ancient *zanni* syndrome, but the great clowns have perpetuated it to a greater degree.

Red Skelton, like Jackie Gleason, has created a gallery of inimitable, memorable characters. These hilarious creations range from Freddie the Freeloader to Clem Kadiddlehopper, Sheriff Deadeye, Willie Lump Lump, Cauliflower McPugg, San Fernando Red, and

the Mean Widdle Kid. Ed Wynn, a dean of the comedic art, once stated that Skelton, Lucille Ball, Jimmy Durante, Martha Raye, and a few others were "natural-born comedians." He added, "I think to be an eccentric comedian—to be like Red Skelton—I would say that it is born in him." The Perfect Fool had few, if any, dissenters.

Joseph Skelton, a former clown with the Hagenback-Wallace Circus, and his wife, Ida Mae Skelton, had three sons, Denny, Paul,* and Chris. Then on Friday, July 18, 1913, their fourth son, Richard Bernard Skelton, was born at Vincennes, Indiana. Two months after the birth of their fourth son, Joseph died. Ida Mae, who could neither read nor write, found work as a charwoman at $12 a week at an F. B. Keith's vaudeville theatre. After surviving the third grade, young Richard left school to sell newspapers and worked in the receiving section of J. C. Penney's department store. At the age of 10 he left home to join the traveling

---

* Paul Skelton later became a master carpenter at Twentieth Century-Fox studios.

medicine show of "Doctor" Reynolds Lewis. He had become fascinated with show business, especially the comedy turns he had witnessed at Keith's theatres on passes secured by his mother.

The Lewis Medicine Show paid Red $10 a week (when he got it) as a general flunky and to help Doc Lewis pitch the elixir called Hot Springs System Tonic. Red's entrance into comedy came in the two years spent with the medicine show doing pratfalls. Finally, discouraged by Doc Lewis' erratic weekly stipend, Red joined the Williams' Tent Show as a singer. But he was left stranded from this enterprise. Later he had a brief, inglorious career of one-night stands with the John Lawrence Stock Company wrestling with dramatic dialogue, and losing. Then he became a "mammy" singer with the Clarence Stout Minstrels. Aboard an Ohio and Missouri River showboat, the *Ol' Cotton Blossom,* he played in comedy skits and briefly followed his father's footsteps as a "walk-around" clown with the Hagenback-Wallace Circus. (He had an even shorter experience working with lion tamer Clyde Beatty and his cats.)

Fifteen-year-old Red joined a burlesque troupe doing "Jiggs and Maggie" and "Mutt and Jeff" skits and burlesquing Broadway hits. At Kansas City's Gaiety Theatre he met an usherette, Edna Stillwell, who was an undertaker's daughter. Red, 17, married 15-year-old Edna in 1931, borrowing two dollars from her for the marriage license. Edna, a one-time winner in a Kansas City Walkathon contest, suggested they team up for a tour of the freak-craze Walkathon circuits. From the marathon madness, the young Skeltons advanced to vaudeville. Edna wrote their material, managed their finances and, for three years, had her husband tutored in a high school correspondence course. Red received a high-school diploma in Chicago in 1938.*

The Skeltons had a booking at Loew's Montreal Theatre which developed into a 26-week outing. The management was as enthralled as the audience with Red's doughnut dunking act. Like many of his later famous routines it was based on Skelton's premise

that "people like to laugh at themselves." After a brief airing on Cincinnati's WLW "Avalon Hour," Red was signed for his New York vaudeville debut in July 1937 at Times Square's Paramount Theatre. His record-breaking 16-week Paramount stint was largely because of his switching from doughnuts to "Guzzler's Gin."* Using his early training from Doc Lewis' Medicine Show, the bit had him start the spoof of a commercial as a smooth-talking, charming pitchman. He would emphasize the delights of his product by liberally sampling the gin. Soon he would be lubricated into a frenzied, reeling, inarticulate growler, using Guzzler's for gargling. At the finale he would collapse into a drunken heap. During his Paramount engagement, on August 12, 1937, Red was heard on Rudy Vallee's radio show and America had discovered a new clown.

RKO signed Red for the role of Itchy, social director of Camp Kare-Free, in *Having Wonderful Time* (1938). The Broadway hit lost most of its pungent charm in the diluted screen version and Skelton's screen debut proved inauspicious. The Skeltons returned to vaudeville in a rather lavish musical revue they wrote and produced. *Paris in Swing* played to enthusiastic audiences, but lost the couple $5,000. A month before *Having Wonderful Time* opened at Radio City Music Hall, Red made his first and last legitimate stage appearance.

On June 3, 1938, the St. Louis Municipal Opera produced a new musical by Jerome Kern with book and lyrics by Oscar Hammerstein II and Otto Harbach. *Gentlemen Unafraid* featured Barry Sullivan, Hope Manning, Ronald Graham, Annamary Dickey, and, in the role of Bud Hutchins, Richard "Red" Skelton. Red sang four of Jerome Kern's songs with actress Vicki Cummings. The show folded after one week.

At Washington, D.C.'s Capitol Theatre in the summer of 1938 Red was master of ceremonies of the initial March of Dimes program for President Franklin D. Roosevelt's campaign against infantile paralysis. On January 31, 1939, he was invited to be master of ceremonies for FDR's 57th birthday

---

* In May 1975 Indiana State University conferred an honorary degree of Theatrical Arts on Red following his commencement address to the year's graduating class.

* The "Guzzler's Gin" was used by Skelton in the movie *Ziegfeld Follies* (1946), retitled "When Television Comes."

party. He would return to Washington each year thereafter for the annual celebration as the guest of President and Mrs. Eleanor Roosevelt.

A few Vitaphone short subjects (including *Seein' Red*) in 1939 failed to generate a Hollywood contract for Red. However, Mickey Rooney, impressed by Red's performing at President Roosevelt's birthday celebrations, enthusiastically recommended Skelton to Louis B. Mayer. For his screen audition he performed his vaudeville routines, and did impressions of James Cagney, Errol Flynn, and an Indian with rigor mortis. MGM was significantly impressed with the zany audition and signed him to a contract. The pact was the first MGM player agreement permitting performing in radio and television. (Astute Edna was the one who insisted on the insertion of a radio and television clause.)

For his first assignment on his $2,500 weekly salary, Red was cast by producer J. Walter Ruben and director Frank Borzage in *Flight Command* (1940). Red played the relatively straight role of Lieutenant "Mugger" Martin. MGM further tested the Skelton talent in its Blair General Hospital series, *The People vs. Dr. Kildare* (1941) and *Dr. Kildare's Wedding Day* (1941). He was assigned the recurring role of dim-witted hospital orderly Vernon Briggs. Red temporarily replaced the series book character, interpreted usually by Nat Pendleton.

Metro's Arthur Freed production of *Lady Be Good* (1941) was not. The charm and glow of the Gershwin Broadway hit was oddly absent in MGM's screen version. Even odder was an interpolated song by Jerome Kern and Oscar Hammerstein II, "The Last Time I Saw Paris." It won the Academy Award as the year's Best Song.

Although Red was being hailed as "The Comedy Find of 1941," it was his fourth Metro picture that brought him stardom. Cautious MGM had been aware of Red's comedy potential but had been dubious of his ability to carry a sustained role in a feature. But in its inexpensively mounted remake of *Whistling in the Dark* (1941), MGM decided to give the contract player a break. Red was cast as amateur radio crime detective Wally Benton, known as "The Fox." His expert clowning in the comic mystery led *Photoplay* to judge, "Mr. Skelton is a comic that will give all other comics a first-class run for their money." MGM was so pleased with the box-office results to *Whistling* that it would reteam Red with Ann Rutherford and Rags Ragland for two sequels: *Whistling in Dixie* (1942) and *Whistling in Brooklyn* (1943). Skelton had proved to be Metro's answer to Paramount's Bob Hope.

Between his starring *Whistling* comedies, Red brought a good deal of life and laughter to *Ship Ahoy* (1942), with Bert Lahr as his stooge and Eleanor Powell as his tap-dancing leading lady. On the other hand, the comedian's talents were wasted in a programmer of pure corn, *Maisie Gets Her Man* (1942). MGM mauled its screen version of Cole Porter's massive Broadway hit, *Panama Hattie* (1942). The plot was reshuffled to give more screen time to the roles of three sailors (Red, Rags Ragland, and Ben Blue) and less to the title figure (played by Ann Sothern).

Skelton's increasing popularity with the movie-going public was vastly increased with the 1941 debut of "The Red Skelton Radio Show" on NBC. His Mean Widdle Kid character became as famous on radio as Fanny Brice's "Baby Snooks" and his oft-said "I dood it" became a national phrase. The Kid skits were cleverly written and deftly performed by Red as the precocious, crisis-prone brat. Red would remain among the 10 top rated radio stars for over a decade. At one point his "Scrapbook of Satire" placed third behind Bob Hope and Fibber McGee and Molly.

MGM's revamping of another Cole Porter Broadway hit, *DuBarry Was a Lady* (1943), was eminently more successful than its reworking of *Panama Hattie*. Rubber-faced, dimpled-cheeked Red mugged through the fantasy as King Louis XV, an unlikely role that Bert Lahr had played to perfection in New York. The Madame Pompadour of the piece was another redhead (actually pink), Lucille Ball. The film was a hit and Skelton's best picture to date.

The national popularity Skelton had gained through his motion pictures and his hit radio series was evident in a record-breaking return to vaudeville with his wife and vivacious Lupe Velez. Then on February 11, 1943, Edna was telling Judge Harry R. Archbald that Red stayed out late and came home early in the morning, using such ex-

With John Carroll, Ann Sothern, Robert Young, and Eleanor Powell in a publicity pose for Lady Be Good (1941).

cuses as "I got stuck all night on Sunset Boulevard waiting for a red light to change." The judge regarded the statement as grounds for divorce. Edna would continue writing scripts and acting as Red's business manager for many years. In 1945 she married director Frank Borzage, who had given Red his MGM start.

Metro alternately announced Bert Lahr, Wallace Beery, and Red Skelton as the star of Jack McGowan's screenplay, *Oh, You Kid.* However, the picture was never made. Instead Red was one of many MGM stars in the musical revue *Thousands Cheer* (1943). Also that year he was top-billed over Eleanor Powell in a Vincente Minnelli–directed comedy, *I Dood It.* Next, paired with Esther Williams in *Bathing Beauty*, he offered satirical sequences in tutu and ballet shoes impersonating a ballerina. It remains one of the highlights of his film career.

In 1944 Red had filed for a marriage license, planning to marry model Muriel Morris. The license was never used, nor the change in plans explained. He had also joined the army. During a 14-day leave, on March 9, 1945, he would marry Georgia Maureen Davis at the Beverly Vista Community Church. After entertaining troops in nearly four thousand camp shows, Red returned to Los Angeles on September 28, 1945. He told the press, "I was the only celebrity who went in and came out as a private!"

Skelton was among the MGM contract stars who appeared in the opulent *Ziegfeld Follies* (1946), but the studio then gave Red an assignment that was beyond his acting competence. In the remake of George Kelly's *The Show-Off* (1946) he was the obnoxious braggart Aubrey Piper. Red tried hard but the role of Piper eluded him and the picture was generally off-key. Another remake of *Merton of the Movies* (1947) was no improvement over previous productions and did little for Skelton's movie career.

Skelton's penchant for screwball comedy was given full rein on loan-out to Columbia for *The Fuller Brush Man* (1948). He returned to MGM for the hilarious Civil War spoof *A Southern Yankee* (1948). The film was rescued by the imaginative sight gags devised by onetime MGM great, Buster Keaton, then employed by the studio as a "comedy consultant" for $100 weekly. It was Keaton who suggested to Louis B. Mayer that he be allowed to form a small comedy company within the studio structure to produce, write, and direct his own pictures with Skelton as the star. The proposal was turned down. (Two years later MGM did cast Skelton in a remake of a Keaton picture, *The Cameraman*, retitled *Watch the Birdie* [1950]. But the slapstick second edition did not have the imaginative sight gags and taut timing of Keaton's 1928 silent version.)

Esther Williams' *Neptune's Daughter* (1949) was a sunny success brightened with the teaming of Red and Betty Garrett. The duo followed a straight rendition of the song "Baby, It's Cold Outside" with a rollicking burlesqued version that they repeated at the Academy Awards ceremony when the song won an Oscar. In 1949 it was announced that Red would star in the MGM-Arthur Freed

comedy with music *How To Win Friends and Influence People*, but the venture did not materialize. That same year Red made his television debut on the "Milton Berle Show," thanks to the sagacious Edna, who had insisted on a TV clause in his movie contract.

In 1950 Red was seen as accident-prone inventor Red Pirdy in *The Yellow Cab Man*. In another MGM ersatz film biography of songwriters, Red gave a muted, pleasant performance as Harry Ruby to Fred Astaire's Bert Kalmar in *Three Little Words*. Skelton also made a token appearance in Esther Williams' *Duchess of Idaho*. In 1951's *Excuse My Dust*, Red invented the horseless carriage and he held together a stereotyped Esther Williams musical, *Texas Carnival* (1951), with his expert clowning. Mervyn LeRoy's pedestrian remake of *Roberta* emerged as a second-string affair called *Lovely to Look At* (1952). Red's performing of one sketch was dismissed as "surprisingly unfunny."

The year 1953 was Red's final one at MGM and he made three undistinguished pictures on the lot. *The Clown* was a sloppily senti-

With Mike Mazurki in Neptune's Daughter *(1949).*

With Dorothy Stickney and Arlene Dahl in The Great Diamond Robbery *(1953).*

mental remake of Wallace Beery's Academy Award-winning *The Champ*, with Red as a drunken ex-Ziegfeld star reduced to playing second-rate amusement parks. Skelton was uneasy in a straight role in *Half a Hero*, and after playing good-hearted boob Ambrose C. Park in *The Great Diamond Robbery*, his MGM contract expired.

Although he was forced to relinquish a $150,000 MGM pension fund to enter television, his 20 years in the new medium would provide more than adequate artistic, public, and financial compensation. "The Red Skelton Show" debuted on TV on September 30, 1951. Red won an Emmy as the Best Comedian on television in 1951 and his show was named the Best TV Comedy Show of the season. Over the years he would occasionally break free from the format of his program to try sustained comic and/or dramatic roles. On September 8, 1955, Red gave a comic performance as Rusty Morgan on "Climax" in *Public Pigeon No. 1*.* On November 8, 1956, he appeared on "Playhouse 90" in *The Big*

Slide, giving stature to a serious role as an unsuccessful vaudeville comic who finds success in silent films.

Behind the masks of many clowns lies a syndrome of torment, despair, frustrations, anxieties, and fears. Red Skelton was no exception. He has been a chronic worrier, a hypochondriac, and a long-standing insomniac. Deeply religious, Red brooks no gap in faith and owns a Masonic emblem (he is a 33-degree Mason), a St. Christopher Medal, a Hebrew mezuzah, a carved Buddha, and a Quaker medallion. Beyond all this is the scar of tragedy.

Red and his wife were told that their son Richard (born: May 1948) had leukemia. Replying to Richard's question of what happened to people when they die, Red told his son, "They join a parade and they start to march." Hoping to brighten the child's last days, the Skeltons left on a world tour with their son and 11-year-old daughter, Valentina Maris.* The journey was a nightmare of ruthless reporters besieging them with per-

---

* RKO filmed *Public Pigeon No. 1*, which was released by Universal in 1957. The movie version proved of very little passing interest to anyone.

* On July 14, 1969, Valentina married Carlos Jose Alonso and in August 1970 made Red a grandfather with the birth of Sabrina Maureen Alonso.

sonal questions. It was all climaxed in England when the journals suggested that Richard's illness was questionable and that the tour was simply prearranged world publicity for Skelton. The horrified Skeltons returned to California. There, after a week at UCLA Medical Center and a few days before his 10th birthday, Richard died on May 10, 1958.

Hiding behind his clown's mask, Red plunged into a marathon period of performing. Most of his work was on television or for charity events. Over the years he would occasionally do a comedy bit in a feature film. He played a drunk in *Around the World in 80 Days* (1956), and was a "client" in Warner Bros.' *Ocean's 11* (1960). He contributed the best gag and laughter as the Neanderthal Man trying to become a flying bird in *Those Magnificent Men in Their Flying Machines* (1965).

Red's domestic situation has had its complexities over the years. Red and former photographer's model Georgia had separated briefly in 1952. Another separation, on August 4, 1971, was final, and in November, at Indio, California, they divorced. Earlier, in 1966, Georgia had "accidentally" shot herself in the chest in a Las Vegas hotel room. On Monday, May 10, 1976, the 18th anniversary of the death of her son, Richard, she fatally shot herself in the head with a .38-caliber revolver. Ill and despondent for several years, Georgia had required the services of a full-time nurse.

On October 9, 1973, in San Francisco, at the First Unitarian Church, Red married Lothian Toland, the daughter of one of Hollywood's best cameramen, Gregg Toland.

During 1973 Red attained considerable acclaim as an artist outside the performing arts. His paintings of clowns and still-life canvases had successful showings in the United States.* His work was part of an 11-

* His famous paintings of clowns (W. C. Fields, Carol Burnett, Emmett Kelly, "Freddy the Freeloader," et al.) are very much in demand. (Red's originals have ranged from $6,000 to $20,000.)

In a publicity shot for Public Pigeon No. 1 *(1956).*

In Those Magnificent Men in Their Flying Machines *(1965)*.

minute film, *Celebrity Art*, sponsored by the Franklin Mint and featuring canvases painted by Kim Novak, Dinah Shore, Richard Chamberlain, Candice Bergen, Tony Bennett, and Henry Fonda. Franklin Mint reproduced 750 prints of one of Red's famous clowns, a Pagliacci type. Red personally signed all copies of the print despite constant, chronic pain in his right hand. He explained, "There's bone on bone. The cartilage has just been destroyed from all the years of falling."

Beyond his expertise as an artist, Red writes delightful children's books, like the adventures of *Gertrude and Heathcliffe* (two wacky seagulls), designs coloring books for children (*Clown Alley* and *Frog Follies*), and composes music that has been recorded by the London Philharmonic. He rationalizes these talents, saying he wants "to leave something behind me. No one's going to have a trace of me as a clown after I'm gone. But I like to think that people will see my pictures, and read my stories, and hear my music when I'm gone."

Over the years Red has plied his craft in many successful Las Vegas and other nightclub outings. Not too long ago, he signed a four-year million-dollar contract with Sparks' Nugget Club in Reno, Nevada, and in mid-1977 he agreed to a two-million-dollar pact with the Sahara Hotel in Las Vegas. Fittingly, during National Clown Week in August 1975, with his old friend and circus clown Emmett Kelly opening the act, Red was exemplifying his stature as "America's greatest clown." Reviewers noted that the Skelton talent has, if anything, increased with the years. One observer added, "Red Skelton is a unique and magnificent performer. All by himself, he can keep an audience totally enthralled for two hours, a feat virtually no one else can achieve."

It has been reported of his new club act, "He can seemingly do anything with his face and body, running the gamut of practically every emotion, achieving his results with a nuance, a grimace, a smile, as well as with total bodily involvement in a character. He closes his act with a magnificently poignant 'Old Man at the Parade,' a stunning combination that combines tears and smiles and earned a well deserved and thunderous standing ovation."

To this day Skelton is not sorry that he turned down a leading role in the film of *The Sunshine Boys* (1975). He was appalled when he discovered the script would have had him call then signed co-star Jack Benny a son-of-a-bitch. As it turned out neither famous clown made the Neil Simon screen version. Benny died. George Burns and Walter Matthau inherited the comedy, with Burns winning a Best Supporting Actor Oscar.

After nearly 40 years Red returned to New York City professionally to appear "in concert" at Carnegie Hall on Saturday, March 12, 1977. To a wildly enthusiastic audience he was in top form and Richard F. Shepard in the *New York Times* wrote, "He is as hilariously rubbery as ever, nimble legs, facile hands, plastic-putty face and expressive eyes." The *Hollywood Reporter* detailed of the occasion, "With his ever-present hat molded into many shapes and backed by a 17-piece band playing his own music, Skelton brought to mimetic life a juggler and a strongman, a lonely old man who builds a snowman and then brings it indoors New Year's Eve to assuage his loneliness, and a man struggling up the Eiffel Tower. . . . His Guzzler's Gin

routine broke up the audience as Skelton waltzed through this funny, yet pathetic turn. . . . Skelton was back and New York had him, but all too briefly."

At the annual Academy Awards presentation on March 28, 1977, Red proved his immense talent by adding great (and much needed) hilarity in presenting the 1976 Sound Award. The same week he co-hosted the Mike Douglas TV Show, performing his old routines, and charmingly reminiscing about his long career.

Red has hopes to make another film, *Shadow Horse*, in which he would play a medicine man, patterned, he says, after old Doc Lewis with whom he started in show business six decades ago puffing the dubious glories of Doc's Hot Springs System Tonic. The increasingly busy Mr. Skelton has recently taken to performing TV commercials and, having sold both of his Palm Springs abodes, has constructed a new home in the Santa Rosa mountains. On January 28, 1978, Skelton received the Cecil B. DeMille Award from the Hollywood Foreign Press Association; a month later he set a new record at a sold-out performance at the Towson Center in Baltimore, Maryland; TV guest spots such as his appearance on Bob Hope's annual Christmas outing (NBC-TV, December 17, 1978) demonstrate yet again that Skelton has not lost any of his knack for comic timing.

These days, gone is the entourage of business managers, lawyers, secretaries, and leeches. In more somber moments, Skelton will relate how bad advice and faulty management cost him an estimated $6 million. He now travels alone (or only with his wife) when he plays his Nevada engagements, state fairs, universities, etc. Skelton explains, "I pay my own bills [now] and I don't have any investments to worry about—except things . . . [I was set up in]."

When asked to describe the basis of winning comedy, the very conservative (politically and morally) Red confides that the idea is "to start out, get in trouble, and get out of it." On another occasion he amplified on the state of comedy, and possibly humanity, "We're all on a throne of wax. What happens when it melts?"

It is ironic that despite the popular acclaim he has received over the years, very few American critics have ever taken Red seriously. Had he been performing in France, for example, he undoubtedly would have received the same stunning accolades thrust at fellow pantomimist Marcel Marceau. Red, in any country, belongs in the front ranks of the world's best clowns.

FEATURE FILMS

Having Wonderful Time (*RKO 1938*)
Flight Command (*MGM 1940*)
The People vs. Dr. Kildare (*MGM 1941*)
Lady Be Good (*MGM 1941*)
Whistling in the Dark (*MGM 1941*)
Dr. Kildare's Wedding Day (*MGM 1941*)
Ship Ahoy (*MGM 1942*)
Maisie Gets Her Man (*MGM 1942*)
Panama Hattie (*MGM 1942*)
Whistling in Dixie (*MGM 1942*)
DuBarry Was a Lady (*MGM 1943*)
I Dood It (*MGM 1943*)
Whistling in Brooklyn (*MGM 1943*)
Thousands Cheer (*MGM 1943*)
Bathing Beauty (*MGM 1944*)
Ziegfeld Follies (*MGM 1946*)
The Show-Off (*MGM 1946*)
Merton of the Movies (*MGM 1947*)
The Fuller Brush Man (*Columbia 1948*)

A Southern Yankee (*MGM 1948*)
Neptune's Daughter (*MGM 1949*)
The Yellow Cab Man (*MGM 1950*)
Three Little Words (*MGM 1950*)
Duchess of Idaho (*MGM 1950*)*
Watch the Birdie (*MGM 1950*)
Excuse My Dust (*MGM 1951*)
Texas Carnival (*MGM 1951*)
Lovely to Look At (*MGM 1952*)
The Clown (*MGM 1953*)
Half a Hero (*MGM 1953*)
The Great Diamond Robbery (*MGM 1953*)
Susan Slept Here (*RKO 1954*)*
Around the World in 80 Days (*United Artists 1956*)
Public Pigeon No. 1 (*Universal 1957*)
Ocean's 11 (*Warner Bros. 1960*)*
Those Magnificent Men in Their Flying Machines (*20th Century-Fox 1965*)

* Unbilled guest appearance.

Alison Skipworth

Supported by a credo of never giving a sucker an even break, W. C. Fields' aggression against most of the human race had few contemporary counterparts on the distaff side. But in Alison Skipworth, irascible W.C. found an exemplary confederate in the art of the con game. The portly, well-trained actress of regal bearing could create striking portrayals of middle-aged demimondaines flushed with a lust for larceny, surveying an unsuspecting world with twinkling, beady eyes, and provoking laughter in pursuit of willing victims and her own tarnished, if undaunted, dignity.

Off screen Miss Skipworth was feisty, often cantankerous and as opinionated as her sometime screen vis-à-vis, Mr. Fields. Her associates (and especially novice interviewers) were often taken aback at her free-wheeling candid conversations. Yet despite her many eccentricities, she was admired by all of her friends and associates, to whom she was ever the beloved "Skippy." In a vehemently Fieldsian tirade she would declare her deep-seated dislike of children, vowing

they irritated and bored her to death. On the other hand, she delighted in babbling baby talk to Baby LeRoy on the Paramount sound-stages and basked in the admiration of moppet Douglas Scott during the filming of *Devotion* (1931) for Pathé.

According to an old rhyme, "Saturday's child works hard for a living," and Alison spent a lifetime verifying the rhyme. She was born Alison Mary Elliott Margaret Groom on Saturday, July 25, 1863, on North Audley Street in London, England, to Richard Ebenezer Groom and his wife, Elizabeth (Rodgers) Groom. While in her teens she married a well-known artist, Frank Markham-Skipworth, and later reflected, "Every day I posed for my artist-husband. I was both his model and inspiration but we were very poor and we couldn't make enough to pay the grocery bills, so I set out to earn some money. All I had was a good singing voice, and because I wanted to eat I marketed my voice." She made her stage debut at Daly's Theatre in London in *The Gaiety Girl* in September 1894 and recalled, "I was lauded far and wide for

With George Raft in a pose for Night after Night *(1932).*

my beauty and contralto voice. In spite of this, my husband and I could barely exist."

Britisher George Edwardes signed her as understudy for Marie Tempest in *An Artist's Model* and American producer Daniel Frohman engaged her for the leading role in the Broadway version of the operetta. "My boat docked at noon," said Skippy, "and the opening matinee was scheduled for two o'clock that afternoon [December 23, 1895]. Well, I made it. I was a beautiful girl in those days and I guess everything went off pretty well for the papers next morning called me 'The Toast of Broadway.' Svelte figure, peach-blossom complexion, youth, and sex appeal—and I had a generous share of all of them—never got me anywhere, at least financially." Skippy later reminisced, "I remained with the Frohman stock company for nine years, glorious years and a grand era—we lived at top speed. We had a marvelous time. These are my most precious memories."

Alison played with most of the great stars of the theatre: James K. Hackett and Mary Mannering in *The Princess and the Butterfly*, John Drew in *Captain Dieppe* (1903), Henry Miller in *Man's Proposes* (1904), a season performing in Shakespearean repertory with Viola Allen, and with James K. Hackett in *The Prisoner of Zenda* (1908). Happily, she was seldom out of work. After playing 160 performances in Rachel Crothers' play *39 East* (1919) she was engaged to repeat her Broadway role in Paramount's 1920 film version, along with the show's star, Constance Binney.

For Lewis Selznick's movie drama *Handcuffs and Kisses* (1921) Alison played Miss Strodd, but found acting in the flickers to be degrading. She returned to the stage for the next nine years and appeared in at least three good plays. She was fine in *Lilies of the Field* (1921), starring Marie Doro, and in the summer of 1922 at the Savoy Theatre in Asbury Park, New Jersey, she created one of her most famous characters. The role was that of Mrs. J. Duro Pampinelli, the little-theatre producer and banner-waver in *The Torch Bearers*. The part was a perfect mating of actress and author (George Kelly). Skipworth played Mrs. Pampinelli, spouting, among other pronouncements, "There will be actresses when husbands are a thing of the past!" She played the role for 135 perform-

ances on Broadway, joined Mary Boland in an excerpted second act of the play for vaudeville's two-a-day at the Palace Theatre in the spring of 1923, and joyously re-created her torchbearing culturist on film for Fox's version called *Doubting Thomas* (1935).

Ferenc Molnar's *The Swan* (1923) with Eva LeGallienne and Basil Rathbone gave Alison a showy role as Princess Maria Dominica. It ran for 255 performances and was virtually Alison's last long-lasting Broadway show. Although constantly employed thereafter, she was in a long string of flops. Years later, when she returned to Broadway, Alison was quoted as saying, "After years of success, I was in 20 consecutive failures on Broadway! Now, at least, 18 of these were fine productions and should have had long-run records. But the Depression killed them before they could really get started. I enjoyed playing in *The Swan* but I didn't come on until everyone else had the play well under way. And I used to stand in the wings longing to be on. I don't want someone else to get all the applause before I go on. Of course, *The Torch Bearers* will ever be my fondest memory. It is written across my heart in letters of flame. If George Kelly revives it I shall drop whatever I am doing to play Mrs. Pampinelli again."

Alison's love of the theatre was equaled only by her love of land. During the summer months she cultivated strawberries on her farm at Smithtown, Long Island. "I have two great interests in life," she said. "One is the stage and the other is the land. Had I not attained a modest success in the theatre I would have turned the greater part of my time to farming. As it is I devote considerable time in the summer to making a comfortable living out of my place on Long Island. America has given me the opportunity to make money enough to buy a farm and to cope on an equal plane with men toward the goal of success."

But her farming was more productive than her time in the theatre. She was imposing in the unsuccessful *The Enchanted April* (1925) with Helen Gahagan, and she shone in the short-lived *The Grand Duchess and the Waiter* (1925) with Elsie Ferguson and Basil Rathbone. Among her more notable flops was *Pay to Bearer*, which opened in Chicago in September 1926 and closed in early October on Broadway despite a powerful cast that included Laura Hope Crews, Reginald Owen, Shirley Booth, and Thurston Hall. Changing the title to *Buy, Buy, Baby* did not help. For 82 performances Alison delighted in playing an aging cabaret dame and philanthropic louse supporting a young gigolo (Donald Cook) in *New York Exchange* (1926). She was replaced in *Spellbound* (1927), starring Pauline Lord, and had a brief life in George M. Cohan's production of *Los Angeles* (1927). A musical, *Say When* (1928), occupied her for 24 performances, and critics thought, "Of all the principals, Alison Skipworth contributed the most genuinely hilarious moments of the evening."

Looking back on a parade of Broadway disappointments, Alison was sure the Shuberts' musical *The Right Girl* (1928) would succeed after its reception on the out-of-town tryout circuit. But when the show, retitled *Angela*, starring Jeanette MacDonald, opened at New York's Ambassador Theatre on that December 3, the production closed after 40 performances. Next Miss Skipworth was seen as Tomassa, proprietress of *Cafe De Danse* (1929), a Continental melodrama with music that lost most of its zip in a translation from the French. Gregory Ratoff, also in the cast, staged the import, which died in 31 airings. Alison opened and closed in shows of lesser longevity until Gilbert Miller's production of Marcel Pagnol's *Marseilles* (based on his Marius, Fanny, Cesar trilogy) offered her a showy role as Fanny's mother, Honorine. But audiences of 1930 were not prepared for Mr. Pagnol. Thus Alison, with a weathered eye on prospective Hollywood gold, left the *Marseilles* waterfront for the Pacific coast. At an age when many performers look toward retirement, Alison Skipworth, age 67, started her real film career.

No admirer of Hollywood or the film industry, she intended to return to Broadway after her four-week contract to play Lady Catherine Champion-Cheney (Kitty) in *Strictly Unconventional* (1930). This remake of Somerset Maugham's *The Circle* found little favor with the public or with critics. When the filming of that feature was completed in three weeks she was signed for the role of Lady Melrose, foolishly fascinated with Ronald Colman's *Raffles* (1930). This sophisticated adventure film was for United Artists, as was her appearance in Norma

Talmadge's *Du Barry, Woman of Passion* (1930). Over at Warner Bros. she played the affected socialite, Mrs. Cliveden-Banks, in *Outward Bound* (1930).

Her fifth film for 1930 reunited Alison with Jeanette MacDonald in Fox's strangely fluffy spoof of burglary and opera *Oh, for a Man!* In 1931 Skippy gave sparkling performances in William Powell's first Warner Bros. picture, *The Road to Singapore,** and the *New York Times* found her playing of Nancy Carroll's impoverished, tarnished mother, Countess von Martini in *Night Angel*, well conceived: "Alison Skipworth interprets the reprehensible Countess with some of her usual savoir faire." For Gloria Swanson's *Tonight or Never* (1931) Alison was the Marchesa, the aunt of opera impresario Melvyn Douglas despite appearances of opulently supporting him as her gigolo. Signed to a studio contract by Paramount, the substantially solid Alison was Carole Lombard's mother in *Sinners in the Sun* (1932).

In these fledgling years of the talkies, Hollywood had recruited many aging actresses whose enormous talents had weathered years of theatre training. Marie Dressler's outstanding success at Metro led to the renewed professional interest in May Robson, Louise Dresser, Emma Dunn, and others. For high-class wickedness, ladies of royal lineage, or slightly tarnished madames, Alison Skipworth was well cast. She infused her portrayals with spry humor and, like most of her generation, shamelessly stole most of her scenes from the picture's star.

George Raft was enraged at Skippy's ability to steal the limelight in *Madame Racketeer* (1932). Here she was laughably diverting as the ersatz "Countess of Auburn," an engaging con artist who fleeces the unsuspecting between excursions to jail. Although the film released Alison from supporting roles to a leading part, Raft received top billing through Paramount's strenuous build-up of that wooden actor. Raft was given supporting-cast approval on his future films. Yet despite his rage at Alison's ability to dominate scenes he was wise enough to recognize her talent and selected her as the first of his supporting players for his next picture.

* She also played Mrs. Miller in Powell's fast-paced run of confusion, *High Pressure* (1932).

Night After Night (1932) remains historically classic, thanks to another Raft recommendation for the casting of Maudie Triplett. He wanted his old friend Mae West. Next to Mae and Alison, the other players in this romantic drama paled. The Skipworth-West scenes were gems of flashy, comedic playing, but Alison was edgy and wary of iconoclastic Mae. Later Alison would extol Mae as "one grand actress and a very clever person." But during the filming of *Night After Night*, their scenes together were a tug-of-war between two seasoned troupers trying to dominate the action. It culminated in Alison's announcement, "I'll have you know I'm an actress." Mae responded quietly, "It's all right, dearie, I'll keep your secret."

In *Night After Night*, Alison's portrayal of Mrs. Mabel Jellyman, employed by Raft to teach him the social graces, was delightful. Especially vivid were her scenes with undulating Mae, who not too successfully teaches the old gal how to drink liquor. Alison's slow, penetrating, deliberate timing threw Mae off pace. To combat the situation Mae stepped up her timing and delivery. As a result La West not only dominated what she termed "Alison's good many fat scenes" but also walked off with the entire picture. Skippy had met her match.

If I Had a Million has survived through the years as the best of Hollywood's forays into the multistory, episodic conglomerate exercises in filmmaking. The best section of the picture was the Charlie Ruggles-Mary Boland episode. Racing for second place in the segmented film was the Norman Taurog-directed segment with Alison and W. C. Fields as retired ham actors scrimping to buy a new roadster only to have it wrecked by a road hog on its first outing. When they receive a million dollars from philanthropist Richard Bennett, they buy a fleet of cars. They hire a squad of bullish drivers and pompously lead their crew into an onslaught of vengeance against road hogs. The two portly players were well teamed, with Alison twitteringly pleased as her spouse in flowery terms responds to her with "my little chickadee" and "my tomtit" and other unlikely diminutives.

Paramount kept Miss Skipworth busy as Grand Duchess Emilie in the Claudette Colbert-Fredric March feature *Tonight Is Ours* (1933). And as English Lady Beulah Bonnell in *A Lady's Profession* (1933) she helps her brother (Roland Young) run a Manhattan speakeasy. For *He Learned About Women* (1933) Alison was craftily humorous as ex-actress Mme. Vivienne Polidor, who plots a fancy extortion scheme for millionaire Stuart Erwin.

After completing Rouben Mamoulian's beautifully filmed dud, *Song of Songs* (1933), Alison appraised her performance as Frau Rasmussen, "You won't like me. I don't like myself, for I'm a shrewish old aunt who messes up Marlene Dietrich's romances. Next I'm to do *Don't Call Me Madame*, and it will be the first time Mary Boland and I have been together since our run in *The Torch Bearers*. I know we'll have a swell time!" The proposed *Don't Call Me Madame* was not made but the two actresses did get together in *Six of a Kind* (1934), a very broad comedy bash directed by Leo McCarey. In it Alison was W. C. Fields' saloonkeeping friend Mrs. K. Rumford and Boland and Ruggles were celebrating a second honeymoon in the West. The fast-paced comedy was dominated by Fields and only the Ruggles-Boland team registered. (George Burns and Gracie Allen completed the film's sextet.)

Tillie and Gus (1933) reteamed Alison and W. C. Fields as the Winterbottoms. Tillie is the ex-proprietress of a bordello in China and W.C. is a cardsharp in Alaska. Both return to America seeking an inheritance and posing as, of all things, missionaries. Veering strongly into slapstick, both Fields and Alison were capable of expert clowning with grim seriousness. Mordaunt Hall (*New York Times*) tersely capsulized the film: "Insane as are the doings in this concoction, they succeed in being really funny. It is the sort of thing admirably suited to Mr. Fields' peculiar genius. Miss Skipworth rivals Mr. Fields in arousing laughter." Tillie Winterbottom was a strenuous comedy role for 70-year-old Skippy but she played it to the hilt. (The same year another wonderfully talented senior citizen was lighting up the cinema skies in *Lady for a Day*—May Robson, who was older than Alison.)

Following her Duchess in Paramount's all-star *Alice in Wonderland* (1933), Skipworth made a series of programmers for her home studio. She was tarnished Mother Bright in

With Marlene Dietrich
in Song of Songs
(1933).

With W. C. Fields in a
publicity pose for
Tillie and Gus
(1933).

Wharf Angel (1934) and was Señora Perez in Marlene Dietrich's *The Devil Is a Woman* (1935).

In the mid-Thirties Alison began freelancing. She was Miriam Hopkins' sponsor, Miss Crawley, in the Technicolor RKO release *Becky Sharp* (1935). Over at Warner Bros. she was well cast as a former Floradora girl and Bette Davis' landlady, teaching Bette social refinements in *The Girl from Tenth Avenue* (1935). In Davis' award-winning *Dangerous* (1935), she was effective as Franchot Tone's disgruntled housekeeper.

Alison's last work for Paramount was as Carole Lombard's conniving, portly, dignified companion in *The Princess Comes Across* (1936). One of the character actress' glittering bits of screen exposure came thereafter in a dismal remake of *The Maltese Falcon*. The 1936 version was retitled *Satan Met a Lady* and Alison played Madame Barabbas, a reworking of the menacingly charming male role of Kaspar Gutman, smartly played by Dudley Digges in the 1931 version and by Sydney Greenstreet in the 1941 classic. If the Warner Bros. *Falcon* remake did not finish Alison's movie career, the rest of her films managed that feat.

Two pictures with Polly Moran (made by Republic) tried to rekindle the Dressler-Moran magic of yore, but Alison, capable performer though she was, could not recapture the charisma of the great Marie. Skipworth's last screen appearance, *Ladies in Distress* (1938), was Republic's obvious attempt to duplicate the success of the Dressler-Moran MGM picture *Politics* (1931). The rehash cast Alison as Mayor Josephine Bonney cleaning up a politically corrupt town with Polly Moran as her sister.

That Alison Skipworth survived the Thirties in Hollywood is remarkable when one considers her candid, outspoken rage that could explode: "Pictures! I don't like motion pictures and never did!" She found life rosy-hued in comparison with her early struggles and thought it amusing that "not until I began to get old and funny-looking did I get a

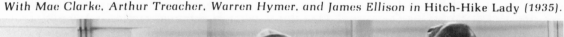
With Mae Clarke, Arthur Treacher, Warren Hymer, and James Ellison in Hitch-Hike Lady *(1935).*

financial break. The comedy producers took me up and my salary began to soar. Rather a joke that now, after the years have taken so much from me, I've been photographed as I act. What I might have been on the screen at 22!"

Alison once told an interviewer that the reason she became an actress was "to keep from starving to death. I want to keep right on acting on either stage or screen as long as I can. Why, I'll hobble around in character parts to my last breath, if they will only let me. What in the world would I do if I stopped *acting?*"

When no further screen roles were forthcoming, she returned to Broadway to play the lead in a feeble farce called *Thirty Days Hath September* (1938). When it folded after 16 performances, she told the press, "I thought it was a good play, but one critic declared I should have been spanked for appearing in it, and another ran my picture with the caption, 'They Done Her Wrong.'"

On December 25, 1939, Alison was starred (with J. C. Nugent, Tom Powers, and Ann Andrews) in J. B. Priestley's comedy *When We Are Married,* playing the part of a belligerent charwoman "with a kind of bullying aggressiveness—very amusing at times" (*New York Times*). She played Mrs. Northrup for 156 performances in the Priestley play, which was one of the first complete shows to be televised by NBC. At 76 Alison was still bursting with joy for being back on Broadway. She allowed to the press (after admonishing reporters that she hoped their questions would be slightly intelligent), "Please say that I am definitely through with motion pictures. They ruined my eyes with their horrible lights. In fact, they ruin almost everybody's eyes. Bill Powell is half blind now as the result of working in the awful glare from seven in the morning until six at night. I've never seen a picture of myself that I really liked very much. Practically every time I've seen myself in a finished picture I've left the theatre so bad tempered that nobody dared speak to me for 48 hours. Sometimes I didn't dare talk to myself.

"They waste so much money out there. I was in pictures for eight years, although I went out [to Hollywood only] for three weeks. There's many a film in which I've seen them spend $100,000 for one scene, then throw it out. Now, they have to be more careful and economical because they haven't the world markets anymore. The war has ended that. I think it's a good thing. They'll have to use brains instead of money and plan their stories carefully so there won't be the enormous waste there has been in the past." She graciously offered both Hollywood and England to the press with her compliments and insisted that the only place in the world fit for decent living was between 40th and 50th Streets on the island of Manhattan.

In the summer of 1940, Alison took to the eastern summer circuit in the play *Criminal-at-Large,* and on January 5, 1941, she was starred with Taylor Holmes and James Bell in an unfortunate comedy, *First Stop to Heaven,* which survived for eight performances. But the title, for Alison, was prophetic. *Lily of the Valley* in 1942 was her last stage appearance and the score of rich portraits she created on stage and screen were to remain a memory.

On Saturday, July 5, 1952, Alison Skipworth, long since retired, died on her beloved isle of Manhattan at the age of 88 at her apartment at 202 Riverside Drive. There were no relatives alive at the time of her death.

FEATURE FILMS

39 East (*Paramount 1920*)
Handcuffs or Kisses (*Select 1921*)
Strictly Unconventional (*MGM 1930*)
Raffles (*United Artists 1930*)
Du Barry, Woman of Passion (*United Artists 1930*)

Outward Bound (*Warner Bros. 1930*)
Oh, for a Man! (*Fox 1930*)
Virtuous Husband (*Universal 1931*)
The Night Angel (*Paramount 1931*)
The Road to Singapore (*Warner Bros. 1931*)
Devotion (*Pathé 1931*)

Tonight or Never (*United Artists 1931*)
High Pressure (*Warner Bros. 1932*)
Unexpected Father (*Universal 1932*)
Sinners in the Sun (*Paramount 1932*)
Madame Racketeer (*Paramount 1932*)
Night After Night (*Paramount 1932*)
If I Had a Million (*Paramount 1932*)
Tonight Is Ours (*Paramount 1933*)
A Lady's Profession (*Paramount 1933*)
He Learned About Women (*Paramount 1933*)
Midnight Club (*Paramount 1933*)
Song of Songs (*Paramount 1933*)
Tillie and Gus (*Paramount 1933*)
Alice in Wonderland (*Paramount 1933*)
Coming Out Party (*Fox 1934*)
Six of a Kind (*Paramount 1934*)
Wharf Angel (*Paramount 1934*)
Shoot the Works (*Paramount 1934*)
The Notorious Sophie Lang (*Paramount 1934*)
Here Is My Heart (*Paramount 1934*)

The Captain Hates the Sea (*Columbia 1934*)
The Casino Murder Case (*MGM 1935*)
Doubting Thomas (*Fox 1935*)
The Devil Is a Woman (*Paramount 1935*)
Becky Sharp (*RKO 1935*)
The Girl from Tenth Avenue (*Warner Bros. 1935*)
Shanghai (*Paramount 1935*)
Dangerous (*Warner Bros. 1935*)
Hitch-Hike Lady (*Republic 1935*)
Stolen Holiday (*Warner Bros. 1936*)
The Princess Comes Across (*Paramount 1936*)
Satan Met a Lady (*Warner Bros. 1936*)
Two in a Crowd (*Universal 1936*)
The Gorgeous Hussy (*MGM 1936*)
White Hunter (*20th Century-Fox 1936*)
Two Wise Maids (*Republic 1937*)
King of the Newsboys (*Republic 1938*)
Wide Open Faces (*Columbia 1938*)
Ladies in Distress (*Republic 1938*)

In The Duchess of Buffalo *(1926)*.

Constance Talmadge

Time has strangely diminished the luminous glow and prominence of Constance Talmadge as one of the foremost comediennes of the silent screen. During the late Teens and throughout the Twenties she was *the* star of comedy when silents were golden. Her pictures did extremely well at the box office and should be reviewed today. Unfortunately, most of her best pictures (on nitrate stock) are gone to dust. Today only a few of her films remain for rewarding reappraisal.

Film historians, justifiably, extol Mary Pickford's unique artistry in playing both comedy and drama, the comedic genius of Mabel Normand, Dorothy Gish's effervescent clowning, and Colleen Moore's buoyant comedy. In recent years there has been critical reappraisal of Marion Davies' considerable gifts as a deft light comedienne. But for the slick, polished, sophisticated (at their point in time) screen portrayals of Constance Talmadge, documentation is sparse. (Perhaps Anita Loos' new biography, *The Talmadge Girls*, 1978, will alter the situation.

Lack of proper historical recognition would not have bothered Constance, who was constantly surprised that audiences found her films so humorously beguiling. An unrelenting realist, she was truly the girl of the moment, dismissing yesterday and only casually glancing at tomorrow. Anita Loos—who with her husband John Emerson wrote many of Constance's screenplays—regarded the brown-eyed, 5'6" vivacious blonde as one of the few genuine femmes fatales she ever knew. On screen Constance played exaggerated comic variations of the sultry, ensnaring woman who vigorously engaged in the battle of the sexes. She underscored her sexual motifs with clowning and, by the last reel, permitted the man she loves to subdue her extroverted, willful ways. It was a plot ploy that recurred in many of her pictures.

Constance Alice Talmadge was born on Wednesday, April 19, 1899, in Brooklyn, New York, to Frederick and Margaret Brown Talmadge. The youngest of the three Talmadge daughters, she became the tomboy of the family, nicknamed "Dutch" because of her blonde hair and rosy complexion. Outgoing, carefree Constance was a marked contrast to serious, moody, firstborn Norma and to ef-

611

ficient, methodical Natalie. With the leave-taking of Mr. Talmadge, the three daughters and mother became a closely knit unit, as cohesive as the Musketeers.* Mother Margaret, known to everyone—including her daughters—as "Peg," raised her brood, sent them to Public School 9 and to Brooklyn's Erasmus High School. Peg prodded Norma into pursuing a career in the new medium of moving pictures at Brooklyn's Vitagraph Studio. There the photogenic, lovely young girl became a member of the stock company and was soon playing leads.

Norma's filmmaking career fascinated Constance. But basking in her sister's reflected glory did not appease her desire to be part of what she thought the funniest place in the world, a movie studio. Throughout her career she would retain the concept that "screen actors are the funniest people in the world. I adore them!"

Vitagraph director Ralph Ince, having seen Constance's impromptu, expert impersonation of the studio's comedienne Flora Finch, arranged for her to work as a $5-a-day extra. Within a short time she was playing bits in Vitagraph comedies with Paul Kelly (*Buddy's First Call* and *Buddy's Downfall*) and opposite Billy Quirk (*The Maid from Sweden, Our Fairy Play,* and *Father's Timepiece*). She essayed serious roles opposite her movie idol Maurice Costello in *The Moonstone of Fez* and *The Mysterious Lodger.* With Flora Finch she was in *Fixing Their Dads* and had a pivotal role in sister Norma's *The Peacemaker* (1914).

Peg Talmadge approached life with a good deal of zest, astute business sense, and earthy realism. In Peg, Anita Loos found the

germination of many of the wise and witty lines for *Gentlemen Prefer Blondes.* If Peg inspired Miss Loos' character of wisecracking Dorothy, the prototype of blonde Lorelei Lee was not fun-loving, anything but man-chasing Constance.

"Dutch," with her casual, happy air about everything (hiding professionalism and devotion behind a mask of laughter), was blasé on the subject of l'amour. By October 1923 *Photoplay* magazine would be calling her "The Most Engaged Girl in the World," and with good reason. Her legion of suitors included: Richard Barthelmess, Jack Pickford, Kenneth Harlan, singer John Charles Thomas, socialite millionaire William Rhinelander Stewart Jr., movie director Robert G. Vignola, and author Michael Arlen. Another of her many suitors, songwriter Irving Berlin, dubbed her "A Virtuous Vamp," a title Anita Loos would use for the first screenplay she would write for Constance.

Irving Thalberg was greatly enamored of Constance and wanted to marry her. But his mother, Henrietta, deemed the candidate too flighty for a brilliant, rising movie mogul. Actor Buster Collier amorously basked in Constance's shimmering shadow for several years. Dorothy Gish would recall, "Constance was always getting engaged—but never to less than two men at the same time." Miss Talmadge would eventually marry four times, but not to *any* of her most publicized ardent admirers or to anyone within her chosen profession.

On August 2, 1915, the Talmadge clan embarked for California, where Peg had secured contracts for Norma and Constance with a new studio, National Film Corporation. Constance played a bit in Norma's *Captivating Mary Carstairs* (1915) and had leads in two-reel comedies opposite "Smiling Billy" Parsons in *Beached and Bleached, You Can't Beat It,* and *The Little Puritan.*

D. W. Griffith rescued the sisters from the floundering National studio and signed them for his Fine Arts-Triangle productions. In Griffith's scenario, written under his pseudonym of Granville Warwick and directed by Lloyd Ingraham, they appeared in Triangle's *The Missing Links* (1915). When Griffith was casting his masterpiece, "a sun play of the ages," he realized there was more than superficial clowning in Constance's playing. For

* When his daughters were little more than babes in arms, Frederick Talmadge left home one evening to visit a local saloon and never returned. He followed a career of drifting from odd jobs to cheap bars. Years later, when Norma and Constance had acquired fame and considerable fortune, the family discovered him on a bench in Central Park. Peg had their chauffeur stop their Cadillac and said to the daughters, "If you girls care to know who that tramp is, he's your father."

Constance, who stood in awe of no one and whose natural charm and nonchalance were equally distributed, bounded from the car. She said, "Hello, Fred, how'd you like to meet your family?" With equal insouciance, Fred accepted his rediscovered family's largess. But odd jobs at the studio had less inspiration for him than the Third Avenue saloons, to which he retired only to emerge for his weekly payroll check. When the Talmadge female clan relocated to California, Fred (still unimpressed with their ambience) went West, where he died in 1925.

the most spectacular of the four interwoven episodic stories, *The Fall of Babylon*, he cast Constance in the star-making role of the Mountain Girl in *Intolerance* (1916).* She proved to be superb as the rough, onion-eating, rambunctious Mountain Girl who loves Prince Belshazzar (Alfred Page) and who drives a chariot to warn her beloved ruler of impending massacre. In the story line she dies during the siege of the city.

Peg Talmadge recalled that during the filming of *Intolerance* Constance was "determined and tireless. She worked hard to project Griffith's conception of the Mountain Girl, learning to drive a chariot and manage the horses until she was black and blue with bruises that sister Natalie nightly rubbed with oils."

Nothing intimidated Connie. Griffith always held Constance's unique and malleable talents in high regard and, with Clarine Seymour, she became one of his two favorite actresses (despite his appreciation of the talented Lillian Gish). Peg probably best summed up much of Griffith's admiration of Constance:

> Part of Constance's value to Mr. Griffith lay in the fact that she amused him, just as she had amused Mr. Ince and the others back in the Vitagraph days. She made him laugh largely because of her absolute disregard of his importance, in contrast to the awe and respect and head-bowing accorded him by all the others.

Griffith frequently sent for Constance just to make him laugh with her stock greeting, "Well, here I am. Your Majesty may begin at once!" And the great director was tolerant when she lost the padding placed in her ragged, homespun fabric Mountain Girl costume designed to compensate for a noticeable lack of voluptuousness. At the time he told her, "If you please, Miss Constance, half of your figure is missing again. Do you think I want a lopsided heroine?"*

During the Griffith days, Constance and impish Dorothy Gish became close, kindred companions. Their friendship endured with a mutual declaration that if they ever married, it would be a double-wedding ceremony to bolster each other's courage. On Sunday afternoon, December 26, 1920, they maintained their vow when Connie wed handsome Greek tobacco importer, John T. Pialoglou of New York City, and Dorothy married actor James Rennie. In less than a year marriage had paled for Constance and in 1922 she and Norma were touring the continent of Europe. Abroad she was presented to the Duke of York at London's Marble Arch Theatre and was received by Colonel Harvey at the American embassy. In Paris she met British army captain Alastair William MacIntosh of the Seaforth Highlanders. He was a personal friend of the Prince of Wales. In June 1923 Constance divorced Pialoglou and resumed her pursuit of laughter.

Actually it was Norma's fortuitous marriage in October 1916 to powerful movie magnate Joseph M. Schenck that became the turning point in the fortunes of the Talmadge family. Schenck's sponsorship never wavered and he soon established Norma in her own studio at 318 East 48th Street in New York City and the Constance Talmadge Film Company at 332 East 48th Street. With Schenck's astute guidance, the sisters retained stardom throughout the Twenties and amassed large fortunes. Schenck arranged to have their pictures released by Lewis J. Selznick's Select Pictures.

Constance's first Selznick-Select film, *The Lesson* (1917), was withheld until a better made comedy, *Scandal* (1917), went into release. The latter film, which proclaimed to the public, "You will be for her from the very first reel," was found to be a light and frothy comedy that delicately skirted risqué situations. Constance's acting was compared to that of Madge Kennedy, a far better actress who never gained the public adulation of the Talmadges.

---

* In 1919 this segment of *Intolerance* was reissued with a refilmed happy ending in which the Mountain Girl and the Rhapsode are reunited. *Variety* found that her star-making performance in the reissue was still the finest thing she had done on screen and that "she has never exceeded that performance." (Certainly none of her comedy parts in which she starred had the depth or scope or magnitude of the Griffith classic. But it was in these typecast assignments that she made her cinema fame.)

* Constance also played Marguerite de Valois in the French episode of *Intolerance*. In this segment she was billed as Georgia Pearce. While at Triangle she was also Douglas Fairbanks' leading lady in *The Matrimaniac* (1916).

With Alfred Paget in Intolerance *(1916).*

Several of Constance's Selznick releases were screen adaptations of successful Broadway marital comedies in which she registered effectively. Billie Burke's 1911 hit *The Runaway* became Connie's *The Studio Girl* (1918). She was seen on the screen in the stage roles of Margaret Illington in *Mrs. Leffingwell's Boots* (1918), of Grace George in *Sauce for the Goose* (1918), and of Laura Hope Crews in *Romance and Arabella* (1919). From 1918's *Goodnight Paul* to her final Selznick release, *Happiness a-la-Mode* (July 1919), Harrison Ford was her leading man in 10 consecutive pictures. If the Select comedies did little toward advancing comedy as screen art, they were entertaining and popular with the public.

After severing the Select association, Joseph Schenck completed negotiations with Associated First National to release the Talmadge sisters' pictures. He also arranged with writer/actor/director John Emerson and his wife, Anita Loos, to take on Constance's film projects. Presenting his proposition to

Emerson, Schenck said, "I'd like to turn Dutch over to you and have Anita do the same thing for her that she did for Doug Fairbanks; write her into some films that will satisfy Peg and get that woman off my neck!" The Emersons met the challenge by turning out well-constructed scenarios measured to Constance's irrepressible natural comedy.

The first Loos-Emerson script, *A Temperamental Wife* (1919), was credited as an adaptation of Jane Cowl and Jane Murfin's Broadway play *Information Please* and was well received. Although several of their scenarios for Dutch were originals, others were adaptations of tested Broadway comedies. Clyde Fitch's *The Bachelor* became *A Virtuous Vamp* (1919); *The Man from Toronto* was retitled *Lessons in Love* (1921); whereas *Mamma's Affair* (1921) and *Wedding Bells* (1921) reached the screen under their original identification.

The combination of Dutch, Loos, and Emerson produced financial rewards at the box office and Schenck, appreciative of what he deemed a "gold mine," gave the writers a $50,000 bonus. Critics delighted in Constance's radiant clowning and found her performance as a chorus girl in the Loos-Emerson adaptation of the play *At the Barn*—called *Two Weeks* (1920) on the screen—brightly amusing. The reviewers noted that she was more than simply Norma's sister and that she had a definite talent for amusing pantomime. Her playing of the innocent coquette in *In Search of a Sinner* (1920) was applauded and there was general rejoicing for her *Polly of the Follies* (1922).

Mother Peg probably pinpointed Constance's wide appeal as well as any critic: "It has always been my fond private thought that the very zest of life which is so wholeheartedly Constance is a great part of her charm and the best reason for her magnetism. One feels that love of life in all her pictures." Public acceptance of the Talmadge sisters was reflected in the 1921 National Exhibitors Poll when Norma was voted the top female star of the year and Constance placed second.

There were occasional misses for Constance. In 1922 the *New York Times* tagged Frances Marion's screen adaptation of *The Divorcee*—retitled *The Primitive Lover*—"dull and witless and a waste of Constance Talmadge's talent for bright comedy." On the other hand, when Frances Marion wrote the screenplay to the hit Broadway comedy *East Is West* (1922), it became one of Constance's greatest hits. *Motion Picture World* reported, "*East Is West* in film form should equal if not exceed the stage version in popularity. Frances Marion's scenario, Sidney Franklin's direction, an extraordinarily fine performance by Constance Talmadge—a delight as Ming Toy, realizing every possibility, latent or obvious, that the unusually rich role contains. For sheer sparkle she exceeds anything she has done before in comedy or dramatic work, and a large percentage of the picture's wide appeal is derived from her winsome personality and the manner in which she draws the character of the indomitable little Chinese girl who finally turns out to be an

In In Search of a Sinner (1920).

615

The star.

American. Superb performance from Warner Oland as Charlie Yong."

The *Washington Post* headed its review of this film with, "A New Constance Talmadge Revealed to Packed Houses," and wrote, "Constance Talmadge has brought many interesting character studies to the screen, ranging from a cleverly burlesqued Cleopatra to the most deadly type of a modern flapper, but never has she done anything to approach her portrayal of Ming Toy, the Americo-Chinese central figure in the elaborate picturization of *East Is West*." Throughout this period of success, Constance remained modest and was telling eager listeners, "Some day people will wake up to what a joke I am."

George S. Kaufman and Marc Connelly's lively comedy *Dulcy* opened on Broadway in 1921 and was saved by Lynn Fontanne's stunning performance. Anita Loos and John Emerson adapted the play as a screen vehicle for Constance, casting Dutch as the amiable dumbbell who nearly wrecks her husband's career. The *New York Times* found her "most

adorable. In place of the beautiful nitwit, however, audiences saw a delightful and charming actress bring the full perfections of her talents to a most ungrateful part." (Marion Davies, who was Constance's lifetime close friend and whom she nicknamed "Daisy," made *Dulcy* as a 1930 MGM talkie called *Not So Dumb*; Ann Sothern had the lead in Metro's 1940 re-remake.)

Constance's last 1923 release was a turgid affair set in 17th-century England. In *The Dangerous Maid* she was unable to overcome the labored story and the best she could do was to be sweet and sympathetic. Constance was not delighted with the picture and declared, "I am through with costume pictures forever! Hereafter I am going to stick to American roles, American wardrobes and American fun, and the more American they are, the better. There is enough laughter around us to fill a hundred films, so why go abroad or delve into the days when knights were bold and ladies wore hoopskirts?" About her fencing scenes in the picture she

616

said, "I can make more conquests with the flash of an eye or a long worked-over dimple than I can with a sword. It took me six weeks to learn how to fence for six seconds in *The Dangerous Maid*. In that same six weeks I could have knocked several of 'em cold without resorting to steel if I had been playing in a modern picture." She conceded that sister Norma, Mary Pickford, and her friend Marion Davies could get away beautifully with powdered hair, flouncy costumes, and swashbuckling lovers. But she was not the type.

By 1924 both Norma and Constance were filming an average of two pictures a year. *The Goldfish*, a play in which Marjorie Rambeau had starred on Broadway, was Constance's first 1924 entry, and was dismissed by the *New York Times* as "refreshing and quickly forgotten other than for Constance Talmadge's clever playing and charm." Unbilled, both Talmadge sisters did cameo roles of would-be vamps trying for the star part in a movie in *In Hollywood with Potash and Perlmutter*. In the story, Betty Blythe won the part. As Constance's final offering of the year she co-starred with Ronald Colman in *Her Night of Romance*. She played heiress Dorothy Adams disguised as an old maid and Colman was an impoverished nobleman. Miss Talmadge was cited for appearing "gay and charming, affectionate and coy, always making the most of her expressive eyes."

The last script written for Constance by Anita Loos and John Emerson was *Learning to Love* (1925), with Constance, again, as a flirt fatale, this time teamed with Antonio Moreno. *Photoplay* appraised, "Constance Talmadge, in her unique manner, endeavors to show modern girls the various ways to capture a husband, and, as a result, we have a comedy that is filled with screamingly funny situations."

Her Sister from Paris (1925) became one of Constance's best films, a showcase for her comedic talents and knack of wearing stunning clothes (designed by Adrian). *Photoplay* selected the film as one of the best of the month and Constance's performance as one of the six best. Here she played a dual part, that of a dull wife posing as her volatile, sexy, and dashing sister. Ronald Colman was again her leading man and won praise for his smooth handling of comedy. (So popular was the story line that Hollywood would use it at least twice again: in 1934's *Moulin Rouge* with Constance Bennett and in 1941's deplorable *Two-Faced Woman* with Greta Garbo.)

On February 27, 1926, Constance married Captain Alastair William MacIntosh (the Seaforth Highlander she had met in Paris in 1922) in a civil ceremony at the home of Jean de St. Cyr in San Mateo, California. One of her innumerable former swains, William Rhinelander Stewart Jr., was best man, sister Norma was her bridesmaid, and Natalie and Buster Keaton (who had married Natalie in 1921) were in attendance. The MacIntoshes moved to London and Constance announced she was giving up her career. Plans to star her in a comedy, *Silky Ann*, and a Graustarkian adventure entitled *East of the Setting Sun* were abandoned. But Constance soon found the highly social life of London boring. By mid-summer 1927 she had announced plans for a divorce, charging desertion. In August when she left for Paris she told reporters, "I might get a divorce, if I find time."

By September she had found time to file for divorce at the Edinburgh, Scotland, Court of Session, charging her husband with misconduct during a fling in June at Brighton. While she was shedding MacIntosh, her only 1926 picture, *The Duchess of Buffalo*, was wobbling along at the box office. Neither her performance nor that of rather wooden Tullio Carminati helped matters. The following year her interpretation of an Italian thief, Carlotta, who swims the canal in *Venus of Venice*, was rated competent. *Breakfast at Sunrise* (1927) allowed Constance to parade a sumptuous wardrobe and was helped by Marie Dressler's portrayal of the queen, but little more.

Joseph Schenck again guided the Talmadge sisters into a new film deal, this time with United Artists. The last four pictures of Norma's career were United Artists releases. Plans for Constance included a comedy treatment of Madame Pompadour, but Dorothy Gish's successful English film, *Madame Pompadour* (1927), precluded Constance's excursion into the French court. Schenck then hired F. Scott Fitzgerald to write a story groomed to Constance's talents with a collegiate background. Fitzgerald's marathon drinking bouts canceled the proposed *Lipstick*.

With Ronald Colman in Her Sister from Paris *(1925).*

With Antonio Moreno in Venus of Venice *(1926).*

618

In Venus (1929).

The ogre of sound and the new demon of the "talkies" hovered over both Talmadges. Constance removed herself from the sound revolution to make a picture on the French Rivera. It was a trifle called *Venus*. It would be her last picture and her only United Artists release. It was withheld from distribution until 1929 and by then the screen was babbling its head off and silents were doomed. Constance announced she would never make another picture and she kept her word. On May 8, 1929, she married for the third time.

The Reverend James Lash of the Hollywood Congregational Church married Constance to Chicago sportsman Townsend Netcher at the home of Buster Keaton. Sisters Norma and Natalie went through their roles as attendants. The Netchers moved into an ocean-front home at Santa Monica, a residence the bridegroom had built for them. The marriage was beset with separations and recriminations; it ended in divorce. Anita Loos summarized it: "Dutch took as her third hus-

band a Chicago playboy and millionaire whose first and last claim to fame was that he had annexed Dutch, just as his brother had earned headlines for having married one of the playful Dolly sisters. Dutch enjoyed her husband's way of life until his persistent jealousy began to spoil her fun and she once more sought relief in divorce."

Constance was one of Hollywood's most wealthy women, her status having resulted from her own earnings (thanks to Schenck's business acumen) and the fortunes inherited from others. In 1939 she wed her fourth and last husband, Walter Michael Giblin, a New York City stock exchange broker who was then vice president of Blyth & Co. During World War II while Giblin served overseas with the OSS, Constance spent the war years as a practical nurse in New York City hospitals.

At no time did she contemplate returning to the screen and was appalled when reporters would ask if she planned a "comeback." The marriage with Giblin endured through the early Sixties, with the couple making their home at the Carlton House on Madison Avenue in Manhattan. On May 1, 1964, Walter Giblin, age 62, died at St. Luke's Hospital. Nine years later, on Friday, November 23, 1973, Constance died at a Los Angeles hospital at the age of 74.*

* Peg Talmadge had died in the mid-Fifties; Norma had died December 24, 1957; and Natalie had died June 19, 1969.

FEATURE FILMS

Captivating Mary Carstairs (*National Film Corporation 1915*)
The Missing Links (*Triangle 1915*)
The She-Devil (*Mutual-Reliance 1916*)
The Matrimaniac (*Triangle 1916*)
Intolerance (*D. W. Griffith 1916*)
The Microscope Mystery (*Triangle 1916*)
The Girl of the Timberclaims (*Triangle 1917*)
Betsy's Burglar (*Triangle 1917*)
Scandal (*Select 1917*)
The Lesson (*Select 1917*)
The Honeymoon (*Select 1917*)
The Shuttle (*Select 1918*)
The Studio Girl (*Select 1918*)
Up the Road with Sally (*Select 1918*)
Goodnight Paul (*Select 1918*)
A Pair of Silk Stockings (*Select 1918*)
Sauce for the Goose (*Select 1918*)
Mrs. Leffingwell's Boots (*Select 1918*)
A Lady's Name (*Select 1918*)
Who Cares? (*Select 1919*)
Romance and Arabella (*Select 1919*)
Experimental Marriage (*Select 1919*)
The Veiled Adventure (*Select 1919*)
Happiness a-la-Mode (*Select 1919*)
The Fall of Babylon (*Griffith 1919*)
A Temperamental Wife (*Associated First National 1919*)
A Virtuous Vamp (*Associated First National 1919*)
Two Weeks (*Associated First National 1920*)
In Search of a Sinner (*Associated First National 1920*)
The Perfect Woman (*Associated First National 1920*)

The Love Expert (*Associated First National 1920*)
A Good Reference (*Associated First National 1920*)
Mamma's Affair (*Associated First National 1921*)
Lessons in Love (*Associated First National 1921*)
A Dangerous Business (*Associated First National 1921*)
Wedding Bells (*Associated First National 1921*)
Woman's Place (*Associated First National 1922*)
Polly of the Follies (*Associated First National 1922*)
The Primitive Lover (*Associated First National 1922*)
East Is West (*Associated First National 1922*)
Dulcy (*Associated First National 1923*)
The Dangerous Maid (*Associated First National 1923*)
The Goldfish (*Associated First National 1924*)
In Hollywood with Potash and Perlmutter (*Associated First National 1924*)
Her Night of Romance (*Associated First National 1924*)
Learning to Love (*First National 1925*)
Her Sister from Paris (*First National 1925*)
The Duchess of Buffalo (*First National 1926*)
Venus of Venice (*First National 1927*)
Breakfast at Sunrise (*First National 1927*)
Venus (*United Artists-French 1929*)

The Three Stooges

The medium of television has performed many miraculous tasks. But few have been as awesomely dramatic as its resurrection of a worn, weathered comedy team known as the Three Stooges. They were transported from limbo in 1958 to the limelight in 1959.

In 1958 Moe Howard, Buster Brown-coiffured bossman of the Stooges, and Larry Fine, wild-haired flunky, had split up to seek professional employment as solos. Both Curly and Shemp Howard were dead. Joe Besser's short-lived tenure as the third Stooge had fizzled. Columbia Pictures, home base for the Stooges for over two decades, had put the slapstick specialists out to pasture. The team's style of raucous, rough-neck shenanigans* seemed fatally passé.

Then in 1958 Screen Gems, the television branch of Columbia Pictures, acquired the rights to 78 Three Stooges short subjects. Placed into distribution, the Stooges became a favorite with new generations of viewers. Soon the surviving members (plus the new third member, Joe DeRita) were enjoying the greatest celebrity status of their 30 years of performing. Nightclubs, television spots, and feature films suddenly became available to the Stooges. A whole new generation was able to view and laugh at the sometimes controversially rough physical humor of the comics. (The United States once refused to rent Three Stooges shorts to the USSR when it was learned that the Soviets intended to play up the gouged eyes and plucked noses as examples of basic American barbarianism.)

The Three Stooges' method of mayhem was certainly not for everyone. But they were dedicated, hard-working clowns who practiced the ancient comedy of the physical in the forums of vaudeville, Broadway shows, and motion pictures. Although devotees of sophistication have reveled in smart-cracking critiques of the comedians' work, there is no denying the cheers of the children who loved their visual scampering or the guffaws of adults who surrendered willingly and laughed at their childish antics.

---

* *Films in Review*, in a retrospective on the Stooges, described their humor as "a minimum of plot and character, a maximum of fast action and sight gags; no sex, no thinking, no complexity, no logic; [and the ability to] turn every situation into a laugh."

Larry, Moe, and Joe DeRita in The Three Stooges Go Around the World in a Daze (1963).

The history of the Stooges begins really with the birth of Moe Howard (born Moses Harry Horwitz) in Brooklyn, New York, on Saturday, June 19, 1897 (1905 was the usual year listed in publicity handouts, but Moe validated his real age in a 1973 interview on the Mike Douglas TV program). There were three other brothers: Irving (born 1892), Shemp (born 1895)—actually named Samuel, and Jerome (born 1903)—later known as Curly. Their parents were Solomon Horwitz, a clothes cutter, and Jennie Horwitz, who later tried her skill at real estate.

School (P.S. 101 at Bath Beach) did not particularly engage the interest of Moe. In the spring of 1909 he jaunted over to the Vitagraph Studio on East 16th Street in Brooklyn where he earned his entree into filmmaking by running errands "for no tips" for such performers as Maurice Costello. It soon led to small screen roles for the youngster, playing with the likes of Costello, John Bunny and Flora Finch, Herbert Rawlinson, and Earle Williams.

In the summer of 1909 Moe first met Charles Ernest Lee Nash (born October 1, 1896, in Houston, Texas) who would become better known as Ted Healy. Moe and Healy would become good friends and together in mid-1912 they joined Annette Kellerman's aquatic act as swimming girls (!). This job lasted for a season.

Always adventuresome, Moe escaped the confines of Brooklyn tenement life in March 1914 when he ran away to join a performing troupe on the "Sunflower," a Mississippi riverboat. There he quickly learned the exaggerated technique of melodramatics. By the end of his second season with the troupe he was earning $100 weekly.

After the riverboat trek, Moe associated with various touring stock companies, during which period he was frequently involved in Shakespearean productions. Meanwhile, younger brother Shemp was reaching maturity. The two brothers formed a blackfaced vaudeville act which disbanded briefly when Shemp was drafted into the army during World War I. He was discharged after only a few months of duty (the military discovered he was a bedwetter) and he rejoined Moe in vaudeville.

It was during this period that the boys' parents acquired a 116-acre farm in Chatham, New York, where the sons would spend a good deal of time helping with farm chores. In 1917 Shemp and Moe played their comedy act on both the Loew's and RKO circuits, managing to be retained by the rival outfits through a ruse: they played a black-faced routine for RKO and a whitefaced one for Loew's. The Howards would continue in the stage medium through 1922 learning a great deal from the assorted buffoons with whom they shared bills.

The winter of 1922 found Moe renewing acquaintanceship with Ted Healy, whom he had not seen in nearly a decade. At this point Healy was successfully performing on the vaudeville circuit with his wife Betty and their dog Pete. Healy hired Moe and Shemp on a temporary basis to back up his comedy package. They got along so well on stage that the partnership solidified and they remained together—with some breaks—for almost ten years. (Since Healy produced his traveling vaudeville unit and he had the "name," he demanded and received the lion's share of the group's weekly salary.) At one point in their touring the troupe was billed as Ted Healy and His Southern Gentlemen.

In 1928* the act, which was known as Ted Healy and His Racketeers and sometimes as Ted Healy and His Stooges, acquired the talents of Larry Fine.** The latter was born on Saturday, October 4, 1902, in Philadelphia, the son of Joseph and Fannie Feinberg. Larry had toured extensively in the act Haney Sisters and Fine. In that group Larry clowned and played the violin; off stage he wed one of the Haney girls (Mabel) in 1927 and they had a daughter Phyliss.

Healy and his revamped Stooges act played the plusher vaudeville establish-

* In 1925 Moe married Helen Schonberger, a cousin of Harry Houdini; and that same year Shemp wed Gertrude Frank (nicknamed Babe), the daughter of a Bensonhurst, Brooklyn, builder. Moe and Helen became the parents of Joan (1928) and Paul (1935).

** Before Larry Fine joined the Healy-Stooges menagerie, there was an original third stooge. Kenneth Lackey had worked briefly with Healy in vaudeville before being added to the partnership of Moe and Shemp and Healy. Two years later he quit the team to join Earl Carroll's Vanities. After several years he returned to his home in Indiana, where he served as a district court clerk. He eventually retired to Columbus, North Carolina. There he became president and producer of the Tryon Little Theatre. He died in Columbus on April 16, 1976, after a lengthy ailment.

ments and then frolicked on Broadway in the Shubert Brothers' *A Night in Venice* (Shubert Theater, May 21, 1929) after tryout engagements in New Haven, Atlantic City, and Akron.* The expansive revue, with 25 skit scenes, was directed and choreographed by Busby Berkeley and provided Ted Healy (especially) and the Stooges with an ample theatrical showcase. The *New York Times* reported of Healy's clowning trio that they were "three of the frowziest numbskulls ever assembled." The show lasted 175 performances and then went on tour. When the Depression closed the road engagement, Healy and the gang returned to the vaudeville circuit, opening at Loew's Capitol in Washington, D.C.

In 1930 Healy and the Stooges attracted Hollywood interest. Heeding a job call from the Fox Film Corporation, the team went west to play in the 65-minute feature *Soup to Nuts* (1930). They were billed as Ted Healy and His Racketeers. (There was a fourth Racketeer, comic Fred Sanborn.) The movie utilized the comedians as part-time firemen who aid Healy in crashing a highbrow affair. While the feature was not remarkable in any way, it did lead Fox to offer the team members seven-year contracts. However, the pending deal was suddenly cancelled. Only later did the Stooges learn that Healy—always thinking of his own interests—had tried to dissuade Fox from hiring the Stooges along with him. The annoyed executive committee instead hired none of the group. (For *Soup to Nuts* Healy had been paid $1250 weekly, while each of the Stooges earned only $100 apiece for each of the five weeks of shooting.)

This uneasy situation led to a temporary split between Healy and the Stooges. The latter, booking themselves under the act name of Howard, Fine, and Howard—Three Lost Souls, performed on the West Coast and worked their way back to New York. In 1931 the Stooges hired straight man Jack Walsh to become part of their act. Meanwhile Healy had revamped his stage turn to include three new knockabout comics, none of whom equalled the Stooges in any professional way. At a career low ebb and drinking far

more than usual, Healy continued his machinations to ruin his former partners' professional standing (e.g. trying to woo one or another of the trio away from the act; making it difficult for the boys to utilize sketch material from past seasons, etc.). Finally in 1932 Healy and some of the Stooges made peace. Shemp would have *no* part of a reunion with Healy and decided to strike out on his own.*

Thus Moe recruited his brother Jerry—known professionally as Curly (making a joke out of his deliberately shaved head)—to join the act.** After a tour of major vaudeville houses, Metro-Goldwyn-Mayer employed Healy and the Stooges both in tandem and separately. Their first joint released effort at MGM was *Meet the Baron* (1932) in which the comic task force aided an array of established screen funsters: Jimmy Durante, ZaSu Pitts, and Edna May Oliver. They supported Lee Tracy and Mae Clarke in *Turn Back the Clock* (1933), and then provided comedy relief in the very classy *Dancing Lady* (1933), an MGM blockbuster starring Joan Crawford (singing and dancing), Clark Gable, Franchot Tone, Nelson Eddy, Robert Benchley, and a new cinema face, Fred Astaire. The major production featured the Stooges as musicians—terrible musicians—whom mischievous Broadway director Gable employs to destroy Crawford's singing audition.

Metro used the Stooges with Healy in *Fugitive Lovers* (1934), the Robert Montgomery-Madge Evans predecessor to *It Happened One Night*, and then spotted them in the abortive hodgepodge, *Hollywood Party* (1934), along with Jimmy Durante, Laurel and Hardy, Charles Butterworth, Polly Moran, Lupe Velez, Mickey Mouse, et al. During these two years, the Stooges and

* In 1927 Healy and Shemp, along with Betty Healy, Phil Baker, Sid Silvers, Helen Kane, and others, appeared in the Shubert Brothers' Broadway revue *A Night in Spain.*

* After assorted vaudeville work and making short subjects, Shemp Howard settled in Hollywood in the late Thirties. He found a nice berth at Universal City where he appeared as a solid foil for a number of established comedians. He played the bartender of "The Black Pussy" in W. C. Fields' *The Bank Dick* (1940), worked with Olsen and Johnson in *Hellzapoppin* (1941), and performed in a number of Abbott and Costello outings, including *Buck Privates* (1941), *In the Navy* (1941), *Hold That Ghost* (1941), *It Ain't Hay* (1943), and *Africa Screams* (1949). Sometimes Shemp appeared in "straight" films, such as Universal's *Pittsburgh* (1943), starring Marlene Dietrich, Randolph Scott, and John Wayne.

** Over the years Curly would marry and divorce four times, and have two children.

624

Curly Howard. Moe Howard. Joan Crawford. Ted Healy. and Larry Fine in Dancing Lady *(1933).*

Healy would appear in a quartet of two-reel musical shorts: *Beer and Pretzels* (1933), *Hello Pop* (1933), *Plane Nuts* (1933), and *The Big Idea* (1934).

According to Moe Howard's posthumously published book, *Moe Howard and The Three Stooges* (1977), it was in May 1934 that the final confrontation with Healy occurred. Howard said to Healy who had been featured in several films *without* the Stooges, "Ted, I saw your latest film, *Death on the Diamond* [1934] . . . and at least four times during the picture you extended your arms as if you were pushing us back. You always did that when we worked with you as Stooges. Only this time we weren't there and it made you look very awkward. . . . In all honesty, Ted, you really don't need us any longer. You're doing great on your own. Let's sign a paper right here stating that, as of this date, we will go our separate ways." Healy and his agent agreed and the act was split apart.*

* Healy continued to make pictures and appear in vaudeville through 1937 when he died on December 20 as a result of a brain concussion suffered in a brawl with three nightclub patrons.

What happened next could only occur in the Hollywood of the Thirties, when competition, confusion, and productivity were at their peak. According to Moe, he was stopped one day by Walter Kane, a young agent, who announced he could get the Stooges a Columbia contract. Moe was soon being ushered in to meet the studio chief, Harry Cohn, and his production head, Sam Briskin. Cohn offered the trio a one-picture deal; if the two-reel comedy was successful, a long term contract would be signed. The boys would be paid $1500 for the first short. Meanwhile Larry was approached by Joe Rivkin, another young agent, who took him to Universal where Carl Laemmle Jr. signed the trio to a term contract. When the three performers met later that day and discovered their dual deal, it was decided that whichever contract was signed earlier would be honored. Thus Columbia won the Three Stooges.

The trial short for Columbia was *Woman Haters*, made in late June 1934. (Walter Brennan had a bit as a train conductor in the film.) It was a musical, accomplished in rhymes, with Archie Gottler serving as scripter and director. Moe, Curly, and Larry appeared in the film in separate roles, not as a team. The Columbia agreement had provided a 60-day waiting period before the studio decided if it wished to exercise its option on the Stooges. However, when Moe promptly scripted a story, *Punch Drunks*, it so pleased Columbia executive Ben Kahane that he in turn talked with Cohn and Briskin and soon the trio had signed the Columbia pact ahead of schedule. While the deal gave television and other media use of the Stooges' voices and likeness to Columbia (which precluded royalties for later TV showings of the Stooges' short subjects), the contract provided that the boys would make eight two-reel comedies in a 40-week period, with 12 weeks off (which could be used for any sort of work except in the cinema field) at a salary of $60,000 a year. Any income derived from the 12-week layoff time belonged to the actors. It was the start of a three-decade tenure at Columbia, during which time the group made 191 shorts for the studio and appeared in several features, the first being *The Captain Hates the Sea* (1934), with John Gilbert, Alison Skipworth, Leon Errol, Victor McLaglen, Akim Tamiroff, Donald Meek, and many others.

A follow-up to the very successful *Woman Haters* was *Men in Black* (1934), a satirical short poking fun at MGM's then popular drama of the medical profession, *Men in White*. It proved a powerhouse as a "curtain raiser" and was nominated for an Academy Award as the Best Short Subject of 1934. (Despite the popularity of the team over the years—they were the top two-reel money-makers for several years in the early Fifties—Columbia craftily convinced the comedians that they were doing the players a favor keeping them on the payroll, managing almost every time option renewals came up to bargain down the salary increases requested by the boys.)

As Moe would evaluate later of their comedy style, "People want to laugh with their mouths, not their minds. Audiences want belly laughs. Rarely will a subtle line or a cute phrase get them into a laughing jag. It takes the old pratfall, a pie in the face, a good chase, or a bop on the casaba to keep a laugh going. That's what we give 'em." Indeed they did: Moe, the bullying "brains" of the madcap group; Larry, the hopelessly nurdy man-in-the-middle; and the quite incredible Curly, with his amazing repertoire of wildly mugging rubber faces and a collection of hysterical wheezes, growls, screams, and coos. Soon the trio became entrenched in Depression-bound America as filmdom's most raucously slapstick comedians.

If the Stooges' celluloid product appeared totally unrehearsed and inorganic, it was not. Like all the major comic talents of the Thirties, the Stooges were actually strict disciplinarians who fully thought out their routines before performing on camera. In another interview, spokesman Moe explained that the group worked in the areas of "deflation and sound." As he viewed it, "When we hit an elegant lady in the squash with a pie, it deflates her. We're called 'sight' comics, but we're also 'sound' comics. When I belted Curly with a mallet, you heard a cringing, bell-like sound. And when Larry runs a comb through his hair, you hear a crackling sound, like someone had exposed a live wire."*

Although the Stooges proved to be immensely popular in many circles—much preferred to the screen antics of Wheeler and Woolsey and that ilk—there were often adamant cries that their brand of comedy was too childish, silly, and overly brutal. In 1937 the *Motion Picture Herald* observed that movie audiences are "to be divided roughly into two groups, one composed of persons who laugh at the Three Stooges, and the other made up of those who wonder why."

Off the Columbia soundstages, the Stooges made many lucrative personal appearance tours. A favorite routine for their new theatre act was their singing of "She Was Bred in Old Kentucky, but She's Just a Crumb up Here." A highlight of their annual forays into stage mayhem was a mid-1939 trek to Europe. Their two week engagement at the London Palladium was extended; thereafter they met with equal success in their appearances in Blackpool, Dublin, and Glasgow. When they returned to the United States they went into rehearsal for *George White's Scandals*, which tried out in Atlantic City and opened

---

* Strangely, while the word *slapstick* comes immediately to mind in reference to the Stooges' comedy work, Moe never accepted that term as a definition of their work: "Actually, we are farcical comedians. Slapstick belongs to the world of the circus, portrayed by the wonderful circus clowns."

in New York at the Alvin Theatre on August 28, 1939, for 120 performances. The cast included Willie and Eugene Howard, Ella Logan, Ben Blue, and a young tap dancer named Ann Miller. One of her two specialty numbers, "Mexicongo," was a nightly show-stopper. As for the Stooges, a highlight of their on-stage shenanigans was "The Stand-In," a sketch written by Matty Brooks and Eddie Davis, in which there was a very messy pie-throwing sequence. Reported Burns Mantle (Robert Coleman) (*New York Daily Mirror*), ". . . [The Stooges] come through with flying colors and faces dripping with gooseberry pies. . . . They lured laughter from the first nighters like a wringer does water from a damp shirt."

Thereafter the boys returned to Columbia where their shorts continued to be filmed at an approximate cost of $27,000, with each entry usually lasting 18 minutes of screen time. The studio would occasionally cast them in a feature film as dragged-in comedy relief: in *Start Cheering* (1938) they had supported Jimmy Durante and Walter Connolly; in the low-budget *Time Out for Rhythm* (1941) they aided stars Rudy Vallee and Ann Miller; and in the high-caliber *My Sister Eileen* (1942) they bolstered Rosalind Russell, Brian Aherne, and Janet Blair. But the trio remained principally short-subject luminaries.

Several directors steered the Stooges on screen: Del Lord, Preston Black, Charlie Chase, Jules White, and Edward Bernds. By the time Bernds took over control in the mid-Forties, the quality of the Stooges' output was very standard, and sometimes not even of that caliber. In Leonard Maltin's *Great Movie Shorts* (1972), Bernds is quoted as saying, "We'd usually have a kind of bull session in which the boys would wander all over the place, ad-libbing routines, reminiscing, and I would make notes. I would borrow from old scripts too, but mostly I listened. I would stockpile routines, devise some sort of framework for the boys to hang onto. I would then write a rough-draft script and call them in. They would go through the first draft; it would give them other notions, and I would make cuts and additions, and somehow hammer out a further draft so that it was pretty much agreed upon by the time it got into the final draft."

During the World War II years, the Stooges made frequent tours of military bases to entertain the troops. Abbott and Costello might have been the number one comedy team on the screen, but the G.I.s were extremely appreciative of the diverting knockabout humor provided by the Stooges. One tour, sponsored by Coca-Cola, paired the Stooges with entertainer Morton Downey and found the troupe touring the entire East Coast.

By the mid-Forties, the professional situation was changing for the Stooges. Besides the shriveling of their creativity (understandable, given their vast output) and the growing apathy of Columbia toward their screen work, the Stooges faced the problem of Curly's declining health. It was on May 14, 1946, during the shooting of *Half-Wits' Holiday* (1947), a remake of their very well-regarded *Hoi Polloi* (1935) short, that Curly suffered a stroke. Shemp Howard rushed in to replace his ailing younger brother. Curly would make one final, brief gag appearance in a Stooges short, *Hold That Lion* (1947). It was the only occasion in which all three of the brothers appeared in one film together. In subsequent years, Curly suffered additional strokes, and on January 18, 1952, he died. He was survived by his wife, Valerie, and daughter Janie.

Shemp was a talented comedian but lacked the fetching insanity of Curly. The Stooges continued their professional fall. In the decade following they appeared in three features: *Rockin' in the Rockies* (1945) for Columbia, *Swing Parade of 1946* for Monogram, and United Artists' Western *Gold Raiders* (1951) starring George O'Brien, Fuzzy Knight, and Sheila Ryan. Occasionally there was a special something that made the public laugh a little louder at the filmed mugging of the Stooges. In 1953 they appeared in two 3-D shorts, *Spooks* and *Pardon My Backfire*. (The latter was not released in the third-dimensional process because that gimmick faded too quickly.)

Death again plagued the Stooges. On November 23, 1955, Shemp Howard died of a heart attack. The trio had just signed their 23rd annual Columbia contract for eight short subjects. Joe Besser, a veteran comic, became the third Stooge.* But it was too late

* Besser was memorable as Stinky, the Little Lord Fauntleroy-suited brat of the Abbott and Costello TV series.

An advertisement for Micro-Phonies (1945).

to halt the creative decline. *Sappy Bull-fighters* (1958), the 191st Stooges' short, marked the end of their Columbia tenure. They left the lot and went their separate ways, convinced that the Three Stooges were a dead commodity.

Nobody would have predicted that the Stooges were actually on the threshold of the greatest popularity of their careers. Audiences of all ages (but, not surprisingly, small children mostly) became addicted to the Stooges when Screen Gems distributed the shorts to TV stations across the country. In mid-1958 a Pittsburgh nightclub offered an engagement to the Stooges. Moe and Larry reformed the act, signing plump Joe DeRita to become "Curly Joe." The Three Stooges performed early evening shows for children and did capacity business with the adult crowd as well. Ed Sullivan signed them to appear on his Sunday night TV variety showcase. Soon

the veteran comics found themselves with more personal appearance bookings and video offers than they could handle.

The new public endorsement created new demand for the Stooges on the Hollywood scene. In 1959 Moe, Larry, and Curly Joe appeared in Columbia's *Have Rocket, Will Travel*. David Lowell Rich directed, and *Variety* wrote, "Strictly for the juve market. . . . It's a silly hash of sight gags and sound effects loosely organized around a funny enough theme." The box office loved it! In 1960 there appeared *The Three Stooges Scrapbook*, a Norman Maurer production blending animated work with some old Stooges footage, and *Stop! Look! and Laugh!*, a Columbia release mixing together Paul Winchell and Jerry Mahoney and Knucklehead Smiff, the Marquis Chimps, and old Stooges screen scenes. In 1961 Twentieth Century-Fox released *Snow White and the Three*

Stooges, with 1960 World Olympic Skating Champion Carol Heiss (of New York) as Snow White. The discriminating *New York Times* reported, "It's not bad. No kidding. . . . Even if it all sounds pretty gruesome—a Snow White on skates and a trio of slapstick comedians who usually run wild—it isn't. . . . The Stooges, never more subdued . . . do quite nicely as sideline sponsors of the hero and heroine." Meanwhile the Stooges engaged in an array of lucrative personal appearance engagements.

Also well received was *The Three Stooges Meet Hercules* (1962), a modestly budgeted Columbia release directed by the comics' old mentor Edward Bernds.* It was a rather witty satire of the then popular Italian spectacles in which Hercules (Samson Burke) is portrayed as a moronic fool. The *New York Times* saluted, "Credit Moe, Larry, and Curly Joe with stepping on the gas and knowing what to step on for fun, if not art. Hurry back, boys, and don't forget the pies." Bernds also directed Columbia's *The Three Stooges in*

Orbit (1962), in which the boys confront the Martians Ogg and Zogg.

In 1963 the Stooges cameoed in Stanley Kramer's United Artists comedy spectacle, *It's a Mad, Mad, Mad, Mad World*, and went over to Warner Bros. for the Frank Sinatra-Dean Martin-Anita Ekberg-Ursula Andress farce *4 for Texas*. Also that year they starred in yet another Columbia feature, *The Three Stooges Go Around the World in a Daze*. Of this *Variety* wrote, "Considering the fact that 33 years have elapsed since their first film, Moe Howard and Larry Fine, who date back to the original, demonstrate remarkable physical endurance. Relative newcomer Joe DeRita is a fine foil and effective replacement for the late Shemp Howard. . . ."

The final Stooges feature was *The Outlaws IS Coming!* (1965), a Western featuring Adam "Batman" West and the lovely Nancy Kovack (as Annie Oakley). The *New York Herald-Tribune* decided, "Well the Three Stooges IS here, in *The Outlaws IS Coming!* and for Stooges buffs it ARE a lot of fun . . . corny, silly, but danged if you don't find yourself laughing, just as you did when you were a kid. Remember?"

* The Stooges formed Normandy Productions to package their feature films.

Larry Fine, Moe Howard, Curly Howard, and Bud Jamison (right) in Stop! Look! and Laugh! (1960). [compilation feature]

629

Larry. Curly Joe. and Moe in The Outlaws Is Coming! *(1965).*

By the mid-Sixties the new cycle of Three Stooges popularity had nearly run its course. The comics supplied their own voices for 106 five-minute cartoons in 1965, but virtually retired thereafter.* In 1971 the comedians decided to reteam for a TV series entitled "Kook's Tour" which would match the boys with Moose, a black Labrador retriever. But then after shooting location footage in the Pacific northwest, Larry suffered a stroke. He would be hospitalized for a good deal of the subsequent years until his death at the Motion Picture Country House on January 24, 1975; he was survived by his daughter Phyliss. He was buried at Forest Lawn Cemetery.

* The team had appeared infrequently on TV talk programs such as "The Joey Bishop Show" and Moe appeared alone in *Don't Worry. We'll Think of a Title* (1966) and later *Dr. 'Death: Seeker of Souls* (1973). Always the most ambitious and articulate member of the group, Moe had appeared solo in Twentieth Century-Fox's *Space Master X-7* (1958) and was associate producer of Columbia's *Senior Prom* (1959).

After the retirement of the Stooges, Curly Joe DeRita was permitted to do personal appearances with Paul "Mousie" Garner and Frank Mitchell in simulated Three Stooges routines, but the act fell flat. In his last years (as had Larry), Moe often received mail and frequent visits from devoted fans. In 1974 Columbia issued *The Three Stooges Follies*, a compilation feature containing extracts from the team's film work as well as bits and pieces from other studio products (including Kate Smith singing a patriotic song and scenes from a Batman and Robin chapterplay).

Moe, who lived with his wife in a West Hollywood domicile above the Sunset Strip, continued making appearances on the college lecture circuit throughout 1974. When he died on May 4, 1975, of lung cancer he was in the midst of taping his memoirs.*

* Before their final ailments prevented their participation, the surviving Stooges were to have appeared in the Western sex spoof *Blazing Stewardesses* (1975). They were replaced by the surviving brothers of another great comedy trio, the Ritz Brothers.

He was buried at Hillside Memorial Park in Los Angeles.

Moe's death at age 77 marked the end of the history of the original Three Stooges. In many ways the end of a comic era had occurred.

FEATURE FILMS

With Moe, Shemp, and Larry and Ted Healy:
Soup to Nuts (*Fox 1930*)

With Moe, Larry, and Curly and Ted Healy:
Meet the Baron (*MGM 1932*)
Turn Back the Clock (*MGM 1933*)
Dancing Lady (*MGM 1933*)
Fugitive Lovers (*MGM 1934*)
Hollywood Party (*MGM 1934*)

With Moe, Larry, and Curly:
The Captain Hates the Sea (*Columbia 1934*)
Start Cheering (*Columbia 1938*)
Time Out for Rhythm (*Columbia 1941*)
My Sister Eileen (*Columbia 1942*)
Rockin' in the Rockies (*Columbia 1945*)
Swing Parade of 1946 (*Monogram 1946*)

With Moe, Larry, and Shemp:
Gold Raiders (*United Artists 1951*)

With Moe, Larry, and Curly Joe DeRita:
Have Rocket, Will Travel (*Columbia 1959*)
The Three Stooges Scrapbook (*1960*) [compilation of old footage and animated sequences]
Stop! Look! and Laugh! (*Columbia 1960*) [compilation feature with Jerry Mahoney as host]
Snow White and the Three Stooges (*20th Century-Fox 1961*)
The Three Stooges Meet Hercules (*Columbia 1962*)
The Three Stooges in Orbit (*Columbia 1962*)
It's a Mad, Mad, Mad, Mad World (*United Artists 1963*)
4 for Texas (*Warner Bros. 1963*)
The Three Stooges Go Around the World in a Daze (*Columbia 1963*)
The Three Stooges Follies (*Columbia 1974*) [compilation of old footage]
The Outlaws IS Coming! (*Columbia 1965*)

Moe alone:
Space Master X-7 (*20th Century-Fox 1958*)
Don't Worry, We'll Think of a Title (*United Artists 1966*)
Dr. Death: Seeker of Souls (*Cinerama 1973*)

The comedienne.

Thelma Todd

Beauty is rarely a deterrent in the performing arts, but it is *seldom* a requisite for comedy. Generally, comediennes are unlikely candidates for Miss or Mrs. America. Yet the striking beauty of such talented zanies as Carole Lombard, Lucille Ball, and Rosalind Russell highlighted their farcical follies. One of the screen's loveliest players, a striking blue-eyed blonde, Thelma Todd, was one of the great beauties in Hollywood motion pictures. And she was a remarkably clever funster.

Miss Todd's career spanned a brief 10 years, beginning at Paramount's Astoria, Long Island, acting school and ending with her mysterious, inexplicable death four miles north of Santa Monica, California.

She was born on Saturday, July 29, 1905, in Lawrence, Massachusetts, the daughter of John Shaw Todd and his wife, Alice. Thelma Alice Todd graduated from the Lowell (Massachusetts) Normal School and for two years would teach sixth grade students the rudiments of geography, history, and English literature.

There was no doubt that this schoolmarm was a beauty. She had been selected Miss Massachusetts of 1924 in an Elks' Beauty Contest and reigned as beauty queen over a ball sponsored by the brotherhood. Her pulchritude and a desire for something different in life led her to dream of a career in motion pictures.

At about this time Jesse L. Lasky founded an acting school at Paramount's Astoria studio in the belief that acting could be taught to photogenic photoplay aspirants possessed of a reasonable degree of malleable talent. Utilizing Paramount's various state film exchanges to screen applicants' qualifications, two dozen young applicants were finally selected nationwide for the Lasky-Astoria experiment. Transportation and living expenses were to be paid to the students and the six-month course would include a whirlwind curriculum of studies in dramatics, deportment, makeup, social graces, dancing, fencing, riding, swimming, and exposure to the wonderland of filmmaking.

Thelma was among those who won admission to the first (and only) class of Paramount's school of acting. When the class of '26 commencement was held at a dinner party at Manhattan's Ritz Carlton Hotel on March 2, 1926, the 20-year-old Miss Todd was one of the final 16 graduates who received diplomas and one-year Paramount player contracts with options. The 16 "Junior Stars of 1926"* were assigned roles in a specially written picture, *Fascinating Youth* (1926), directed by Sam Wood.

Considering its intent and structure, *Fascinating Youth* had a mild success with Charles "Buddy" Rogers as the hero and Ivy Harris as the heroine. Thelma was assigned a supporting part as Lorraine Lane, Josephine Dunn's sister. To spark the picture's box office, Paramount featured several of its top stars (Clara Bow, Richard Dix, Lois Wilson, Thomas Meighan, Lila Lee, et al.) as "themselves." For the picture's opening at Broadway's Rivoli Theatre on May 9, 1926, John Murray Anderson staged a prologue, *Alice in Movieland,* in which the eight young girls and eight young men appeared in person and introduced themselves in song backed by a stage setting strikingly re-creating a studio set.

But Mr. Lasky's pioneering acting college folded. He later wrote in *I Blow My Own Horn* (1957), "What I failed to take into consideration was that looks and talent and training aren't enough by themselves. More important than all three is personality—and that's something you can't turn out by factory methods. To be sure, Buddy and Thelma benefited amazingly from the school, but they had personality galore, and untapped dramatic ability as well. . . ." A few members of the class survived briefly in minor screen roles. Josephine Dunn had a moderately successful screen career and later went on the stage. Jack Luden, after playing a spate of juveniles, drifted into Westerns and Charles "Buddy" Rogers became one of Paramount's top stars. His fine performance in the first Academy Award Best Picture category, *Wings,* is still memorable.

* The lucky sixteen were: Charles "Buddy" Rogers, Thelma Todd, Josephine Dunn, Jack Luden, Ivy Harris, Walter Goss, Claude Buchanan, Mona Palma, Thelda Kenvin, Jeanne Morgan, Dorothy Nourse, Irving Hartley, Iris Gray, Charles Brokaw, Gregory Blackton, and Robert Andrews.

As for Thelma, her career was a series of fits and starts, alternating leads with supporting roles. She had promising ventures into drama that too often veered into mere atmospheric, if glamorous, background. It would take some time before her talent for comedy found fulfillment on the screen.

Paramount cast several of its acting school graduates, including Thelma, in *The Popular Sin* (1926) and *God Gave Me Twenty Cents* (1926). Her first important screen time was the female lead in Ed Wynn's movie debut, *Rubber Heels* (1927), in which she played Princess Aline trying to sell the family's crown jewels in Manhattan. A minor part in *Fireman, Save My Child* (1927) was offset by playing the love interest, sought and contested by villain William Powell and hero Gary Cooper, in Zane Grey's *Nevada.* She was Richard Dix's leading lady in *The Gay Defender* (1927), regarded as a "cheery little heroine." After that, Paramount did not renew her contract.

It seemed as if Thelma's career was taking an upswing when Howard Hughes cast Thelma in the original silent-screen version of his *Hell's Angels.* But when the initial film was scrapped and remade, Thelma and femme lead Greta Nissen were replaced. More concretely, Thelma made a series of features for First National, ranging from a supporting role in Richard Barthelmess' *The Noose* (1928) and Louise Fazenda's daughter in *Heart to Heart* (1928), to her first adventure with satire, *Vamping Venus* (1928). In the last film she played Madame Vanezlus, doubling as a lusciously sensuous, alluring Venus. In *The Crash* (1928) she was Milton Sills' actress wife, saved by the stalwart hero from a train wreck if not the picture. Thelma's first feature with talking sequences was *Seven Footprints to Satan* (1929), in which she had the female lead.

The year 1929 was a fortunate one for Thelma. She signed a contract with producer Hal Roach to appear in his lively comedies, while permitted to freelance in features. On April 27, 1929, Thelma recorded "Let Me Call You Sweetheart," "If I Had You," and "Honey" for RCA Victor records. For Roach, she was seen on the screen in Laurel and Hardy's first talking short, *Unaccustomed as We Are.* She played the wife of explosively jealous cop Edgar Kennedy. It was she who

With Chester
Conklin and
Barbara Bedford in
Haunted House
(1928).

had her skirt burned off while cooking for Stan and Ollie. As Roach maneuvered his other top clowns in their two-reeler talkie debuts, Thelma was enlisted to support Charley Chase in *Snappy Sneezer* and baby-face Harry Langdon in *Hotter Than Hot*. In the eight Roach-produced Langdon comedies, Thelma appeared in six and within three years made a dozen comedies with amusing Charley Chase.

First National's *Her Private Life* (1929) gave Thelma a showy role as Walter Pidgeon's card-cheating sister. In her first Technicolor feature, Paramount's *Follow Thru* (1930), she was radiantly beautiful as a golf champion. Tay Garnett's *Her Man* (1930), with Helen Twelvetrees and Phillips Holmes, cast Thelma as a watered-down Nellie Bly. That same year she helped Laurel and Hardy through another short, *Another Fine Mess*.

Thelma's Yankee perseverance should have resulted in better feature assignments than her fiercely independent freelancing brought. As Lasky had discerned, she had an abundance of personality, considerable talent, and a reservoir of potential. She also possessed a fine sense of humor that was

apparent in her pursuit of laughter in the Roach comedies. Not to be easily overlooked was her coolly detached, ever feminine beauty. But as Hollywood found its screen voice, there were newcomers of vast talents, scintillating personality, and beauty—all waiting in the wings. Thelma's original sponsor, Paramount, was grooming Nancy Carroll, Claudette Colbert, Carole Lombard, Miriam Hopkins, Sylvia Sidney, and the fabulous Marlene Dietrich. No major studio was touting Todd.

In 1931 United Artists signed Thelma as Chester Morris' leading lady in what the studio regarded as a milestone in cinema adventure. For *Corsair* director Roland West suggested that her name, associated with low comedy, be changed to Alison Loyd. He felt a glossy, starlit name such as that would be more in keeping with her new status as a glamorous leading lady. But *Corsair* was dismissed as "just another adventure movie" and Thelma's playing of wealthy Alison Corning was passed off as "merely amusing." Alison Loyd expired with *Corsair* and Thelma returned to Todd.

In Vamping Venus *(1928).*

Prior to the *Corsair* fiasco, Thelma had good supporting roles in Joe E. Brown's *Broad-Minded* (1931) and as Iva Archer in Warner Bros.' first pursuit of *The Maltese Falcon* (1931). The same year she also had her first encounter with the mad Marx Brothers, in *Monkey Business;* she whirled through a wild tango with Groucho.

In the spring of 1931, Hal Roach, hoping to create a distaff counterpart to his successful Laurel and Hardy team, signed screen veteran ZaSu Pitts to co-star in a series of two-reel comedies with Thelma. It was a felicitous choice. The two laughmakers worked well together. More often than not, the duo rose above maudlin scripts that usually followed a formula of sleek, smart gal Thelma untangling ZaSu's innocently provoked crises. Their 17 comedies as a team began with *Let's Do Things* (the first and only three-reeler, released June 6, 1931) and ended with *One Track Minds* in the spring of 1933.

Spacing other work with her Hal Roach comedies, Thelma started 1932 in Tiffany's 11-minute short, *Voice of Hollywood.* With John Wayne as an announcer, Thelma was Miss Information. She was seen to good advantage playing the wife of javelin thrower Cary Grant in Paramount's *This Is the Night. Time* magazine compared Frank Tuttle's tongue-in-cheek direction of the picture with that of Ernst Lubitsch, "He even uses a Lubitsch touch at the very beginning when a lady (Thelma Todd) gets her evening gown caught in a door of a limousine and the crowd on the sidewalk turns the incident into a song—'Madame Has Lost Her Dress.'" Thelma was also effective over at MGM in *Speak Easily* (1932), a comedy with Buster Keaton and Jimmy Durante.

Her second safari with the Marx Brothers was in *Horse Feathers* (1932). Here she played college widow Connie Bailey, who is Zeppo's love. She did a hilarious love scene in a rowboat with Groucho, falling into the lake screaming, "Throw me a lifesaver." Resourceful Groucho finds a roll of candy "lifesavers" in his pocket and obligingly tosses

With Roland Young
in This Is the Night
(1932).

With Chico Marx and
Groucho Marx in
Horse Feathers
(1932).

With co-player ZaSu
Pitts (c. 1932).

her one. The Marx Brothers never had a
cinematic comedy foil as lovely as Thelma,
nor one who sensed and elaborated on their
frenetic sprees as she did—with the exception
of dignified (and very funny) Margaret Dumont, a matronly actress who was hardly
eligible for pinup girl honors.

On Sunday, July 10, 1932, Thelma was
married to wealthy Pasquale DiCicco, a
sportsman and an actors' agent. The union
took place at Prescott, Arizona, before a justice of the peace. On March 2, 1934, she received a divorce from Pat DiCicco on a charge
of extreme cruelty. Between marriage and divorce, Thelma was never lovelier on the
screen than as Lady Pamela Rocburg in The
Devil's Brother, MGM's version of the comic
opera Fra Diavolo. Jeanie MacPherson's
lighthearted adaptation of the work suited
the talents of Laurel and Hardy and provided
Thelma with a picturesque display of her
beauty in 18th-century costumes. As James
Finlayson's philandering lady, she dallies
with highwayman Dennis King. He is almost
as beguiled by her deep-dimpled, seductive
smile and décolletage as by her money and
jewels.

Like many Hollywood performers, Thelma
took advantage of an offer from British filmmakers to make a movie in England. She
made her English screen debut in You Made
Me Love You (1933), a modernized musical
version of Shakespeare's The Taming of the
Shrew, adapted by and starring Stanley Lupino. As the up-to-date version of the shrewish Katherine, Thelma performed rather well.
The New York Times would headline its
review of the film with "A Beautiful Shrew."
The Times thought Thelma was properly
ferocious in the harum-scarum farce and that
"Miss Todd, who does not forget that a vixen
may be beautiful, does quite well with her
role." Thelma's friendship with Stanley Lupino would continue over the next two years;
in fact, she would make her last public
appearance at a party given in her honor by
Lupino.

In the summer of 1933 ZaSu Pitts left Hal
Roach's studio to further her expansive career; Patsy Kelly, a perky Irish brunette
nurtured in vaudeville, was signed to replace
her. Loud, boisterous, wisecracking Kelly
was an even better teammate for refined "ice
cream blonde" Todd. Within two and one-

half years the girls would make 21 two-reel comedies for Hal Roach, from *Beauty and the Bus* (September 16, 1933) to *All-American Toothache* (released in January 1936). The Kelly-Todd shorts were zestful, enthusiastic, and fast-paced. If an occasional weak, ill-defined script crept in, the girls were ever pleasing—and funny.

When not preoccupied at the Roach film factory, Thelma continued to accept outside assignments. In Universal's fine screen adaptation of *Counsellor-at-Law* (1933) she received good notices (as did the entire cast) for her playing of John Barrymore's client. In Paramount's musical *Sitting Pretty* (1933), she shone as predatory Gloria Duvall, a top Hollywood star pursuing Jack Oakie. United Artists' *Palooka* (1934) had Thelma in the minor role of Trixie. She then shuttled to Fox to play in *Bottoms Up* (1934), which featured Spencer Tracy and John Boles and exploited the talents of Pat Paterson who would marry Charles Boyer that year.

Wheeler and Woolsey enjoyed a reign as RKO's resident comedy team during the Thirties. Many of their films were fast, raucous, and forgettable. But two, *Hips, Hips, Hooray* (1934) and *Cockeyed Cavaliers* (1934), were bolstered by Thelma's presence. As Robert Woolsey's love interest in *Hips, Hips, Hooray*, Thelma joined the madcap boys and their perennial girlfriend, Dorothy Lee, in a highly amusing ersatz ballet. *Cockeyed Cavaliers* was a festive affair that returned Thelma to exquisite period costumes. She followed these comedy parts with another thrust at drama in a screen adaptation of Earl Derr Biggers' *The Deuce of Hearts*, entitled *Take the Stand* (1934). For RKO she was caught up in a weak and uninspired murder mystery with Ben Lyon and "Skeets" Gallagher, *Lightning Strikes Twice* (1935).

Paramount's *Two for Tonight* (1935) was one of Bing Crosby's lesser musical efforts but had the advantage of two comic performances from two blonde and gifted comedi-

With James C. Morton, Eddie Foy Jr., Patsy Kelly, Alphonse Martell, and Charles Rogers in the short subject Maid in Hollywood *(1934).*

ennes: Mary Boland and Thelma Todd. Thelma was cast as Crosby's girlfriend and the star of his planned musical comedy. The lackadaisical musical was Thelma's last stint at Paramount, where 10 years before she had been given perfunctory preparation for stardom.

Hal Roach's earlier success with the opera spoof, *The Devil's Brother*, encouraged him to produce the 1843 opera *The Bohemian Girl* (1936), which was revitalized for his royal kings of comedy, Laurel and Hardy. Thelma was bewitching in a black wig, an open-laced bra, and tight, clinging skirt as the gypsy queen's daughter. She soloed the picture's first song, "Song of the Gypsies." It was her final screen appearance.

On Tuesday, December 17, 1935, the nation's newspapers carried the tragic news of Thelma Todd's death. The front page of the *New York Times* read:

Thelma Todd dead, found in garage. Actress, discovered in auto after 18

hours, was monoxide *victim*, surgeon says. *Friend's* story differs. Actor's wife says Miss Todd phoned her long after hour of death set by autopsy.

The bizarre story unfolded in a mounting cloud of confused and conflicting versions of Thelma's final hours. And the case would terminate in a smog of perplexity, dissatisfaction, and inconclusiveness.

Ida Lupino was hostess for her father Stanley's small dinner party at the Trocadero nightclub on Sunset Boulevard on Saturday night, December 14, 1935. Thelma Todd was guest of honor. The get-together was not a bash, but a decorous and festive party. Ernest O. Peters, an auto livery chauffeur, drove Thelma home in a rented limousine to her beach sidewalk cafe (known as Thelma Todd's Roadside Rest—or "Thelma's Place").* The car arrived at the Coast High-

* Thelma Todd's Cafe was shown in Columbia's *Screen Snapshots #3* (1935) with Patsy Kelly as a patron.

In 1935.

way dining spot, four miles north of Santa Monica, at 4:20 A.M. He was the last person reportedly to see her alive.

Above the cafe Thelma shared a home with Roland West, who had directed her (and changed her name briefly to Alison Loyd) in *Corsair*. They were also co-owners of the cafe. From the highway, Thelma climbed 270 steps to 17531 Posetana Road. In the darkness before dawn (as was later theorized), unable to arouse West, she went into the garage adjacent to his quarters. She started her cabriolet sports car and settled in to await morning. Sunday morning at 10:30 Thelma's maid, May Whitehead, found her slumped over the wheel of her car, dead.

County autopsy surgeon, Dr. A. F. Wagner, certified that Thelma died of carbon monoxide poisoning at approximately five o'clock Sunday morning, December 15, 1935, from fumes "that she breathed accidentally." There were no signs of violence. Thelma was wearing a matched pearl necklace, diamond rings, and, over her mauve and silver evening gown, a full-length mink coat—and unblemished satin slippers. Blood on her face, and on the running board of the car, was dismissed by Dr. Wagner as occurring when her head struck the steering wheel. If her slightly disarrayed clothing indicated a brief struggle, it was seemingly inadmissible.

By Monday, Martha (Mrs. Wallace) Ford was telling authorities she had talked with Thelma on the telephone on Sunday afternoon when the effervescent blonde had called to request permission to bring a "new, handsome friend from San Francisco" to the Fords' cocktail party. Actress Jewel Carmen West, Roland's estranged wife, stated that she *saw* Thelma a day after her reported death driving her car with a handsome, dark male companion. Authorities rigidly defended their theories of accidental death and the officially reported time of death. But amidst increasing and reasonable doubt, a grand jury investigation was opened on Wednesday, December 18.

The grand jury summoned for testimony various guests who had attended the Lupino party. Rumors of Thelma being drunk and having passed out in her car were squelched by several friends. Ida Lupino recalled, "Thelma drank a cocktail before dinner and a little brandy and champagne during dinner."

The testimony of Harvey Priester, Arthur Prince, and Sid Grauman (who had called Roland West to tell him Thelma was on her way home from the party) added nothing theretofore unknown.

But the tabloids had a field day when it was disclosed that Thelma's ex-husband, Pat DiCicco, was at the Trocadero that night with actress Margaret Lindsay. The scandal sheets immediately tagged Miss Lindsay as "ex-hubby's girlfriend." DiCicco returned to California from his home in Smithtown, New York, but added nothing new to the grand jury's probe. Miss Lindsay was subpoenaed but could add little information beyond the less than sensational aspects of having dinner with her close friend, DiCicco, with whom Thelma was on mutually friendly terms.

ZaSu Pitts, who had last seen Thelma the previous Wednesday, testified, "I never saw Thelma happier in her life. We had a leisurely lunch and she was gay. We went shopping and Thelma bought a lot of Christmas wrappings and seals, and I am sure she intended to be alive and observe Christmas." According to Roland West's testimony, he had heard nothing and assumed Thelma had decided to spend the night in Hollywood. He claimed he slept through the entire tragedy, but did admit that he and Thelma had had a lover's quarrel prior to her leaving for the Lupino party.

The investigation led in many directions. There was conjecture of it being a gangster-oriented murder. On the other hand some insisted that Thelma's death was tied in to the extortion letters she had received from Edward Schiffert, a psychopath of Astoria, Long Island. (He was committed to the Manhattan State Hospital for the Insane the day the grand jury began its investigation into Thelma's demise.) One persistent juror climbed the 270 steps to the Todd-West home in a pair of satin slippers similar to those worn by Thelma. She found the shoes were torn, frayed, and badly scuffed after her effort. Thelma's slippers were not.

By January 3, 1936, with no further evidence, the grand jury closed the case, divided on the cause of Thelma's death. Most of the 18 jurors expressed a belief she committed suicide. Not one believed her death was accidental. The case was closed, to become another of California's unsolved mysteries.

Forty years later her friend and co-star Patsy Kelly told reporters inquiring about the strange end of Thelma Todd, "She had a fight with her lover at a party that night. I wasn't there but friends of mine were and they told me about it. There were a lot of suspicious things surrounding her death that never got explained. She most certainly wasn't drunk. Thelma used to nurse one drink for a whole evening and she never touched drugs of any kind. She was a strong New England woman with a powerful sense of humor and a wonderful zest of life. I always figured God wanted another angel. She was too young and too beautiful. . . ."

On Thursday, December 19, 1935, Thelma, clad in blue satin lounging pajamas—looking radiantly younger than her brief 30 years—was viewed by some 12,000 within five hours at the chapel of the Wee Kirk o' the Heather in Glendale, California. Funeral services were private and she was buried in Forest Lawn Memorial Park. In a will, dated September 19, 1933, she left $1 to Pat DiCicco and the balance of her estate (slightly in excess of $10,000) to her mother, Alice.

Today, like Roscoe "Fatty" Arbuckle's, Thelma's screen work is clouded by scandal and the unsolved, poorly explained circumstances of her death. She was an effervescent, delightful comedienne, who in her brief time brought abundant joy to many moviegoers.

FEATURE FILMS

Fascinating Youth (*Paramount 1926*)

The Popular Sin (*Paramount 1926*)

God Gave Me Twenty Cents (*Paramount 1926*)

Rubber Heels (*Paramount 1927*)

Fireman, Save My Child (*Paramount 1927*)

Nevada (*Paramount 1927*)

The Gay Defender (*Paramount 1927*)

The Shield of Honor (*Universal 1927*)

The Noose (*First National 1928*)

Vamping Venus (*First National 1928*)

Heart to Heart (*First National 1928*)

The Crash (*First National 1928*)

The Haunted House (*First National 1928*)

Naughty Baby (*First National 1929*)

Seven Footprints to Satan (*First National 1929*)

Trial Marriage (*Columbia 1929*)

The House of Horror (*First National 1929*)

Careers (*First National 1929*)

Her Private Life (*First National 1929*)

The Bachelor Girl (*Columbia 1929*)

Follow Thru (*Paramount 1930*)

Her Man (*Pathé 1930*)

Command Performance (*Tiffany 1931*)

Aloha (*Tiffany 1931*)

Swanee River (*World Wide 1931*)

The Hot Heiress (*Warner Bros. 1931*)

Broad-Minded (*Warner Bros. 1931*)

Monkey Business (*Paramount 1931*)

The Maltese Falcon (*Warner Bros. 1931*)

Corsair (*United Artists 1931*) [billed as Alison Loyd]

This Is the Night (*Paramount 1932*)

Speak Easily (*MGM 1932*)

Horse Feathers (*Paramount 1932*)

Klondike (*Monogram 1932*)

Big Timer (*Columbia 1932*)

Call Her Savage (*Fox 1932*)

Air Hostess (*Columbia 1933*)

Deception (*Columbia 1933*)

The Devil's Brother (*MGM 1933*)

Cheating Blondes (*Equitable 1933*)

Mary Stevens, M.D. (*Warner Bros. 1933*)

Counsellor-at-Law (*Universal 1933*)

Sitting Pretty (*Paramount 1933*)

Son of a Sailor (*Warner Bros. 1933*)

You Made Me Love You (*British 1933*)

Palooka (*United Artists 1934*)

Hips, Hips, Hooray (*RKO 1934*)

Bottoms Up (*Fox 1934*)

The Poor Rich (*Universal 1934*)

Cockeyed Cavaliers (*RKO 1934*)

Take the Stand (*Liberty 1934*)

Lightning Strikes Twice (*RKO 1935*)

After the Dance (*Columbia 1935*)

Two for Tonight (*Paramount 1935*)

The Bohemian Girl (*MGM 1936*)

A publicity pose.

Ben Turpin

Good taste would seem to dictate that physical impairment never be made the subject matter of comedy. But throughout the history of motion picture comedy there have been numerous exceptions to this rule; even in the Seventies we have witnessed the big-screen stardom of walleyed Marty Feldman. To the silent-screen audiences, the excessive weight of Fatty Arbuckle and the cross-eyes of Ben Turpin would make for automatic parody whenever these actors were placed in a part or situation that demanded sophistication. For all the talk among cinema historians and critics about comic craft or insight, the *mere* visual incongruity of these actors was what provided the silent screen with its funniest moments. For Ben Turpin, like Greta Garbo, the fortune was in the face.

Benjamin T. Turpin was born of French extraction in New Orleans, Louisiana, on Friday, September 17, 1869. His father was a candy shop owner. Very little is known about the details of his childhood (he was an intensely private man throughout his life), aside from the fact that the Turpins moved to New York when Ben was seven years old. The family resided on Manhattan's Lower East Side.

According to one recurrent version, when Turpin was in late adolescence, his father gave him $100 to make his way in life. The young man kept the funds until Jersey City where he lost it gambling. Thereafter, the ashamed youth snuck aboard a freight train and ended up in Chicago where he learned the ways of hobo life.

Eventually he entered vaudeville, where his slight height (5′4″) and slender frame (140 pounds) lent themselves to various comedy sketches with Sam T. Jack's Burlesque Company at $20 weekly. According to researcher Barry Brown in a *Films in Review* career study of the comedian, he was first in partnership with another novice, and then later on his own, developing a character called Happy Hooligan. Says Brown, "He also developed considerable acrobatic skill, including the execution of a '180,' a trick which starts from a standing position, with the acrobat throwing himself backward and landing on his feet. Turpin learned to modify this for laughs, landing on his face or back or any part of his anatomy that got the biggest audience response. There are many versions of the origins of his strabismus, ranging from the story that he crossed his eyes so much during the balancing-a-card-on-his-nose part of his act that one day they remained so, to the more plausible contention that it was caused by damage to an optic nerve through repetition of these brutally masochistic backward somersaults." At any event, normal vision was never restored. Although he would appear in several melodramas during his later vaudeville engagements, it was this accident that set Turpin on the course of pursuing a comedy career. (He would later have his famous eyes insured for over $20,000.)

Like so many pre-Chaplin comics at the turn of the century, he developed a "tramp" act and later joined the Mabel Paige Repertory Company at $15 weekly, performing in such traditional melodramas as *East Lynne* and *Tennessee Partner*. The range of his early theatrical experiences extended even to light opera, a circus (where he worked as a clown—of course), and county fairs (as a taffy puller) around the Chicago area.

In 1907 Ben married Carrie LeMieux and for most of their marriage Carrie was incapacitated one way or another. (Among other ailments she lost her hearing after a bout with influenza.) Still pursuing a theatrical career, Ben and Carrie settled in the Chicago area. His early adventurous careers made him amenable to the possibilities of the still fledgling film industry.

It was in 1907 that G. M. "Broncho Billy" Anderson and George K. Spoor founded their Essanay Films in Chicago and hired Turpin for their film shorts. According to Brown in his *Films in Review* and the filmography to the piece prepared with Richard A. Braff, Turpin's first work was in a one-reeler, *Ben Gets a Duck and Is Ducked,* filmed at South Park, Chicago. Another of his early shorts is *Midnight Disturbance,* made for Essanay in 1909.

In 1909, Turpin went to California on behalf of Carl Laemmle's Independent Motion Picture Company (IMP), helping with the supervision of the construction of a studio near Edendale. Not long afterward,

Ben returned East for unspecified reasons.

It was during this year that Turpin told *Moving Picture World* that moviemaking "... is a great life.... I must say I have had many a good fall and many good bumps and I think I've broken about 20 barrels of dishes, upset stoves, and also broken up many sets of beautiful furniture, had my eyes blackened, both ankles sprained and many bruises." However, Turpin decided to abandon the cinema and for 4-5 years he returned to theater circus tours, again performing as Happy Hooligan.

By 1914 he was back with Essanay—at $25 weekly—appearing in one-reelers with Broncho Billy Anderson (in his Snakeville series) and Wallace Beery.

Ben's first important movie part was with Charlie Chaplin in *His New Job* (1915), a comedy short which chronicles Chaplin's rise from janitor-office boy to comic star. (Since Turpin had performed in those menial tasks, the irony and inspiration of the situation were not lost on him.) Gloria Swanson was an extra in the picture. Although Turpin worked well with Chaplin in this and other shorts, he always disliked him and resented his own supporting roles in the Chaplin entries. (At this time he was still functioning as both actor and janitor/factotum at Essanay.) Later Turpin would say, "I have since proved that I could work without him. I am now the star of Keystone, and my films make lots of money."

Yet when Chaplin left Chicago for Essanay's Niles, California, studio, Turpin had gone with him, making such shorts as *A Night Out, By the Sea,* and the famous four-reeler, *Charlie Chaplin's Burlesque of Carmen* (1916). Despite his pronounced dislike of Chaplin, Ben worked well with the star and their interaction in *A Night Out* suggested the closest Chaplin ever came to having a true screen partner.

By April 1916 Turpin had left Essanay and signed with Mutual (where Chaplin was in residence). He headlined one of the two troupes making the Vogue comedies. Many of the films fell into a pattern: some with comic Paddy McGuire (as two hobos) and the others with Rube Miller as his co-star and director.

The Vogue pictures were a downward slide for Turpin and fortunately George Stout, Mack Sennett's business manager, made the

With Charles Chaplin in His New Job (1915).

effort to bring Turpin into Sennett's fold. It was Sennett who was the first overtly to exploit Ben's cross-eyes (they had *not* even been commented upon by reviewers of Chaplin's films) and to recognize the possibilities of casting Ben in outrageously improbable roles. His first effort for Sennett was *A Clever Dummy* (released in 1917) and his earlier experiences in melodrama prepared him for such elaborate film parodies as *East Lynne with Variations* and *Uncle Tom without a Cabin.* He even got to play John the Baptist in *Salome Versus Shenandoah,* a two-reeler that juxtaposed a Civil War spy yarn with a Biblical tale à la *Intolerance.* It featured most of Sennett's then (1919) repertory company including Chester Conklin, Phyllis Haver, Charles Murray, and Heinie Conklin. A five-reeler, *Yankee Doodle in Berlin* (1919), with approximately the same cast, was a spoof on German militarism with Ben as a field marshal. Turpin also appeared in other Sennett five-reelers, including *Down on the Farm* (1919) and *Married Life* (1921).

The Turpin pictures remembered most affectionately by critics and audiences were the parodies of well-known films: for example, *The Shriek of Araby* (1923) in which he spoofed Valentino, and his send-up of Erich von Stroheim in *Three Foolish Weeks* (1924). James Agee in his well-regarded 1949 *Life* magazine article on silent-screen comedy noted, "The reader may remember how upright and wandlike old Ben Turpin could stand for a Renunciation Scene, with his lampshade moustache twittering and his sparrowy chest stuck out and his head flung back like Paderewski assaulting a climax and the long babyish back hair trying to look lionlike, while his Adam's apple, an orange in a Christmas stocking, pumped with noble emotion."

Considerably less enthusiastic was Walter Kerr's appraisal of Turpin's value in *The Silent Clowns* (1975): "Turpin—with crossed eyes and the permanently stunned expression of a haddock on ice—became popular because his affliction defined him immediately: like fat comics, like tall comics, he could be detected at any moment in a chase. No camera had to pause for him. When it did pause—he wound up at Sennett, which is surely where he belonged—he offered it very little. I am sorry to say that I have never seen him do anything at any time that made me laugh."

Indeed, full-length features starring Turpin are hard to imagine, but brief cameos and excerpts from Turpin shorts, like those in the Robert Youngson silent comedy compendiums, still provide laughs to new generations of moviegoers.

Perhaps the most reasonable analysis of Turpin's parodies was provided by Raymond Durgnat in his book *The Crazy Mirror* (1969): "Slapstick parody can work up a fine satiric charge, as in Ben Turpin's mockery of Valentino and von Stroheim. In fact, Turpin's fussy gestures and wild squint are relevant to every human emotion, activity, or state of soul."

The popularity of these parodies, as well as the demise of Roscoe Arbuckle's stardom, made Ben the most successful* two-reeler comic working in the early Twenties, often playing the character of Rodney St. Clair. As Sennett's leading star, he was frequently temperamental (director Robert Florey characterized him as "a foul-mouthed vulgarian") and his newly found wealth made him often eccentric and generally egotistical. Legend had it that he never deposited his money in a bank but concealed it in a mattress. According to Sennett, when he entered public places he would exclaim loudly, "Ben Turpin! Three thousand dollars a week!"

Sennett managed to pacify his money-maker by agreeing to his demands and even starring him in the seven-reel *A Small Town Idol* (1921), in which he was co-starred with Phyllis Haver and James Finlayson (another famous squinter). The *National Board of*

---

* It should be remembered how perilous Ben's profession was; all of his on-camera antics were physically abusive to his body and landed him in the hospital scores of times. Turpin would recall, "One time they got me on a rope over a canyon, and somebody let go the rope. I've been bit by a peevish lion, and chased by temperamental dog actors. In one of the Mack Sennett comedies, the villain was to hit me with a trick statuette. He grabbed up one made of solid marble by mistake. I just remember everything turned black; then I got mad and socked the guy. He let out a yell and I found out it was my wife. I had been in bed a week."

Review magazine reported, "Mr. Sennett makes Ben Turpin, a little shrimp of a man, do the same stunt (as a Tom Mix or William S. Hart) while giving us a cross-eyed wink." In 1922 Ben made a personal appearance on the stage of the Capitol Theatre in Manhattan.

Success continued with the five-reel *The Shriek of Araby*, but in December of 1924 Ben announced his retirement from the screen in order to care for his terminally ill wife. He informed the press, "What's the good of all the money I got if it can't make my wife well? She's all that counts. As long as she needs me, the movies can go hang. I'm tired of acting anyhow." In a desperate attempt to forestall the inevitable, he took Carrie to Ste. Anne de Beaupré near the city of Quebec in Quebec, Canada. He also planned to take her to Lourdes in France. But on October 1, 1925, she died at the age of forty-three and was buried in Forest Lawn Cemetery.

Ben's own poor health—he suffered from asthma—was also a determining factor in his retirement plans. While a patient at Santa Barbara Hospital in 1925, he met his second wife, Babette Elizabeth Dietz of Bismarck, North Dakota. A year later, on July 7, 1926, Ben and Babette were married at the Church of the Good Shepherd in Beverly Hills. His second marriage seemed to provide him with renewed confidence. Although he was now a millionaire and did not need the salary, he decided to resume his film career on a part-time basis.

Keystone, by this point, was in decline, so he made comedy shorts for Pathé. He also appeared in several silent features, more or less in cameo roles. Without Sennett's guidance, Turpin was smart enough to realize that he would have difficulty sustaining an entire feature. But his name still meant something, and in the case of *The College Hero* (1927) at Columbia, he received star billing for what amounted to an extraneous guest role.

The advent of sound on a commercial basis in films generated its own nostalgia for silent comedy. Like former Keystone colleagues Chester Conklin and Hank Mann, Turpin frequently withdrew from retirement to accept small film parts. Often he appeared playing a bartender or a "lackey," as he was billed in Ernst Lubitsch's *The Love Parade* (1929). Whatever his minuscule assignment,

*With Eddie
Gribbon and
Phyllis Haver in*
Small Town Idol
(1921).

*With Natalie
Kingston in* **The
Daredevil** *(1923).*

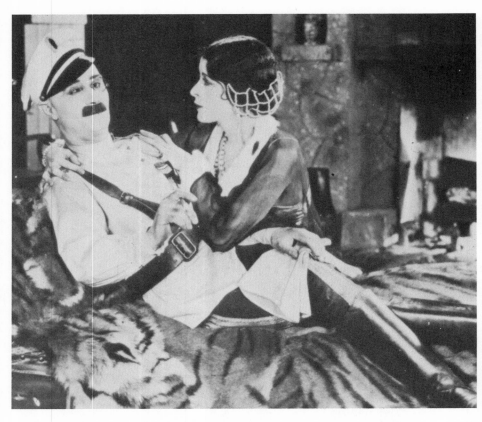

In Three Foolish Weeks *with Madeline Hurlock (1924).*

his mere appearance was enough to guarantee a chuckle. (His low, unremarkable voice suggested that he was fortunate to have earned his fame when he did.)

In 1929 he was reunited with the Conklin Brothers in Warner Bros.' review picture, *The Show of Shows,* in which they engaged in a brief blackout skit. In *Swing High* (1930), starring Helen Twelvetrees, at Pathé, Turpin performed as a bartender. The following year, he played in MGM's *Our Wife,* a two-reeler, and then made a quick entrance-exit in Wheeler and Woolsey's *Cracked Nuts* (1931) at RKO. For Paramount in 1932 he made what were perhaps his two best sound features. In *Make Me a Star,* a revamping of *Merton of the Movies,* Ben instructed Stuart Erwin in the fine art of pie throwing. Also that year Ben played a sinister-looking stranger dressed in black who takes notes on the odd goings-on in the surrealistic *Million Dollar Legs.* A blatant Jack Oakie and a more subdued W. C. Fields were the stars of this Paramount opus.

Donald McCaffrey in *The Golden Age of Screen Comedy* (1971) has described Ben's curious role in the picture: "In the opening scene, George Barbier, playing the role of a brash manufacturer, declares: 'I want to get out of this country. I have a feeling I'm being spied on.' Told not to worry because spying could not be possible in Klopstokia, the magnate doesn't see, pressing close behind him, the cross-eyed Ben Turpin, with obvious cloak and dagger garb—a large brimmed black hat and a long cape. In such dress, he appears periodically throughout the picture taking notes on the proceedings—a mute specter of the silent screen comedy."

During the same year, Ben also appeared in a series of short subjects for Paramount, but they were halfhearted attempts, certainly not in the same league with the Sennett pictures. Turpin also performed in an edition of the short-subject series, *Hollywood on Parade.*

The ultimate nostalgic tribute to the type of comedy that Ben did best came in 1935. This was *Keystone Hotel,* directed by Ralph Staub as a sort of pilot for a projected Keystone Kop renaissance to be produced at Warner Bros. Ben, Ford Sterling, Hank Mann, Marie Prevost, and Chester Conklin were contracted for this one film, in which Ben was cast as dapper Count Drewablank. When audience reaction to the short subject proved very favorable, the comics' agents demanded three times the salary discussed for the series. Mogul Jack Warner in anger vetoed the series idea. That same year Turpin also worked in an Educational Pictures short, but it lacked the polish of the Warner Bros. enterprise.

Ben's next feature came in 1939 with Twentieth Century-Fox's color entry, *Hollywood Cavalcade*. It was a sentimental film, a clef tribute to Ben's former boss, Mack Sennett, who also appeared in the picture as himself. It starred Alice Faye (in a Mabel Normand-like character) and Don Ameche (as a film-director copy of Sennett); Ben's brief cameo consisted of playing a bartender in a Western film-within-a-film, in which Chester Conklin was a cowboy. There were guest bits in the picture by Al Jolson, Buster Keaton, and Rin Tin Tin, adding up to a fascinating chronicle of the first four decades of the movies. It is indeed odd that so many of Ben's films (*His New Job, A Small Town Idol, Hollywood, Make Me a Star, Hollywood Cavalcade*, and even the parodies) were about Hollywood and the movies. And it is ironic that movie stardom could be conferred on so strange a figure as Ben. His mere appearance in these pictures suggested a joke on the star system itself.

Ben's final film came in 1940. It marked a reunion with Laurel and Hardy whom he had played with in the MGM/Hal Roach two-reeler *Our Wives* (1931). The 57-minute *Saps at Sea* also marked the end of a comedy era as it was that comedy team's final association with the Roach studio. Billed as a "mixed-up plumber," Ben's contribution to the proceedings consisted of listening to the many complaints of apartment dwellers on maintenance and exclaiming, "It looks all right to me!" The slapstick sequences were beyond his seventy years.

A month after *Saps at Sea* was released, in June of 1940, Turpin suffered a heart attack and later was hospitalized in Santa Monica. On July 1 he suffered another attack and died. Some 300 people were present at Turpin's funeral at the Church of the Good Shepherd in Beverly Hills. Among those present were: Buster Keaton, Andy Clyde, Jimmy Finlayson, Charlie Murray, and Al St. John. Charlie Chaplin provided a seven-foot spray of red roses for his former co-worker.

Over the years the unique Mr. Turpin would be seen again in countless documentary celebrations of silent-screen comedy such as Sennett's own *Down Memory Lane* (1949) and the several Robert Youngson compendiums. His appearance would still automatically signal audience laughter.

Perhaps the best summation of Turpin's bizarre screen fame comes from filmmaker Frank Capra in his autobiography, *The Name Above the Title* (1971), in which he relates an anecdote from one of Sennett's gag writers: "'Hear what happened about Turpin?' a writer cracked. 'As a gag Johnny Grey calls up Sennett and tells him Turpin was going to a doctor to get his eyes straightened. The old man roared like a wounded buffalo and threatened to shoot every doctor in Hollywood.'"

FEATURE FILMS

Charlie Chaplin's Burlesque of Carmen (*Essanay 1916*)
Yankee Doodle in Berlin [a.k.a. The Kaiser's Last Squeal] (*Lesser 1919*)
Down on the Farm (*United Artists 1919*)
Married Life (*First National 1919*)
A Small Town Idol (*Associated Producers 1921*)
Home Talent (*Associated Producers 1921*)
Hollywood (*Paramount 1923*)
The Shriek of Araby (*Allied Producers and Distributors 1923*)
Hogan's Alley (*Warner Bros. 1925*)

Steel Preferred (*Producers Distributing Corporation 1926*)
The College Hero (*Columbia 1927*)
The Wife's Relations (*Columbia 1928*)
The Show of Shows (*Warner Bros. 1929*)
The Love Parade (*Paramount 1929*)
Swing High (*Pathé 1930*)
Cracked Nuts (*RKO 1931*)
Million Dollar Legs (*Paramount 1932*)
Make Me a Star (*Paramount 1932*)
Hollywood Cavalcade (*20th Century-Fox 1939*)
Saps at Sea (*United Artists 1940*)

In Chitty Chitty Bang Bang *(1968)*.

Dick Van Dyke

Even if Dick Van Dyke performed nothing more than his five-season TV run as comedy writer Rob Petrie on CBS's "The Dick Van Dyke Show" and his Bert the chimney sweep in Disney's classic *Mary Poppins* (1964), most contemporary audiences would award him a niche in the pantheon of great comedians. With a handsome face and a lanky frame of rubber, the comedian rose to national prominence in the early Sixties. His emergence was welcome, for it came at a time when Hollywood comedy was becoming increasingly bitter, nasty, and often ugly. In direct contrast, Dick appeared as an irresistible funnyman who can sing, dance, pantomime, mug, and deliver comic dialogue in a deliciously cheery, comic style.

However, Van Dyke has not been forced to lean on past credits, and has offered enough solidly fun credits in recent years (including the underrated musical feature *Chitty Chitty Bang Bang!* [1968] and a lauded 1975 NBC-TV special) to offset some definite professional pitfalls (his two recent TV series) and personal problems (a bout with alcoholism).

Richard Van Dyke was born on Sunday, December 13, 1925, in West Plains, Missouri. His father was a trucking agent. (Brother Jerry would be born on July 27, 1931, in Danville, Illinois.)* During his childhood Dick got plenty of pratfall practice. "It's my firm belief that real humor comes from pain," he once analyzed. "Up to age 10, I had no instinct for self-protection, no instinct to put my hands up to stop a fall. So I had to lose teeth, [and get] bumps on my forehead and a smashed nose. So what did I wind up doing for a living? Falling on my nose! I learned early to laugh my way out of predicaments."

While a small boy, Dick moved with his family to Danville, Illinois. There he later became active in high school plays and civic theatre, and for a time contemplated becom-

---

* Jerry Van Dyke would begin his show-business career in nightclubs, later guesting on his brother's weekly TV show, and still later headlining his own short-lived video series, "My Mother the Car." He appeared in such feature films as *McLintock!* (1963), *Palm Springs Weekend* (1963), *The Courtship of Eddie's Father* (1963), *Love and Kisses* (1965), and *Angel in My Pocket* (1969).

ing a Presbyterian minister. He also fell in love with cinema comedy, especially the art of Stan Laurel. "I first saw Laurel and Hardy when I was about six or seven years old. Thereafter I'd go to the movies every Saturday to see them, sitting right through all afternoon and evening performances until my mother'd come and get me out. Believe it or not, when I was a child I looked exactly like Stan Laurel. Maturity has changed me, but then we were identical. Indeed my father looked like Stan too, same ears and all. Everybody in our family did impressions of Stan. And it just happened that I married a woman with a long chin, with a smaller nose than mine, who looked quite a lot like Stan. Obviously I didn't marry her for that reason, but our four children look rather like Stan too. So there are still a lot of Laurel impressions in our family."*

During World War II Dick served in the air force. After his discharge he opened an advertising agency in Danville with friend Wayne Williams. The business soon declared bankruptcy. For a very brief spell he was a radio announcer on WDAN in Danville. In 1947 he gave in to his ambitions to become a real part of show business and joined an act entitled The Merry Mutes, touring nightclubs with Philip Erickson. They later became Eric and Van. The act frequently had dry periods such as the time it was dropped from a Hollywood club date after three nights. At one point Van Dyke was ousted from a rooming house for failure to pay his rent. Still the team lasted for six years, playing from coast to coast. It provided an entree when Van Dyke maneuvered into local television in Atlanta, Georgia. He became the M.C. of the daytime programs "The Merry Mutes Show" and "The Music Shop." After two years he moved to New Orleans and starred on the locally televised Monday–Friday variety program "The Dick Van Dyke Show." He performed with such style on the two-hour daily show that the CBS-TV network summoned him to New York and presented him with a seven-year contract.

* Van Dyke would later meet Stan Laurel in Hollywood. He would do an impression of Laurel on an episode of "The Dick Van Dyke Show" with Henry Calvin doing Ollie. It was Van Dyke who gave the eulogy at Laurel's Forest Lawn funeral. Dick's CBS-TV special (November 23, 1965) was a salute to Stan Laurel.

To the surprise of everyone, including CBS, Dick insisted upon performing on daytime television, reasoning that it would provide him with needed additional experience. He first followed in the footsteps of Walter Cronkite, Jack Paar, and John Henry Faulk by becoming master of ceremonies of CBS's "The Morning Show," on which he specialized in comic monologues and telling children stories. On September 20, 1956, he began a series entitled "Joe and Mabel" for his network, and the same year became the M.C. of the evening time "Cartoon Theatre."

CBS by now had firm plans to build Van Dyke into a major personality and saw fit to remove him from daytime television. The network spotted him as a guest player on various evening series, such as on "The Phil Silvers Show" in the episode *Bilko's Cousin* (January 28, 1958). Dick was unhappy with this situation and later told the *New York Herald-Tribune* "I kept asking for a daytime show and they kept saying I ought to have a nighttime comedy show and when I said 'Okay' they told me it was a bad time for comedy. I just got tired of waiting for comedy to come back. It's not that I'm ambitious. I just want to work." As a result, Van Dyke asked for and received a release from his CBS contract.

As a freelancer, Dick was busy. He appeared on ABC-TV's "The Andy Williams Show" and in October 1958 joined that network as the host of the daily panel show "Mother's Day," aimed at housewives. "I want to stay with the housewives," he had said earlier of his burgeoning career. "I can't think of a more delightful way to make a living." Van Dyke, meanwhile, had a housewife of his own, Marjorie Willett Van Dyke, his childhood sweetheart, whom he wed on the "Bride and Groom" radio show on February 12, 1948. Four children followed: Christian (born June 13, 1950), Barry (born July 31, 1951), Stacey (born January 7, 1955), and Carrie Beth (born October 18, 1961).

Van Dyke continued adding to his resumé. In 1959 he became M.C. of NBC's "Laugh Line," an ad-libbed weekly comedy show that featured Elaine May, Mike Nichols, Orson Bean, et al., and next hosted "Flair," an ABC weekday radio show which premiered in October 1960. He also made guest appearances on CBS's "Alfred Hitchcock Presents"

(*Craig's Will*, 1960) and NBC's comedy revue of November 1960, *No Place Like Home* (with Rosemary Clooney, José Ferrer, and Carol Burnett), as well as on other programs.

While his career was progressing on television and radio, Dick set his sights on a Broadway success. His first foray came on November 2, 1959, at the Alvin Theatre in the musical revue *The Girls Against the Boys*. The show starred Bert Lahr, Nancy Walker, Shelley Berman, and Van Dyke. The *New York Times* dubbed Van Dyke "an amiable performer" and the *New Yorker* reported, "A versatile comic named Dick Van Dyke adds color to a lot of drab spots." The show folded after only 16 performances.

However, Dick's next stage role proved to be the key to success. The show was the musical *Bye Bye Birdie* (Martin Beck Theatre: April 14, 1960) and Dick played Albert Peterson, the mama's boy promoter of singing sensation Conrad Birdie (Dick Gautier). With direction and choreography by Gower Champion, the show's cast included Chita Rivera as Albert's secretary and love interest, Kay Medford as his bullying mother, Susan Watson as the small-town girl (Kim) who wins the nationwide contest to give Birdie his farewell kiss on the "Ed Sullivan Show" before he enters the service, and Paul Lynde as Kim's hysterical father.

Although the *New York Times* had faint praise for the show itself ("It needs work"), it approved of Van Dyke as "a likable comedian, who has India-rubber joints." John Chapman enthused in the *New York Sunday News*, "Dick Van Dyke, whose affable mugging and gentle joking have entertained daytime television watchers, is a most attractive and sincere agent—and he has nimble feet." Van Dyke sang in the show numbers "Everything Is Rosy" and "Put on a Happy Face." The latter song became something of a theme song for the star. *Bye Bye Birdie* found enthusiastic audiences and ran for 607 performances. In May 1960 Dick won a Theatre World Award as the most promising young actor of the season.

During the spring of 1960 Van Dyke had completed a pilot for a proposed new CBS-TV series. The half-hour show, "The Trouble with Richard," dealt with the misadventures of a good-natured bank teller and co-starred Parker Fennelly as Gramps. It was shown during the summer of 1960 on an anthology show entitled "New Comedy Showcase" but failed to find a sponsor willing to launch it as a full-time show.

In 1961 comic talent Carl Reiner was developing a comedy series for CBS, designing the show as a vehicle for himself.* He would play a television comedy writer who faces trials and tribulations with his egotistical boss. However, after viewing a performance of *Bye Bye Birdie*, Reiner decided to vacate the leading role and cast Dick Van Dyke as Rob Petrie, head writer for "The Alan Brady Show." Added to the cast was Morey Amsterdam as Buddy, the co-writer of the endless one-liners; Rose Marie as Sally, the man-hungry secretary; Richard Deacon as Mel Cooley, Brady's hapless producer; and Mary Tyler Moore as Rob's wife Laura.

"The Dick Van Dyke Show" premiered on CBS-TV on October 3, 1961. Though the series has become a classic airwave domestic situation comedy, the program initially was not a hit with critics or with the public. *Variety* reported the show as being "about par" as a TV comedy entry, and the ratings were not good. Before the show premiered Van Dyke told the *New York Herald-Tribune*, "I feel optimistic about our chances for success. We have a believable premise and situations that are alternately warm and funny." Though the show began winning a responsive audience thanks to Reiner's script and directing élan and the contributions of the irrepressible cast members, CBS-TV almost canceled the show the first year.

But on May 23, 1962, "The Dick Van Dyke Show" won the Emmy for Best Comedy Program of the season. By this time the *New York Post* had saluted the comedy half-hour as "the best cast situation comedy on the air." The show would settle down to run four more very popular seasons, landing in the Top 10 Poll of TV programs in October 1962.

In the meantime, Columbia Pictures purchased the screen rights to *Bye Bye Birdie*. Dick was signed to re-create his stage role of Albert Peterson. He was quick to remark that he was not the first choice for the film assign-

* Reiner actually made a pilot (aired the summer of 1960) for the show, with himself playing Rob Petrie, Barbara Britton his wife, Morty Gunty and Sylvia Miles his comedy writers, and Jack Wakefield the comedian boss.

With Maureen Stapleton, Paul Lynde, and Bryan Russell in Bye Bye Birdie (1963).

ment. "I understand Laurence Harvey didn't have time to play the role and some other guys weren't interested, or something like that." The movie version retained Paul Lynde in his priceless portrayal of Mr. MacAfee, but replaced dynamic Chita Rivera with a black-wigged Janet Leigh, overbearing Kay Medford with equally overbearing Maureen Stapleton, hip-swinging Dick Gautier with a toned-down Jesse Pearson, and quaint Susan Watson with curvaceous Ann-Margaret (ludicrously if awesomely cast as the 16-year-old Kim). When the George Sidney–directed feature appeared in the spring of 1963, *Variety* noted, "Colorful, imaginative, amusing musical comedy.... Van Dyke displays a show biz knowhow far more extensive than his current television outings would communicate." Despite all its faults, the picture tallied a healthy gross of $6,200,000.

In between his television work, Dick continued to make films. His next screen part was in the shamelessly opulent *What a Way to Go!* (1964) at Twentieth Century-Fox. In the broad comedy Shirley MacLaine—abetted by lavish costumes, wigs, and jewelry—tells psychiatrist Bob Cummings of her assorted marriages (Paul Newman, Robert Mitchum, Dean Martin, Gene Kelly, and Van Dyke). Dick was her first spouse, a small-town merchant who begins to prosper after wedding Shirley, but later works himself to death.

Van Dyke attained cinema stardom with his next film role, that of Bert the chimney sweep in *Mary Poppins*, the feature based on the P. L. Travers stories of the unorthodox nanny (played to Oscar-winning perfection by Julie Andrews). The musical version boasted a score by Richard M. Sherman and Robert B. Sherman, and a delightful cast which included Glynis Johns, David Tomlinson, Ed Wynn, Jane Darwell, Arthur Treacher, and Elsa Lanchester. "Mr. Van Dyke is joyous," wrote the *New York Times* reviewer of the film. The *New York Herald-Tribune* added, "Dick Van Dyke's Bert reveals that this young performer's gifts have never been truly exploited before—obviously because they're limitless." Besides offering a large helping of his personable interpretation of the hero, Van Dyke did some charming singing and dancing—"Chim-Chim-Cheree," "Jolly Holiday," etc. In fact, his hoofing with the animated penguins from that latter number is shown at Disneyland as part of "The Walt Disney Story." *Mary Poppins* still ranks high on the list of all-time box-office champions, grossing over $42,000,000, some $8,000,000 more than the movie *My Fair Lady*, which defeated *Poppins* in the Oscar race for Best Picture.

While Dick continued his television show,* regaling loyal audiences with such oft-repeated adventures as Laura's first meeting with Rob's parents, their courtship and mishap-filled wedding, and his sporadic encounters with monstrous Alan Brady (played by a mugging Carl Reiner), he accepted film offers as his schedule permitted. His next starring cinema role came in *The Art of Love* (1965) at Universal, with Van Dyke as a painter in France, Elke Sommer as his starry-eyed girl, and such co-stars as James Garner, Angie Dickinson, Carl Reiner, and Ethel Merman (as a singing madam!).

* In 1964 and 1965 both Dick Van Dyke and Mary Tyler Moore won Emmies for their series' work on "The Dick Van Dyke Show."

In the late spring of 1966—shortly after Mary Tyler Moore's character blurted out the news on the show that Alan Brady wore a toupee (perhaps the series' most famous episode)—"The Dick Van Dyke Show" left the air. It was a unique situation for a still top-rated program to quit while ahead, but Van Dyke was insistent that it happen this way.

That summer Walt Disney's *Lieutenant Robin Crusoe, U.S.N.* (1966) appeared, featuring Van Dyke in the title role, Hawaiian location shooting, comely Nancy Kwan, a boisterously hammy Akim Tamiroff (as a native headhunter), and a very talented chimp named Floyd. Critics huffed at the piece—*Variety:* "Van Dyke's comedy is overly broad but he handles his assignment diligently for what it is"; *New York Times:* "Only for the very very young and for television fans who think Mr. Van Dyke can do no wrong." Nevertheless, the comedy feature was a huge hit with summertime audiences, grossing $7,950,000 in domestic rentals, $350,000 more than the well-remembered *Georgy Girl* released that same year.

With Julie Andrews and Karen Dotrice in Mary Poppins *(1964).*

In The Art of Love (1965).

Columbia's *Divorce American Style* (1967) required a little more sophistication from Dick the actor. It was produced by Norman Lear and directed by Bud Yorkin, and co-starred Debbie Reynolds, Jason Robards, Jean Simmons, and Van Johnson. Judith Crist on the "NBC Today Show" called the opus "a really, funny, sophisticated adult comedy," and *Time* said, "For Debbie Reynolds and Dick Van Dyke, the film represents a new direction. Together they provoke laughter whenever they should, but for the first time both are unafraid to appear unattractive and even unsympathetic in roles that show them at play and at bay."

Time was less excited about Van Dyke's *Fitzwilly* (1967), which cast Dick as Fitzwilliam, a butler who is actually a robbery gang leader. His co-stars were Barbara Feldon, Dame Edith Evans, and John McGiver. *Time* reported, "An uneasy amalgam of *Miracle on 34th Street* and the Marx Brothers' *The Big Store, Fitzwilly* is not helped by the surpris-ingly flaccid performance of Dick Van Dyke and Barbara Feldon. . . . All in all, the family night out might better be spent at the bowling alley."

Chitty Chitty Bang Bang! (1968) followed for Dick. It was United Artists' $10,000,000 splash of escapism based on a collection of children's stories by Ian Fleming. It featured a score by the *Mary Poppins* composers Richard M. Sherman and Robert B. Sherman, and a cast including Sally Anne Howes, Lionel Jeffries, and Gert Frobe. As Caractacus Potts, Van Dyke transforms a 1908 flivver into the flying machine that gives forth the title sound. In the course of the 142 minutes, Dick displays his musical talents via such songs as "Hushabye Mountain" (a lullaby), "Me Ol' Bam-Boo" (with a male chorus), and the title song. *Saturday Review* judged *Chitty Chitty* as entertainment that "can be recommended for children and is also reasonably bearable for adults," and wrote that Van Dyke "is creating such a cheerful image for himself that he may soon be able to run for governor of California." Nevertheless, the splashy production failed to generate the same kind of enthusiasm that surrounded *Mary Poppins* and it proved to be a box-office disappointment.

On a lower key was Walt Disney's *Never a Dull Moment* (1968), directed by Jerry Paris, who had helmed some of "The Dick Van Dyke Show" episodes. The film co-starred Edward G. Robinson and Dorothy Provine, with Dick as a struggling actor who becomes embroiled with Robinson's gangster pack. A far less engaging vehicle was *Some Kind of a Nut* (1969), written and directed by Garson Kanin. It supplied Van Dyke with Angie Dickinson as his leading lady and the role of Fred Amidon, a lifelong conformist whose life changes wildly after he grows a beard.

One of the more ignored films to deal with the subject of Hollywood has been *The Comic* (1969). It was produced, directed, and written by Carl Reiner, who also played a bit in the proceedings. It was a pet project of Reiner and Van Dyke, and supposedly inspired by

the lean last days of Stan Laurel, whom both men idolized. Dick played Billy Bright, a comedian whose story is unfolded in flashback, ranging from his vaudeville days to silent comedies to his decline and onward to his later rediscovery by TV personality Steve Allen (who appears in the film). Michele Lee was conventionally cast as a starlet who weds Billy Bright and then leaves him. Mickey Rooney gave a most captivating performance as a character called "Cockeye" (based on Ben Turpin). It was a lovingly turned-out, but stringent, study and Columbia Pictures was unsure how to package the product. In typical fashion it decided to toss it onto the release market and it failed to gain the public's attention.

It was two years before Van Dyke appeared in another feature, *Cold Turkey* (1971), produced, directed, and written by Norman Lear as an attack on middle-class American attitudes and values. The money-making comedy concerned a promotional sharpie (Bob Newhart) who offers any town $25,000,000 if it can collectively give up

With Joe Flynn in Divorce American Style *(1967).*

659

In The Comic (1969).

cigarette/cigar/pipe smoking. Van Dyke played the Reverend Clayton Brooks, who greedily encourages the scheme. The wild satire grossed $5,500,000 in distributors' domestic rentals, but neither critics nor audiences were totally ready to accept the ingratiating Van Dyke as a loathsome preacher who sleeps in hair curlers.

About this time several announcements were made in the trade press that Van Dyke would star in a cinema version of *I Do! I Do!*, the 1966 Broadway musical that had starred Mary Martin and Robert Preston. The song-filled property, based in turn on *The Four-poster*, was shelved, as far as motion pictures was concerned.

In the meantime, Van Dyke had moved his family from the Mandeville Canyon sector of Los Angeles to a ranch near Phoenix, Arizona. When Carl Reiner formulated the idea for a new comedy series for CBS-TV, the network was agreeable if Van Dyke would star in the package. Dick agreed to the assignment, but insisted the show be lensed in Arizona. Results: "The New Dick Van Dyke Show," a half-hour color series which premiered on September 18, 1971. The prime-

time Saturday night offering featured Hope Lange as the star's wife, and cast Dick as a TV talk-show host. The new offering was something of a disappointment to most viewers, who now expected all TV comedy programs to follow the "All in the Family" format. Van Dyke seemed intent on recapturing his success of the past and it was not working in the new setup. At the end of the second season Reiner restyled the show. Dick's character became an unemployed actor trying to land roles in Hollywood. When "The New Dick Van Dyke Show" returned on September 10, 1973, audiences were more pleased with the revamped format. However the entry still failed to tally impressive ratings. After a total of three chaotic seasons, "The New Dick Van Dyke Show" was no more. It failed to match even the popularity of the reruns of the original "Dick Van Dyke Show" running nationwide in syndication.

Privately, this was a trying period for the star and his family. His years in a turbulent profession had pushed him into alcoholism. He explained later: "My excuse for drinking was the pressure of my career. I tried to tell myself that I was a passive person, that this business was too difficult for me. I told myself I wasn't an alcoholic because I didn't drink in the morning or at work. I had all the excuses in the world, and they were all baloney. It took a long time to prove to myself that I couldn't drink. I just wouldn't admit it could happen to me." In August 1972, as his second difficult season started with his new weekly show, Van Dyke entered Saint Luke's Hospital in Phoenix, Arizona, and at his own request was treated in a ward rather than in a private room. His self-discipline assisted him in a quick treatment. When he left, his wife entered the hospital for treatment of the same problem. "My wife began drinking to keep me company," Van Dyke said later. "We'd sit up until three or four in the morning, talking and drinking in the bar at our home. We both became alcoholics." About their recovery Van Dyke says, "It's like getting out of prison. I've been sober long enough to know I've still got a lot to learn. . . . I was lucky. But you never really have it licked. As they say, it's one day at a time."

Artistically, Van Dyke's alcoholic treatment led to perhaps his greatest acting performance to date—as Charley, the problem drinker who guzzles away a lucrative writing post and an attractive family, in *The Morning After* (ABC-TV, February 13, 1974). "Maybe this movie will help the person who's beginning to be a little bit worried about his drinking," said Van Dyke to *TV Guide.* "When I saw the script, I said to myself, 'The good Lord meant this for me.'" Many viewers who still watched reruns of his old series and who had not seen a Van Dyke film performance since *Mary Poppins* were aghast to witness Van Dyke on camera punching his wife (Lynn Carlin) and screaming along a beach with delirium tremens. But nobody could deny that he gave the most powerful portrayal of a hopeless alcoholic since Ray Milland in *The Lost Weekend* and Jack Lemmon in *The Days of Wine and Roses.* Since making the film, Van Dyke has joined such public figures as Mercedes McCambridge, former Senator Harold Hughes, and former Representative Wilbur Mills in projects sponsored by the National Council on Alcoholism, which attempts to aid the more than 10 million American confirmed heavy drinkers. Van Dyke appeared in a 90-minute TV interview with Dick Cavett discussing the problem drinker. According to Van Dyke, his public acknowledgment of having been an alcoholic has not harmed his image with the public.

As a result of *The Morning After,* ABC-TV network offered Dick a lush contract which provided that he would star in a special, a TV movie, and a new situation comedy series. On October 30, 1975, he was seen in a showcase special (Mary Tyler Moore was his prime guest) which had mixed reaction from the critics and the public. But there was no doubt for Dick that his new pilot, "MacLeish and the Rented Kid," was a half-hour of video junk. Van Dyke and ABC-TV came to a parting of the ways. Says Dick, "I . . . found out that it's OK to say No, when that's how you feel. Doesn't everybody know that? I didn't." The chronic people pleaser was no more.

After the ABC-TV fiasco, NBC wooed Dick with a lucrative pact for a weekly variety show, which emerged as "Van Dyke & Company." The 60-minute format lavished Dick with opportunities to do what he does so well—situation humor, comic singing and dancing, and pantomime. During the fall of 1976 NBC shifted the program into various time slots, hoping to offset the critics' predictions that the too conventional show would not last. On December 30, 1976, the final installment of the wheezing series was telecast. It departed the scene quietly and was hardly missed. A philosophical Van Dyke mused shortly before the show's cancellation, "The reason I said yes to it [the series] in the first place was that I couldn't bear the thought of being 65 and looking back and kicking myself for never having tried a variety show. So I've done it, and now I'm liberated from that obsession. I'm still sober and I couldn't be happier."

If Van Dyke no longer had his own series, he was still seen frequently on TV in repeats of his old programs and in a slew of new commercials (toothpaste, amusement parks, home safety, and toys—the latter as part of a long-term deal as corporate spokesman for Gabriel Industries, a manufacturer of games, hobbies, toys, crafts, and home playground equipment). The lanky comic could also be seen in company with Julie Andrews and Carl Reiner in a syndicated variety special in January 1977 and then as co-host of the

"People's Choice Awards" (CBS-TV, February 10, 1977).

Shortly after Carol Burnett agreed to star in the stage comedy *Same Time, Next Year* at the Huntington Hartford Theatre (April 12-May 15, 1977), it was announced that Dick would be her co-star in front of the footlights. The long-running Broadway hit found equal success on the West Coast where it grossed $554,341. Burnett could not resist adding a scene to the end of Bernard Slade's established fun fest, in which a pair of "Carol Burnett Show" characters of extreme age chase one another about and finally fall into bed—to sleep.

Even before the popular stage venture completed its lucrative run, Burnett contracted Dick to appear as a regular on her Saturday night TV series. It was emphasized in the press that Van Dyke was not to be considered a replacement for long-time regular and "second banana" Harvey Korman who had departed for other projects. (Ironically Van Dyke's son Barry was in Korman's ABC-TV pilot which failed to find a sponsor for the then upcoming season.)

On Saturday, September 24, 1977, "The Carol Burnett Show" began its eleventh season. For any seasoned TV watcher it was soon evident that the show's producers were unable to showcase Van Dyke properly and that his brand of comedy did not mesh with Burnett's style sufficiently to endure over-exposure in weekly segments. In October it was openly rumored that the Burnett program was in serious rating trouble. A month later Van Dyke admitted to the press he was leaving "The Carol Burnett Show," stating that commuting from his ranch in Cave Creek, Arizona, to Hollywood was too much. Less rosy reports indicated that in view of the format's low viewer ratings, it was decided Van Dyke's weekly $25,000 salary could be dispensed with and that perhaps a time change to Sunday evening would be sufficient to restore Burnett's video standing. (It was not and the variety program departed the TV scene at the end of the 1977-78 season.)

In the summer of 1978 Van Dyke took time out from his full schedule of filming TV commercials to star in Stanley Kramer's *The Runner Stumbles* (1979), which was shot on location in Roslyn, Washington. Based on a play by Millan Stitt, it featured Van Dyke as a priest who falls in love with a nun (Kathleen Quinlan). Tammy Grimes co-starred in the outing which producer-director Kramer described as ". . . a love story from change of life to dotage and an examination of what faith is and what love is and the meaning in either or both."

Dick, now a grandfather (he allowed his hair to go gray in the late Sixties), and his family reside in both Arizona and Coronado, near San Diego (where he indulges in his passion for boating). The star has written two humorous books (*Faith, Hope and Hilarity* and *Those Funny Kids*) and occasionally strives to be a guiding force on the entertainment scene. He says of his craft, "I think it's a mistake even to try to figure out a definition of comedy. You could lose your sense of humor in the attempt. A guy who feels good and then tries to find out why he feels good may soon find he has no reason for it and wind up feeling miserable."

FEATURE FILMS

Bye Bye Birdie (*Columbia 1963*)
What a Way to Go! (*20th Century-Fox 1964*)
Mary Poppins (*Buena Vista 1964*)
The Art of Love (*Universal 1965*)
Lieutenant Robin Crusoe, U.S.N. (*Buena Vista 1966*)
Divorce American Style (*Columbia 1967*)
Fitzwilly (*United Artists 1967*)

Chitty Chitty Bang Bang! (*United Artists 1968*)
Never a Dull Moment (*Buena Vista 1968*)
Some Kind of a Nut (*United Artists 1969*)
The Comic (*Columbia 1969*)
Cold Turkey (*United Artists 1971*)
The Runner Stumbles (*Stanley Kramer Productions 1979*)

In The Remarkable Mr. Pennypacker *(1959).*

Clifton Webb

"I've destroyed their formula completely. I'm not young. I don't get the girl in the end and I don't swallow her tonsils, but I have become a national figure!"

Thus spoke Clifton Webb to *Life* magazine in 1949, following his resounding success as Lynn Belvedere, the intellectual babysitter not above dumping oatmeal cereal on the head of a troublesome tyke, in Twentieth Century-Fox's *Sitting Pretty* (1948). For the acerbic Webb, fame in motion pictures occurred when he was in his fifties. It followed a sterling stage career as a farceur schooled in Noël Coward and a lithe dancer who boasted such stage partners as Libby Holman, Mae Murray, and Jenny Dolly. The cinema was a welcome medium for Webb. While he was typed almost invariably as the waspish, priggish, polished, upper-crust insufferable, it was a typing he relished—for he was playing the real-life Webb in doing so.

Indeed, lanky Clifton Webb was rather singular in Hollywood circles. When he moved west permanently in 1944, he had crossed the Atlantic Ocean 38 times, owned 65 expensive suits, and been acclaimed "the most versatile of all American revue artists." But he was also of note in show-business circles for being unabashedly padlocked to his mother's apron strings and an uncloseted homosexual, a man who armored himself against the world with an acidic exterior.

He was born Webb Parmalee Hollenbeck in Indianapolis, Indiana, on Thursday, November 19, 1891. (The year 1896 became the usually publicized year of birth.) He was the son of a wildly ambitious stage mother, Mabel Parmalee, who spelled her name "Maybelle" and who would become her son's inseparable companion almost his entire life. Mr. Hollenbeck never rated a mention from either mother or son. As Maybelle would explain, "Clifton's father was not interested in the theatre." Her stage ambitions kindled, Mrs. Hollenbeck moved to New York City with her child when Clifton was just three.

Once in Manhattan, Clifton was soon enrolled at P.S. 87, where upon commencing to recite "Spartacus to the Romans at Capua" for an assembly, he promptly forgot his lines. But he fared much better at Palmer Cox's Lyceum's Children's Theatre, which he joined at age eight. He was quickly assigned roles such as Oliver Twist, and as Sid Sawyer in *Huckleberry Finn.* Actually his debut with the Cox company was as "Cholly" Boutonierre in the producer's *The Brownies.*

Under the ever watchful gaze of Maybelle, Clifton developed into quite the artistic young teenager. Besides theatrical skills, he was also adept at art. As he summed up his early years of creative development, "I held my first exhibition when I was 14, and one of the critics was so reckless as to call me a juvenile genius. But I tired of painting and went on to study voice. I made my debut in grand opera with the Aborn Opera Company in Boston, singing the role of Laertes in *Mignon.* I was 17 at the time. After I'd mastered some 24 operatic roles, in various languages, the dance craze came along. I ditched the opera to make a reputation as a dancer."

On April 7, 1913, Clifton made his Broadway debut in *The Purple Road* at the Liberty Theatre. He played a bridegroom named Bisco, and doubled in the role of Vestris, a dancing master. Mother Maybelle was also in the cast. After touring clubs and vaudeville with Bonnie Glass in a ballroom-dancing act (then the rage, courtesy of Irene and Vernon Castle), Clifton teamed with Mae Murray. They performed their dance routine on March 16, 1914, at Broadway's Palace Theatre. Their engagement was so successful that they were held over for a third week. On October 14, 1914, Clifton opened at the Winter Garden Theatre in *Dancing Around*; played a very successful dance engagement in Paris in 1916; starred in Jerome Kern's *Love o' Mike* (Shubert Theatre: January 15, 1917); and continued a very steady pace of professional work in the Broadway theatre and at vaudeville houses.

Besides his growing success in America, Webb was quite a drawing card in Europe. He played two seasons in London: opening in October 1921 in *Fun at the Phayre* (London Pavilion Theatre) and in August 1922 in *Phi-Phi* (London Pavilion Theatre). In the latter he sang the only Cole Porter song in the show, "Pipes of Pan." In 1923 his pal Elsa Maxwell signed Clifton to dance at her new Paris club, Les Acacias, where he performed with Jenny Dolly (of the famous Dolly Sisters) for six weeks. When he returned to Broadway for a

leading comic role in *Meet the Wife* (Klaw Theatre: November 26, 1923), he acquitted himself so nimbly with the witty repartee that critics agreed he would never need to dance again—so adroit was he as a comic actor. (The star of *Meet the Wife* was Mary Boland; a minor player in the cast was Humphrey Bogart.)

In the meantime, Clifton made a brief foray into motion pictures. His screen debut was as Clay Cullum in Metro's *Polly with a Past* (1920), starring lilting Ina Claire. In Vitagraph's Pauline Frederick vehicle *Let Not Man Put Asunder* (1923), he supported the lofty star as Major Bertie. In 1925 he was seen in two First National releases: *Heart of a Siren,* starring Barbara LaMarr (he was Maxim), and *New Toys,* a domestic comedy in which he played an ungallant Broadway figure named Tom Lawrence. The star of that film was Richard Barthelmess and in a featured role was Mary Hay. With the latter Clifton danced at New York's Club Ciro in May 1925 and he later would reteam with her in vaudeville and Broadway shows.

Webb continued his stage career to great acclaim. Among his credits were: *Sunny* (New Amsterdam Theatre: September 22, 1925), a Jerome Kern–Otto Harbach–Oscar Hammerstein II musical; *The Little Show* (Music Box Theatre: April 30, 1929), starring Webb, Fred Allen, and Libby Holman (Clifton staged, directed, and appeared with Miss Holman in the famed "Moanin' Low" number; Clifton also appeared in the George S. Kaufman sketch "The Still Alarm" and sang the Arthur Schwartz–Howard Dietz hit "I Guess I'll Have to Change My Plans"); and, most impressively, Irving Berlin–Moss Hart's *As Thousands Cheer* (Music Box Theatre: September 30, 1933), which was Clifton's greatest stage success.* Critic John Mason Brown reported, "Mr. Webb continues to grow in versatility from one season to another. In addition to his dancing and his sure instinct for comedy, he has now become a master of makeup; his Mahatma Gandhi, his Douglas Fairbanks Jr., his elder Rockefeller, and his waiter who has modeled himself on Noël

---

* Webb and Fred Allen made a 1930 short subject of *The Still Alarm* sketch. In October 1933 Webb would record "Easter Parade," "Not for All the Rice in China," and "How's Chances?" from *As Thousands Cheer* for Victor Records.

Coward are astonishing achievements in greasepaint and mimicry."

If Clifton was the most discussed performer along Broadway at this time, he was also the subject of much of the gossip. He was inseparable from Maybelle ("You see, my mother isn't a bit like Whistler's Mother"), sharing a residence with her at 455 East 57th Street in New York. Together they doted on their menagerie: a French poodle named Ernest, and a talking parrot, Goo-Goo, that delighted Clifton by insulting guests. While Clifton's strong attachment to his mother left little room for serious romantic relationships, he was the subject of much speculation concerning assorted homosexual affairs which the actor (surprisingly for the times) took little effort to conceal. This hardly fazed the columnists' affection for linking him with beautiful ladies: in 1918 he was reported engaged to Jeanne Eagels and later to Libby Holman; and shortly after *As Thousands Cheer* closed, Louella O. Parsons noted that he was about to marry Princess Natalie Paley after her divorce from French dress designer LeLong. Instead she wed John C. Wilson, Noël Coward's good friend; she would appear in Katharine Hepburn's film *Sylvia Scarlett* (1935).

In 1933 Clifton had been offered a dancing role in Joan Crawford and Clark Gable's *Dancing Lady* at MGM, but he demanded too large a salary and the role eventually went to Fred Astaire. Then after *As Thousands Cheer* closed (after 390 performances), the November 29, 1934, issue of the *Hollywood Reporter* broke the news, "Clifton Webb has been signed by Metro-Goldwyn-Mayer on a long-term deal that will divorce him from the musical comedy stage for quite a period." Clifton, Maybelle, and their assorted pets, converged on Culver City, where Louis B. Mayer did indeed have lavish plans for his newest star. The studio was preparing a property called *Elegance,* which would weave the life of the famous dancer Maurice* with a *Pygmalion* plot, in which he raised a 10-cents-a-dance girl to ballroom splendor and stage notoriety. The girl was to be played by Joan Crawford.

---

* At Paramount George Raft made *Bolero* (released in February 1934) with Carole Lombard. It was another thinly veiled account of the rise and fame of ballroom performer Maurice.

Webb would recall later, "I learned upon my arrival that a sinister malady called story trouble had afflicted the picture. It was a dreadfully long siege, lasting, in fact, for 18 months, after which the project quietly expired." The star did not relate that, in addition to story problems, there was co-star discord. When Webb encountered Miss Crawford for dance rehearsals, there was an immediate air of incompatibility. Miss Crawford was not impressed by Clifton's rather effete manner, nor did she care for the fact that her role was secondary to his. Webb diverted himself for most of the 18 months of "vacation" by swimming at Malibu Beach, going to parties, and flaunting his skills with a fish fork at various coastal restaurants. Meanwhile, he was drawing a $3,000 weekly salary from MGM. The actor finally tired of the tedium, requested his contractual release, and received it. He departed Hollywood with the statement, "The only thing I can really chide the movie industry for is its negligent attitude toward the actor's chief assets—time and talent."

Returning to New York, Clifton was deluged with scripts from theatrical producers and he soon returned to the stage. He starred in *And Stars Remain* (Guild Theatre: October 12, 1936), *You Never Know* (Winter Garden Theatre: September 21, 1938), and *The Importance of Being Earnest* (Vanderbilt Theatre: January 12, 1939). His co-star in the Oscar Wilde classic was Estelle Winwood.

Then in 1939 Monty Woolley opened in *The Man Who Came to Dinner,* the George S. Kaufman-Moss Hart spoof of iconoclastic Alexander Woollcott. When a touring company left New York that fall, Clifton was cast as the poison-tongued Sheridan Whiteside. For a year and a half the star toured the country in the role. The *Chicago Tribune* reported, "The whole play is Mr. Webb's, and he's taken remarkable possession." Clifton followed his triumph in the national company by playing wheelchair-bound Whiteside in summer theatres in August 1941.*

It was Noël Coward's *Blithe Spirit* (Morosco Theatre: November 5, 1941) which provided Clifton with his longest run. The delightful comedy co-starred Peggy Wood, Mil-

---

* After toying with the idea of casting John Barrymore in the lead role, Warner Bros. starred Monty Woolley in the film version of *The Man Who Came to Dinner* (1941).

dred Natwick, and Leonora Corbett as Elvira the blithe spirit. The *New York Times* enthused, "Clifton Webb can turn a line with as much neat dexterity as Mr. Coward can write it." Webb's performance in the sophisticated romp fully rounded his stage appeal. Since his return from Hollywood he had developed into an actor who no longer needed dance routines to be an audience pleaser.

Blithe Spirit ran for 650 performances. During this period, on February 22, 1942, Clifton appeared at the 60th Annual Actors' Fund Benefit, entertaining at the Imperial Theatre with such stage figures as Peggy Wood, Olsen and Johnson, Eddie Cantor, George Jessel, Bill Robinson, and Danny Kaye. On September 6, 1943, *Blithe Spirit* would reopen for a limited engagement of 32 performances.

Clifton enjoyed his celebrity status as always. He was still inseparable from mother Maybelle and spent as much free time as possible at his estate, High Acres, in Connecticut. He described his daily pattern there as "up at seven every morning, out in the garden, and up to my neck in ferns and fertilizer. Nails dirty, dungarees, literally—smelly!"

He had no idea that his career was in for yet another major metamorphosis. In early 1944 Twentieth Century-Fox, under the aegis of Darryl F. Zanuck, was preparing a cinema version of Vera Caspary's bestselling mystery, *Laura*. Originally the film was to star Jennifer Jones as the mysterious Laura, Dana Andrews as detective Mark McPherson, and Laird Cregar as venomous Waldo Lydecker, a radio celebrity who raises Laura to a refined status and, in a surprising denouement, reveals his desire to murder her. Rouben Mamoulian was to direct. However, studio intrigue intervened. Jennifer Jones departed the project and was replaced by Fox contractee Gene Tierney. Mamoulian then vacated his post and was replaced by Otto Preminger, the producer on the venture. Zanuck and Preminger clashed over the casting of Cregar as Lydecker. Preminger thought that Cregar was so stereotyped as a villain that it would spoil the story line's mystery. Zanuck argued that he could think of no better actor for the part. (Surprisingly, George Sanders, then frequently acting at Fox, was not mentioned for the role. In the

mid-Sixties, he would play Lydecker in an ill-fated TV version starring Princess Lee Radziwell.)

While Zanuck and Preminger argued, Clifton came to Los Angeles to play an engagement of *Blithe Spirit*. Preminger saw a performance of the Coward comedy and informed Zanuck that Webb was ideal for the role. Zanuck retorted that the actor "flies." Preminger argued that while Clifton was indeed effeminate off stage, he was not "that way" in performing. Webb won the part.*

Cifton proved to be very smooth, witty, debonair, and, ultimately, very chilling in *Laura* (1944). Even as he played his role, the off-camera disagreements continued with the result that the feature was shot with two endings. In the closing preferred by Zanuck and most of the obliging Fox executive force, Lydecker discovers that he imagined the whole story. The *released* version cast him as the *actual* murderer. Fox released *Laura* with surprisingly little fanfare, but it became the "sleeper" hit of the year. Clifton snared many of the best reviews. The *New York Times* described him as "sophistry personified" and New York's *PM* printed, "Clifton Webb, in his movie debut [*sic*], steals most of the honors as Lydecker. Webb, a kind of romantic Monty Woolley, knows how to make a wisecrack sizzle even if he does not pass muster as a murder suspect." When the Oscar nominations for Best Supporting Actor were announced for the year, Clifton was in the running. His competitors were: Hume Cronyn (*The Seventh Cross*), Barry Fitzgerald (*Going My Way*), Claude Rains (*Mr. Skeffington*), and Monty Woolley (*Since You Went Away*). Barry Fitzgerald proved to be the winner.

Fox was very impressed by Clifton's screen work. The studio had a roster of elegant "cad" types, with George Sanders and Vincent Price regularly playing such assignments. When major character star Laird Cregar died on December 9, 1944, Webb, who had replaced him in *Laura*, was reviewing with the

* Webb had never made a Hollywood screen test and saw no reason why he should now, especially with a relative "newcomer" like Gene Tierney. Since Zanuck demanded to see a filmed audition of Webb, Preminger solved the dilemma by taking a camera crew to the Biltmore Theatre in Los Angeles where Webb was performing. Webb was filmed performing the famous monologue from the play.

front office the terms of a lucrative long-term contract. It provided for time off for theatre work and promised not to overexpose Webb's attractively bitchy persona.

Webb's new contract allowed such a degree of freedom that it was over a year before the actor began work on another picture. *The Dark Corner* (1946), another mystery, co-starred Lucille Ball, Mark Stevens, and William Bendix. Henry Hathaway directed Clifton as treacherous art dealer Cathcart. The *New York Times* jibed, "If Mr. Webb doesn't change his style soon, his admirers are likely to grow impatient." Then came a showcase for Webb via Fox's lavish 146-minute *The Razor's Edge*. The Edmund Goulding-directed feature was primarily packaged as a gala comeback for ex-marine Tyrone Power. Clifton was at his insufferable best interpreting the role of Elliott Templeton, the titanic social tyrant who dies a pathetic figure. Once again, he was nominated for a Best Supporting Oscar, along with Charles Coburn (*The Green Years*), William Demarest (*The Jolson Story*), Claude Rains (*Notorious*), and Harold Russell (*The Best Years of Our Lives*). Russell won.

After his triumph in *The Razor's Edge*, Clifton took advantage of his loosely constructed film contract and returned to Broadway to star in his friend Noël Coward's *Present Laughter* (Plymouth Theatre: October 29, 1946). The *New York Times* praised the star's ability to be "vain without being precious, overbearing without being fatuous." The play ran for 158 performances. After it closed Clifton returned to Hollywood—never to return to the Broadway theatre, though the liberty to do so remained in his various studio agreements.

Back in the revitalizing climate of Southern California, Clifton admitted to enjoying cinema stardom. But he did confide, "My only concern is, where does an actor go from here? Heaven knows that I've had all that Broadway and Hollywood can do for one actor. When he has been professionally associated with Coward, and Maugham, the two top-ranking literary figures of his generation, what is there left for him to do that isn't anticlimax?"

He soon had an answer. Fox cast Clifton as Lynn Belvedere, a yoga-practicing intellectual who becomes a babysitter of uncanny repute, in *Sitting Pretty* (1948), in which the best billing went to Robert Young and Maureen O'Hara. "The night *Sitting Pretty* was sneak-previewed," Clifton quipped to *Photoplay* magazine, "I had a sneaking suspicion that those in the audience who had previously seen me on the screen were quite sure that I was going to start right in by murdering the baby. But, when they began to laugh uproariously, I had nothing to worry about." Indeed, audiences found Clifton irresistible, slightly spoofing his professional austerity, gracefully wiping splattered oatmeal from his eye, and retaliating by dumping the bowl on a surprised baby's dome. *Life* magazine would exult, "Played flawlessly by Clifton Webb, Mr. Belvedere is a piece of pure Americana."

The role of Belvedere performed box-office magic for Clifton. It transformed him from a major character player to a star who would rate top billing in the grade A features he starred in for the next nine years. Hollywood rapidly circulated the story of how Clifton, dining with cronies at Romanoff's restaurant, was greeted by a producer with the words, "Ah there, Webb, I don't suppose you'll be speaking to us small fries now that you've had this big success." Clifton icily retorted, "My dear man, I have *always* been a success. One more will not unsettle me."

Now a star in the film colony, Clifton—referred to by his less-ardent industry admirers as the "Queen Bee"—began disgorging an array of witticisms that only increased his reputation as the waspish duenna of Hollywood. Regarding the ambience of Bel Air Webb said, "A delightful acreage that might tentatively be described as the Forest Lawn of the living." He and Maybelle preferred Beverly Hills, where the star began a campaign of transforming a house at 1005 North Rexford Drive into a dream home. "I bought an adobe house, changed it into a Mediterranean villa. Walls knocked out, you know—arches removed—when will it be finished? Dear, it *will* be finished one of these days—and I'll be wheeled in." During Clifton and Maybelle's reign on Rexford Drive, neighbors included: Edward G. Robinson, Mickey Rooney, Jane Wyman, Boris Karloff, and Marlene Dietrich.

So successful was Clifton as Lynn Belvedere in *Sitting Pretty* that he received his

With Maureen O'Hara and Robert Young in Sitting Pretty *(1948).*

third Oscar nomination—this time as *Best Actor.* His competition included: Lew Ayres (*Johnny Belinda*), Montgomery Clift (*The Search*), Dan Dailey (*When My Baby Smiles at Me*), and Laurence Olivier (*Hamlet*). Olivier was the winner.

Fox promptly placed Clifton back into his applauded characterization in *Mr. Belvedere Goes to College* (1949), with Shirley Temple and Tom Drake in support. Though not comparable to the initial entry, it enjoyed a healthy box-office reception. Clifton remarked, "Belvedere, you see, has become a beloved character, and I now have an entirely new audience—housewives, truck drivers— literally millions who had never seen me before. I think that's a sign of a healthy career." Happy though he was with the headlines of cinema stardom, the actor vowed to *Life* magazine, "I don't want people to think of me only as Belvedere. I have always refused to be pigeonholed. So in my next picture I'm going to play the goddamnedest, most murderous, most terrifying creature

who ever drew breath. I assure you I will make that Richard Widmark look like a nursing baby."

But such was not the case. Instead, he portrayed Frank Bunker Gilbreth in *Cheaper by the Dozen* (1950), with Myrna Loy as the mother of his 12 children, including lovely Jeanne Crain. The *New York Times* reported of this period comedy that he "plays with the sweeping assurance of not only an authoritarian but a special star." Fox then placed Clifton, its number one character star, in a variety of formats, all allowing him to display his famous haughtiness and all affording him top billing.

For Heaven's Sake (1950) cast him as Charles the Angel sent to hasten the arrival of the daughter of Robert Cummings and Joan Bennett. A comic highlight of the film was Webb's masquerading as a westerner, complete with a hilariously incongruous cowboy hat and drawl. In 1951 he starred in two releases. *Mr. Belvedere Rings the Bell* placed the character in an old folks home. It was his last outing as the oddball fellow who won him major stardom. In *Elopement* Clifton was the harassed father of Anne Francis, taking off in pursuit of his little girl when she elopes with William Lundigan.

One of Webb's more amusing portrayals was as Thornton Sayre, a silent-film star turned Midwest college professor, in *Dreamboat* (1952). He is aghast when his old flickers are shown on TV. His co-star of the silent silver screen was Ginger Rogers, and the two players proved very adept at satire as they enacted scenes from a World War I drama, a Foreign Legion adventure, and a costume epic. In *Stars and Stripes Forever* (1952) Webb was John Philip Sousa, the famed marching band composer and conductor, with support from Robert Wagner, Ruth Hussey, Debra Paget, and a fleet of rousing marches. The *New York Times*, piqued by Webb's first color feature, penned, "Mr. Webb is unable to project any more than a chin-whiskered dandy who makes tart wisecracks and looks down his nose through pince-nez specs."

Clifton did a commendable about-face in his interpretation of Richard Sturges, the elegant socialite who pursues his fleeing wife (Barbara Stanwyck) and children (Audrey Dalton and Harper Carter) aboard the fateful luxury liner *Titanic* (1953). It was a thrilling and well-executed account of the infamous ocean tragedy on the night of April 15, 1912. The part allowed Webb to reveal more sympathetic shadings than did many of his recent predictable assignments. In the scenes where he bids goodbye to his family there were actually tears in the eyes of the allegedly icy actor.

Plans for Clifton to be loaned to MGM for the producer's role in Fred Astaire's *The Band Wagon* dissolved when Clifton made too many contractual demands. The part, instead, went to Britisher Jack Buchanan. It left Clifton free to lend his comedic talents to *Mister Scoutmaster* (1953) at Fox. Early in the filming of this picture, Webb became sarcastic with child performer George "Foghorn" Winslow and the tyke reciprocated by

With Lotte Stein, Clancy Cooper, and Jeff Chandler in Mr. Belvedere Goes to College *(1949).*

671

With Harry Hines in Mr. Belvedere Rings the Bell *(1951).*

With Ginger Rogers in Dream Boat *(1952).*

672

nearly stealing the picture from under Webb's arched nostrils.

By this time Clifton was in his early 60s (and his mother was in her mid-80s). He was now a staunch defender of the comfortable Hollywood lifestyle. In 1953 he informed *Cosmopolitan* magazine, "As a film actor, you become a human being. While you are working at your profession, you do not have to do the same thing day after day. You are continually in different scenes with different people. Then, between pictures, you have time to travel, to be social, or vegetate, or to be a citizen who can be home at voting time." In the meantime, the veteran star revealed *no* penchant for the burgeoning medium of television. He felt himself both too old and too temperamental to adjust to the demanding video schedules.

The very mature leading character man continued his employment at Fox. In 1954 he was top-billed in the plush CinemaScope production, *Three Coins in a Fountain*, playing expatriate author Shadwell amidst the Rome and Venice location shooting. Also that year Clifton starred as a motor corporation president in *Woman's World*, in which he invites couples Cornel Wilde and June Allyson, Fred MacMurray and Lauren Bacall, and Van Heflin and Arlene Dahl to his offices and home, watching the women to decide which man gets the promotion. The feature followed MGM's all-star *Executive Suite* by some four months. The *New York Times* snapped at the Fox effort, "A better title would be Executive Sweeties."

In 1956 he played Lieutenant Commander Ewen Montagu in the slick spy adventure *The Man Who Never Was*, but the actor's overly familiar loftiness was deemed more a liability than an asset to the World War II espionage thriller. In *Boy on a Dolphin* (1957) Webb was forced to surrender top billing to Alan Ladd. Webb is the determined art collector Victor Parmalee in a quest for the title statue amidst a Grecian setting. (Captivating Sophia Loren, in her American film debut, garnered most of the audience interest.) It appeared Webb's charm had run its cinema course. The *New York Times* carped, "The urbane Mr. Webb, who tries in a restrained, superior fashion to be funny, is not."

There were no Clifton Webb releases in 1958, but in 1959 Clifton was top-starred in two touted movie adaptations of Broadway hits. The first was Fox's *The Remarkable Mr. Pennypacker*, with Clifton in the title role of a businessman scion of two families and 17 children. Despite an agile supporting cast (Dorothy McGuire, Charles Coburn, and Jill St. John), *Variety* labeled the film "disappointing" and the *New York Times* branded it "gross and distasteful." Better received was *Holiday for Lovers*, with Clifton again a family man, this time taking his wife (Jane Wyman) and daughters (Jill St. John and Carol Lynley) on a South American vacation. The *New York Herald-Tribune* called the picture "delightful" and reported of the star, "Webb has lost, fortunately, I think, some of that Belvedere character that has typed him for so long. . . . He unbends considerably in this role." But at 68 Clifton was not in the best emotional position to unbend or revamp his screen image.

On October 17, 1960, Maybelle died at Hollywood's Cedars of Lebanon Hospital. She was 90 years old. Clifton was crushed. Friends wondered if he could recover from the trauma. Noël Coward, who would quip later, "You realize this makes Clifton the oldest orphan in the world!" called his bereaved friend from Jamaica. Coward insisted that Webb's secretary Helen Matthews pack his things and send him to Coward's for Christmas. Clifton greeted Noël's call with such wailing that Coward finally clucked, "My dear boy, if you go on like this I shall be forced to reverse the charges!"

Clifton, much the worse for the ordeal, recovered sufficiently to make one more film for Twentieth Century-Fox, *Satan Never Sleeps* (1962). It was a misguided missionary story in which he was billed between William Holden and France Nuyen. He played Father Bovard, a self-sacrificing priest described by *Variety* as "a wry, caustic version of Barry Fitzgerald's Father Fitzgibbon." The film was badly received.

Now in his 70s, Clifton was in poor health, both emotionally and physically. In January 1963 he underwent two hours of surgery in Houston for an abdominal aneurysm. Thereafter he remained secluded in his Beverly Hills home. He was said to be a rather miserable old man. For one thing, he refused to send a biographical sketch to the editors of the 1964 *Who's Who of the Theatre*. In May

With Doro Merande in The Remarkable Mr. Pennypacker.

1966 the actor again entered the hospital for an operation to rectify an intestinal blockage. Then on Thursday, October 13, 1966, at 9:00 P.M., Clifton died of a heart attack in his Rexford Drive home.

Strangely enough, Hollywood had not heard (nor seen) the last of Clifton Webb. In 1967 columnist Joyce Haber and her husband Doug Cramer purchased the Webb estate—and they vowed that Webb was haunting the house! "One night I saw Webb's ghost in my bedroom stark naked," insisted Miss Haber. "He was singing and dancing around the room. I know all this sounds like nutty time, but I'm only telling it the way it truly happened." When the ghost continued to appear in various forms (including that of a woman with an hourglass figure), the owners, in 1970, summoned famous psychic Sybil Leek from Florida to exorcise the ghost from the house. Recalls Mr. Cramer, of the exorcism,

"Sybil's voice became that of Clifton Webb. And she told us a number of facts about him during the séance. The exorcism lasted two hours and I think it was successful. On several occasions, however, I've seen gray, ectoplasmic shapes around the house."

Many critics and film scholars have wondered why Clifton Webb was artistically satisfied to settle in Hollywood and reprise his bitchy, precious persona in film after film after so sterling and varied a stage career. The answer is obvious. The aging actor found a perfect outlet for his own true self. As he confided to *Cosmopolitan* magazine, "I have never believed in the so-called 14-year-old mentality of filmgoers. I have never patronized any audience by trying to play down to it. When I read my fan mail today, and realize that in a single film evening, I reach more people than I would in two years in a Broadway play, I am very happy."

Feature Films

Polly with a Past (*Metro 1920*)

Let Not Man Put Asunder (*Vitagraph 1923*)

Heart of a Siren (*First National 1925*)

New Toys (*First National 1925*)

Laura (*20th Century-Fox 1944*)

The Dark Corner (*20th Century-Fox 1946*)

The Razor's Edge (*20th Century-Fox 1946*)

Sitting Pretty (*20th Century-Fox 1948*)

Mr. Belvedere Goes to College (*20th Century-Fox 1949*)

Cheaper by the Dozen (*20th Century-Fox 1950*)

For Heaven's Sake (*20th Century-Fox 1950*)

Mr. Belvedere Rings the Bell (*20th Century-Fox 1951*)

Elopement (*20th Century-Fox 1951*)

Dreamboat (*20th Century-Fox 1952*)

Stars and Stripes Forever (*20th Century-Fox 1952*)

Titanic (*20th Century-Fox 1953*)

Mister Scoutmaster (*20th Century-Fox 1953*)

Three Coins in the Fountain (*20th Century-Fox 1954*)

Woman's World (*20th Century-Fox 1954*)

The Man Who Never Was (*20th Century-Fox 1956*)

Boy on a Dolphin (*20th Century-Fox 1957*)

The Remarkable Mr. Pennypacker (*20th Century Fox 1959*)

Holiday for Lovers (*20th Century-Fox 1959*)

Satan Never Sleeps (*20th Century-Fox 1962*)

In Myra Breckinridge *(1970).*

Mae West

"It's not the men in my life that count, it's the life in my men" . . . "Beulah, peel me a grape" . . . "I used to be Snow White, but I drifted" . . . "Between two evils I always picked the one I never tried before" . . . "It's better to be looked over than overlooked" . . . "There are no withholding taxes on the wages of sin" . . . "Is that a gun in your pocket or are you just glad to see me?"

These famous morsels of lascivious verbal Americana arrived courtesy of Mae West, the blonde perennial paragon of cinema sex.* Ironically, for all her celebrated (and profitable) ribaldry, she probably did more to promote carnality as a *healthy* preoccupation than any other screen personality. When she wiggled into Hollywood in early 1932, after years as a legend of vaudeville and Broadway, Mae purred to the press, "I'm not a little girl from a

little town makin' good in a big town. I'm a big girl from a big town makin' good in a little town."

As Mae began employing her trademarks—swaying hips, rolling eyes, and repertoire of naughty witticisms—before the cameras, the Hearst newspaper chain denounced her as a "menace to the sacred institution of the American family," the Roman Catholic church created the Legion of Decency (largely to combat her), and America's Sweetheart, Mary Pickford, openly condemned her. Yet, despite her offending the sacred cows and pundits, Mae helped to rescue Paramount Pictures from bankruptcy. More important, she evolved promptly into one of the screen's greatest original comediennes.

Over four decades have passed since an already mature Mae caused delighted audience gasps in such movie classics as *She Done Him Wrong* (1933) and *I'm No Angel* (1933). Yet Mae is still very much a household word. As she once explained to reporters, "Sex and I have a lot in common. I don't want to take any credit for inventing it—but I may say, in my own modest way, and in a

* It is interesting to note Mae's reflection on the evolution of her comedienne status. "My comedy was a gradual thing. I didn't start putting in the wisecracks until the censors started taking out the drama. They were weakening my play, so I used humor to get over the sex, exaggeratin' my gestures and such."

manner of speaking—that I have rediscovered it."

Mae West was born on Wednesday, August 17, 1892, in Brooklyn, New York, the daughter of prizefighter John Patrick West and German immigrant mother Matilda Delker Doelger, a corset designer. For a time Mae joined the neighborhood kids at Brooklyn's P.S. 123, but her interests were always in performing.* At age five she sang "Ring Out, Wild Bells" at a church social and at seven was attending "Professor" Watts dancing school. Her professional bow came on the stage of the Royal Theatre on Fulton Street in Brooklyn in a song-and-dance act. At age six she was the resident child star of the Hal Clarendon Stock Company at Brooklyn's Gotham Theatre. In her four years there, Mae played such characters as Lovey Mary in *Mrs. Wiggs of the Cabbage Patch*, Little Eva in *Uncle Tom's Cabin*, and the Angel Child in *Ten Nights in a Barroom*. She followed this engagement by becoming a strongwoman in a Coney Island acrobatic act. At the age of 15 she toured with William Hogan in a vaudeville act as Huck Finn's girlfriend.

The always precocious Mae early on set her philosophy of life. "I've never been without a man for more than a week since I was 13 years old." Mae recently revealed that she lost her virginity with her music teacher ("I was 13, and he must have been 21"). As she relates it, "It happened one night on the stairs in our house, in the vestibule. . . . He was afraid, so I told him I had done it before. I wanted to see what it was like. . . . My mother and father were upstairs, but they couldn't tell what was going on. If one of them opened the door and came down the hall upstairs, I would have been able to hear them. And they wouldn't be able to see anything because I had my fur coat wrapped around me. The underwear was that long kind with a string tied at the waist and a slit

down the front that folded over. That was pretty convenient. . . ."

As Mae's career continued, so did her interest in men. On April 11, 1911, she married jazz singer Frank Wallace in Milwaukee, Wisconsin, with the vows pronounced by Civil Court Judge Joseph E. Cordes. The bride was 18, and says today, "I was tricked into getting married—I did it because I was scared—and I never had the slightest interest in having children. That was the last thing I would want to do. What did I need that for? I had to concentrate on myself. And I'm still concentrating on myself." (Mae and Wallace would be separated several months later, and were never to be reunited, although the divorce did not occur till 1943, after Wallace had made quite a stir announcing he was wed to the legendary sex symbol.)

It was also in 1911 (September 22) that Mae made her Broadway stage debut at Jesse L. Lasky's dinner theatre, Folies-Bergere, in a production entitled *A la Broadway.*

Mae rapidly earned a reputation in vaudeville and the theatre as a risqué avant-garde entertainer. Almost from the start, audiences and critics alike were unsure whether to take Mae's come-on act as a sex symbol seriously. Granted, in her earlier years as an entertainer her substantial hourglass figure was much more in keeping with the erotic tastes of the times. But as Mae grew more mature and thicker about the waist (and her hair and wigs became more bleached), it was hard to accept her by contemporary sexual standards. But whether or not from the start Mae was mocking the public's sexual-erotic tastes, there was never any doubt that Mae was a crowd pleaser. More important, Mae always took herself very seriously as a performer.

In 1912 she toured with the Gerard Brothers (Bobby O'Neil and Harry Laughlin). In October 1913 she appeared at New York's Fifth Avenue Theatre in her act, "Mae West and Beverly." (Beverly was her younger sister, born in 1897.) In 1916 and 1917 Mae was a vaudeville headliner on the Loew's circuit, billed as "The Baby Vamp" and "The Original Brinkley Girl." On October 4, 1918, she opened at the Shubert Theatre in the Arthur Hammerstein musical *Sometime*. The star of the show was Ed Wynn, but Mae became the production's most discussed performer via

---

* Mae freely admits to a life-long involvement with vanity; her favorite subject is always herself. As one interviewer analyzed the matter, "What would seem offensive in anybody else becomes charming in her because she is totally honest about her ego-love." West has noted, "Even when I was a little girl, I was terribly vain. There were these windows, see, near the house where I lived, and I would walk back and forth, back and forth, looking at my reflection. A person could never get me to carry a package. Never! I thought it would ruin my appearance."

her interpretation of Mayme Dean, a Hoboken whore who dances "The Shimmy" in the number "The Shimmy Shawabble." Mae also sang "Any Kind of Man" and "All I Want Is Just a Little Lovin'," which were both crowd pleasers. The show ran for 283 performances. After it closed, Mae toured the vaudeville circuit reprising her famous "Shimmy." When public response to the dance was at times starched, Mae squelched complaints thus: "I just told them it was some kind of Polish folk dance."

On October 24, 1919, Mae helped open the Broadway Capitol Theatre; she appeared as part of Ned Wayburn's *Demi-Tasse Revue*, singing "Laughing Waters" and "Oh, What a Moanin' Man." Mae almost made her screen bow in 1920 when she tested at Pathé for the lead opposite Jack Dempsey in the serial *Daredevil Jack* to be directed by W. S. Van Dyke. She did not make the chapterplay. In 1922 Mae developed a vaudeville act with pianist Harry Richman (he was later replaced by "Whispering" Jack Smith) and embarked on tours of the Pantages vaudeville circuit. By now the enterprising Mae was writing her own material and further developing her good-natured seductive style that became her stock-in-trade. The act was booked into the *Ginger Box Revue* at the Greenwich Village Theatre in 1923.

Mae reached a plateau of stage notoriety in 1926. Director Edward Elsner ("he looked like something out of an Edgar Allan Poe story dusted off") had cast her in a new play. "I would do things and he'd say, 'Do it that way again—it's so sexy.' I didn't know what he meant. Like he'd tell me to sit on a guy's lap. I didn't just plop down. I didn't wait for the guy to get set either. I just sort of moved over . . . and used my knee to open his knees. It drove Elsner crazy.

"He said, 'You reek with sex. It's in your eyes, your mouth, your voice, the way you move.' I was just acting nonchalant. Like I did in vaudeville. It was just natural to me. He said I had a low sex quality—and that sounded better than high."

The result was *Sex*, which opened at Daly's Theatre on April 26, 1926. The play became a Broadway phenomenon, running 375 performances before outraged social groups succeeded in having Mae arrested and sentenced to jail on Blackwell's Island for 10 days. She

was also fined $500. She was released after eight days of incarceration and told the press, "The warden was very nice. He used to take me out driving every night." Upon her release, irrepressible Mae, an early champion of gay liberation, produced *The Drag*. The show, with an all homosexual cast, tried out in early 1927 in Paterson, New Jersey, but never reached New York City.

Mae next wrote and starred in *The Wicked Age*. That show opened on November 4, 1927, but ran only 19 performances. However, her next theatrical venture was a winner. It was *Diamond Lil* (Royale Theatre: April 9, 1928). With Mae in the title role, the show featured three songs that have become an integral part of the West legend: "Easy Rider," "A Guy What Takes His Time," and "Frankie and Johnny." "I'm her and she's me and we're each other," analyzed Mae of her Lil characterization, the 1890s vamp of the Suicide Hare Saloon. The impressive show ran for 323 performances. Her follow-up, *Pleasure Man* (Biltmore Theatre: October 1, 1928), featured female impersonators and was promptly shut down. Mae was escorted back to court. After extricating herself from that censorial hassle, Mae toured in *Diamond Lil* and returned to Broadway in *The Constant Sinner* (Royale Theatre: September 14, 1931, 64 performances).

In the meantime, a pick-up collector of one of Mae's underworld backers had made it big in Hollywood. His name was George Raft and he encouraged Paramount to feature Mae in a romantic drama he was to star in called *Night After Night* (1932). The financially hard-pressed studio acquiesced and lured the lady to Hollywood, offering her a $5,000 per week contract with a 10-week guarantee. (She was a replacement for another Raft pal, Texas Guinan.) When Mae arrived at the studio she was unhappy with the script. Paramount, in a rather unprecedented move, allowed her to write her own material (as she would do in most of her subsequent films). Her first appearance on screen was as Maude Triplett and the characterization has become a classic. Dripping with diamonds, she slowly struts before an agog hatcheck girl who sighs, "Goodness. What beautiful diamonds!" Mae retorts in her slow drawl, "Goodness had nothing to do with it, dearie!" Though billed fourth in *Night After Night* (beneath Raft,

Constance Cummings, and Wynne Gibson), Mae, in Raft's words, "stole everything but the cameras."

Paramount was about to cave in, caught in the financial chaos of the Depression. Despite the presence on the lot of exotic Marlene Dietrich, pert Carole Lombard, sophisticated Kay Francis, and charming Claudette Colbert, the studio was in dire money trouble. Some 1,700 Paramount theatres were destined to be converted into office buildings and the lot itself was about to be sold to Louis B. Mayer's MGM facilities.

However, when Paramount executives studied the box-office returns on *Night After Night* and audience reception to Mae, the studio offered her over $100,000 to appear in another picture. She demanded that the project be a film version of her *Diamond Lil*. Besides providing the screenplay (earning a bonus of $25,000), Mae selected the leading man as she saw him walking across the Paramount lot. His name was Cary Grant. Producers argued he had insufficient experience. Mae reasoned, "Call him over. If he

can talk, I'll take him. He'll do for my leading man." (This is Mae's version of the account. Actually Grant had already appeared in eight features, receiving top billing over Nancy Carroll in *Hot Saturday*, and as the leading man in Sylvia Sidney's *Madame Butterfly*. While there is no question that the terrific success of West's film exposed Grant to a larger number of filmgoers, his career was already well established and he would have gotten where he did in the profession *if* he had *never* made the two West pictures. There is some indication that Grant is annoyed by her claims on this score.)

The film, retitled *She Done Him Wrong*, premiered at New York's Paramount Theatre on February 9, 1933, and earned some $2 million in distributors' domestic grosses (10 times its cost) within three months. Audiences whooped at the saucy exchanges between Mae and handsome Grant. At one point in the story line, Mae's Lady Lou is arrested by law enforcer Grant, and she is handcuffed.

With Cary Grant in She Done Him Wrong *(1933).*

WEST: Are those absolutely necessary? You know, I wasn't born with them.

GRANT: No. A lot of men would have been safer if you had.

WEST: I don't know. Hands ain't everything!

With Mae again warbling her "Frankie and Johnny" and other Diamond Lil tunes, *She Done Him Wrong* gave Paramount a new financial lease on life.

The studio rushed Mae into another sex comedy, *I'm No Angel* (1933) with 41-year-old Mae as Tira the lion tamer (she entered the cage herself—no doubles!). She sang "They Call Me Sister Honky Tonk" and other tunes, and told her on-camera leading man (Grant), "When I'm good, I'm very good, but when I'm bad, I'm better." *I'm No Angel* broke box-office records when it bowed at Manhattan's Paramount Theatre.

As a result of her trio of Paramount films, Mae was number eight in the top 10 box-office attractions in North America. The studio awarded their mature heroine a new contract, promising her $100,000 per picture plus an additional $100,000 per scenario.

It was easy to understand Mae's commercial appeal. At a time when sex was a subject more giggled about than discussed in most polite and not so polite circles, Mae bluntly put the facts forth with good humor. The sexual aura of Greta Garbo, Marlene Dietrich, and Dolores Del Rio was treated by the cinema as if their charms were rich opium, intoxicating men to decadent depths. But jaunty Mae was good-humored, brutally candid, and fully able to enjoy the pleasures of a lover without her entire life suffering. As critic Don Herold would later assess, "Mae West burlesques sex, kids it, and I prefer that as moral fare for young American junior misses to the overserious consideration of sex suggested by Garbo, Dietrich, Joan Crawford, and others."

Yet the majority of the country's social watchdogs despised and feared Mae and all that she represented. When her next Paramount feature, *It Ain't No Sin,* opened in early 1934, Catholic priests paraded under the marquee with signs that read, "It *Is.*" It was retitled *Belle of the Nineties,* and featured Roger Pryor and Johnny Mack Brown as her co-stars, and contained one of Mae's most sagacious sayings, "A man in the house is worth two in the street." *Belle* was her only release that year, yet she rose to the number one spot on the popularity polls, her only potent female competition (ironically enough) being super-wholesome Janet Gaynor of Fox Films.

In 1935 Mae starred as footloose Cleo Borden in Paramount's *Goin' to Town.* In it she sang (quite well) the operatic aria "My Heart at Thy Sweet Voice" from Saint-Saens' opera *Samson and Delilah.* Of Delilah Mae said, "I have a lot of respect for that dame. There's one lady barber that made good." The film was anathema to the Hays Office and the Legion of Decency. Even the more worldly *New York Herald-Tribune* huffed, "There are times when Miss West fairly outdoes herself as a rather vulgar retailer of indelicate wise-cracks." Nevertheless, Mae finished 11th in that year's box-office tally and reported an income of $480,833.

In her next film, *Klondike Annie* (1936), Mae was the Frisco Doll who becomes, through a twist of fate and plot manipulation, a soul saver in the frozen north. She delivered the song "It's Better to Give Than to Receive" and mouthed lines like, "Any time you take religion as a joke, the laugh's on you." The newspaper critics who had once endorsed her were now becoming satiated with Mae's brand of screen comedy. "There is no place anywhere," snarled a *New York Times* reviewer, "for the stupid substitute that Miss West is now trying to pass as comedy." Yet, for all the furor her comedy caused, Mae appeared to be a permanent Hollywood superstar with the public.

While Mae was combating the critics, she also had problems on her home lot. Ernst Lubitsch's reign as production chief at Paramount had left a sour taste in Mae's mouth. He lamented publicly, "Her films are vehicles built around her, and I, personally, cannot make a good picture unless I am dealing with someone more pliable." Lubitsch reportedly informed Mae, "In every story there must be parts for two players, like *Romeo and Juliet,*" to which Mae responded, "That was Shakespeare's technique, but it ain't mine." Though Lubitsch vacated his post early in 1936 and a new executive hierarchy took control, Mae noted, "Paramount didn't seem like home to me any longer."

She filmed two more features for Paramount. *Go West, Young Man* (1936) presented Mae as movie star Mavis Arden who lives by the code "A thrill a day keeps the chill away" and who finds a very unlikely romantic partner in the form of Randolph Scott.* Her Paramount stay ended with *Every Day's a Holiday* (1938), with Mae as con artist Peaches O'Day who masquerades as Mademoiselle Fifi (with an assist from a black wig).

Off screen Mae led a very discreet private life, keeping a Hollywood apartment, a ranch at Sepulveda, and a beach mansion—all decorated in her favorite color, white. She was the subject of infinite speculation regarding her affairs, but lived by the credo suggested in one of her famous lines:

INGENUE: Oh, Miss West, I've heard so much about you!

* Many feel that this property was a great mistake for Mae in that it revealed her limitations as an actress. When done on Broadway by Gladys George in October 1934 (for a 501-performance run), the stage star brought great variety to the role, using several different voices over a seeming two octave range. The film version was the first occasion since *Night After Night* that Mae had *not* written her own part, and it cruelly exposed her limitations as a screen actress.

WEST: Yeah, honey. But you can't prove a thing!

In December 1937 Mae caused the greatest controversy of her steamy Hollywood career when she guested on the Sunday evening Edgar Bergen-Charlie McCarthy Chase and Sanborn Hour on NBC network radio. In the "Garden of Eden" skit (penned by Arch Oboler) Mae purred to Charlie, "Would you, honey, like to try this apple sometime?" with such suggestive nuance that church groups denounced her for publicly performing lasciviously on a Sunday. Radio decided that Miss West was persona non grata and she remained off the airwaves for a dozen years when she returned to the airwaves on Perry Como's "Chesterfield Supper Club" program.

Mae suffered temporary defeats in other arenas. In 1938 an advertisement in *Motion Picture Herald* listed her on a "Box Office Poison" chart (along with Katharine Hepburn, Fred Astaire, Marlene Dietrich, et al.). If the movies were out of bounds for the time being, audiences still flocked to see Mae when she returned to the stage with a 46-minute act. She performed at Loew's State Theatre in New York and other entertain-

With Randolph Scott in Go West, Young Man *(1936).*

With Victor McLaglen in Klondike Annie (1936).

ment houses. Although she had formed her own film producing company, Empire Picture Corp., it was for Universal Pictures that she returned to the screen.

The project became the classic *My Little Chickadee* (1940) and her second-billed co-star was another ex-Paramount comedian, W. C. Fields. If their teaming caused fans to hold special memories of Flower Belle Lee and Cuthbert J. Twillie, Mae does not share them. She recalls that the bulbous-nosed laughmaker reworked some of the lines she wrote for him. She also recalls, "I had been a little worried about Bill's fondness for dipping into the sauce. . . . I had a clause inserted into my starring contract stating that if he should show up on the set intoxicated, he was to be removed immediately. . . . The fourth week of shooting began with Mr. Fields beautifully stoned, and I had to invoke that protective clause. . . . Some people have gotten the quaint idea that I made more than one film with W. C. Fields. No way, baby. Once

was enough." Fields himself carried no great fondness for the equally iconoclastic Miss West and enjoyed referring to her as "my little brood mare." At the time of its release, *My Little Chickadee* received only lukewarm reviews. ("It's one thing to burlesque sex and quite another to be burlesqued by it," snorted the *New York Times*.) Mae, then 47, was noticeably beefy and obviously bewigged.

Though Mae's professional output slowed down in the Forties, her notoriety remained intact. In 1941 the RAF named their life-saving jacket after Mae, who replied, "I've been in Who's Who and I know what's what, but it'll be the first time I ever made the dictionary." Her last picture for almost three decades was Columbia's low-budgeted *The Heat's On* (1943), with Victor Moore and Xavier Cugat & His Orchestra. She wore contemporary costumes and appeared quite hefty in the process. The *New York Herald-Tribune* called the West wisecracking style "outdated" and Mae herself later admitted

683

With Victor Moore in
The Heat's On (1943).

that *The Heat's On* was a film "I made against my better judgment."

If Mae could no longer compete with such up-to-date Hollywood pinup queens as Betty Grable, Lana Turner, Veronica Lake, and Hedy Lamarr, she was still an attraction on stage. She had long hoped to make a film on Russia's great Catherine, and now revamped the project into a play. *Catherine Was Great* opened at Broadway's Shubert Theatre on August 2, 1944, running 191 performances. The show contained her famous curtain speech, "Catherine was a great empress. She also had 300 lovers. I did the best I could in a couple of hours." After a U.S. tour of *Catherine*, Mae toured the 1946 summer stock circuit in *Ring Twice Tonight*, took *Diamond Lil* to England in 1947, and then toured that play for four years in the United States. (She made two return stopovers to Broadway with the show, in 1949 and in 1951.)

In 1952 Miss West again performed on the strawhat circuit, this time in *Come on Up . . . Ring Twice*. Two years later in July 1954 she made her Las Vegas nightclub debut at the Sahara Hotel with nine muscle men. She opened the entertainment with the song "I Wanna Do All Day What I Do All Night." The chorus line of beefcake included the former Mr. California of 1948, Charles Krauser, Mickey Hargerty (who would later wed Jayne Mansfield), and Mae's long-time companion Paul Novak. The unique act went on to play New York's Latin Quarter club and, in 1955, Chicago's Chez Paree. Miss West made sure there was considerable publicity concerning the backstage fights among the musclemen for her affections.

After a 1956 summer stock tour of *Come On Up . . . Ring Twice*, Mae allowed herself to be lured by television. On March 26, 1958, she appeared on the NBC network Oscar telecast, singing "Baby It's Cold Outside" with Rock Hudson and definitely stopping the show. On May 3, 1959, she guested on ABC-TV's "Dean Martin Show," dueting with the host and trading cracks with Bob Hope. On October 16, 1959, she taped a "Person to Person" television interview with Charles Collingwood for CBS, but the show was censored because of Mae's too frequent double entendres. The line that really caused the censors to veto the segment occurred when Collingwood asked Mae why there were so many mirrors in her bedroom. Her reply, "I like to see how I'm doin'." Mae later spoofed this experience on March 1, 1960, when she guested on CBS-TV's "Red Skelton Show." It was four years before she appeared in the medium again, this time—of all places—on NBC-TV's "Mr. Ed." She swapped racy repartee with the celebrated talking horse.

Meanwhile, Mae made some LP albums and in July 1961 opened a new play, *Sextette*, at Chicago's Edgewater Beach Playhouse. Her co-star was Jack LaRue, who had appeared with Mae in her original production of *Diamond Lil*, and Alan Marshal (who died during the tour). Occasionally the movies bid for West's services, but she rejected the roles as too subordinate or not right for her brand of humor. Among the parts she refused were the Rita Hayworth role in *Pal Joey* (1957), the Barbara Stanwyck circus owner role in Elvis Presley's *Roustabout* (1964), and the Ethel Merman "madame" role in *The Art of Love* (1965).

Eventually Mae—who had survived most of her contemporaries—did return to the screen.* It was in a film, *Myra Breckenridge* (1970), that she (and most everyone else) would prefer to forget. For 10 days of work and for writing her own material, Mae received $350,000 and joyously feuded with sexpot Raquel Welch, who played the title figure. In her complex contract Mae stipulated that she alone be allowed to wear white, and invited gossip when she purred, "Today you have sex symbols without sex personalities." At the New York premiere gala, Mae upstaged Raquel totally, strategically arriving after Raquel and entering the theatre as some 10,000 fans mobbed and screamed for her. Sixty policemen on foot and six mounted police did their best to prevent the crowd from engulfing the 78-year-old-lady. For all these hi-jinks, the much ballyhooed film was a disaster. The *New York Times* reported that Mae "has finally been done wrong by getting a short shrift." Fortunately, some of Mae's more tasteless scenes were deleted before general release. (At one point in the preexpurgated version, a Vietnam war veteran complains that his artificial arm and leg

* In 1969 Mae filmed—in part—a planned TV special at the Warner Bros. facility; Cary Grant was a guest performer. The show was never televised.

both unscrew; to which Mae replies, "Well, come up and see me some time and I'll show ya how to screw your head off.")

Now in her mid-80s, Mae still keeps professionally busy. On April 5, 1976, she was the special guest of a Dick Cavett CBS-TV special devoted to Hollywood. In her interview segment, for which she was paid $30,000, she traded witticisms with straight man Cavett and sang "Frankie and Johnny" and "After You've Gone." She told *Variety* she did the show "because of the dullness of the bicentennial. I thought I'd take a little starch out of the year." Her memoirs, *Goodness Had Nothing to Do with It*, had been updated in 1970 and are still being distributed. Her novel, *Pleasure Man*, was published in 1976.

More recently, Mae won great publicity as she maneuvered through her twelfth feature film, *Sextette*, produced by Daniel Briggs and Robert Sullivan (both in their twenties) and filmed at Paramount. Mae was paid $250,000 (plus a percentage-of-the-profits agreement) for her participation in the $4.2 million color feature based on her 1961 play.* She selected Timothy Dalton for her leading man after screening his performance as Heathcliff in the 1971 remake of *Wuthering Heights*. Other actors pitted against Mae in this venture are Ringo Starr, Dom DeLuise, George Hamilton,

* When interviewed during the lensing of this feature, Mae told the press, "It's got sex and comedy. It's my personality. I put in all the things the public expects of me.

"Yet it's different. None of my stories is the same. I never use anything I've done before for the basic plot. If you've seen one of my pictures you haven't seen them all. I always forget everything I've ever done and start from scratch.

"I make my notes, and I know just what I want to do. I have a secretary—he's been with me quite a long time—and he takes down everything I say. I get up and act it out, and he puts it down.

"Making the movie, that's the easy part. It's the writing that's the job. But I got to write it to do it right, so I've got double work. Most stars have it written for them, but this star has to write for herself!

"Now, I've studied my audience, and I know what they want me to do. I don't think people who don't write can really satisfy an audience unless they got writers who know exactly what the audience wants.

"I believe in treating sex with comedy, in having laughs with it to keep it from becoming too serious. I don't go too far. I've had some of these new sex pictures brought up to the apartment to see what they look like—I wouldn't want anyone seeing me going into a theatre to see such pictures! Now I'd never show the sexual act on the screen. I think that would be too crude. But there certainly is an audience for it."

Keith Moon (of The Who), Walter Pidgeon, and George Raft. Said DeLuise, "She never looked a day over 50 and, on good days, she looked 40. She was on the set at 8 A.M., and still going strong at 5:30 P.M., and she never once said, 'I'm tired.'" One of the six musical numbers in the feature has West singing "Happy Birthday 21." Although the film was completed in May 1977 there was great resistance among picture distributors to acquire the offbeat property for release. Warner Bros. test-screened *Sextette* in a few engagements in southern California, but thereafter refused to commit itself to handling the motion picture.

Meanwhile, on May 13, 1977, platinum-wigged Mae was the center of attention at a party held at the Beverly Wilshire Hotel where she received *After Dark* magazine's Ruby Award. It is given annually "for distinguished work in the entertainmant field." In presenting the tribute to Miss West, the sponsors cited, "Always up, always funny, always glamorous, Mae West is undisputedly one of the most important women of the century." On August 17, 1977, she celebrated her birthday with a party for 30 of her closest friends; "mostly men," she quipped. Later in the year it was reported that she had rejected a $250,000 offer for a week's engagement at the Tropicana Hotel in Las Vegas.

A great believer in mysticism, Mae today insists that her deceased brother and pet monkey have both appeared to her from the beyond, and that "several groups of handsome young men have come and stood beside my bed. I extended my hand to them . . . and they disappeared." Mae has never been a smoker or a drinker, and traces her still impressive figure to the fact that she massages her breasts with cocoa butter every night (sometimes in the morning too) and sprays them with cold water. "This treatment kept them right up where they were supposed to be."

Mae's opinions of other sex goddesses are indeed cavalier. Of Jean Harlow she says, "She was before me" (Harlow was some 19 years younger than Mae and made her hit in *Hell's Angels* two years before Mae's feature bow) and describes the platinum blonde star as offering merely "schoolgirl sex" (a term she also uses to dismiss Marilyn Monroe). As for Barbra Streisand, who attempted a Mae Westian delivery in the screen version of *Helly, Dolly!* (1969), Mae announced, "She's got nothin' much of her own. I don't care for her doin' that imitation of me she tries. It's a compliment to be mimicked, but when she's makin' her *livin'* at it? She wants to be sexy is why she does it. Every studio wanted a Mae West, they never found one 'cause my technique's my own—it can't be copied."

FEATURE FILMS

Night After Night (*Paramount 1932*)
She Done Him Wrong (*Paramount 1933*)
I'm No Angel (*Paramount 1933*)
Belle of the Nineties (*Paramount 1934*)
Goin' to Town (*Paramount 1935*)
Klondike Annie (*Paramount 1936*)

Go West, Young Man (*Paramount 1936*)
Every Day's a Holiday (*Paramount 1938*)
My Little Chickadee (*Universal 1940*)
The Heat's On (*Columbia 1943*)
Myra Breckenridge (*20th Century-Fox 1970*)
Sextette (*Crown International 1978*)

"It's not the pictures in my life, but the life in my picture . . ."

$72,258

Exclusive engagement at Pacific's Cinerama Dome.

SEXTETTE

Briggs and Sullivan present **MAE WEST** in SEXTETTE
Co-Starring **TIMOTHY DALTON** • **RINGO STARR** • **GEORGE HAMILTON** • Special Guest Star **TONY CURTIS**
Special Appearance by **ALICE COOPER** • **DOM DeLUISE** as Dan Turner
Cameo Appearances by **RONA BARRETT** • **VAN McCOY** • **KEITH MOON** • **REGIS PHILBIN**
WALTER PIDGEON • **GEORGE RAFT** • **GIL STRATTON** • **HARRY WEISS**
Executive Producer **WARNER G. TOUB** • Screenplay by **HERBERT BAKER** • From the Play by **MAE WEST**
Produced by **DANIEL BRIGGS** and **ROBERT SULLIVAN** • Directed by **KEN HUGHES**

687

In Babes in Toyland *(1961).*

Ed Wynn

Several generations of audiences delighted in "The Perfect Fool's" ludicrous comedy and grew accustomed to his high-pitched lisping voice punctuated with a contagious giggle. For three decades he romped through vaudeville and Broadway musical comedies where his unique, inventive comedy remained unequaled for hilarious fantasy. He seemed to be forever cavorting in outlandishly weird costumes amid his distinctive, if bizarre, laugh-provoking inventions. He went on to delight America as one of its first radio and television stars.

Wynn's enormous talent eluded Hollywood. Early attempts to capture the essence and mercurial madness of his comedy failed. Not until he was 70 years old did he realize success on the screen. Then, except for a few gossamer glimpses of his great comedic gifts, it was as a fine character actor that he made a burst of success in the cinema.

The future Ed Wynn was born on Tuesday, November 9, 1886, at 460 North Second Street, Philadelphia, to storekeeper (later hat maker) Joseph Leopold and his wife, Minnie. He attended Central High School with an-other future famous classmate, Alexander Woollcott. At the age of 15 he ran away from home and joined the Thurber-Nasher Repertoire Company, making his professional stage debut in Haverhill, Massachusetts, on August 8, 1902. To spare his family embarrassment from his being on the stage, Isaiah Edwin Leopold would change his professional identification by splitting his middle name and substituting a "y" for the "i" and affixing a second "n" at the end, thereby becoming Ed Wynn.

Doubling as a utility boy on stage and passing out handbills off stage, he stayed with the troupe until it folded 21 weeks later in Bangor, Maine. The following year he played vaudeville circuits in a sketch, "The Boy with the Funny Hat," and for the next two years teamed with Jack Louis as vaudeville's "Rah, Rah, Rah Boys." Criss-crossing the United States in a variety of vaudeville sketches, he was playing the Orpheum Theatre in Winnipeg in 1912 in a two-a-day sketch "Joy and Gloom" when he met his future wife. Hilda Keenan was then playing on the show circuit in a sketch with her father Frank, who would make something of a name as a silent-screen star. In a civil ceremony on September 4, 1914, Hilda became Mrs. Ed Wynn.

Without notice by the press Wynn rushed from a Chicago engagement to substitute in the opening bill of New York's Palace Theatre on March 24, 1913. His act was billed as "The King's Jester," a farce by Ed Wynn & Co. "The Boy with the Funny Hat" had written the book, music, and lyrics and "& Co." included Frank Wunderlee, William Sadler, and Robert Jones. His next Broadway venture was in the *Ziegfeld Follies of 1914*, which opened on June 1, 1914, for 112 performances. It was a more prestigious engagement than his Broadway legitimate stage debut in *The Deacon and the Lady*, a trifle that collapsed in two weeks after opening October 4, 1910, at the New York Theatre.

The New Amsterdam Theatre's June 21, 1915, opening of *Ziegfeld Follies* was Ed's second and last *Follies* and the first for a bulbous-nosed juggler up from vaudeville, W. C. Fields. In the 1915 edition, Fields did his famous billiard-table routine. Untimely laughter bewildered Fields, until he caught Ed under the table flycatching and furiously mugging at the audience. Never one to take interference with his performing lightly, Fields threatened homicide. But when the show reached Boston, unscheduled rippling merriment raced through the house. Fields reversed his billiard cue, swung it like Babe Ruth, and knocked Ed cold.

When the Ziegfeld 1915 production completed its road tour, Ed signed with the Shuberts. On June 22, 1916, he opened at the Winter Garden Theatre in the *Passing Show of 1916*. Before the show opened, as a concession to the staunch Catholicism of the Keenan family, and Hilda's desire to remain in the Church, he remarried his wife before a Catholic priest. While he was on stage in the *Passing Show*, on Thursday, July 27, 1916, he announced to the audience the birth of his son. Hilda determined to raise her half-Jewish son in the Catholic faith. To touch all bases, she named him for four Catholic saints: Francis-Xavier Aloysius James Jeremiah Keenan Wynn.

Ed was back at the Winter Garden Theatre on October 18, 1917, with Frank Tinney and the Duncan Sisters in *Doing Our Bit*. He left that musical to replace T. Roy Barnes in

Sigmund Romberg's wartime revue *Over the Top*, in which Fred and Adele Astaire made their Broadway stage debut. *Sometime* (October 4, 1918) featured Ed, with Mae West and Francine Larrimore in support, and ran for 283 performances.

The increasingly popular clown had become one of the Great White Way's best known musical comedy comics. In July he headed the *Shubert Gaieties of 1919*. On August 6, 1919, when the first Actors' Equity strike in history was called, Ed unwittingly became its most vociferous and dedicated leader, along with Ethel Barrymore, Marie Dressler, and Mary Boland. On Times Square he vehemently lashed into the deplorable working conditions and unreasonable demands of the producing managements and ended with an emotional declaration that he would *never* again do a Broadway show if the actors lost. "I'd rather sell peanuts and popcorn in the circus," he shouted. His speech was so enthusiastically received that he was carried through the streets atop the shoulders of sympathizers.

The actors won. Wynn lost.* He was boycotted on Broadway. With the remarkable resilience that continued throughout his career, Ed wrote his own show. He opened *Ed Wynn's Carnival* at the New Amsterdam Theatre on April 5, 1920. Marion Davies, after several unremarkable films, returned to the stage as Ed's comedy foil and was grandly ignored by the critics. It was Davies' farewell appearance on Broadway.

The success of that production led to *The Perfect Fool* (November 7, 1921), with book, music, and lyrics by Ed Wynn. Here he continued to parade an insane wardrobe, augmented by his collection of funny hats. His trademark was still his eyebrows made into dark arches resembling question marks, accented by horn-rimmed glasses. The newest all-Wynn show was a resounding hit. Later he wrote a complete comedy carnival and presented himself again in *The Grab Bag* (October 6, 1924), doing a devastating impersonation of Will Rogers. While bewilderingly pacing the stage holding a rope Ed would

---

* The Lambs' Club and Actors' Equity Association presented Ed with a Scroll of Honor signed by 1,800 grateful performers for his dedicated leadership in their victorious strike.

In Rubber Heels *(1927).*

inform the audience, "Either I've found a rope, or I've lost a horse!"

Paramount signed Ed for $125,000 to make his screen debut in an original screenplay, *Rubber Heels* (1927). He played amateur detective Amos Wart, shuttling between jewel thieves and a Princess (Thelma Todd), the latter trying to sell the crown jewels. The farce ended with Ed going over Niagara Falls in a chest. It was a destination he prescribed for the silent picture which he intensely disliked. He claimed he was "de-Ed Wynnized" in the Astoria-made farce. He offered to return his salary to Paramount if they would shelve the comedy. When they refused he left for Europe before the film opened on Broadway. He told reporters, in denial of the studio's assertion that he was imitating Harold Lloyd, "When I wore the first pair of amber-colored, horn-rimmed glasses seen in this country, which had been sent to me from Germany, Harold Lloyd was 8 years old!"

If the silent screen did not reflect the buffoonery and scope of Ed's comedy, the talking screen seemed more likely to accomplish the transition of his clowning from stage to film. His lisping falsetto voice and zany comedy seemed a natural for the early talkies' constant transferring of Broadway musicals to the screen.* Paramount selected his Broadway hit *Manhattan Mary* (1927) for his talking screen debut.

The project was retitled *Follow the Leader* (1930) and Ed reprised his Broadway role of Crickets, an ineffectual kidnapper assigned to spirit away the star (Ethel Merman) of a Broadway show so her understudy (early Ginger Rogers) can play the part. The Long Island-filmed musical was no milestone, but did garner some praise for the star. "This affable comic with his fund of laughable

---

* Ed Wynn was the first actor heard on radio in a complete Broadway show; on June 12, 1922, over station WJZ in New York City he broadcast *The Perfect Fool.*

In Follow the Leader
(1930).

inventions is another player who benefits distinctly by being heard as well as seen, for it is plain that his gags could never be pictured to such advantage in a silent film" (*New York Times*). But even *Photoplay's* rave, "Ed Wynn, no howl in silent pictures, is a scream in this, now that talkies gives us his apologetic, squeaking voice," did not agitate Paramount to extend his picture career.

The Paramount picture was sandwiched between Ed's starring role in Ziegfeld's production of *Simple Simon* (February 18, 1930). That show was a frothy fantasy heightened by Rodgers and Hart's score and Ruth Etting's memorable singing of the show's hit song, "Ten Cents a Dance." Critics stumbled in print trying properly to place Ed within the world's six funniest men, if not *the* funniest. The *New Yorker* magazine, while deploring the banality of the fairy tale musical, decreed that his comic genius turned the whole show into a riot of rich comedy nothing short of legerdemain. In the spring of 1931, Ed, following a long road tour in the show, returned to Broadway in *Simple Simon* as both producer and star.

The Laugh Parade (November 2, 1931) was his next Broadway showcase. Brooks Atkinson (*New York Times*) would later define the Wynn comedic eloquence: "There was a winning purity about Ed Wynn—purity of method as well as material. He made a point of innocence, and won his audiences with beguiling nonsense; he did not try to conquer them with wit." During the run of *The Laugh Parade* he frescoed the lobby walls of the Imperial Theatre with several of his inventions, including a miniature guillotine ("A French Cure for Dandruff"), and installed crazy, curved mirrors to amuse audiences.

His rousing success in *The Laugh Parade* was compounded when in 1932 he signed a $5,000 weekly contract to become radio's beloved "Fire Chief" for Texaco. If the screen had failed to make Ed Wynn known to the hinterlands, radio made him a household word. He was the first of radio's great comedians to work in makeup and costume in front of an appreciative audience and the first humorously to deprecate his sponsor's product. His ludicrous, lunatic tales began with Wynn's self-conscious giggle and an aside to straight man/announcer Graham MacNamee ("Oh, Graham, this is so silly"). Ed would punctuate this opener with a piping, falsetto "Soooooo" and continue on to the tag line. Wynn would lisp through several years as radio's "Fire Chief" and would have a brief reign on the airwaves as "King Bubbles."

Ed's national acclaim as a radio star was not lost on Hollywood. MGM, eager to capitalize on his new career and popularity, signed him for a picture. The studio furthered its opportunistic enterprise by titling the film *The Chief* (1933). The *New York Times* properly appraised Metro's less than altruistic effort: "Mr. Wynn is more than a funny man. He is lovable. It is impossible not to feel affection for him even in the moment that one is laughing most heartlessly at the bewildered saucer eyes behind the horn-rimmed spectacles, the foolish agitation of his hands, the apologetic hiccough, the strained falsetto and the collapsible forehead. In a perfect world there would be unmentionable penalties for gag men who weighed him down with the bewhiskered slapstick that has found its way into *The Chief*. What it all comes down to is that Mr. Wynn is genuinely funny and *The Chief* is not."

After the Hollywood preview of *The Chief* Ed refused to continue constant retakes on the Metro dud and the studio shot additional plot footage around him, trying to salvage a total loss. On Tuesday, October 31, 1933, Ed returned to the airwaves as Texaco's "Fire Chief."

In the Thirties, son Keenan would say of Ed, he "reached the heights as a clown and the depths as a bedeviled husband and father." In the early Thirties Ed's marriage floundered. He separated from his wife and moved into an apartment at the Hotel Berkshire on West 52nd Street in Manhattan. On May 10, 1937, Hilda Keenan Wynn filed a divorce suit in Reno, Nevada, requesting alimony of $1,500 weekly and restoration of her maiden name. Ed contested the petition, charging his wife with habitual intoxication (son Keenan described his grandfather, Frank Keenan, as a "monumental drunk"). But on May 13, 1937, Hilda won a divorce decree that restored her maiden name and provided her with $300 a week for life. She died three years later.

On June 16, 1937, Ed was married in the New York City Municipal Building chapel by his friend Deputy City Clerk Philip E. Hines to Freida Louise Mierse, a 26-year-old divorcée from Denver, Colorado. The honeymoon was spent on Ed's yacht, *The Sea Wynn*, moored at the foot of East 26th Street. Two years later they would be divorced.

In early 1936 Ed had produced his first straight dramatic show, *Alice Takat*, which closed on Broadway within a week. On December 1, 1937, he was back on Broadway in the Shuberts' production of *Hooray for What!* The satirical book by Howard Lindsay and Russel Crouse was a spy spoof, blessed with Harold Arlen's music and staging by Lindsay and Vincente Minnelli (who also did the settings). The show provided a stunning showcase for the wacky antics of Ed Wynn as inventor Chuckles, helped considerably in comedy and song by Vivian Vance. (In the middle of these Broadway outings he turned down the role of the title figure in MGM's *The Wizard of Oz*, 1939, claiming the part was too small.) Ed would return to Broadway in his own production of *Boys and Girls Together* (October 1, 1940). *Life* magazine judged the show as Ed's balmy best, particularly when he was accompanying singer Jane Pickens perched atop the piano of his invention, the pianocycle. *Life* added, "Wynn is a perfect fool, but owes his success to his portrait of a friendly man having a wonderful time."

A concoction of vaudeville, *Laugh, Town, Laugh*, occupied Ed's time at New York's Alvin Theatre in 1942. In 1943 he was one of many Broadway stars featured in cameo roles in United Artists' *Stage Door Canteen*.

On July 31, 1946, at the Little Church of the West in the Last Frontier Hotel in Las Vegas, Ed was married to Dorothy Elizabeth Nesbitt. (This marriage would end in divorce in 1955.) Another vaudeville stint, *Ed Wynn's Laugh Carnival*, opened on the West Coast and expired at St. Louis' American Theatre on January 22, 1949. Others in the cast were Phil Baker, Pat Rooney, and Allan Jones.

Ed's career had a resurgence with his debut in television. "The Ed Wynn Show" (October 6, 1949 to July 4, 1950) won Emmy Awards at the second annual award presentation as the Best Live Show and a second Emmy for Ed as the Most Outstanding Live Personality. In 1950 Ed alternated with Jimmy Durante,

Danny Thomas, and Jack Carson on television's "Four Star Revue." For Walt Disney's animated cartoon feature, *Alice in Wonderland* (1951), Ed was wonderfully right and hilarious as the voice of the Mad Hatter.

Ed never considered retirement; in the Fifties, his career at low ebb, he was playing nightclub engagements in Las Vegas, telling audiences, "My name is Ed Wynn. If you don't know who I am, I'm Keenan Wynn's father. And if you don't know who Keenan Wynn is, he is the guy who, when Esther Williams dives in the pool, gets splashed."

In 1956, before he reached his threescore and 10, The Perfect Fool entered a new career as a warm and capable character actor. After both Hume Cronyn and Burgess Meredith had turned down the role of Paul Beaseley in José Ferrer's Universal picture *The Great Man* (1956), Wynn was hired for the part of the small-town radio station owner, largely at the suggestion and coaxing of son Keenan, who was already signed for the picture. Ed gave an incisive characterization (winning the *Film Daily* Award). However, his untapped capabilities as a straight actor were more acclaimed on television.

Rod Serling's powerful TV drama *Requiem for a Heavyweight* was telecast on "Playhouse 90" on October 11, 1956—live. At the ninth annual television awards, *Requiem* won six Emmy Awards. Ed was nominated for his role in *Requiem* as the trainer of has-been prizefighter Jack Palance. (Keenan Wynn was also in the sterling cast.) Four years later the director of *Requiem*, Ralph Nelson, wrote, produced, and directed a filmed one-hour drama, telecast on the "Desilu Playhouse" (April 15, 1960). It was a documentary based on the behind-the-scenes frustrations and trials of and personal interplay between father and son, Keenan and Ed, during the production of the 1956 dramatic hit. Advertised as "the true story of 'The Perfect Fool's rise to dramatic stardom,'" *The Man in the Funny Suit* documented Keenan's concern and fear that his father would not perform as he should in a dramatic role. The telecast reconstructed the trauma of the '56 show and included peripheral participants Red Skelton, Rod Serling, Maxie Rosenbloom, and Ed's understudy, Ned Glass. Ed Wynn was again nominated for an Emmy Award for his *The Man in the Funny Suit.*

Now in his seventies, Ed began guesting on several variety shows. He would tell the TV audience, "Ladies and gentlemen, I'm happy to be here. At my age, I'm happy to be anyplace!" About his renewed career, he would say, "Pretty good for a guy who has morticians tip their hats to him every time he walks down the street." Proof that his dramatic debut was not a lark was verified by his performance in *The Great American Hoax* on "The 20th Century-Fox Hour" (May 15, 1957) and in the *Protege* episode (May 19, 1957) of "The Alcoa Hour." Critics reported, "In *Protege*, Ed gives a sensitive, understanding, and at times deeply moving performance, and once again proves that as long as he wants to be a serious and dedicated dramatic actor, he can be one of the best." Wynn added to his laurels, on November 17, 1957, with his playing of the old man fending off death in *On Borrowed Time* on "Hallmark Hall of Fame."

In 1958 he received the *Film Daily* Award for his splendid playing of Uncle Samson in Warner Bros.' *Marjorie Morningstar*. In George Stevens' stern screen translation of *The Diary of Anne Frank* (1959), Ed was excellent as the bachelor Mr. Dussell. He received a well-earned Academy Award nomination as the Best Supporting Actor of the Year, but lost to Hugh Griffith's Sheik Ilderim in *Ben-Hur*.

After the abortive "The Ed Wynn Show" (NBC-TV, September 25, 1958-January 1, 1959) in which he played a retired businessman and widower, Ed shone as a lovable grandpa to Jane Powell, Jeanne Crain, and Patty Duke in a two-hour CBS special (April 26, 1959) of the musical *Meet Me in St. Louis*. He joined the girls in the title song and soloed in "When You Were Sweet Sixteen." On November 27, 1959, Ed was Kris Kringle on NBC's color telecast of *The Miracle on 34th Street*. If he was less effective than Edmund Gwenn in the screen version, he gave a telling performance. On Ford's "Startime" in 1960 Ed was joined with another funster, Bert Lahr, in the episode *The Greatest Man Alive*.

With the new decade, Ed continued his new filmmaking career, unhampered by the increasing tremors that caused his head and hands to shake. He was a likely fairy godfather in Jerry Lewis' *Cinderfella* (1960). In 1961 he signed with Walt Disney to play the Fire Chief, who arrives to rescue his flubber-

With Everett Sloane
and Natalie Wood in
Marjorie
Morningstar (1958).

With Richard
Beymer, Shelley
Winters, Gusti
Haber, Millie
Perkins, and Diane
Baker in The Diary
of Anne Frank
(1958).

With Dick Van Dyke
in Mary Poppins
(1964).

bouncing son Keenan, in *The Absent-Minded Professor*, and he brightened Disney's pedestrian remake of *Babes in Toyland* (1961) as the toymaker. For Disney's television one-hour *Golden Horseshoe Revue*, filmed at Disneyland in color, Ed returned to his glorious theatrical past by reviewing his sixty years in show business. He peddled his pianocycle and sang "Shine on Harvest Moon" and "Tea for Two."

The veteran performer had a walk-through part in *Son of Flubber* (1963) and a cameo role in Jerry Lewis' *The Patsy* (1964). These wasteful assignments were forgotten when contrasted to his appearance in Disney's *Mary Poppins* (1964), in which he was uninhibited Uncle Albert, unable to control his laughter as he floats around the ceiling of his living room. In George Stevens' sprawling *The Greatest Story Ever Told* (1965) Ed was Old Aram. In Twentieth Century-Fox's *Dear Brigitte* (1965) Ed as an old captain introduced the main characters.

His last television appearance was on a segment of "Bonanza." On camera he had roles in Disney's *Those Calloways* (1965) and *That Darn Cat* (1965) and supplied the voice of the Emperor in a cartoon feature of Hans Christian Andersen tales, *The Daydreamer* (1966). He completed his screen career with a role as the 1,100-year-old king of the gnomes in Disney's *The Gnome-Mobile* (1967).

On Sunday, June 19, 1966, Ed Wynn died at his Beverly Hills apartment, less than five months before his 80th birthday. He had undergone the removal of a malignant neck tumor that January.

Ed's definition of a comedian has been used, misused, and reused by many of his predecessors: "A comedian is not a man who says funny things. A comedian is a man who says things funny."

696

FEATURE FILMS

Rubber Heels (*Paramount 1927*)

Follow the Leader (*Paramount 1930*)

The Chief (*MGM 1933*)

Stage Door Canteen (*United Artists 1943*)

Alice in Wonderland (*RKO 1951*) [voice only]

The Great Man (*Universal 1956*)

Marjorie Morningstar (*Warner Bros. 1958*)

The Diary of Anne Frank (*20th Century-Fox 1959*)

Cinderfella (*Paramount 1960*)

The Absent-Minded Professor (*Buena Vista 1961*)

Babes in Toyland (*Buena Vista 1961*)

Son of Flubber (*Buena Vista 1963*)

The Sound of Laughter (*Union 1963*) [narrator]

The Patsy (*Paramount 1964*)

Mary Poppins (*Buena Vista 1964*)

The Greatest Story Ever Told (*United Artists 1965*)

Dear Brigitte (*20th Century-Fox 1965*)

That Darn Cat (*Buena Vista 1965*)

Those Calloways (*Buena Vista 1965*)

The Daydreamer (*Embassy 1966*) [voice only]

The Gnome-Mobile (*Buena Vista 1967*)

Staff

JAMES ROBERT PARISH, Los Angeles-based free-lance writer and management executive, was born in Cambridge, Massachusetts. He attended the University of Pennsylvania and graduated as a Phi Beta Kappa with a degree in English. He is a graduate of the University of Pennsylvania Law School and has been the president of Entertainment Copyright Research Co., Inc., as well as a reporter for Manhattan film trade papers. Among the books that he is author of are *The Great Movie Series, The Fox Girls, Hollywood's Great Love Teams, The Jeanette MacDonald Story, Hollywood Character Actors,* and *The Hollywood Beauties.* He is the co-author of *The MGM Stock Company, The Debonairs, Film Directors Guide: The U.S., The Leading Ladies,* and many other books on the media. Mr. Parish is also a contributor to national magazines.

WILLIAM T. LEONARD, former Research Director for the Theatre Collection of the Free Library of Philadelphia, has spent many years in theatrical and cinema research, contributing articles to several publications including *Films in Review* and *Classic Film Collector.* During World War II he wrote and appeared in his play *Hurry Up and Wait.* He has written reports for proposed culture centers, including Lincoln Center for the Performing Arts, and was one of the principal contributors of data for the American Film Institute's catalog volume, *Feature Films: 1921–30.* Books he has co-written include *Hollywood Players: The Forties* and *Hollywood Players: The Thirties.* His book *Theatre: Stage—to Screen—to Television* will soon be published.

GREGORY W. MANK is a graduate of Mount St. Mary's College, with a B.A. in English. He has written several articles for *Films in Review* and *Film Fan Monthly* and has been associated with Mr. Parish on *Hollywood Players: The Forties, Hollywood Players:* *The Thirties, The Tough Guys, Great Child Stars, The Hollywood Beauties,* and others. Mr. Mank lives in Pennsylvania with his wife, Barbara, and daughter, Jessica, and is active in theatre as a performer and a teacher.

CHARLES HOYT is currently a film booker for Warner Bros. in Boston, Massachusetts. He is a graduate of the University of Massachusetts and received his M.A. in English from the University of Oregon. He has worked on *The Fox Girls* and *The Hollywood Reliables* (the latter to be published by Arlington House in early 1980).

JOHN ROBERT COCCHI was born in Brooklyn where he currently resides. He is one of America's most respected film researchers and has worked as research associate on *The American Movies Reference Book: The Sound Era, The Fox Girls, Good Dames, The Swashbucklers, The Leading Ladies, Hollywood Character Actors* and *The Hollywood Beauties.* He has written cinema history articles for *Film Fan Monthly, Screen Facts,* and *Films in Review.* He is the author of *The Western Picture Quiz Book* and is co-founder of one of New York City's leading film societies.

FLORENCE SOLOMON was born in New York City, attended Hunter College, and then joined Ligon Johnson's copyright research office. Later she was director of research at Entertainment Copyright Research Co., Inc., and she is currently a reference supervisor at ASCAP's Index Division. Ms. Solomon has collaborated on such works as *The American Movies Reference Book, TV Movies, Film Actors Guide: Western Europe,* and many others. She has worked as a research associate on *The Leading Ladies, Hollywood Character Actors,* and *The Hollywood Beauties.* She is a niece of the noted sculptor, the late Sir Jacob Epstein.

Index

Numbers in italics indicate that a picture of the performer is on the page indicated. A letter "n" after a number indicates that the reference is to a footnote.

Astor, Gertrude, *574*
Astor, Mary, 322, 446
At the Barn, 615
At the Circus, 50, 472
At War with the Army, 455
Atkinson, Brooks, 101, 116, 126, 253, 383, 553, 692
Atlantic Adventure, 404
Atoll K, 414
Atwill, Lionel, 15, 125, 482, 533, 534
Au Pied, au Cheval et Par Spoutnik, 71
Auction Block, The, 478
Auctioneer, The, 574
Auer, Anthony, 66
Auer, Leopold, 63, 64
Auer, Mischa, *62*, 63–73, *65, 66, 67, 68, 69, 71*, 333n, 360, 522
Auntie Mame, 57
Austen, Jane, 504
Austin, Albert, 178, *181*
Autobiography, 546
Autry, Gene, 159, 213, 237
Avalon, Frankie, 58, 374
Avanti!, 426
Avenging Trail, The, 530n
Avery, F. H., 391
Aviator, The, 322
Awakening, The, 353
Awful Truth, The, 310
Axelrod, George, 256
Ayres, Agnes, 508
Ayres, Lew, 404, 509, 670

Babbling Brook, The 144n
Babes in Toyland, 411, 499, *688*, 696
Baby Mine, 45, 278
Baby Peggy, 321
Baby Quintanilla, *164*
Baby Sandy, 68
"Baby Snooks," 523, 593
Bacall, Lauren, 59, 335, 673
Baccaloni, Salvatore, 301
Bachelor, The, 614
Bachelor Daddy, 327
Bachelor in Paradise, 314
Back Stage, 39
Back to the Woods, 488
Backus, Jim, 204, 334
Baclanova, Olga, 391
Bacon, Frank, 35
Bacon, Lloyd, 178
Bad Bascomb, 446
Badger, Clarence, 488, 543
Baer, Max, 362
Bailey, Pearl, 216, 313, 525
Bain, Conrad, 218
Bainter, Fay, *337*
Baker, Belle, 49
Baker, Benny, 333
Baker, Diane, *695*
Baker, George, 221
Baker, Josephine, 49, 157, 308
Baker, Kenny, 90, 472, 531, 581
Baker, Phil, 126, 157, 623n, 693
Balanchine, George, 70
Ball, Desirée, 76, 84

Ball, Henry, 76
Ball, Lucille, 57, 74, 75–85, *79, 80, 81, 83*, 91, 96, 107, 204, 212, 219, 238, 239, 295, 298, 312, 316, 372, *385*, 438, 448, 470, 493, 586, 591, 593, 633, 669
Ball of Fire, 78n, 335
"Ballad of Louie the Louse, The," 585
Ballard, Kaye, 25, 58, 239
Ballyhoo, 266
Ballyhoo of 1932, 307
Baltake, Joe, 422, 423
Baltimore News-American, 31
Balzer, George, 90
Bananas, 23, 28, 33
Bancroft, Anne, 420, 426
Band Wagon, The, 671
Bandolero!, 459
Banjo Eyes, 170
Bank Dick, The, 270, 624n
Bankhead, Tallulah, 70, 76, 300, 362
Banks, Leslie, 322
"Banyon," 390n
Bara, Theda, 123
"Barbara Whiting Show, The," 206
Barber, Bobby, *102, 183*
Barber Shop, The, 266
Barbier, George, 650
Bardot, Brigitte, 71
Barefoot in the Park, 58, 363
"Baretta," 260
Bargain of the Century, 194
Barnes, Binnie, 133, 533
Barnes, Clive, 106, 216, 428, 586n
Barnes, T. Roy, 690
Barnett, Vince, 246
Barnacle Bill, 445
Barnum and Bailey, 591
Barnyard Flirtations, 37
Barrie, Elaine, 531
Barrie, James, 488
Barrie, Wendy, 445
Barry, Don "Red," 255
Barry, Carol Ann, 184
Barry, Gene, 421
Barry Jack, 29
Barry, Joan, 183, 184
Barry, Philip, 255
Barrymore, Ethel, 101, 112, 123, 124, 222, 223, 265, 300, 447, 690
Barrymore, John, 96, 123, 202, 222, 235, 265, 269, 361, 531, 639, 667n
Barrymore, Lionel, 91, 123, 222, 228, 265, 411, 546, 581
Barrymore, Maurice, 222
Barthelmess, Richard, 353, 612, 634, 666
Bartholomew, Freddie, *268*
Bartlett, Michael, 562
Barton, James, 126
Basie, Count, 25
Bassermann, Albert, 562
Bat, The, 513, 514
Bataan, 77n
Bates, Barbara, 336
Bates, Florence, 566
Bath House Blunder, A, 478
Bathing Beauty, 594
"Batman," 107

Burke, Edwin, 512
Burke, John, 35
Burke, Samson, 629
"Burke's Law," 354, 515, 557
Burlesque, 384, 399, 444
Burnett, Carol, 83n, 84, 493, 526n, 597n, 654, 662
Burnham, Eunice, 276
Burns, Bob, 91, 520, *520*, 521
Burns, George, 84, 91, 92, 95, 96, 97, 114, 141–154, *142,*
    146, 147, 148, 150, 151, 152, 195, 204, 254, 309, 315, 316,
    520, 575, 599, 605
Burns, Robert, 158, 162
Burns, Ronnie, 145, 149
Burns, Sandra, 145
Burns and Allen in Lambchops, 144
Burr, C. C., 497
Burrows, Abe, 460
Busch, Mae, 321, 410, 478, 487
Business and Pleasure, 546
Business Before Pleasure, 572
Buster Keaton Rides Again, 354
Buster Keaton Story, The, 353
Buswell, Karl, 404
Busy Izzy, 569, 571
Busy Izzy's Boodle, 571
Busy Izzy's Vacation, 571
Butcher Boy, The, 39, 346
Butter and Egg Man, The, 134
Butterflies Are Free, 58
Butterworth, Charles, 159, 235, 359, 404, 555, 624
Buttons, Red, 248n, 379, 526n
Buy, Buy, Baby, 604
Buzzell, Eddie, 165, 472
Buzzi, Ruth, 199
Buzzin' Around, 45n
By the Sea, 646
Bye Bye Birdie, 655, 656, *656*
Byington, Spring, 202, 563, *565*
Byrne, George, 307

Cab Waiting, 88n
Cabanne, William, 489
Cabot, Bruce, 391
Cactus Nell, 478
Caddy, The, 456, *458*
Cadell, Jean, *268*
Caesar, Irving, 237
Caesar, Sid, 25, 240, 370, 589
Cafe De Danse, 604
Caged, 299
Cagney, James, 113, 285, 313, 335, 414, 422, 446, *560*, 593
Cahill, Marie, 223
Cahn, Sammy, 582
Cahn, William, 439
Caine Mutiny, The, 374
Calamity Jane, 523
Calhern, Louis, 334
California Pictures, 438
Call Again, 321
Call Me Bwana, 314, *315*
Callahans and the Murphys, The, 224, 479
Calleia, Joseph, 534
Calling All Stars, 157, 158, 520
Calloway, Cab, 145
Calvet, Corinne, 338, *452, 455*

Calvin, Henry, 654n
"Camel Caravan," 237
Cameraman, The, 349, *350*, 595
Cameron, Hugh, 574
Camille, 222, 265
Campanella, Joseph, 260n, 303
Campbell, Eric, 178
Campbell, Flo, 580
Campbell, Glen, 239n, 316
Camping Out, 41
Campus, The, 37
*Can Hieronymus Merkin Ever Forget Mercy Humppe
    and Find True Happiness?*, 106, *106*
Canary Cottage, 165, 166, 552
Canby, Vincent, 32, 33, 187, 347
Cancel My Reservation, 314
Candido, Candy, 19
"Cannon," 440n
Cannonball, 162
Canova, Anne, 155, 157, 158
Canova, Diana, 162
Canova, Henrietta, 155, 157
Canova, Joe, 155, 157
Canova, Judy, 49, 92, *138*, 155–162, *156, 158, 160, 161,*
    202, 308, 489n, 580
Canova, Pete, 155, 157
Canova, Zeke, 155, 157, 158
Canterville Ghost, The, 325
Cantinflas, 373
Cantor, Eddie, 18, 45, 76, 77, 91, 96, 100, 109n, 123, 144,
    163–173, *164, 168, 169, 171, 172,* 202, 203, 231, 278,
    279, 308, 454, 479, 480, 545, 668
Cantor, Edna, 166
Cantor, Ida, 165, 166n, 172, 173
Cantor, Janet, 167
Cantor, Marilyn, 166
Cantor, Marjorie, 165, 173
Cantor, Natalie, 166
Capp, Al, 362
Capra, Frank, 66, 68, 77, 221, 323, 326, 371, 397, 399, 400,
    401, 402, 574, 651
Capri Productions, 338
Captain and Tennille, The, 151
Captain Dieppe, 603
Captain Hates the Sea, The, 626
Captain Is a Lady, The, 445
Captain Jinks, 132
Captain Jinks of the Marines, 132
Captivating Mary Carstairs, 612
Capucine, 26, 373, *374*
"Cara Williams Show, The," 326
Carey, Macdonald, 333
Carlin, Lynn, 661
Carlisle, Kitty, 469, 470
Carminati, Tullio, 617
Carnegie, Hattie, 76
Carney, Art, 25, 82, 425, 586
Carnival, 77, 235, *236*
"Carol Burnett Show, The," 662
Carol, Sue, 390
Carolina Cannonball, 161
Carousel, 326, 558
Carp, Betty, 468n
Carr, Alexander, 572, 575
Carr, Frank B., 165

728

734